D1281579

BY DUMAS MALONE

~·~·~·~·~·~·~·

JEFFERSON AND HIS TIME
(*of which the following volumes have been published*)

JEFFERSON THE VIRGINIAN

JEFFERSON AND THE RIGHTS OF MAN

JEFFERSON AND THE ORDEAL OF LIBERTY

JEFFERSON THE PRESIDENT
FIRST TERM, 1801–1805

JEFFERSON THE PRESIDENT
SECOND TERM, 1805–1809

Jefferson the President

Second Term, 1805 – 1809

THE "MEDALLION PROFILE" OF JEFFERSON
Portrait by Gilbert Stuart, 1805

JEFFERSON AND HIS TIME

VOLUME FIVE

Jefferson the President

Second Term, 1805 – 1809

BY DUMAS MALONE

With Illustrations

Boston

LITTLE, BROWN AND COMPANY

D

Library of Congress Cataloging in Publication Data

Malone, Dumas, 1892-
    Jefferson and his time.

    Includes bibliographies.
    CONTENTS: v. 1. Jefferson the Virginian.--
v. 2. Jefferson and the rights of man.--v. 3. Jefferson and the ordeal of liberty.--v. 4. Jefferson
the president, first term, 1801-1805.--V. 5. Jefferson the president, second term, 1805-1809.
    1. Jefferson, Thomas, Pres. U. S., 1743-1826.
I. Title.
E332.M25   973.4'6'0924 [B]   48-5972

Published simultaneously in Canada
by Little, Brown & Company (Canada) Limited

PRINTED IN THE UNITED STATES OF AMERICA

Illustrations

Contents

Introduction

THE present volume, the fifth in the series *Jefferson and His Time*, completes the story of his presidency that was begun in the fourth. Not only does it carry him through his second term but also to the end of an official career that spanned some forty years. He afterwards rendered memorable public service, notably in education and architecture, and he enriched American thought and literature by means of fascinating letters, but he did so as a private citizen. As there was poignancy in his last years as a human being so there was in his final official period. It was certainly not the most glorious of his public life, and his second quadrennium as chief executive must be compared unfavorably to his first. That seems to have been the rule rather than the exception in presidential history, but in this detailed narrative I seek to show how and as best I can why it came about under his particular circumstances.

In the introduction to the previous volume I went to some pains to point out that I was not attempting to write a history of the United States during Jefferson's presidency. Well aware of the necessary limitations of my presentation, I thus sought to guard myself against criticism for having left important things out. At the same time I reminded my readers, as I keep reminding myself, that this is a study of a man while President and that it is supposed to center on him. Keeping it centered on him has proved even more difficult in this volume than in its predecessor because his actions were taken to a greater degree in response and reaction to the doings of others. It would appear that his image loomed largest in the public mind in the months immediately following the report of the Louisiana Purchase; and, just as his triumphant re-election in 1804 marked the zenith of his presidential career, so did the partial repeal of the embargo and the rejection of his final appointment mark not only its end but also its nadir. During the last congressional session of his first term, when John Randolph and Justice Samuel Chase usurped the domestic stage, he lost the initiative. In the area of foreign affairs he regained it, and not until his last months in office did he lose it, but except in his continued but futile efforts to acquire West Florida, he was essentially on the defensive against the aggressions of the chief warring powers of the Old World; and as Aaron Burr provided most of the drama on the domestic scene, so on the foreign front did the British sea lord who caused the *Leopard* to fire on the *Chesapeake* off the Virginia Capes.

Jefferson's activism was manifested in characteristic form in his patronage of the Lewis and Clark expedition, and until the last session of his presidency, while keeping out of sight, he continued to receive a high degree of co-operation from Congress. During most of his second term he remained the major unifying factor in his party, the government, and the country, but factionalism increased at home along with aggression from abroad. On his second presidential voyage seas were rougher and winds less favorable than on his first. As we sail it with him we shall have abundant opportunity to judge his actions in particular situations, but first we may profitably inquire into the seaworthiness of his vessel and ask about its desired destination. That is, we should ask just what sort of government this was at this time, what it could be fairly expected to do, and what he himself expected of it.

Nothing could be more absurd than to equate him with the government, although his opponents, with the exaggeration so common in politics, often did just that. It was a divided government, based on the principle of the separation of powers.[1] The purpose of the Fathers was to obviate, or at least minimize, the danger of tyranny by dividing power among "rival interests," and the constitutional separation was reflected and accentuated in the residential and social pattern of the governmental community in Washington. Legislators lived on Capitol Hill, executives in the neighborhood of the President's House, and members of the federal judiciary, when in town, associated almost exclusively with one another. As has been well said: "The 'separation of powers' became the separation of persons."[2] Divisiveness was further increased by the legislators' practice of living in boarding-houses in sectional groupings. The situation was not conducive to co-operation between the separate branches of the government or to the development of leadership on the part of the President or within Congress itself.

[1] It is described as a government of "separated institutions *sharing* powers" by R. E. Neustadt in *Presidential Power, the Politics of Leadership* (1960), p. 33. While this seminal work deals primarily with conditions in the middle of the twentieth century, it illuminates the whole of presidential history.

[2] J. S. Young, *The Washington Community, 1800–1828* (1966), p. 78. The theme is elaborated in this illuminating study; see ch. IV in the present connection. The social separation increased rather than diminished in the period studied.

While Jefferson, who had members of Congress to dinner almost every day when they were in town, did more than anybody else to bridge the social gap between legislators and executives, he does not appear to have questioned the doctrine of separation. When in opposition, he had strongly emphasized the danger of executive tyranny and the necessity of distrust. In the Kentucky Resolutions of 1798, written in protest against the Alien and Sedition Acts and presidential action under them, he said that "confidence [in rulers] is everywhere the parent of despotism — that free government is founded in jealousy, and not in confidence; . . . In questions of power then, let no more be heard of confidence in man, but bind him down from mischief by the chains of the Constitution."[3] Since his authorship of the resolutions was known to only a few people at the time, these particular words could not be flung at him when, as the responsible chief executive, he sought to promote social harmony, inspire confidence, and make a divided government work. Even so, he was repeatedly charged with hypocrisy by his political enemies, and he could hardly have failed to give an impression of ambivalence. It might be said that throughout his presidency he strove to reconcile the irreconcilable, and there may have been more conflict within his own breast than he gave outward sign of. It seems indisputable, however, that in his first term, working within constitutional limitations that he himself honored and in a political community marked by more than constitutional divisiveness, this foe of consolidation achieved genuine though incomplete success in his efforts to unite the country and render its government sufficiently effective to perform such tasks as he thought appropriate to it. Before entering into a consideration of his second term we may remind ourselves of the more favorable conditions and circumstances, both at home and abroad, under which he operated in his first.

Along with his own personal persuasiveness and that of his Cabinet members, especially Gallatin, the means on which Jefferson most relied to minimize divisiveness and attain co-operation with the Legislature was his political party. The term "party" was something of a misnomer at a time when the affiliations of members of Congress were not a matter of record, and organization was rudimentary from our point of view. Parties were loose groupings without legal sanction or formal leadership. The struggles of the Republicans in opposition, however, had imparted to them considerable cohesion, and among them Jefferson had no rival. (Burr read himself out of the party at an early date.) There is no way to measure his public popularity with any precision,

[3] Ford, VII, 504–505.

nor to determine what effect this had on the minds of legislators, but there is no more doubt that it was great and growing than there is that congressmen and senators were aware of it. The skill he displayed in his dealings with the congressional majority and the notable influence he had on legislation during his first term are abundantly illustrated in my previous book. He worked through leading legislators of his own party, carefully avoiding the appearance of dictation – in respect for congressional sensitivity and in deference to the principle of separation of powers.

This was not party government in a strict sense. When have we ever had that in the United States? But what was enacted could be described not inaccurately as a party program. Furthermore – and this is very much to the point in any comparison between the legislation of the two terms – laws based on a policy of peace, economy, and tax reduction lightened burdens and called for no sacrifice on the part of the public. A few members of the federal judiciary suffered as a result of an early Jeffersonian law, but the purchase of Louisiana was effected without the imposition of fresh taxes. The legislation of the period when the President and Congress were in fullest co-operation – roughly during his first three years in office – certainly need not be regarded as unmeritorious because it was relatively painless, and it seems likely that Jefferson wanted little more at the time. But, quite clearly, presidential leadership in legislative matters had not yet been severely tested.

Warning signs could have been perceived in the last congressional session of Jefferson's first term. The events of that session illustrate the perils of political prosperity and demonstrate that in the absence of effective leadership in or over Congress confusion is inevitable and chaos may ensue.[4] The President himself may have been lulled into a false sense of security by his electoral triumph in 1804, and Republican factionalism unquestionably increased as Federalist opposition weakened. Toward the end of the previous session, in writing to Caesar A. Rodney, who had decided not to stand for re-election to the House, Jefferson said: "I had looked to you as one of those calculated to give cohesion to our rope of sand."[5] Divisiveness of spirit was much more pronounced in the session of 1804–1805, when John Randolph, whose past co-operation had been so useful, conspicuously displayed his genius for obstruction and prevented a compromise settlement of the highly controversial Yazoo claims. Apart from legislation regarding the government of Louisiana, the President had no real program in this

---

[4] *Jefferson the President: First Term*, esp. ch. XXIV.
[5] TJ to Rodney, Feb. 24, 1804 (Ford, VIII, 296).

session. The Yazoo question came up as a matter of unfinished business, and in the bitter controversy over the proposed settlement that John Randolph precipitated, the President played a passive role. Even if he had felt more comfortable with the proposed compromise than he probably did, he may have been wise in remaining above a conflict which was sharply dividing his own partisans and, since the alignment tended to follow sectional lines, was threatening to divide the country.

The behavior of John Randolph was an augury of what might be expected in the first congressional session of Jefferson's second term, and actually this was marked by an open revolt of that avowed constitutional purist against presidential leadership. Jefferson reasserted this on issues in foreign affairs, a field in which his initiative was relatively unresented; and with great skill he contained the revolt, preserving the essential unity of his party and even strengthening his position as its head.[6] Early in that session John Quincy Adams recorded this prediction in his diary: "If a really trying time should ever befall this administration, it would very soon be deserted by all its troops, and by most of its principal agents."[7] The Senator from Massachusetts afterwards showed considerably less political sensitivity in his own presidency than Jefferson did in his, and if this direful prophecy was ever borne out, it was certainly not until the latter's last months in office. He maintained his position of leadership at least until his successor was elected.

While he was notably successful in bridging the gap between the executive branch and Congress until almost the end of his troubled second term, the chasm between the judiciary and the other two branches appeared to be impassable. Indeed, there was great uncertainty in the public mind whether there should be any attempt to bridge it. From the acquittal of Justice Samuel Chase at the very end of Jefferson's first term it appeared that federal judges, however partisan and irresponsible they might be, were untouchable unless proved to have been criminal. In view of Jefferson's belief that the existing judiciary constituted in effect an arm of the Federalist party, his attitude toward it could hardly have failed to be affected by partisan considerations throughout his presidency. But, quite clearly, he was baffled by the problem of reconciling judicial independence with the sovereignty of the people; and his own actions can be interpreted as designed, not to attain dominance over the judiciary, but to prevent it

---

[6] See chs. V, VII, IX, X, below.
[7] Feb. 7, 1806, in *Memoirs*, I, 404.

from encroaching on the prerogatives of the executive and obstructing the necessary operations of the government.

Although the Burr conspiracy, along with the resulting trial, bulks large in the domestic story in this volume, I do not claim to have given a rounded account of that highly controversial and still-mysterious episode. My concern has been to ascertain Jefferson's relations with the principals, Burr and General James Wilkinson, and his response to specific events as they were reported to him. The main point to be emphasized here is that he was convinced that the security and unity of the country were imperiled. In the light of present knowledge he appears to have been gullible with respect to Wilkinson, and he erred gravely in stating publicly that Burr's guilt was indubitable, but apart from that it is hard to see how he, as the responsible head of the government, could have done any less than he did in connection with Burr's prosecution. His personal participation in the legal procedure was grossly exaggerated at the time by Burr's counsel and his own political enemies. They charged him with personal vindictiveness, and from the speeches in court one might suppose that he, rather than Burr, was on trial. On the other hand, he and his own supporters believed that Chief Justice Marshall, who presided over the trials, abetted the enemies of the administration, and, by his construction of the law, made conviction of treason virtually impossible. The anomalies of this episode can best be perceived in the course of the detailed narrative, but it is important to call attention here to the sharp division within the government between the executive and the judiciary. Without attempting at this point to assess the relative blame for this situation, I merely say that the problem was not solved and may have been insoluble. Perhaps the best that could be hoped for was the avoidance of direct confrontation.

In the conduct of domestic affairs Jefferson was inhibited by the devotion to separation and the distrust of power which were shared by the overwhelming majority of his countrymen and were not only reflected but aggravated in the divided political community of Washington. He undoubtedly felt freer in the conduct of foreign affairs since this was clearly delegated to him by the Constitution. He did not forget that congressional support had to be gained, but he was in position to take the initiative, and the difficulties he sought to overcome were chiefly owing to the actions and policies of other nations. By the same token his options were limited by external circumstances he could not control. His bargaining power, though not precisely proportionate to his country's power and stature, was certainly dependent on them. Though potentially a giant, the American Republic was then only a stripling among the powers — an awkward lad, very lightly armed against foreign foes. Furthermore, to the vast body of Americans danger from abroad seemed remote and they were much occupied with their own affairs.

Throughout his presidency Jefferson controlled foreign policy to a greater degree than domestic, but the difficulties he had to meet and the limitations under which he labored turned out to be much greater in his second term than in his first. Fortunately for him the quarrel with France that had plagued and sharply divided the country in the administration of John Adams was resolved, or virtually so, by that President before Jefferson took office. During the two middle years of his first term the world was at peace; otherwise he could hardly have proceeded on his popular policy of economy. During these two years the interests and security of the United States were gravely endangered at New Orleans, the gateway to the Mississippi and its valley, but in the end, surprisingly, the young Republic acquired the imperial province of Louisiana. Credit should certainly not be denied the administration and its representatives for this magnificent acquisition of territory, whereby Jefferson made his most memorable contribution to the physical greatness of his country, but Bonaparte would not have sold Louisiana but for the setback to his colonial ambitions in St. Domingo and his determination to reopen the war in Europe. Out of the troubles and quarrels of the Old World a vigilant administration gained vast benefits for the New. These were not unmixed, to be sure. Fresh troubles were acquired along with fresh territory; and try though he might Jefferson could not exploit the international situation further by rounding out the "empire for liberty" by acquiring the Floridas. The renewed war imposed on American maritime interests great and growing dangers, but during his first term American commerce thrived, to the great advantage of the national economy. On the whole, the young country was well served by the times in which it lived.

Such a concatenation of circumstances as that which facilitated the purchase of Louisiana could not have been expected to recur; and, in fact, the external situation went steadily from bad to worse throughout Jefferson's second term. At the outset the administration gained a minor success in the relatively favorable settlement of the war with Tripoli, but there were to be no more diplomatic successes of any note. The period was marked by successive frustrations and it ended in the recognized failure of hopes. Since fairness requires that actions be viewed in their particular settings, the wisdom of Jefferson's policies and the skill with which they were pursued by him and his associates can be best adjudged in the light of particular events and circumstances. I have sought to describe these one by one in this book and the facts should speak for themselves, though it is not to be supposed they will say the same thing to everybody. Without attempting to summarize them here and without anticipating all of my own judgments, I should like to view the situation in its larger setting.

Early in the negotiations with the French regarding Louisiana, Jefferson observed to his Secretary of State: "An American contending by stratagem against those exercised in it from their cradle would undoubtedly be outwitted by them."[8] He was thinking about his minister, Robert R. Livingston, who was certainly no Talleyrand, and he was to find out that James Monroe was no match for the British Foreign Secretary, George Canning. The American Secretary of State had never been abroad and was alleged by his critics to have been more aware of the niceties of international law than of the wiles of diplomats. The President himself had had better opportunity to observe these wiles than anybody else in the administration, but he was often charged with gullibility. As observed from the chancellories of the Old World the Americans may have appeared to be rank amateurs, and their conduct of foreign affairs was undoubtedly marked by some bungling, but their errors should be attributed far more to slowness of communication and lack of information than to deficiency in expertise. Monroe might never have made his futile trip to Spain if he had been able to consult his government beforehand.

Policies were formulated in Washington on the basis of information that was already obsolete, and instructions to American representatives abroad were often out of date before they were delivered. Jefferson himself was not without blame for the inadequacy of information, since he had considerably reduced the foreign service for reasons of economy, but the major difficulties of communication, which affected the Americans far more than they did the British or the French, were in fact insuperable. We may wonder if, under such conditions, effective diplomacy was really possible. Because of the time lag tactics were often faulty, and an ill-informed administration could easily commit itself to a strategy which had already become unrealistic.

Jefferson never wholly gave up hope that by playing the major powers against each other he could gain advantages for his own country. This persistence was nowhere better illustrated than in his efforts to acquire West Florida. His thought was that the French would

8 Nov. 19, 1803 (*Jefferson the President: First Term*, pp. 298–299 and note 40).

prefer this territory of their Spanish satellite to pass into American hands rather than into those of the British, who could easily have taken it if they had wanted to, but Napoleon proved unwilling to bring pressure to bear on his proud and reluctant ally. The devious methods Jefferson employed in this connection are described in this book, along with the domestic difficulties that ensued. The long-drawn-out episode is mentioned here chiefly because it affords an example of methods which appear to have been ill-timed in the first place, and which were unquestionably employed too long.

Meanwhile, the struggle between the major powers increased in intensity and ruthlessness, and as a consequence the diplomatic efforts of the Republic had to be directed, not to the gaining of territorial or any other positive advantages, but to the safeguarding of its own rights and interests. These were chiefly imperiled upon the seas, where its commerce had thrived, and it was chiefly victimized by the British, whose maritime supremacy was unquestionable after Trafalgar, as was that of Napoleon on land after Austerlitz. A policy of neutrality was enjoined by American tradition and predominant sentiment, as well as by Jefferson's conviction that it was to the interest of his country to keep wholly out of this conflict. Thus he was confronted with the problem of both maintaining neutrality and protecting his country's interests in what amounted to a world war.

It may now appear that he was slower than he should have been in recognizing how ruthless the rulers of the contending nations actually were — how indifferent to the rights of others and how inaccessible to reason. He may have sought more assurance and consideration than any neutral could hope to gain during such a war. Convinced that time was his young country's greatest need, he may have been over-disposed to procrastinate. In his efforts to avoid impalement on any of the horns of his successive dilemmas he no doubt gave an impression of indecisiveness. In his final choice of commercial coercion as the best available weapon, he may have erred, as he undoubtedly did with respect to the willingness of some of his countrymen to endure the hardships entailed by the embargo. But no fair judgment of any of his actions can be made without considering the options available to him at the time. In fact these were painfully few, and under existing conditions no one in his position could have been reasonably expected to be fully successful. The only real chance was to mitigate the ills and reduce the dangers that beset his country.

In retelling the story of this administration and its declining fortunes, I have sought, by paying strict regard to chronology and the circumstances attendant on the decisions and actions of this President, to determine as best I can what he did on particular occasions and why he did it. I must confess that even with the benefit of hindsight I have often found it extraordinarily difficult to arrive at a defensible judgment as to what he *ought* to have done, and no one can do more than speculate on what he *could* have done. Besides a stronger impression of his difficulties, I have gained a fresh one of the weakness of his bargaining power vis-à-vis the diplomats of the Old World. Some of this may be attributed to his frequent reference to his desire and that of his countrymen for peace. His expressions were designed in part for domestic consumption, no doubt. I am of the opinion that he never dismissed the possibility of war as a last resort, and I regard his official position as a better reflection of his judgment that war was not a viable option under existing conditions than of any theoretical pacifism. It is abundantly clear, however, that in the foreign offices of Europe the likelihood of American resort to force was adjudged to be remote.

The inadequacy of armed neutrality in the face of British seapower was strikingly illustrated in 1807 when the sea lords bombarded Copenhagen and seized the Danish fleet; and Jefferson's opinion, especially after Trafalgar, that a strong sea-going navy would have been an utter waste was not as silly as certain later enthusiasts for sea-power were to claim.[9] At one stage both Jefferson and Gallatin perceived that additional frigates would have been desirable for defensive purposes; and, although always fearful of a strong naval and military establishment, the President was generally more realistic with respect to national defense than the legislative body as a whole. A very large share of the blame for the unpreparedness of the country must be borne by Congress. But such pressure as he brought to bear on that body was belated, and if he ever thought of armed might as an aid to diplomacy he greatly minimized its value. One may doubt if anything the country could have done, in the last half of his second term, to build up its armed strength would have significantly improved its international situation, but, when seeking to play one great power against the other, as he had done previously and continued to want to do, his hand at the bargaining table would have been strengthened if he had had more to offer. It now appears that, except perhaps in his first years as President, a policy of rigid economy was less imperative than he and his Secretary of the Treasury supposed. He might have rearranged his priorities before his second term began. There is no assurance, however, that he could have got any significant military or naval program through Congress while danger seemed remote and the public

[9] See ch. XXVII, below.

was apathetic; and he was a better judge of what could be hopefully attempted than we at this distance can expect to be. His means of appealing to the public were very limited, and he would unquestionably have been taunted with inconsistency if he had strongly urged preparedness for war while proclaiming the blessings of peace. We need not be at all surprised, therefore, that what was done was so little and so late.

I hope that in my effort to show the increasing difficulties under which Jefferson labored in his second term I have not exaggerated them. It seems to me not far from the truth to say that in the domestic field he was seeking to reconcile the irreconcilable, and in the foreign field to solve the insoluble. On the home front the chasm between the executive and the judiciary was certainly not bridged, but there was grave doubt whether this ought to be; and, while Jefferson regarded the judiciary as obstructive in the case of Aaron Burr, rarely did it affect the ordinary operations of the government. The President was not able to unify the society of the capital despite his dinners and social virtuosity. Yet, while the presidential violinist and the congressional orchestra were not always in harmony, and the resulting concerto was often ragged, their performance as a whole was marked by surprisingly few discords until the final movement and these were somewhat muted even then. It would seem that only a political maestro could have effectively exercised the sort of leadership that Jefferson did. His leadership was distinctly personal; it was not formally recognized, and, because of dominant doctrine and prevailing sentiment, it probably could not have been overt. That it lasted as long as it did may seem surprising. Presidential popularity and power do not often last through eight full years of office. A decline in his political fortunes might have been expected anyway, but the one that actually occurred cannot be dissociated from the unfavorable course of foreign relations and the domestic opposition to the successive and increasingly restrictive embargo laws.

I have given as much attention to the embargo as I very well could without marring the proportions of this narrative, but my account of it makes no pretense of being full-bodied or well rounded. Inevitably the story here must center on the administration. I hope it will contribute something to the understanding of Jefferson's attitude. Since the embargo laws imposed on the economic freedom of individual Americans restrictions such as they had not known since the winning of independence, the policy these laws represented may seem wholly uncharacteristic of Jefferson, who advocated a maximum of individual liberty in all fields. This policy, like all others, should be viewed in its setting of time and circumstance, not in a vacuum. He adopted it in the first place as the only alternative to war or submission. It imposed on his countrymen greater hardships than he had anticipated, but he never ceased to believe that these should be borne in the spirit of patriotism, as supposedly the greater hardships of conventional war would have been. Until almost the last, the policy received overwhelming support in Congress, and in administering the laws he and Gallatin exercised authority that had been specifically given them by legislation. He regarded violators of the regulations as lawbreakers, and had no patience whatever with smugglers and profiteers. Believing the embargo to be a great national enterprise, he regarded those opposed to it as unpatriotic obstructionists. But he sought no restraint on expressions of unfavorable opinion. While limiting freedom of enterprise under what he regarded as wartime conditions, he maintained freedom of speech, which he regarded as of more fundamental importance. He expected too much of patriotism, and he himself did too little to arouse it. He did not allow sufficiently for the self-interest of mortal men, but he never doubted that the government was acting in the national interest.

It has been beyond my purpose to describe and weigh the effects of the embargo on the different sections of the country except as Jefferson became aware of them. To his mind and that of Gallatin direct opposition was largely confined to the Northeast, and it was there that they faced the major problems of enforcement. To a greater degree than I anticipated when I began this study, their difficulties were concentrated in Massachusetts. There were more ships belonging to that state than to any other, and political foes of the administration gained control of the legislature. Jefferson was disposed to blame his troubles chiefly on them. Considering the seacoast of that state, which then included Maine, one would suppose that the enforcement of the embargo there, against an unwilling people, would have been virtually impossible. Through the summer and fall of 1808, however, the government received strong support from members of Jefferson's party in New England, and Gallatin believed that, except for the Canadian border, the embargo was being reasonably well enforced everywhere else. But, before the beginning of the last congressional session of Jefferson's presidency, it appeared to have failed thus far as a measure of economic coercion, since it had had no perceptible effect on the policies of the British and the French against which it was directed.

Any summary of the last months of Jefferson's presidency, which coincided with this session, would rob them of their poignancy. After the election of Madison as his successor, when he was weary and temporarily discouraged, he concluded that he should loosen his grip, and thenceforth he seems to have left the major decisions to others. Opposition to the embargo intensified when an even more stringent law was passed, and the ruling party was weakened thereafter by the defection of many of its northeastern members. Consequently, the congressional leaders decided on a modification of the restrictive policy, and at the last they concurred in the partial repeal of the embargo. Jefferson always regretted that the measure was not retained in full force a little longer, but, to the outward view at least, his policy, though modified, had not been repudiated. Neither had he himself been repudiated by his countrymen, especially in the South and West, but the Legislature had virtually taken over the government and was to continue to dominate it for at least a score of years.

Jefferson's last months in office were anticlimactic; he was unimpressive during them, and his exit was characteristically undramatic. But the sort of leadership he had exercised during more than seven-eighths of his presidency was not to be revived in his lifetime, if it ever was. The power he wielded was to an exceptional degree personal and little institutionalized. This could not be transmitted, nor was it to be expected that his countrymen would look on his like again.

DUMAS MALONE

Alderman Library
University of Virginia
June, 1973

Chronology

1805

Mar. 4   TJ is inaugurated President for the second time.

11   He gives James Wilkinson an *ad interim* appointment as governor of the Territory of Louisiana.

14   He leaves Washington for Monticello.

Apr. 17   He returns to Washington.

During the month Aaron Burr begins a western tour.

June   During the month Gilbert Stuart paints the Edgehill portrait and the Medallion profile of TJ.

July 1   TJ privately acknowledges improper conduct toward Mrs. John Walker and denies all other charges of immorality.

13   He receives reports from Lewis and Clark on their journey up the Missouri.

15   He leaves Washington for Monticello.

25   James and Dolley Madison leave for Philadelphia, where she has medical treatment.

26   TJ leaves Monticello for a brief visit to Poplar Forest.

During the month "Queries" respecting Aaron Burr's purposes appear in the newspapers.

Aug. 7   TJ offers John Breckinridge appointment as attorney general.

By this date he is aware of the failure of Monroe's mission to Spain.

22   "Vindication of Mr. Jefferson" begins in the Richmond *Enquirer*.

Sept. 6   TJ is informed of the peace treaty with Tripoli (dated June 4).

24   By this date Madison is aware of the alarming seizures under the *Essex* decision (May 22).

During the month the Dearborns are guests at Monticello.

Oct. 3   TJ arrives in Washington from Monticello.

21   The battle of Trafalgar is fought (reported in Washington about Dec. 20).

James Stephen's pamphlet, *War in Disguise,* appears in England about this time (sent to America by Monroe on Nov. 1).

23   By this time TJ has given up the idea of a British alliance.

Late in the month, Madison returns to Washington from Philadelphia.

Dec. 3   Napoleon defeats a Russo-Austrian army at Austerlitz.

TJ sends his fifth annual message to Congress.

5   By this date his daughter Martha is in Washington for the winter.

6   He submits a confidential message on Spain.
    General Miranda comes to Washington.

1806

Jan. 16   The two-million-dollar bill passes the House.

17   TJ sends Congress a special message on neutral commerce.
     James Madison Randolph is born in the President's House.

23   William Pitt dies in England.

27   The Senate consents to James Wilkinson's appointment as governor of Louisiana Territory.

29   The Gregg Resolution is presented in the House.

Feb. 6   TJ sends Congress a confidential message on Great Britain.

7   The two-million-dollar bill passes the Senate.

8   TJ receives a letter from Joseph H. Daveiss about intrigues with the Spanish.

10   The Ministry of All Talents, with Fox as foreign secretary, is formed in Great Britain.
     The Nicholson Resolutions are presented in the House.

Mar. 5   A speech of John Randolph in the House opens a breach with the administration.

17   John Armstrong's appointment as commissioner to treat with Spain (along with James Bowdoin) is confirmed by the vote of the Vice President.

20   TJ sends Congress a special message on Spanish boundaries.

29   The act authorizing construction of the Cumberland Road is approved.

Apr. 12   The Senate consents to the treaty with Tripoli.

15   TJ makes a memorandum of his conversation with Burr a month earlier.

18   TJ approves the non-importation bill.

19   He nominates James Monroe and William Pinkney as commissioners to Great Britain.

21   First session of Ninth Congress ends.
     About this time the Connecticut libel cases begin.

May 3   TJ drafts a proclamation concerning the *Leander*.

6   He leaves Washington for Monticello.

June 7   He returns to Washington.
         He learns of the poisoning of his old mentor, George Wythe, who dies the next day.

23   He urges Thomas Mann Randolph not to engage in a duel with John Randolph.

July 15   Captain Zebulon M. Pike sets out on an expedition to the Southwest.

21   TJ leaves Washington for Monticello.

Aug. 15   The first of John Randolph's "Decius letters" appears.
          In the latter part of the month TJ is at Poplar Forest.

Sept. 13 Charles James Fox dies in England.

During the month TJ receives the first credible news of the Burr conspiracy.

Oct. 4 He returns to Washington from Monticello.

22–25 The Cabinet deliberates on the actions and purposes of Aaron Burr.

24 TJ learns of the arrival of Lewis and Clark in St. Louis (Sept. 23). Several weeks earlier he had learned of the failure of the Freeman expedition up the Red River.

Nov. 3 David M. Erskine, successor to Anthony Merry as the British minister, is presented to TJ.

5 General Wilkinson signs the "neutral-ground" agreement with Colonel Herrera.

21 Napoleon issues the Berlin decree, beginning his Continental System.

25 TJ receives communications from Wilkinson revealing a projected expedition against the territories of Spain. He holds a meeting with his Cabinet. Wilkinson reaches New Orleans.

27 TJ issues a proclamation warning against an illegal expedition against Spanish possessions.

Dec. 2 He sends his sixth annual message to Congress.

3 He sends a special message to Congress on Great Britain.

5 A Kentucky grand jury denies a true bill against Burr.

9 On orders of the Governor of Ohio, boats and supplies for Burr's expedition are seized at Blennerhassett's Island.

27 Burr joins the expedition at the mouth of the Cumberland.

28 Meriwether Lewis arrives in Washington.

31 The Monroe-Pinkney treaty is signed in England.

During the winter, TJ receives many requests that he accept a third term as President.

1807

Jan. 7 British Orders in Council are issued, closing coastal trade between French ports and forbidding neutral ships to trade in ports closed to the British.

16 TJ nominates Caesar A. Rodney as attorney general.

17 Burr surrenders to the civil authorities in Mississippi Territory.

22 Unaware of this, TJ sends Congress a special message on Burr.

23 Bollman and Swartwout, Burr's agents, reach Washington in military custody.

The Senate passes a bill suspending the writ of habeas corpus for three months in certain cases (defeated in the House).

Feb. 2 The Cabinet reaffirms the position of the administration regarding impressment.

6 TJ receives the text of Napoleon's Berlin decree.

10 TJ sends Congress a special message on gunboats.

11 He replies to citizens of Hartford about libel cases.

21 The Supreme Court discharges Bollman and Swartwout.

Mar. 2   The act prohibiting the importation of slaves after Jan. 1, 1808, is approved.

       The Senate by resolution asks Gallatin to prepare a report on roads and canals.

   3   Second session of the Ninth Congress ends.

       A copy of the Monroe-Pinkney treaty reaches the British minister, Erskine, and is transmitted to TJ (original is received Mar. 15).

  31   The Portland ministry, with George Canning as foreign secretary, assumes authority in England.

Apr. 7   TJ leaves Washington for Monticello.

May 16   He returns to Washington.

  20   Madison sends fresh instructions to Monroe and Pinkney.

  22   The trial of Aaron Burr begins in Richmond.

  29   TJ acknowledges the receipt of a medal for his moldboard.

June 11   He writes John Norvell about newspapers.

  14   The French army defeats Russians and Prussians at Friedland.

  15   A subpoena, ordered by the court on the motion of Burr, is served on TJ.

  22   The *Leopard-Chesapeake* affair occurs (reported in Washington, June 25; in London, July 25).

July 2   TJ issues his *Chesapeake* proclamation.

   7   Napoleon and Tsar Alexander I agree to the treaties of Tilsit.

  31   TJ calls Congress to meet Oct. 26.

Aug. 1   He leaves Washington for Monticello.

  26   A court-martial is held at Halifax on seamen taken from the *Chesapeake*.

  31   Monroe receives instructions about the *Chesapeake*.

Sept. 1   Burr is acquitted of treason.

   7   Copenhagen capitulates after British bombardment.

  15   Burr is acquitted of misdemeanor.

  18   An official French statement is made that the Berlin decree applies to neutral vessels without exception.

Oct. 3   TJ returns to Washington.

  16   In England, a royal proclamation calling for vigorous impressment is issued.

  27   TJ sends Congress his seventh annual message.

Nov. 3–4   Demonstrations against Burr occur in Baltimore.

  11   British Orders in Council, declaring a blockade of the Continent, are issued.

  19   France invades Portugal.

  23   TJ sends Congress a copy of the proceedings in the trial of Burr.

  30   By this date he is informed of the British position on the *Chesapeake* affair.

       About this time the Portuguese King and fleet escape Napoleon.

Dec. 7   TJ sends a confidential message to Congress on the *Chesapeake* affair.

  10   He explicitly states that he will not serve another term as President.

14 The Non-Importation Act goes into effect.
    By this date the administration is aware that the Berlin decree
    is being applied to the United States.
17 Napoleon issues his Milan decree.
18 TJ recommends an embargo to Congress; Congress authorizes
    188 gunboats.
22 The embargo is approved.
    James Monroe reaches Washington.
31 In the House, John Randolph introduces a resolution calling for
    inquiry into the conduct of General Wilkinson.

1808

Jan. 1 The prohibition of the importation of slaves becomes effective.
      2 A court of inquiry into the conduct of General Wilkinson is
         initiated, though no public announcement is made.
      9 An act supplementary to the Embargo Act is approved.
     13 George H. Rose arrives in Washington from England to nego-
         tiate about the *Chesapeake*.
     23 A Republican congressional caucus nominates Madison for
         President and Clinton for Vice President.
Feb. 2 TJ transmits to Congress the British Orders in Council of Nov.
         11, 1807.
     11 A bill to punish treason is introduced in the Senate.
     27 An act supplementary to the Non-Importation Act is approved.
Mar. 2 A bill to punish conspiracies to commit treason is introduced
         in the House.
      7 TJ sends Congress a message on public defense.
     12 The act in addition to the Embargo Act is approved.
     17 TJ reports Napoleon's Milan decree to Congress.
     21 Timothy Pickering's letter attacking the embargo is reported in
         Washington.
     22 Following the failure of the Rose mission, TJ sends Congress a
         special message on British negotiations.
     25 TJ transmits the report of the Surveyors of Public Buildings,
         which leads to severe criticism of a deficit.
Apr. 3 He reports ten days of headache.
      6 A bill to punish treason is passed by the House.
         Gallatin's report on roads and canals is communicated to the
         Senate.
     19 TJ issues a proclamation calling for enforcement of the embargo
         laws on Lake Champlain.
     22 The act authorizing the President to suspend the embargo is
         approved.
     25 The act to enforce the embargo is approved.
         The first session of the Tenth Congress ends.
May   6 TJ leaves Washington for Monticello.
June 10 He returns to Washington.
     23 John Quincy Adams resigns his seat in the Senate.

	28	Wilkinson is exonerated by a court of inquiry (verdict is approved by TJ on July 2).
July	20	TJ leaves Washington for Monticello.
		About the same time Gallatin goes to New York, whence he views the operations of the embargo in the Northeast.
Aug.	26	TJ begins to reply to petitions from New England towns against the embargo.
Sept.	17	His granddaughter, Anne Cary Randolph, is married to Charles Lewis Bankhead at Monticello.
Oct.	22	He arrives in Washington accompanied by his grandson, Thomas Jefferson Randolph, who soon proceeds to school in Philadelphia.
	29	He receives word that the American diplomatic overtures have been rebuffed by Britain and ignored by France.
Nov.	7	Second session of the Tenth Congress begins.
	8	TJ sends his eighth annual message to Congress.
	18	Beginning with this date TJ is confined to the house with a diseased jaw for six weeks.
	21	By or before this date the election of Madison as President is assured.
	22	G. W. Campbell submits report on foreign relations to the House (debated Nov. 28–Dec. 17).
Dec.	8	Senator Giles reports a bill "making further provision for enforcing the embargo."

1809

Jan.	6	The House after an all-night meeting passes the embargo enforcement bill. TJ signs the law on Jan. 9.
		Formal protests against embargo policy increase in New England during this month and February.
	30	Debate begins in the House on the Nicholas resolution.
		The act is approved altering the time for the next meeting of Congress to the fourth Monday of May.
Feb.	3	The House approves the first clause of the Nicholas resolution, recommending that the embargo be repealed on March 4. The second clause, which recommends letters of marque and reprisal, is defeated on Feb. 7.
	21	A bill to interdict commercial intercourse with Britain and France is passed in the Senate.
	24	The House amends the non-intercourse bill, striking out its provisions for letters of marque and reprisal. The next day, it further amends the bill, postponing the partial repeal of the embargo from March 4 to March 15.
	27	Nomination of William Short as minister to Russia is rejected by the Senate.
	28	The act is approved freeing from postage all letters and packets to TJ.

Mar. *1*   TJ signs the act to interdict commercial intercourse with Britain
            and France.

    4   Madison is inaugurated President.

      The Tenth Congress adjourns.

  11   TJ leaves Washington for Monticello, arriving March 15.

  15   Embargo laws are repealed except as they relate to Britain and
            France, and their dependencies.

In Public and Private

[I]

Presidential Re-entry

WHEN Thomas Jefferson was inaugurated as President of the United States for the second time — on Monday, March 4, 1805 — the echoes of the impeachment trial of Justice Samuel Chase, which ended on the previous Friday, had not yet died away. And the capital city was still talking of the extraordinary valedictory of Aaron Burr on Saturday, which had reduced the senators to breathless silence and left many a strong man in tears.[1] The acquittal of the Justice was far more dramatic and the exit of the Vice President much more moving than the re-entry of the President, which had so long been taken as a matter of course. Though he had received, only a few months before this, an electoral majority that was not to be matched by any successor of his for upwards of a century, he entered upon his second term under rather unpropitious circumstances. His inauguration would have been a more triumphal occasion if it had occurred in January, as is the case today. Apart from the inaugural address, the occasion and the meetings in celebration of it in other places received relatively little attention in the newspapers, which continued for weeks to be filled with details of the Chase trial.[2]

The President could hardly have wished that his inauguration should be thus overshadowed, but, disliking ceremony as he did, he undoubtedly wanted it to be unpretentious — as it unquestionably was. He did not walk to the Capitol from his nearby lodgings as he had done four years before, but on his ride from the President's House a mile away, he was accompanied by only his secretary and a groom. He took the

[1] Burr's address was well described by Senator S. L. Mitchill in a letter of Mar. 2, 1805, to his wife (*Harper's New Monthly Mag.*, LVIII [1878–79], 749–750). The Chase trial is described in *Jefferson the President: First Term*, pp. 458–483.

[2] *National Intelligencer*, Mar. 13, 20, 1805, spoke regretfully of the necessity of omitting details of these celebrations. It gave few descriptive details about the inauguration itself.

oath of office from Chief Justice Marshall and delivered his address in a crowded Senate chamber, but no quorum of either House was present. By or shortly before half past nine on the previous night, Congress had adjourned *sine die* after the stormiest and most unproductive session of his administration thus far. At its end the President himself, according to his custom, was in a committee room in the North Wing signing bills. Before noon on Monday the congressional exodus was well under way.[3]

There was no spectacle to miss and little to hear, for Jefferson's second inaugural address, like his first, turned out to be only partly audible. Commentators should have made some allowance for the poor acoustics of the chamber, but the President spoke in a low voice. He had once expressed satisfaction at being able to pursue a noiseless course; he was virtually doing that now, wittingly or unwittingly. But the address, printed in advance of its delivery by the *National Intelligencer* as his first one had been, was quickly available, and it was better read than listened to anyway. No doubt it was read afterwards by many of the President's auditors, but in the meantime everybody proceeded by common accord to the big house at the other end of the unpaved road known as Pennsylvania Avenue to pay him compliment. A young British diplomat, more sympathetic than his superior, Anthony Merry, noted with apparent approval that Jefferson was dressed in black, with black silk stockings, and was in high spirits. But this aristocratic and by no means uncritical observer described the company as very mixed and some of it as uncouth, while in his view the procession on the road was composed of "low persons."[4] This had been formed in the Navy Yard by the mechanics there, who presented the President with an address of congratulation. They expressed gratitude that they lived in a land "where the honest industry of the mechanic is equally supported with the splendor of the wealthy."[5] The support of such "low persons," who regarded the President as the symbol and champion of the liberty and equality they prized, undoubtedly gratified him far more than the grudging plaudits of a foreign observer could have.

Outside Washington the details of the day's happenings may have been little known, for they were not extensively reported. More was said, in newspapers and private letters, about the inaugural address, but

---

[3] Senator Plumer took the mail stage at 11 P.M. on Sunday and rode northward all night (Mar. 3, 1805; *Memorandum*, p. 315). J. Q. Adams described the end of the session in his *Memoirs*, I, 370.

[4] A. J. Foster, in *Jeffersonian America* (1954), p. 15.

[5] Address dated Mar. 4, 1805 (LC, 23739).

this attracted no such attention as the one delivered by Jefferson four years earlier, and it has no such historical significance.[6] The author himself described it as an account of performance, rather than a statement of profession and promise. His critics now taunted him, as in fact they had long been doing, with failure to live up to his own declaration that his fellow citizens were all republicans, all federalists — a saying they interpreted as a promise that no member of their own party should be removed from office except for malfeasance. The justice or injustice of this allegation can be determined only in the light of the policy of removals and appointments, which we have discussed at length in the previous volume and which should be viewed on the background of the intense political partisanship of the times on both sides.[7] It seems safe to say that on the whole the President, harassed by both friends and foes, had conducted himself with wisdom and moderation while maintaining high standards of administration.

That he had reduced taxes and practiced economy while preserving the peace could not be denied. He touched on foreign affairs only lightly in his address, and could not have been expected to admit that he had been lucky. We can now see that his luck had already begun to turn, though few of his political enemies appear to have recognized the trend as yet. The maintenance of peace with honor was to prove more difficult and more costly in his second term than in his first. He did not boast of the acquisition of Louisiana, as he would have been warranted in doing. Instead, he recognized the apprehensions of some that the enlargement of the nation's territories would endanger the Union. "But," he asked, "who can limit the extent to which the federative principle may operate effectively? The larger our association, the less will it be shaken by local passions; and in any view, is it not better that the opposite bank of the Mississippi should be settled by our own brethren and children, than by strangers of another family?" He spoke as a nationalist against the localists, making no attempt to foresee the ultimate effect of the settlement of the trans-Mississippi region on the position and power of the old states. Actually, he was trying to facilitate settlement east of the river by encouraging the Indians to move to the west of it.

In this address he devoted what he himself recognized as dispropor-

[6] The inaugural address of Mar. 4, 1805, with TJ's own notes and memoranda from Madison, dated Feb. 8 and 21, is in Ford, VIII, 341–348. Various drafts by TJ are in LC, 25711–25716; 27135. Gallatin's remarks of Feb. 12, 1805, are in his Writings, I, 227–228.

[7] See, especially, ch. V of Jefferson the President: First Term. A good example of recurrent criticism is provided by the discussion of the President's speech in Washington Federalist, Mar. 13, 1805.

tionate attention to the Indians. His policies with respect to them cannot be divorced from considerations of national defense and the interests of white settlers, and they may seem irreconcilable with his claim that the sad history of the aborigines had inspired in him commiseration for them. But few of his American contemporaries were so deeply interested in the Indians over so long a period as he, if indeed anybody was; and, while seeking to effect the peaceful removal of as many of them as he could before the irresistible tide of white settlement should engulf them, he had followed a supplementary policy aimed at preparing them for the settled agricultural life he regarded as necessary for their survival. He wanted to make citizens of them in the end and was seeking to "humanize" his fellows toward them. In discussing their plight and problems on this occasion, however, he had an ulterior motive. By condemning hostility to them and obstructions to their progress toward civilization, he sought by inference to condemn antisocial and unprogressive attitudes of which he disapproved but which he preferred not to attack directly. This oblique approach may not commend itself to the present-day reader, but the end result was one of the most striking condemnations of the ultra-conservative mind he ever penned, and as such it marks a contrast with his customary public moderation. Speaking of "crafty individuals" who, to maintain their own position in the existing order, imposed obstacles to necessary changes in Indian society, he drew a pen picture which approaches timelessness and universality:

> These persons inculcate a sanctimonious reverence for the customs of their ancestors; that whatsoever they did, must be done through all time; that reason is a false guide, and to advance under its counsel, in their physical, moral, or political condition, is perilous innovation; that their duty is to remain as their Creator made them, ignorance being safety, and knowledge full of danger; in short, my friends, among them [the Indians] is seen the action and counteraction of good sense and bigotry; they, too, have their anti-philosophers, who find an interest in keeping things in their present state, who dread reformation, and exert all their faculties to maintain the ascendency of habit over the duty of improving our reason, and obeying its mandates.

This passage, in which he set reason above tradition and appeared as a thinly disguised champion of progressive change, created little noise, but the contrast between Jefferson's bold words and prudent actions was not lost on his political enemies of that time, and it offered them ground to charge him with hypocrisy. To resolve all the apparent contradictions in this complicated man would be difficult indeed, and he would lose much of his fascination if reduced to stark simplicity, but a distinction can be made between what John Marshall referred to as the "general cast" of his political and social theory and his working philosophy as a responsible statesman. The latter he well summed up in a private observation at the beginning of his presidency, that "no more good must be attempted than the nation can bear."[8] His zeal for reform and progress was tempered by his assessment of the actualities of a particular situation. By the same token, he has been described as both a visionary and an opportunist. Since both of these terms are in ill repute we hesitate to apply either of them, but they suggest qualities commonly found in elected officials in varying proportions. Like others, Jefferson oscillated between the two extremes. Mistakes in judgment were to be expected of him as of everybody else, and in the pursuit of immediate objectives he may at times have lost sight of long-range goals. Interpreters may be expected to differ about the precise proportions in the mixture, but his statecraft was marked on the one hand by rare vision and on the other by unusual sensitivity to public opinion and by extraordinary patience.

His patience may be attributed in part to his congenital optimism and his unshakable confidence that time was fighting on the side of the causes he most valued. But he had schooled himself in self-restraint, disciplining his exuberant imagination and generally denying himself in public the extravagances of speech he not infrequently indulged in private. Early in this year, John Quincy Adams, after dining with him, noted that his "itch for telling prodigies" was unabated — that he actually knew better but loved to excite wonder.[9] He appears to have enjoyed pulling the leg of the humorless New Englander. He might have found wicked pleasure also in shocking certain hostile clergymen whom he regarded as self-righteous and self-seeking and on whom he vented his wrath in private letters. When charged with being an infidel, it was hard for him not to dilate on the dangers of clerical influence in affairs of state. Among the passages in his speech that he toned down for prudential reasons on the advice of Gallatin was the one dealing with religion. In this he contented himself with saying that his government, in accordance with the Constitution, had had nothing to do with religion. He made no mention of the specific things that he as President had refrained from doing — such as proclaiming a Thanksgiving Day. Nor did he make public reference here or anywhere else

[8] See *Jefferson the President: First Term*, pp. 22, 27.

[9] Jan. 11, 1805 (*Memoirs*, I, 330–331), referring particularly to TJ's report of an incredibly cold winter in Paris.

to his personal generosity to religious groups. This was well exemplified in the next few months, when he subscribed liberally to the building funds of Presbyterian, Baptist, and Episcopal churches in the Washington district.

The counsel of Gallatin and Madison may also have caused him to moderate his comments on the licentiousness of the press. The three paragraphs he devoted to the press and its freedom constitute the most eloquent section of his speech and the part of it that has been most quoted. Since we have already discussed this in connection with specific attacks on him and the reaction to these, we need say little about Jefferson's famous utterance here beyond reminding the reader of its immediate setting.[10] He claimed with what appeared to be sufficient warrant that his countrymen, by pronouncing their verdict at the polls, had shown that his government could not be "written down by falsehood and defamation." But, judging from their actions, his assailants had not learned that lesson. Hostile newspapers had been firing at him furiously since the electorate had overwhelmingly approved his administration, and the reverberations had not died away by the time of the inauguration. The malicious charges originally made by James Thomson Callender had been exhumed in Massachusetts and exhibited in the legislature there amid the gloatings of the Federalist press.[11] No one of these charges bore on Jefferson's conduct as President; all were directed against his character and morals, and nearly all related to events of a score of years before. In irrelevance and indecency this exhibition is probably without parallel in presidential history.

Almost always Jefferson followed a policy of ignoring personal attacks, and if he was tempted to depart from it on this occasion, Gallatin and Madison counseled otherwise. He made no reference to private morals, nor did he intimate that the attacks on his own character reflected the desperation of foes who had been unable to assail him effectively on public grounds. He did say that the "artillery of the press" had been leveled against the administration with the purpose of disturbing it. Obviously he was referring to the Federalist newspapers, the most partisan of which had often appeared to be obstructive. The charge of licentiousness that he made was no exaggeration, though in times past it could have been as appropriately applied to certain Republican papers, and actually it was being applied to William Duane of the *Aurora* by members of his own party at that very time. This was an era of journalistic irresponsibility as well as of extreme political partisanship.

10 See *Jefferson the President: First Term*, pp. 233–235.
11 *Ibid.*, pp. 206–220, with references.

Though Jefferson was not and could not have been expected to be a disinterested observer of this scene, he spoke as a timeless philosopher when he said: "These abuses of an institution so important to freedom and science, are deeply to be regretted, inasmuch as they tend to lessen its usefulness, and to sap its safety." His advocacy of freedom for the press was subject to certain qualifications. He believed that falsehood and defamation could and should be punished under state laws. But he claimed that his administration, conducting itself with zeal and purity in the true spirit of the Constitution, had left discussion wholly free, relying not on governmental power but on the force of public opinion. Essentially, his claim was warranted, and up to this point the experiment had been successful. He noted it, therefore, as proof that

> since truth and reason have maintained their ground against false opinions in league with false facts, the press, confined to truth, needs no other legal restraint; the public judgment will correct false reasonings and opinions, on a full hearing of all parties; and no other definite line can be drawn between the inestimable liberty of the press and its demoralizing licentiousness. If there be still improprieties which this rule would not restrain, its supplement must be sought in the censorship of public opinion.

This can be best regarded as an expression of faith — a faith which was to be tested further in a period of continuing journalistic irresponsibility and increasing disillusionment.

Jefferson made no mention here of his determination that his second term as President should be his last. Judging from an early draft of his address, he was disposed at one time to refer to it, but Madison and Gallatin disliked the idea and he dropped it. Shortly after the election, John Taylor of Caroline urged his continuance in office. So did John Tyler after the inauguration, and John Randolph said in semi-jest that Jefferson was "again seated in the saddle for four years, with a prospect of reelection for life."[12] Following the counsel of his friends, the President had made no public announcement, but he let his intentions be known in private. Therefore, rumors of them spread and, according to the sagacious Speaker of the House, these were pleasing to the Federalists, who believed the Republicans could not agree upon a

[12] Tyler to TJ, Mar. 17, 1805 (LC, 25789–25790); John Randolph to J. H. Nicholson, Apr. 30, 1805 (Nicholson Papers). Taylor's letter of Dec. 26, 1804 (LC, 25334), and TJ's reply of Jan. 6, 1805 (Ford, VIII, 338–340), have been previously referred to.

successor.[13] The Federalists continued to believe this, and, while unable to capitalize on Republican dissension to the degree they hoped, they rightly recognized that no one could approach Jefferson in ability to hold the discordant party together. At a Fourth of July celebration, he was toasted by an admirer as "the brightest star in the heaven of republicanism," and he might have been described as the sun in this particular celestial system.[14] John Randolph, who was in a pessimistic frame of mind after the congressional session and recognized little merit beyond his own, feared that the enemies of the man and his principles would take advantage of "the easy credulity of his temper." There was little ground for the assertion of Gouverneur Morris that the President's supporters realized his "incapacity," although that critic approached the truth when he said the party had no one else to run.[15] Such had been the case in the last three presidential elections, and it might still be so in the next one.

John Taylor presented less partisan and more philosophical arguments when he urged Jefferson's continuance, describing objectives in terms highly congenial to that gentleman himself. These, he said, were "to subdue tyranny by intellect," and to exhibit republicanism to the world in an experiment that was "fair, full and final." To Taylor, as to Jefferson, this was an experiment in limited and moderate government, with prime emphasis on the individual and (more in his case than Jefferson's) on the states. He did not want its success to be hazarded and saw no one else into whose hands he would willingly commit it. Like John Randolph, though not to the same degree, he distrusted Madison.

In the flush of his electoral victory, when declining the diadem which, in John Taylor's opinion, was his for the asking, Jefferson had said:

> The danger is that the indulgence & attachments of the people will keep a man in the chair after he becomes a dotard, that re-election through life shall become habitual, & election for life follow that. Genl. Washington set the example of voluntary retirement after 8 years. I shall follow it, and a few more precedents will oppose the obstacle of habit to anyone after a while who shall endeavor to extend his term. Perhaps it may beget a disposition to establish it by an amendment to the constitution.

13 Nathaniel Macon to J. H. Nicholson, June 7, 1805 (Nicholson Papers).
14 Toast of July 4, 1805, in Jefferson's Scrapbook (UVA).
15 June 2, 1805 (*Diary and Letters*, II [1888], 465–466).

The present-day reader may not be aware of the full significance of the analogy with George Washington. Jefferson and Madison believed that the first President suffered a diminution of his powers *before* his retirement, which was at a lesser age than Jefferson himself would reach by the end of his second term. At sixty-two in the spring of 1805, he was in excellent health; but, while his difficulties thereafter may provide a sufficient explanation, his effectiveness declined. He gave the impression, soon after his re-election, that he could count on popular support for another term if he wanted it. But he could conceive of only one circumstance that would induce him to continue in office: the prospect of the succession of a monarchist — that is, of an ultra-Federalist — and he regarded the eventuality as unthinkable.

He had other reasons for desiring relief than fear of dotage. Few public men ever disliked discord more, or strove more consistently to compose it, but he had recognized long since that there could be no quarter between him and Federalist irreconcilables and, somewhat more recently, that dissension might be expected to increase among Republicans as they assumed unquestionable preponderance. Hitherto he had been virtually invulnerable within his own party, both because of his indispensability and his wise abstention from local and factional disputes, but the danger of being caught between two fires was growing and the painfulness of his position as head of the party might be expected to increase. While never ceasing to deplore intra-party dissension, he recognized its inevitability and as a rule viewed it with philosophic calm. Apparently he thought that if he could not compose it he could endure it during one more term, but a man of his temperament could not have been expected to do so any longer than he had to.

Since the continued personal attacks on him by his irreconcilable foes could be attributed to desperation, they were relatively undisturbing from the political point of view. But they rankled all the more because of their irrelevance, impropriety, and unfairness. They were particularly shocking to Jefferson, not only because he was in fact a highly moral man, but also because he made a sharp distinction between public and private matters and regarded the latter as an improper subject of public discussion. He does not appear to have referred, even in private letters, to the carnal sins of Hamilton, which John Adams denounced so vehemently;[16] and such criticisms of his presidential predecessors as he voiced or approved related to their official conduct, not their personal characters — which in fact he highly esteemed.

[16] On his attitude towards the Hamilton-Reynolds affair, see *Jefferson and the Ordeal of Liberty*, pp. 330–331.

Certain comments of his in private letters, early in his second term, revealed more fully than any public utterance the pain he suffered from the attacks on his personal morals and opinions. He appeared to be more sensitive than he had been when Callender first launched the scurrilous charges which had been so recently revived for such unmistakable partisan purposes. Sadly disillusioned, this exponent of rationality who deeply cherished personal privacy had come to regard personal abuse as one of the perquisites of his office. Responding to a letter of congratulation from a friendly clergyman, living in a notably hostile district, he remarked that the administrators of the government must submit to a "fiery ordeal" — that "their character must be offered on the altar of the public good."[17] He was especially appreciative of support from ministers in New England because he was so often denounced from pulpits there. At just this time the Reverend William Bentley of Salem was recording in his diary that Mr. Parish (whom he called "the mean little Parish") of Newburyport had calumniated the President in a sermon and that his invective was to be reprinted, since the Federalists had found that they profited much from "pulpit declamations." The President might have been gratified if he had known that Bentley thought the cleric in question deserving of a sound whipping, and he would unquestionably have found a later entry in this diary extremely interesting: "I am informed that my friendship for Mr. Jefferson will subject me to great evils."[18] The New Englander knew that he would be accused of defending an immoral infidel.

Among the bitterest comments of Jefferson on the personal attacks to which he had been subjected were those made by him to a Republican leader in Massachusetts who, as he correctly predicted, was destined to become governor of that Commonwealth when it had been restored to "the general body of the nation." After congratulating James Sullivan on the advance already made, he said:

You have indeed received the federal [i.e. Federalist] unction of lying & slandering. But who has not? Who will ever again come into eminent office, unanointed with this chrism? It seems to be fixed that falsehood & calumny are to be their ordinary engines of opposition; engines which will not be entirely without effect. The circle of characters equal to the first stations is not too large, & will be lessened by the voluntary retreat of those whose sensibilities are stronger than their confidence in the justice of public

17 TJ to Rev. Thomas Allen of Pittsfield, Mass., Mar. 12, 1805 (LC, 25767).
18 William Bentley, Diary, III (1911), entry of Sept. 20, 1805. Entries of Mar. 3, 10, 19, and Apr. 14, 1805, bear on the actions and merits of Mr. Parish.

opinion. I certainly have known, & still know, characters eminently qualified for the most exalted trusts, who could not bear
up against the brutal hackings & hewings of these heroes of Bil-
lingsgate. I may say, from intimate knolege, that we should have
lost the services of the greatest character of our country, had he
been assailed with the degree of abandoned licentiousness now
practised. The torture he felt under rare & slight attacks, proved
that under those of which the federal [Federalist] bands have
shewn themselves capable, he would have thrown up the helm in
a burst of indignation.[19]

He was correct in saying that the attacks on George Washington
were relatively rare, but some of them could not properly be described
as slight. Had Jefferson conveniently forgotten what Benjamin Franklin Bache and Thomas Paine had said? He would have been on safer
ground if he had declared that he himself had been subjected to far
more attacks than the first President and that these had been far more
personal. Also, he could have safely predicted that Washington would
never have endured equivalent punishment from either Federalists or
Republicans. As a party leader — which Washington never was — he
was absolving his own partisans and blaming his enemies, who at this
particular time were in fact highly censurable. Also, he was seeking to
encourage the faithful in a region where they were still in the minority. Continuing, he said:

Yet this effect of sensibility must not be yielded to. If we suffer
ourselves to be frightened from our post by mere lying, surely
the enemy will use that weapon; for what one so cheap to those
of whose system of politics morality makes no part? The patriot,
like the Christian, must learn that to bear revilings & persecutions
is a part of his duty; and in proportion as the trial is severe, firmness under it becomes more requisite & praiseworthy. It requires,
indeed, self-command.

Despite the unquestionable persecution to which followers of his
were subjected in certain regions where his political enemies were
most strongly entrenched, the parallel he drew between New England
Republicans and Christian martyrs does not commend itself to posterity. In the light of generations of American history we can readily
perceive that in the struggle for the control of government, which is
the essence of politics, contenders on both sides don the mantle of
patriotism and the armor of self-righteousness. Also, our history seems

[19] TJ to James Sullivan, May 21, 1805 (Ford, VIII, 354–356).

to warrant the observation that a President who is the major symbol and recognized leader of a party is more exposed to attack than an administrator of more neutral hue. Jefferson, who belongs in the former category, could no more have escaped attack than he could have avoided ambivalence. And his psychological difficulties were accentuated by his unwillingness to admit, or his inability to perceive, that he was playing a dual role which was in fact without American precedent. Despite the occasional extravagance of his language in private letters he played his political role with restraint, generally exerting a moderating influence within his party while keeping out of sight. He was the most conspicuous figure on the political horizon, nevertheless, and by fair means or foul his political enemies sought to bring him down. Specifically, the partisan attacks on his personal as well as his public character that had been widely publicized in the winter were renewed in the summer after his second inauguration.

One of his Baptist supporters in New England, Elder John Leland, memorable for his association with the "mammoth cheese," remarked in an oration on the Fourth of July that all the President's misdeeds, as recently alleged in Massachusetts, fell between the years 1776 and 1791 — a period when he himself was living in Virginia at no great distance from Monticello. Yet he had never heard of any of them until he read about them in the Federalist newspapers, and he regarded the testimony of James Thomson Callender as insufficient evidence.[20] Though Jefferson had a few neighbors whom he regarded as hostile and malicious, his reputation in his own locality was almost as exalted as his house. Nevertheless, there had been some talk of the Walker affair before Callender first publicized it, as Jefferson himself reported. He assigned the episode to the period before his own marriage, and apparently his neighbors had virtually forgotten it until it was indecently exhumed for political ends. The disinterment and exhibition of it in the legislature of Massachusetts during the winter had served no public purpose and was actually inhumane. Reviving a personal quarrel which seemingly had been settled months before, it brought fresh pain to the persons most involved. The episode was again being publicized when Jefferson wrote a private letter to one of his department heads in which he admitted the impropriety of his conduct toward Mrs. Walker as a young man, while flatly denying all the other charges of immorality that had been brought against him.[21] There appears to be

20 Speech of July 4, 1805, at Cheshire, Mass., birthplace of the famous cheese (Leland's *Writings*, p. 286).

21 TJ to Robert Smith, July 1, 1805 (Bixby, pp. 114–115). For details and further references bearing on the Walker affair, see *Jefferson the President: First Term*, ch. XII.

no record of his ever having made specific mention of the grossest of the latter, relating to an alleged slave mistress, and this seems to be the only reference to the Walker affair from his own pen that has survived. It should not be supposed that, even in this case, he was confessing to all he had been accused of, and in the absence of detailed information we are left in doubt as to the precise nature of his offense. But he was admitting to the members of his official family not previously in his confidence that his conduct had been improper. Beyond that he did not go. In connection with a personal episode of a former generation, this grandfather recognized no obligation on him or his "particular friends" to take any sort of public action.

Within a few weeks, however, Thomas Ritchie published in the Richmond *Enquirer* a powerful defense of him, entitled "Vindication of Mr. Jefferson."[22] The immediate occasion for this was the publication, in a Boston paper and elsewhere, of a letter from a Virginian named Thomas Turner. Written in response to certain "interrogatories," the letter seemed to substantiate the charges against the President's private and public character that had been discussed in the legislature of Massachusetts. Of Ritchie's seven installments only the last bore upon the question of personal morals. Primarily concerned with Federalist allegations that had better claim to relevance, he gave chief attention to Jefferson's conduct as chief executive of Virginia during the American Revolution. Turner asserted that Jefferson timidly abandoned the seat of government during Arnold's invasion of the state and was a "dastardly traitor" at the time of Tarleton's raid, when he fled precipitately from Monticello.[23] Such allegations had not been made at the time of the events themselves, but they had been current in Federalist circles since the campaign of 1796. The man whom Jefferson's friends charged with first voicing them publicly was afterwards appointed by President Adams to a lucrative federal office, and from this President Jefferson had not removed him.[24] While well aware of the circumstances of their promulgation, Ritchie recognized that, from the public point of view, these charges were much more important than those of immorality. From them it might be inferred that Jefferson lacked the necessary qualities of leadership, that his conduct as

[22] Richmond *Enquirer*, Aug. 23, 27, 30; Sept. 6, 13, 17, 27, 1805.

[23] Extract quoted in Richmond *Enquirer*, Aug. 23, 1805. Turner's letter, which was undated, appeared in Boston *Repertory*, May 31, 1805, and was widely reprinted. Among the replies to it was one by Thomas Paine, under a pseudonym (Foner, *Complete Writings* [1945], II, 980-988). This is amusing on the Walker case.

[24] Charles Simms of Alexandria, whose name was spelled "Symmes" by Ritchie. See *Jefferson and the Ordeal of Liberty*, pp. 279-282, and footnotes.

governor demonstrated his unfitness to perform the larger task of administering the affairs of the nation. The President could have been more properly judged on the basis of his performance during four years in that office, to be sure, but his enemies might say that he was only a fair-weather sailor. Furthermore, the charge of personal cowardice, though utterly unfair, was damaging. The best answer to it and the other allegations was an account of actual events and a record of contemporary impressions.

The "Vindication" was based on documentary materials that were collected by Jefferson's friends. Their efforts, beginning in 1796 in response to similar charges regarding his conduct as war governor, were renewed in 1805. The person most active in this connection was the President's secretary, William A. Burwell, who had been on leave for some months, both because of the state of his health and his duties as a member of the General Assembly of Virginia.[25] The acting secretary, Isaac Coles, also attested certain documents. Jefferson's knowledge of this activity and his approval of its purpose may therefore be assumed. He was highly sensitive to criticism of his conduct as governor, and the unwarranted charges of personal cowardice could not have failed to rankle in his breast. Undoubtedly he welcomed this effort to vindicate him.

There is no need for us to insert here even a summarized account of his actions during the British invasions of Virginia when he was governor.[26] The narrative and documents published by Ritchie constitute a valuable historical contribution, but he stated that his purposes were limited and did not extend to the depiction of Jefferson as a hero. Indeed, this defender may be charged with conceding rather too much to the prosecution in some of his comments on Jefferson as a nonmilitary man. But Ritchie amply demonstrated that the onetime Governor was not a "dastardly traitor," and that his conduct was not "dictated by timidity." The former charge was so obviously a preposterous partisan exaggeration that it could not have been expected to persist, but in one form or another the latter has been long-lived. This fact may be cited as proof of the old adage that when much mud is

[25] Concerning Turner's letter, Burwell wrote in his Memoir (LC): "I conversed with Mr. Jefferson and received an assurance of its falsity, referring me to sources from which I could establish the reverse. I immediately wrote to Ritchie the Editor of the Enquirer contradicting the statements of Turner, pledging myself to prove them untrue." Burwell, therefore, may have been the author of the "Vindication," although it was printed as an editorial.

[26] See *Jefferson the Virginian*, chs. XXIV, XXXV. In that work I availed myself of the account in the Richmond *Enquirer* and made use of many of the same documents.

thrown, some of it will stick. Or it may suggest that the "Vindication" has not been widely read, even by historians.

The publisher of another journal, who was critical of the President, read it to advantage. While questioning Jefferson's heroism, the *Norfolk Ledger* conceded his patriotism in the American Revolution and saw "much to praise and nothing to censure" in his conduct while governor and thereafter "until the adoption of the *present revolution*."[27] With commendable candor this journal admitted that the real cause of its opposition lay in the present situation. The *Enquirer* itself sounded a note of realism in its final words to Thomas Turner. Speaking of Jefferson's accomplishments as President, Thomas Ritchie asked if there could be "any better proof of the energy of an officer than the success of his measures."[28] Whatever else might be said, this President unquestionably had a record of substantial achievement behind him as he entered upon his second and last tour of official duty.

[27] Quoted in Richmond *Enquirer,* Sept. 17, 1805. Italics added.
[28] Sept. 27, 1805.

[II]

Blessed Interim

IF the attacks on his character temporarily robbed Jefferson of the serenity which was his hallmark, he found, during the months immediately following his second inauguration, many private compensations for the ordeal of public prominence. He always regarded the period between congressional sessions as a "blessed interim"; and a number of circumstances contributed to his joy of living in the spring and summer of 1805. For one thing, he spent more time than usual in the company of his own family away from the seat of government. For another, he promptly availed himself of the temporary lull in official business to catch up with his non-political correspondence, and, by giving attention to things that most interested him, restored his mind to a happier balance. Mention may be made here of some of the private activities of this extraordinarily resilient and resourceful man.

In this respite one of the things he first turned his mind to was the "moldboard of least resistance," by means of which he had sought to increase the effectiveness of the plow — already the most useful of human instruments, in his opinion.[1] His invention was now more than a decade old and he had communicated it to certain savants and agriculturists before he became President. Meanwhile, he had designed a sharp toe as an alternative to the original square toe. Some months had elapsed since Dr. James Mease, who had published an account of the moldboard in his *Domestic Encyclopedia*, requested a pattern that might be used for casting. In the ten-day interval between the inauguration and his departure for Monticello for a month Jefferson sent this gentleman in Philadelphia two models, along with a block of wood

---

[1] For the earlier history of this invention, see *Jefferson and the Ordeal of Liberty*, pp. 214–217. The most important documents for the full story are in *Farm Book*, pp. 47–64.

showing the method of making them.[2] He had long had the matter in mind, but had been unable to take half a day off with a workman. Also, he sent a box with similar contents and a copy of the *Domestic Encyclopedia* to John Strode of Culpeper, with whom he had so often lodged on journeys between Monticello and Washington but whom he did not expect to see on his next trip, when he would be going by a drier road. To this rural friend he admitted that he took disproportionate pride in his invention, saying that men often value themselves most for what they actually know least about. Elated by the gift, John Strode responded by predicting that the name of its eminent donor would endure after time had obliterated those of presidents, emperors, and kings.[3] The "great approbation" with which, as Jefferson came to believe, his sharp-toed moldboard was received, was extended in this instance to the inventor himself. About six weeks after the inauguration, when he had found a bearer, he sent a model to the agriculturist William Strickland in York, England; at the same time he sent one to the Board of Agriculture in London, which had received a squaretoed model some years before.[4]

It was in recognition of this earlier model, rather than the one with a pointed toe, that the Société d'Agriculture du Département de la Seine awarded him a gold medal. Writing him in May, Du Pont de Nemours described this action as "homage rendered to the Philosopher-Statesman of your country by the planters of mine." Though the award received some mention in American newspapers, the official notice of it was long delayed — so long that Jefferson inquired of Du Pont about it. And, just to make sure that the French were brought up to date, he sent this friend models of the moldboard in its two forms. He was midway in his second term before he got the medal, but the association thus begun with the French society was long continued and led to a subsequent exchange of plows. Meanwhile, he learned that his moldboard had been declared by French authority to be "mathematically exact, and incapable of further improvement."[5] Much of his gratification was to come later, but in the spring of 1805 his cherished inven-

---

[2] Jas. Mease to TJ, Mar. 28, 1804; TJ to Mease, Mar. 11, 1805 (*ibid.*, pp. 53–54). Apparently no cast was made until some years later.

[3] TJ to John Strode, Mar. 11, 1805 (LC, 25755; largely in *Farm Book*, p. 54); Strode to TJ, Mar. 25, 1805 (LC, 25819–25820).

[4] TJ to William Strickland, Apr. 25, 1805 (*Farm Book*, pp. 54–55 from LC, 25951); TJ to Tunnicliff, same date (Bixby, p. 113).

[5] Du Pont to TJ, May 12, 1805; TJ to Du Pont, Feb. 12, 1806 (*J.-D. Correspondence*, pp. 82–83, 88–89); TJ to M. Silvestre, acknowledging the medal, May 29, 1807; D. B. Warden to TJ, Oct. 21, 1807 (*Farm Book*, p. 57).

tion diverted his mind, and the reception of it then and thereafter by the sort of people he valued most — farmers and savants — warmed his heart.

Among the latter he continued to maintain cordial relations with the group centering on the American Philosophical Society in Philadelphia. Because of one of his most intimate friendships there, however, he found himself in a delicate situation regarding what he viewed as a technical appointment: the directorship of the mint in that city, which was less than a full-time job. Late in April, 1805, anticipating the resignation of Elias Boudinot, who had succeeded David Rittenhouse, he offered the directorship to Professor Robert Patterson of the University of Pennsylvania, saying also that he did not want this distinguished mathematician to leave his academic post. About the same time his good friend Dr. Benjamin Rush offered himself for the position. In his reply to this unexpected and embarrassing suggestion Jefferson could have contented himself with reporting his prior commitment to Patterson, but he chose to justify his action on other grounds. Saying that the duties of the office required the best mathematical talents that could be found, he cited as precedents the appointments of Sir Isaac Newton in England and David Rittenhouse in the United States. In this case, as in others, he took counsel with the other members of the administration and associated them with his decision. Also, he went to great pains to explain the grounds of it to Dr. Rush, whose technical qualifications lay in another field. Employing a metaphor which this particular friend would immediately recognize as appropriate, he emphasized his own necessary impersonality. "I am but a machine," he said, "erected by the Constitution for the performance of certain acts according to laws of action laid down for me, one of which is that I must anatomize the living man as the surgeon does the dead subject, view him also as a machine and employ him for what he is fit for, unblinded by the mist of friendship."

This striking description of executive responsibility, which deserves recognition as a classic, was destined to be unrevealed to the public eye for generations. While expressing entire satisfaction with Jefferson's letter, Rush asked that his friend keep his application secret. Jefferson had already sent a copy of his letter to Rush to another scientist in Philadelphia, whose understanding he also sought, but there is no reason to believe that privacy was afterwards invaded or that a notable friendship was in any way impaired.[6]

[6] TJ's letter of June 13, 1805 (LC, 26208) is quoted in part in the editorial note on Rush's letter of June 15 (Butterfield, II, 896–897); see also Rush to TJ, Apr. 29, 1805 (ibid., II, 894). Other letters are TJ to Robert Patterson, Apr. 27, 1805 (LC,

Among medical men he specially honored was Dr. Benjamin Water-house, whose crusade for Jennerian vaccination he strongly supported by both precept and example. The dauntless physician, an enemy to all the physical ills of men, delivered to the medical students of Harvard in the autumn of 1804 a lecture warning them against tobacco and spirituous liquors. This appeared in printed form and turned out to be the most popular of Waterhouse's writings. Believing that the President was indifferent to nothing that concerned human welfare, Water-house sent him a copy about two weeks before the inauguration. Replying shortly after that event, Jefferson began his brief letter, sur-prisingly, by quoting the sentence with which Ovid introduced his book *The Remedy of Love*. In this the god of love is reported to have exclaimed, after reading that title: "War, I see, is being prepared against me." A lecture against tobacco, said Jefferson, might be ex-pected to excite the same sort of alarm in a Virginian who raised it. But he went on to say that, being "a friend neither to its culture nor consequences," he wished the doctor success in his opposition to "this organ of Virginia influence," as well as to everything else that was injurious to "physical, moral or political well being."[7]

Delighted with Jefferson's "Ciceronian epistle," Waterhouse wished that he could write a history of men and parties in his part of the country in the spirit of Tacitus. "Then," he wrote, "perhaps you and others in the South would see that the men among us most distin-guished for talents, character and years abhor that odious vapour of calumny, which has appeared among us, and even tainted the walls of some of our Temples." Since he himself was under the "black imputa-tion of being a moderate man, or a lukewarm Federalist," he had long been excluded from "the solemn feasts and *clamorations* of the out-rageous party men." But, when opportunity offered, he never failed to denounce "this odious, this wicked calumniating spirit" — which was so much worse than "Virginia influence."[8] Such words were a balm to the spirit of the first citizen of the Republic and of that state.

Though passionately devoted to his native region throughout his life, Jefferson was never uncritical of Virginia; and the influence he sought to exert on the state and wanted it to exert on the Republic went far beyond the realm of politics, as New Englanders like Dr.

25959); to B. S. Barton and to Patterson, June 13, 1805 (LC, 26207, 26209). Patterson served as director of the mint throughout the rest of the administration, and in 1819 became one of TJ's successors as president of the American Philo-sophical Society.

[7] Waterhouse to TJ, Feb. 20, 1805 (LC, 25643); TJ to Waterhouse, Mar. 9, 1805 (LC, 25743).

[8] Waterhouse to TJ, Apr. 7, 1805, received Apr. 17 (LC, 25881).

Waterhouse and the Reverend William Bentley well knew. He was fully aware of the needs of his own region, as well as those of the undeveloped West, when he remarked to Gallatin that the gratifying increase in the public revenue was hastening the moment when they could begin on canals, roads, colleges, and so forth.[9] The hope he thus expressed was to prove vain, but in the meantime hope had arisen that the legislature of Virginia would institute a university on a liberal plan. After Littleton W. Tazewell had informed him of the prospect during the winter, he wrote a long letter on this favorite subject despite frequent interruptions which, he said, prevented him from keeping his ideas rallied on it. Nothing came of this cherished project as yet, but his letter is an important document in his history as an educational statesman.[10] It reflects his abiding concern for the enlightenment of the people generally — without which he believed that the present state of American liberty would be short-lived. But, since education at the higher rather than the lower levels was under present contemplation by the legislature, he addressed himself to that. Many of his specific proposals strikingly anticipated those he was to advance successfully after his own retirement from public life. We need not concern ourselves with them at this point, but we can at least note certain comments of his, in mid-career as President, on the state of science — which, as he used the term, meant human knowledge as a whole. "Science is progressive," he said. "What was useful two centuries ago is now become useless." In his opinion Oxford, Cambridge, and the Sorbonne were that far behind the age. He wanted Virginia's projected university to be in pace with the knowledge of the times. Not only so, he set standards and prescribed qualifications for professors and members of the governing board, especially the latter, which might well have been regarded as unattainable in his generation. He could not offer himself as yet, but he suggested an important personal contribution:

Should this establishment take place on a plan worthy of approbation, I shall have a valuable legacy to leave it, to wit, my library, which certainly has not cost less than 15,000 Dollars. But its value is more in the selection, a part of which, that which respects America, is the result of my own personal searches in Paris for 6 or 7 years, & of persons employed by me in England, Holland, Germany and Spain to make similar searches. Such a collection on that subject can never again be made.

[9] TJ to Gallatin, May 29, 1805 (Ford, VIII, 357).
[10] TJ to L. W. Tazewell, Jan. 5, 1805 (UVA).

BLESSED INTERIM   23

He did not sufficiently anticipate the industry and zeal of later collectors, but he did not overestimate the scholarly worth of his own library.[11]

At this stage of his career he claimed that he had no time to read books, but this insatiable bibliophile had certainly not ceased to collect them. One manifestation of his omnivorous appetite might have astounded his clerical foes if they had been aware of it. He was assembling editions of the New Testament in various languages and from these he was to compile, when he had leisure, the multi-lingual work he called "The Life and Morals of Jesus of Nazareth."[12] While his own morals were being attacked in Massachusetts and Justice Chase was being tried in Washington, he was procuring Greek and English versions of the words of the lowly Nazarene from Mathew Carey in Philadelphia and a French version from J. P. Reibelt of Baltimore. The latter bookseller, after writing many animated letters in French to the "Vénérable Chef des Républicains," visited Monticello late in the summer, although, as Jefferson explained, the place was too crowded and he himself too busy to give this guest the attention he deserved.[13] To what extent the venerable party chieftain, in this era of partisan bitterness, was able to reflect on the moral maxims of the ancients and the timeless teachings of Jesus we have no way of knowing, but the chances are that he often gave thought to them in his last waking hours.

He did not boast about his books on religion as he did about his American collection, which included rare materials bearing on the history of his own state. He was equally notable for his care in preserving these and his generosity in making them available. About two months after the inauguration he received from John Daly Burk, who was writing a history of Virginia, a request to see his collection of laws and newspapers. These were in his library at Monticello, locked up when he was away, as he was at the time. Responding to this request and giving a general account of this collection, he described arrangements whereby this author could avail himself of it. A rare volume of laws was to be sent to Governor John Page in Richmond under carefully prescribed safeguards, and thus made accessible not only to Burk but to such lawyers as might want to see it. Burk was to be allowed to take the newspapers to Petersburg. Meticulous instructions were sent

[11] It was this collection that afterwards went to the Library of Congress, before the University of Virginia was established.
[12] See *Jefferson the President, First Term*, pp. 204–205.
[13] TJ to Carey, Feb. 3, 1805 (UVA); Carey to TJ, Feb. 20, 1805 (MHS); TJ to Carey, Mar. 7, 1805 (UVA); Reibelt to TJ, Oct. 1, and TJ to Reibelt, Oct. 12, 1805 (LC, 26694, 26731).

Thomas Mann Randolph, who was to unlock the library and ship the box, and to Governor Page, who was to receive it, as well as to the writer who was to avail himself of its contents.[14] The episode may be said to illustrate antiquarianism at its best.

A major contribution of his own to Virginiana was the book he had not really intended to publish and of which he often spoke lightly — his *Notes on Virginia*. Toward the end of his first term, as on a number of other occasions, he expressed the wish that he could find time to revise it. In response to the letter of a friendly critic of the nineteenth chapter, in which he decried manufacturing while singing a hymn of praise to agriculture, he frankly admitted that he would like to review this in the light of the "wonderful changes" in America since he wrote it nearly a quarter of a century before. What he then feared was an industrial population like those in European cities, but he was now of the opinion that Americans engaged in manufacturing were no less moral and independent than tillers of the soil. He believed that they would continue to be so as long as there were vacant lands for them to resort to; and among the "wonderful changes" he was probably thinking less of the growth of manufacturing, which was still on a relatively small scale, than of the vast acquisition of fresh land. His heart was still with the farmer, whose future he believed he had assured.[15] From this same man he received further critical comments on the chapter on manufacturing that he had never got around to revising. Along with them, however, he got words of praise — for his candor in describing the society of his native state, among other things. Also, he received from this non-political correspondent an exhortation, written on inauguration day: "I hope you will never think of retiring. I wish you to remain long enough to give a tone and stability to the republican system that all men may be convinced that it is not merely the dream of Philosophy."[16]

If by philosophy this writer meant abstract speculation, Jefferson himself rarely indulged in it, whatever his enemies might say. Very often when he used the term he meant "natural philosophy," best translated into our idiom as "science." Presumably it was in this sense that it was used in the summer of 1805 by Dr. Samuel Latham Mitchill,

14 TJ to Burk, June 1, 1805 (Ford, VIII, 357–359); to T. M. Randolph, June 2, and to John Page, June 2, 1805 (LC, 26164 [copy], 26155). On TJ's physical care of this collection, see *Jefferson and the Ordeal of Liberty*, pp. 253–254.

15 TJ to J. Lithgow, Jan. 4, 1805 (LC, 25434); L. & B., XI, 55–56, incorrectly designating the recipient as "Mr. Lithson."

16 Lithgow to TJ, from Philadelphia, Mar. 4, 1805 (LC, 25723–25724). Lithgow was a minor literary figure and secretary of the Society of Artists and Manufacturers in that city.

onetime professor of natural history, chemistry, agriculture, and botany at Columbia, who as Senator from New York, though a Republican, had voted for the acquittal of Justice Chase on all counts. Writing
the President about a chemical analysis, he deferred to him as one
"whose love of general science, and whose labors to illustrate the history of Virginia, have rendered him famous not only in his own
country, but throughout the civilized world abroad."[17]

This love of all knowledge led Jefferson, during the spring and
summer, to engage in correspondence ranging from ornithology to the
distillation of seawater, and to write elaborately about a new sort of
meteorological chart as well as about changes in English orthography.
The chart, he suggested, could be a table which would note, for every
day of the year in every coastal state, the appearance of flora and fauna
and any other indicators of the progress of the seasons, so that it would
be possible for the observer to mark the movement of these with
precision. In his mind this lover of warmth and sunshine would go
southward in measured steps with the autumn and northward with the
spring.[18] Responding to a letter recommending a change in the alphabet, he held that, while desirable, this could not be sudden or drastic.
There had been progress toward the phonetic since Anglo-Saxon days,
he said, along with the unfortunate loss from the alphabet of two
useful characters. "Thus, we are leaving out the *u* in favor, honor, etc.,
the *gh* in tho, thro, ect., the *w* and *d* in acknolege, altho' the dictionary
makers have not yet ventured to admit it."[19] Actually, he himself was
inconsistent in his spelling, being relatively indifferent to it except in
his formal writing, but quite obviously he believed that language was
made for man, just as government was, not man for language.

As a humanist he was a foe to any sort of pedantry, and in the
physical sciences he was notably utilitarian. When asked that summer
whether a general work on chemistry was needed, he replied that he
was less qualified than his questioner to judge of that, but that he had
no doubt whatever of the importance of turning chemistry to household uses. "The common herd of philosophers [meaning scientists, as
we use the term] seem to write only for one another," he said. "The
chemists have filled volumes on the composition of a thousand sub-
stances of no sort of importance to the purposes of life; while the arts
of making bread, butter, cheese, vinegar, soap, beer, cyder, etc., remain

[17] S. L. Mitchill to TJ, July 1, 1805 (LC, 26310).
[18] No brief description can do justice to TJ's elaborate one in his letter to
Nicholas King, Apr. 21, 1805 (LC, 25917).
[19] TJ to Samuel R. Demaree, May 6, 1805, sending a report from a committee of
the American Philosophical Society (LC, 26022).

totally unexplained. . . . Good treatises on these subjects would receive general approbation." Rightly regarding these expressions as
consistent with the humane acts which had characterized his life, his
correspondent fully recognized the benevolence which led him "to
promote the interest of the people in general."[20]

In an age which to almost any American of our day would seem
appallingly devoid of conveniences, he was enormously interested in
labor-saving devices or gadgets of any sort. In this period the one that
continued to fascinate him most — or about which he wrote most
often, at any rate — was the polygraph. An incredibly prolific penman
who liked to keep legible copies of everything he wrote, he had found
this exceedingly useful; and, after he had employed it for more than a
year he sought to bring others within the circle of this delight by
making gifts of the machine to them.[21] It required a "degree of
mechanical attention," as he admitted to more than one of the beneficiaries of his generosity, and as his own extended correspondence with
Charles Willson Peale about defects and improvements clearly showed.
This was, in fact, a major reason why the machine did not come into
more general use, although no deterrent to an inveterate tinkerer like
Jefferson. Also, the polygraph was for that day an expensive item; he
had previously paid Peale sixty dollars for each of three machines. In
this period, besides ordering for himself a portable model which did
not work very well and had to be returned for correction, he ordered
three others. One was for his secretary, another was for the French
philosopher Volney, and the third was for Commodore Edward
Preble.[22]

He received this letter about chemistry late in the summer at Monticello, where he had no secretary but his polygraph. He wrote his own
letters and, even when at home, spent his morning hours in his study.
The three and a half months he was away from the seat of government
during the spring and summer of 1805 — in one stretch of four weeks
and another of ten — could not be properly described as a vacation.
Though the burden of official business was lightened it was not removed, and there were troublesome private affairs which must be at-

20 TJ to Dr. Thomas Ewell, Aug. 30, 1805, and Ewell to TJ, Sept. 10 (LC,
26597, 26632).
21 For his previous relations with the polygraph and his correspondence with
Charles Willson Peale about it, see *Jefferson the President: First Term*, pp. 410–421.
22 TJ to Volney, Feb. 8, 1805 (L. & B., XI, 67–68); TJ to C. W. Peale, July 12,
1805 (LC, 26355), and Oct. 6, 1805 (LC, 26704); Account Book, Jan. 28, 1805,
showing payment of $180 for three machines.

tended to. One immediate problem this year was that of finding an overseer for Monticello to replace Gabriel Lilly, who could not read but had served him well for five years. Lilly may have had other than financial reasons for leaving. There had been a serious rupture, some months earlier, between him and John H. Craven, who had leased five of Jefferson's fields across the Rivanna. But the ostensible reason was a demand for more pay than Jefferson felt warranted in giving him. Another overseer was hired at the old rate late in the summer, but he proved unsatisfactory and lasted little more than a year. His successor, Edmund Bacon, became a fixture.[23]

Problems that had necessarily been sidetracked while Jefferson was in Washington crowded upon him when he returned to his own acres, but to a man of his domestic tastes visits home were particularly rejuvenating, and to his nostrils no air was so refreshing and revivifying as that on his little mountain. His spirits, though generally sanguine, were much affected by climate, and no doubt this was one reason for his lifelong interest in that subject. While recognizing that people are disposed to like what they have become accustomed to, he left no doubt that he much preferred the American climate to that he had experienced in northern Europe. "I think it a more cheerful one," he said to a French friend. "It is our cloudless sky which has eradicated from our constitutions all disposition to hang ourselves, which we might otherwise have inherited from our English ancestors."[24]

During the winter he had just gone through the skies must often have been gray in Washington, and, according to his own report, the cold surpassed anything he had experienced since his last winter in Paris. In the first letter he got from his former Attorney General after the latter's return to Massachusetts, he learned that Levi Lincoln, buried in snow, was disposed to agree with him about the advantages of a temperate climate.[25] Jefferson always claimed he had this at his elevated seat in his native region, and he could count on a full measure of sunshine. The Hessian fly destroyed his son-in-law's wheat crop in June, but in mid-August he reported that the weather had been "extremely seasonable" in his quarter, and that better crops had never

[23] J. Holmes Freeman began work Aug. 22, 1805; Bacon, who had previously operated the toll mill, became overseer ("manager" in TJ's language) Sept. 29, 1806 (Account Book). Besides a list of overseers, there are brief biographies in *Farm Book*. Among the letters relating to Lilly are TJ to TMR, Oct. 28, 1804 (MHS), June 5, 1805 (LC, 26182).
[24] TJ to Volney, Feb. 8, 1805 (L. & B., XI, 64).
[25] TJ to Martha, Jan. 7, 21, 28, 1805 (*Family Letters*, pp. 265-267); Lincoln to TJ, Mar. 9, 1805, from Worcester (LC, 25747).

been seen. After that they needed rain, but other districts suffered more from drought than his did. In the end there may have been too much sunshine, but Nature was generally beneficent.[26]

He spoke not only of good crops but of good health. His daughter Martha, who was closest to him of all living beings, had been "gravely indisposed" by a stomach complaint during the winter. So concerned was he about the physical state of this normally robust young matron that he would have hastened to her bedside, he said, had Congress not been in session. It would have been an exceedingly difficult trip in January if the cold was as severe as he said it was. He admonished her to take as good care of herself as she did of others and, whether she did or not, she was improved by the time he reached home for his visit of a month after the inauguration. She was wholly recovered by midsummer when he got there for his long stay, and in the meantime the children got through the mumps.

Matters of health figured largely in his correspondence with members of the family at all times, as they did in most people's personal correspondence in those days. But he and his grandchildren talked about all sorts of things in the letters that passed between them when he was away. His oldest granddaughter, now in her early teens, solemnly informed him of her decision to change her name to Anastasia, but he continued to address her as Anne, and he paid no heed when Ellen, aged nine, signed herself as Eleonora. Along with continuing concern for the physical well-being of his grandchildren he showed unabated interest in the development of their minds, laying more emphasis on imagination than might have been expected of one who was in so many ways utilitarian. He had been sending bits of poetry to the older girl for a scrapbook she was making; and, when he concluded that this was about full, he started sending them to the younger, that she also might have a collection. This he did on inauguration day, when he availed himself of the departure of her father to send Ellen a brief letter. He brought the children a batch of books when he himself went home ten days later. On the Fourth of July, when he was back in Washington, Ellen wrote him that they had not half got through these. As far as she had got she was very much interested, however, and they were "going on with great spirit."

According to Anne, whose judgment of her junior need not be taken at face value, Ellen was the laziest girl she ever saw and the slowest dresser, but the nine-year-old was not lacking in intellectual

[26] Quotations from various letters in August in *Garden Book*, p. 304; TMR to TJ, June 16, 1805 (E-R Papers, UVA), referring to Hessian fly.

and artistic curiosity, as an inquiry in this same letter showed. She knew about six of the fine arts, she said — painting, sculpture, architecture, music, poetry, and oratory — but neither she nor her mother could recollect what the seventh was, and she hoped that her grandfather could tell her. In his reply the President of the United States solemnly observed that there was no general agreement on this question — that, in fact, there was no perfect definition of what a fine art is. He reported, however, that some people coupled rhetoric with oratory, and, citing Lord Kames as authority, suggested that gardening, not as horticulture, but as the "art of embellishing grounds by fancy," might possibly be added to the list.[27] That art was to occupy more of his attention a little later.

He made no entries in his Garden Book this year, but early in the spring he had four thousand thorns, such as he had observed growing abundantly around Washington, set out as a hedge around his orchard. He expected this living fence, while serving a practical purpose, to be also an embellishment. Planted when he was at home in March, many of the thorns died, and had to be replaced in another year, but one of his granddaughters informed him, shortly before his return in July, that the others were flourishing.[28]

For half a dozen years his daughter's family had been living at Edgehill, three or four miles from Monticello on the other side of the Rivanna, but during the weeks that he was at home they customarily joined him on the little mountain. The main house there was much more commodious than their cramped quarters. He set a painter to work during his visit in the spring and with difficulty secured lead, linseed oil, and spirits of turpentine in quantity, along with coloring materials in great variety. The scope of the operation is suggested by a supplementary order for five hundred pounds of white lead that he made in May. He did things in a big way when he finally got around to them, and he showed more regard for economy in the conduct of the government than in his private building operations. From one memorandum it appears that four coats of paint were to be applied to the woodwork of his house, inside and out. At the same time that his granddaughter wrote him about his thorn hedge she reported that the house looked much better now that it was painted. We may doubt that the job was wholly done but may assume that the rawness of which Mrs. William Thornton had complained had largely disappeared from

[27] For this entire period, see *Family Letters*, pp. 267–278.
[28] Account of the thorns by Betts in *Garden Book*, p. 299, and in note to letter of Martha to TJ, Apr. 19, 1805, in *Family Letters*.

the mansion house, which was the central unit in the architect's full plan.[29]

The timing of the painting was good, for the wedding of Thomas Mann Randolph's younger sister Virginia (Jenny) took place late in August.[30] Jefferson, while in Washington, played a part in procuring wedding clothes and certain ornaments that were particularly desired by his daughter. Dolley Madison acted as his agent in this matter, although that lady's movements soon became severely limited because of a tumor on her leg. This prevented the Madisons from making their customary summer visit to Montpelier and occasioned their going instead to Philadelphia, where she could receive medical attention. Early in the summer Jefferson wrote his daughter that her commission gave him the greatest pleasure. "My wishes are always to do what would be pleasing to you," he added; "but knowing nothing of what would be proper or acceptable, I do nothing." He saw to the sending of a number of feminine garments by stage, and among the articles he took home with him were a comb that cost seven dollars and some earrings that cost thirty-five.[31]

He timed his visit to his Poplar Forest estate so as not to conflict with the wedding. The main purpose of his visit to Bedford County was to lay out a tract of land for his Eppes son-in-law in behalf of one of Maria's children.[32] He had not yet begun to build the house at Poplar Forest that young Francis Eppes was to inherit, but in his mind he may already have begun to plan it. Meanwhile, a visit to Monticello was expected from the little boy and his father in the later summer, though the records leave some doubt whether they got there for the wedding.

Before he left Washington for his own long visit the third President of the United States sat to Gilbert Stuart ("Stewart" in his spelling) for two portraits that were destined to become famous. The first of these, which eventually hung for three-quarters of a century at Edgehill, remained in the artist's studio so that he could paint replicas from it. The official likeness of Jefferson, as it appears on paper money and postage stamps, derives from one of the replicas. The "Edgehill" Stuart

[29] Account Book, Mar. 28, 1805, saying that a painter, Richard Barry, had begun work; various items in Monticello Construction File for this period, including a rough estimate from the painter, and a number of TJ's letters and orders.

[30] Aug. 28, 1805, to Wilson Jefferson Cary. The approaching wedding is referred to in *Family Letters*, pp. 273, 277.

[31] Letter of June 12, 1805; Account Book, July 12, 1805.

[32] Correspondence with JWE, Mar. 25-26, 1805 (*Huntington Library Quarterly*, May, 1943, pp. 337-338), and May 27, 1805 (Randall, III, 136).

and its replicas are the most stylized of his major portraits, along with the earlier one by Mather Brown. The "medallion profile" done by Stuart in June, 1805, "à la antique" as Jefferson said, is the portrait his own family liked best. Perhaps it is too classical — especially the nose — but it was said to show, better than any other likeness, the shape and characteristic pose of the head. It may lack the nobility of the Houdon bust, but, better than any other likeness, it suggests his sensitivity. For the rest of his term it was in the President's House, and it was then moved to Monticello.[33] His daughter and grandchildren saw it for the first time when they visited him in Washington the winter after it was painted.

[33] An excellent account of the "Edgehill" portrait and the "medallion profile," with references, is in A. L. Bush, *Life Portraits of Thomas Jefferson* (1962), pp. 71–77.

Unsettled Weather

[III]

A Minor Success: The Navy and Tripoli

AT the time of his second inauguration, Jefferson supposed that he had restored to normal strength what he called "our executive family," and that he had effected a shuffle which would be advantageous to the Department of the Navy. Things did not go as planned, but in the end he arrived at a relatively satisfactory situation.

All year he had faced the problem of replacing Levi Lincoln as attorney general. The degree of loyalty he inspired in those who worked most closely with him is suggested by what Lincoln said when offering his resignation, as it is also by the language of William A. Burwell, when, early in the year, he asked for temporary relief from his duties as private secretary. This young man referred to the "uniform benevolence" that had been shown him, just as the Attorney General did to Jefferson's goodness, contrasting this with the malignity of his foes. Burwell's inability to return to what he described as the most pleasurable employment of his life created no grave problem, for an Albemarle County neighbor of the President's, Isaac Coles, assumed this unexacting position.[1] The attorney-generalship was still only a part-time position, and, according to the hostile press, Levi Lincoln actually did very little in it, but Jefferson took the problem of his replacement seriously.

He asked and received suggestions from other members of what was beginning to be called the Cabinet. On Gallatin's list appeared the names of John T. Mason, then living in Georgetown, and Senator John Breckinridge of Kentucky. He regarded the former as the best person yet proposed and the latter as very good, but was doubtful of acceptance in both cases. Agreeing with the appraisal, Secretary Robert

[1] Levi Lincoln to TJ, Dec. 26, 1804, and TJ to Lincoln, Dec. 28 (LC, 25331–25332, 25337); comment on Lincoln in *Washington Federalist*, Oct. 17, 1804; W. A. Burwell to TJ, Jan. 18, 1805, and TJ to Burwell, Jan. 8 (LC, 25482, 25517); TJ to Isaac Coles, Sept. 20, 1805 (LC, 26678).

Smith said that, if neither would accept, he himself would find the office more congenial than the one he then held. "I have not yet been able to acquire a taste for the details of the Navy Department," he admitted, adding that he knew of three people who could fill his office. This suggestion surprised Jefferson, who believed it would be easier to find an attorney general than a secretary of the navy, but he would have been warranted in welcoming it, for the appointment of Smith had been a makeshift in the first place. Accordingly, he asked Smith to name the three he had in mind. One of these, presumably, was Congressman Jacob Crowninshield of Massachusetts, a former sea captain, for he was promptly sounded out. After declining the offer he decided, toward the end of the congressional session, to accept it. Accordingly, the President sent to the Senate the nominations of Crowninshield as secretary of the navy and Smith as attorney general, and these were promptly confirmed. No doubt this disposition of the matter seemed desirable from the political point of view since it might have been expected to gratify New Englanders. Shortly after the nautical Congressman got back to Salem, however, he decided that the health of his wife precluded acceptance.[2]

The executive officer most disappointed by this turn of events was undoubtedly the Secretary of the Treasury. When he sent Jefferson an account of expenditures for the first five months of 1805, Gallatin complained of the excessive cost of the navy, in which there had been no extraordinary construction during this period. Since the Department of War had made a better showing, he concluded that either it was better organized, or that naval business could not be "conducted on reasonable terms." Continuing, he said: "Whatever the cause may be, I dare predict that whilst that state of things continues we will have no navy, nor shall progress towards having one." He thought that after so much expenditure Jefferson's government should have had an increased fleet rather than an impaired one. Gallatin had maintained silence on this subject, he said, "for the sake of preserving perfect harmony in your counsels."[3] Distrust of Robert Smith was one of the ties between Gallatin and John Randolph. Whether or not Crowninshield, who continued in Congress but died within three years after some months of precarious health, would have been a more effective administrator can only be speculated, but it is conceivable that this able and informed New Englander might have bettered the naval situation.

[2] Gallatin to TJ, received Jan. 3, 1805 (LC, 27149); Robt. Smith to TJ, Jan. 2, and TJ to Smith, Jan. 3, 1805 (LC, 25420–25421, 25423); Jacob Crowninshield to TJ, Jan. 24, 1805 (LC, 25495), and Mar. 27, 1805 (LC, 28528–28529).
[3] Gallatin to TJ, May 30, 1805 (*Writings*, I, 233–234).

At all events, a seemingly rational plan failed and Gallatin was left to put up with Smith for the rest of the administration.

Meanwhile Jefferson, whose forebodings about the naval portfolio were thus justified, renewed his search for an attorney general. He received two declinations before he got an acceptance. Rebuffed by John T. Mason, he offered the post to John Julius Pringle, then attorney general of South Carolina; and when that gentleman declined he again sought Mason, who declined on the ground that he had to devote himself to his personal affairs. Then Jefferson turned to John Breckinridge, whom he was reluctant to lose from the Senate but who, he said, would bring into the executive councils knowledge of western interests and circumstances they often lacked. Whether or not the President gained more than he lost by this transfer of a loyal supporter, Breckinridge was destined to serve only a year; he died in December, 1806, at the age of forty-six.[4] All the rest of the executive family served with the President to the end. Gallatin was never reconciled to Robert Smith, and that less than businesslike official was not always wise in the conduct of his department, but, judging from results, the young navy was adequate to its tasks in the Mediterranean. In June, 1805, a treaty of peace brought to an end the war with Tripoli.

Before he learned of this in September, the unnautical President had faced an embarrassing situation that was unwittingly created by the most noted naval commander to emerge from this conflict, Commodore Edward Preble. The Tripolitan War, into the details of which we cannot go here, lasted about four years altogether; and, on looking backward, almost anyone could see that the arrival of this able and aggressive commander in the Mediterranean toward the end of the summer of 1803 marked the turn in American fortunes. Also, it could have been claimed that, but for a couple of unfortunate developments thereafter, the war could have ended sooner than it did. The first of these unfortunate events was the grounding of the frigate *Philadelphia* (October 31, 1803) and the capture of Captain William Bainbridge and his crew — more than three hundred men altogether. (At a later time Bainbridge was fully exonerated.) Thereupon the Pasha, Yusuf, set a ransom price of three million dollars on the prisoners. At the instance of Preble, the *Philadelphia* was destroyed a few months later (February 16, 1804) by Americans led by Stephen Decatur in what was described by Lord Nelson as the "most bold and daring act of the age." Though Preble's force was greatly weakened by the loss of the frigate

---

[4] TJ to J. J. Pringle, June 15, 1805 (LC, 26217); TJ to Henry Dearborn, July 14, 1805 (LC, 26373); J. T. Mason to TJ, July 20, 1805 (LC, 26898); TJ to John Breckinridge, Aug. 7, 1805 (LC, 26473).

he denied the enemy, he made a succession of assaults on the city of Tripoli in the summer, and he might have been expected to continue to follow an aggressive course when reinforcements came. Dispatched from America before news of the attacks on Tripoli had been reported there, these included four frigates and, of the officers, two ranked Preble, who was now recalled. No reflection on him was intended. He was highly regarded by the administration even before his latest exploits, but there seemed to be no way to get around the obstacle of seniority. Unfortunately, Commodore Samuel Barron, who superseded Preble, suffered from bad health. Within a year he gave way to John Rodgers, who commanded the most impressive fleet yet gathered under the American flag.[5] Meanwhile, Preble returned to America, where he was treated like the hero he was. Communicating a report of his to Congress, the President said: "The energy and judgment displayed by this excellent officer . . . and the zeal and valor of his officers and men . . . cannot fail to give high satisfaction to Congress and their country, of whom they have deserved well."[6]

This excellent officer, whom his countrymen delighted to honor, had brought from Sicily a hogshead of Marsala wine, and he sent this by sea to the President a few weeks after he was extolled in Congress. Jefferson's desire to procure some of this wine, which as he understood resembled Madeira, had been recently expressed, but, as he wrote the Secretary of the Navy, he found the gift painfully embarrassing. His rule had been to reject any present of value, but he recognized that such rejection might suggest that he regarded the motives of the donor as impure, and he did not want to run the risk of offending Preble, who had been recalled under such unfortunate circumstances. Therefore, he decided to send him a counter-present of equal cost — namely, a polygraph. In his letter, without mentioning the expense, he said:

> You write much, move about much, and must of course find convenience in a portable secretary, which will copy all your letters and keep secret their contents. . . . Your turn for mechanics will render pleasing to you those little attentions necessary in the use of the instrument. You are not one of those who will not take

[5] These events and others in the war are well described by Gardner W. Allen, in *Our Navy and the Barbary Corsairs* (1905), especially chs. X–XV. Naval affairs also enter into the study of R. W. Irwin, *Diplomatic Relations of the U.S. with the Barbary Powers* (1931); see especially chs. IX, X. The letter of May 22, 1804 (quoted by Allen, pp. 198–199), announcing reinforcements and Preble's recall, was received by him early in August and he was relieved about a month later. In the excellent biography by Christopher McKee, *Edward Preble: A Naval Biography, 1761–1807* (1972), see chs. X–XV, XVII.

[6] Feb. 20, 1805; *Annals*, 8 Cong., 2 sess., p. 62. McKee, *Preble*, pp. 312–316.

time to learn what will save time. I have used one the last 18 months and can truly say that it is an inestimable invention.

The recipient's gracious letter of acceptance and thanks closed an episode which had been robbed of embarrassment and invested with charm by tact and generosity. Meanwhile, the connoisseur who headed the government had made a welcome addition to his wine list.[7]

The report that a treaty had been made with Tripoli reached Jefferson at Monticello. It was transmitted by the man who almost became secretary of the navy. Jacob Crowninshield wrote him in late August that news of an "honorable peace" had been borne by a brig just arrived in the port of Salem. Official dispatches were sent him a few days later by Robert Smith.[8] Secretary of War Dearborn and his wife, who were described by Jefferson as being "without ceremony," were his guests at the time — as were the President's old collegemate, John Page, now governor of Virginia, and his wife Margaret. Returning the papers to Robert Smith, Jefferson described the peace as "a subject of satisfaction." Margaret Page was less moderate. The verse she composed was equally marked by fervid patriotism and adulation of the President. One of the stanzas still reposing in his papers reads:

> *To Thee* exulting Friendship turns,
> Blest cause of All! immortal Man!
> *For Thee* the blaze of Glory burns,
> Whose Mind exhaustless form'd the Plan![9]

Congratulating him less effusively, a friend in Richmond wrote: "Your enemies now admit that your administration has been *very fortunate*. The people believe that such a *run of luck* must be the result of wise deliberations and prudent arrangements."[10] The settlement with Tripoli did not escape criticism, however. It was promptly attacked by Federalist newspapers and defended by Republican, and not for a long time did it gain the consent of the Senate.[11]

[7] Preble to the Secretary of the Navy, May 18, 1805 (LC, 26084); TJ to the Secretary of the Navy, May 31, 1805 (LC, 26156); TJ to Preble, July 6, 1805 (LC, 26328); Preble to TJ, July 30, 1805 (LC, 26435). TJ referred to his desire for Marsala wine in several letters.

[8] Jacob Crowninshield to TJ, two letters of Aug. 28, 1805 (LC, 26584, 26587), received Sept. 6 and 9 respectively; TJ to Robert Smith, Sept. 18, 1805 (LC, 26672), returning "Tripoline papers."

[9] LC, 26641; inscribed "Monticello, September 12th, 1805," and received that day.

[10] Meriwether Jones to TJ, Sept. 18, 1805 (LC, 26675).

[11] The partisan debate in the newspapers in the fall is described by Irwin, pp. 155–159.

The treaty of which the President learned in September and which he communicated to the Senate in December was negotiated by Tobias Lear, former secretary of George Washington and now consul general at Algiers.[12] Most welcome to the public at home was the provision for the release of the American prisoners, which was promptly put into effect in return for a ransom of $60,000. This sum amounted to one-fiftieth of the Pasha's original demand and represented a very considerable scaling down of later ones, but competent scholars of our own century have held that, in view of the growing strength of the American position, the payment of ransom could have been wholly avoided if Lear had waited a little longer.[13] On the other hand, the ranking naval officer, Commodore John Rodgers, would have been willing to pay more if necessary; and fear for the captives was a major reason for the conclusion of peace at the earliest possible moment. The prisoners may have overestimated their peril, but, as the Secretary of the Navy reported to the President, they were convinced that if they had not been ransomed they would have been murdered by the Pasha, who "again and again was heard to say that having killed his father and a brother he could not have any scruples in killing a few infidels."[14] Lear had been instructed to pay no ransom if he could avoid doing so, but, for all its economy-mindedness, the government could not object to the valuation of the captives at $200 a head, and this particular provision offered little ground for criticism. Also, there was occasion for rejoicing in the fact that no tribute was required, even though the understanding was that each new American consul would bring a substantial present. As treaties with Barbary powers went, nearly all of the provisions of this one were satisfactory if not positively gratifying.

The chief uncertainties and embarrassments arose from the third article. This required the evacuation of Derne on the Tripolitan coast, which had been taken by a motley force commanded by William Eaton after an incredible desert march from Egypt. It also required the effort to procure the withdrawal of Hamet Caramalli, elder brother of the reigning Pasha, Yusuf, by whom Hamet had been exiled and whom he was seeking to supplant. Eaton, whose official status was that of

---

[12] Treaty dated June 4, 1805, though actually executed June 10. English text in Hunter Miller, *Treaties and Other International Acts of the U.S.A.*, II (1931), 529–535, followed by Arabic text. It was communicated to the Senate on Dec. 11, 1805, along with Lear's instructions and his letter of July 5, 1805, describing the negotiations. These and other documents afterwards communicated are in *A.S.P.F.R.*, II, 695–725.

[13] Both Allen, who discusses the treaty in ch. XV, and Irwin, who does so in ch. X, take this position.

[14] Robert Smith to TJ, Sept. 19, 1805 (LC, 26677).

navy agent, had been authorized to co-operate with him and the two men had signed a convention. Commodore Barron would sanction no promise that the United States would place Hamet on the throne and, as time went on, he became increasingly impressed with the weakness of that unfortunate man's character.[15] Eaton had promised too much. The hero of the most fantastic operation of the war was bitterly disappointed by the turn of events and afterwards said that he himself was prepared to perish with Hamet before the walls of Tripoli or to triumph with him within them. All that was promised in the treaty was that in return for Hamet's withdrawal from Derne his brother would deliver over his wife and children, who were being held as hostages. The reigning Pasha made a demand for time to which Lear acceded. Nobody in the United States yet knew how long this was to be, but it could be argued that Hamet had been let down and his plight naturally aroused sympathy.

Disregarding for the moment more important developments in the winter of 1805–1806, we shall carry the story of relations with the Barbary powers through the congressional session and a bit beyond it. Hamet Caramalli presented his case to the American people in an address which Jefferson duly presented to Congress, along with numerous documents and a statement regarding the position of the government.[16] From the latter it appeared that Eaton had never been authorized to assure Hamet of his forcible restoration to the throne, and that a land war — that is, an attack on the city of Tripoli from Derne — was never contemplated. Although the President was careful not to impugn Eaton's motives, that frustrated agent, who continued to believe that Hamet had been badly treated, himself aroused sympathy which could readily be turned into condemnation of the government. Rightly acclaimed as a hero when he got home, he was almost inevitably taken up by Jefferson's political foes. Argument about the treatment of the luckless Hamet consumed most of the time the senators gave to the consideration of the treaty, when they finally got around to it at the very end of the session. One of them, who was no friend of the administration, told John Quincy Adams that the affair of Hamet had taken up two or three days when it might have been expected to take only that many minutes.[17]

[15] The most important documents are the Convention of Feb. 23, 1805, and Barron to Eaton, Mar. 22, 1805 (*A.S.P.F.R.*, II, 706–708).

[16] Hamet to the People of the U.S.A., Sept. 1, 1805, communicated Jan. 13, 1806 (*A.S.P.F.R.*, II, 696, 719).

[17] Senator J. A. Bayard, Apr. 2, 1806, in J. Q. Adams's *Memoirs*, I, 426.

The attempt to make ratification contingent on the return of his family was defeated, as was a motion to postpone action until the next session, and at length the Senate consented to the treaty on April 12, 1806, by a vote of 21 to 8. The division was largely though not wholly on party lines, for John Quincy Adams and William Plumer, who described the final debate as animated but mostly irrelevant, favored the treaty, while Robert Wright of Maryland, a Republican and the most vociferous champion of Hamet, was among its opponents.[18] Carrying on the sad story of that Tripolitan, for whom in fact virtually everybody wanted to do something, we must report that his wife and family were not soon delivered to him for reasons which were rumored earlier but did not come within official cognizance until after a new American consul appeared in Tripoli in May, 1807, and learned that Tobias Lear had made a secret agreement with Yusuf that allowed him four years to carry out his part of the bargain. If this information had been available at the time, it might have occasioned the defeat of the treaty. Jefferson communicated it to the Senate, with appropriate expressions of regret early in the next session of Congress.[19] The new consul, George Davis, had already persuaded the Pasha to make the return, and the government proceeded to make all the honorable amends it could. Hamet, who received financial aid from Commodore Rodgers and subsequently from Congress, lived about three years after his wife and children were restored to him, finally dying in exile in Egypt.[20]

"In operations at such a distance," said Jefferson to Congress, "it becomes necessary to leave much to the discretion of the agents employed; but events may still turn up beyond the limits of that discretion."[21] While disowning neither Eaton nor Lear, the government wisely declined to support them when they overstepped the line, as both did. The former received public acclaim for courage and generosity. After news of the secret agreement got out, the latter was charged by one Federalist with base treachery, and until our own day he has been blamed for letting his anxiety to attain peace becloud his judgment.[22] His major error was not soon revealed, but for a variety of reasons the treaty he negotiated with the Pasha did not redound to the credit of the administration to the extent that it deserved. At the

18 *Senate Exec. Procs.*, II, 31–32; Plumer, *Memorandum*, pp. 481–483; Adams, *Memoirs*, I, 433.
19 Nov. 11, 1807 (*A.S.P.F.R.*, II, 696–697).
20 Sketch of events in Allen, pp. 263–265.
21 Jan. 13, 1806 (*A.S.P.F.R.*, II, 696).
22 Charge by Timothy Pickering, quoted by Irwin, p. 159.

time, Senator William Plumer rightly described it as a good treaty, which "we are bound by the principles of justice and the welfare of our Country to ratify." But most of his colleagues viewed it with partisan eyes, and both he and John Quincy Adams questioned the trustworthiness of the President and his Secretary of State.

The uncertainties of these two senators, which may have been accentuated by their congenital suspiciousness as New Englanders, centered on what was known as the Mediterranean Fund. This had been set up a couple of years before to finance the operations off North Africa by the addition of a small import tax, and under the terms of the act it was to expire three months after the ratification of a treaty with Tripoli unless at that time the country should be at war with another Barbary power. Some of Jefferson's critics attributed to this consideration the delay of the Senate in acting on the treaty. He himself was said to have viewed with equanimity the prospect that action would be withheld until the next congressional session.[23] But, whatever alternatives he may have weighed as the person ultimately responsible for the solvency of the government, the treaty was accepted as a measure of the administration by what amounted to a partisan vote, and other means were found to meet the financial situation and provide for future contingencies. After reporting difficulties with Tunis, Jefferson suggested that Congress consider the expediency of continuing the Mediterranean Fund for a limited time, and Congress promptly did so until the end of the next session.[24]

The trouble with Tunis arose from the American seizure of a Tunisian vessel when it was attempting to run the blockade into Tripoli. The Bey loudly demanded its return, which Commodore Rodgers sternly refused; and, after futile conferences, an ambassador, Mellimelni by name, was sent to the United States to negotiate the matter. This emissary could enter into conversation only through an interpreter and proved to be an intractable negotiator. He made such exorbitant demands and acted so capriciously that his departure from the country was a relief. The danger of war was more remote than his threats implied, but this matter was not finally settled until January,

---

[23] Comments of Plumer, Apr. 2, 1805 (*Memorandum*, pp. 465–468); see also Apr. 3 (p. 472) and Adams, *Memoirs*, I, 434.

[24] For the Act of Mar. 26, 1804, setting up the Mediterranean Fund, see *Annals*, 8 Cong., 1 sess., pp. 1301–1303; for TJ's message of Apr. 14, 1806, see *Annals*, 9 Cong., 1 sess., pp. 237–238. By the Act approved Apr. 21, 1806, the first section of the original Act was continued (*ibid.*, p. 1274). John Randolph sought at the same time to get rid of the tax on salt, but we do not enter into that complication here.

1807, when Tobias Lear persuaded the Bey to accept $10,000 for the vessel.[25] After that, American naval forces were gradually withdrawn from the Mediterranean. There were further troubles with Tunis and Algiers, and not until the War of 1812 was the Barbary menace fully removed. We shall concern ourselves no more with it beyond saying that, while Jefferson's government did not wholly dispose of this problem, it did more, by force and diplomacy, than any previous administration or any European power had done and deserves credit for a minor success. But there were more serious problems in the international sphere, and other developments there had already raised grave doubts that his run of luck would continue.

[25] Developments are described by Irwin, pp. 161–167.

[IV]

Paris, Madrid, and Washington

1804 - 1805

EARLY in August, 1805, while at Monticello, Jefferson learned that James Monroe's mission to Spain had completely failed. For several months he had anticipated bad news from that quarter, but this report was even worse than he had expected and it quite took the edge off the good news that arrived from Tripoli a few weeks later. Spanish affairs were his chief concern while he was preparing for the next congressional session and dominated the early part of that, arousing violent controversy within his party. For a time this problem obscured that of relations with Great Britain, which became increasingly urgent as the European war took on new dimensions and American commerce incurred greater dangers. From the American point of view the futile negotiations in Madrid marked the beginning of a period of unsettlement which did not end while Jefferson remained in office. Thus the episode assumes major importance.

After signing the treaty whereby Louisiana was surprisingly ceded to the United States by France while still in Spanish possession, Monroe did not proceed to Madrid as he was authorized to do. Having received intimations from French officials that circumstances were unpropitious in Spain, where there was great annoyance over the cession, he wisely went instead to England, where his country was without a minister after Rufus King's return home. In the following spring (1804), after the United States had come into peaceful possession of Louisiana without knowing just what its boundaries were, his government instructed him to proceed to Spain to reach a settlement of the matters at issue with that country. His immediate departure was not required, however, if the state of American affairs in Britain, or European events yet unreported in his own land, should not permit.

Monroe did not feel warranted in leaving England until the following autumn. Despite some disagreeable experiences he gained a general impression of British attitudes which was not unfavorable: he believed that the British would grant more in practice than they would willingly admit in theory. But, becoming convinced that the government had no present intention of negotiating a treaty dealing with commercial matters and impressment, he left for the Continent, arriving at Paris early in November, 1804.[1] He had also been left at liberty to make his departure for Madrid contingent "on the prospect of active co-operation or favorable dispositions from quarters most likely to influence the counsels of Spain," and had been told by Madison that it would be of "peculiar importance to ascertain the views of the French government."[2]

While Monroe was given considerable leeway in the matter of timing, the objects of his negotiation were explicitly stated in the instructions Madison had drafted in the previous spring and slightly supplemented in the summer. Monroe was in full agreement with these, but they left him little freedom to maneuver. The main concern of the administration was to settle the question of boundaries, which had been left so vague in the treaty of cession; and, besides gaining Spanish recognition of the Perdido River as the eastern boundary of the purchase, to acquire the remainder of the Floridas, thus extinguishing Spanish rule east of the Mississippi. The claim to the Perdido boundary (between the present states of Florida and Alabama), far from being regarded as a mere arguing point, had become a fixed idea with Monroe, Jefferson, and Madison.[3] To the elaborate arguments based on historical events and old treaties that had already been advanced Madison added a very practical consideration: since the cession of Louisiana to the United States much of the most valuable land between the Mississippi and the Perdido had been granted by Spanish officials. The American government wanted to void these titles. With the lands to the southwest it was less concerned. Madison referred to the claim that the Río Bravo (Rio Grande) was the boundary, but this could have been regarded as a bargaining point or the matter left unsettled. On that side Monroe had some room to maneuver. Besides that of boundaries, there was the unsettled question of spoliation claims

[1] Monroe's judgments of the British are well set forth in his letter of July 1, 1804, to Madison (S.M.H., IV, 218–219).
[2] In Madison's letter of instructions, Apr. 15, 1804. This, with a draft of a convention and observations, and a further letter of instructions addressed to Monroe and Charles Pinckney, July 8, 1804, is in Hunt, VII, 141–156; quoted words on p. 141.
[3] See *Jefferson the President: First Term*, ch. XVIII.

for injuries to American shipping in the course of the recent European war. These were based on the actions of Spanish vessels, and also on those of French vessels which had used Spanish ports. A convention, signed in 1802 before the cession of Louisiana, provided for the adjudication of the claims arising from the former and for future consideration of the latter. The United States finally ratified this convention in 1804, after the acquisition of Louisiana and before Monroe's departure from England, but the Spanish declined to do so unless it were modified in ways that the American government regarded as unnecessary and undesirable.[4] Further complicating an already extremely complicated matter was the American claim to damages to shipping from the temporary removal of the right of deposit at New Orleans, which occurred after the negotiation of the convention of 1802.[5] The validity of all these claims of a commercial nature would have been hard to establish, but they added up to an impressive total.

As bargaining went, the American purpose amounted to an attempt to balance them against territorial claims and desires. In return for the recognition of the "right" to the Perdido and the cession of the rest of the Floridas, the United States would pay, *to its own citizens* to whom damages should be awarded, a sum of money as yet unspecified. Conceivably there could be territorial concessions on the western border and some modification of claims not provided for in the convention of 1802; but no money was to be poured into Spanish coffers. Anything that might go there could easily be seized by Napoleon's government, to which that of Spain was indebted and subservient; but the American proposals as described by Monroe to Talleyrand and others offered no monetary gain to France or any of her officials. And, unfortunately, Livingston had already heightened French appetites by suggesting that the United States might make a large "loan" to Spain. That the French would be the financial beneficiaries of this was as probable as its repayment to the United States by Spain was unlikely.

[4] The convention of Aug. 11, 1802, first communicated to the Senate, Jan. 11, 1803, is in *A.S.P.F.R.*, II, 475-476. The delay in ratifying it was occasioned by the unsuccessful attempt of Charles Pinckney to persuade the Spanish to make specific provision for the claims arising from the actions of French vessels. TJ recurred to the convention Dec. 21, 1803, communicating the correspondence (*ibid.*, II, 596-606). The Senate consented to the convention later in the session, but these claims were not surrendered. A major Spanish demand, made after the passage of the Mobile Act, was for further disavowal of the disrespect for the sovereignty of His Catholic Majesty allegedly shown in that measure. See the exchange of letters between Yrujo and Madison, Oct. 13, 15, 1804 (*ibid.*, II, 624-626). Madison's reaffirmation of assurances already given would appear to have been sufficient if the Spanish had really been disposed to reach a settlement with the United States.

[5] See *Jefferson the President: First Term*, pp. 240, 260, 281.

Annoyed by Livingston's officiousness and shocked by French venality, Monroe quickly let it be known that he would sanction no measure contemplating a payment of money to Spain.[6] Relying on the rightfulness of his country's claims, both commercial and territorial, he was sticking to the letter of his instructions. He was also relying on the offer of French good offices, made toward the end of the negotiations for Louisiana, which he and Livingston had seized upon at the time and which Jefferson and Madison had not sufficiently discounted. He was not disposed to pay the French for the help which, as he believed, they had voluntarily promised. Their unwillingness to give it to him now he attributed to the "project" of Livingston, and he afterwards asserted that the failure of his mission to Spain was "entirely owing to the misconduct of that individual."[7] Without justifying the interposition of Livingston, or condoning the rapacity of Napoleon and the venality of French officialdom, we may wonder what the United States and its virtuous representative had to offer that was wanted by either Spain or France. The likelihood was great that the potential Giant of the West would ultimately take over the Floridas by peaceful penetration, but the Spanish minister, the Marqués de Casa Yrujo, of whose troublesome presence the American government was not to be rid for several years longer, had reported that the threat was not likely to be backed by force. The case of the Floridas, even West Florida, was different from that of New Orleans.

The dilemma of the administration arose from the fact that, while determined to possess the Floridas, it was neither ready to fight for them nor content to let Nature take its course. Furthermore, the administration was obsessed with the idea of economy. Monroe appears to have shared that obsession, although he seems to have regarded his principals at home as being more belligerent than they were. As in the past, Jefferson was seeking to exploit the troubles of Europe to the advantage of his own country. One argument that continued to be advanced was that in case of Spanish involvement in the war on the side of France (which became a reality before Monroe got to Madrid) the British could seize the Floridas if they wanted to. Possession by the United States, presumably, would be more agreeable to Napoleon, just as friendly relations between that country and his vassal Spain would be to his advantage. So the President argued, but Napoleon, having removed the most likely cause of Franco-American conflict by ceding Louisiana, perceived no American threat sufficient to warrant an

[6] He described his experiences in France in a letter of Dec. 16, 1804, to Madison (S.M.H., IV, 277-297).

[7] Monroe to Madison, July 6, 1805 (S.M.H., IV, 302).

affront to Spain. Meanwhile, no doubt, Talleyrand and others continued to believe that money would be forthcoming.

Under these circumstances it is not at all surprising that the results of Monroe's stay of more than a month in Paris were negative. Livingston was still there, though he had asked to be relieved early in the year, and his replacement had finally arrived in the person of his brother-in-law, John Armstrong. That gentleman lacked official status while waiting to be presented to the Emperor. Monroe's own status was dubious, as Livingston did not fail to point out, and he got his case to Talleyrand only in a letter.[8] Though he did not receive a reply to this until after he reached Madrid, he was left in no doubt that the French refused to concede the American "right" to the Perdido boundary, that they denied the American spoliation claims arising from the actions of French ships and were indifferent to the others, and that they saw no hope of successful American negotiations without the offer of money. Since they were in position to call the tune, it now seems clear that there was no point in Monroe's proceeding to Spain.

In that era, when America was weeks rather than hours away from Europe and communication could be only by letter, American diplomacy was conducted under difficulties which modern men can scarcely imagine. On the occasion of his fruitless visit to Paris in the autumn of 1804, Monroe could not talk with Jefferson and Madison across the air waves. It is a great pity that he could not have asked them whether or not he should go to Spain. In the spirit of his instructions he might have abandoned, and undoubtedly could have postponed, the mission as soon as he became convinced that the French government would not support it, but it was a responsibility that anybody in his position would have hesitated to assume, and such a confession of failure would have been peculiarly embarrassing to him because of his sensitiveness and his relations with Livingston. The administration itself, having so strongly put itself on record, might have hesitated to instruct him to return to England, but they could have acted with better grace than he. Or, while instructing him to go to Madrid, they might have enlarged his powers by authorizing him to make a more attractive financial proposal. Judging from what he wrote home, however, he himself would have advised against that. At any rate, being unable to consult his superiors and distrustful of Livingston, he had to follow his own counsel.

His decision may be attributed in part to his temperamental perti-

---

[8] Monroe to Talleyrand, Nov. 8, 1804 (S.M.H., IV, 266–274).

nacity. He was not one to turn back from a difficult task. Furthermore, the ardor of his patriotism was increased, not diminished, by the rebuffs he received in Paris. The enthusiasm he had felt and manifested for the French cause when he was minister there a decade earlier was entirely dissipated, and he became increasingly desirous that his own country should pursue an independent course. Events were to show that he was far from undisposed to employ force against Spain in pursuit of claims he regarded as rightful, but he was not disposed to offer money, and least of all to engage in any species of bribery of Napoleonic France and her officials. As a diplomat Monroe was unfortunate, but he was a brave, upright, and thoroughly patriotic man. On his three-week journey to Madrid in December, 1804, he suffered considerable inconvenience, even hardship, and he faced possible complications there in the presence of Charles Pinckney, who had confused the situation by premature negotiations and had been at odds with the Spanish officials. In fact, his return to America was desired both by him and by the Spanish government, and James Bowdoin of Massachusetts had been named as his successor.[9] However, Pinckney, whose temperamental faults as a diplomat were recognized by Monroe as well as by the administration, remained in Spain throughout this mission and the two men got along very well.

Monroe arrived on New Year's Day, 1805. Nearly six months later he and Pinckney regretfully reported that the negotiation with which they had been charged had failed "in all its objects," notwithstanding their "unwearied and laborious exertions, for so great a length of time."[10] Not only had they failed to gain Spanish recognition of the Perdido boundary on the east and the cession of the rest of the Floridas; they had elicited a Spanish claim on the other side of the Mississippi which would have left the United States a mere string of land on the western bank of the river. Far from gaining Spanish recognition of further spoliation claims, they could not get them to accept the convention of 1802.

Commenting sagely on this failure soon after he learned of it, Albert Gallatin said: "The demands from Spain were too hard to have expected, even independent of French interference, any success from the

---

[9] Bowdoin was appointed Nov. 28, 1804, but did not sail till spring. Arriving in Europe in the summer of 1805, he went to London because of the unpropitious situation in Madrid, and afterwards to Paris.

[10] Monroe and Pinckney to Madison, May 23, 1805 (*A.S.P.F.R.*, II, 667–669). Their official correspondence with the Spanish government begins on p. 636 of that volume. The negotiations are described in detail in I. J. Cox, *West Florida Controversy* (1918), ch. IV; in Henry Adams, *History*, III, ch. II; and in Harry Ammon, *Monroe* (1972), ch. XIII.

JAMES MONROE
Engraving from an Original Painting by Alonzo Chappel
From E. A. Duyckinck, *National Portrait Gallery of Eminent Americans* (1862)

negotiation."[11] But the lack of candor and consideration the two envoys perceived in the Spaniards, and the imperiousness in the tone of the latter, may be attributed to the tacit support of the French government, which allowed the Spanish to give vent to their injured pride. Furthermore, on the basis of representations by Yrujo, the Spanish were confident that the United States would not push matters to extremes and that they themselves were safe in conceding nothing. The American assault on the court of Spain has been compared to that of Don Quixote on the windmill, and Monroe's stubborn reliance on the rightfulness of his country's cause gives point to the analogy.[12] But if this prosaic man was ever a knight, he was a sadly disillusioned one at the end of the negotiations. He then saw no recourse except to force, as was clearly shown by the private letter he and his colleague sent to Madison, along with the official report of their defeat.[13]

Monroe was wholly convinced that Spain would not pay a farthing toward spoliation claims, and that she would not cede a foot of territory or relinquish any of her "pretensions" except under compulsion. He regarded France as disposed to foment disagreement as long as she had any hope of profiting from it. By "shrinking before France and inviting her pressure," the United States would greatly weaken its position. Therefore, rather than submit to "injuries and insults," he and Pinckney recommended that the United States take possession of both of the Floridas and the whole region west of the Mississippi to the Río Bravo (Rio Grande), or at least to the Colorado. Believing such a course of action more likely to succeed than any other, they claimed that it could be pursued in "a spirit of moderation, of justice, and love of peace" by the nation in whose hands lay the destiny of the New World. But the seizure of these territories could not have failed to be regarded as a hostile act which would lead to war if not acceded to.

A couple of months before this letter was written, Jefferson, on the strength of reports from Armstrong in Paris, had anticipated that the Monroe mission would fail of its objectives. And, shortly before the mission ended, Madison set forth the position of the administration with respect to the alternatives it must now face. Writing to Monroe and speaking of war, he said: "As it is a question which belongs to Congress, not to the Executive, that consideration alone forbids any step, on the part of the latter, which would commit the nation, and so

[11] Gallatin to Madison, Aug. 6, 1805 (*Writings*, I, 238).
[12] It is suggested by Cox, p. 103.
[13] Pinckney and Monroe to Madison, May 25, 1805 (MP, 3:595).

far take from the Legislature the free exercise of its power."[14] These scruples were in full accord with the constitutional theory of pure republicanism, as they were with domestic political reality at a time when Congress was not in session and the country in no obvious peril. Of more immediate concern was the reference to the essentials of the moment for the maintenance of the peace: namely, a forbearance on the part of both countries to augment their settlements or to strengthen their military establishments in the "controverted limits," and on the part of Spain not to obstruct communication from the United States through the rivers to the Gulf. At the express direction of the President, Madison instructed Monroe to seek these safeguards.[15] This instruction had not reached Monroe when that minister wrote Jefferson from London four months later, saying he was "utterly at a loss" as to the present wishes of the government respecting Spain,[16] but Madison had enjoined him previously to the same effect.

In early instructions the Secretary of State had said that if no territorial settlement should be attainable, the immediate object should be to provide for the free use of the rivers. The United States could never be satisfied without Spanish admission of this right, and no representation short of war could be stronger than the case merited.[17] An even more specific injunction was included in the instructions addressed to Monroe and Pinckney in the summer of 1804. Madison then said that on entering into conference — that is, at the very first — they should "propose and press . . . in the strongest manner" that the military situation between the Iberville and Perdido should be strengthened by neither country and that the navigation of the Mobile should not be interrupted. If Spain should be unwilling to consent to this, the United States would be impelled to strengthen its own military forces in that quarter and to exert its right to navigation through Mobile. The latter was so essential that a refusal of Spain to acquiesce in it "must commit the peace of the two nations to the greatest hazard."[18] If Monroe had followed these instructions at the very beginning, he conceivably might have gained a *modus vivendi*. Or, if met by a refusal, he could have suspended the negotiations and returned to England. It is possible, however, that there was a breakdown in communication and that Monroe did not receive these final instructions until he was in the

[14] Madison to Monroe, May 23, 1805 (*A.S.P.F.R.*, II, 633).
[15] TJ's attitude is shown in his letters of Mar. 23 and Apr. 1, 1805, to Madison (MP, 28:100, 104) and of Apr. 3, 1805, to Gallatin (Ford, VIII, 350).
[16] Monroe to TJ, Sept. 26, 1805 (S.M.H., IV, 335).
[17] Madison to Monroe, July 29, 1803 (*A.S.P.F.R.*, II, 627).
[18] Madison to Monroe and Pinckney, July 8, 1804 (*ibid.*, II, 630–631).

midst of the negotiations.[19] At any rate he did not propose the maintenance of the *status quo* at the beginning of his mission, and apparently
he concluded that there was no point in doing so afterward. The
Spanish might have found the proposal unacceptable at any time, but
Jefferson and Madison had perceived an alternative between war and
submission which their representative had not even suggested to the
Spanish.[20] Monroe appears to have been unaware of any failure on his
part to follow his instructions, and his principals neither asked nor
received an explanation. Thus imperfect communication contributed
to the misunderstanding which had begun to cloud his relations with
Jefferson and Madison, and especially Madison.

During the month he spent in Paris on his way back to London
from Madrid, Monroe became more than ever convinced that the
French were counting on financial gain from any agreement between
the United States and Spain. Meanwhile, Madison, in response to information previously received from John Armstrong and speaking for the
President, had expressed strong disapprobation of "the venal suggestions emanating from the French functionaries."[21] Assuming a high
moral tone, he wrote: "The United States owe it to the world as well
as to themselves to let the example of one government at least, protest
against the corruption which prevails." Believing that the destinies of
no country could be injured by "adherence to the maxims of virtue,"
he confidently predicted that events would ultimately demonstrate the
wisdom of pursuing virtue's plain path. The Secretary of State, who
had had no firsthand experience with the courts of Europe, appears
here as a strict and upright official in a wicked world. He gave no sign
of relaxing the theoretical claim to West Florida but supported it anew
by elaborate reasoning. And he described the attitude of France as
inexplicable since she ran the risk of driving the United States to the
British side by wholly taking the part of Spain.

Armstrong was less disposed to await the ultimate triumph of
morality. Like Monroe, he had concluded that in the case of Spain the
proper recourse was to force. But his counsel, as given a little later, was
to disregard the Floridas and assail the Spanish posts west of the Missis-

19 According to Ammon (pp. 242, 621-622), Monroe did not receive Madison's
letter of July 8, 1804, until March, 1805.
20 While blaming Monroe, Brant (in *Madison*, IV, 263) holds that the proposal
was one-sided, since the process of settling adjacent American territory, and
thereby strengthening the American position, would have been unimpeded.
21 Monroe to Madison, July 6 and Aug. 6, 1805 (S.M.H., IV, 302-309); Madison
to Armstrong, June 6, 1805 (Hunt, VII, 183).

sippi. He believed that, if the United States should also threaten a commercial embargo against the Spanish, the French would interpose in order to prevent an open conflict with their ally.[22] Armstrong's anticipation of the Emperor's reaction may have been overly optimistic, but in the light of subsequent events it can be argued that Jefferson would have run relatively little risk and have saved much later trouble if he had followed the recommendation of his representatives abroad that he employ force at this juncture.[23] Had he been a Napoleon Bonaparte or even an Alexander Hamilton or an Aaron Burr, conceivably he might have taken military steps as a result of which his country would have gained speedy possession of territories it was destined to acquire later by means which were not wholly diplomatic. By ranging the United States, in effect, on the side of Great Britain in the international conflict he might have greatly reduced, though he could hardly have wholly obviated, later commercial difficulties with that country. He might have prevented the War of 1812 and hastened the downfall of Napoleon, whom he actually detested. Unlike the historian, however, he was unable to take a retrospective view. We must judge his policies in the light of the immediate circumstances, the information available to him, his attitudes toward constitutional republicanism, and his estimate of both the international and the domestic political situation.

ii

When, in August and September, he saw the dispatches from abroad, Congress was not in session and not scheduled to meet until December. His little group of advisers was widely scattered. During this period the Secretary of War visited him at Monticello, but Madison, instead of being in a neighboring country, was in Philadelphia with his ailing wife. Gallatin was in New York and Robert Smith in Baltimore. Jefferson caused the crucial dispatches to be circulated among them, inviting their comments, and summoned them to a meeting in Washington in the beginning of October. There was no grave national danger requiring immediate executive action so far as any of them could see; and Jefferson, Madison, and Gallatin were at one in the desire to infringe in no way on the constitutional prerogatives of Congress, the body in

---

[22] Armstrong to Madison, July 3, 1805 (quoted in Adams, *History*, III, 40); comment of TJ on the proposal in letter to Madison, Sept. 16, 1805 (Ford, VIII, 379).

[23] Adams, *History*, III, 80–81, referring particularly to Armstrong's proposal.

which the authority to declare war was vested. As the Secretary of the Treasury said, it was the duty of the Executive to do nothing in this interim which would put the peace of the country in jeopardy.[24]

Jefferson's first thought, which was echoed by Madison and Gallatin, was of the desirability of securing express assurance that the *status quo* would be maintained, a thing that Monroe and Pinckney had failed to get, but he soon recognized, and his advisers agreed, that further direct negotiations with Spain were impracticable. He did not yet know that the newly appointed minister to that country, James Bowdoin, had decided to proceed to London rather than Madrid, but he readily acquiesced in this action, as he did in Bowdoin's subsequent move to Paris. On the arrival in Madrid of Bowdoin's secretary, George W. Erving, to serve as chargé, Charles Pinckney left for home in the autumn. Though diplomatic relations with Spain were not broken, they were largely deprived of meaning. Madison reported from Philadelphia, where he saw Yrujo, that the generally obstreperous envoy was surprisingly friendly. He concluded that the Spanish did not want war, but neither he nor any other high executive official saw any present point in negotiating with them.

Viewing the situation from the American side, Jefferson promptly expressed the opinion that Spanish actions in themselves did not warrant war. Nonetheless, he went so far as to say to Madison at the height of his frustration in mid-August: "I do not view peace as within our choice."[25] Not even Gallatin ruled out the possibility of eventual war with Spain, but at this particular moment the President went beyond his most trusted advisers in referring to it as inevitable. The reason for this was not merely the obduracy he perceived in the Spanish government, but even more the hostility he sensed in the attitude of the French, which boded ill for the future. Therefore, his mind quickly turned to France's irreconcilable enemy, Great Britain. He never ceased to believe that it was to the interest of his own country to maintain full neutrality and complete independence. But, as he had observed to Madison a year earlier, both of these inveterate foes must always recognize that the United States might be driven into the

---

[24] Gallatin, after writing Madison, Aug. 6, and TJ, Aug. 17, sent extensive observations on Spanish affairs to TJ, Sept, 12, 1805 (LC, 26536; *Writings*, I, 238, 241–254). Robert Smith wrote him at considerable length, Sept. 10 (LC, 26633–26637). Madison's chief letters are referred to hereafter in connection with TJ's to him. The dialogue is described in Brant, IV, ch. XXI.

[25] TJ to Madison, Aug. 17, 1805 (LC, 26531).

scale of one of them by "unjust conduct" on the part of the other.[26] In the late summer of 1805 the disregard of American "rights" and interests of which he was most aware was that of France.

In fact, French policy toward the United States had been hardening since the acquisition of Louisiana; and it was now well symbolized by Napoleon's minister, General Louis Marie Turreau. This man of "ferocious disposition and brutal manners" could be readily contrasted with the friendly Pichon, who had done so much to facilitate the transfer of Louisiana.[27] Turreau had his first audience with the President on November 23, 1804; and Pichon, who was a general favorite, went home a few months later, after having served briefly as consul general in Philadelphia. William Plumer, recording his impressions of Turreau, explained the rise of this lowborn soldier on the ground that his sanguinary and brutish qualities made him useful to Napoleon.[28] His magnificent mustache, military bearing, splendid equipage, and elaborate dinners made considerable impression on Washington society, but he occasioned more talk by his flagrant visits to a "woman of easy virtue" and his gross maltreatment of his wife, who was said to have been also of low origin and to have brought the manners and language of the kitchen into the parlor. The pompous little British minister, Anthony Merry, who made so much of social propriety, reported this connubial brawling to his home office.[29] It became a matter of less concern in the summer of 1805, when the General and his family were in the country near Baltimore, but, at just the time that the President and Secretary of State were poring over the depressing dispatches from Spain, Turreau occasioned another sort of annoyance. This was in connection with the arrival in America of General Jean Victor Moreau, a French military hero who had been banished by Napoleon and to whom the Emperor did not want a conspicuous reception to be accorded. Regarding as highly offensive the letter in which Turreau sought to tell how this visitor to the United States should be treated, Jefferson told Madison that it offered an opportunity to inform the government of France that this country was "not of those powers who will receive and execute mandates." Then, referring to the Spanish question, he said: "I am strongly impressed with a belief of hostile and treacherous intentions against us on the part of France,

[26] TJ to Madison, Aug. 15, 1804 (MP, Rives Coll., 3:545).
[27] Quoted description from Plumer, *Memorandum*, p. 636; good account of Turreau in Brant, IV, ch. XX.
[28] Dec. 8, 1805 (*Memorandum*, p. 345).
[29] Merry to Mulgrave, June 30, 1805 (FO, 5:45, pp. 109–110).

and that we should lose no time in securing something more than a mutual friendship with England."[30]

The attitude of imperial France to the United States at this time might have been better described as one of contemptuous indifference; and even in his most fearful moments Jefferson did not regard the danger from that quarter as immediate. But, perceiving a shift in the international balance, he was concerned to redress it while the British were in need of allies. That is, he wanted to exploit the possibilities afforded by the European war and to avoid the danger of diplomatic isolation after the peace. He had no way of knowing that peace would be a decade in coming. At the moment he was also thinking in terms of the ensuing session of Congress. If an alliance with Britain was to be sought, he wanted to get negotiations under way so that he could have something to present or report to that body before it broke up in the spring. But if there was an uncharacteristic note of impatience in the dialogue he carried on with Madison in the late summer, this was not because he anticipated immediate hostilities with anybody. He was thinking of a provisional treaty of alliance which would become effective only *if and when* the United States should go to war with France or Spain or both.[31]

Madison, who was accustomed to Jefferson's proneness to exaggeration in private discourse with trusted friends and often supplied the necessary corrective, promptly took the sensible position that no agreement would be acceptable to the British if it was not reciprocal. "An eventual alliance with G.B.," he said, "if obtainable from her without inadmissible conditions, would be for us the best of all possible measures; but I do not see the least chance of laying her under obligations to be called into force at our will without correspondent obligations on our part." That is, as he said in another letter, the United States would either have to join her in the war or grant special commercial privileges or "concessions on points in the Law of Nations." Presumably he himself was opposed to benevolent neutrality as well as to overt belligerency; and unquestionably he believed that no formal proposition should be made at this time, whatever might be

---

[30] TJ to Madison, Aug. 25, 1805 (Ford, VIII, 376). The Moreau episode is in Brant, IV, 272-273. TJ seems to have found an earlier letter about Moreau's reception inoffensive. Writing DeWitt Clinton, Oct. 8, 1804, he advised against public display, saying that it would be injurious to Moreau and to American harmony with France.

[31] Besides the letters already cited, he wrote Madison on Aug. 25, 27, 1805 (Ford, VIII, 376-378); Sept. 16, 1805, referring to Armstrong's proposal (Ford, VIII, 379-380); Sept. 18 (LC, 26671); Oct. 11, still talking of a provisional alliance (Ford, VIII, 380). By Oct. 23 he had given up this idea (Ford, VIII, 380n.).

done later. Instead, he thought that "frank but informal explanations" should be made of the state of things between the United States and Spain.[32] In fact, that is just what was done, as Anthony Merry reported to his own government. Describing a conversation that took place in the middle of October, he said the President spoke with "great frankness." While Jefferson believed that, in the event of hostilities with Spain, the conquest of the Floridas and even of Cuba would be easy, he said that "his individual voice would constantly be for the preservation of peace with every Power, till it could no longer be kept without absolute dishonor."[33] This report was hardly calculated to terrify British policy-makers; nor was it likely to arouse their hopes that the cautious President would lead his country into the war on their side. It was about this time, in fact, that he dropped the idea of a provisional alliance with Merry's country. Late in August, he had said that the "first wish of every Englishman's heart" was to see Americans once more fighting beside them against the French, and that no public act could be more popular than an alliance with the United States.[34] A few weeks afterwards he would have been greatly embarrassed if this highly optimistic private assertion had been made public. But, whatever accuracy or inaccuracy there may have been in his assessment of British opinion in a period of frustration and disillusionment with the Spanish and the French, he had to face the grim realities of British *official* policy. And, after his return to Washington, he began to perceive the effects on American shipping, and on American public opinion, of the more rigorous efforts of the British to control commerce to their own advantage in their intensified conflict with Napoleon.

Actually, these may be dated back to the replacement of the Addington government by that of William Pitt in 1804, or even to resumption of the European war the year before, but the most conspicuous turning point was the decision in the *Essex* case in the late spring of 1805.[35] Invoking her own "Rule of 1756," that trade forbidden in times of peace might not be carried on in wartime, the Mistress of the Seas sought to prevent the use of neutral shipping in trade between her enemies France and Spain and their colonies.

[32] Madison's views are well set forth in his letters of Aug. 20 and Sept. 1, 1805 (LC, 26552–26553, 26608).

[33] Merry to Mulgrave, Nov. 3, 1805 (FO, 5:45, pp. 159–160—Secret No. 45).

[34] TJ to Madison, Aug. 27, 1805 (Ford, VIII, 378).

[35] Excellent brief account of the case in Bradford Perkins, *The First Rapprochement* (1955), pp. 177–180. He points out the uncertainty about the exact date of the decision but thinks May 22, 1805, the likely one (see his note 24 on p. 218). Official confirmation was not sent Madison by Monroe until Oct. 18, 1805.

American vessels had participated increasingly in this profitable business while the British navy was clearing the seas of enemy ships. The device employed was that of the "broken voyage," which had been permitted under an earlier British decision. In the case in question the *Essex*, en route to the West Indies from Spain, had put in at Salem, Massachusetts, and paid a nominal duty there. According to the decision, such a subterfuge was no longer permitted, but actual transshipment after the full payment of duties was required. From the British point of view this interpretation may have seemed logical as well as advantageous, but the Rule of 1756 was a unilateral pronouncement which they themselves had not consistently adhered to.[36] What is more, the policy based on it was carried into effect by naval officers in the summer without advance notice, and dozens of American vessels, engaged in trade they had good reason to regard as permissible, were seized and condemned. The consequent dismay can be easily imagined. Whatever grounds there may have been for the policy of the British, unquestionably they were arrogantly contemptuous of the United States.

On the day he reached Washington, Jefferson learned from Madison in Philadelphia that merchants were alarmed over late Admiralty decisions of the British. Madison conjectured that several millions of property were afloat, subject to capture under the doctrine now in force. And, following the meeting of the Cabinet the next day, the President reported to the absent Secretary of State that the question of a British alliance could not be decided without his presence and counsel.[37] In fact, Jefferson reached a decision against such an alliance before Madison's return late in October. Further reports from Europe entered into the reasons for this. Americans learned that Austria had joined the Third Coalition against Napoleon; and this news, with other reports of the spread of the war, led Jefferson to predict that it would be prolonged beyond his previous expectation.[38] He wrote Madison: "This gives us our great desideratum, time. In truth it places us quite at our ease." If the United States should be forced into the war, he said, it might be better — and without much doubt he was already convinced that it would be better — to do so without the embarrassment of an alliance and with the freedom to retire when the desired objects had

[36] See below, ch. VII, for Madison's arguments against it.

[37] Madison to TJ, Sept. 30, 1805, received Oct. 3 (LC, 26693); TJ to Madison, Oct. 11, 1805 (Ford, VIII, 380–382), after meeting of Oct. 4.

[38] Reference will be made hereafter to TJ's fascinating correspondence with the Tsar of Russia, beginning in 1804 (see below, ch. XXIV). It does not fit into the narrative at this point.

been obtained. Also, he had concluded that he now had time to make another effort for a peaceable settlement with Spain.[39]

Two days before the President of the United States wrote this letter, Lord Nelson, by defeating the fleets of France and Spain at Trafalgar, effectually removed the danger of the intervention of either of those powers in the affairs of the New World. Almost simultaneous with this memorable event was the appearance in London of a pamphlet that was highly significant at this particular time: *War in Disguise; or the Frauds of the Neutral Flags*, by James Stephen. This strongly supported, and was destined greatly to popularize, the current British commercial policy of ruthlessness toward neutrals. Since Jefferson and his chief advisers did not learn of them until a couple of months after they happened, these events did not influence the decision on Spain that he and his Cabinet reached in the middle of November.[40] Had he known about them he might have concluded that the United States could now with relative impunity occupy the territories disputed with Spain. He might have assumed British territorial indifference despite commercial ruthlessness and have decided to seize the Floridas and Texas when they were not looking.

But he and his major colleagues had already expressed the opinion that the United States did not have a just cause for war. Gallatin, who described the possible alternatives more fully than anybody else, and who for many reasons advocated persistence in a "pacific policy," put the matter impressively when he wrote:

> The high station which America and, I flatter myself, Mr. J's administration now occupy in the eyes of other nations, is principally due to the opinion which is entertained of their wisdom, justice, and moderation; and I think it (exclusively of every reason derived from duty) of primary importance that nothing should be done to weaken those favorable impressions; and that if war must be ultimately resorted to, we should previously place the controversy on such ground as will evidently put Spain in the wrong.[41]

One advantage that he saw in resuming negotiations was that a Spanish rejection of reasonable proposals — which in his mind meant

<hr/>

[39] TJ to Madison, Oct. 23, 1805 (Ford, VIII, 380*n.*).

[40] News of the battle of Trafalgar (Oct. 21, 1805) appears to have reached Washington about Dec. 20, and TJ learned of the pamphlet even later. The Cabinet met Nov. 12, 1805, after Madison's return (Ford, I, 308).

[41] Gallatin, *Writings*, I, 244, in his long discussion of Spanish affairs, sent TJ on Sept. 12, 1805.

somewhat modified American demands — would put the American cause on undeniably just ground. However, a temporary arrangement might be arrived at; and, in any case, the United States would gain delay and a chance to grow in strength. That consideration always carried great weight with Jefferson, and it goes far to explain his proneness to temporize and procrastinate. A complete cessation of negotiation would have amounted to a confession of utter failure and might have been interpreted as an abandonment of American claims, including those for spoliations.[42] Furthermore, it would have been politically embarrassing. Therefore, if negotiation offered any hope at all he thought it should be pursued in some way.

Gallatin seems to have been the first of the inner group to say that, under existing circumstances, they would have to negotiate with France. From Jefferson's private expostulations in the late summer, when he was flirting with the idea of a British alliance, one would assume that he then regarded the French as too hostile to be approached. But by late October, on the basis of the European news then available to him, he had concluded that the Emperor, confronted with a more formidable coalition of enemies than hitherto, would not want his ally Spain to be faced with foreign difficulties. Also, Napoleon might be supposed to be in greater need of money. That he had already gained a victory at Ulm the distant President did not know; and that he was to gain a greater one at Austerlitz Jefferson could not have been expected to foresee.

Aware only that the war had attained new intensity and that the British were treating neutral commerce more ruthlessly, Jefferson proposed to his advisers, informally in late October and formally in mid-November, that another effort be made for a peaceful settlement with Spain — not at Madrid, but at Paris, with France as the agent or mediator. To this proposal they agreed.[43] Now fully informed by his Secretary of the Treasury of the direct and indirect costs of war, he was willing to pay a higher price than hitherto for a peaceful settlement. Before the Cabinet meeting he wrote Madison that they "need not care" who would get the money, and that the increase might be "the bait to France." Whether this experienced diplomat was less scrupulous than Monroe and Madison, or more realistic, is a question.

---

[42] In a letter to Senator James Logan, Apr. 7, 1806 (LC, 27659), TJ said that, but for the spoliation claims, they would have been willing to let territorial matters take their natural course. If, however, they came forward with one complaint they had to bring forth all others, lest these be considered under international law as abandoned.

[43] TJ to Madison, and to Gallatin, Oct. 23, 1805; to Robert Smith, Oct. 24 (Ford, VIII, 380–382). Memo. of Cabinet meeting of Nov. 12 (Ford, I, 308–309).

But at this juncture he could have readily assumed that France could take anything she liked from Spain, and he gave no hint of yielding to the venality of French officials. He hoped to soothe the Spanish by setting the western boundary line in the middle of present Texas. The American payment for territories was now to exceed that of the Spanish for spoliations and could be made sooner. The figures remained flexible, but the American government was now agreeable to a payment of $5,000,000, of which it expected to get $4,000,000 back.

Within a week Madison received a coded letter from John Armstrong which served to strengthen the impression that they were on the right track.[44] The Minister enclosed a copy of a note, received by him in Talleyrand's handwriting from an unnamed intermediary, along with notes of his own on a subsequent conference relating to it. Devious and circumspect procedure was characteristic of Talleyrand, in Armstrong's opinion, but the American Minister thought that these papers represented French policy of the moment on the subject of relations between the United States and Spain. In his opinion the presentation of it might have been hastened somewhat by expected developments in the war and the desire to raise money. At all events, Talleyrand was now saying that the good offices of France should be reclaimed, and that pressure should be brought to bear on Spain, since a rupture with the United States was inevitable if Spain should persist in deciding arbitrarily the questions of boundaries, and so on. "The more you refer to the decision of the Emperor," Talleyrand said, "the more sure and easy will be the settlement." Then he set forth acceptable conditions on which Spain should part with the Floridas. Regarding territorial limits the stipulation was that on the west the boundary should be the Colorado (in mid-Texas) and that thirty leagues on each side of this river should remain unoccupied forever. With respect to finances it was proposed at first that the United States should pay Spain $10,000,000 but Armstrong got the figure whittled down to $7,000,000 before reporting it.

When Jefferson and his advisers considered Talleyrand's proposals on November 19 they stuck to the figure of $5,000,000 while agreeing to all the other provisions.[45] Presumably they did not regard these as particularly disadvantageous to their own country. What advantage France and her officials might gain, however, was another question.

[44] Armstrong to Madison, Sept. 10, 1805, with enclosures (NA, Diplomatic Dispatches, France).

[45] Memo. of Nov. 19, 1805 (Ford, I, 309); undated memo. of heads of articles to a proposed treaty with Spain (LC, 26862). The latter document appears in Ford, VIII, 383-384, with the conjectural date of Nov. 14, 1805, which seems a few days too early.

That was to be raised many times before any fresh negotiations could get started, but the details of the settlement the administration was now willing to seek were not a matter of public knowledge. And, having reached a decision regarding foreign policy, the next question the President must answer was just what to say to Congress. He had to reckon with the body that held the purse strings.

[V]

The Spanish Question Before Congress

1805 – 1806

THE first congressional session of Jefferson's second term turned out to be the most difficult of his presidency thus far. In the autumn of 1805 he may have anticipated that his annual political ordeal would be more severe than usual, and he always dreaded the social demands of his "winter campaign." But there was at least one pleasure he could look forward to: the company of his daughter Martha and her children in the barnlike President's House. They would serve as an antidote to the contentious legislators and disgruntled diplomats.

These children now numbered six, ranging in age from two to fourteen years, and a newcomer was well on the way — destined to be the first child born in that house. The health of the mother, which was exceptionally good as a rule, had occasioned Jefferson some alarm in recent weeks, and she herself wanted to avoid a lonely accouchement in the country, where she no longer had a sister to keep her company while their men were occupied with the public business in Washington. At her request her father commissioned Mrs. Madison to procure for her certain articles — a fashionable wig, a set of combs, a "bonnet shawl and white lace veil, for paying morning visits." Mrs. Madison sent the articles from Philadelphia, where she remained several weeks after her husband's return, and Jefferson paid sixty dollars for them. His daughter was much concerned over the expense of her visit, at a time when her husband's finances were in a parlous state, but Jefferson was only too glad to assume the whole of it. He sent her a hundred dollars to cover the costs of her journey and dispatched a carriage to meet her at Centerville. Vehicles were hard to find at a time when so many representatives and senators wanted them, but the President's coachman, Joseph Dougherty, got hold of one, and the arrival of his daughter and grandchildren coincided almost exactly with the opening of Congress.[1]

Exactly a week after the session began, John Quincy Adams dined at the President's. The Senator noted that Mrs. Randolph and her daughter were the only ladies present. Anne Cary, not yet fifteen, would undoubtedly have been pleased if she had known that she had been elevated to the status of a lady. Jefferson's two sons-in-law and his secretary were there as usual. Adams was the only representative of his party, and the Federalists are said to have blamed the President for not having them as dinner guests in December — so much so that hardly any of them observed the custom of paying their respects to him on New Year's Day.[2] His seeming neglect of them may have been owing to a temporary curtailment of hospitality occasioned by the advanced state of his daughter's pregnancy, for he had numerous Federalist guests after her deliverance.[3] There is political significance, nonetheless, in the fact that the company at this early dinner consisted largely of Republican legislators, whose support was important and some of whom it would have been most unfortunate to offend even unwittingly. Included among the latter were Joseph H. Nicholson and John Randolph, who was noted both for his vanity and his extraordinary capacity for inflicting wounds on others.

About a month before he set out from the place that was so appropriately named Bizarre, Randolph wrote Gallatin that his health, which was generally precarious, was so improved that he proposed to brave another Washington winter. "I look forward to the ensuing session of Congress with no very pleasant feelings," he continued. "To say nothing of the disadvantages of the place, natural as well as acquired, I anticipate a plentiful harvest of bickering and blunders; of which, however, I hope to be a quiet, if not an unconcerned, spectator."[4] Quietness was not to be expected of him, but he gave no sign of ill will toward the President. "I regret exceedingly Mr. Jefferson's resolution to retire," he said, "and almost as much the premature annunciation of that determination. . . . If I were sure that Monroe would succeed him, my regret would be very much diminished." That is, he was against Madison; and his willingness to imply as much was not a good omen at a time when the most important matters to be presented to

---

[1] The correspondence preceding the visit is in *Family Letters*, pp. 279–284; financial items are in TJ's Account Book. Congress convened Dec. 2, 1805.

[2] J. Q. Adams, *Memoirs*, I, 378; Plumer, *Memorandum*, p. 363.

[3] As on Feb. 25, 1806 (Adams, *Memoirs*, I, 415). Her child, James Madison Randolph, was born Jan. 17, 1806.

[4] Randolph to Gallatin, Oct. 25, 1805 (Adams, *Gallatin*, pp. 331–333).

Congress by the administration lay within Madison's field of foreign affairs. Randolph had previously inquired of Gallatin how long Monroe would remain in London, and it was afterwards rumored that he would have liked to succeed that emissary.[5] Whether or not he harbored this ambition, it was hardly a major consideration when he returned to Congress. Nonetheless, the congressional leader who had blocked the Yazoo compromise, for which his old friend Gallatin was chiefly responsible, and had mismanaged the impeachment trial of Justice Chase, was in a restless state of mind and an anomalous position. By right he should not have expected recognition as the congressional spokesman of the administration, but anyone who knew him could have foreseen that he would bitterly resent any challenge of him as majority leader of the House.

Randolph had assumed this role by virtue of his chairmanship of the Ways and Means Committee, a post to which he was appointed by the Speaker. Direct interference by the President in either the election or the appointing power of the latter would not have been tolerated by the House of Representatives and would have been quite out of line with Jefferson's customary procedure. He sedulously avoided participation in intra-party contests of any sort. There was one in the House over the speakership at the very beginning of the session. The re-election of Nathaniel Macon, who was liked by virtually everybody and opposed by fellow Republicans only because of his intimacy with John Randolph, was contested in behalf of Joseph B. Varnum of Massachusetts, who was supported by the northern Republicans. John Randolph was reputed to despise them, while Jefferson had sought from the beginning of his presidency to build up their wing of the party. The re-election of Macon on the third ballot was described in Federalist quarters as a blow to the friends of the administration, and undoubtedly it was a disappointment to the northern Republicans. We cannot believe that Jefferson would have raised a hand or uttered a word against Nathaniel Macon, whom he greatly liked and deeply respected, but the reappointment of John Randolph as chairman of the Ways and Means Committee, which quickly followed, could hardly have failed to disquiet him. Probably it was true at this time, as it unquestionably was a little later, that he would have preferred the appointment of Barnabas Bidwell of Massachusetts, which might have

---

[5] Gallatin reported the inquiry about Monroe in a letter of Oct. 17, 1805, to TJ (LC, 26749). W. A. Burwell in his Private Memoir (LC) reports and tends to discount the rumor about the mission to Great Britain. Brant, IV, 310–311, takes it rather more seriously.

been expected of Varnum despite the fact that this lawyer from Stockbridge was a new member.[6]

Bidwell, who was strongly commended to Jefferson by his New England sentinel, Levi Lincoln, was presented to him by Varnum a few days before the session began and reported to his wife that he received a very polite reception.[7] That might have been said by almost any visitor to the President, however, and unfortunately the details of his "easy and sensible" conversation were not reported. Within a few weeks the new congressman was given the name of "sworn interpreter of executive messages." Since Bidwell was resented by both the Randolph faction and the New England Federalists, who affected to despise him, their slighting comments must be discounted. William Plumer, who was relatively objective, thought highly of his abilities, just as the New England Republicans did.[8] He appears to have gained Jefferson's confidence at the outset, but it seems impossible to ascertain what part, if any, the President had in his initial maneuvers in the House in which John Randolph's authority was vainly challenged.

On the opening day of the session this authority seemed to be established. Besides being named chairman of the Ways and Means Committee, Randolph headed the committee that reported to the President the presence of a quorum. After the annual message of the latter had been received next day, there was a contest over the question whether the parts of it relating to the conduct of the belligerent powers with regard to neutral commerce should be referred to Ways and Means or to a select committee. Outmaneuvering Bidwell, Nicholson proposed the former before the newcomer could propose the latter, and his resolution prevailed. It was to be more than six weeks, however, before Jefferson sent a special message on neutral commerce; and after some quibbling and skirmishing this question was referred to the Committee of the Whole.[9] The important consideration at the outset was that the displeasure of the contemptuous Majority Leader was aroused against one whom he regarded as an upstart; and that, whatever the facts may

[6] An account of the contest over the speakership, which is not suggested in the report of the proceedings in *Annals,* 9 Cong., 1 sess., p. 254, and of the immediate aftermath is given by A. B. Lacy in his dissertation, "Jefferson and Congress" (1963), pp. 157–160, with full references. Most of the details come from accounts by Federalists, especially William Plumer (*Memorandum,* pp. 337–338) and Josiah Quincy (*Life,* pp. 94–95). Most of the Federalists supported John Cotton Smith of Connecticut, but Quincy and a few others ultimately voted for Macon, assuring his election.

[7] Barnabas to Mary Bidwell, Nov. 28, 1805 (courtesy of Richard D. Birdsall).

[8] See Samuel Taggart's comment of Jan. 12, 1806 ("Letters," p. 173) and Plumer's entry of Mar. 8, 1806 (*Memorandum,* p. 446).

[9] Actions, respectively, of Dec. 4, 1805, and Jan. 29, 1806 (*Annals,* 9 Cong., 1 sess., pp. 258–262, 412). TJ sent his special message on neutral commerce Jan. 17.

have been, he probably believed that Jefferson was party to a plot to disarm if not to depose him. Thus he was in a highly suspicious state of mind when the matter of most immediate concern to the administration came up — namely, the renewal of negotiations with Spain.

Jefferson himself regarded the infringement on neutral rights by the maritime powers as a greater "enormity" than the intransigence of Spain, and he commented on it first in his annual message to Congress, without referring to the British by name. He deliberately adopted a strong tone in this public document. "The message is more energetic and warlike than any he ever sent to Congress," said Senator William Plumer.[10] Hostile critics accused him of blustering in order to gratify the public, but, so far as his references to Spanish relations were concerned, he said privately that his major purpose was to impress the French. And, having concluded, after reading an early draft, that he had been too soft on the British, he toughened the passages relating to them in order to effect a better balance. He did not indicate what precise "injuries" he had in mind — whether from the British on the water or from the Spanish on the border — when he said that some of these were "of a nature to be met by force only." But, while deferring to the wisdom of Congress, he made recommendations and suggestions regarding the organization of the militia and the augmentation of the navy.

His efforts in matters bearing on national defense may have been insufficient, but the events of this session were to show that his concern exceeded that of the majority in Congress. He strongly recommended a classification of the militia on the basis of age, so as to make an effective body of young men available for service anywhere in the country, but this reform proved too much for upholders of the existing archaic and localized system.[11] For the defense of harbors he pointed out the desirability of increasing the number of gunboats and providing cannon for land batteries. Here he was keeping within the

[10] Plumer, *Memorandum*, p. 339. TJ's draft of the message, showing changes, is in Ford, VIII, 384–396, along with extracts from his correspondence with his executive officers about it. His note of Nov. 24, 1805, to Gallatin is of special interest.

[11] Draft of a bill for classifying the militia is in Ford, VIII, 409–412. Similar reforms had been advocated by Knox when secretary of war. This matter is discussed more fully in ch. XXVIII below. TJ also sought to establish a naval militia (Ford, VIII, 403–409). The Act for establishing rules and articles for the government of the armies (Apr. 10, 1806; *Annals*, 9 Cong., 1 sess., pp. 1238–1253), revising the Articles for the first time since 1776, resulted from a resolution of Varnum in the House, Dec. 6, 1805 (*ibid.*, p. 264); discussed Jan. 2, 1806 (*ibid.*, pp. 326–327). Dearborn's connection with this has not been established and TJ appears to have played no part in it except to sign the measure.

range of congressional approval. But he also reminded the legislators that materials for the construction of ships of the line had been collected under previous authorization and could be utilized if Congress should so determine. The augmentation of the navy by building ships of this class had been strongly recommended by Robert Smith and was even favored by economy-minded Gallatin as an ultimate policy. Getting ahead of the story, we may report here that resolutions calling not only for gunboats and the fortifying of harbors but also for the building of six ships of the line were duly introduced in the House. The latter proposal, however, was supported by less than a third of that body.[12] After Congress had adjourned, writing to the man he had wanted as his secretary of the navy, Jefferson said: "That we should have a squadron properly composed to prevent the blockading our ports is indispensable." He then believed that if the measure should be brought forward in a moderate form the country would come to it, "notwithstanding the repugnance of some on the subject being first presented."[13]

The President might have been able to force through some or all of the defense measures that he and his major advisers favored if he could have found better human instruments to work with and had put his own prestige on the line. But, besides having to depend on such men as were available, he was handicapped by the unmistakable fact that he was seeking a peaceful solution of his gravest problems. If he erred in tactics, his major fault lay in his choice of priorities. The Spanish question came first in point of time and seemed to him less controversial than that of British relations; but, in the effort to gain the means to pursue what proved to be a fruitless negotiation, he aroused a domestic storm which endangered other objects. As a leader he survived this storm handily, but the diplomatic gains did not match the struggle.

He sent a confidential message on Spain to the two houses of Congress three days after his secretary brought them his public message.[14] He candidly reported the complete failure of the Monroe

---

[12] Resolutions of Dec. 23, 1805, introduced by John Dawson of Virginia, acted on, Mar. 25, 1806 (*Annals*, 9 Cong., 1 sess., 302, 842–848).

[13] TJ to Jacob Crowninshield, May 13, 1806 (Ford, VIII, 453).

[14] Dec. 6, 1805 (Ford, VIII, 397–402, with pertinent materials in the notes). TJ's correspondence with Gallatin about the message and proposed resolutions is in fuller form in the latter's *Writings*, I, 275–282. The message is also in *A.S.P.F.R.*, II, 613. It is followed there by diplomatic documents and by a further batch of papers transmitted by TJ on Dec. 10 (pp. 669–695). The latter, which were not confidential, bear upon Spanish depredations on American shipping, the imposition of import and export duties at Mobile, military threats on the border, and the like.

mission and submitted abundant evidence of the unsatisfactory state of affairs on the southern border. At the same time he informed the legislators of his belief that France was disposed to bring about a settlement of the Spanish question which would be acceptable to the United States and promised to remove all future grounds of controversy. He could not have been expected to imperil such a settlement by revealing its terms in advance, nor to have realized as yet the extent to which his own hopes were exaggerated. But the optimism of his tone contrasted sharply with the forebodings he had voiced in his public message. It was more in character with his sanguine nature, but he may have deliberately assumed it in the effort to be persuasive. Urging that the opportunity to effect a settlement be immediately seized upon, he said that formal war was neither necessary nor probable. Thus he took the edge off the rather belligerent passages in his public message and elicited from certain congressmen charges of double-talk. By the same token he dulled the demand for measures of national defense. He pointed out that the desired diplomatic course would require money; and, without mentioning the Floridas by name or suggesting a specific sum, he committed everything to the wisdom of Congress.

After full allowance is made for the constitutional authority of the legislature in financial matters, and for the fact that in his age the presidency had gained no such prestige or power as it was to enjoy in the twentieth century, it would appear that he erred on the side of deference. Also, desirable as secrecy is in diplomacy, he appears to have erred on the side of vagueness. Gallatin, who was so wise in legislative matters, objected to the tenor of the message on the ground that it did not "explicitly declare the object in view" and might therefore be "cavilled at as having induced Congress into a mistaken opinion of that object."[15] Jefferson's procedure was approved by Gallatin as well as by the other ministers, however, and in important respects was guided by his counsel. What the President and his advisers wanted Congress to do was to pass a set of resolutions describing Spanish offenses and stating American objectives in general terms, which could be made a matter of public record; and then, by secret action, to authorize the use of a specific sum of money. The purpose of the appropriation, as Gallatin put it privately, was to permit partial payment for the desired territory as soon as possession of it was assured, without waiting for the ratification of a treaty by the Senate, an action which might be dangerously delayed. He thought $2,000,000 would be enough, though he was somewhat fearful lest a false impression be given that no more would be required. The course he now recommended and Jefferson adopted was precisely the one that had been followed in connection with Louisiana before Monroe set out for France. Then, after the adoption of resolutions that were introduced by John Randolph and in due course became public, an appropriation was made whose specific purpose remained confidential. In fact, the appropriation at that time was for exactly the same amount now asked for. Gallatin argued that a course following this precedent would be "the smoothest mode of doing the business in Congress."[16] But, unhappily, John Randolph's relations with the administration were not the same as they had been a couple of years earlier. That egotistical and vitriolic congressman now deplored the sort of approach to Congress which had been made in the past and had then had results more gratifying than anybody expected.

The precise course of events is difficult to determine, since little record remains of what went on behind the scenes. Gallatin delivered to his kinsman Joseph H. Nicholson, a member of the committee which would consider the Spanish business, a paper containing the resolutions the President had drawn and his advisers had agreed to, but these were never presented to Congress. On the same day John Randolph sought, and on the next day had, a conference with Jefferson. Then, according to his own account, written months later, he was informed that the President desired an appropriation of $2,000,000 for negotiations for the Floridas.[17] He reported that he rejected the proposal — partly because he frowned on the negotiations themselves, but chiefly because the President had not stated in his message precisely what he wanted and what he wanted it for. In Randolph's expressed opinion, Jefferson was seeking to evade responsibility and to fix it on Congress. To those viewing this episode from the vantage point of later years, it might appear that, at a time when a sharp demarcation between the executive and the legislature was dictated by republican theory, the President was going to extreme lengths to avoid the very appearance of encroaching on the prerogatives of Congress. He may be said to have resorted to indirect means through force of necessity, being able to escape from the shackles of republican ideology in no other way. The President had to tread warily in a period when his own partisans admitted that they were sometimes embarrassed because he was not "sufficiently *scrupulous* in the concealment of his opinions."[18]

[16] *Ibid.*, 179; see *Jefferson the President: First Term*, pp. 268, 270–272.

[17] He reported this in the first of his Decius letters to the Richmond *Enquirer*, Aug. 15, 1806; summary in Bruce, *Randolph*, I, 225–226.

[18] "Reflections upon Decius," in Richmond *Enquirer*, Sept. 2, 1806.

In this particular instance he might have pursued a wiser course, from the tactical point of view, if he had been as specific in his official message as he was in private conference, but it may seriously be doubted if any procedure would have satisfied John Randolph's suspicious mind.

He was not mollified by the President's hospitality and yielded none of his scruples because of his friendship with the Secretary of the Treasury. He afterwards reported that, while this matter was still pending in committee, Gallatin put into his hands a paper with the heading, "Provision for the Purchase of Florida." This he spurned, declaring that he would not vote a shilling. According to his further report, Gallatin then hedged by saying that he did not want to be understood to be recommending the measure, but that he had devised a plan to raise the money if Congress should decide to authorize it.[19] Like Jefferson, Gallatin was caught between the upper and nether millstones of republican dogma and what he believed to be a realistic appraisal of an actual situation.

Randolph also reported an early, and to his mind fateful, conversation with Madison. On the floor of Congress months after the event, referring sarcastically to the head of what was supposed to be the first executive department, he said he was informed in this conversation that money must be paid France before she would permit Spain to come to any accommodation with the United States. Whether this was a "declaration," as he designated it, or his own inference, he vividly described his reaction to it: "I considered it a base prostration of the national character, to excite one nation by money to bully another out of its property, and from that moment . . . my confidence in the principles of the man entertaining those sentiments died, never to live again."[20]

In view of his proneness to distortion and to the impugnment of the motives of those who disagreed with him, he cannot be regarded as an objective reporter. And the morality of the executive officers should be adjudged in the light of the totality of the complicated circumstances and the alternatives open to them. Randolph, who approached public problems as a purist and talked in terms of absolutes, was not the man to concede that a government might be faced with a choice between evils; and he assumed a tone of moral superiority which did not comport with his personal (verbal) cruelty toward those who differed from him in matters of policy or tactics or who affronted his vanity. Whatever may be said about the policy and tactics of the

[19] Bruce, I, 227, from DECIUS letters.
[20] Apr. 5, 1806 (*Annals*, 9 Cong., 1 sess., p. 947).

administration in this instance, he was grossly unfair in laying the chief blame for either on the Secretary of State, who was already the object of his special detestation.

The presidential message and accompanying documents were referred to a special committee of which John Randolph was chairman and Barnabas Bidwell a member, and after about a month the former presented a report.[21] This may be described as ambiguous and in certain respects pusillanimous. It expressed indignation at the hostile spirit and specific actions of the Spanish, asserting that these in themselves constituted ample cause for a declaration of war. Jefferson's most trusted advisers had not gone that far. In tone, however, this report was far from bellicose. Few could object to the statement that "to a Government identified with its citizens, too far removed from the powerful nations of the earth for its safety to be endangered by their hostility, peace must always be desirable, so long as it is compatible with the honor and interest of the community." That was, in fact, a good statement of Jefferson's own position. But Randolph's insistence that belligerency should be shunned until the national debt had been discharged went beyond any position that the economy-minded President and his economy-minded Secretary of the Treasury had taken. It might have been expected to bring comforting assurance to actual or potential foreign foes, who could infer that to the American mind the *summum bonum* was freedom from taxation. And the reference to "reaping the rich harvest of neutrality" was hardly a noble utterance. The committee believed that the present state of international affairs was "peculiarly favorable" to the peaceful pursuit of the best interests of the country, and it indulged the hope that an amicable settlement could be reached with Spain. But John Randolph made only one positive proposal. He offered a resolution authorizing the immediate raising of such number of troops as the President might deem sufficient to protect the southern frontiers from Spanish "inroad and insult." Beyond that he would have had Congress assume no responsibility whatsoever.

Barnabas Bidwell made no minority report, but he immediately introduced a resolution calling for the appropriation that the President desired, thus challenging the Chairman. The issue was joined between these two resolutions. This is not to say that it lay between military preparedness and diplomacy, for, on the day the debate began, Varnum, as chairman of the committee to which the former matter had been referred, introduced a bill authorizing the President to call

21 Jan. 3, 1806 (*Annals,* 9 Cong., 1 sess., pp. 1117–1118).

into service militia up to 100,000 and appropriating $2,000,000 for that purpose. This bill was adopted by the House three weeks later by a rising vote.[22] Meanwhile, the debate on the proposed appropriation of a like amount for undefined diplomatic purposes took place behind closed doors. Since this was not officially reported we must rely on secondhand accounts of John Randolph's impassioned oratory and on his own later statements, but we cannot doubt that he violently objected to the proposal. This was partly because he did not want to "grease the fists of Napoleon with American gold," as he is reported to have said, and partly if not more because he resented the secretive tactics of the administration. But the adoption of the Bidwell resolution marked his defeat; and on the next day the President could also rejoice in the birth of a grandson, who, by interesting coincidence, was named for James Madison.

This was about ten days after the issue was joined. The debates and parliamentary maneuvers in the two houses extended over a period of about a month, at the end of which time Jefferson signed an act giving him just what he wanted. Some six weeks later the injunction of secrecy was removed by the House of Representatives. The proceedings and votes, without the speeches and the presidential message, then became in the full sense a matter of *public* record.[23] This action could be regarded as a vindication of Randolph, who had protested violently against the secrecy of this business; and, according to William Plumer, the unanimous support of it by the Federalists was attributable to their belief that the publicity of the measure would damn the popularity of the President. But the Senator from New Hampshire himself believed that the first exclamation of those reading the published proceedings would be "*Is this all?*"[24] In fact, the most important bits of information had leaked out already.

Following a long conversation a few days after the House gave publicity to the objective of the appropriation, Plumer recorded that

[22] Presented Jan. 6, 1806; adopted Jan. 27 (*Annals*, 9 Cong., 1 sess., pp. 333–334, 398–408). It was passed by the Senate Apr. 14. For the final act, see *ibid.*, pp. 1265–1266.

[23] Supplemental Journal in *Annals*, 9 Cong., 1 sess., pp. 1117–1144. The main debates in the House were between Jan. 6 and 16, 1806, when the bill passed. The Senate concurred Feb. 7 and TJ signed the Act on Feb. 13 (*ibid.*, pp. 1226–1227). The injunction of secrecy was removed Mar. 31, and the matter was discussed further in a debate on John Randolph's unsuccessful motion to publish the President's message also, Apr. 5–7, 1806 (*ibid.*, pp. 946–993). Plumer gives an account of the debate in the House as he heard of it (*Memorandum*, pp. 367–371) and describes the debate in the Senate at some length in his entries from Jan. 21 to Feb. 7.

[24] *Memorandum*, p. 465.

Jefferson regretted the action, believing that it would do no good and might do harm. But the President added that the House was responsible for its own measures. "I then observed," said the Senator, "that our form of government appeared to me better calculated for the management of our own internal concerns than to regulate our relations with other nations." Jefferson replied that the observation was "perfectly correct" — a judgment which was unquestionably borne out by his experience as President. In the effort to overcome the difficulties arising from the division of powers, he kept diplomacy in his own hands as fully as possible, never doubting that it was an executive function. At the same time he set high value on a divided and limited government and was profoundly concerned to preserve republican institutions. Inevitably, therefore, he sometimes appeared ambivalent. "Our constitution is a peace establishment — it is not calculated for war," he said. "War would endanger its existence."[25] That was a major reason for his persistent attempt to find peaceful solutions for his country's international problems.

The measure that had been signed by him and was now revealed to the public left his hands untied. It appropriated $2,000,000 "towards defraying any extraordinary expenses that may be incurred in the intercourse between the United States and foreign nations." The bill that was transmitted to the Senate after its passage by the House had that title, but it was accompanied by a statement that it was actually designed to support negotiations for the purchase of Spanish territory.[26] The House put itself on further record as preferring specific to general language in a resolution that was revived under Randolph's spurring. He had the pleasure of presenting this to the President, along with another resolution declaring that a settlement with Spain based on an exchange of territory would meet the approbation of the House.[27] The first of these may be regarded as an intended rebuke, and the other as an attempt by the House to intrude in the treaty-making process. But the fact remains that on the crucial question of the appropriation and the language of the act itself Jefferson received the necessary support from his own party. All the Federalists went along with Randolph in his obstructive course and some of the best of them were now showering praise on him. To James A. Bayard it seemed that he had behaved "very handsomely" in the field of foreign relations. "His conduct has been candid, decided, and manly," said that Senator, who described the administration as weak and hypocritical by contrast.

25 Interview of Apr. 2, 1806 (ibid., p. 470).
26 Annals, 9 Cong., 1 sess., p. 1133.
27 Ibid., pp. 1137–1138.

"What they are ashamed of they transact before the two houses with closed doors. And the President, speaking one language, is endeavoring to pursue opposite measures in order that he may be judged by the world by his speeches, and the responsibility of the measures thrown on other persons."[28] Like John Randolph, he was putting the worst possible construction on Jefferson's language. But Randolph was able to carry only a few of his fellow Republicans with him. The party loyalty of the northern representatives and senators was specially notable, for they were relatively uninterested in the Floridas. But they were devoted to Jefferson, especially the New Englanders whom he had tried so hard to encourage, and they had abundant reason to dislike John Randolph, who now, more than ever, lashed them with whips of scorn.

[28] Comments in letters of Jan. 30, 31, 1806 ("Correspondence" in *Annual Report A.H.A. 1913*, II, 164–165).

[VI]

Troublemakers and Frustrated Diplomats

FROM the point of view of the President and his Secretary of State the chief gadfly of this season was the attenuated, shrill-voiced congressman from Bizarre in their own Virginia. And, as we shall see, John Randolph got more not less obstreperous as the session proceeded. But there was another of lesser note with a wholly different background who, for entirely different reasons, harassed the administration and sought to circumvent its Spanish program. Shortly before the House passed the Two-Million-Dollar Act and transmitted it to the Senate with what the President regarded as an entirely unnecessary explanation of its purpose, the Marqués de Casa Yrujo arrived in Washington from Philadelphia. This was an unpleasant surprise to Jefferson and Madison, who had long been seeking to rid themselves of that turbulent Spanish envoy. In the fall of 1804, more than a year earlier, a request that another minister be substituted for him had been decided on, and this had been delivered to the Spanish court by Monroe on his arrival in Madrid.

The decision was precipitated by Yrujo's improper advances to a Federalist editor, with a view to enlisting him against the policies of the government, and by his own recourse to the newspapers.[1] Though the undiplomatic conduct of this violent and irrepressible young nobleman has received no such indignant attention in American historical writing as that of Citizen Edmond Charles Genet in Washington's administration, it was comparable to Genet's in insolence and it extended over a much longer period. Yrujo's own government took the position that, since he had already asked for and received permission to return home, he should be allowed to do so without a formal recall, and the American government agreed to this. But he showed no disposition to leave

[1] Yrujo's advances to William Jackson and other actions, as well as the response of the American government, are described in Brant, IV, 209–212.

the country, and, if Anthony Merry is to be believed, the administration blamed Spanish intransigence on the misrepresentations and exaggerated reports he communicated from Philadelphia.[2] Madison, whom he appears to have disliked as much as John Randolph did, saw him there under reasonably amicable circumstances in the early autumn of 1805, but if the Secretary of State did not then discourage him from coming to Washington he did so afterwards, receiving in return a violent attack on Jefferson for alleged misstatements about Spain in the presidential message to Congress. This letter Yrujo subsequently gave to the Federalist press. Like Anthony Merry, but even more flagrantly, he sought to bring comfort to the enemies of the government.

Jefferson was not willing to tolerate him on the presidential doorstep. On the day of his arrival Madison informed Yrujo that it would be "dissatisfactory'" to the President for him to remain in Washington, and that his departure from the United States would be expected after the inclement season had passed. In the first of his two replies to this letter Yrujo asserted his intention of remaining in the city as long as it might suit the interest of his King or his personal convenience. He referred to the administration in slighting if not insulting language and promised no more than that he would communicate Madison's letter to his own government. Perhaps angered by Madison's failure to respond, he wrote another letter in which he asserted that the Minister of His Catholic Majesty took no orders except from his own Sovereign. Describing the style and tenor of Madison's letter as indecorous, he claimed that it violated his diplomatic rights and privileges and declared that he would transmit the entire correspondence to the other diplomats in Washington. He circularized them first and then carried out his full threat.[3]

No doubt these actions pleased the political enemies of the President and the Secretary of State, but they occasioned Senator John Quincy Adams to introduce a bill empowering the President to send ministers of foreign nations from the country under certain conditions. The failure of this to pass can probably be attributed to Jefferson's belief that he already had that power.[4] He did not choose to exercise it in the case of Yrujo, who remained in the country more than a year longer and managed to stir up further trouble, some of it in the next few

---

[2] Merry to Mulgrave, Aug. 4, 1805 (FO, 5:45, pp. 119-120).
[3] The Madison-Yrujo correspondence of Jan. 15-19, 1806, is in *Annals*, 9 Cong., 1 sess., pp. 1221-1224. It was seen in Washington by Feb. 8, as Plumer's entry for that date shows (*Memorandum*, pp. 426-427). Plumer saw the circular and the letter about TJ on Jan. 30 (*ibid.*, pp. 398-399). The episode is in Brant, IV, 323-325.
[4] Plumer, *Memorandum*, p. 435, note 104 with references; also p. 445.

weeks, by representations to the French Minister and others. Since the American government wholly ceased dealing with him, diplomatic relations with Spain were virtually suspended in both Washington and Madrid at just the time Jefferson was seeking to renew negotiations with that country. The situation was complicated further, both at home and abroad, by the actions of a Spanish-American revolutionary who had a far more appealing personality than Yrujo but who also abused the hospitality of the United States.

Early in February, midway in the troubled congressional session, word reached the Department of State and was quickly relayed to the President that General Francisco de Miranda, who had been a visitor in the country for about three months, had set sail from New York. His ostensible destination was a port in the West Indies, but Jefferson and Madison had good reason to believe that this dauntless man was on his way to Caracas in an attempt to free his native Venezuela from Spanish rule. Later events showed that this was indeed the case. The *Leander*, the American-owned vessel on which he sailed, was armed and carried military stores, along with a complement of 180 to 200 men, including a considerable number who were recruited for this particular enterprise. Some of the men were aware of Miranda's objectives but others appear to have been deceived.[5]

After getting the news, Madison, on Jefferson's instruction, promptly requested the United States Attorney in New York to see if any federal laws had been violated. The tough French minister, General Turreau, who had learned of the expedition from Yrujo in Philadelphia, expostulated with Madison next day and was then informed of this action. It mollified him only slightly at the time, and he afterwards requested and received further explanations, but it signified the determination of the administration to prevent the Miranda episode from becoming an international incident and endangering the projected negotiations with Spain through France. Furthermore, the President had a constitutional responsibility to enforce the laws of his own land. The equipping of an American vessel for hostile action against a nation with which the United States was at peace, and the enlistment of Americans for such a purpose, were clearly illegal. As a result of the

[5] The best treatment I have seen of the Miranda episode as it related to the conduct of the American government is in Brant, IV, ch. XXIV. This corrects and supplements the account of Henry Adams, who did not have access to important documents that afterwards became available and does not appear to have been wholly fair in using those he had (*History*, III, 189–196). The letters and memoranda in King, IV, ch. XXXII and App. IX, are important sources.

investigation ordered by the President, two men were arrested in New York and brought before the federal district judge for examination. They were Samuel G. Ogden, owner of the *Leander* and the heaviest investor in the enterprise, and William S. Smith, surveyor of the Port of New York, who chanced to be the son-in-law of John Adams. Formal indictments by a federal grand jury followed a few weeks later at the April session of the circuit court. Before that time, however, the President removed Smith from office. He would have preferred to delay this action until the results of the trial were known, but his hesitancy was overcome by the strong arguments of Gallatin, who held that Smith's own admissions warranted his ouster and that the peace and honor of the country required it. It was agreed to at a Cabinet meeting and the successor who was promptly nominated was quickly confirmed by the Senate.[6]

Weeks before the trials occurred in the summer the government was charged with base persecution and a mean attempt to cover up its own errors. The charges had an unmistakable political coloration: they were circulated with obvious relish among High Federalists. Also, at a time when many were profiting from risky trade of doubtful legality, there was much sympathy in commercial circles for the persons who had involved themselves in this hazardous undertaking, and, in fact, for the ill-fated enterprise itself. The alleged justification for accusing the government, however, was that its spokesmen had assured Miranda that, while they could not sanction his plans, they would not obstruct them. This claim was based on the undeniable fact that on a visit to the capital in December he had conferred with Madison and dined with Jefferson, and upon the highly questionable report that he himself made orally to a number of people and which they in turn repeated. Madison gave his version of the conference in a letter to John Armstrong in Paris, but this did not reach the public eye. In private, Jefferson flatly denied that he had sanctioned the expedition, but he issued no official statement.[7] The administration would probably have hesitated to report on a private interview bearing on international relations even if the diplomatic situation had been less delicate. At all events, there was a communications gap and the administration was judged by

[6] Gallatin to TJ, Mar. 11, 1806 (*Writings*, I, 293–295); TJ's memo. of the Cabinet meeting of Mar. 14 (Ford, I, 310); nomination of Peter A. Schenck sent to the Senate Mar. 17, agreed to Mar. 21 (*Senate Exec. Procs.*, II, 30). Smith and Ogden were examined by Judge M. B. Talmadge on Mar. 1, indicated Apr. 7, and tried in July (*Trials of William S. Smith and Samuel G. Ogden* [1807]).

[7] Madison to Armstrong, Mar. 15, 1806 (Hunt, VII, 202–204); TJ to William Duane, Mar. 22, 1806 (Ford, VIII, 433).

its known actions. These were generally interpreted according to the predilections of the viewers — that is, their faith in or distrust of the President and the Secretary of State.

Miranda had come to New York in November, bearing a letter to Rufus King, whom he had known in England and whose basic sympathy with his purposes he rightly assumed. This letter was from Nicholas Vansittart, a member of Parliament who regretted that the present British government was not disposed to aid the would-be liberator as predecessors of theirs had done, and this despite the fact that Britain was at war with Spain. King, who had recently written Madison about Miranda, saying that his object was one toward which they could not be indifferent, sent this letter to him for the President's perusal. On the strength of it they were warranted in seeing Miranda in order to gain a fuller understanding of British thinking and policy with respect to Spanish America, if for no other reason.[8] Before he left New York for Washington, Miranda claimed that two armed vessels were ready (they sailed soon after his return) and that he needed only military stores and a little money; these he was seeking through Christopher Gore in Boston, whom he also knew to be sympathetic. Stopping in Philadelphia, he captivated Benjamin Rush and got from the Doctor effusive letters to Jefferson and Madison in which he was described as a friend of liberty and a believer in governments conducted in the interest of the people.[9]

Madison afterwards told Armstrong that in Washington Miranda "was treated with the civilities refused to no stranger having an ostensible title to them." Since Jefferson extended his hospitality to all visitors of any consequence, his entertaining the General at dinner might have been expected, even if the handsome Venezuelan had been less notable for love of liberty. But his personal friendliness was often misinterpreted, and both he and Madison appear to have been insufficiently aware of the impression Miranda's cordial reception might make on his prospective supporters in New York. The minds of the latter, it may be added, were filled with hopes not merely of the liberation of colonial peoples but of financial gains commensurate with the risks of the undertaking.

Madison also told Armstrong that Miranda disclosed his revolutionary purposes in "very general terms," that he had in mind the possibility of war between the United States and Spain, and that he

[8] Vansittart to King, Aug. 14, 1805; King to Madison, Oct. 15, Nov. 25, 1805; King to C. Gore, Nov. 29, 1805; Madison to King, Dec. 4, 1805 (King, IV, 518–526).
[9] Miranda to Gore, Nov. 27, 1805 (King, IV, 523–524); Rush to Madison, Dec. 3, 1805, with a useful editorial note (Butterfield, II, 910).

JAMES MADISON

Portrait by Gilbert Stuart, 1804. This portrait hangs in the Conference Room of the
Capitol at Williamsburg

would have welcomed positive encouragement. He never claimed that he got this and he must have been disappointed to learn that the government expected to remain in amity with Spain and to maintain the position of honorable neutrality in the current war. Shortly after this visit Anthony Merry reported to his government the general opinion in Washington that Miranda's purpose was to offer his services in the event of a break with Spain. The British Minister believed, however, that the American government did not place confidence in him and that his visit had been "attended with no material result."[10]

Miranda may have been misled by expressions of sympathy, on the part of both the Secretary of State and the President, for the colonials under Spanish rule. Jefferson would have been untrue to his own past if he had disapproved of a popular revolt against an imperial master, though he would hardly have picked this particular time to encourage one in Venezuela. As Madison afterwards told Monroe, the government faced a delicate situation: it had to observe its legal obligations to Spain; and, by not going beyond them, to avoid making itself "a party against the people of South America."[11] It intended to enforce the laws of the United States, but did not need to object to actions of individuals that fell within them. We may guess that the exportation of arms to be used by rebels at some undetermined future time would not have been objected to; it may even have been expected by the government. But if Madison is to be believed, the attempt to raise an American military corps was not at all anticipated. To accept in its entirety the oral report made by Miranda to Rufus King, and recorded by that confidant weeks later from memory, would require extraordinary credulity. Even in that version certain crucial expressions show that Miranda was relying on inference and interpretation. Thus he is reported to have said that Madison *intimated* that "whatever might be done should be discreetly done" and that his own *understanding* was that "although the Government would not sanction, it would wink at the Expedition."[12] This sort of understanding was necessary if he would retain the support of his prospective backers, and the ardent revolutionary conveyed it to them for their reassurance.

Several weeks after the *Leander* sailed, Rufus King, in a private letter to Christopher Gore, said that his statement of what passed between the government and Miranda rested solely on the latter's report to him, but that he fully credited this. By that time he had no

10 Merry to Mulgrave, Jan. 3, 1806, No. 2 (FO, 5:48).
11 Madison to Monroe, Mar. 10, 1806 (quoted from MP, Rives Coll., in Brant, IV, 333).
12 From the account in King's papers, said to have been written Mar. 5, 1806 (King, IV, 580–581).

doubt that the conduct of the government in the affair had been unworthy. His correspondent, who was of similar political persuasion and likewise shared Miranda's confidence, spoke even more severely of the highest officials of his country: "Their baseness and meanness seem only to be exceeded by their extreme weakness," he said.[13] King had recorded another sort of judgment at a time when the political opportunities afforded by this episode were less obvious. On the back of an importunate letter from Miranda about a week after the latter's return from Washington he summarized the reply he made verbally. This was to the effect that the steps previously agreed upon could not be taken, since the government, though given an opening to do so, had not intimated in confidence to him or any of his friends even that supplies might be provided in discretion. At that date he himself was unwilling to rely on Miranda's "understanding" about non-interference, and it seems a pity that he did not communicate his doubts to those who did take the risks to their own subsequent injury.[14] The complete failure of the enterprise was not owing to the actions of the administration, but as a result of it some people lost a lot of money.

About ten days before he sailed, Miranda showed King his parting letters to Madison and Jefferson, of which he afterwards sent him copies. Certain artful expressions in these, especially in the one to Madison, could have been interpreted to mean that he was acting in complete accord with the authorities in Washington and that they were well aware of his secret plans.[15] It is much easier to believe, however, that their awareness of these plans was distinctly limited, and a safe guess that it was very much less than that of Rufus King. Surprisingly, that distinguished former diplomat and his old colleague Christopher Gore, both of whom were thoroughly familiar with international obligations, appear to have seen no impropriety in the alleged assurances to Miranda. What they blamed the administration for was reneging. They would have come closer to truth and justice if they had charged Madison and Jefferson with gullibility in assuming that a dedicated revolutionist like Miranda would be concerned to maintain American neutrality or be mindful of American legalities.

Since the government avoided a confrontation with Spain, we may dismiss this episode from further consideration in connection with foreign affairs. In the sphere of domestic politics, however, there were

[13] King to C. Gore, Mar. 9, 1806; Gore to King, Mar. 26, Apr. 15, 1806 (*ibid.*, 529–531).
[14] Notation of Dec. 30, 1805, on the back of a letter of the same date (*ibid.*, 526–527).
[15] Letters dated Jan. 22, 1806, and sent later (*ibid.*, 583–584).

additional efforts to exploit it to the discredit of the administration and especially of Madison. During this congressional session, William Plumer, after noting that only two Federalists besides himself attended the funeral of Senator James Jackson, a Republican, penned this male-diction in his private record: "Cursed be the spirit of party! Its blind, baleful, malevolent, degrading effects cease not with the grave."[16] That baleful partisanship did not vanish when Miranda's ship crossed the three-mile limit, and when supposed collaborators of his had been indicted, was strikingly manifest at the very end of the congressional session. Extraordinary memorials from Ogden and Smith were then presented to both branches of the Legislature. They claimed that if they were guilty of the alleged offense against the laws they had been "led into error by the conduct of the officers of the Executive Government," who were now seeking to make sacrificial victims of the accused "in expiation of their own errors, or to deprecate the vengeance of foreign Governments." The memorialists also claimed that they had suffered injustice in the conduct of the prosecution (referring particularly to their examination by the judge) and prayed such relief as the wisdom of Congress might grant them.

As an appeal to the legislature against the two other co-ordinate branches of the federal government this would be difficult to match in the history of the country and it met the repudiation it deserved. There is no official record of what happened in the Senate except that, on the last day of the session, that body voted to expunge from its journal everything bearing on these memorials; but there is record of a lively and illuminating discussion in the House on the same day.[17] A little earlier Senator John Quincy Adams, writing Smith, who was his brother-in-law, said that he was not competent to pass judgment on what passed between Miranda and the President and Secretary of State. But he added this statement: "That he [Miranda] misunderstood or misrepresented their real intentions I have no doubt."[18] By contrast, Josiah Quincy, the Federalist leader who presented the memorials to the House, asserted that gentlemen on the floor could corroborate the statement that the Executive "had been advised of the fitting out of the *Leander* in time to have prevented her sailing." After he had been reproached for this reckless assertion he retracted his words, saying that he had not meant to criminate the administration. But obviously

[16] Mar. 20, 1806 (Plumer, *Memorandum*, p. 460). I have presumed to make a minor correction in the indignant Senator's grammar and to supplement his punctuation.
[17] Apr. 21, 1806 (*Annals*, 9 Cong., 1 sess., pp. 250, 1085–1094).
[18] J. Q. Adams to W. S. Smith (*Writings*, III, 139).

he could have had no object except the discrediting of the President
and his appointees, since there was no way in which Congress could
properly provide relief for men facing trial under prescribed legal
procedure. The extreme impropriety of intervention in a pending case
was recognized by the unanimous vote by which a resolution to that
effect was adopted.

Actually this was the third of the four parts of the resolution the
legislators adopted, voting on these separately. The first of them stated
that, in the opinion of the House, the charges in the memorials were
wholly unsupported by evidence criminating the executive branch in
any degree. This was adopted by the overwhelming vote of 75 to 8,
only Josiah Quincy and a handful of die-hard Federalists being against
it. The second, stating that the memorials appeared "to have been
presented at a time, and under circumstances insidiously calculated to
excite unjust suspicions" in the public mind against the administration,
was approved by a slightly smaller margin (70 to 13). John Randolph
stood with the Federalists on this. The final part of the resolution
called for the return of the memorials to the persons from whom they
came. Thus Congress, rallying in defense of the President, the Secretary of State, and a federal court, dismissed from its consideration
charges that it deemed improper and associated with political partisanship.

Nonetheless, these charges were exploited further in connection
with the trials, which took place in midsummer and resulted in the
acquittal of the two defendants.[19] The verdict may be attributed
chiefly to personal sympathy for them and to the difficulty of proving
that they were fully apprised of Miranda's plans, but it is most unlikely
that the efforts of the counsel for the defense to embarrass the administration were solely due to their professional zeal for their clients. They
caused subpoenas to be issued to the members of the Cabinet to appear
as witnesses, probably expecting to fail in this attempt, as they did, but
managing to keep suspicions alive in the meantime.[20] Jefferson privately recorded the opinion that the defendants and their friends had
contrived to make this prosecution "a Government question" in which

[19] The trials ended July 26 with the acquittal of Ogden, after the previous
acquittal of Smith.
[20] Reply of Madison, Dearborn, and Smith, July 8, 1806 (*ibid.*, pp. 6–7). Gallatin, who was out of town when the subpoenas were brought to Washington, did
not receive one. He wrote the U.S. attorney, however, that the enforced attendance of department heads would create a dangerous precedent, not because they
occupied a privileged position but because such actions if repeated might paralyze
the entire conduct of the government. Gallatin to Nathan Sandford, July 9, 1806
(*Writings*, I, 302–304.)

the administration and the judge were "tried as the culprits instead of themselves." Convinced that the marshal, John Swartwout, a loyal supporter of Aaron Burr and an intimate friend of William S. Smith, had packed the jury panel with bitter Federalists, he removed him from office. After the trial was over, Jefferson said that the decision was reached weeks before it was put into effect.[21] He was not dissatisfied with the outcome of the case. He had no feelings of any sort about Ogden, but expressed compassion for the other man. "I had no wish to see Smith imprisoned," said Jefferson, who had made a friend of him when he was secretary to the embassy in London; "he has been a man of integrity and honor, led astray by distress."[22]

Reflecting on the Miranda episode in the summer, when enjoying another blessed interim between congressional sessions, he was disposed to think that it did little harm.[23] In some minds, however, it left a residue of bitterness and suspicion.

ii

The actions of the would-be liberator of Venezuela and the unwelcome envoy from Spain may be regarded as only minor harassments, but Jefferson's project with respect to the latter country, which had been conceived in the fall and had survived John Randolph's vehement objections in the winter, had other serious difficulties to overcome on Capitol Hill before it could even get started. The hope of "reclaiming" the good offices of France had been strengthened by the suggestions of Talleyrand, as reported by John Armstrong months earlier. Jefferson's mind naturally turned to him as the crucial agent in this business — along with the newly appointed minister to Spain, who had betaken himself instead to London and then to Paris. Since Monroe had failed, since American diplomatic material was scarce, and precious time had already been lost, the choice of John Armstrong and James Bowdoin as commissioners must have seemed little short of inevitable. But the nomination of the former, which Jefferson sent to the Senate shortly after the passage of the Two-Million-Dollar Act, created a storm in that body. The leader of the fight against the nominee was

---

[21] TJ's memo. of the Cabinet meeting of May 1, 1806 (Ford, I, 315–316). Also, TJ to Madison, May 23, 1806 (Ford, VIII, 454).

[22] TJ to Gallatin, Aug. 15, 1806 (Ford, VIII, 464).

[23] Writing him from New York, Aug. 7, 1806, Gallatin expressed the opinion that the manifest injustice of the verdict had reacted against the Federalists, who "promoted" that event (*Writings*, I, 305–306).

Samuel Smith of Maryland, brother of the Secretary of the Navy, who was supported by numerous Republicans and all the Federalists. Timothy Pickering said that Armstrong had been guilty of "base conduct"; John Quincy Adams described the appointment as "one of the most disgraceful acts of Mr. Jefferson's administration"; and even the relatively moderate William Plumer regarded the appointee as disqualified.[24]

The harshness of these senatorial comments probably exceeded the presidential expectation, but before Jefferson submitted the nomination he was well aware that a "terrible tempest" had been excited against Armstrong.[25] This was occasioned by reports that he had interfered in the case of the *New Jersey*, an American vessel that had been captured by the French half a dozen years earlier and for which indemnity was claimed under the convention of 1800 with France. In the first instance this claim was disallowed. American merchants and underwriters were alarmed by the principle Armstrong was alleged to have laid down in this connection — namely, that the benefits of the convention did not extend to insurers. Jefferson's opinion that they extended to underwriters who had paid the loss of the original owners was reported by Madison in a letter of inquiry that he sent Armstrong, and from the minister's reply it was clear that, whatever his original objection may have been, he had withdrawn it.[26] Unfortunately, however, an early letter of Armstrong's bearing on this issue and taking a position that he afterwards modified had got into print in a pamphlet and in the newspapers.[27] Armstrong's more severe critics claimed that he had originally tried to block this large claim in order that more money would be left in the fund for other claimants, notably the Livingstons, to whom he was related by marriage, and persons whose

[24] Comments from Adams, *Memoirs*, I, 421, and Plumer, *Memorandum*, pp. 422, 455-458.

[25] TJ used these words in a letter of Feb. 14, 1806, to Armstrong (Ford, VIII, 423), and he had been aware of the criticism of the Minister at least since the late summer or early autumn of 1805.

[26] Madison to Armstrong, Aug. 25, 1805; Armstrong to Madison, Nov. 26, 1805; transmitted to the Senate, with a couple of other documents, Mar. 5, 1806 (*A.S.P.F.R.*, II, 774-775).

[27] In his communication of Mar. 5, 1806, to the Senate, TJ mentioned voluminous printed memorials in French, by the agent of those interested in the *New Jersey*. This was Du Pont de Nemours (see Ambrose Saricks, *Pierre Samuel Du Pont de Nemours* [1965], pp. 323-324). Writing TJ on Sept. 8, 1805, he referred heatedly to Armstrong's "error" and "incomprehensible opposition" to the *New Jersey* claim (see my edition of their *Correspondence*, pp. 83-85). TJ did not refer to this matter in his reply of Feb. 12, 1806, but it should be noted that he wrote Armstrong on Feb. 14.

interests they favored.[28] Such a charge, on the other hand, might have been attributed to political partisanship or to rival economic interests.

At all events, Jefferson sent Armstrong's nomination to the Senate, along with that of Bowdoin. While it was pending, John Randolph, speaking in the House with denunciatory vigor that exceeded his own high average, castigated the "unfaithful, dishonest agents" of the United States in France. He was referring to Livingston, no doubt, as he unquestionably was to Armstrong, and was implying that the government had not called the latter to account because of his powerful connections.[29] Senator William Plumer, who had long had difficulty in making up his mind about Jefferson but who at length had concluded that he was a man of integrity (a concession which Senators Timothy Pickering and Uriah Tracy would hardly have made), was disposed to attribute the President's "errors" to his credulity. To this New Englander, Jefferson seemed insufficiently suspicious. Of his loyalty to his own appointees and his disposition to regard them as innocent until proved guilty there could be no doubt; but, on the other side, the acceptance at face value of the charges against Armstrong was also a form of credulity. Jefferson was well aware that there were valid criticisms of the way the claims convention had been administered, but the documents he submitted to the Senate on request made a good case for Armstrong in the episode of the *New Jersey*, and the charges of "base conduct" on that official's part remained unproved.[30]

The nomination was approved by the narrowest possible margin. It was reported that one Republican senator left his seat in order to avoid voting and that others manifested their consent with faltering voices.[31] The vote was a tie, 15 to 15, which was broken by Vice President George Clinton on the last day this elderly man was in attendance during the session. By common consent a poor presiding officer, he rendered at least this service to the administration and to Armstrong,

[28] Brant (IV, 361–362), while saying that he found nothing in the official record to support Senator Smith's specific charges against R. R. Livingston in this instance, refers to efforts of Armstrong, at one time or another, in behalf of the notorious James Swan, whom his brother-in-law had previously favored.

[29] Plumer (*Memorandum*, p. 444) thus interpreted a passage in Randolph's speech of Mar. 6, 1806 (*Annals*, 9 Cong., 1 sess., pp. 603–604).

[30] Besides the correspondence between Madison and Armstrong already referred to, TJ communicated the copy of a letter of Feb. 26, 1806, from Henry Waddell to Messrs. Nicklin and Griffith, owners of the *New Jersey*. This persuasive document, exonerating Armstrong of virtually everything except minor indiscretion, probably brought no little relief to the President's mind, which may have been previously upset by the representations of Du Pont de Nemours.

[31] According to J. Q. Adams (*Memoirs*, I, 421). Plumer gave the same report about Senator John Adair of Kentucky, saying that he "absconded" (comments and record of the vote in *Memorandum*, pp. 456–457).

whom he regarded as an honest man though he did not care for the
family he had married into.[32] No doubt Jefferson was correct in his
judgment that Republican leadership in the Senate at this stage was
inferior to that provided by Uriah Tracy and James A. Bayard on the
other side, but a number of his own loyal followers were dubious
about the projected negotiations, and, as he himself recognized, a
"cloud of dissatisfaction" rested on General Armstrong in many
minds. For that reason he flirted briefly with the idea of adding
another man to the commission to increase public confidence and
tentatively sounded out his friend and neighbor Wilson Cary Nicholas.
That rural gentleman begged off for personal reasons, however, and
Jefferson was left with the pair whom it had seemed so logical to select
in the first place. They proved to be jealous and suspicious of each
other and the enlargement of the duo into a trio would probably have
served only to make matters even more difficult.[33]

Getting ahead of the domestic story, let us follow the course of this
ill-fated mission to a logical stopping point. The envoys were well
briefed for a situation that never arose. The draft of a convention to be
presented to the Spanish if the French could induce or compel them to
negotiate, and the accompanying instructions, closely adhered to the
plan that had been adopted by Jefferson and his Cabinet before the
legislators met and began to wrangle.[34] Perhaps it was because of the
fears of "bribery" voiced in Congress that Gallatin tightened the
financial provisions, with a view to making *douceurs* to French officials
and stockjobbery impossible.[35] But these safeguards could not have
enhanced the desirability of the settlement in the eyes of Talleyrand,
and the total now offered, for territories and claims, fell considerably
below the figure he had mentioned as acceptable. Recognition of the
Perdido boundary as an American right was not absolutely insisted on,
but the envoys were instructed to get it if they could. Actually, they
would have offended the Spanish even by broaching the subject.

[32] TJ nominated Armstrong and Bowdoin on Feb. 28, and the vote was taken on
Mar. 17 (*Senate Exec. Procs.*, II, 25, 29). Senator John Smith made a detailed
report of the vote to him that day (LC, 27571), The documents previously
referred to were sent by TJ on Mar. 5. The session lasted until Apr. 21.
[33] TJ to Nicholas, Mar. 24 and Apr. 13, 1806 (Ford, VIII, 434–436).
[34] See above, ch. IV, 37–40; Gallatin to Madison, Mar. 1, 1806 (*Writings*, I,
291–293); TJ to Madison, Mar. 5, 1806 (Ford, VIII, 427–428); Madison to Armstrong and Bowdoin, Mar. 13 (Hunt, VII, 192–200); Brant, IV, 362–363.
[35] The initial payment, not to exceed $2,000,000, was to be made after delivery
of the desired territories was unquestionably assured and was to be in a lump sum.
Stocks were not to be sold below par as they were in the case of the Louisiana
Purchase (Gallatin, *Writings*, I).

It has been suggested on high scholarly authority that the differences between Armstrong and Bowdoin in themselves would have wrecked the negotiations.[36] But they were in an unhappy situation, and we may wonder if the proposals they were authorized to make would have been acceptable even at the most propitious moment — that is, when Talleyrand suggested in the previous autumn that the good offices of France might be available. His sincerity might have been doubted even then, and Armstrong may be blamed for not viewing his proposals more critically, but that was the psychological moment if there ever was one. Under the conditions of American governmental procedure and the limitations of communication, the United States could not strike when the iron appeared to be hot. The obstructive tactics of John Randolph and others in Congress, while serving to gratify their *amour-propre*, delayed matters further, but the inability of the American envoys to get negotiations started can be sufficiently explained by changes in the European situation. They could gain no footing in those shifting sands.

Before the summer of 1806 Madison instructed Armstrong and Bowdoin that, if they should fail to obtain their territorial objectives, as he now thought likely, they should seek the sort of *modus vivendi* that Monroe had been instructed to seek in the first place but had not asked for. This would include maintenance of the *status quo,* navigation of the Mobile, and ratification of the claims convention of 1802, and would insure "the increase of the relative power of the United States for which time alone is wanted."[37] That is, Madison was back where he had started and where, as it now appears, the government might just as well have stayed. But even these instructions were no more than so many words on paper, for the Spaniards could be neither lured nor driven to serious discussion.

Jefferson did what he could to inspirit the newly commissioned envoys. In a friendly private letter he told Armstrong that success in the matter he was charged with would render the next meeting of Congress one of "gladness and reconciliation" and would bring "ineffable satisfaction" to the American people. A few weeks later he made a characteristically generous gesture to Bowdoin, informing him

---

[36] I. J. Cox, *West Florida Controversy* (1918), p. 246. Bowdoin, who was not accredited to France, believed that Armstrong did everything possible to keep him out of things and suspected his colleague of connivance with Daniel Parker, a financier of speculative bent with whom Armstrong was in fact too intimate and whose schemes Armstrong did not report to his own government. (Brant makes numerous references to Parker.) Armstrong in turn regarded Bowdoin as an indiscreet interloper.

[37] May 26, 1806, quoted by Cox, p. 257.

that a polygraph would be sent him shortly and describing in detail the portable private secretary of whose discretion there could be no question. Among other things he said that the procurement of Florida and a good western boundary would "fill the American mind with joy." In his next annual message to Congress, however, while explicitly stating that he had nothing to report about negotiations with Spain, he had something to say regarding troubles on the border.[38] About a month later he got a letter from Bowdoin showing that, far from being joyous in mind, that frustrated minister was miserable and hopeless.[39]

Jefferson was never able to report to Congress any negotiations looking to a settlement of the Spanish question, and this became overshadowed by the question of neutral rights in an accelerated war. The effort to buy Florida, which was already lagging badly, was suspended in the summer of 1807, when it was feared that the money might be needed for war with the British, and the envoys were instructed not to draw on the appropriation. Bowdoin, after a breach with Armstrong, had already asked if he might come home, as he did in the next year.[40] Thus ended a joint mission which now appears to have been futile from its inception.

Why was it undertaken? Like any other historical action it must be viewed in the circumstances under which it was conceived and initiated. It may be said to have been the last of a series of steps based on successive mistakes in judgment, starting with the claim to a legal title to West Florida as far as the Perdido. It may be cited as a historical example of the compounding of error. But allowance must be made for the inadequacy of information and slowness of communication in that age, for the vast uncertainties of international developments, and also for the exigencies of politics. West Florida was an obsession with Jefferson, but the desirability of possessing it cannot be denied, and he would probably have been subjected to severe criticism if he had attempted no positive steps to that end. Furthermore, he could not have been expected to give up the spoliation claims. He can hardly be blamed for believing that even a faint hope of settling the Spanish question peaceably should be seized upon. Perhaps he might have got

[38] TJ to Armstrong, May 30, 1806 (LC, 27870); to Bowdoin, July 10, 1806 (L. & B., XI, 118–121); message of Dec. 2, 1806 (Ford, VIII, 483 ff.).

[39] Bowdoin to TJ, Oct. 20, 1806 (cited by Cox, p. 265). TJ got the letter Jan. 4, 1807. Cox (pp. 236–265) carries the complicated diplomatic story into the fall of 1806, continuing it through the rest of TJ's administration and into Madison's in the following chapter.

[40] Madison to Armstrong and Bowdoin, July 15, 1807, following the *Leopard-Chesapeake* incident (Hunt, VII, 460–462); TJ to Bowdoin, July 10, 1807 (Ford, IX, 104–105) and May 29, 1808 (L. & B., XII, 68–70).

the Spanish to agree to a *modus vivendi* if his successive representatives had not sought so much more, but there is no certainty that he could have; and he could assume that time was working to the American advantage in any case, as in fact it continued to do. The immediate effects of the policy were chiefly felt in domestic politics. They complicated his efforts to meet Anglo-American problems and put his party leadership to the most severe test it had yet encountered.

[VII]

Foreign Aggressions and a Domestic Revolt

"UNQUALIFIED submission to France and unqualified defiance of Great Britain are indeed the two pillars upon which our measures are to rest," wrote Senator John Quincy Adams to his father the ex-President in the midst of the congressional session.[1] At that moment he appears to have been more aware of the significance of Austerlitz than of Trafalgar. "The continent of Europe . . . is not only prostrate at the feet of France, but to all appearance irretrievably subdued," he said. "How long the insular situation of Great Britain and her naval force will enable her to bear up against this universal suppression, is not easy to say; but that she too must sink sooner or later under such a mass and impetus of force can hardly be questioned." Jefferson's judgment of the world situation, at a time when Adams believed that the doom of Britain's isle was sure, was well expressed in a private letter the Senator from Massachusetts did not see. Recently the President had written:

> What an awful spectacle does the world exhibit at this instant, one man bestriding the continent of Europe like a Colossus, and another roaming unbridled on the ocean. But even this is better than that one should rule both elements. Our wish ought to be that he who has armies may not have the Dominion of the sea, and that he who has Dominion of the sea may be one who has no armies. In this way we may be quiet; at home at least.[2]

That he regarded the maintenance of a balance of power in the western world as highly desirable, even as indispensable to American security, cannot be doubted. Furthermore, this appears to have been

[1] J. Q. Adams to John Adams, Feb. 11, 1806 (*Writings*, III, 134–135).
[2] TJ to Thomas Lomax, Jan. 11, 1806 (LC, 27225).

the prevailing judgment among his own countrymen at the time.[3] As the guardian of his country's interests he tended to oppose, at any particular moment, the power that seemed to him most threatening to these interests. In this restricted sense, throughout most of his public life he could have been regarded as anti-British, but he had flirted with the idea of a British alliance only a few months before, and at no time during his presidency could he have been properly described as pro-French. In seeking the good offices of France in connection with the projected resumption of negotiations with Spain he may have been chasing a will-o'-the-wisp, but at the time he decided on this procedure he could see no other way. And, given the existing circumstances and the safeguards Gallatin prescribed, it was a gross exaggeration on the part of John Randolph and others to say that the purpose of the two millions was to bribe France to bully Spain. After all, the United States could have seized the disputed territory from that feeble nation.

Another charge of catering to Napoleon, even of subservience to him, arose from the prohibition of American commerce with the part of the island of St. Domingo that was in rebellion against the French. This trade was protested against by Turreau in the fall and winter, but he got little response from Madison. The chief American mover in the business was Senator George Logan, a Quaker pacifist, who introduced a bill to prohibit this commerce. The measure was opposed in the Senate by Adams and the Federalists, some at least of whom espoused the interests of eastern merchants; and many of its supporters, including Jefferson's son-in-law, Congressman John W. Eppes, appear to have been motivated by fear of slave uprisings, inspired by success in St. Domingo, far more than by any desire to conciliate France. In Madison's opinion the bill, passed by overwhelming majorities, went beyond American obligation under international law and was not attributable to French requisition, though he thought they would be grateful for it. Ironically, Turreau afterwards regretted it, saying that it had resulted in the transfer of virtually all the trade with the island to British vessels.[4] In any case, if this was a pro-French gesture it was a

---

[3] See the excellent discussion in Bradford Perkins, *Prologue to War* (1963), pp. 52–66; also, L. S. Kaplan, "Jefferson, the Napoleonic Wars, and the Balance of Power" (*W. & M.*, April 1957, pp. 196–217). It should be borne in mind that we are dealing here with the situation before Napoleon's Berlin decree and the British Orders in Council of 1807.

[4] Complying with a request of Dec. 27, 1805, TJ communicated to the Senate on Jan. 10, 1806, the documents relating to French complaints (*A.S.P.F.R.*, II, 725–727). The bill passed the Senate Feb. 20, by a vote of 21 to 8; and the House Feb. 25, by the margin of 93 to 26; it was approved Feb. 28 (*Annals*, 9 Cong., 1 sess., pp. 138, 515–516, 1228–1229). Madison commented on it to Armstrong, Mar. 15, 1806 (Hunt, VII, 200–201); as did Plumer at various times (*Memorandum*, pp.

very slight one for which the administration itself bore little or no responsibility, and the country that was really trying to drive Americans from the profitable carrying trade was Great Britain. The United States had commercial grievances against the French and Spanish — they had privateers and their cruisers followed modes of search that Madison described as irregular and unwarranted — but Napoleon became increasingly dependent on American shipping as his own vessels were driven from the seas. Inevitably, at this stage, the United States as a neutral nation and a commercial power had its chief difficulties with the British, and the government would have been untrue to its responsibilities if it had not sought to resolve these.

As we have seen, Jefferson, whose information about European developments was generally from six to eight weeks behind the events themselves, did not become aware of the intensified actions against neutral shipping until he got back to Washington in the early fall of 1805. It was then that he abandoned all thought of even a tentative alliance with the British. Meanwhile, James Monroe, who had reached London late in July after his futile mission to Madrid, had quickly learned of the actions against American vessels in the wake of the *Essex* decision, though he had not been officially informed of the ruling itself.[5] He estimated that fifty were seized and brought to London during the summer and supposed that as many more suffered a similar fate in the West Indies. Months before this, Madison had briefed him well, not only about the impressment of American seamen, which was a continuing grievance, but also about the Rule of 1756, which the British were now vigorously reviving in their ruthless effort to prevent any participation by neutrals in trade between their enemies and the colonies of the latter.

Monroe believed they were emboldened to do this by their success in forming the Third Coalition, which enabled them to disregard the remaining neutrals. He found Lord Mulgrave more assertive of Britain's "rights" and maritime interests than his predecessors, and, while wanting no open breach with the United States, similarly disposed to dilatory tactics. Recognizing the gravity of the situation, Monroe, who had expected to return home, concluded that he should remain in England through the winter. Besides sending reports that eventually reached his superiors in Washington, he strongly presented the American case against the Rule of 1756 in a letter to Mulgrave, a

---

414, 435, 540–541). Brant discusses it in *Madison*, IV, 274–275; Henry Adams (*History*, III, 90 and elsewhere) exaggerates its significance, in my opinion.

[5] On the decision, see pp. 59–60, above. Harry Ammon describes Monroe's actions in ch. XIII of his biography.

copy of which the President included in the documents he afterwards transmitted to Congress.[6]

The argument to which the administration consistently adhered may be summarized briefly. The doctrine that trade forbidden in time of peace should not be permitted in time of war was not recognized by the law of nations but was assumed by Great Britain unilaterally, "under the auspices of a maritime ascendency," with a view to her particular interests. It was neither reasonable nor right and it had been disregarded by the British themselves. Furthermore, it had been specifically overruled by British decisions of recent years on which Americans were warranted in relying. Monroe, aware of a drastic change in policy which Madison had feared, properly claimed that it had been made without any sort of warning. To him it appeared as an act of contemptuousness rather than one of desperation.

About the time that Jefferson got back to Washington, Anthony Merry, writing Lord Mulgrave from Philadelphia where Madison still was, reported a "great degree of irritation" among American merchants who had been engaged in trade with colonies of His Majesty's enemies but had regarded themselves as "perfectly secured" by official assurances previously given them. The "sensation and clamor" excited by "totally unexpected" events had caused the insurance on such cargoes to be raised fourfold. The Secretary of State had not mentioned the matter to the British envoy as yet, however, presumably because he lacked official information about it from Monroe.[7] A couple of months later, Merry reported to his home government that Madison now viewed the situation much more seriously. Commercial groups in the seaports had held public meetings on this subject; and, if Merry may be believed, the public prints most reflective of the opinion of the government had largely lost sight of their complaints against Spain and were seeking to excite the "whole national indignation" against Great Britain.[8]

In fact the protests were spontaneous, and pressure was being exerted *on* the government, not *by* it. Memorials were pouring in from merchants and underwriters all along the coast, and the departmental offices were assembling these, together with lists of vessels and cargoes

[6] Monroe to Mulgrave, Sept. 23, 1805. Also, Madison to Monroe, Jan. 5, 1804, dealing with impressment, and Apr. 12, 1805, about the case of the brig *Aurora* (*A.S.P.F.R.*, II, 730–737). This vessel, whose cargo had been brought from Havana to Charleston and reshipped to Barcelona, was seized by a British cruiser and her cargo condemned by an Admiralty court in Newfoundland. The case was appealed to Great Britain, and Madison apprehended that the sentence would not be reversed.

[7] Merry to Mulgrave, Sept. 30, 1805, No. 40 (FO, 5:45, pp. 142–145).

[8] Merry to Mulgrave, Dec. 2, 1805, No. 50 (FO, 5:45, pp. 176–178).

captured by belligerent powers. Occasional captures by the French and Spanish were recorded, but the captors were nearly always British. The attitude of the merchants was well expressed in a generally restrained memorial from Philadelphia:

> Could the judgment, or even the charity, of your memorialists see, in the new doctrines of the British court nothing but the revival and enforcement of an ancient and established principle, which friendship had relaxed or favor permitted to slumber, they might regret the departed good, but could impute no injustice to the hand that withdrew it. They are struck, however, with the novelty of these doctrines; their unequivocal hostility to neutral interest and rights; their inconsistency with former declarations of their ministry and decisions of their courts, and with the extraordinary time and manner of their annunciation.[9]

Jefferson transmitted to Congress an impressive collection of these memorials, along with relevant letters of Madison and Monroe. This was the day after the House passed the bill providing the money he was seeking in connection with the projected reopening of negotiations with Spain.[10] That business had proved more controversial than he had expected and it was by no means in the clear as yet, but the pressing question of British relations would admit of no further delay. That delay had not been without its uses, however, in the accumulation of pertinent materials.

Among these was an anonymous pamphlet, admittedly by Madison, which was placed on the tables of the senators the day before they got Jefferson's special message. It was made available to the representatives in quantity at that time or soon thereafter. The designation of it as a pamphlet does scant justice to its bulk, for it contained some seventy thousand words. It was, as its author told Monroe while preparing it, a "pretty thorough investigation" of the principle on which the British were now proceeding, the Rule of 1756.[11] Anyone who attempts to

---

[9] *A.S.P.F.R.*, II, 740. The position taken with respect to neutral rights in this memorial, which also protested against certain French actions and could not be properly described as anti-British in spirit, was virtually identical with the official position as described by TJ and Madison.

[10] Message of Jan. 17, 1806, with documents transmitted at the time or soon thereafter, in *A.S.P.F.R.*, II, 727–773. The message itself may be seen in Ford, VIII, 416–417, and elsewhere.

[11] "An Examination of the British Doctrine, Which Subjects to Capture a Neutral Trade, Not Open in Time of Peace" (Hunt, VII, 204–375, with incorrect note about the date); referred to, Madison to Monroe, Sept. 24, 1805 (Hunt, VII, 191); discussed in Brant, IV, ch. XXII.

read this learned treatise can but agree with the comments of Senator
Plumer on it and its author: "He extends the discussion too far — 'tis
too prolix for common use."[12] Others besides the Senator from New
Hampshire found it inordinately fatiguing, and an occasional partisan
critic saw nothing but weakness in it, but it was generally approved by
John Quincy Adams and was in full accord with the contentions of the
American mercantile group. In his annual message to Congress, Jefferson had asserted that new principles had been "interpolated into the
law of nations founded neither in justice nor the usage or acknowledgment of nations" and Madison elaborately portrayed the most dangerous of these. Whatever may be said of his references to Grotius,
Pufendorf, and Vattel, there could be no real doubt that he fully
exposed the inconsistency of Britain in denying to her enemies the
right to relax their laws of trade in wartime while relaxing her own,
and in trading with her enemies and their colonies while denying to
neutrals the right to do so.[13] To Madison, as to Jefferson, this was "an
inconsistency at which reason revolts," and quite obviously it was
contrary to the American interest at the time.

After Madison's treatise was written but before it was off the press,
he and Jefferson received from Monroe copies of the pamphlet by
James Stephen, *War in Disguise*, in which the British "interpolation"
they most objected to was advocated on grounds of commercial advantage and as a means of driving Americans from the carrying trade.
Admittedly, the seizure of American vessels on the basis of the resuscitated Rule of 1756, while a war measure, was designed to secure British
commercial advantage. It was a policy of expediency, backed by force.

The interpretation of British policy that the President and Secretary
of State had already arrived at was supported by a letter recently
received by Madison from Monroe, who had reported so optimistically
on the attitude of the government before he went to Spain. This letter
Jefferson submitted to Congress "separately and confidentially" because its publication might discourage frank communication between
ministers and their own government. After it was read in the Senate, it
was delivered to the President's secretary and communicated to the
House, whence it was returned to Jefferson. A little later the Senate

[12] Plumer's account of the transmission of the pamphlet and his comments on it
are in *Memorandum*, pp. 387–389. Brant quotes various comments (IV 301).

[13] See, especially, Hunt, VII, 269. C. E. Hill, in *American Secretaries of State*,
ed. by S. F. Bemis, III (1927), 107–111, summarizes American attitudes on this
question at that time and thereafter. As he says, the United States applied the
doctrine of continuous voyage during the Civil War, adding to it as a corollary
the doctrine of ultimate consumption. The changes in attitude accompanied and
reflected the growth of American naval power.

asked to see it again, an action which was opposed by James Logan, who said the letter breathed "a spirit of war and blood." Not only was Monroe convinced that the seizure of American vessels was a deliberate policy of the British government; in his opinion their intention was to subject American commerce then and thereafter "to every restraint in their power." Regarding the growing importance of the United States as unfavorable to them, they were seeking "to check if not to crush it." He himself viewed the recent actions as an experiment to determine just how much the United States would bear, and he favored strong resistance.[14]

With all this documentary support, Jefferson could well afford to make his own message brief. While assuring Congress that the government, through its minister in London, would insist with renewed vigor on rights of neutral trade "too evident and too important to be surrendered," and would continue to remonstrate against the impressment of American seamen, he called the attention of the legislators to the gravity of the situation without making any specific recommendation. He undoubtedly wanted them to take some action. Otherwise, as he told John Quincy Adams a few weeks later, Americans must abandon the carrying trade, since the British would never yield on this point unless something should be done "in aid of negotiation." He appears to have avoided private suggestions such as he and Gallatin had made in connection with the Spanish question. Perhaps discouraged by his experiences with John Randolph, he was more strictly observing the principle of separation of powers that was so dear to the hearts of the constitutional purists in his own party, though he was destined to be accused of indecisiveness by that orator because he was *not* specific. He probably believed that he could safely anticipate the line legislation would take if any should be enacted. Some form of economic reprisal was to be expected. This was in the tradition of the Continental Association of the American Revolution, which in his opinion at the time did not go far enough, and of the retaliatory legislation against Great Britain that he had favored as secretary of state and Madison had proposed in the House in 1791 and 1794.[15] Conditions had changed during the intervening years — the British had increased their mastery

[14] Monroe to Madison, Oct. 18, 1805 (S.M.H., IV, 352–365); *Annals*, 9 Cong., 1 sess., pp. 54, 71 (Jan. 17, 24, 1806); Plumer, *Memorandum*, pp. 380, 389; TJ to Senate, Jan. 26, 1806 (LC, 27305), returning letter and expressing confidence that it would not be made public. On Feb. 6, he sent a letter from Monroe dated Nov. 26, 1805 (LC, 27378; *Annals*, 9 Cong., 1 sess., p. 86).

[15] See *Jefferson the Virginian*, p. 191; *Jefferson and the Rights of Man*, p. 335; and *Jefferson and the Ordeal of Liberty*, pp. 157–159.

JOHN RANDOLPH
Silhouette drawn from life by William Henry Brown
From W. H. Brown, *Portrait Gallery of Distinguished Americans* (1846)

of the seas — but he and most of the Republicans still regarded economic pressure as a feasible alternative to war and a helpful adjunct to
diplomacy.

While the President, in what appeared to be a favorable climate of
opinion, chose to leave the legislators to their own devices, he could
hardly have failed to be sympathetic to the efforts of his more loyal
supporters in the House to bypass John Randolph. The reader will
recall that at the beginning of the session the part of the presidential
message dealing with infringements on neutral commerce had been
referred to Randolph's Ways and Means Committee, despite the efforts
of Barnabas Bidwell and other northern Republicans, whose commercial concern, actually, was much greater than that of this rural Virginian.[16] Jefferson himself wanted to postpone consideration of
grievances against the British until he was assured of the desired
approbation for the renewal of negotiations with Spain; and it was
partly for that reason, no doubt, that Madison delayed his response to
Randolph's request for documentary materials bearing on neutral
rights. But supporters of the administration had good reason for wanting to remove this matter from his imperious and capricious control,
and, within a couple of weeks of the submission of Jefferson's special
message on neutral commerce, the Ways and Means Committee was
discharged from further consideration of this question and it was referred to the Committee of the Whole.[17]

There appears to be no evidence that the administration played any
overt part in this maneuvering, but during the most heated period of
the congressional session Jefferson was informed by the editor of the
Aurora, William Duane, of a report that was circulating in Pennsylvania: "It is said here that you have thrown yourself into the arms of a
New England party, and given them your exclusive confidence; that
the sturdy and independent republicans of the South are treated by
you with coldness and reserve." Replying to this, Jefferson said that in
fact he had had less communication with the eastern Republicans
during this session than in times past, and that his "reserve" had consisted of no more than his avoidance of participation in "the divisions
among our friends."[18] But the rumor in Philadelphia was in full accord
with John Randolph's suspicions and contentions. And, deprived of the
direction of this particular business as committee chairman, he vociferously opposed on the floor the proposals of all others.

[16] See pp. 68–69, above.
[17] Action of Jan. 29, 1806 (*Annals,* 9 Cong., 1 sess., pp. 409–412); see also
Randolph's statement of Jan. 30 (*ibid.,* pp. 415–416).
[18] Duane to TJ, Mar. 12, 1806 (*Procs. MHS,* 2 ser., XX, 1907, p. 282); TJ to
Duane, Mar. 22, 1806 (Ford, VIII, 431–432).

One unfortunate result of the abstention of the President from a specific recommendation, under what now appears to have been an undue regard for the doctrine of the separation of powers, and of his inability as yet to set up a line of communication comparable to the one previously established through John Randolph, was that the House gave first attention to an extreme individual proposal that the administration did not favor. On the same day that the question of neutral commerce was referred to the Committee of the Whole, Congressman Andrew Gregg of Pennsylvania submitted a resolution calling for the exclusion of *all* British imports until equitable and satisfactory arrangements should be made respecting impressment and the actions against American commerce. Federalist Senator Bayard, who described this as little short of a declaration of war against Great Britain, thought it probably a measure of the administration.[19] He doubted its passage, however, and regarded the House of Representatives as "completely disorganized, having no man to lead them, and being split into twenty different opinions." John Randolph, the onetime majority leader who had assumed the part of chief disorganizer, unlimbered his forensic artillery against this resolution. But that was not for about five weeks, during which time Gallatin, at the request of the House, collected and transmitted statistical information regarding imports. This was anybody's ammunition.

Meanwhile, the more sedate Senate adopted a couple of resolutions, couched in general terms, that were strongly anti-British in tone and marked by great concern for American commercial interests. Though presented by Samuel Smith, they were drafted by John Quincy Adams.[20] The first of these, which was unanimously approved, strongly condemned the actions of the British and contested their interpretation of the law of nations. The second, adopted by an overwhelming majority that included several Federalists, requested the President to *demand* the restoration of confiscated property and the indemnification of American citizens for losses. (The words *and insist upon* were stricken out by a vote of 16 to 15.) According to Senator Plumer, this business was "managed with great address" by the President and his friends, but such supporters of the action as Timothy Pickering and Uriah Tracy could hardly have been numbered among

---

[19] Text of Gregg resolution of Jan. 29, 1806 (*Annals,* 9 Cong., 1 sess., p. 413); Bayard's expressions of opinion in letters of Jan. 30, 31 (*A.H.A. Report,* 1913, II, 164–165).

[20] Resolutions of Feb. 12 and 14, 1806 (*Annals,* 9 Cong., 1 sess., pp. 91, 112; J. Q. Adams, *Writings,* III, 133–134; Plumer, *Memorandum,* pp. 428–434). Action on a third resolution, calling for a restriction of British imports, was postponed, pending developments in the House.

the latter, and we may doubt if Jefferson relished the phraseology of the second resolution even though modified.[21] Plumer himself opposed it on the ground that such a request was an infringement on the prerogatives of the President, whose function it was to initiate and conduct negotiations on his own responsibility. While recognizing that Jefferson had sufficient authority, other senators held that he would not negotiate without a resolution — either because of temperamental indecisiveness or unwillingness to endanger his popularity. Thus this action may be interpreted as an effort to exert pressure on him.

In fact, the administration, through the representations of James Monroe, had already made its position clear on the chief points at issue. But it had not authorized him to negotiate a new commercial treaty, and in view of the turmoil excited by Jay's treaty, Jefferson may well have hesitated to embark on such a hazardous undertaking wholly on his own accord. What some of his critics interpreted as concern for his popularity, however, might have been regarded as a desire to maintain unity within the federal government in the face of a grave national crisis. His determination to retain full control of diplomatic matters, as was so manifest in connection with the Spanish negotiations, arose from pragmatic as well as constitutional considerations. Basically, the question of British relations was more controversial, and in this connection he was more dependent on the support of Congress and the public. At all events, the Senate expressed itself strongly, and he appears to have shown no resentment at any infringement on his authority. He had far more reason to be offended by language that was soon heard in the House.

Speaking in opposition to the Gregg resolution on March 5, John Randolph delivered what William Plumer described as "the most bitter, severe and eloquent philippic" he had ever heard. The next day, after hearing from the same orator another speech almost as long (two hours) and similarly devastating, the Senator privately declared that Randolph had passed the Rubicon — that neither the President nor the Secretary of State could longer be on terms with him since he had "set them and their measures at defiance."[22] Randolph claimed that he could not tell what the administration was really for, but in fact this was not one of its measures. And, although he made frequent sarcastic

---

[21] S. F. Bemis regards the passage of these resolutions as "Adams's first triumph as a nonpartisan Senator" (*John Quincy Adams and the Foundations of American Foreign Policy* [1949], p. 137).

[22] Comments of Mar. 5, 6 in Plumer's *Memorandum*, p. 444; Randolph's speeches of those days in *Annals*, 9 Cong., 1 sess., pp. 555–574, 592–605. W. C. Bruce (*Randolph*, I, 233–285) gives a lengthy account of this entire episode and Randolph's breach with the administration, including extensive quotations from the speeches.

references to the secretive and underhand influence of the executive branch on legislation, he now charged it with impotence. While bitterly opposing the Gregg resolution on its merits, he availed himself of the opportunity to hurl verbal darts at the administration, aiming chiefly at Madison. He continued to do so after the Republican majority shelved the Gregg resolution in order to consider a much more moderate one introduced by his intimate friend Nicholson. After it appeared that relatively few members of his own party were willing to cross the Rubicon with him, he resorted to tactics of delay, and he absented himself from the decisive vote on that resolution.[23]

Avowedly sympathetic to the British in their duel with the French, the perfervid orator denounced the latter in a way that must have pleased Federalist Anglophiles. At the same time, however, he sprayed epithets on the merchants and shipowners who had been profiting from the wartime carrying trade, and, speaking for agricultural America, asked if the nation was to be ruled by the Atlantic seaports. Thus he sought to widen the gap between the southern and western Republicans and the more commercially minded representatives of the party from the Northeast, whom he treated with undisguised contempt. Commercial cupidity may have deserved rebuke, but Randolph's assumption of moral superiority could not have failed to be infuriating. As for the administration, after voicing innuendos about "backstairs influence" and invisible, inscrutable, and unconstitutional procedures, he asserted: "*There is no longer any Cabinet.*" By this he meant that Gallatin was without influence in it and that Madison was supreme. The embittered disorganizer was trying to drive a wedge between the Secretary of the Treasury and the Secretary of State. That the latter was the special object of his abomination was shown by his sneering references to Madison's book. This, he asserted, actually conceded the "principle of necessity" for which the British contended in *War in Disguise.*[24] It is not surprising that the speaker was quoted approvingly in England.

Though Randolph left little doubt of his judgment that Jefferson had failed as a "political Messiah," and though he heaped scorn on alleged claims of executive infallibility, his attacks on the President were generally indirect. Robert Smith and Gideon Granger were occasional objects of his wrath and Madison always a major one, while Gallatin was singled out for praise. In one of his later speeches, after

23 The Nicholson resolution, proposed Feb. 10, 1806, was considered after a vote on Mar. 13 *not* to consider the Gregg resolution, and was adopted Mar. 17 by a vote of 87 to 35 (*Annals,* 9 Cong., 1 sess., pp. 451, 769, 823).

24 *Ibid.,* pp. 565–566.

the shelving of the Gregg resolution had removed that target, Randolph renewed the charge that the head of the Treasury Department had been ousted from the Cabinet.[25] According to this allegation, important foreign dispatches had been withheld from that vigorous, commanding, and practical statesman (as well as from Randolph himself) and policies had been determined without the benefit of his sage counsel. In this instance the faultfinder was following the divisive tactics of quoting, or seeming to quote, one member of the Cabinet against another. He did the same sort of thing a little later in connection with his unsuccessful effort to make public the secret message of the President on the Spanish situation. Then, on the basis of hearsay, he said in thinly veiled language that, according to Gallatin, Madison had sought to secure from the Treasury money for these negotiations before Congress had authorized the desired appropriation. From the heated exchange in the House and Gallatin's own explanation, it appears that an unwarranted inference had been drawn from what Gallatin actually said, the purpose being to injure Madison.[26]

The Yazoo question had come up again a few days earlier, when the House majority, following Randolph's lead in this controversial matter as in the past, rejected a bill from the Senate calling for the payment of the much-disputed claims. Speaking of the original measure, he said: "This bill . . . is the head of the divisions among the republican party; it is the secret and covert cause of the whole."[27] Since this controversy was in important respects sectional, and since it served to alienate the more doctrinaire from the more pragmatic Republicans, such may indeed have been the case. But the major architect of the settlement that the "Virginian Saint Michael" spurned as a base compromise with evil was the Secretary of the Treasury. Gallatin's maintenance of intimate personal relations with John Randolph after the attack on his handiwork was a credit to his forbearance. This may be attributed in part to his awareness of the importance of rapport with the Chairman of the Ways and Means Committee and his respect for the latter's abilities. But the irate orator had now made friendship of the old sort impossible without disloyalty to the administration, and at this point it may be said to have ended.

Rumors about the Cabinet, which Randolph's public utterances seemed to corroborate but which may have been set in motion by him

[25] Mar. 13, 1806 (*ibid.*, p. 771).
[26] Apr. 7, 1806 (*ibid.*, pp. 985, 987–988, 995); Gallatin to George Clinton, Jr., Apr. 5, 1806 (*Writings*, I, 295–297).
[27] Mar. 29, 1806 (*Annals*, 9 Cong., 1 sess., p. 909). On the earlier history of the controversy, see *Jefferson the President: First Term*, ch. XXIV.

and his coterie in the first place, spread beyond the House of Representatives. William Duane reported from Philadelphia that in some Republican quarters it was alleged that Madison, alone among his ministers, supported the President. The Secretary of the Navy was said to act with his brother, the Senator from Maryland, to thwart him in naval matters; and the Secretary of War, "secretly governed by the Postmaster General," was represented as doing the same in military matters. Most serious of all was the report that the Secretary of the Treasury did not approve of Jefferson's policies and that, not being consulted about them, Gallatin was threatening to resign.[28]

Jefferson couched in general terms his private reply to these wild rumors of executive dissension and confusion. There were differences between Gallatin and Robert Smith to which he avoided reference, but the innumerable communications that passed between him and his department heads in this period and throughout his presidency bear out the essential accuracy of his statement. To Duane he said:

> That there is only one minister who is not opposed to me, is totally unfounded. There never was a more harmonious, a more cordial administration, nor ever a moment when it has been otherwise. And while differences of opinion have been always rare among us, I can affirm, that as to present matters, there was not a single paragraph in my message to Congress, or those supplementary to it, in which there was not an unanimity of concurrence in the members of the administration. The fact is, that in ordinary affairs every head of a department consults me on those of his department, & where anything arises too difficult or important to be decided between us, the consultation becomes general.
>
> That there is an ostensible cabinet and a concealed one, a public profession & concealed counteraction, is false.[29]

In this confidential letter Jefferson said that there must be an enemy who was trying to sow discord among the Republicans, and there is record that he expressed the same thought to a few others, but neither here nor anywhere else does he appear to have indulged in recrimination against the chief troublemaker in Congress. He contented himself with an acknowledgment of John Randolph's attack and a brief statement of the position the administration had taken. "We were not disposed," he said, "to join in league with Britain, under any belief that

28 Duane to TJ, Mar. 12, 1806 (*Procs. M.H.S.*, 2 ser., XX, 282).
29 TJ to Duane, Mar. 22, 1806 (Ford, VIII, 432–433).

she is fighting for the liberties of mankind, and to enter into war with Spain, and consequently France. . . . We are for a peaceable accommodation with all those nations, if it can be effected honorably." Also, after observing that, whatever the administration might do, it was liable to criticism by those who wanted to misrepresent it, he presented the alternatives with grim precision. If the President publicly recommended measures, he could be charged with issuing edicts; if he expressed opinions in private, he could be said to have "back-door counselors"; if he said nothing, he could be charged with having "no opinions, no plans, no Cabinet." Jefferson did not need to point out that John Randolph had sought to deny him *all* of these alternatives. "In truth it is the fable of the old man, his son and ass, over again," he sagely said.

Jefferson recognized that there may have been other grounds for Randolph's alienation from the administration than his disagreement with it regarding public policy, but he did not press the point. He knew by this time that this brilliant but erratic leader had failed to create a schism in the congressional majority. A crucial vote on the Nicholson resolution had already shown that Randolph could rally very few Republicans in his effort to defeat what had come to be regarded as a party measure. A few weeks later he read himself out of the party by openly declaring that he could not co-operate with the administration but would continue to oppose it.[30] He did not renounce the name Republican, but thenceforth he could resort only to guerrilla tactics.

The net result of weeks of acrimonious debate on the means to be employed against British commercial aggression was the passage of what came to be known as the Non-Importation Act.[31] This was based on the resolution introduced by Nicholson, and insofar as it reflected the influence of the administration, this must have been exerted by the Secretary of the Treasury, his kinsman by marriage and intimate friend. Recognizing that the cutting off of all imports would drastically reduce the government's revenue and deprive Americans of accustomed articles they could not themselves produce, Nicholson drew a list of articles and commodities which, in his opinion, they could produce. The result was a mild measure which was not to be-

[30] Apr. 7, 1806, when urging the publication of TJ's confidential message about Spain (*Annals,* 9 Cong., 1 sess., p. 984).

[31] Bill passed by the House, Mar. 26, 1806, by a vote of 93 to 32; by the Senate Apr. 15, by a vote of 19 to 9; approved Apr. 18 (*ibid.,* pp. 877–878; 240, 1259–1260).

come effective until November 15, 1806, and which would therefore permit both the spring and fall importations. John Randolph, who had characterized the proposal of Gregg as absurdly and dangerously strong, ridiculed the act resulting from the proposal of his friend Nicholson for its weakness, and, because of their quotability, his pungent words have reappeared in many a history book: "What is it? A milk and water bill, a dose of chicken broth to be taken nine months hence. . . . It is too contemptible to be the object of consideration or to excite the feelings of the pettiest state in Europe."[32]

As allowance must be made for John Randolph's rhetoric, it must also be made for the opinions of the British minister, Anthony Merry, which so often reflected what Federalist critics of the administration told him. In his view as reported to his home office, the American government and the majority of Republicans believed that this partial non-importation would not be "resented in a hostile manner" by His Majesty's government, but that it would have an effect on British merchants and manufacturers and thus lead to concessions.[33] Such concessions, he held, would redound to the popularity of the President at home, and in the meantime the latter would have accomplished the further object of pleasing the French by this effort to curtail British and promote neutral trade. Adhering to the Federalist party line, Merry attributed Jefferson's policies to his desire to maintain his popularity. War would destroy that popularity in Merry's judgment and he reported that the idea of war was deprecated in Congress and throughout the country. Therefore, American threats need not be taken very seriously.

There is ample reason to believe that the country, like the President, was in no mood to go to extremes, and the Non-Importation Act in itself may be recognized as a feeble instrument. But what Jefferson wanted from Congress was its support of negotiation, and at this stage he regarded legislation as merely a supplement and aid to diplomacy. Even John Randolph, who fiercely deprecated war and loudly praised Monroe while castigating Madison, relied on that. Logically this opponent of strong action should have been pleased with the Non-Importation Act because of its moderation. By the time it emerged from the turmoil in Congress, hopeful signs had appeared on the diplomatic horizon and induced in Jefferson a mood of optimism. Shortly before the bill passed the House he sent Congress an encouraging letter from

[32] Mar. 26, 1806 (*ibid.*, p. 851).
[33] Merry to Mulgrave, No. 15, Mar. 19, 1806 (FO, 5:48, pp. 65–71).

Monroe, and he told William Plumer a little later that the prospects of settling the differences with the British were "very flattering indeed" — that he had no doubt whatever that these would be accommodated to the "entire satisfaction" of the United States.[34]

Events were to prove that he was much too sanguine, but at the moment the situation appeared to have improved greatly because of changes in the British government. The death of William Pitt had been followed by the formation of the Ministry of All Talents, so-called, and Charles James Fox had become foreign secretary. It was not to be known during the congressional session that one of the new secretary's early acts was the recall of Anthony Merry, but Fox was widely regarded as friendly to the United States. Under these circumstances the limited congressional action, which was in accord with the temper of the country, seemed to the President to be adequate to the situation.

Writing James Monroe the day after the crucial vote on the Nicholson resolution, Jefferson reported that he had never seen a House of Representatives "more solidly united in what they believed to be the best for the public good." He added that no better proof could be afforded than "the fact that so eminent a leader should at once and almost unanimously be abandoned." Only eight other Republicans had joined John Randolph and the Federalists in opposition.[35] Far from disrupting his party, he was abandoned by it several weeks before he publicly renounced the administration (April 7, 1806). Soon after he did that, he lost his chief lieutenant. He was not present on April 9, when the Speaker laid before the House a letter of resignation from Joseph H. Nicholson, but he wrote that cherished recent colleague that he greeted the news with tears. Nicholson had accepted appointment to a high post in the judiciary of Maryland and was thus removed from the national public scene. The reasons for his withdrawal appear to have been chiefly financial. Contrary to the assertion frequently made in works of history, Jefferson did not get Nicholson out of Congress by giving him a federal appointment; but, apparently aware of the financial situation, he offered him one about six months after Nicholson became a judge. This was the collectorship of the Port of Baltimore, which Nicholson declined in a cordial and appreciative

---

[34] Entries of Mar. 24 and Apr. 2, 1806, in Plumer's *Memorandum*, pp. 462, 470. The former reference is to Monroe's letter of Jan. 28, 1806, to Madison (S.M.H., V, 45; *Annals*, 9 Cong., 1 sess., p. 199).

[35] TJ to Monroe, Mar. 18, 1806 (Ford, VIII, 428–429), a letter which did not reach Monroe as intended, but which nonetheless reflected TJ's interpretation of events (see note 42, below).

letter. It would appear, therefore, that friendly relations between the two men were maintained, in form at least.[36]

Of the Republican senators only Dr. George Logan, whose pacific principles colored his views of all aspects of foreign policy, voted against the non-importation bill. About a month earlier, in a letter of protest against Jefferson's "errors in conducting the exterior relations of our country," this senator had offered advice which suggested his uncritical acceptance of some of John Randolph's allegations in the House and some of the reports that were circulating in his own state of Pennsylvania. He had urged the President to call together his "long neglected Council" and intimated that he had been improperly secretive. Jefferson promptly invited this old friend to a private conference. He also invited Nathaniel Macon to an uninterrupted evening of conversation, saying that some unknown enemy was sowing tares among the Republicans and expressing at the same time his unqualified confidence in the Speaker of the House, who in times past had been so intimate with John Randolph. Since we do not know what happened at either of these meetings, or even if they occurred, we mention them here merely as examples of his persistent efforts to maintain friendly relations and understanding with leading Republicans and to reduce dissension within the party.[37] Sometimes he over-played his part, but his good will was genuine and his tolerance of minor differences within his own following was great. One of the most successful, perhaps the most successful, of party leaders in presidential history, he was notably forbearing — he left John Randolph enough rope to hang himself. He himself described this session of Congress as "long and uneasy," but at its end he concluded that his party had gained, not lost, in solidarity, and declared that his own confidence in the "solidity and permanence" of the American government had increased.[38] Viewing the domestic scene, he was warranted in that judgment, but it remained to be seen if

---

[36] Nicholson's letter of resignation was read Apr. 9, 1806 (*Annals,* 9 Cong., 1 sess., p. 996). On Mar. 26, he had been commissioned as chief judge of the Sixth District of Maryland, and as such he became a member of the Court of Appeals of that state (C. T. Bond, *Court of Appeals of Maryland* [1928], pp. 104–106). The error in Adams, *History,* III, 166–167, is repeated in Bruce, I, 252, and in even more recent writings. TJ offered the collectorship Oct. 11, 1806, and Nicholson declined Oct. 14 (LC, 28349). That Nicholson's position in Congress had become equivocal is suggested by the fact that while he introduced the resolution that historically bears his name and voted for it, he went along with Randolph in seeking to delay action on it.

[37] George Logan to TJ, and TJ to Logan, Mar. 12, 1806 (LC, 27550, 27547); also TJ to Logan, Apr. 7, 1806 (LC, 27659), showing continued disagreement about Spanish relations; TJ to Nathaniel Macon, Mar. 26, 1806 (Ford, VIII, 439).

[38] TJ to John Tyler, Apr. 26, 1806 (Ford, VIII, 441–442).

the means approved by him and by Congress would be effective in dealing with other countries in a desperately warring world.

He himself said afterwards that his original preference was to leave negotiations with the British in the hands of James Monroe, although the common practice of the United States had been to meet crises in foreign relations by setting up extraordinary commissions.[39] We may speculate that he might have changed his mind anyway, but, according to his own report, he did so under pressure from members of both houses of Congress, beginning with the senators. The committee that conveyed to him the Senate resolutions of February (Smith of Maryland and Mitchill of New York) informed him that virtually every member of that body favored an extraordinary mission.[40] The matter was subsequently taken up by individual members of the House, including some of the best friends of Monroe and of the President himself, according to the latter. These took the position that, in case of possible failure to secure a redress of American grievances, the responsibility would be too heavy on both of them if the almost-unanimous judgment of the legislators had been disregarded. Probably it was not very difficult for Jefferson to yield his opinion graciously to that of the "national council," and he acted on the decision with haste that would have surprised the members of that body had they known about it. Before the House had voted to consider the resolution of Nicholson instead of that of Gregg, he sounded out the man he wanted to nominate as joint commissioner with Monroe and learned that William Pinkney of Baltimore would accept with pleasure.

This noted lawyer had served eight years in London as joint claims commissioner under the Jay treaty (with Christopher Gore) and more recently had written for the merchants of his city a strong memorial against the Rule of 1756.[41] Time was to show that Pinkney was less successful in diplomacy than at the bar, where he was pre-eminent, but on the basis of the existing record he was an admirable choice. Jefferson sought to inform Monroe of it promptly, in a letter which contained a veiled warning against being drawn unwittingly into the campaign against Madison being waged by John Randolph. He wrote Monroe, of whose personal plans he was still uncertain, that Pinkney

[39] TJ to Monroe, Mar. 10, 1808 (L. & B., XII, 3-5).
[40] On the resolutions, see pp. 104-105. Plumer comments on senatorial attitudes in his *Memorandum*, pp. 393, 429.
[41] Pinkney to TJ, Mar. 13, 1806, written after he had received through Jacob Wagner, clerk of the State Department, TJ's confidential views about the special mission (LC, 27552); received by TJ Mar. 16.

was authorized to succeed him as resident minister whenever he should decide to return home. This letter, which unfortunately did not reach Monroe, was meant to be reassuring and reflected Jefferson's great concern to prevent Republican dissension.[42] But if Pinkney's appointment had any domestic political purpose it was to promote the unity of the nation, not that of the party.

The President sent the Senate the nominations of Monroe and Pinkney as joint commissioners toward the end of the session, after the non-importation bill had been duly passed and the treaty with Tripoli consented to.[43] The naming of Pinkney was a special shock to Senator Samuel Smith, also of Baltimore. At the time Jefferson made this choice, without consulting the Senator or his brother Robert, the former, for reasons which appear to have been far from disinterested, was still trying to defeat the nomination of John Armstrong as commissioner, and he had been hoping that he himself would be sent either to England or France.[44] Smith's high hopes of appointment as envoy extraordinary to Great Britain were recognized or suspected by a number of his colleagues and were admitted by him in a letter to his brother-in-law, Wilson Cary Nicholas, after he learned — from his brother, no doubt — that Jefferson had been engaged in private correspondence with the intended appointee.[45] This intriguing senator deserved rebuke. Other Republicans, designating Pinkney as a Federalist, expressed regret at his nomination. Doubt as to his political complexion persisted, but when his name came up nobody in the Senate voted against him.[46] Sober judgment confirms the opinion of William Plumer that this appointment was "a stroke of sound correct policy."

Before Pinkney set sail, about a month after his confirmation, Charles James Fox had sent Anthony Merry instructions to inform the American authorities of British good will and the desire to enter into a

42 TJ to Monroe, Mar. 16, 1806 (LC, 27562). On the circumstances attending Monroe's failure to get this letter see p. 149, below. He received the longer letter TJ wrote him May 4, when Congress was in recess and TJ had more time (Ford, VIII, 447-450).

43 Apr. 19, 1806 (Senate Exec. Procs., II, 35).

44 Armstrong was confirmed Mar. 17, 1806; on Mar. 13 Pinkney signified his willingness to accept the appointment.

45 Samuel Smith to Nicholas, Apr. 1, 1806; quoted in Adams, History, III, 169-170, from Nicholas MSS.

46 Plumer, Memorandum, pp. 489, 491-492. He reported J. Q. Adams as saying that Rufus King might have been appointed if he had been left "unfettered with particular restrictions," but if TJ was well informed of King's part in the Miranda episode this seems unlikely.

treaty with no more delay than was absolutely necessary.[47] Previous to the receipt and communication of this message, however, great excitement was created in New York by a naval incident which reflected no spirit of British good will. His Majesty's Ship *Leander,* off Sandy Hook, firing a shot to cause a merchant vessel to come to and submit to search, killed a man in another vessel. This was in American waters and the offense was aggravated by the presence of a couple of other British vessels in the same general locality. Eight days later Jefferson issued a proclamation charging the Captain of the *Leander* with murder, enjoining his apprehension for trial if ever he should set foot on American territory, and ordering the three vessels out of American waters, never to return.[48]

Writing afterwards to a congressman from New England who unlike himself was seagoing, and describing the act of the British officer as "an atrocious violation of our territorial rights," he said that one suggestion considered by the government in this difficult situation was to send three frigates to New York harbor. But these were not immediately available, and in the meantime the government had been assured by Merry that the three British vessels that had converged on New York had done so by accident and were not expected to remain. "We concluded therefore," said Jefferson, "that it was best to do what you have seen in the proclamation, and to make a proper use of the outrage and of our forbearance at St. James's, to obtain better provisions for the future."[49] It can be truthfully said that American naval weakness restricted his freedom of choice — in this very letter he recognized the need for more capital ships than Congress had been in the mood to make provision for. It can also be said that he knew in advance that by ordering the British ships away he was not likely to offend their government. Nonetheless, his limited action was a wise one in the existing diplomatic situation. The firing of the cannonball could not properly be blamed on the present British ministry, which had given signs of friendliness and with which he was hoping that Monroe and Pinkney could negotiate successfully.

Events were to show that his faith in the good will of Charles James Fox was warranted. The Foreign Secretary, describing the *Leander* episode as a "melancholy transaction," promptly promised an investigation of it; and, during the few weeks of service left to him, he did all

---

[47] Fox to Merry, Apr. 7, 1806 (*I.B.M.,* p. 221). Merry acknowledged this June 1, saying that he read it to Madison, No. 29 (FO, 5:49).

[48] Proclamation of May 3, 1806, draft in Ford, VIII, 445-446. Merry reported events to Fox, May 4, 1806, No. 24 (FO, 5:49).

[49] TJ to Jacob Crowninshield, May 13, 1806 (Ford, VIII, 451-453).

he could to prevent its occasioning enmity or distrust. Not until another year did Jefferson learn of the disappointing outcome of Captain Whitby's trial.[50] Meanwhile, he properly sought to safeguard the negotiations of Monroe and Pinkney in England. Writing the former the day after he issued his proclamation, he said that he could have done no less than he did, after the late "unparalleled outrage" but that this action was not directed against the present British ministry.[51] What was more, he strongly implied that if they had been in office earlier his own administration would have followed a different course. "We had committed ourselves in a line of proceedings adapted to meet Mr. Pitt's policy and hostility, before we heard of his death, which self-respect did not permit us to abandon afterwards," he said. It is not clear whether he was referring to the Non-Importation Act or to the effort to gain the good offices of France in the hope of acquiring Florida.

At all events, he was more hopeful of accord between his country and Britain than he had been since the actions of the latter against American commerce had caused him to abandon the idea of an alliance. "No two countries upon earth have so many points of common interest and friendship," he said; "and their rulers must be great bunglers indeed, if, with such dispositions, they break them asunder." He saw no possible rivalry except upon the ocean, but leaned to the opinion that British ascendancy there was safer for his country than that of France. Although he did not resurrect the idea of an alliance, he wanted to be truly neutral and hoped the British would permit him to be so. But he was now pinning his hopes on the uncertain life of one man and he never allowed sufficiently for the necessities of war as perceived, rightly or wrongly, in England. Furthermore, communication with the Old World was so slow that his information was always out of date. For a number of reasons this patriotic opportunist was too sanguine in viewing the diplomatic scene.

On the domestic side, however, and especially in matters of party politics and public opinion, about which he was thoroughly informed, he was notably perceptive and his major success during this troubled legislative session was achieved at home. On the same day that Jefferson wrote Monroe, Anthony Merry made a prediction in a letter to Charles James Fox. The opposition which had been shown to the

---

[50] Fox's immediate response is shown in his letter of June 6, 1806, to Merry (*I.B.M.*, p. 223). Months later Captain Whitby was acquitted. For an excellent account of these events, see Perkins, pp. 106–108. We shall recur to them in connection with the Monroe-Pinkney negotiations (see below, ch. XXII).

[51] TJ to Monroe, May 4, 1806 (Ford, VIII, 449–450).

measures of the government, he said, and the exposure of its general weakness, submissiveness to France, and duplicity of conduct, would probably have the effect of considerably diminishing its influence throughout the country.[52] But the President seemed virtually invincible when Congress met again. One member of that body then remarked that "if he should recommend to us to repeal the Gospels of the Evangelist, a majority of Congress would do it."[53]

[52] Merry to Fox, May 4, 1806, No. 22 (FO, 5:49).
[53] Dec. 11, 1806, Gen. Stephen R. Bradley of Vermont, quoted by Plumer (*Memorandum*, p. 527).

The Great White Father

[VIII]

Paterfamilias and Friend

BY describing the late congressional session as "squally," Jefferson
virtually admitted that it had brought him personal discomfort, for
he particularly disliked rough seas. Indeed, enemies and critics claimed
that this was a basic weakness of his. But he had the satisfaction of
realizing that as a party leader he had survived a mutiny, and that on
the whole Congress had been responsive. The second *Leander* episode
of the year occurred shortly after the adjournment, but it does not appear to have marred his equanimity. After he had issued his proclamation and written Monroe, and Madison had made the appropriate
formal protests, he could do nothing more about British relations. The
issue lay with his envoys extraordinary, from whom he could not expect a conclusive answer for many months. Nor could he expect to
hear soon from Armstrong and Bowdoin, whose confirmation had
been so long delayed. The forcible ejection of Yrujo, who was still in
Philadelphia, did not seem wise while there was any hope of restoring
negotiations with his country. Therefore, it appeared that for the
present this unwelcome visitor should remain undisturbed.

If, in early May of the year in which he reached the age of sixty-
three, circumstances did not warrant euphoria they at least permitted
temporary relaxation. He said he hoped to "unbend" during a few
weeks' visit to Monticello, but apparently he began to do so before he
left Washington. His daughter and her children had been with him
throughout the season, and the wife of the editor of the *National
Intelligencer* left a glowing account of a visit she and her husband paid
the presidential family on the Sunday before their departure. Seeing
Jefferson at play with his grandchildren, Mrs. Smith "could scarcely
realize that he was one of the most celebrated men now living"; and
she was enraptured to find him in "one of his most communicative and
social moods." In the evening, after the children had gone to bed, he

talked delightfully on his favorite topics — not politics or diplomacy, but agriculture and gardening in various climes and countries. As they parted he gave her some winter melon seed from Malta, though doubtful of the effect of early American frosts on this plant from the Mediterranean.[1]

Her horticultural host was in no position to read this ecstatic account of a friendly visit, but he had in his files a request for another from a versifying New Englander. We record it here as a sort of antidote to the political abuse with which these pages have been sprinkled and the affairs of state with which they have been weighted. Several months earlier a hitherto unknown bard had thus addressed the President:

> Philanthropist, Illustrious Sage;
> The Pride and Glory of our Age;
> An Audience grant I pray.
> Vermont Sam Harrison has come
> From Chittendon to Washington
> To Visit the Great Jefferson:
> A lengthy tedious waye.[2]

Since he was accessible to all, the Illustrious Sage may be presumed to have received Vermont Sam Harrison. He undoubtedly saw a visitor from New York, a onetime playwright and theatrical producer who had recently taken up his brushes and, while in Washington, occupied himself in some part in making a copy of Jefferson's portrait by Gilbert Stuart. For the benefit of his wife and ultimately of posterity, William Dunlap reported that he had "seen, touched, and heard the great man." Having noted on a sultry February day that the frogs had already commenced their town meetings, though their orators were not in full voice as yet, he mentioned this observation to Jefferson only to learn that "the great man" had heard the croaking ten days earlier and duly recorded the event. Seemingly unchagrined, the artist when recounting the wonders of Washington gave a sympathetic description of the main one:

And first — Thomas Jefferson, is a tall man, say 6 feet & thin. His hair which has been red & is now grey, is worn in negligent disorder, tho not ungracefully. His complexion is ruddy & his eye (a hazle) very animated. He converses with ease & vivacity, possessing true politeness, which places his guests perfectly at their

[1] Margaret Bayard Smith to Mrs. Kirkpatrick, May 4, 1806, in *First Forty Years of Washington Society* (1906), pp. 49–50.
[2] Feb. 12, 1806 (LC, 27403).

THOMAS JEFFERSON

The "Edgehill" portrait, painted from life by Gilbert Stuart,
shortly before June 7, 1805, in Washington

ease. During the short period which we past with him, rendered shorter by the uncertainty of having interrupted him in study or Business (for he came into the room *en dishabille* & slippered) he talked of the early approach of spring, of gardening French & English, preferring the latter & praising their great taste in laying out their ground . . .[3]

On the very day that the Senate passed the Two-Million-Dollar Act, this host sent a letter to his overseer at Monticello urging that Jerry, one of the servants attached to the place, set off as soon as possible for Washington with the light cart and two mules, in order to carry home a load of trees to be planted. Jerry and the mules arrived a couple of weeks later, and toward the end of February they went home. In the heavily laden cart were an indeterminate number of young fruit trees for the orchard and some forty bundles that contained upwards of ten thousand thorn plants. Sending his overseer a plan of the grounds and full instructions about the planting, Jefferson urged him to set his entire force to work immediately when the cart arrived. He was strictly economical in his conduct of the federal establishment but in no sense niggardly in planning for his beloved estate. The chief costs were for labor, which he often figured in hours and days and less often translated into dollars and cents. The thorn plants, which he got from Thomas Main's nursery three miles from Washington, cost him six dollars a thousand. He had procured two thousand in the previous autumn and with these his hedge had been started along Mulberry Row. As now designed, it was to enclose not only his garden but the enlarged and freshly planted orchard.[4]

When he got home in May of this year for a visit of about a month, the region was suffering from a severe drought. They had a copious rain before he returned to Washington, but when he got back home in late July for his customary long visit, the streams in Albemarle and neighboring counties were drying up and the springs were failing.[5] Either because of the drought or for other reasons he had to replenish his stock of thorns before another year rolled around and he continued to set out fruit trees. About a year after he talked about grounds and gardens with William Dunlap he sent to Monticello by cart (now guided by Davy instead of Jerry) four thousand more thorn plants, along with some bundles of trees, and in the autumn of that year he

[3] Feb. 19–25, 1806 (*Diary of William Dunlap*, II [1930], pp. 387–388).
[4] This account is based primarily on the *Garden Book*, pp. 310–329, dealing with the year 1806 and containing pertinent correspondence. See especially TJ to John Freeman, Feb. 7, 26, 1806; Thomas Main to TJ, Feb. 24, 1806; and Plate XXI.
[5] TJ to Madison, May 23, July 26, 1806 (*ibid.*, pp. 319, 322).

purchased two thousand that were somewhat more expensive.[6] Despite the vicissitudes of his hedge, he continued to think highly of this variety of thorn. Speaking of it to a nurseryman in Philadelphia, toward the end of his seventh year as President, he said: "Certainly no thorn in England which I have ever seen makes a hedge any more to be compared to this than a log hut to a wall of freestone." In his later years he expressed some doubts about its strength against cattle but still preferred it.[7]

Among his many cherished non-political correspondents were the chief American nurserymen and horticulturists of his time. One of these was Bernard McMahon of Philadelphia, who in 1806 published *The American Gardener's Calendar.* Jefferson had no doubt that this work would be useful to the friends of an art of great importance which had been too much neglected in the United States. McMahon, informed of his unsuccessful attempts to acquire seeds of tarragon, sent him some roots of that herb shortly before he set out for his May visit to Monticello; and when he was back in Washington in July the horticulturist sent him some tulip roots. In acknowledging these Jefferson intimated that he did not want plants of this sort as yet since he would not be able to attend to them until he went home to stay. Even when he did begin to collect seriously, he would be more inclined to procure "curious and hardy" trees than flowers, he said.[8] He had long been interested in every bud that opens, but hedges, trees, and shrubs were his major concern just now.

He laid no claim to the title of landscape gardener, but in the summer of 1806 he tossed off a little treatise on the subject. This was in the form of a letter to William Hamilton of "The Woodlands," Philadelphia, with whom he had often exchanged seeds, plants, and botanical information and whose grounds were the only ones he had seen in America that rivaled those of England.[9] He anticipated (much too optimistically) that the building operations on his little mountain which had engaged him for so many years would be finished by the end of this one. Therefore, his mind had now turned to the improvement of his grounds. While recognizing that the best models were to

[6] TJ to Edmund Bacon, his overseer, Mar. 12, 1807; Main's bill of Nov. 20, 1807 (*ibid.,* pp. 343, 353).
[7] TJ to William Hamilton, Mar. 1, 1808; to J. C. Cabell, July 13, 1816 (*ibid.,* pp. 365, 559).
[8] Correspondence of April–July, 1806 (*ibid.,* pp. 313, 318–319, 321, 322).
[9] TJ to William Hamilton, after July 11, 1806, when he got Hamilton's of July 7 (LC, 28121, largely in *Garden Book,* pp. 322–324). TJ had been corresponding with him at least since the spring of 1800, when he himself was in Philadelphia as Vice President.

be found in the mother country, as a realistic observer he clearly perceived that he could not transform his mountaintop into an English landscape. The lower slopes were still largely in their majestic native woods with thick undergrowth and he was disposed to leave them so. His chief problem there was one of roads. Several times during the year he mentioned the road from the Shadwell ford to the top of the mountain on the north side that was finished in May, and in this letter he spoke of the encircling walks near the summit and of others of easy ascent that intersected these. At the highest level the grounds were largely open, though there was a dense thicket of Scotch broom to the southward. The disposition of his ground, he said, "takes from me the first beauty in gardening, the variety of hill and dale, and leaves me as an awkward substitute a few hanging hollows and ridges." Describing his subject as unique and at the same time refractory, he modestly remarked that "to make a disposition analogous to its character would require much more of the genius of the landscape painter and gardener" than he could pretend to. Therefore, a visit from William Hamilton would be most welcome.

While looking to the best available models elsewhere for inspiration, Jefferson was no more a copyist in landscape gardening than in architecture. Speaking of the English, he said: "Their sunless climate has permitted them to adopt what is certainly a beauty of the first order in landscape. Their canvas is of open ground, variegated with clumps of trees distributed with taste. They need no more wood than will serve to embrace a lawn or glade." Under the Virginia sun, on the other hand, shade was a necessity and this called for many trees. Believing that an impression of openness was desirable, this Virginian broached an idea he was never able to carry into effect. This was that the ground be filled with very tall trees, trimmed as high as feasible but united at the top so as to yield dense shade. In this open wood, shrubs should be planted in clumps much the way the English grouped trees. Thus it would be possible to have shade and a diversity of vistas at the same time. Except for his thorn hedge and orchard, he was doing little planting as yet, but in the meantime he found much to delight his eye at Monticello.

Of prospect I have a rich profusion and offering itself at every point of the compass. Mountains distant & near, smooth & shaggy, single & in ridges, a little river hiding itself among the hills so as to shew in lagoons only, cultivated grounds under the eye and two small villages. To prevent a satiety of this is the principal difficulty. It may be successively offered, & in different portions

through vistas, or which will be better, between thickets so disposed as to serve as vistas, with the advantage of shifting the
scenes as you advance on your way.

i i

The writer of this fascinating letter may have shown lack of political
sagacity in saying so much, even in private, about his still-distant retirement, and he undoubtedly gave considerable rein to his imagination
when anticipating its joys. During this very summer his hopes for
future happiness were clouded for a time by fears for his son-in-law,
Thomas Mann Randolph, and his daughter's family. Martha's high-
tempered husband again got himself into trouble by his impetuosity.
On the last day of the congressional session he had tangled with his
cousin John Randolph, and a duel between the two men had been
narrowly averted. When Jefferson was at home in May he thought the
incident closed, but after he got back to Washington in June he
learned from the newspapers that the quarrel had been reopened and
the threat of armed combat revived. Then he wrote his son-in-law a
deeply moving letter.

The trouble started in the House of Representatives, where the
Chairman of the Ways and Means Committee, who was making a final
and futile attempt to repeal the duty on salt, was charged with being
primarily motivated by a desire to embarrass the administration. There
was merit in the charge, but it chanced to be made by Congressman
Findley of Pennsylvania, who had availed himself of a brief recess for
dinner to imbibe spirituous liquors. To John Randolph's defense came
David R. Williams of South Carolina, who had declined a dinner
invitation from Jefferson earlier in the year on the ground that acceptance might compromise his independence.[10] Offended by his language, a number of representatives tried to call Williams to order.
Among them was Thomas Mann Randolph, who rarely spoke and
whose congressional career thus far had been undistinguished. Soon
thereafter John Randolph himself took the floor.

From the recorded words of this master of epithets and artist in
innuendo it is difficult to determine just whom he was aiming at. After
inquiring whether it was the dinner they had just eaten that had
brought them to such heat, he expressed the hope that no gentleman
who had hitherto kept "the noiseless tenor of his way" had now "permitted his passions to indulge" in an asperity not previously mani-

[10] Williams to TJ, Jan. 29, 1806 (Bixby, pp. 127–128); TJ to Williams, Jan. 31, 1806 (LC, 27350).

fested. He used the term "contumely" in speaking of former occasions, but he was speaking of this one when he referred to "the splenetic temper of age or youth." Since the effects of the recess were most visible in Findley, who was in his middle sixties and might perhaps have been regarded as old, there could be little doubt that the orator had him in mind. But it could also have been supposed that he was taunting the President's son-in-law. That young gentleman thought so, at any rate. If the reference to "the noiseless tenor of his way" was not intended for him, it undoubtedly fitted him as a public man, and he rose to this bait.[11]

His psychological state can be easily imagined. The embarrassments incident to his relationship with Jefferson might have been expected to increase rather than diminish during the years he was a congressman in Washington, living in the President's House, overshadowed more than ever by that towering figure and more than ever dependent on his father-in-law's overwhelming generosity. In a household that was not his own he was necessarily a secondary figure, even when his wife and children were there, for Jefferson was the undisputed head of this establishment. Although the President habitually abstained from political discussions in the family circle and scrupulously avoided interference with the congressional activities of his two sons-in-law, they were inevitably charged with echoing his opinions. In fact, they sometimes differed with him, but Thomas M. Randolph was a more obscure member of Congress than John W. Eppes, and no doubt this high-spirited, thin-skinned young man was painfully aware that he had achieved less than had been expected of him. The contrast he now drew was not between himself and his more effective brother-in-law, however; it was with the arrogant kinsman who had infuriated him, and his tirade against John Randolph was also a confession and an apologia. As such it was a distressing exhibition. If unable to maintain the silence he now sought to explain, he would have done better if he had registered a dignified protest against expressions he believed to have been pointed toward him, or had inquired into the speaker's meaning and intentions. It is entirely possible that the Orator would have denied their applicability to his interrogator, though it is hard to believe that he would have foregone a tone of contemptuousness.

Admitting that he himself had hitherto made little noise, Thomas Mann Randolph said John had made too much — an assertion that could not be easily contested. Needlessly acknowledging his inferiority in talents and intellectual elevation, he claimed that of the two he was the better patriot. Offended by the word "contumely" and other terms, and charging the other gentleman with using language in the House that he would not employ outside it, he said that, whenever honor should require, he was willing to resort to lead or steel. After issuing a virtual challenge to a duel, he pronounced John Randolph "forever bankrupt as a popular statesman." These words were probably quoted more often afterwards than anything else in this speech. The final section, in which he attributed to diffidence the noiseless tenor of his own course, must have been extremely embarrassing to his friends. Many another man may have feared to launch his little bark on the tempestuous seas that John Randolph had done so much to agitate, but he bared his soul unnecessarily when he made the public statement that he had determined to "hug the land and hold a safe though inglorious course." He now threw prudence to the winds, he said, rather than ignore what he regarded as an insult and have his disgrace reported by a hundred colleagues as they dispersed through the country.

It appears that, on this same day, he received the other Randolph's emissary, Congressman James Mercer Garnett of Virginia, who demanded an apology or satisfaction; that he named Isaac A. Coles, his father-in-law's secretary, as his own second; that he gained from Garnett the impression that the objectionable expressions were not directed to him and said that, if they were not, he would make honorable amends; and that, while Garnett was seeking from his principal an express statement (which actually was refused), Thomas Mann Randolph was informed by a half-dozen other members that he was not the object of the offensive remarks. As the session was nearing an end and time was running out, the young man who had yielded hastily to one impulse did so to another. Concluding that his honor was unimpaired, he returned to the floor of the House and expressed regret at having used "very severe and harsh language" which was improper in such a place. This performance was creditable to him as a gentleman, and few may have perceived that he again bared his soul unduly, since he spoke in a very low voice. John Randolph seemed undisposed to do anything more about the matter, and there it probably would have ended if politics had not continued to intrude into the private lives of individuals.

In the last minutes of the congressional session the Chairman of the Ways and Means Committee, whom so many of his colleagues found insufferable, received a buffeting in comparison with which he may have regarded the attack by his outraged young kinsman as a mere impertinence. Striking at the base of John Randolph's power, Congressman James Sloan of New Jersey introduced resolutions calling for the election of standing committees by the House and of chairmen by the committeemen, and requiring weekly reports from them. These resolutions were not acted on at this session, but the speech preceding their presentation led Speaker Nathaniel Macon to believe that Sloan was going to move the expulsion of John Randolph from the House.[12] It was a blistering attack, charging him with flagrant abuses of his position and the privileges of the House. These charges by Sloan, which now seem generally justifiable, along with those made on the same day by Findley and Thomas Mann Randolph, led to the counter-charge that the three men had conspired to ruin John Randolph. The alleged conspiracy was described by a contributor to the *Aurora* under a pseudonym and was accepted as fact by a later biographer of the gentleman who was said to have been its object.[13] This wild shot was followed by a verbal battle in the newspapers over the quarrel. The main question at issue was which gentleman backed down first? Under these circumstances, Jefferson's son-in-law became unsure that his honor had been vindicated and there was again talk of a duel. In faraway Massachusetts, John Quincy Adams heard that one had been set for June 28.[14] Jefferson learned of this danger by June 23, when he was back in Washington after a brief visit home.

Apparently he had been apprised by neither his son-in-law nor his secretary of all that had gone on, and at the moment he was not sure just where the former was. He did not want his daughter to see the letter he wrote her husband; if uninformed of the situation she might as well continue to be so, in his judgment. Accordingly, he sent the letter under the cover of one to an Albemarle County neighbor, James Ogilvie, a school-master living in Milton who was obligated to him for many kindnesses, including permission to make free use of his library at Monticello during the months he was away. The earlier correspondence of the two men, besides illustrating Jefferson's generosity, conveys much information about how he cared for and arranged his

[12] Macon to J. H. Nicholson, Apr. 21, 1806 (quoted by Lacy, "Jefferson and Congress," p. 174, from the Nicholson Papers). The speech is in *Annals*, 9 Cong., 1 sess., pp. 1107–1115.
[13] H. A. Garland, *Life of John Randolph of Roanoke*, I (1874), pp. 247–250. Article in *Aurora* signed "A Citizen." The letter of George W. Randolph, Feb. 6, 1856 (Randall, III, 165–167), while giving the tradition in TMR's family, refers to contemporary sources and seems a fair statement.
[14] J. Q. Adams to his wife from Quincy, July 13, 1806 (*Writings*, III, 152). He doubted that it had taken place.

books. He knew where every one of them belonged.[15] He had great respect for Ogilvie, to whom he had sent his grandson for schooling, and he undoubtedly included this teacher in the "thinking part" of mankind who regarded the settlement of differences by duel as "absurd and immoral."

Jefferson told his son-in-law that he took up his pen with an aching heart, and there was an undertone of deep emotion in the letter he wrote that proud and sensitive young man. He justified his "interference" in a private matter on grounds of solicitude for the well-being and happiness of "our whole family," but in his reasoned appeal there was no trace of recrimination, no rebuke whatsoever for past rashness. He told James Ogilvie that only fear of the opinion of the world led men to engage in duels. To his daughter's husband he presented the same idea in gentler terms. "Certainly I would not wish you to do what might lessen you in the esteem of the world," he said, "but I wish you to estimate correctly the public opinion in such a case, and not to volunteer beyond what that might require or approve." Convinced that the other party had no desire to go any further, he saw no need for his son-in-law to do anything more than calmly correct false statements, if such had been made and if rectification of them was really important. There must be no display of emotions. "The least expression of passion on the one side draws forth a little more on the other, and ends at last in the most barbarous of appeals," he said.

Having given this sensible counsel and made these wise observations, he proceeded to remind the husband and father of his responsibilities.

How different is the stake which you two would bring into the field! On his side, unentangled in the affections of the world, a single life, of no value to himself or others. On yours, yourself, a wife, & a family of children, all depending for all their happiness & protection in this world on you alone.

This statement was hard on John Randolph and would scarcely have been made by the President in public, but the contrast in personal responsibilities was real and Jefferson's dominant concern was to save Thomas Mann Randolph for personal, not public, reasons.

Should they lose you, my cares for them, a poor substitute at any time, could continue, by the course of nature, but for a short time.

[15] James Ogilvie to TJ, Jan. 26, 1806 (LC, 27320); TJ to Ogilvie, Jan. 31, 1806 (Ford, VIII, 417–418). TJ's letter of June 23, 1806, to TMR (E-R Papers, UVA) was enclosed in one of the same date to Ogilvie (*Papers, MHS,* pp. 116–117).

Seven children, all under the age of discretion & down to infancy, would then be left without guide or guardian but a poor broken-hearted woman, doomed herself to misery the rest of her life. And should her frail frame sink under it, what is then to become of them?

The mother, though unwell at this time, was in fact a strong woman who might have been expected to be stouthearted in adversity, but the grandfather was wholly warranted in asking: "Is it possible that your duties to these dear objects can weigh more lightly than those to a gladiator?" The gladiatorial parallel was much on his mind. "If malice and levity find sport in mischief," he said, "rational men are not therefore to exhibit themselves for their amusement." The laws of dueling were made for lives of no consequence to others, not for fathers of families. "The valuable part of society," he was convinced, "condemn in their hearts that knight-errantry which, following the *ignis fatuus* of an imaginary honour, bursts asunder all the ligaments of duty and affection and assigns to misery and ruin innocent and helpless families."

Therefore, he urged that his son-in-law take no step in this business but on the soberest reflection, that he consult his rational and prudent friends, that he take his time, suppress his passion, and exercise his good sense. Whether or not it was owing to Jefferson's counsel, Thomas Mann Randoph kept his head. Within two weeks the President in Washington, having received a letter from him and read the Richmond papers, was assured that he would do nothing rash and convinced that he did not need to do anything. Writing him in mid-July, Jefferson said: "I find but one sentiment prevailing (and I have that from very many) that the thing may stop where it now is with entire honour to yourself."[16] Jefferson believed that great care would be taken by John Randolph not to revive it. In his opinion that gentleman, while declining to retract or explain his own past utterances, had shown himself not to have the "ravenous appetite for unnecessary risk" that some people had ascribed to him and had probably not intended to test his young kinsman's sensibility anyway.

Speaking of the family, Jefferson said that peace of mind and happiness had been restored to "us all," but his letters to the children and their mother and theirs to him do not remotely suggest that they had been involved in any danger. As usual he was concerned about their health, and he informed one of his granddaughters that he had never

---

[16] TJ to TMR, July 13, 1806 (Ford, VIII, 459). He had received on July 7 TMR's letter of July 5 and Richmond *Enquirer* of July 4.

found Washington so dull and never been so tired of it. The day before he had reassuring news from her husband he wrote his daughter Martha:

> Absence from you becomes every day more and more insupportable and my confinement here more disgusting. I have certainly great reasons for gratitude to my constituents. They have supported me as cordially as I could ever have expected; and if their affairs can preserve as steady a course for two years to come, and I can then carry into retirement the good will they have hitherto bestowed on me, the day of retirement will be the happiest I have now to come. It will relieve me from a load of care too burthensome for my time of life, and will restore me to those domestic scenes where alone I can be happy.[17]

His daughter and her growing flock were central in his life as a domestic being, but normally he included John Wayles Eppes, as well as Thomas Mann Randolph, in "our whole family." He still regarded that young widower as his son-in-law, though Eppes was planning to remarry. A month before Jefferson became so alarmed for his other son-in-law he wrote this one: "That at your period of life, you should doom the rest of it to a dreary celibacy was not to be expected, nor desired. Nature and reason equally condemned so useless a penance. I have counted on it and be assured that that measure can never lessen my affections to you. You have many years of life to come, which could not have been made happy in any other way. You will have other children, who will be entitled to an equal portion of your love, and of your property."[18] This did not mean that he himself was not particularly concerned for his dead daughter's son, little Francis. Nor was he now disposed to build a house at Pantops, as he had been when he thought it would be occupied by Maria. Judging from what he said later, he had given her husband only a lifetime interest in the place. He now said he was pleased to learn that Eppes was thinking of spending the whole or a part of his time there, and he gave a further reason why he could not build the house. He had fallen so in arrears in Washington that he could not afford it. He repeated an earlier offer, however, and this was a generous one. Leveling would have to be done at Pantops, as had been done at Monticello; and if Eppes could hire as many hands as

[17] TJ to Martha, July 6, 1806 (*Family Letters*, pp. 287–288). Other family correspondence precedes this.
[18] TJ to JWE, May 24, 1806 in Norma B. Cuthbert, "Poplar Forest: Jefferson's Legacy to His Grandson," *Huntington Library Quarterly*, VI (May, 1943), p. 339. He was replying to a letter of May 16 from Eppington.

would do the work in a year, he would meet the expense of their pay and subsistence.

As things turned out, Eppes did not get the lady, whose name remains unknown. After a brief visit to Albemarle County to look after his affairs, he accompanied his father-in-law when that gentleman reluctantly returned to Washington in June. Then, after a night in the President's House, he proceeded on a Sunday to Annapolis. He was back on Tuesday, "all that matter being entirely broken off," as Jefferson reported to his daughter. "I understand it was from the disagreement of the mother, solely, who has some other match for her daughter in her eye, more to her mind," he said.[19] He may have been more relieved than he would admit. Although he had told Eppes that the latter and his new wife would be "a much valued addition to our family society" if they should establish themselves at Pantops, and although he undoubtedly enjoyed the young man's company, as Maria's father he obviously took a dim view of the prospect. He had intimated that Eppes should not make a final decision about a place to live until after he had learned whether or not his companion could "relinquish city habits and enjoyments for those of the country" — adding, of course, that as country situations went this one could compete with any other. But the test was not to be applied. The companion his son-in-law acquired some three years later came from rural North Carolina and he established a home in Buckingham County rather than Albemarle.[20] Jefferson could not know that as yet, but there was now no immediate likelihood that a house would be built at Pantops.

When he wrote Eppes in May that he had to suspend every unnecessary expense, he must already have been planning fresh building operations. At the very time that he reported to his daughter the ill-fated trip of her brother-in-law to Annapolis, he stated that he himself would have to spend a week or ten days in Bedford County in August in order to lay the foundations of a house at Poplar Forest. Perhaps he had already gone too far with his plans to draw back. Perhaps he regarded engagement in an architectural enterprise as essential to his happiness. At all events, being in sight of the end at Monticello, though by no means there as yet, he was starting a house at Poplar Forest. Though well worth talking about, it need not concern us here since it was not habitable until the end of his presidency and far from com-

19 TJ to Martha, June 16, 1806 (*Family Letters*, p. 284).
20 In 1809, Eppes married Martha Burke Jones of Halifax, N.C., and he resided thereafter at Millbrook, Va. Neither place could have been properly described as metropolitan.

pleted then. It provided him with diversion and a place of refuge in old age. In the present context, the most pertinent fact is that he cherished and guarded it as a legacy for Maria's only surviving child.[21]

iii

In the death of his beloved teacher, George Wythe, Jefferson suffered his greatest personal loss since the death of his daughter Maria. He had not seen much of this very old friend in recent years and could not have expected Wythe, who had already reached eighty, to live indefinitely. But the death of this former mentor, collaborator, and colleague meant the severance of a deeply cherished tie with the past; and, what is more, it occurred under most extraordinary and most painful circumstances.[22]

On the very day that the President got back to Washington after his short visit to Monticello in May, he received from William DuVal, a neighbor of the revered Chancellor in Richmond, a letter saying that the latter was at death's door as the result of poison, presumably administered by his grandnephew. Soon thereafter Jefferson learned from the same correspondent that their "venerable, great, and pious friend" had died after days of suffering. Before he got that news, Wythe's remains had been conveyed to the state capitol by order of the Governor and Council of Virginia and his funeral oration had been pronounced by William Munford.[23] (Under modern conditions of transportation Jefferson would have been there as the chief mourner.) Also poisoned were Wythe's three servants, all of whom he had freed and for all of whom he had made provision in his will. Two of these survived, but the boy Michael Brown, whom he had commended to the care of Jefferson in his will, died before he did. The grandnephew, George Wythe Sweeney (who also appears in the records of the time as Swinney) had been the residuary legatee. Undoubtedly a forger, he was believed by virtually everybody to have poisoned the entire family.

The letters from William DuVal, who besides being a devoted neighbor to the universally esteemed jurist was the executor of his will,

---

[21] See Norma B. Cuthbert, "Poplar Forest," *Huntington Library Quarterly*, VI (May, 1943), 333–356. This consists largely of correspondence between TJ and JWE.

[22] There are numerous references to TJ's early association with Wythe in *Jefferson the Virginian*, especially in chs. V, XIX.

[23] William DuVal to TJ, June 4, 8, 1806; received June 7, 12 (LC, 27874, 27882). William Munford to the Governor (William H. Cabell), June 8, 1806 (H. W. Fournoy, ed., *Calendar of Virginia State Papers*, IX [Richmond, 1890], 487.

GEORGE WYTHE
Portrait by J. F. Weir after John Trumbull

constitute an invaluable source of information about this macabre episode, but we do not enter here into the details of the shocking affair except as these relate to Jefferson and his reaction.[24] He was horrified that such a man should have fallen by the hand of a parricide. "Such an instance of depravity has been hitherto known to us only in the fables of the poets," he said.[25] Perhaps it was because of the horror that he did not mention the matter in the letter he wrote his daughter a couple of days later or, apparently, in any of his family letters in this period. To his mind such things were no more for the ears of women and children than duels were. But, while we cannot be sure, it would appear that he spoke of it only to those who spoke to him about it first. He was characteristically reticent about matters on which he felt most deeply. Years later he said things about George Wythe, especially in the statement he made on request to the author of a book on the Signers of the Declaration of Independence, which have been quoted ever since.[26] The pen pictures he occasionally drew of his contemporaries lead us to regret that he never essayed to be a Plutarch. He now said that no purer character than Wythe had ever lived. At a time when the virtues of the old Chancellor were on so many lips eulogy was superfluous, but what he said about his own relations with the man who introduced him to the law casts light on both of them:

> He was my antient master, my earliest & best friend; and to him I am indebted for first impressions which have had the most salutary influence on the course of my life. I had reserved with fondness for the day of my retirement, the hope of inducing him to pass much of his time with me. It would have been a great pleasure to recollect with him first opinions on the new state of things which arose soon after my acquaintance with him [that is, the struggle for and winning of American independence]; to pass in review the long period which has elapsed since that time, and to see how far those opinions had been affected by experience & reflection, or confirmed and acted on with self approbation. But this may yet be the enjoyment of another state of being.

---

[24] The most authoritative account is *The Murder of George Wythe* (1955), consisting of essays by J. P. Boyd and W. E. Hemphill, reprinted from *W. & M.*, 3 ser., XII (Oct., 1955). The first essay draws extensively on the correspondence between DuVal and TJ in the Library of Congress, which remains unpublished but which I have read. The second contains the official record of the examination of George Wythe Swinney (or Sweeney) at a court of hustings, June 2, 1806.

[25] TJ to DuVal, June 14, 1806 (LC, 27898).

[26] TJ to John Sanderson, Aug. 31, 1820 (S. K. Padover, *Complete Jefferson* [1943], pp. 927–928).

Clerical foes of the writer of this passage might have been surprised by the last sentence, or have claimed to be, but nobody who knew Wythe doubted *his* belief in immortality or *his* piety. His former neighbor, William DuVal, said in a later letter: "His great desire, he told me, was to be holy and innocent." He thought faith unavailing without good actions and that God was no respecter of persons. "Charity, as described by high authority, seemed to be ingrafted in his soul." There must have been people who were saying at this time that the Virginian Aristides, as he was often called, was too charitable, that this guileless man was easily taken in. No doubt he himself would have protested, saying that more often than not his faith in human beings was well rewarded. His neighbor was sure he felt that way about his most famous pupil. Thus DuVal wrote to Jefferson:

> I believe that the great & good Mr. Wythe loved you as sincerely as if you had been his Son; his attachment was founded on his thorough knowledge of you, personally. Some years ago he mentioned that if there was an honest man in America, T.J. was that person; everything that he said has been verified.[27]

In a later letter DuVal, who himself was obviously a great admirer of the President, made this gratifying statement: "I know from what Mr. Wythe often said, that you were dearer to him than any relation he had — that his attachment arose from that impulse that unite[s] great minds, the sincere love of virtue."[28]

Although himself notably charitable in spirit, as befitted one who had felt Wythe's benign influence in his impressionable years, Jefferson expressed the hope that the dear old man had had time to alter the disposition of his will as to the ingrate who had "brought it prematurely into force." He afterwards received an authenticated copy of that will, including the codicil drafted (presumably by Edmund Randolph) at the dying man's bedside, in which all the provisions relating to George W. Sweeney were revoked. He probably cherished more the copy of an earlier testament made by Wythe himself and directed to him. DuVal found this in the old jurist's papers and promptly sent it to him.[29] This is in large-sized manuscript writing and it discloses Wythe's penchant for the lower case. Jefferson may have picked up this idiosyncrasy from his old teacher; he did not

[27] DuVal to TJ, June 29, 1806 (LC, 27970).

[28] Nov. 21, 1806 (LC, 28475).

[29] The authenticated copy of the will, including the codicils of Feb. 24 and June 1, 1806, is in LC, 27971-27972; the earlier copy of the will of Apr. 20, 1803, with codicils of Jan. 19, 1806, is in LC, 22615.

commonly write the personal pronoun "i" as Wythe did in the pre-
amble to this document, but he did begin sentences with small letters.
The document, which is sprinkled with Latin words and phrases, ends
with a prayerful English poem and a bit of Greek. The spelling is
individualistic, like Jefferson's, though the phraseology has a whimsical
quality he never achieved. Wythe declared this will to be his testament, "probably the last."

Because of the death of Michael Brown, Jefferson was, to his regret,
relieved of the responsibility of overseeing the life and education of
this "freed boy" who was said to have been not unlike Wythe in
goodness and humility and would have been a living reminder of him.
Jefferson himself was remembered in another provision, couched in
Wythe's distinctive language:

> I give my books and small philosophical apparatus to Thomas
> Jefferson, president of the united states of America, a legacie con-
> sidered abstractlie perhaps not deserving a place in his museum,
> but, estimated by my good will to him, the most valuable to him
> of anything which I have power to bestow.

The "legacie" was not all that the testator intended, for the spend-
thrift grandnephew had sold the terrestrial globe and some of the
books, but none other could have been more fitting or more welcome.
In another codicil he left to the same man, now described simply as his
friend, his silver cups and gold-headed cane. These things the "president of the united states of America" received in due course and he
immediately sought to obtain a portrait. During the summer he was
sent a profile belonging to Lydia Broadnax, Wythe's faithful servant;
and, after having a copy made, he returned the original to her, though
she had offered to let him keep it. This copy was made by Charles
Willson Peale with the assistance of his son Rembrandt. DuVal also
informed Jefferson that he had a miniature profile of Wythe taken by
physiotrace in 1804; he was having a copy of this made and Jefferson
might have either this or the original. Saying that every trace of his old
friend would be dear to him, Jefferson stated that he would be thank-
ful to get either. DuVal sent him the original.[30]

---

[30] The most important letters bearing on the profiles are: DuVal to TJ, July 12,
1806 (LC, 28044); TJ to DuVal, July 17, 1806 (LC, 28061); DuVal to TJ, Nov. 21,
1806 (LC, 28475); C. W. Peale to TJ, Nov. 26, 1806 (LC, 28488); TJ to DuVal,
Dec. 4, 1806 (LC, 28523); DuVal to TJ, Dec. 10, 1806 (LC, 28553); TJ to Peale,
Dec. 21, 1806 (LC, 28572). Despite the plethora of references, I remain somewhat
uncertain which profile Peale copied.

Apparently Jefferson never received from DuVal the account of the final legal proceedings in this notorious case, but he was undoubtedly aware that after preliminary hearings that seemed to leave Sweeney's guilt unquestionable he was acquitted when put on trial. Since there appears to be no recorded comment from Jefferson on this amazing verdict, we need not discuss it here. It has been explained on the ground that, despite the almost universal belief that the grandnephew was guilty, the evidence actually presented against him was circumstantial and, from the legal point of view, insufficient. It has also been noted that the testimony of Negroes — including that of Lydia Broadnax — was inadmissible.[31] That such testimony would have led to a different verdict cannot be proved, but the outcome was most ironical, for the provision of the statute forbidding it had been taken from the old law of Virginia and incorporated into the new by Jefferson himself, with the concurrence of Wythe, when they drafted their famous and in many ways notably progressive Revisal a generation earlier.[32]

i v

Writing his daughter in the October after George Wythe died, the President lamented the dreariness of his private life in Washington in characteristic manner and employed even stronger language than usual. "Having been so long in the midst of a family," he said, "the loansomeness of this place is more intolerable than I ever found it. My daily rides too are sickening for want of some interest in the scenes I pass over: and indeed I look over the two ensuing years as the most tedious of my life."[33] He had been away from Monticello for three weeks. His secretary, Isaac Coles, who was said to resemble him in physique and features, lived with him and sometimes accompanied him on his unexciting rides, though Jefferson generally made them alone.[34] The tedium of his life was relieved considerably in late November and early December by the return of the congressmen and senators, although their presence as a group never contributed to his peace of mind. A new member was his former secretary, William A. Burwell, who had been elected to a vacant seat in the Virginia delegation and continued

31 In *The Murder of George Wythe,* Boyd emphasizes this point (pp. 29–31). Hemphill, while not overlooking this claim, lays major emphasis on the inadequacy of the medical testimony and the general circumstantiality of the evidence (pp. 58–64).

32 For the provision as drafted by TJ, see Boyd, *Papers of TJ,* II, 471, with the editorial comment accompanying it.

33 TJ to Martha, Oct. 20, 1806 (*Family Letters,* p. 289).

34 Plumer, entry of Dec. 30, 1806 (*Memorandum,* pp. 550–551).

to be intimate with him. His two sons-in-law again had rooms in the President's House and he continued to be on the best of terms with both of them. So at least he thought, but as the winter wore on he began to perceive that there was a "difference" between them. He did not know what caused it and did not want to know, but he supposed that it did not amount to much. Therefore, he had a rude shock in February, when Thomas Mann Randolph moved out.

Without informing Jefferson in advance, the moody young man betook himself to the boarding-house of Frost and Quinn on Capitol Hill, where William Plumer and a few other Federalists lodged. The political complexion of the place probably lent color to the rumor that he had quarreled with the President, a few of whose actions and policies he had recently criticized or seemed to oppose. But Plumer, who liked him and often talked with him, quickly dismissed this explanation, saying that he spoke of Jefferson with great cordiality. By the end of his first week at Frost and Quinn's, indeed, he had visited his father-in-law and had dinner with him.[35]

Shortly after his move he wrote Jefferson a letter which overwhelmed the man who claimed to love him like a son and had supposed that his actions showed it. This letter revealed that Randolph was at odds with Eppes, as had been rumored, but the disclosure that troubled Jefferson most was something that nobody else appears to have suspected. Randolph believed that his father-in-law preferred Eppes to him. The underlying cause of this opinion probably was his own realization that his brother-in-law deserved greater admiration than he as a member of Congress, but the immediate occasion for his expression of it was an invitation that Jefferson gave Eppes without including him. Jefferson afterwards described his own action as unpremeditated, saying that he quickly regretted it but could not undo it. Its precise nature remains unknown, but obviously a hypersensitive man exaggerated a trivial matter.

Although Jefferson manifested pained surprise, there was no more recrimination in his prompt reply than in the one he had sent him in the summer, in the effort to dissuade him from a duel.[36] While seeking to convince Randolph that the latter's "separation" had been produced by things which had either not existed or been misconstrued, and while

---

[35] Plumer so reported in his entry of Feb. 23, 1807, when TMR had been his fellow boarder for a week (*Memorandum*, pp. 622-623). He described the boarding-house at the beginning of the session on pp. 523-524. On the immediate political circumstances, see below, ch. XVI, pp. 281-288. Gaines describes the episode in *Thomas Mann Randolph*, pp. 65-67.

[36] TJ to TMR, Feb. 18, 1807 (MHS); Feb. 19 (E-R Papers, UVA). I have not discovered TMR's letter but its tenor can be judged from TJ's reply.

intimating that he had been too sensitive, Jefferson neither blamed nor reproached him. He said that he could have no part in any disagreement between his two sons-in-law, both of whom had and merited his warm affection — that far from having any such preference for Eppes as Randolph supposed, he had feared that the contrary might be suspected because of his attachment to his surviving daughter. He may have been indulging in pardonable exaggeration when he declared that there was no man on earth for whom he had, or had ever had, such affection as for Randolph. He appears to have been quite truthful, however, when he said that nobody recognized and valued Randolph's virtues more, for it may be doubted if anybody else valued them as much. Within his own family group Jefferson tended to be uncritical. He would regard the loss of this son-in-law as a great misfortune, he said, even if they had not had a "particular connection." But when he considered their connection through Martha and her children, he could regard his own separation from the husband and father as nothing less than a calamity. The implication was that it would involve his own separation from them, and this thought he could not tolerate. We may guess that Martha would have stayed with her father if she had had to make a choice, but he did not want to face or have her face that alternative.

This letter and a second one, in which he blamed himself for taking too much for granted and not expressing his feelings more, and also assured Randolph that he had never called him a Federalist or resented his minor criticisms of the administration, seem to have had an appreciable effect on the absentee. Not only did he dine at the President's House; soon thereafter he rode with Jefferson to Main's nursery to get more thorn plants. This was an unfortunate ride, for he was insufficiently clad on a raw day, and was taken that night with a chill and fever.[37] William Plumer, at the boarding-house, feared that Randolph's illness would terminate fatally. The Senator from New Hampshire was now entirely sure that he had not come to Frost's because of any personal dissatisfaction with the President. "No man could pay greater atttention or discover more anxiety for Mr. Randolph than Mr. Jefferson has," he said, adding that Mr. Eppes had not visited his brother-in-law.[38] Congressman Burwell and Secretary Coles were most attentive, and the vigil of Dr. Jones at the sick man's bedside was shared by Captain Meriwether Lewis, who was back from his journey to the Pacific and was staying at the President's House. About a week

37 TJ to Martha, Mar. 2, 1807 (*Family Letters,* p. 297); TJ to TMR, Feb. 28, 1807 (LC, 29081).
38 Entry of Mar. 4, 1807 (*Memorandum,* p. 642).

after the adjournment of Congress, Jefferson was pleased to report to his daughter that her husband's fever was past and he had been moved back to that house.[39] He remained there as a convalescent for a month; then he and his father-in-law went back to Albemarle County together. He did not expect to return to Washington, as Jefferson must, for he had wisely decided not to offer himself again for Congress.

Jefferson wrote his daughter by every post during her husband's illness and convalescence.[40] The latter lasted longer than he had anticipated and the day of departure was again and again postponed. "It has always seemed to be about a week off," he said; "but, like our shadows, it walks before us, and still keeps at the same distance." During most of the month of March he himself was in no condition to make a journey which would have been unusually difficult at that season. Urging his delay, Martha forewarned him that he would have to pass through a sea of mud. She reported that in the vicinity of Orange Courthouse, nine horses had been put to one wagon, and that, when one of these mired down, the wagon had to be unloaded and the horse prized out. About the time that Randolph's fever abated, Jefferson picked up one of his rare colds; and this was followed a few days later by one of his periodic headaches (probably what we should call migraine). His "fits," as he called them, were not as severe as in times past, but they lasted from nine to five everyday at first, and he was not wholly recovered for about three weeks.

Whether or not this spell may be designated as psychosomatic, he had been under great stress of mind with respect to his son-in-law after a difficult congressional session. We have not yet described the labors and problems of the period and he himself avoided reference to them in his family letters. Several times in recent weeks, however, his granddaughter Ellen, his most assiduous correspondent among the children, reminded him that he was falling behind in his account with her. He solemnly observed to her that the tide of business, like that of the ocean, would wait for nobody; and she graciously admitted that he had more to do than she. Meanwhile, Martha Randolph, who had been so anxious on account of her husband, manifested her great concern about her father.

Pray take care of your self [she wrote]. Your constitution is not adequate to the labours of your place. I look forward to the 2

[39] TJ to Martha, Mar. 9, 1807 (*Family Letters*, p. 299). Dr. Jones moved in with him, but was expected to leave next day. Eppes had gone home after Congress adjourned. TJ described this illness in the household in a letter of Mar. 21, 1807, to him (UVA).
[40] *Family Letters*, pp. 297–306.

remaining years with more anxiety than I can express. Those past with what joy shall I hail that return which will be followed by no separation. I make no exception when I say the *first* and most important object with me will be the dear and sacred duty of nursing and chearing your old age, by every endearment of filial tenderness. My fancy dwells with rapture upon your image seated by your *own* fire side surrounded by your grand children contending for the pleasure of waiting upon you.[41]

If Thomas Mann Randolph had seen this expression of filial devotion, no doubt he would have regarded it as excessive, and he may have wished that his father-in-law's devotion and generosity to him had not been so overwhelming. But neither he nor any other member of this family could doubt who was and would continue to be its head.

[41] Mar. 20, 1807 (*ibid.*, p. 303).

[IX]

The Head of the Party

JEFFERSON was the first President of the United States who was also the head of a party, and, until this writing, his extraordinary success in the latter role has been matched by few of his successors in the first office, if indeed it has by any of them. It was not a role that could have been openly acknowledged in that era of beginnings without arousing resentment, and this particular President would have been out of character if he had claimed it, but it was implicitly recognized by Republican leaders. The sensation created by John Randolph's revolt in the first session of the Ninth Congress was partly owing to the vividness of his language and personality. He was ostensibly condemning Jefferson's methods in the employment of presidential power and authority rather than his conduct in the unofficial role of party leader. At the same time, Randolph was directly attacking one who, to use his own words, had been set up by the party as a "political idol." In the language of our own day, one of the objects of his attack was the "personality cult." At the outset of the administration, though highly admiring of Jefferson, he privately expressed disgust at the "spirit of personal attachment" evinced by some of the President's supporters, asserting that the idea that salvation depends on a single individual is "the essence of monarchy." Five years later, after he had led a corporal's guard of Republicans across the Rubicon, he said: "The colossal popularity of the President seemed to mock at all opposition."[1]

While the charge of one-man rule was often made by members of the Opposition in this period, as it was destined to be in later years against other famous presidents, Jefferson himself liked monarchy no better and craved power for its own sake no more than when he was

[1] John Randolph to J. H. Nicholson, July 26, 1801 (quoted in N. K. Risjord, *The Old Republicans* (1965), pp. 35–36; letter of DECIUS in Richmond *Enquirer,* Aug. 15, 1806.

inveighing against King George III or voicing to George Washington his deep distrust of Alexander Hamilton. His shunning of ceremonial occasions, the informality of his dinners, and his indifference to dress, while not inexplicable on other grounds, reflected a concern to avoid the trappings of royalty that amounted almost to an obsession. It could have been claimed that he avoided the appearance of power while grasping the reality, but his procedure, especially in his dealings with the legislative branch, can be best explained as an expression of his desire to make the government work and the American experiment succeed. The indirection that Randolph particularly deplored, while partly attributable to Jefferson's temperament, may be also regarded as a concession to the sensitiveness of the legislators.

While colossal, Jefferson's popularity was not universal, as George Washington's virtually was through most of his administration — that is, as long as the first President was recognized as being above party conflict. Jefferson wore an unmistakable party label. Furthermore, the inveterate civilian in the President's House was no national hero, as Washington had been and Andrew Jackson was to be. Though Thomas Ritchie's defense of his conduct as the wartime governor of Virginia had vindicated his courage, it had not even attempted to establish his heroism. He was a symbol, however, and was to remain one — Herald of Freedom, Man of the People, and, to a relatively small but deeply devoted group, Apostle of Enlightenment. To him as a political man, and to his party, his public image was a priceless asset. Besides that, his policies, with their emphasis on economy and peace, which he and his advisers regarded as of the first importance in this early stage of the country's development, were widely popular since they tended to decrease the burdens on the public, not to increase them. In terms of statesmanship, he may be open to criticism for not asking more of his countrymen. But his political antennae were acutely sensitive, and he recognized that politics is the art of the possible. His popular appeal was owing chiefly to his symbolism and his policies, for he had very slight personal contact with the public. He did not make speeches except on inauguration day and to visiting Indian delegations. He made no presidential tours and, far from seeking personal publicity, he avoided it. His direct political activities were largely limited to his personal relations with individuals. While seeking to keep these as amicable as possible in all cases, he worked through the leaders of his party, and in so doing realized upon his own amiable personality and talent for conciliation.

In his political scrapbook, which is still preserved in the University he fathered, is a newspaper clipping containing the words of a song for

July 4, 1806, which was sung to the tune of "Yankee Doodle." To quote all of its many verses, allegedly descriptive of Jeffersonian America, would be to waste paper and affront the reader's intelligence, but one of them may tickle somebody's humor:

> America's a *dandy* place;
> The people are all brothers;
> And when one gets a pumpkin pye,
> He shares it with the others.[2]

Whatever may have been true of the country generally, the spirit of brotherly love had not dominated the recent congressional session and did not prevail in certain circles of the Republican party. Pennsylvania continued to provide a conspicuous example of its absence. There the Duane-Leib wing of the party, which had come to constitute a majority, completely broke with Governor Thomas McKean and nominated Simon Snyder to replace him. Nonetheless, with the support of the Federalists, McKean was re-elected in 1805. It was in this connection that the term "Tertium Quid" entered the political vocabulary, signifying a group that occupied an ambiguous position between the two major parties.[3] Jefferson, who disliked discord of any sort, and especially in his own party, regarded the schism in Pennsylvania as an instance of men's letting their passions get the better of their reason and patriotism. Deploring the fusion with the Federalists, he blamed both Republican factions for it.[4] As we have already seen, he kept aloof from such factional quarrels. Both sides sought to bring his name into the campaign, but he said that both deserved scolding. He continued to keep on good terms with leaders in both camps, nevertheless. Before the McKean faction joined forces with the Federalists he probably preferred it, but he retained the personal loyalty of William Duane, who was critical of Madison as well as Gallatin and took an equivocal stand with respect to John Randolph at first.[5] But there was

[2] Alderman Library (UVA). Some member of TJ's may have pasted this in the Scrapbook, but we are presuming that he saw it.

[3] Cunningham, in *Jeffersonian Republicans in Power*, pp. 218–220, and in "Who Were the Quids?" (*Miss. Valley Hist. Rev.*, Sept., 1963) says that in no strict sense should the term be applied to John Randolph and his followers, though it often has been. For details about Pennsylvania politics in 1805 and 1806, see S. W. Higginbotham, *The Keystone of the Democratic Arch* (1952), chs. IV, V.

[4] TJ to C. A. Rodney, Oct. 23, 1805 (LC, 26772).

[5] Writing TJ on Nov. 2, 1806, Duane said: "My opinions and sentiments on particular men and circumstances I know cannot be agreeable to you, tho' from my soul I believe that in so doing I am acting more faithful to my attachment to you, than if I forbore from *scotching the snakes* that trouble your path" (*Procs. M.H.S.*, 2 ser., XX, 285).

no real rapport between Randolph and either faction in Pennsylvania. Nor was he in accord with the Federalists as a group, except in his pro-British sentiments and his hostility to the administration. Jefferson soon learned, however, that he had supplied them with campaign materials that they used with some effect in New England.

To his loyal supporters in that region the President was an unfailing fount of encouragement and inspiration. They had made considerable progress in their effort to attain majority status but were still struggling, especially in Massachusetts and Connecticut, against entrenched establishments. Writing him about recent elections in the former state, Levi Lincoln said that the Federalist combination extended "from the Governor, through all the grades of office, down to the tithingman of the parish, with the clergy as an appendage."[6] Jefferson's own zeal was no whit diminished by the reminder that the dominant clergy were against him. James Sullivan had previously written him from Boston in considerable discouragement over the situation in the state and had suggested his own availability for federal office. In reply Jefferson said he doubted if it would be for the public good to withdraw this Republican leader from a scene where he was so necessary, even if a suitable office were in sight. None was at the moment. To these tactful words he added others of encouragement: a little more time could place Sullivan where he ought to be (that is, in the governorship, which he actually attained the next year) and give his enemies "leisure to repent of their useless wickedness." Gratefully acknowledging this letter, Sullivan said that he had needed comfort and support.[7] Reporting on the elections, in which the Republicans while zealous and united had not done as well as they had hoped, Lincoln said that the speeches of John Randolph had been "weapons in the hands of the adversary." They must have been sent in buckets from Washington, he said, for they were spread like locusts through the land. According to this report, then, the former majority leader aided the enemy in New England and slowed the march of his own party somewhat. It may be safely assumed, however, that he had caused the leading Republicans of that region, whom he held in such low esteem, to support Jefferson and the party more zealously than ever.

Much the same can be said of the effects of his actions on the Republicans in Congress. His ferocious attacks on the administration served to consolidate the majority and strengthen the hand of the President. In his own branch of the government, John Randolph de-

[6] Levi Lincoln to TJ, June 17, 1806 (LC, 27908–27909).

[7] TJ to James Sullivan, May 26, 1806 (LC, 27856), replying to Sullivan's letter of Apr. 21; Sullivan to TJ, June 20, 1806 (LC, 27927–27928).

feated himself by his excess. For a time, though, circumstances favored him in his attempt to alienate the Minister to Great Britain from the Secretary of State and even from the President.

The effort to denigrate Madison in the interest of Monroe, which Jefferson quickly perceived, aroused his deep concern on both political and personal grounds. Besides recognizing this as a threat to the unity of the government and the party, he was sincerely devoted to both men. They were associates of very long standing whom he had ever viewed, as he afterwards said, as "two principal pillars" of his happiness. The move to set up Monroe as a rival to Madison for the presidential nomination pained him deeply, and he believed that association with Randolph would work to Monroe's political disadvantage, as in fact it did. Before the decisive defeat of the censorious orator in Congress but at a time when Jefferson was confident of it, he said in a letter to Monroe in England: "Some of your new friends are attacking old ones out of friendship for you, but in a way to render you great injury." Promising to write less enigmatically at a later time, he urged his friend to be cautious about what and to whom he wrote. Also, he stated that he intended to join William Pinkney to Monroe as his associate in his negotiations, with the authorization to succeed him as minister whenever he should feel compelled to come home. Jefferson added that it would be to Monroe's political benefit to do so before the next congressional session.

Unfortunately, this considerate and solicitous letter, with its timely warning, was not picked up in Norfolk by the man who was expected to take it to England. Along with another brief letter written to Monroe a couple of days later, it was returned to its author some three months after he dispatched it. We are here afforded a striking example of the difficulties of transatlantic communication which so fatefully affected Monroe's diplomacy and his relations with his superiors at home.[8] If he had been forewarned and reassured as Jefferson intended, John Randolph's approaches to him might have been less beguiling and his suspicions of his superiors less easily aroused.

At the time Randolph was on cordial terms with Monroe because of the latter's great kindness to his deaf nephew, St. George Randolph,

[8] TJ to Monroe, Mar. 16, 1806 (LC, 27562). The fortunes of this letter and of the one of Mar. 18 (Ford, VIII, 428–429) were described in TJ's of Apr. 11, 1808 (Ford, IX, 181–184n.). He sent Monroe both letters at that later time. He learned of their miscarriage in June, 1806, and did not inform Monroe of it then presumably because he had written him more explicitly about Randolph in the meantime and did not suspect that Monroe resented Pinkney's appointment, or because he expected Monroe to be sailing home before a letter could reach him.

who had been sent to England and placed under the minister's special care. Monroe, after keeping this unfortunate boy in his own family for months, placed him in what appeared to be the best available school — serving, in his solicitous uncle's words, as another father to him. Months after Randolph entered into an undercover campaign to nominate Monroe for the presidency, he said that his most intimate friends had no reason to believe that their correspondence related to any other subject than the welfare of his nephew.[9]

His political purpose was recognized in Washington nonetheless, and in a private letter, written a few days after the undelivered one from Jefferson, Randolph avowed it to Monroe himself.[10] After intimating that the latter's wise recommendations had not been followed by the government, and charging it (especially the Department of State) with "paltry finesse and bungling stupidity" in connection with certain of his dispatches, Randolph asserted that the "principles" of the administration had materially changed. Everything was now made "a business of bargain and traffick," with the ultimate object of raising Madison to the presidency. Speaking primarily for the "Old Republicans," he said they could not countenance this and were united in support of Monroe. He implied that the principles to which the party had adhered in its years of opposition had been yielded to unholy compromise with the enemy. The "open rupture" with Madison that he now reported had other causes, as we have seen, but it reflected a lingering suspicion that Madison had leanings toward Federalism. He was not enough of a localist for the Old Republicans of his own state.[11] Randolph did not make specific charges against Madison in his letter, and he castigated the administration chiefly for its methods. He appealed to Monroe to demonstrate that the government could be conducted on "open, upright principles, without intrigue or any species of disingenuous artifice."

Writing again just after the adjournment of Congress, he said that the "Anti-Ministerialists" had been proscribed. Among these he named Nicholson, who had retired "in strong disgust." He predicted that the Speaker and many others, including himself, would do likewise for similar reasons.[12] In fact neither he nor Nathaniel Macon did so. After

9 Bruce, *Randolph*, I, 330–331, referring to a letter of July 20, 1804, to Monroe; Monroe to Randolph, Feb. 20, Nov. 12, 1806, and Randolph to Monroe, Sept. 16, 1806 (S.M.H., IV, 414–416, 485–486, 488).
10 Randolph to Monroe, Mar. 20, 1806 (Bruce, I, 333–334).
11 N. K. Risjord, in *The Old Republicans*, pp. 2–5, summarizes the doctrinal position of the group for whom Randolph claimed to speak.
12 Randolph to Monroe, Apr. 21, 1806 (Bruce, I, 334). On the circumstances of Nicholson's retirement, see above, pp. 111–112.

giving the impression that the dissidents were more numerous than they actually were, he warned Monroe against any "compromitment" of himself to persons in whom he could not *wholly* confide. Obviously the President of the United States was not included among the faithful and trustworthy, and this warning may have been one of the reasons why Monroe did not unbosom himself at this juncture to the most important of his friends.

This extremely sensitive man actually wrote a long and revealing letter to Jefferson, but this he did not send. For it he substituted another which was much briefer and relatively unrevealing; and between the two was sandwiched his reply to John Randolph.[13] In the unsent letter he manifested his dissatisfaction with the state of his country's foreign affairs, which he discussed at great length. His main objection to the course being followed was that a forceful policy was not being pursued with respect to *both* Spain and Great Britain. His recommendations regarding Spain and his warnings against the French had not been heeded and, so far as those countries were concerned, he had, in fact, been left largely in the dark by his own government during recent months. In his first letter he voiced strong suspicions of John Armstrong, but in his second letter to Jefferson (the one he sent), he refrained from critical comment on the Minister to France; and he also omitted his extended comments on foreign policy. Even in the unsent letter he said that he was far from believing that "any essential much less fatal error" had been committed and he expressed his entire willingness to go along with the present plan.

In the light of later events the most important difference between the two letters to Jefferson lay in Monroe's references to the effects on his own mission and status of the appointment of William Pinkney as joint commissioner. In the first letter he left no doubt of his wish that matters had been left wholly in his own hands. In his second he contented himself with saying that his business had been necessarily delayed. In both cases he gave assurances of co-operation such as might have been expected from such a thoroughly patriotic man. He was facing the same sort of situation that his own appointment as envoy extraordinary to France had created for Livingston, and, judging from his correspondence with his government, he had previously recognized

---

[13] Monroe to TJ, June 15, 1806; to John Randolph, June 16, 1806; to TJ, June 20, 1806 (S.M.H., IV, 450–472). Among the letters he had received by this time from persons who may be designated as Old Republicans were ones from Congressman James Mercer Garnett (May 19, 1806) and John Taylor (Feb. 27, 1806). The latter gentleman, however, though suspicious of Madison, went to no such extremes as John Randolph and was quite unwilling to break with Jefferson.

the desirability of a special mission to Great Britain under existing circumstances.

Not even in his own letter that miscarried did Jefferson describe the congressional pressure on him to dispatch an additional commissioner, as he did a couple of years later and would almost certainly have done much sooner if he had been aware of Monroe's growing misgivings. If he erred in taking Monroe's unquestioning loyalty too much for granted, this would have been an easy mistake to make in view of the past relations of the two men. For more than a quarter of a century they had been intimate friends, and, while Jefferson was always disposed to treat his chief political associates as peers, it would not have been improper to describe Monroe as his disciple.[14] But that minister, on the defensive because of his failure in Spain and unable to share in the intimate deliberations of the government because of distance and imperfect communication, had become increasingly restive as the spring wore on. Thus the seeds of discord that were sowed by John Randolph fell on fertile ground.

Nearly the whole of Monroe's reply to Randolph's recent letters was devoted to foreign affairs.[15] His discussion of these with a man who had broken with his government was of questionable propriety, and he implied his dissatisfaction with the current policy toward Spain. But he revealed no such doubts of its success as Randolph had expressed in Congress and showed much greater fear of further restrictive actions by the British than was manifested by his correspondent. His emphasis on increased military and even naval strength was not in accord with Randolph's purely defensive position and extreme insistence on economy. Regarding the American system of government as by no means secure from danger, Monroe believed that "an union of all the talents, virtue and force of its friends" was required to preserve it against its foreign and domestic foes. The domestic foes he most feared were the Federalists, and he manifested no sympathy here with Republican disaffection.

Towards the end of a letter which upon its face might have been expected to disappoint its recipient, he expressed disapproval of the suggestion regarding his candidacy for the presidency against Madison:

My own opinion then is, that the idea had better be relinquished: — that by such relinquishment, the cause of free government

14 On the beginnings of their association, see *Jefferson the Virginian*, pp. 324–325.
15 He referred to Randolph's letters of Mar. 20 and Apr. 25.

would be more essentially served, than by pursuing it. There are older men, whom I have long been accustomed to consider, as having higher pretentions to the trust than myself, whose claims it would be painful to me to see rejected; and . . . the person, who seems to be contemplated by others, is in that class.

To enter into such controversy, he said, would be to put into opposition men who had long labored together in the cause of free government; it would be to tear old friendships by the roots; it would involve the danger of promoting the success of the other party. Therefore, he believed that more service would be rendered the country by withdrawing him from the contest than from embarking him in it. Declaring that he had expressed his sentiments on this subject to nobody else, he asked that his letter remain confidential.

The letter did not constitute a rebuff of John Randolph, however. Saying that they would have later opportunity to confer about this matter and that a course of action could then be decided on, Monroe gave the distinct impression that he wanted to keep the door open. He said that he would like to hear from Randolph frequently, especially if his stay in England should be prolonged. He was not denying himself a channel of political information which, as he soon found out, Jefferson regarded as polluted. The dissident Congressman wrote him during the summer, warning him of machinations against him and urging that he be on guard.[16] Of greater interest to us at this point is the response he gave to Monroe's letter several months later. After describing it as "very interesting and acceptable" (though in fact it actually contained views at considerable variance from his own), he said that the very arguments Monroe had adduced to dissuade his friends from supporting him for President formed with *him* "an invincible motive for persisting in that support," since they exhibited "the most irrefragable proof" of Monroe's superior merit. He himself would now have no difficulty in determining who was the "most disinterested and virtuous" individual he had known. Combining fulsome praise of Monroe with highly critical and unjust comments on Madison, he was continuing the campaign the former had not sufficiently discouraged.[17]

Whether or not Monroe would have responded differently to Randolph's approaches if he had waited a few days longer, and had had the benefit of the counsel he then got from Jefferson in a private letter written shortly after Congress adjourned, is a matter of sheer specula-

16 Randolph to Monroe, July 3, 1806 (Bruce, I, 335).
17 Randolph to Monroe, Sept. 16, 1806 (S.M.H., IV, 486–488n.; partially in Bruce, I, 336–337).

tion.[18] In this Jefferson did not enter into any explanation of Pinkney's appointment, presumably regarding his previous (unreceived) statement about it as sufficient, but he spoke at greater length and with more freedom than hitherto of John Randolph's recent conduct in Congress and its political implications.

> His course has excited considerable alarm. Timid men consider it as a proof of the weakness of our government, & that it is to be rent into pieces by demagogues, & to end in anarchy. I survey the scene with a different eye, and draw a different augury from it. In a house of Representatives of a great mass of good sense, Mr. R's popular eloquence gave him such advantages as to place him unrivalled as the leader of the house; and, altho' not conciliatory to those whom he led, principles of duty & patriotism induced many of them to swallow the humiliations he subjected them to, and to vote as was right, as long as he kept the path of right himself. The sudden defection of such a man could not but produce a momentary astonishment, & even dismay; but for a moment only. The good sense of the house rallied round it's principles, & without any leader pursued steadily the business of the session, did it well, & by a strength of vote which has never before been seen.

Apart from the implied identification of the "right" with the policies favored by the administration and the party, this passage gives a fair picture of the situation in Congress, as it also does of the state of his own mind. With this reassuring statement, however, he coupled an admonition. After referring obliquely to the question of the nomination of his successor and reaffirming the determination he had expressed in his undelivered letter to adhere sacredly to a policy of neutrality in the presidential contest, he said: "But it is unfortunate for you to be embarrassed with such a *soi-disant* friend. You must not commit yourself to him." And, as a further demonstration of his continued solicitude for Monroe, who was in an uncomfortable financial situation and needed a salary, he reported his readiness to appoint him to the governorship of either the Territory of Orleans or that of Louisiana. Since he was renewing a tentative previous offer which Monroe had shown some disposition to accept, this need not be regarded as an attempt to get him out of Madison's way, as has been alleged. Nonetheless, Jefferson may be assumed to have regarded his

18 TJ to Monroe, May 4, 1806 (Ford, VIII, 447–450). In his letter of July 8, 1806, to TJ (S.M.H., IV, 477–478), Monroe said he got this on July 24 and had not received TJ's of Mar. 16.

Secretary of State as the more fitting successor to himself on grounds of seniority, experience, and demonstrated statesmanship. In fact that was Monroe's own opinion until Madison's critics and enemies excited his suspicions.

He declined on personal grounds Jefferson's reiterated offer of a territorial governorship, implying in no way that it had been made for an ulterior motive.[19] In his brief letter he assured the President that he would continue to exert his best endeavors to carry to a successful conclusion the negotiations with which he had been entrusted — sincerely desiring to promote the credit of the administration as well as the interest of the country. But, with respect to the most significant passages in the letter to which he was replying he was evasive, claiming that because of the hazards to which communication at such a distance was exposed he forbore to enter into such "delicate topicks." They could discuss matters when he got home, which he hoped would be in the autumn.

Though Monroe was committed to further discussions with John Randolph, against whom his old friend Jefferson had warned him, he does not appear to have communicated so freely with anybody else. By this time, however, he had received from Joseph H. Nicholson, now out of Congress but still under Randolph's spell, a disquieting report which seems not to have reached Jefferson. This was that some people believed that the appointment of Pinkney was quite unnecessary and that its real intent was to take from Monroe the credit for settling the differences with Great Britain.[20]

Of all the canards circulated by those who were seeking to sow seeds of discord in Monroe's mind and wean him from the administration, this was perhaps the most reprehensible and probably the most effective. Nicholson also made this statement: "The canker of Federalism I fear is eating the heart, I almost said the head, of the body politick." Monroe must have been baffled by the conflicting testimony he received that summer. Republican James Sullivan wrote him from Boston that the leading Federalists were "openly clamorous for a monarchy, and a division of the nation."[21] Confusion was confounded when John Beckley, while urging him to do nothing against the

[19] *Ibid.*

[20] Nicholson to Monroe, May 5, 1806, quoted by Risjord, p. 74, and in part by Ammon, p. 255. The former author implies that this influenced Monroe's unsent letter of June 15 to TJ, but in view of Monroe's statement that he did not get TJ's of May 4 until June 24, it seems unlikely that he got Nicholson's nine days earlier.

[21] Sullivan to Monroe, May 9, 1806, printed as a footnote to his reply of Aug. 29 (S.M.H., IV, 482–483).

nomination of Madison, which was the will of the party, expressed the personal opinion that Monroe was better qualified for the presidency than the Secretary of State, who was timid, indecisive, and too forbearing toward Federalists.[22] It would appear that Madison was not sufficiently partisan for Beckley.

Resuming his dialogue with Monroe in September — in the letter already mentioned in which he addressed that discontented gentleman in terms of excessive praise — John Randolph blamed Madison for "that strange amalgamation of men and principles" that had distinguished certain recent acts of the administration.[23] Without specifying the acts, he now laid emphasis on the departure from "principles." Those for which the Old Republicans had contended had, to their immeasurable disgust, been "neutralized at the touch of a cold and insidious moderation." Under the "baneful counsels" of the Secretary of State, the government was relapsing into the "system" of its predecessors. It was standing aloof from its tried friends and hugging to its bosom men of highly equivocal character along with some who were actually hostile to the "cause." If he was referring to the New England Republicans, the responsibility for embracing them lay with Jefferson rather than with Madison. The Secretary of State could not have been fairly blamed for the domestic policies the Old Republicans most objected to. They wanted no Yazoo President, said Randolph, nor anybody who had mixed in the "intrigues" of the last few years in Washington. He reached the height of unfairness in his reference to the Secretary's "unfortunate matrimonial connexion." Whatever reflection on Dolley Madison he may have been seeking to convey by this innuendo, it was unworthy of the high code of honor he professed so vociferously.[24]

In his response in mid-November to this letter, Monroe went further than he had gone previously in frankly owning that he was dissatisfied with the treatment he had received from the administration during his stay abroad.[25] Circumstances had occurred which were calculated to

[22] Beckley to Monroe, July 13, 1806, quoted by Ammon, p. 255. This author also refers to a letter from William Wirt to Monroe, June 10, 1806, saying that both men were obviously prompted to write by TJ. I know of no basis for this opinion but in their emphasis on party unity they were at one with him.

[23] Randolph to Monroe, Sept. 16, 1806 (S.M.H., IV, 486–488*n.*).

[24] Without claiming to explain this ungentlemanly remark, Bruce mentions in connection with it a slighting remark Mrs. Madison is alleged to have once made about Monroe (*Randolph*, I, 338). Brant says that Randolph had picked up Federalist whispers against the morals of Dolley Madison and her sister (*Madison*, IV, 322).

[25] Monroe to John Randolph, Nov. 12, 1806 (S.M.H., IV, 485–494).

hurt his feelings, he said, and actually had hurt them. These might produce a change in his relation with the persons in power at home unless satisfactorily explained. Thus he admitted to Randolph (though to nobody else, he said) that there were personal grounds for his discontent. And, since he did not forbid that gentleman to continue his efforts to procure the presidential nomination for him, he might have been assumed to approve it. But, irrespective of his own interests, he discouraged attacks on the administration, and if his words may be taken at face value he was quite willing to view with indulgence its conduct under the pressure of crises and regarded its sins as venial. Recognizing in it no such criminality as the extravagant language of John Randolph would suggest, he expressed his basic approval of it:

> It is incorruptible to foreign influence; it is respectful of & watchful over the public rights; it is friendly to free government; it is honest in the administration of the publick money. It is certainly desirous of avoiding foreign wars, & securing to our virtuous people the blessings of peace.

This was not at all like what John Randolph had been saying. Monroe's observations abroad had made him more aware than ever of the importance, to the cause of freedom and self-government everywhere, of the success of the American government. He was not one to attack it when it was at least "tolerably successful." Nor did he favor attacks on Madison, even on grounds of self-interest, believing that they would do himself more harm than good. He regarded as inconsiderate the appointment of Pinkney, which Randolph and his coterie had made so much of, but said that his relations with his associate had been quite satisfactory. So far as his immediate situation was concerned, he had withstood the distracting and divisive influence of John Randolph. About his political course after his return to America, however, he remained uncertain.

Obviously he regarded the administration with a divided mind, but he gave no sign that he perceived any difference between himself and Jefferson, or even between himself and Madison, on "principles." The policies with which he had expressed dissatisfaction were those relating to Spain and France, and he probably would have been much less dissatisfied with these if they had been more fully explained to him. Nor did he give any sign of disagreement with the administration on British policy. Thus it seems clear that the major reason for the discontent of this deeply patriotic and characteristically loyal man was that his *amour-propre* had been wounded. It seems equally clear that such would not have been the case, at least to the same degree, if communication with his government had not broken down.

Before that could be fully restored, the course of the negotiations with the British, which we shall consider hereafter, created further misunderstanding between Monroe and his old political friends and imposed further obstacles to his resumption of his function as a chief pillar of Jefferson's happiness. Meanwhile, after the President got back to Washington in the autumn of 1806, he added to a letter to Monroe a paragraph relating to the estate of Albemarle County to which the Minister would eventually return. Seeking to prepare the absentee owner in advance and thus to minimize depression, he made a candid statement about a bad situation. His action was that of a good neighbor. With it may be contrasted a letter that John Randolph wrote this same man in the winter, cautioning him again "*how and to whom*" he should write.[26] Among those Randolph had in mind must have been that neighbor.

[26] TJ to Monroe, Oct. 26, 1806 (Ford, VIII, 478); Randolph to Monroe, Jan. 2, 1807 (Bruce, *Randolph*, I, 338).

[X]

Rallying Round the Leader

THE extraordinary hold that Jefferson maintained on his local constituency was one of the most important factors in his public career. Although he had powerful political enemies in Virginia — such as John Marshall and his coterie — there were not many of them; and, except during the months immediately following his governorship, he had never been without honor in his own country. His base in the Old Dominion, still the most populous of the states, had always been strong. The Federalists there were not numerous, and the revolt of John Randolph was all the more sensational because of the remarkable unity that the Republicans had previously presented on national issues. Randolph's actions constituted a continuing threat to that unity because of the widespread admiration of his talents and fear of his invective, but he had slight success in his efforts to undermine Jefferson's base. At this time these efforts took the form of private representation and communications to the press. Organization was not his forte.

Shortly after Randolph's return to Virginia from Congress he reported privately that individuals who had been informed by him of what actually had happened in Washington agreed that the conduct of the Republican minority had been right, and he was confident that Southside Virginia was for Monroe. He claimed, however, that the party press everywhere was closed to critics of the administration.[1] He had given up hope of the *Aurora* but believed that he had shaken the faith of Thomas Ritchie of the Richmond *Enquirer*. Events showed that such was not the case. In May, Ritchie asserted that, while it was ridiculous to claim that the administration could do no wrong, a careful consideration of the proceedings of the last Congress had added strength to his first impressions. "We feel our confidence in the virtue

[1] Randolph to J. M. Garnett, May, 1806, and June 4, 1806 (Randolph-Garnett Letterbook, UVA).

and watchfulness of our present Chief Magistrate completely undiminished," he said. He opened his columns to John Randolph, nonetheless, publishing the first of the Decius letters in August. While at Monticello, Jefferson read and commented on this letter and on Ritchie's reply to it a couple of weeks later.[2]

In it Randolph appeared in character, professing to be a man of utter candor who followed unswervingly the dictates of his own conscience and independent judgment without compromise of principles. In opposing the administration the minority were pursuing a forlorn hope, he said. In questioning the "infallibility" of the party's idol (Jefferson), they had to be prepared to bleed. They had nothing to gain and everything to lose by refusing to acquiesce in measures they condemned, but they did not choose to swim with the current of the day "in ignoble security." This sort of self-characterization, so typical of Randolph, colored his public image, especially in his own state, where, more than elsewhere, his contemporaries were disposed to tolerate his idiosyncrasies and admire his personal independence. Ritchie had previously described him as a knight "*sans peur et sans reproche.*" He may have been without fear, but no one could be above reproach who was guilty of such misrepresentation.

Under an easily penetrated disguise he presented to the public his version of the events of the recent congressional session with particular reference to the controversial Spanish question. Thomas Ritchie in Richmond and Thomas Jefferson at Monticello were chiefly interested in the part of his long communication (six columns) that bore on the conduct of the Chief Executive. As the former summed this up in his reply (three and a half columns), the charge was that Jefferson had followed "a wavering, a doubtful, an unconstitutional course." Ritchie himself took the position that even if the facts were admitted they did not warrant the conclusions. Believing that Randolph's major objection was to Jefferson's methods, he himself was chiefly concerned to justify their constitutionality. Randolph had strongly condemned the President's private recommendation of measures looking to the purchase of Florida which he had not requested in his official message. The Congressman's contention was that everything must be in the open and that strict regard must be had for the separation of powers. Ritchie sought to resolve the alleged contradiction between public silence and private utterance by saying that in this instance, according to Randolph's own testimony, the President's personal opinions were offered

---

[2] Richmond *Enquirer*, May 13, Aug. 15, Sept. 2, 1806. See also C. H. Ambler, *Thomas Ritchie* (1913), pp. 34–36.

only on request. Ritchie's statement that the President would deserve condemnation if he presented his individual opinions without being asked shows that his own view of the executive role was sharply limited and distinctly unrealistic, but he met John Randolph on his own ground of strict construction. Jefferson himself described this answer to the chief Republican critic of the administration as judicious, and as an appeal to the constitutional purists of his state it may be regarded as effective. He made no reference to Ritchie's admission that he sometimes embarrassed his friends by not being sufficiently scrupulous in the concealment of his opinions. It would appear that, while some regarded him as secretive, others thought him too outspoken. There was no pleasing everybody, but the man to whose "unsullied virtues" and "ingenuous character" Thomas Ritchie referred had retained the loyalty of the editor of the most influential Republican newspaper in Virginia.

Ritchie, who fully shared Jefferson's desire to maintain party unity, had asked the President's former secretary William A. Burwell, now a candidate for Congress to fill a vacancy, to answer the letter signed Decius. Burwell wrote Jefferson, but his letter was delayed until after the publication of Ritchie's own answer. Along with Madison and Dearborn, both of whom were then guests at Monticello, the President read Ritchie's article with care and then wrote Burwell that while it had now been shown "in a very masterful manner" that the interferences of Decius were unjustified even if his facts were admitted, these were actually far from true. Thereupon he provided materials for the correction of a number of them.[3] Most of his comments related to diplomatic matters about which the Chief Executive had more precise information than anybody else. The one of greatest interest in the present context bears on the "double set of opinions and principles" that Randolph had alleged; "the one ostensible, to go on the journals and before the public, the other efficient, and the real motives to action." Jefferson flatly denied this duality in connection with the Florida business, and, by asserting that private communications of the President were as official as public ones and equally legitimate, he showed that he acquiesced in no such delimitation of presidential utterances as his loyal supporter Ritchie had suggested. He appears to have eschewed profanity, but in one of his comments on Decius, whom he had unmistakably identified with John Randolph, he showed less restraint than he had hitherto manifested in any of his recorded private words about that exasperating person:

[3] TJ to Burwell, Sept. 17, 1806 (Ford, VIII, 468–472; Cunningham, pp. 257–258).

He speaks of secret communications between the executive and members, of backstairs' influence, &c. But he never spoke of this while he and Mr. Nicholson enjoyed it almost solely. But when he differed from the executive, in a leading measure, & the executive not submitting to him, expressed it's sentiments to others, the very sentiments (to wit, the purchase of Florida) which he acknoleges they expressed to him, then he roars out upon backstairs' influence.

Jefferson sent his corrections of fact (actually seven in number) to Burwell to be used as that devoted supporter might see fit, without letting the source of information be made known. As President he had not maintained the policy of never writing for the newspapers under a pseudonym, a policy that he had followed scrupulously when in Washington's official family, but his indulgence in anonymous publication was rare, considering the prevalence of the practice, and he was generally disposed to communicate by means of suggestions. In the present instance he thought it would probably be best that the corrections should appear "under the mask" of a member of Congress — presumably unnamed. Actually, they appeared under the heading, "Important Facts," as though they came from the editor; and strong approval of his position was expressed at both the beginning and the end of this ostensible editorial. The author drew to some extent on an essay by CATO (Barnabas Bidwell) in the Boston *Chronicle*, which was republished in this same issue of the Richmond paper. Also, in what appears to have been a genuine editorial, Ritchie, replying to Federalist contentions, denied that his paper was either set up or supported by Jefferson.[4] There is no more reason to doubt this statement than there is to question Ritchie's loyalty to the President and his concern for party unity.

Though he thought John Randolph deserving of condemnation, this advocate of conciliation opposed the move in the Virginia General Assembly to censure the Republican critics of the administration. Nothing came of that move, which in Ritchie's opinion would actually have served to exaggerate the importance of the opposition. Although he regarded this opposition as trivial, he believed that some expression of approval of the administration was desirable. Upon its face, the action of the Legislature in this regard was somewhat equivocal. In December the House of Delegates adopted by overwhelming vote a resolution expressing "the highest confidence in the wisdom, firmness,

---

[4] Richmond *Enquirer*, Oct. 24, 1806. TJ's seven corrections appeared here as six, with only slight modification of his language. See also Nov. 18, 21, 1806.

and patriotism of the President." Though Randolph's supporters were relatively more numerous in the Senate, that body adopted this resolution without debate or division — partly, one may guess, because it seemed innocuous. Certain regular Republicans in the lower House, desiring something stronger, caused another resolution to be adopted by a huge majority. This stated that the Legislature continued to view "with the highest approbation the firm, just, and liberal policy" which characterized the conduct of the government towards foreign nations. But the Senate, by a majority of one, virtually rejected this by voting to postpone action on it.[5] A partial explanation of this surprising and generally unpopular action may be that approval of Madison was implied in the resolution of the House. Very few Republicans in Virginia were willing to put themselves on record as being opposed to Jefferson, at any rate.

As a result of the elections to the Tenth Congress, Randolph's following in the Virginia delegation was to be weakened in that body; and because of the outcome of a by-election that of the administration was strengthened in the second session of the Ninth. In the district including Poplar Forest, Burwell was chosen to succeed a supporter of John Randolph who had resigned. This was Christopher Clark, who had tried to get Randolph appointed minister to Great Britain. (Clark voted for the Non-Importation Act, however.) The outcome of Randolph's undercover campaign in behalf of Monroe as a presidential candidate against Madison remained to be seen, but by fall it appeared that his praise of Gallatin, which Jefferson was not alone in interpreting as an attempt to set that officer at loggerheads with the other members of the Cabinet, had turned out to be a boomerang. The extreme charges of William Duane, who avowed his preference for Jefferson for a third term, "even with *the evil genius of Gallatin in the Cabinet*," gained some currency in Virginia. One contributor to the *Enquirer* drew a disquieting picture of Gallatin's ubiquitous predecessor, Hamilton, which could be regarded as a warning to the man who had consulted so freely with Randolph. And Thomas Ritchie, while declaring that his own mind was not made up about the Secretary of the Treasury, said that his "mysterious tamperings with the Republican minority" had provided "abundant matter for *suspicion*."[6]

Greatly disturbed because such sentiments had been voiced by loyal supporters of his in his own state, Jefferson took occasion to write

[5] Events described in Richmond *Enquirer*, Dec. 18, 20, 1806. The action of the Senate was condemned in an article signed SENECA and by Ritchie himself in an extended discussion of these happenings (*Enquirer*, Dec. 22, 27, 1806).

[6] Richmond *Enquirer*, Oct. 7, 1806, referring to *Aurora*.

Gallatin a reassuring letter. In this he explicitly declared that his confidence and affection were not impaired, and could not be "by means so unworthy the notice of candid and honorable minds." In his reply, Gallatin made illuminating comments on the freedom and indulgence he had enjoyed in his official relations with the President and expressed deep regret at the divisions in the party. He was most aware of the one in Pennsylvania and expected to continue to be attacked unfairly from that quarter. Sending Jefferson's letter to his sister-in-law, he said: "It affords additional proof of the goodness of his heart, and shows that he is much above all those little squabbles."[7]

During the interval between congressional sessions the President engaged in a significant exchange of letters with Barnabas Bidwell, who, more nearly than anybody else, had assumed in the House the role of spokesman for the administration that John Randolph had abandoned. Early in the summer Bidwell wrote Jefferson that he was reluctant to stand for re-election because of the injury to his law practice and the loss of necessary income that resulted from his long absence from his home in Massachusetts. In his lengthy reply Jefferson stated that he deeply regretted Bidwell's disinclination to return to Congress, where everybody was expecting him to take the lead. Also, he set forth more explicitly perhaps than in any other letter he ever wrote his ideas regarding the representation of the measures of the administration in Congress. After stating that there never was a time when men of "talents, integrity, firmness, and sound judgment" were more needed in that body, he said:

> Some one of that description is particularly wanted to take the lead in the H. of R. to consider the business of the nation as his own business, to take it up as if he were singly charged with it and carry it through. I do not mean that any gentleman, relinquishing his own judgment, should implicitly support all the measures of the administration; but that, where he does not disapprove of them he should not suffer them to go off in sleep, but bring them to the attention of the house, and give them a fair chance. Where he disapproves, he will of course leave them to be brought forward by those who concur in the sentiment.

[7] Adams in *Gallatin*, pp. 344–347, gives the letters of TJ to Gallatin, Oct. 12, 1806; Gallatin to TJ, Oct. 13; and Gallatin to Marie Nicholson, Oct. 27. In an earlier draft of his letter to TJ, Gallatin expressed his preference for Madison as TJ's successor, showing his disagreement with John Randolph in this matter.

He illustrated the latter situation by the procedure he followed during the recent session in connection with the bill for the classification of the militia. This he first communicated to Bidwell himself and General Varnum, but he had another bring it forward when he found that they disapproved of it. It failed of passage anyway, to his continuing regret, but that was not the point. The important consideration was that somebody must see that measures of the Executive should not go by default. Because of recent experiences with John Randolph he was fully aware of the objections that might be expected, but he clearly recognized the necessity of liaison between the President and the Congress if the government was to be effective. Thus he said:

> When a gentleman, through zeal for the public service, undertakes to do the public business, we know that we shall hear the cant of backstairs' counsellors. But we never heard this while the declaimer [John Randolph] was himself a backstairs' man as he calls it, but in the confidence & views of the administration as may more properly & respectfully be said. But if the members are to know nothing but what is important enough to be put in a public message, & indifferent enough to be made known to all the world, if the executive is to keep all other information to himself, & the house to plunge on in the dark, it becomes a government of chance & not of design.

This realistic assessment is all the more significant and impressive because of his own past record as a critic and opponent of "monarchical" tendencies in the government when it was under Federalist control, and because of his awareness of the sensitivity of his own following with respect to legislative independence. A major difference between him and the Old Republicans was his greater capacity to learn from experience and willingness to be guided by it. He would not let theories become fetters. He treated the doctrinaires in his own party with respect, however, and neither in spirit nor manner was he dictatorial. With rare discernment and skill he adjusted his words and actions to the vanity of mortals.

In this long letter to Bidwell, which contained references to politics in New England and extended comments on foreign as well as congressional affairs, Jefferson appeared at his best in dealing with a loyal supporter. He left no possible doubt that this congressman had his confidence and was being given his views. But he sought to convince, not to command, and he recognized that he might be charged with impropriety in expressing himself so frankly. "Opportunities of candid explanation are so seldom afforded me, that I must not lose them when they occur," he said. Indulging in no recrimination, he praised the conduct of the majority in the House during the last session. All they needed was a man of business to lead them, he said, adding this appeal: "It is only speaking a truth to say that all eyes look to you." This was something of an exaggeration, to be sure, for the little band of schismatics were not looking in that direction, but as an appeal it was voiced with a maximum of persuasiveness.[8]

Bidwell yielded to it, but in his highly appreciative reply to a letter that he termed flattering he pointed out certain formidable obstacles that would be in his way.[9] While expecting to be attentive to the business of the House and to aid the measures of the administration, he doubted if he could play a conspicuous part. The business of the House was referred to committees and reported on by them. They were controlled by their chairmen, and these were appointed by the Speaker, from whom in the present instance Bidwell could expect no favors. He pointed out, in fact, the serious limitations of the power of any President seeking to improve liaison with Congess and gain its co-operation. While a President could share his confidence with some representative who, in his opinion, could command the support of most of the members belonging to his own party, he could not be entirely sure even of that and had no control over the organization of the legislative body. Any direct effort on his part to influence it was sure to be resented. Jefferson was a master of the oblique approach, but there were sharp limitations to the pressure he could exert on Nathaniel Macon, a constitutional purist whose scruples he respected. Whatever Jefferson's representations to him may have been, when he invited Macon to a private conference toward the end of the last congressional session, they do not appear to have weakened the Speaker's personal loyalty to John Randolph, though the two men saw less of each other than in former days and Macon was far from being a schismatic.

The resolution calling for the election of committees that was presented at the end of the last session of Congress seemed the only way to meet the existing situation short of displacing the Speaker. This question came up again at the beginning of the next session, but the

---

[8] Bidwell to TJ, June 21, 1806 (LC, 27933–27934); TJ to Bidwell, July 5, 1806 (LC, 27995–27996).
[9] Bidwell to TJ, July 28, 1806 (LC, 28111–28112).

move was defeated by a close vote.[10] Since Randolph was not present until after the traditional motion to appoint committees had been adopted, Macon as a strict legalist could not appoint him to his old committee, much as he would have liked to; but, a little later, a member resigned to make a place for him and the committee re-elected him its chairman. Thus the hampering conditions that Bidwell had described to Jefferson continued. So did John Randolph's feud with the administration. The story that Jefferson directly sought to prevent his return to his old chairmanship and that Gallatin favored it rests wholly on Randolph's own report.[11] His reliability as a reporter is questionable, but Gallatin had a high regard for his competence in financial matters, and no doubt he continued to be more respectful of Gallatin than of anybody else in the administration. He did not make the customary call of respect on the President at the beginning of the session and is said to have studiously avoided him during the rest of it.[12]

During the fall and winter of 1806–1807, signs multiplied that Jefferson was strongly supported by Republicans throughout the country. His mail was flooded with addresses, memorials, and resolutions which not only expressed approval of his official conduct but also urged him to permit his name to be presented for a third term.[13] Senator William Plumer, who was a relatively mild partisan on the other side, believed that the meetings in Philadelphia and New York from which many of these documents emerged were designed to "sound the public mind" and assumed that Jefferson approved of them.[14] The very large number of appeals from Pennsylvania and New York give ground for the suspicion that there was concerted action in those two states, but there appears to have been a large element of spontaneity in this movement. It can be most easily explained as a reflection of a widespread desire to maintain the unity of the country and, most particularly, that of the party. There is significance in the fact that Jefferson received most communications of this kind from states and districts where intra-

---

[10] *Annals,* 9 Cong., 2 sess., pp. 110–111, 115. A. B. Lacy describes the events ("Jefferson and Congress," pp. 177–180). On the events at the end of the previous session, see above, pp. 129–130.

[11] Bruce, I, 307–308.

[12] Plumer, *Memorandum,* p. 608 (Feb. 12, 1807).

[13] Upwards of thirty communications of this sort are in his papers in the Library of Congress.

[14] Entry of Nov. 12, 1806 (Plumer, *Memorandum,* pp. 513–514).

party conflict was most intense, including Philadelphia. From that city addresses were dispatched by Republican groups that were warring among themselves. But he had memorials from the legislatures of Vermont, Rhode Island, Maryland, and Georgia as well as from those of Pennsylvania and New York. Also, he received an address of congratulation from the General Assembly of Massachusetts, but this differed from the others in one respect: while voicing the wish that his "public usefulness" be continued for many years, it did not speak specifically of another term as President. That he replied to this, while leaving the others long unanswered, may be attributed to that omission.[15]

All of these memorials were full of praise and claimed to voice general sentiment. The legislators of remote Vermont, who disavowed slavish adulation and might have been expected to avoid it, expressed sincere approbation of the achievements of his administration, adding these words: "We learn that in these sentiments our sister states have almost unanimously coincided, and that, despising the struggles of faction, and the whispers of slander, the public opinion has ripened, from the first grade of favorable expectation, into bold and general applause."[16]

The address of the Democratic Republicans of Philadelphia was less restrained and essayed to be more historical. "Before you ascended the Executive chair," it said, "the doctrines of republicanism and the rights of man were proscribed as heretical, and the fashion was rapidly progressing of contempt for the sovereign people. Representative government was considered as an idle and visionary theory, an Utopian system, unsuited to man's disposition or capacity, and calculated rather for the closet of the philosopher, than the sphere of human fallibility." After saying, among many other things, that Jefferson's administration had revived the hopes of virtue, appalled the enemies of liberty, and demonstrated the excellence of the Republican system, the Philadelphians posed a rhetorical question: "While the work of patriotism and virtue is yet incomplete; while the immortal truths contained in the declaration of independence are hastening to maturity; while the hand of the master is alone wanting to finish the column of liberty, shall we, can we, consent to commit it to other hands?" Jefferson's former landlord Thomas Leiper, sending him this address, made clear

15 TJ to the Massachusetts State Legislature, Feb. 11, 1807, enclosed in letter of Feb. 14 to the President of the Senate and to the Speaker of the House (LC, 28991–28992; printed in S. K. Padover, ed., *Complete Jefferson* [1943], pp. 521–522). The address of Jan. 24, 1807 (LC, 28862–28863) was received by TJ on Feb. 4.

16 Vermont General Assembly to the President, Nov. 5, 1806 (LC, 28409–28412).

the practicalities of the situation. All Democrats wanted him to agree to his re-election, said this old friend, because they could repose no such confidence in anybody else.[17] Also, they could not agree on anybody else. Around him alone could they all rally.

To the addresses that emanated from recognized Republican groups, such as this one, Jefferson appears to have made no reply whatsoever at the time; and of those from legislative bodies he replied only to the one that did not mention a third term. Not until the very end of the year 1807 did he reply to the others and, by explicit action, clear the way for the congressional caucus of the party to choose another candidate.[18]

It should not be supposed that, during the winter of 1806–1807, there was no dissent among Republican leaders with respect to a third term for the President. Among those strongly opposing the idea in his own state was Thomas Ritchie, a loyal supporter who objected to one on principle. Among those who pressed it on him privately was Wilson Cary Nicholas of Albemarle County, whose apprehensions of national insecurity were increased by the strange doings of Aaron Burr in the West. Writing his friend and county neighbor early in 1807, Nicholas said: "Do not I pray you have your countrymen too much dependent upon the virtue of your successor. Many dynasties will pass away before your office will again be filled by one who unites the attachment to liberty and the capacity to govern that you have displayed, and very many before any man will hold the same place in the confidence and affections of your countrymen that you do."[19]

The communications he received that winter should have encouraged him and probably did, but shortly before Nicholas wrote him so beseechingly he himself was bemoaning to one of his compatriots of 1776 that he still had two more years of tedium before him. To John Dickinson he said: "I am tired of an office where I can do no more good than many others, who would be glad to be employed in it. To myself, personally, it brings nothing but unceasing drudgery and daily loss of friends. Every office becoming vacant, every appointment made, *me donne un ingrat, et cent ennemis.* My only consolation is in the belief that my fellow citizens at large give me credit for good intentions."[20] A few weeks later he was reported to have told a senator that he regarded the precedent of George Washington as obligatory and that he himself had consistently favored rotation in public office.

[17] Thomas Leiper to TJ, Nov. 21, 1806 (LC, 28478–28479), sending the address of Nov. 12, which he had hoped to deliver in person (LC, 28439–28441).

[18] Identical reply to the legislatures of six states, Dec. 10, 1807 (LC, 30574).

[19] W. C. Nicholas to TJ, Jan. 26, 1807 (LC, 28832–28835).

[20] TJ to John Dickinson, Jan. 13, 1807 (Ford, IX, 10).

He said he was convinced that if Aaron Burr had been elected, as he might have been in 1801, that adventurous gentleman would have taken measures to prolong his term. Therefore, it was all the more desirable that he himself discountenance the idea of perpetuity in office.[21]

The threat to the Union which many perceived in the strange doings of Burr in the West was one of the underlying reasons for the memorials to Jefferson. We have considered them here chiefly in terms of party loyalty, but there were other grounds for rallying round the Chief at this juncture. Jefferson might have formally rejected the appeals of his supporters at the time he got them, instead of waiting until the end of the year, but he would probably have weakened his own position both in the country and in the party if he had done so. At all events, while expressing his feelings more freely in private than his own supporters liked, he remained the central figure and around him loyalties could still cluster.

21 Plumer's entry of Feb. 6, 1807 (*Memorandum*, p. 603).

[XI]

The Patron of Exploration

A FEW weeks after his return to Washington in the autumn of 1806, Jefferson received "with unspeakable joy", the news that Meriwether Lewis and William Clark had arrived in St. Louis and thus completed the mission to the Pacific coast that he had assigned them.[1] Besides being one of the most important episodes in the early history of the trans-Mississippi region, this expedition constituted the President's greatest success — his only major success, in fact — as a patron and promoter of western exploration. Except in imagination he himself never got farther west than the Warm Springs Valley of Virginia at any time in his long life, but Peter Jefferson's son was always fascinated by maps, and no other American public man of his time did so much to encourage the charting of the waterways of half a continent.

A score of years before he dispatched Lewis and Clark, he asked the latter's elder brother, the redoubtable George Rogers Clark, if he would command an exploring expedition to California. The matter had been only feebly discussed by members of the Continental Congress, of whom Jefferson was one, and he recognized that because of the lack of spirit the prospect was very dim; but, at a time when the territory of the United States had only just been recognized by the British as extending to the Mississippi, his own vision extended to the Pacific.[2] He was disposed to think in long-range terms and may have believed, even at this stage, that the extension of American settlement across the continent was inevitable; but his interest in exploration transcended national interest, as the encouragement he gave John Ledyard in France a few years later clearly showed. It may seem to have tran-

[1] TJ to Lewis, Oct. 26, 1806, replying to Lewis's letter of Sept. 23 (Donald Jackson, ed., *Letters of the Lewis & Clark Expedition* [1962], pp. 350–351). In this chapter and the next I generally cite this admirable collection (referring to it as Jackson) even when letters and documents are printed elsewhere.

[2] TJ to G. R. Clark, Dec. 4, 1783; Clark to TJ, Feb. 8, 1784 (*ibid.*, pp. 654–656).

scended common sense in that instance, for he encouraged the explorer's design to circumambulate the globe, approaching North America from Siberia.[3] Though he was primarily concerned that his own continent be charted, his interest in exploration was more than political. He wanted to expand the bounds of human knowledge in geography, mineralogy, ethnology, and every branch of natural history. The western expedition of André Michaux, originally sponsored by the American Philosophical Society and abetted by him while secretary of state, was supposed to have a scientific purpose. It became entangled with the enterprises of Citizen Genet and did not get beyond the Mississippi, but as planned it anticipated in some sense the Lewis and Clark expedition of the next decade.[4]

In the public mind the latter has inevitably been connected with the Louisiana Purchase, but actually it was authorized by Congress on Jefferson's request at a time when he had no reason to anticipate the cession of the province to the United States and when the region to be traversed was still in Spanish hands. Thus the project was considerably more audacious at the outset than it seemed afterwards. Shortly before the beginning of the congressional session of 1802–1803, the President inquired of Yrujo if the Spanish court would take badly the formation of a small group of travelers to explore the course of the Missouri River and proceed thence to the Pacific. He described the purposes of the projected expedition as predominantly geographical but admitted that these would have to be presented to Congress in commercial guise. As Yrujo put the matter, the Constitution did not authorize Congress to vote funds for a "purely literary expedition." The Spanish Minister was not yet obstreperous, as he became after the cession of Louisiana to the United States, but, despite Jefferson's assurances, he said frankly that such an expedition could not fail to give umbrage to his government. Reporting to Madrid, he voiced his own suspicions:

> The President has been all his life a man of letters, very speculative and a lover of glory, and it would be possible he might attempt to perpetuate the fame of his administration not only by the measures of frugality and economy which characterize him, but also by discovering or attempting at least to discover the way by which the Americans may some day extend their population and their influence up to the coasts of the South Sea.[5]

[3] This episode is briefly referred to in *Jefferson and the Rights of Man*, pp. 67–68.

[4] The Michaux expedition is referred to in *Jefferson and the Ordeal of Liberty*, pp. 104–108. The correspondence is in Jackson, pp. 667–672. For TJ's patronage of science while President, see ch. X of *Jefferson the President: First Term*.

[5] Yrujo to Cevallos, Dec. 2, 1802 (Jackson, pp. 4–6).

Yrujo believed at the time that he had calmed Jefferson's spirit by his recital of useless and fruitless attempts to find a northwest passage, but he did not at all deter the President, who was characteristically tenacious of cherished projects and seems to have concluded that the attitude of Spain did not really matter, since she would soon have to return Louisiana to France anyway. He glossed over the Spanish opposition, but in due course he procured for Captain Meriwether Lewis passports from Great Britain and France. These were issued respectively by Thornton and Pichon, with both of whom he was on the best of terms and both of whom reported, on the basis of conversations with him, that the expedition was to be scientific in character and only nominally commercial.[6] But the appropriation of $2500 that he got from Congress was "for the purpose of extending the foreign commerce of the United States"; and in the confidential message in which he had asked for this he said that the commercial object was primary and the geographical secondary. In the message he described his Indian policy at some length and referred to the potentialities of the trans-Mississippi fur trade.[7] Later events bore out the sincerity of his assurance to Thornton that no articles of commerce would be carried beyond those needed as presents for the Indians, but a major purpose of the expedition was to inquire into the possibilities of future trade along the inland waterways. In his own mind a number of motives were conjoined, as in fact his message to Congress showed, and there is no real point in seeking to determine which was uppermost. At one and the same time he was concerned to promote commerce, to increase national security, to strengthen territorial claims (as in Oregon), and to enlarge the boundaries of knowledge by means of "voyages of discovery." While craftily calling to the attention of others the particular objects that pleased them most, he himself was looking in many directions. He can be more accurately described as ubiquitous than as ambivalent.

He had discussed this expedition with Captain Meriwether Lewis before broaching it to the Congress and had already determined to appoint his secretary as its head. From the time of the Michaux expedition, as he knew, Lewis had panted to engage in transcontinental exploration and the young officer had renewed his solicitations when he learned of this prospect. From his eager secretary the President got an estimate of expenses in advance. The modesty of this may be attrib-

[6] Passports dated Feb. 28, Mar. 1, 1803; letters of Pichon and Thornton to their home offices, Mar. 4, 9, 1803 (ibid., pp. 19–20, 22–23, 25–27).

[7] Message of Jan. 18; act of Feb. 28, 1803 (Annals, 7 Cong., 2 sess., pp. 24–26, 103; Jackson, pp. 10–14). See Jefferson the President: First Term, pp. 275–276.

uted in part to the consideration that the officers and enlisted men would be paid by the army, in part to the characteristic frugality of the President in public matters, in part to the desire of both men to keep the figures so low as not to frighten an economy-minded legislature. Actually, the size of the expedition was increased and it cost considerably more than was anticipated, but it does not appear to have been wasteful.[8]

Meriwether Lewis, now in his twenty-ninth year, came from Albemarle County, a nursery of explorers. Jefferson, besides being well acquainted with his family on both sides, knew that from childhood he was remarkable for "enterprise, boldness, and discretion," and that before "yielding to the ardor of youth for more dazzling pursuits" by embarking on a military career he had shown marked talent for the observation of plants and animals.[9] As Fate would have it, the older man was to write a memoir of the younger a decade later. Jefferson's characterization of the short-lived explorer is so good that anyone writing about him now is impelled to draw upon it.

Of courage undaunted, possessing a firmness & perseverance of purpose which nothing but impossibilities could divert from its direction, careful as a father of those committed to his charge, yet steady in the maintenance of order & discipline, intimate with the Indian character, customs & principles, habituated to the hunting life, guarded by exact observation of the vegetables & animals of his own country, against losing time in the description of objects already possessed, honest, disinterested, liberal, of sound understanding and a fidelity to truth so scrupulous that whatever he should report would be as certain as if seen by ourselves, with all these qualifications as if selected and implanted by nature in one body for this express purpose, I could have no hesitation in confiding the enterprise to him.

This judgment was based, in part at least, on Lewis's actual conduct of the expedition, but in Jefferson's opinion at the outset all he needed was more familiarity with the "technical language of the natural

[8] For Lewis's estimate, see Jackson, pp. 8–10; for the final summation of his account, see pp. 424–431. The Mandan episode, described in the next chapter, may be regarded as excessively expensive.

[9] Details and quotations (punctuation slightly modified) are from the sketch of Lewis in TJ's letter of Aug. 18, 1813, to Paul Allen (Jackson, pp. 586–593). Lewis's given name, derived from his mother's family, occasioned considerable confusion among his contemporaries. It appears on his passports as Merriwether, in correspondence of the time as Merrywether, Merrywhether, and Merryweather, and as if it were his surname, appearing sometimes as Merry.

MERIWETHER LEWIS
Portrait by Charles Willson Peale

sciences" and ability to make the astronomical observations necessary to determine geographical position. To help him overcome these deficiencies the President had him visit leading members of the American Philosophical Society in Philadelphia — Benjamin S. Barton, Caspar Wistar, Robert Patterson, Dr. Benjamin Rush. From these men he got technical advice and suggestions about desirable objects of observation. Dr. Rush gave him a set of rules of health which seem generally sensible, though the efficacy of some of the suggested remedies will be questioned by moderns. Jefferson also commended Lewis to the distinguished astronomer and surveyor, Andrew Ellicott, with whom he took counsel in Lancaster, Pennsylvania, when collecting equipment there.

The initiator and patron of this enterprise gave close personal attention to its scientific aspects, finding occasion to engage in the sort of correspondence that most delighted him. Seizing upon the opportunity afforded by the receipt of a paper by the Comte de Lacépède, he informed that French naturalist of the intended "voyage of discovery," expressing the hope that among other things it would procure them further information about the mammoth and *megatherium*.[10] Nothing could have pleased him more than the prediction of that savant that the expedition would be useful not only for the progress of industry (by which presumably he meant trade, not manufacturing), but also for that of the sciences, especially natural history. Quite unlike Buffon, who had belittled the fauna of the New World, this Frenchman reflected the universality of science when making a prediction that might have come from Jefferson himself. "Hitherto," he said, "the movement of enlightenment has been from east to west. The inhabitants of the United States, if they do not reject their destiny, will one day halt and reverse this movement."[11]

Jefferson himself did not regard the purposes of the expedition as in any sense conflicting, and in planning for it he tried to allow for everything. He had the members of his Cabinet go over the draft of instructions for Lewis that he had made in the spring of 1803, and before putting this into final form sent a copy of it to the Captain, who showed it to his counselors in Philadelphia. It was thoroughly approved by all who saw it, and the recommendations of his advisers were chiefly for additions. The final paper represented a consensus, but except for a few minor details it was the work of Jefferson. It sets

10 See *Jefferson and the Ordeal of Liberty*, pp. 341–345.
11 TJ's letter of Feb. 24, 1803, to Lacépède and the latter's reply of May 13 are in Jackson, pp. 15–16, 46–48. His correspondence with American men of science in this connection can be readily seen in the early pages of that collection.

forth his supplementary purposes, illustrates his unusual capacity for taking pains, and reflects the richly diverse interests of his endlessly inquiring mind.[12]

In describing the geographical objects of this mission of exploration, Jefferson was subject to the limitations of contemporary knowledge and manifested his own inveterate optimism. He hoped that the distance between some one of the sources of the Missouri and the headwaters of one of the streams flowing into the Pacific would be small and that communication with the Far Northwest could be made by a virtually all-water route. Even if that hope should prove vain, however, as in fact it did, precise knowledge of the Missouri and its tributaries could be of great importance to future trade, and he prescribed careful observations of latitude and longitude and the recording of these in several copies. Nothing was more typical of him and nothing of greater ultimate importance than his insistence on the keeping and preserving of records. He even suggested that use be made of birchbark, which was less likely than common paper to be injured by dampness.

Gallatin, who recognized in advance of the Louisiana Purchase that the Missouri country would be settled by Americans in any case, was specially desirous of obtaining all possible information about the entire region. He did not want observation to be limited to the particular branch of the river by means of which communication with the Pacific might be established, but hoped it could be extended to all the principal branches. For practical reasons, no doubt, Jefferson did not go so far as to enjoin that extension. He wanted the explorers to stick to the main course, but he instructed Lewis to find out as much about the lesser streams as he could by inquiry. Gallatin wanted to ascertain if the region could support a large population, and at this stage may have been more of an expansionist than Jefferson, who, with a view to national security, was now stressing the desirability of getting the region east of the Mississippi solidly settled by white men and of inducing the Indians to move to the other side. But no more in him than in Gallatin did frugality in public matters reflect provincial narrowness, and his instructions respecting observation of the country to be traversed gave promise of procuring just the sort of information his Secretary of the Treasury wanted. Notice was to be taken of soil,

[12] The instructions of June 20, 1803, are in Jackson, pp. 61–66. The most important comments that have been preserved were those of Gallatin, Apr. 13, 1803 (*Writings*, I, 120–122; Jackson, pp. 32–34), and Levi Lincoln, Apr. 17, 1803 (*ibid.*, pp. 34–36). See also TJ to Lewis, May 16, 1803; Lewis to TJ, May 29; and other documents (*ibid.*, pp. 49–53).

animals, vegetable products, and minerals. Specially characteristic of him were his references to the remains of extinct animals and observations of wind and weather. The former, at least, indicated an interest going beyond immediate utility.

He did not need to be reminded, as he was by Levi Lincoln, of the desirability of learning everything possible about the Indians. Politically minded Lincoln, fearful of the uses a malignant opposition might make of failure, was especially anxious that there be something to show even if the expedition should not get to the Pacific. Knowledge of Indian ways was of recognized importance for military and commercial reasons and was of great intrinsic interest to Jefferson, who was to be recognized in after years as a pioneer ethnologist, thanks in large part to this very expedition. Included in his comprehensive instructions were references to Indian languages, which were of particular interest to him, and to Indian diseases and morals, about which Dr. Rush submitted special queries to Captain Lewis.

He himself made it abundantly clear that the natives were to be treated in a friendly and conciliatory manner. Insofar as possible he sought to make this a peaceful expedition, as in fact, with only minor exceptions, it turned out to be. At the outset he could not be sure of that, and while he appears to have been much less fearful of its outcome than his Attorney General, he probably agreed with the judgment of that adviser that in case of difficulty the brave Captain would be more likely to push too far than to recede too quickly. At all events Jefferson counseled prudence. "We value too much the lives of citizens to offer them to probable destruction," he said. If their passage should be strongly opposed by a superior force they must return, preserving and bringing back with them the information they had procured. While leaving it up to Lewis to decide what risk should be taken in a particular situation, he enjoined him to err on the side of safety.

The instructions regarding Lewis's conduct on reaching the Pacific show that the President and his advisers were concerned about the fur trade and wanted to learn more about such commerce as was carried on by sea with the northwest coast. Of more human interest is the suggestion that the explorer might send a couple of his men back by sea, along with a copy of his notes, and that, if the return by land should seem too dangerous, he and his whole party should come back by water, either by Cape Horn or the Cape of Good Hope. Recognizing that he would be without money, clothes, and other necessities for such a voyage, Jefferson gave him an unlimited letter of credit. In this, besides authorizing him to draw on the government, the President requested officials and nationals of other countries to honor his drafts and instructed American consuls to do so.[13] Jefferson specifically named some of the latter in far-distant places. Having manifested this foresight, he might perhaps have been expected to send a ship to the mouth of the Columbia to supply, and if need be to rescue, the marooned explorers. If he considered doing so, we can only assume that such action seemed impractical.[14]

As things turned out, Lewis had no more occasion to avail himself of these financial provisions for a remote contingency than he did to employ the cipher furnished him for correspondence with Jefferson. Before he went west, however, he gave Jefferson a promissory note which that gentleman said he forgot about until Lewis's estate was being settled seven years later. As he then correctly recalled, it was for approximately a hundred dollars.[15] Unfortunately the Captain neglected to take his pocketbook with him when he left Washington for the West, but Jefferson sent it to him and he gratefully acknowledged its receipt, writing from Pittsburgh.[16]

Judging from what Lewis wrote William Clark the day before he got his official instructions, which was a couple of weeks before the first news of the signing of the treaty with France reached the capital, the government had "very sanguine expectations" by that time that the entire watershed of the Mississippi would be the property of the United States within twelve months.[17] The unofficial report of the cession came before Lewis set out on July 5, 1803, and Jefferson confirmed it in a letter to him ten days later. But the Louisiana Purchase was by no means a *fait accompli* for a good many months yet, and no reference to it had been inserted in his instructions. Nor was the effort relaxed to maintain all possible secrecy about the objects of his mission. Lewis himself sought to create the impression that he would go up rather than across the Mississippi. Whether or not this degree of secrecy served any important purpose, the fact remains that an expedition destined to be famous was launched without fanfare, and that only a handful of insiders had seen the fascinating instructions by which it was to be guided.

---

[13] TJ to Lewis, July 4, 1803 (*ibid.*, pp. 105–106; see also p. 65).

[14] Bernard DeVoto describes TJ's failure to send a ship as inexplicable (*Journals of Lewis and Clark* [1953], p. 293). Elliott Coues thinks he did not want to arouse the Spanish by so doing (cited by I. J. Cox, *The Early Exploration of Louisiana* [1906], p. 22, note 18).

[15] Actually $103.93, dated June 23, 1803 (see Jackson, pp. 67–68, 495). It is uncertain whether Lewis was covering past obligations or providing for current personal expenses, or doing both.

[16] TJ to Lewis, July 11, 1803; Lewis to TJ, July 22 (*ibid.*, pp. 107, 111).

[17] *Jefferson the President: First Term*, pp. 296–297.

Its purposes as understood by Lewis at this stage, and his plans for it, were admirably described in his letter to William Clark.[18] In this he invited his friend, with whom he had served under Anthony Wayne in the campaign that ended with the battle of Fallen Timbers, to share the leadership of the expedition with him. Jefferson strongly supported this invitation. William was the youngest brother of George Rogers Clark and equally redheaded. Before his birth his family moved from Albemarle to Caroline County, Virginia, and thence to Kentucky, where, resigned from the army, he was now living. Several years older than Lewis, he had had even more frontier experience, and time was to show that the two men admirably complemented each other. Lewis relayed to him Jefferson's promise of a captain's commission, which he clearly rated since he had outranked his friend when they served together. All the President could actually do was nominate him; and, unfortunately, this matter became involved in questions of seniority and entangled with red tape. Thus it came about that instead of a commission as captain in the Corps of Engineers, all Clark got was one as a lieutenant in the Corps of Artillerists. But his pay was to be the same as that of Lewis, who reassured him about his relative position and advised that nothing be said about rank. The two officers did not wear uniforms or insignia in the wilderness, and for the purposes of this expedition Clark was a captain. Though discomfited at the outset, he made little of this mischance afterwards.[19] There is no reason to suppose that he bore any ill will to Jefferson, whom he referred to in his enthusiastic letter of acceptance as "that great Chaructor" and the "Main Spring" of this joint enterprise.[20] The President may be assumed never to have seen that letter, which reached Lewis at Pittsburgh, but he saw many a sample of the inimitable spelling and wise observations of this brave and resourceful man.

ii

Our account of this justly renowned expedition must be limited to Jefferson's direct relations with it and his knowledge of it as this was acquired by him. Not until three and a half years after Captain Lewis left Washington did his friend and patron in the President's House again see him, and in the meantime the amount of correspondence between them varied with the physical difficulty of communication.[21]

18 Lewis to Clark, June 19, 1803 (Jackson, pp. 57-60).
19 Dearborn to Lewis, Mar. 26, 1804; Lewis to Clark, May 6, 1804; Clark to Nicholas Biddle, Aug. 15, 1811 (ibid., pp. 172, 179-180, 571-572).
20 Clark to Lewis, July 18, 1803 (ibid., pp. 110-111).
21 Lewis got back to Washington toward the end of December, 1806.

WILLIAM CLARK
Portrait by Charles Willson Peale

Lewis wrote Jefferson from Harper's Ferry on his way west, as he did from Pittsburgh an hour after he got there on July 15, 1803. That place was only about ten days away from Washington. As Lewis afterwards reported, he was "shamefully delayed" there by the "unpardonable negligence" of a drunken boat-builder. Troubled because he had not yet received a reply from Clark in Kentucky, he gained the consent of Lieutenant Moses Hooke (then at Pittsburgh) to serve; and, through Jefferson, procured the consent of the Secretary of War for this young officer to accompany him if need be. But he soon got a letter from Clark, as Jefferson did almost as soon. That solicitous gentleman took occasion not only to send Lewis his forgotten pocketbook and to inform him of the receipt of the treaty with France, but also to transmit bits of geographical information just received from the Comte de Lacépède in Paris.

The chain of communication lengthened as the explorer dropped slowly down the Ohio. Letters from Wheeling and Marietta were seventeen days in transit, and one from Cincinnati was more than three weeks. The latter, which reached Jefferson in late October, brought him glad tidings of scientific discoveries. Lewis wrote him in detail and with great enthusiasm about the fossil bones already found in the Big Bone Lick and believed to belong for the most part to the mammoth. He himself visited the place and sent Jefferson several "handsome specimens." One of these he described as a grinder of the elephant, another as a grinder of the mammoth, and another as a tusk of an "immence size." Jefferson's appetite, undoubtedly whetted by this report, was to remain unsatisfied, for the big bones, shipped down the rivers, were lost at Natchez and never made the voyage to Richmond and thence to Monticello that he had planned for them. Therefore, William Clark went to Big Bone Lick at a later time.[22]

Lewis, whose progress had been delayed beyond his expectations and who was anxious to keep Congress in a good humor with respect to his expedition, now suggested that he make a horseback tour of the country near whatever winter establishment he should set up. The presumption was that he would make explorations south of the Missouri and he thought that perhaps Clark could be spared from the party to make a similar excursion. By the time Jefferson answered this letter he and his advisers were strongly of the opinion that the explorers should not enter the Missouri until spring, and they were fully decided against the proposed side trip, which they regarded as more

[22] Lewis to TJ, Oct. 3, 1803 (*ibid.*, pp. 126–132, with notes). The correspondence between TJ and Lewis, July–October, 1803, along with other documents of the period, can be readily seen in that work (pp. 106–134).

dangerous than the expedition up the river. It might hazard the main object, which, since the acquisition of Louisiana, interested everybody in the highest degree. "The object of your mission," said the President, "is single, the direct water communication from sea to sea formed by the bed of the Missouri and perhaps the Oregon." Neither he nor Clark should be exposed to risk by going off the line. Jefferson now had plans for exploring the upper Mississippi, the Red River, and the Arkansas. He had only slight success in carrying these out, as we shall see hereafter, but he kept Lewis and Clark on the main track.[23]

His suggestions that the winter be spent on the east side of the Mississippi, so as to avoid possible difficulties with the Spanish, and that efforts be made to gain information at St. Louis, were not needed by the explorer, who came to similar opinions independently. The letters Lewis wrote in December, 1803, from Cahokia were a couple of months getting to Washington.[24] He found the Spanish Governor of Upper Louisiana unwilling to grant him permission to ascend the Missouri, but encouraging about his doing so in the spring. Before Christmas he had selected for winter quarters a site opposite the mouth of the Missouri, and Clark, who had now joined him, was putting up cabins there. All this Jefferson learned at the end of February, receiving at the same time the information Lewis had picked up in St. Louis about the inhabitants of Upper Louisiana.[25]

Meanwhile, Jefferson had sent Lewis a map of the Missouri as far as the country of the Mandans, which was actually as far as the expedition was to get in the following summer. The expedition had now come into the open. "The acquisition of the country through which you are to pass has inspired the public generally with a great deal of interest in your enterprise," he said. "The enquiries are perpetual as to your progress. The Feds. alone still treat it as a philosophism, and would rejoice in its failure. . . . I hope you will take care of yourself, and be the living witness of their malice and folly."[26]

[23] TJ to Lewis, Nov. 16, 1803 (ibid., pp. 136–137). With this letter he sent a printed copy of the account of Louisiana he had submitted to Congress and extracts from the journal of a trader containing information about trans-Misssissippi Indians, along with other documents and articles that had been requested.

[24] Lewis to TJ, Dec. 19, 28, 1803 (ibid., pp. 145–157, received Feb. 27, 1804).

[25] In his letter of Dec. 28, 1803, Lewis discussed at length the possibility, which TJ had talked with him about in Washington, of inducing the inhabitants to move east of the Mississippi and make way for the Indians from that side. He was more optimistic about this than the facts presented by him would seem to warrant. In his opinion, the French settlers would be least disposed to move, and he reported that Americans were coming in at the rate of more than two hundred families a year. To have stemmed this rising stream would have been difficult indeed.

[26] TJ to Lewis, Jan. 13, 1804 (Jackson, p. 163). He sent the map of John Evans (ibid., pp. 135–136, note 3).

In the last letter he wrote Lewis before the expedition started up the Missouri in May, 1804, the President made an addition (apparently the only one he ever made) to the explorer's original instructions. The change in sovereignty permitted a direct offer to the Indians to institute trade with them. They should be reconciled to this change, which involved no diminution of their "rights of occupancy," and their friendship should be sought. Thus the expedition could now candidly assume a more commercial aspect. With this final letter, however, went a reminder of its scientific aspects. Meriwether Lewis was now informed that he had been made a member of the American Philosophical Society.[27] Through his patron the explorer was to make numerous contributions to the collections of that distinguished organization, but these were necessarily delayed.

When departing from St. Louis, Lewis left with Pierre Chouteau, a prominent trader, certain articles to be forwarded to the President. These may be regarded as the first scientific fruits of the expedition.[28] Among the articles was a map of a portion of Upper Louisiana, which was said by Lewis to have had only "small claims to correctness" but had in fact been compiled from the best information yet available to him and Clark. On it he had marked the territories claimed by the Osage nation, from whose "great saline" he sent a specimen of salt which must have been of interest even though it did come from a salt mountain. He sent several specimens of ore and a living curiosity, a horned toad, confined for safety in a small trunk. If Jefferson did not afterwards present this particular creature to the American Philosophical Society, he gave them another like it.

More impressive than anything in this collection were the representatives of the Osage nation whom Pierre Chouteau conducted to Washington to visit the Great White Father. Lewis's invitation to them to do so at public expense accorded with Jefferson's general instructions, and the journey from St. Louis was made with the solicitous co-operation of the Department of War and various officers of the army. According to the President himself, the group that arrived in Washington on July 11, 1804, which chanced to be the day of the Burr-Hamilton duel at Weehawken, consisted of twelve men and two boys. He described the men as the most gigantic he had ever seen and rejoiced that they were wholly unused to spirituous liquor.[29] His brief

27 TJ to Lewis, Jan. 22, 1804 (ibid., pp. 165–166).
28 List, dated May 18, 1804 (ibid., pp. 192–194).
29 TJ to Gallatin, July 12, 1804 (Gallatin, Writings, I, 200); to Robt. Smith, July 13, 1804 (LC, 24598). On TJs' efforts to keep whiskey from the Indians, see F. J. Prucha, Indian Policy in the Formative Years (1962), pp. 104–107.

speech of welcome the next day and his formal address a few days later, after they had had a chance to recover from the fatigue of their long journey, were marked with warmth and touched with the sort of eloquence the Indians expected.[30] Believing that the Osages were the most powerful nation south of the Missouri, as a responsible statesman he was seeking to gain their friendship and their future trade, but his tone was that of a kind father and a humane advocate of peace. It would appear that in the presence of these noble savages he was giving free rein to ineradicable sentiment and describing human relations as they *ought* to be. After telling his auditors that, by late arrangements with the French and Spanish, his countrymen had replaced them as the neighbors, friends, and fathers of the red men, he said in language verging on poetry:

It is so long since our forefathers came from beyond the great water, that we have lost the memory of it, and seem to have grown out of this land, as you have done. Never more will you have occasion to change your fathers. We are all now of one family, born in the same land, & bound to live as brothers; & the strangers from beyond the great water are gone from among us. The great Spirit has given you strength, and has given us strength; not that we might hurt one another, but to do each other all the good in our power. Our dwellings indeed are very far apart; but not too far to carry on commerce & useful intercourse. You have furs and peltries which we want, and we have clothes and other useful things which you want. Let us employ ourselves then in mutually accomodating each other.

Setting forth in part the purpose of the expedition then ascending the Missouri, he said: "I sent a beloved man, Capt. Lewis, one of my own household, to learn something of the people with whom we are now united, to let you know we were your friends, to invite you to come and see us, and to tell us how we can be useful to you." He referred to other explorations he had in mind, spoke of sending an agent to reside among the Osages and serve as an intermediary, and promised that no harm would ever be done them by his nation, while admitting that "all people have some bad men among them whom no laws can restrain." Finally, he invited them to prolong their visit and see other towns and country. Thus they could gain the sort of knowledge of the region east of the Mississippi that he was seeking on the

[30] July 12, 16, 1804 (Jackson, pp. 199–203, with valuable notes). Quotations are from the formal address. A French version of this, an English version, and what appear to be TJ's notes on the reply of White Hairs, are in LC, 24612–24616.

other side. Guides and accommodations would be provided, and they would carry back with them proofs of esteem. As a result of this invitation these chiefs and warriors of the Osage nation visited Philadelphia and went as far eastward as New York. Then, riding "public horses" and duly escorted, they reached Pittsburgh, whence they proceeded to St. Louis on river craft provided by the War Department. Arriving in October, they were unquestionably flattered by the attentions they had received and the gifts they bore.[31] "On your return," Jefferson had said, "tell your people that I take them all by the hand; that I become their father thereafter." The favors shown this particular tribe by him aroused jealousy in others, but as the head of "17 united nations" (that is, the seventeen states), he was prepared to give distinguished consideration to delegations from any of the Indian nations and did not cease to do so while President.[32]

The speech of Meriwether Lewis at Council Bluffs in this same summer breathed the same spirit and was couched in similar language. Addressing the Oto Indians, he spoke for the Great Chief in Washington, "as powerful as he is just, and as beneficent as he is wise, always entertaining a sincere and friendly disposition towards the red people of America."[33] Jefferson's emissary claimed too much, of course, and the Great Chief was certainly not unmindful of the interests of the seventeen white "nations" and their expanding economy. But he still hoped for the eventual incorporation of the red men into an agricultural society, and he saw in the vast trans-Mississippi region ample space for such of them as were determined to remain hunters. Neither he nor anybody else then anticipated the rapidity of the westward movement of the restless and acquisitive whites. His benevolence was genuine, and his messengers admirably reflected his good will. The commercial aspects of this mission may have appealed most to Congress, and its scientific aspects to the savants of the American Philosophical Society, but to the Great Chief in Washington it was also a mission of peace and healing. He may have been naïve in supposing that the warriors could be induced to refrain from fighting with their neighbors, but he was unquestionably sincere in hoping this, as he was that the Indian women should no longer fear the tomahawk of an enemy and that their children should multiply and live long. He in-

31 James Bruff to James Wilkinson, Nov. 5, 1804 (Jackson, p. 215).
32 A useful collection of his Indian addresses is in Padover, The Complete Jefferson, pp. 449–514. For a discussion of the presuppositions and ramifications of Jeffersonian Indian policy, see Bernard W. Sheehan, Seeds of Extinction: Jeffersonian Philanthropy and the American Indian (1973).
33 To the Oto Indians, Aug. 4, 1804 (Jackson, pp. 203–208; quotation from p. 205, spelling slightly modified).

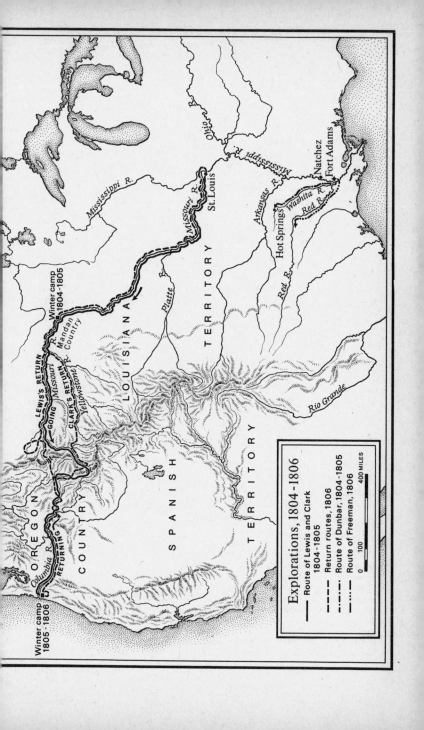

Explorations, 1804-1806

— Route of Lewis and Clark
    1804-1805
----- Return routes, 1806
-·-·- Route of Dunbar, 1804-1805
········ Route of Freeman, 1806

0   100   400 MILES

OREGON COUNTRY

Winter camp 1805-1806

LEWIS'S RETURN

GOING

CLARK'S RETURN

RETURNING

Columbia R.

Missouri R.

Yellowstone R.

Winter camp 1804-1805

Mandan Country

LOUISIANA

TERRITORY

Platte R.

SPANISH

TERRITORY

Rio Grande

Mississippi R.

Missouri R.

Ohio R.

St. Louis

Arkansas R.

Red R.

Hot Springs

Washita R.

Red R.

Natchez

Fort Adams

structed Captain Lewis to take vaccine against smallpox to use among the red men, and Captain Clark won many an Indian heart by his services as a physician.

Although Jefferson got occasional secondhand reports of the progress of the explorers up the Missouri, and anticipated that they would spend the winter in the Mandan country in the present state of North Dakota, he did not receive direct word from them until the following summer (1805). On the same day in April that they resumed their journey, hoping to cross the mountains and reach the Pacific before another winter, Lewis dispatched down the river a barge with a crew of ten able-bodied and resolute men and a cargo containing articles designated for the President of the United States. These had to go from St. Louis to New Orleans and thence by water to Baltimore, and they did not get to Washington until the middle of August, when Jefferson was at Monticello. About a month earlier he got the invoice, along with a letter in which Lewis briefly described the expedition thus far and enclosed Clark's notes on it.[34] Both men apologized for the crudity and incorrectness of this journal, saying they did not want it exposed in its present state, though quite willing for the President and chief executive officers to see it. The chances are that Jefferson was not at all disturbed by Clark's phonetic spelling or by that acute observer's innocence of grammar. There appears to be no record of any comment of his on the journal at the time, but he must have found it fascinating when he got around to reading it. From it he could have learned that discipline was well maintained, that, in the death of Sergeant Charles Floyd (presumably from appendicitis) the expedition had suffered a fatality (the only one, actually), and that by the exercise of firmness and resolution the explorers, without resort to bloodshed, had surmounted the gravest danger they encountered from the Indians — that imposed by the Teton Sioux, whom Lewis designated as "the pirates of the Missouri," and described as "the vilest miscreants of the savage race."[35]

The invoice from Lewis could not have failed to arouse the eager

[34] Clark to TJ, Apr. 3, 1805; Lewis to TJ, Apr. 17, 1805, with invoice; both letters received July 13 (*ibid.*, pp. 231–242, containing extensive notes on the invoice).

[35] I do not enter here into the complicated story of the documents of the expedition, with the fortunes of which TJ was much concerned in later years. The account of the voyage to the Mandan country (for which we have no journal from Lewis) and the winter there is in Vol. I of R. G. Thwaites, ed., *Original Journals of the Lewis and Clark Expedition* (8 vols., 1904–1905). This invaluable work is referred to hereafter as Thwaites. Lewis's comments on the Teton Sioux are in the statistical view of the Indians to which we refer hereafter.

anticipation of such an enthusiast for natural history as Jefferson. It listed animal skins, horns, and skeletons; specimens of minerals and plants; cages containing respectively four magpies, a "burrowing squirel," and a "liveing hen of the Prarie." (By modern standards, Lewis himself was no impeccable speller.) The hen, otherwise described as a sharp-tailed grouse, was not living when the shipment reached New Orleans; and only one of the magpies completed the voyage to Baltimore. According to a newspaper report, this one destroyed the other three. The state of the skins and furs occasioned concern in New Orleans, where they were repacked. Having learned at Monticello in August of their arrival in Washington, Jefferson instructed his steward Lemaire to have them dried and brushed and then done up in strong linen. Also, he requested that special care be given the magpie and the creature described by Lemaire as a kind of squirrel, so that he might see them alive on his return. When he got back to the President's House in early October he sent them, along with a large number of articles, to Charles Willson Peale for that friend's museum. The minerals and plant specimens were designated for the American Philosophical Society, while Jefferson kept the horns, some of the dressed skins, and certain utensils for the Indian Hall he was forming at Monticello. Lewis, saying that he would meet Jefferson there in September, 1806, used the phonetic spelling "Montachello," thus attesting to the traditional pronunciation.[36]

The receipt and distribution of these treasures and the resulting correspondence with fellow enthusiasts undoubtedly gave Jefferson greater satisfaction than he gained from politics. Of more immediate public interest, however, was the large map of the Missouri River and the statistical information about the Indians that Lewis sent the Secretary of War. Jefferson undoubtedly rejoiced in this extension of knowledge, and within a few weeks (February 19, 1806) he reported it to Congress along with discoveries that had been made by other and lesser expeditions up to this time.[37]

[36] On his copy of the invoice, which also appears in Lewis's journal, TJ indicated the disposition of the gifts to Peale and the American Philosophical Society. The remainder he may be presumed to have kept for his Indian Hall. He sent to his horticultural friend William Hamilton some seeds Lewis had enclosed in a letter. Correspondence about the shipment and the distribution can be readily seen in Jackson, pp. 248–269. Lemaire received the shipment Aug. 12, 1805, and TJ returned from Monticello Oct. 4.

[37] *Message from the President of the United States, communicating discoveries made in exploring the Missouri, Red River and Washita, by Captains Lewis and Clark, Doctor Sibley, and Mr. Dunbar; with a statistical account of the countries adjacent. February 19, 1806* (Printed by order of the Senate, Washington, 1806). For other editions of this, see Thwaites, I, lxiii–lxv.

The most interesting thing communicated by the President was the letter in which Lewis summed up his progress thus far and sketched his future plans. One promise the explorer was unable to carry out: he did not send some of his men back from the Great Falls of the Missouri, finding that he needed all of them and that the detachment of some would adversely affect the spirits of the others. Jefferson heard nothing further of the expedition until the fall, when Lewis wrote him from St. Louis. Therefore, his report to Congress was limited to the first stage of the long journey.

The map, copies of which were transmitted to both houses, was to be superseded by the much more accurate one made by Clark after his return from the Pacific, but even in this preliminary form it represented an important addition to geographical knowledge.[38] Heeding Jefferson's instructions and availing themselves of Andrew Ellicott's suggestions, the explorers had made frequent observations of latitude and longitude, and thus were able to show the true course, to the Mandan country at least, of the major waterway they were ascending.

The statistical view of the Plains Indians, running to some sixty pages in printed form, did not have such ethnological value as the informal entries in the explorers' journals, and especially those made on later stages of the expedition. The information given by them here bore directly on questions of trade, but as a description of the various tribes, their location, population, and activities, it surpassed both in scope and reliability anything hitherto available to the American government. Thus the fruits of the expedition that the President now displayed were in accord with its practical purposes as originally presented to Congress. He himself drew no sharp line between science and utility, but this bold undertaking as publicly reported could not be well dismissed as a mere "philosophism."[39]

He was well aware that the friendly advances of the government to the Indians had already caused a good deal of trouble and expense, along with some embarrassment. Lewis's reiterated invitations to them to visit the Great White Father were seized upon with avidity. No fewer than forty-five chiefs of the Missouri nations arrived in St. Louis with the barge he dispatched from the Mandan country, and they were unanimous in their desire to proceed to Washington. American offi-

---

[38] A copy of it, made by Nicholas King in 1806, is reproduced in H. R. Friis, "Cartographic and Geographic Activities of the Lewis and Clark Expedition," *Journal of the Washintgon Academy of Sciences*, XLIV (Nov. 1954), 345. See also pp. 348-349 and notes.

[39] With respect to the Indians, the scientific results of the expedition as a whole are well discussed by V. F. Ray and N. O. Lurie in "The Contributions of Lewis and Clark to Ethnography" (*ibid.*). See also Thwaites, VI, sec. 2, "Ethnology."

cials, fearful of the effects on them of a long journey under climatic conditions to which they were unaccustomed, deterred these tribesmen from an immediate pursuance of their purpose. Many of them, along with others who had come earlier, were sent home with presents. In the late autumn of 1805, however, a delegation set out. Jefferson addressed successive groups early in the new year, voicing characteristic sentiments of paternal good will. They visited eastern centers, as the earlier group of Osages had done, and were interviewed in Philadelphia by Dr. Benjamin S. Barton, who commented on their language. The contacts of the red men with the civilization of the white men were not wholly beneficial. Unfortunately, several of the chiefs died. In Washington the Secretary of War admitted that he had been overwhelmed by Indian delegations of late, and it must have seemed to the President also that governmental hospitality had its inconveniences.[40]

Jefferson had no thought of ceasing to offer it, however, and his desire to procure and disseminate accurate information about the Indians, which was such a distinctive feature of his policy, suffered no diminution. Along with Lewis's statistical survey of the nations of Upper Louisiana, he transmitted to Congress sketches of the tribes of Lower Louisiana that had been sent by Dr. John Sibley.[41] That gentleman, who had left his second wife and family in North Carolina when he moved to Louisiana, had been requested by the President through the Secretary of War to act occasionally as an Indian agent. He was authorized to hold in the neighborhood of Natchitoches such conferences as he should deem necessary to secure the friendship of the natives in that quarter, where Spanish influence had to be contended with. He was instructed to distribute presents among them, being allowed $3000 for that purpose, and was to tell them that if they expected to be treated as "the Children of their Great Father, the President of the United States," they must sever connection with any other power. On his justice and friendship they could rely so long as they conducted themselves in a friendly and peaceful manner.[42] There were local objections to Sibley's appointment on moral grounds — it

[40] I make no attempt here to enter into the details of these visitations. There are numerous references to them in letters and documents in Jackson's collection and notes on these: See, for example, pp. 242–243, 261–262, 280–289, 303–307.

[41] "Historical Sketches of the Several Indian Tribes in Louisiana, south of the Arkansa [sic] River, and between the Mississippi and River Grand" in the President's *Message* of Feb. 19, 1806, pp. 66–86.

[42] Dearborn to Sibley, Dec. 13, 1804 (Carter, IX, 352–353). On Oct. 17, 1805, Sibley was commissioned as Indian agent for the part of the Territory of Orleans west of the Mississippi (*ibid.*, IX, 515–516).

was said that he was trying to marry again — but Jefferson rejected charges that he regarded as unproved. His support of this appointee may be attributed, in part at least, to his gratitude for the information about the Indians that the doctor promptly communicated on request.

In a letter to Sibley, Jefferson showed that his own interest in these Indians transcended considerations of security and trade.[43] As his instructions to Lewis had already shown, it extended to their languages, which to his mind offered the best clues to their origins and to the interrelations of the various tribes. He invited the agent to make a contribution to science — that is, to knowledge. In that age this was relatively undifferentiated, and he himself was at the same time both an ethnologist and a philologist. Since his early years, he said, he had been collecting Indian vocabularies on a plan of his own. He had drawn a blank vocabulary, consisting of a list of objects which might be expected to have a name in every language, and had been entering the names as used by many Indian tribes, including most of those east of the Mississippi and a couple that Sibley had mentioned. He sent that distant agent a number of these blank vocabularies, hoping that Sibley would fill them in.

With the message to Congress that constituted his first report to that body on the progress of the exploration of Louisiana, the President also communicated an account of the Red River by Dr. Sibley, "according to the best information he had been able to collect."[44] This was in lieu of information Jefferson had been hoping to gain from the actual exploration of that stream. From at least the fall of 1803 he had had such an enterprise in mind, but in this connection he suffered a succession of disappointments.

The larger plan, as formulated within a few months after he learned of the treaty whereby France ceded Louisiana, looked toward the exploration of all the main waters of the Mississippi, but he was more immediately concerned with the Missouri, which Lewis and Clark were to ascend, and the tributaries of the Mississippi south of that river, the chief of which are the Arkansas and the Red.[45] His thought was to send an expedition to the source of one of these streams; thence it would proceed by land to the source of the other, and down that to the Mississippi. In the spring of 1804, writing to William Dunbar, who

[43] TJ to Sibley, May 27, 1805 (L. & B., XI, 79–81); Dearborn to Sibley, May 25, and TJ to Claiborne, May 26, 1805 (Carter, IX, 449–453).
[44] Letter of Sibley to the Secretary of War, Apr. 10, 1805 (*Message*, pp. 87–115).
[45] Cox, *Early Exploration of Louisiana*, covers all the expeditions of TJ's administration.

had a plantation a few miles south of Natchez, Jefferson said: "I have thought, if Congress should authorize the enterprise, to propose to you the unprofitable trouble of directing it."[46] Dunbar, the son of a Scottish earl and often referred to as Sir William, was a Renaissance man of the Jeffersonian type — variously described as the "intellectual giant" of the Mississippi Territory, the "pioneer scientist" of the region, and the "most distinguished scholar" in Mississippi's annals.[47] He had been called to the President's attention by Andrew Ellicott, with whom he had surveyed the southern boundary at the thirty-first parallel in 1798, by Governor Claiborne, and by others. Jefferson got him elected to the American Philosophical Society and carried on learned correspondence with him for a decade.

In this particular letter to this kindred spirit Jefferson outlined his full plans. The surveys he had in mind, he said, would enable them to prepare a map of Louisiana which would be perfectly correct in its contour and main waters, giving them "a skeleton to be filled up with details hereafter." Congress approved only part of his proposals, however, making what Dunbar regarded as an inadequate appropriation, and the expedition was further limited by other untoward circumstances.[48] A main one, as perceived by Jefferson in the summer, was that a schismatic group in the Osage nation, recently removed to the Arkansas River, would oppose an expedition up that stream. Furthermore, Dunbar and others believed that the Spanish were likely to oppose by strong military force any expedition going beyond Natchitoches on the Red River. Dunbar had expressed the desire to go some distance up that stream, however, and Jefferson thought it important that the preparations already made should not be wasted. Therefore, while postponing the Red River expedition until a more convenient season, he authorized Dunbar to go wherever he should think best. Thus it came about that, accompanied by Dr. George Hunter of Philadelphia, who had been sent as a scientific reinforcement, he explored the Washita (Ouachita) River to Hot Springs, in the present state of Arkansas.[49]

The expedition set out in the middle of October, 1804, and returned

---

[46] TJ to Dunbar, Mar. 13, 1804 (L. & B., XI, 22).

[47] A. H. DeRosier, Jr., "William Dunbar, Explorer," in *Journal of Mississippi History*, XXV (July, 1963), 165–185, is an informing and spirited modern account. Much of the correspondence is in Eron Rowland, *Life, Letters and Papers of William Dunbar* (1930).

[48] See the Secretary of War to James Wilkinson, Mar. 31, 1804 (Carter, IX, 217–218) with editorial note giving detailed references to the Dunbar expedition.

[49] TJ to Dunbar, July 17, 1804 (LC, 24620); Dunbar to TJ, Aug. 18, 1804 (LC, 24753).

in midwinter, taking more than one hundred days altogether. Jefferson's instructions regarding observations and records were similar to those he gave Meriwether Lewis, and both of the leaders were men of science on whose accuracy he believed he could rely. With his message to Congress a year later he transmitted extracts from Dunbar's observations and the latter's map of the rivers he traversed.[50] Both Dunbar and Hunter kept detailed journals, which, like those of Lewis and Clark, afterwards made their way under the President's guidance to the American Philosophical Society. Dunbar's was published a century later, along with Jefferson's own account of the limits and bounds of Louisiana.[51] Precise information about the course of a lesser river was of relatively slight importance for trade in the near future, and only a portion of the information the explorers gained about the country they passed through was made available to the public. But this was intrinsically interesting and by no means without value; later explorers benefited from the practical experience of these men. Forewarned of the difficulty of navigating shallow and winding streams in boats designed for the Mississippi, they could prepare their own craft accordingly. Time was to show, however, that of all the expeditions President Jefferson dispatched only the minor one to Hot Springs and the major one to the Pacific attained their objectives.

[50] *Message* of Feb. 19, 1806, pp. 116-171. Charts are appended to the publication of that year, but the map is not included. TJ had had extracts made from Dunbar's lengthy journal.

[51] *Documents Relating to the Purchase and Exploration of Louisiana* (1904).

[XII]

Explorers' Return

THE report of the successful exploration of the Washita was good news as far as it went, and Jefferson continued to cherish high hopes of mapping the rivers of the continent. Writing William Dunbar a few months after the return of that scientific gentleman from Hot Springs, he said: "The work we are now doing is, I trust, done for posterity, in such a way that they need not repeat it. . . . We shall delineate with correctness the great arteries of this great country. Those who come after us will extend the ramifications as they become acquainted with them, and fill up the canvas we begin." Because of unfavorable circumstances in the Southwest, however, he modified his original plan. Recognizing more fully than hitherto the difficulty of transporting baggage from the head of the Red River to that of the Arkansas, and being aware of the continuing danger from the unfriendly Osages on the latter stream, he concluded that this would have to remain unexplored for the present. The projected mission, whose purposes he defined anew, must be limited to the Red River, which he described as, next to the Missouri, "the most interesting water of the Mississippi."[1]

Not until another year did the expedition start up this interesting waterway. The delay was not owing to financial stringency such as Dunbar had previously deplored, for Congress made an additional appropriation. Finding a leader was a problem: Dunbar was unwilling to be that in person and Dr. Hunter also had other things to do. The choice fell on Thomas Freeman, an engineer who had served and quarreled with Andrew Ellicott on the southern border but who had been restored to official favor. Dr. Peter Custis, a botanist, was finally

---

[1] TJ to William Dunbar, May 25, 1805 (L. & B., XI, 74–78). He was still clinging to his original design when he wrote Dunbar on Mar. 14, 1805 (LC, 25775), giving the Arkansas the phonetic spelling "Arcansa."

chosen as a scientific assistant. In the effort to minimize the danger of Spanish opposition, Jefferson had Governor Claiborne get a passport for the party from the Marqués de Casa Calvo, who was still in New Orleans as commissioner for his government. The Marqués left the city before the expedition set out, however, and the document issued by him would have carried no weight in any case with Captain-General Salcedo at Chihuahua or with the lesser military commanders on the border. Shortly before Freeman began his voyage in the spring of 1806, Governor Claiborne in a letter to Jefferson voiced the fear that it would be interrupted by "our jealous and ill-disposed Spanish neighbors." Soon thereafter, in response to the Governor's representations, the Secretary of War informed him that measures would be speedily taken to improve the fortifications of New Orleans, and that additional troops were being sent there and to Fort Adams.[2] These actions of the government were designed to meet a military situation that had become precarious, but they afforded no help to the explorers who had already embarked.

The expedition of twenty-four men that set out in April, 1806, was met some six hundred miles above the mouth of the Red River by a large body of Spanish soldiers that had been sent to intercept it. Having been instructed to withdraw if confronted by superior force, the Americans promptly did so. This retirement, while necessary, was not calculated to impress the Indians with American might vis-à-vis the Spaniards, and the latter humbled American pride further by cutting down a flag of the United States that had been set up in a Caddo village. Before the summer ended, the expedition was back where it had started. It was not without significance in the annals of inland navigation, for it overcame considerable physical difficulties, but it added little to geographical knowledge and its experience was a sharp reminder of grave uncertainties on the still undefined southwestern boundary.[3] In the annual message to Congress in which he referred briefly to this disappointing venture, the President reported that the Spanish had encroached on territory to which the United States had clear claim. After advancing to the Red River, however, they had withdrawn their forces to the western side of the Sabine, which the United States had offered to recognize as a temporary line of separation between the armed forces of the two countries, pending the outcome of

[2] Claiborne to TJ, Mar. 26, 1806; Dearborn to Claiborne, Apr. 26, 1806 (Carter, IX, 615–616, 627–628).
[3] For an account of the expedition, including its preliminaries, see Cox, *Early Exploration of Louisiana*, chs. VI, IX.

the negotiations between them.[4] Jefferson could not know that, a decade after he left office, the Sabine would be acknowledged as the boundary, but he recognized that under existing circumstances peace would be endangered if Americans should venture beyond it. He remained confident of the ability of his country to establish its claims to the Red River and its tributaries, and was still concerned about relations with the Indians on the upper Arkansas.

For these reasons his approval of the second expedition of Zebulon M. Pike (1806–1807) was to be expected. This was still in progress and Jefferson did not report on it in his message, but he did refer to an earlier expedition of Pike's (1805–1806), saying that the Lieutenant had made "very useful additions" to their knowledge of the Mississippi by ascending it to its source. This explorer had not really found the source of the Mississippi, and he had actually been dispatched by General James Wilkinson, Governor of the Territory of Louisiana, on the latter's own authority. Even though Jefferson had not sponsored the expedition, he welcomed the additional information about the upper stretches of the great river as contained in Pike's journal and map, information which he expected to communicate to Congress later on. Whatever private schemes with respect to the Spanish Wilkinson may have had in mind when dispatching Pike on an expedition to the Southwest, the ostensible objects of this mission were in accord with the general purposes of Jefferson.[5]

A week before the President sent to Congress the annual message in which he reported on the expeditions of exploration, he had issued a proclamation warning against a conspiracy to set on foot a military expedition against the dominions of Spain.[6] The obvious reference was to Aaron Burr, whose mysterious expedition down the Ohio and the Mississippi was the sensation of the season. Jefferson had received news of it before he learned that Lewis and Clark had returned to St. Louis, and it could not have failed to take the edge off the report in the presidential message that these heroic men had completed their peace-

[4] Message of Dec. 2, 1806 (Ford, VIII, 482–495, especially pp. 483–487, 492).

[5] Donald Jackson, ed., *The Journals of Zebulon Montgomery Pike with Letters and Related Documents* (2 vols., 1966) is the indispensable collection of sources for both expeditions and contains invaluable notes. Cox, *Early Exploration of Louisiana*, chs. X–XIII, and W. E. Hollon, *The Lost Pathfinder, Zebulon Montgomery Pike* (1949), chs. VI–XII, deal with both expeditions. The second is dealt with by T. P. Abernethy in *The Burr Conspiracy* (1954), ch. IX, "Pike's Peek." We consider this expedition in the next chapter.

[6] Nov. 27, 1806 (Ford, VIII, 481–482).

ful and fruitful mission across a continent. He mentioned them first among the explorers, rather than in the order we have followed here, and this was entirely proper since they stand first in their group in the history of his administration, as in fact they do in the history of the country. But his relatively brief reference to them was imbedded in a long message and is notable for its restraint. Of the men who had pursued his purposes with such rare diligence and skill he reported that they had achieved all the success that could have been expected. More specifically he said:

> They have traced the Missouri nearly to its source, descended the Columbia to the Pacific ocean, ascertained with accuracy the geography of that interesting communication across our continent, learned the character of the country, of its commerce, and inhabitants; and it is but justice to say that Messrs. Lewis and Clarke, and their brave companions, have by this arduous service deserved well of their country.[7]

An earlier draft of this passage was twice as long and, besides being rather more laudatory in tone, it referred more specifically to the value and usefulness of the discoveries. The change to a briefer and starker form may perhaps be attributed to the prudence of Madison. Fearing that the Spanish might take offense at the mission, the Secretary of State advised that particulars be avoided and no reference be made to the "uses" of the Pacific country.[8] Perhaps Jefferson himself concluded that he must take care not to claim and promise too much. Actually the explorers had returned a negative answer to the major question. There was nothing approximating an all-water route to the Pacific, and with them ended the agelong quest for a northwest passage.[9] There was no short portage between the headwaters of the Missouri and those of the Columbia. Lewis wrote Jefferson that they had gone 340 miles by land and 140 miles over "tremendious mountains." Time was to show that they had not found the lowest or easiest crossing, and later travelers were to follow the Platte rather than the upper Missouri. For these and other reasons the greatest of American explorations could be fairly judged by no criteria of immediate utility. Actually, the rich fruits of this expedition were not to be fully displayed in Jefferson's administration or even in his century. We can

---

[7] In message of Dec. 2, 1806 (*ibid.*, VIII, 492).

[8] A first and a revised draft are in Jackson, p. 352. For Madison's comments, see Ford, VIII, 484*n.*, under the heading "Missouri."

[9] See comment of DeVoto in his edn. of the *Journals*, p. xlix.

know, better than their own contemporaries did, what the explorers endured and what they accomplished. To say this, however, is not to deny that they received much public acclaim in the weeks immediately following their arrival in St. Louis, dressed wholly in buckskins and looking like Robinson Crusoes.[10] They were prominent in the news until Aaron Burr stole the show, and the diversion created by the most colorful adventurer of the era did not prevent them from receiving generous recognition from the government.

The letter in which Lewis announced the safe return of his party reached the President on October 24, 1806, having been a month in transit. Jefferson's reply to it was couched in terms of personal affection rather than official congratulation. After stating that he had received the news with "unspeakable joy" he said: "The unknown scenes in which you were engaged, and the length of time without hearing of you had begun to be felt awfully." Informed that Lewis, before returning to Washington, was going to Charlottesville, where he hoped to find his mother still living, Jefferson addressed him there in care of his brother Reuben.[11] Of his own letter he said: "Its only object is to assure you of what you already know, my constant affection for you and the joy with which all your friends here will receive you." Also, he sent a message to Sheheke, the great Chief of the Mandans, who was accompanying Lewis, saying that his arms were already opened to receive this friend and suggesting that, while in the neighborhood, the Captain take the Chief to see the Indian Hall being set up at Monticello.

All the information Jefferson yet had of the activities and achievements of the explorers since their departure on the second leg of their western journey, a year and a half before, had been gained from Lewis's letter. He quickly made this available to his friend Samuel Harrison Smith, who published in the *National Intelligencer* a summary of it which may perhaps be regarded as a semi-official report.[12] This was copied by many newspapers and probably provided most readers in the seaboard states with their first reliable information about the latter part of the expedition. It was little more than a brief narrative of events, with dates and estimates of distances covered. The total

[10] Description given in the first of the excerpts from early newspaper notices in Thwaites, VII, 347–350. To these excerpts are attached notes showing where and when these were copied.

[11] Meriwether Lewis to TJ, Sept. 23, 1806 (Jackson, pp. 319–324 from LC, 28299–28301); TJ to Reuben Lewis and to Meriwether Lewis, Oct. 26, 1806 (*ibid.*, pp. 350–351). The latter letter in Ford, VIII, 476–477, is wrongly dated Oct. 20.

[12] *National Intelligencer*, Oct. 27, 1806. The notice in Thwaites, VII, 349, is a reduced version of this.

of 3555 miles from the mouth of the Missouri and back must have
seemed appalling in that slow-moving age, and the length of the land
journey to the navigable portion of the Kooskooske must have been as
surprising as the name of the river itself was strange. (Moderns know
that lovely stream as the Clearwater and can see a tablet near the place
where the explorers took to the water after they had emerged from the
mountains.) There were no heroics or colorful details in this factual
account. Lewis was reported as saying that the regions traversed by
him furnished the most valuable furs in the world, and that some of
these might even be traded with China. There was no reference to his
comments on the designs of the British Northwest Company to
engross the fur trade, or to the difficulties imposed on the navigation of
the Missouri by the unfriendliness of certain nations and bands of
Indians. That was confidential, but hardly anything else in Lewis's
letter to Jefferson was. He expected to see his friend and patron in
Washington.

What he told the President privately after his arrival there toward
the end of December we have hardly any way of knowing, for their
conversations were not recorded. One bit of information from him
that Jefferson communicated to the Secretary of War for the benefit
of future explorers was a list of articles desired by the Indians, in the
order of preference. This began with blue beads, which served them as
money, and was followed by common brass buttons, which were
valued even more than knives, battle-axes, and tomahawks, although
these came next.[13] In due course Lewis made detailed reports to the
Secretary of War regarding the personnel and finances of the expedition, but the nearest thing to a formal report on the latter part of it
that he ever made to the President was the letter he wrote on his
arrival in St. Louis in September. Clear evidence that he had sought to
carry out the scientific objects of his mission was afforded by his
statement that, besides Chief Sheheke, he was bringing with him a
number of animal skins and skeletons, a "pretty extensive collection of
plants," and nine more Indian vocabularies. This news undoubtedly
delighted Jefferson, but it was not communicated to the public by the
National Intelligencer. That paper did report that Captain Lewis had
spoken in most affectionate terms of Captain Clark, declaring that his
colleague was entitled to an equal share in whatever merit might be
ascribed to the success of this enterprise. In view of the earlier difficulty about Clark's rank, it was a good thing that this declaration was
publicized in Washington, where he was much less known than Lewis.

13 TJ to Dearborn, Feb. 14, 1807 (Jackson, pp. 374-375).

Such was not the case in Kentucky, however, and it was there that the first and fullest account of the expedition appeared in print in the form of a letter from Clark.

This was addressed to his brother, who was prevailed upon to release it to the press. Published in the Frankfort *Palladium* on October 9, 1806, it was subsequently copied throughout the country. The *National Intelligencer* ran it about a week after publishing the summary of Lewis's letter to Jefferson. Clark's letter resulted from the friendly collusion of the two explorers, who recognized the likelihood that it would get out first and were concerned that it be in good form. Lewis, who was considerably the more literate of the two, drafted it and Clark copied it.[14] Omitting comments on the fur trade and Indians such as were made in Lewis's letter to Jefferson, it gave details of the journey not to be found in that and is a more colorful account. From it their countrymen, including the President himself, could learn that the portage of the falls of the Missouri was "most laborious," that the three forks of that river, 2848 miles from its mouth (as measured through its meanderings), were named by the explorers the Jefferson, the Madison, and the Gallatin; that they passed "almost inexcessable" mountains; that they subsisted at times on berries and at others on dog meat; that, because of their experience, they had better provisions and suffered less fatigue on the homeward journey than when outward bound. This unvarnished tale could hardly have failed to appeal to their adventurous countrymen, and we may suppose that memorable incidents — such as their encounters with the redoubtable grizzly bears in the Rockies — were recounted by them to friends at various stopping places on their way home.

In St. Louis, while winding things up, they had largely transcribed their rough field notes, but these journals remained unseen by readers of newspapers. In the early accounts there was little or nothing to suggest that the explorers had conducted what may be considered the first American scientific survey on a continental scale. Almost the only contributions to knowledge of which their contemporaries became quickly aware were those in the field of geography. One wonders, indeed, how soon or how fully their patron the President realized what they had seen and done after they left the Mandan

[14] For Clark's letter of Sept. 23, 1806, and Lewis's draft of it, with valuable editorial notes, see Jackson, pp. 325–335. The supposition has been that it was to George Rogers Clark, because of the reference to General Clark in the Frankfort *Palladium*, but Jackson thinks it may possibly have been to another brother, General Jonathan Clark, also of Kentucky. Its eastward movement is shown by its appearance in a Pittsburgh paper on Oct. 28, and in the *National Intelligencer* on Nov. 3, 1806.

country for the Pacific. Lewis must have brought the manuscript journals with him to Washington, when he came there toward the end of December. Jefferson may not have had time to do much reading in them then, but during the Captain's winter visit, when he again lived at the President's House, his host had a good chance to talk with him.[15]

Informing its readers with "high satisfaction" of the arrival of Captain Lewis in the capital, the *National Intelligencer* said that few expeditions had been "conducted with more patience, perseverance, or success." This paper also said, however, that it would give no further notice of the expedition at present since Lewis himself promised to lay an account of it before the public. The editor believed that this would "not merely gratify literary curiosity, but open views of great and immediate objects of national utility."[16] Meanwhile, the Indian visitors to the capital attracted much attention. Accompanying the Captain were the Mandan chief Sheheke and his wife and son, along with an interpreter and his family. There was also a group of Osages that Pierre Chouteau had conducted from St. Louis. Some of the Indians contributed to the entertainment of the theatre-going public on one or more occasions by dancing, prancing, and whooping upon the stage. In times past the Great White Father had witnessed war dances, but there appears to be no record of his doing so that winter.[17] He gave other signs of respect for the two groups of visitors from the Missouri country. He addressed his "children" successively on the last two days of the year, employing the eloquence that befitted such occasions.[18] Whether or not the Indians fully perceived the beauty of the metaphors, as conveyed to their ears by an interpreter, and whether or not they had any thought of heeding the exhortations that they maintain peace not only with their white brethren but also with one another, they could hardly have failed to gain the impression that the Chief of the Seventeen Nations, like his brave but tactful emissaries, was a man of good will.

15 Lewis appears to have arrived on Dec. 28, 1806, and unquestionably was in Washington by Dec. 30. He was at the President's House in the following March, when T. M. Randolph was ill and may be presumed to have stayed there during the entire visit.

16 *National Intelligencer*, Dec. 31, 1806.

17 For a description of the two parties of Indians, see Jackson, p. 325, note 7. Accounts of the Indian visit and dancing are in Foster, *Jeffersonian America*, pp. 27–29, and in Plumer, *Memorandum*, p. 554. If the former's chronology may be relied on, these writers described two different occasions. TJ bought two theatre tickets Dec. 22 and presumably attended before the Indians' arrival. He witnessed the war dances of visiting Osage chiefs in the summer of 1804 (*National Intelligencer*, July 20, 1804).

18 Dec. 30, 31, 1806 (Padover, *Complete Jefferson*, pp. 483–487).

Some of the Indian visitors attended the levee in the President's House on New Year's Day, and Sheheke was at the dinner given by the citizens of Washington to Captain Lewis a couple of weeks later. This was delayed for several days in the expectation that Clark could be present to share the honors, but that redoubtable explorer, detained by personal business of the first importance, did not arrive in Washington until the following week. He had been visiting at Fincastle, Virginia, where he was pressing his ultimately successful suit of the lady for whom he had named a river in present-day Montana, Miss Judith Hancock. On this visit he received from the citizenry and responded to an address of congratulation to him and Meriwether Lewis on the success of their mission.[19]

Since the President's presence was not reported in the newspaper account of the dinner for Captain Lewis, we assume he was not among the "several officers of government" who attended.[20] While no one could have esteemed the guest of honor more, Jefferson abominated such occasions, and he may have believed that his presence would distract attention from the returned hero. But if he did not hear the many toasts, including a good one from Lewis himself, or the songs and instrumental music with which these were interspersed, he was not unaware of the most memorable contribution to the celebration — the "elegant and glowing stanzas" penned by Joel Barlow that were recited by John Beckley. The author had sent Jefferson a copy of the poem the day before, along with the suggestion that the Columbia River be renamed Lewis and one of its principal tributaries be named for Clark. The crucial stanza of the metrical version, which mentioned only one hero, read thus:

Then hear the loud voice of the nation proclaim,
    And all ages resound the decree:
Let our Occident stream bear the young hero's name
    Who taught him his path to the sea.

Reading this and other stanzas in the newspaper, a senator who was himself not without literary proclivities found Barlow's "bombast" unendurable, and, while disclaiming any intention to deprecate the public services of Captain Lewis or to deny him his deserved rewards, wrote a parody of the poem which was duly published in Boston. Though anonymous, it was subsequently attributed to John Quincy

[19] Address and response of Jan. 8, 1807, are in Jackson, pp. 358–360. *National Intelligencer*, Jan. 21, 1807, reported his arrival in Washington. He announced his engagement to Miss Hancock after another visit.
[20] *National Intelligencer*, Jan. 16, 1807, reporting the dinner of Jan. 14.

Adams and at a later stage of his career was used to his political disadvantage. Barlow's bombast, bad rhymes, and mixed metaphors deserved exposure; and it is easy to sympathize with the plea for old Columbus, who had already been defrauded of the name of a hemisphere and was now threatened with the loss of that of a river, but in fact the parody did reflect on

> the mighty deeds
> Achiev'd by Captain Lewis.

Also, without mentioning Jefferson's name, it gave the impression that he was absurdly credulous. The reference to the salt mountain was in line with Adams's comments in his diary on the startling stories the President liked to tell his dinner guests. This reference was relatively innocuous in itself, but in context it suggested that the scientific accomplishments of this mission did not match the claims. The reference to "dusky Sally" was unfair and wholly irrelevant. This bit of doggerel, which revealed more wit than most observers would have expected of the sober Senator from Massachusetts and a more partisan spirit than his public actions showed, may perhaps be dismissed as a mere indiscretion. Adams was one Federalist who might have been expected to express strong approval of a thoroughly national enterprise like the expedition of Lewis and Clark.[21]

Shortly after this dinner, a bill for the compensation of Lewis and Clark and the members of their party was introduced in the House, where some objected to it as extravagant but it was eventually passed by an overwhelming vote. The provision for grants of land to be located west of the Mississippi — 1600 acres to each of the leaders and 320 to each of their followers — caused no immediate drain on the treasury. An appropriation was required, however, to carry out the provision that all members of the expedition should receive double pay, and quite obviously this enterprise was considerably more expensive than had been anticipated at the outset. Without entering into the difficult and complicated question of the total cost, or attempting to translate the figures into their modern equivalents, we can at least say

21 For Barlow's letter of Jan. 13, 1807, to TJ, see Jackson, pp. 361–363, containing in the notes a stanza from the poem and one from the parody. The latter appeared in *The Monthly Anthology of Boston* in March, 1807. Entire poem in *National Intelligencer*, Jan. 16, 1807; entire poem and entire parody in E. A. and G. L. Duyckinck, *Cyclopedia of American Literature* (1856), I, 394–395. See also M. A. DeW. Howe in *Procs. M.H.S.*, XLIII (1910), 237–241; and M. D. Peterson, *The Jefferson Image in the American Mind* (1960), pp. 22, 182, on the political uses of the episode in the Jacksonian era. J. Q. Adams recorded one of TJ's "large stories" Feb. 16, 1807 (*Memoirs*, I, 457–458).

---

that, for all Jefferson's economy-mindedness in public matters, he was as little disposed to haggle or hesitate over costs in connection with this continental enterprise as in his own building operations at Monticello. He regarded this expenditure as an investment in the future of the country, from which there were extra dividends to society in the form of knowledge.[22]

Even before Lewis reached Washington, Jefferson had in mind his appointment as governor of the Louisiana Territory, which had had only an acting governor since General James Wilkinson had left it in the previous summer, three months after he had been ordered to proceed to Orleans Territory to assume command of the military forces there. The nomination of Lewis, which Jefferson sent the Senate toward the end of the session, was welcomed by many as an assurance that the Territory would continue to be spared the presence of Wilkinson. It was promptly approved, but the promotion of Clark to the rank of lieutenant colonel, which Jefferson requested at the same time, was disapproved by a large vote. Though the senators were less aware of his merits than they were of Lewis's, this decisive rejection was not owing to failure to appreciate his services and abilities, but to unwillingness to jump him over other men. For the second time he was blocked by the seniority system.[23]

Clark, who had been known on the expedition and has gone down in its history as "Captain," was on the army roll as a first lieutenant by now. Still in Washington when the senators decided to leave him in that rank, he was aware of the reasons assigned and took the rebuff with his customary good grace. Before he left town, however, he had been commissioned as Indian agent in the Territory of Louisiana, and on his visit to Fincastle he was in a position to inform Judy Hancock that he would have an annual salary of $1500.[24] The lady came to

[22] For the Act of Mar. 3, 1807, along with details about the payments made and the land warrants issued under it, see Jackson, pp. 377–378, 380–383. See also the final statement of Lewis's Account (*ibid.*, pp. 424–431). The bill was introduced in the House Jan. 23, debated Feb. 20 and Feb. 28, 1807, when it was adopted with amendments by a vote of 62 to 23 (*Annals*, 9 Cong., 2 sess., pp. 383, 591, 657–659, 1278). The Senate adopted it without a record vote.

[23] TJ made the nominations Feb. 28, 1807, and the Senate acted Mar. 2. The vote against Clark's nomination was 20 to 9. (*Senate Exec. Procs.*, II, 53, 54). See also Plumer, *Memorandum*, pp. 633, 637. In this vote, as in that on the compensation bill in the House, the Federalists were largely if not wholly in the negative, but its decisiveness precludes the possibility of blaming it on partisanship. Jackson says that the *National Intelligencer*, Apr. 20, 1807, commented on the defeat of Clark's nomination.

[24] Dearborn to Clark, Mar. 9, 1807, and commission dated Mar. 7 (Carter, XIV, 108–110).

terms with him on this visit, as he gleefully reported to Lewis soon thereafter. To his regret he had discovered that her father was a "Fed" instead of being "a good plain republican" as he had supposed. The wedding was set for the next January, and at that time he hoped "to introduce some substantial sincere republicanism into some branch of the family." Meanwhile, he had received from Lewis a commission as brigadier general of the militia of the Territory.[25] Thus he was not without military honor when, returning to St. Louis, he assumed a post for which he was admirably qualified.

He met difficulties in his effort to carry out his instructions to speed the Mandan chief and his family back to their own country. The expedition of fifteen soldiers and upwards of a score of traders that set out with him in the summer had to turn back because of the Arikaras, who, besides being at war with the Mandans, were infuriated with the Americans because of the death of their chief in Washington. Clark learned of this failure in the fall of 1807, while visiting in Kentucky on his way to Virginia for his bride, and the "reconveyance" of Chief Sheheke was not accomplished until after Jefferson had retired from the presidency. Meriwether Lewis was responsible for the costly arrangements that were ultimately made; and the frustrations incident to this episode were to enter tragically into the final stage of his career. The situation was to worsen, but doubts must already have arisen regarding the wisdom of the original invitation to this chief to visit the President.[26]

Meanwhile, in Kentucky in the fall of 1807, General William Clark directed digging (by ten laborers) at Big Bone Lick for specimens for the eminent collector in the President's House. In number the bones procured by the indefatigable explorer and shipped to Washington by way of New Orleans surpassed the expectations of his patron. They belonged chiefly to the mammoth and the elephant, in Clark's opinion. Except for a tusk and femur that Jefferson wanted for a cabinet of his own at Monticello, he had intended these bones to supplement the collection of the American Philosophical Society. But, when most of them turned out to be duplicates, he decided to present these to the Institute of France, to which as a member he thought he ought to contribute something. He sent them in the summer of 1808, along with the horns of a mountain ram and a skin of the "fleecy goat." These had

25 Lewis to Clark, Mar. 18, 1807, and Clark's undated reply (Jackson, pp. 387–388).
26 Clark to the Secretary of War, May 18, 1807 (Carter, XIV, 122–125; Jackson, pp. 411–412); Nathaniel Pryor to Clark, Oct. 16, 1807, announcing the return of the expedition (Jackson, pp. 432–438).

been procured on the great expedition to the West, and the bones from Kentucky may be regarded as a by-product of this.[27]

Writing the French naturalist Lacépède about these gifts, Jefferson expressed satisfaction with the scientific contributions of the explorers. "I can assure you," he said, "that the addition to our knowledge, in every department, resulting from this tour of Messrs. Lewis and Clark has entirely fulfilled my expectations in setting it on foot, and that the world will find that those travellers have well earned its favor."[28] They undoubtedly enjoyed the favor of the savants of the American Philosophical Society (which was to become in effect their residual legatee) and by this time had gained the gratitude of the horticulturists McMahon and Hamilton, who had shared the seeds and roots of indigenous plants Lewis had brought back with him from the other half of the continent. Keeping very few for himself, since he was not in a position to do justice to them, Jefferson distributed them in equal parts. McMahon was the more successful in growing plants from them, and in due course he went to great pains to have accurate drawings of these plants made.[29] Charles Willson Peale was especially in the explorers' debt, and in Jefferson's, for additions to his museum in Philadelphia. Lewis visited that city in the spring after his return and Peale did his portrait with particular pleasure. During the summer Peale mounted the head and horns of the big horn sheep for Jefferson, with whom he corresponded incessantly.[30] This was destined for the hall at Monticello, he said. Not all of the articles intended for that place reached it. Certain boxes that Lewis sent by way of New Orleans arrived in New York and were shipped thence to Washington or some nearby port. Jefferson in turn sent heavy things (including groceries and household goods) to Richmond by water. The vessel carrying one of his shipments stranded, and everything was lost that water could

[27] In letters of Oct. 10 and Nov. 10, 1807, William Clark listed bones shipped to TJ (LC, 30271–30273, 30419–30424). TJ asked for additional specimens that had been left with George Rogers Clark and invited Dr. Caspar Wistar to visit Washington and examine the collection to make sure the American Philosophical Society should get everything it wanted. (To Caspar Wistar, to William Clark, and to G. R. Clark, Dec. 19, 1807 (L. & B., XI, 403–405). Several letters bear on Wistar's visit, into which we do not enter here. H. C. Rice, Jr., "Jefferson's Gift of Fossils to the Museum of Natural History in Paris" (*Procs. Am. Philos. Soc.*, Dec., 1951, pp. 597–627) describes the entire operation and prints the letters.

[28] TJ to Bernard Lacépède, July 14, 1808 (Jackson, pp. 442–443).

[29] TJ's enthusiastic correspondence with Bernard McMahon and William Hamilton in this period can be readily located in Jackson and *Garden Book*. Of particular interest are McMahon to TJ, June 28, 1808, speaking of his success in raising Lewis's plants, and TJ's reply of July 6 (Jackson, pp. 441–442).

[30] C. W. Peale to John Hawkins, May 5, 1807 (Jackson, pp. 410–411); Lewis to TJ, June 27, 1807 (*ibid.*, p. 418).

injure. It could not injure the horns Lewis had brought him, but that explorer thought it peculiarly unfortunate that other articles which had crossed the continent should have been lost in the passage of a small part of the Chesapeake.[31]

Hazards of another sort accompanied a gift to the presiding American scientist by another explorer. In the autumn of 1807 Captain Zebulon M. Pike, who had ventured farther to the southwest than he originally intended, sent Jefferson two grizzly cubs he had captured near the continental divide. If Jefferson had not yet read in the manuscript journals of Lewis and Clark about their encounters with the grizzly, he had learned enough from them in person to recognize this animal as the most formidable on the continent. Nonetheless, he emphasized the gentleness of the cubs when he offered them to Charles Willson Peale, to be exhibited in Peale's museum for the edification of his countrymen. Jefferson reported that while he had them they played happily together, though a little roughly at first, and that when they were caged separately one of them became almost furious. He observed that one of them was much crosser than the other — neglecting to say whether this was the male or the female — but did not believe that they had any idea of hurting anyone. "They know no benefactor but man," he said. Events proved that in this instance he viewed animal nature with unwarranted optimism, as at times he did human nature. Peale, another inveterate optimist, gladly accepted the cubs, but when they grew older and bigger one of them escaped from his cage and terrified the family — with the result that both bears were killed and stuffed. In this harmless form Peale continued to exhibit them.[32]

The tangible scientific fruits of the Lewis and Clark expedition — in the form of seeds, skins, horns, bones, and other articles — were necessarily limited by the lack of facilities for packing and preserving them and by the difficulties of transportation. The reading public had received only brief accounts of the actual events of the long and hazardous journey and was little aware of the additions to knowledge resulting from it. Before the end of the congressional session following

[31] J. L. Donaldson to TJ, Jan. 11, 1807; TJ to Lewis, June 4, 1807, from Monticello; Lewis to TJ, June 27, 1807, from Philadelphia (Jackson, pp. 360, 415, 418). Presumably the two pairs of horns, elk and moose, now over the front door at Monticello, are the ones referred to in this correspondence.

[32] Pike to TJ, Oct. 29, 1807; TJ to Pike, Nov. 5, 1807, and to Peale, Nov. 6; TJ to Peale, Feb. 6, 1808 (Jackson, *Journals of Pike*, II, 275–276, 278–279, 294); Peale to TJ, Jan. 29, 1808 (Jackson, *Letters of Lewis and Clark*, pp. 439–440, with note).

his return, Lewis, who had become aware that spurious and inadequate accounts based on the journals of lesser members of his company might be published, formally announced his intention to prepare an adequate work. He did this in a letter and prospectus which appeared in the *National Intelligencer* and other papers. Soon thereafter, a Philadelphia printer, who went so far as to estimate the cost, issued an impressive prospectus of a work in three volumes. The first of these was to be primarily a narrative and contain a good-sized map; the second was to deal with geography and the Indians; and the third was to be devoted to scientific matters, especially the natural history of the regions visited. When the prospective author was in Philadelphia later in the spring of 1807, after he had helped nurse Thomas Mann Randolph and after Jefferson and Randolph had gone home, he had abundant opportunity to discuss the projected work with the printer, and also with his fellow members of the American Philosophical Society.[33]

No one could possibly have been more pleased by this prospect than Jefferson, and he may have discussed the undertaking with Lewis when they saw each other during the summer. But, after the two men parted in September, the elder received from the younger only three or four letters altogether. The Governor of Louisiana Territory had with him the precious journals in which he and his colleague had recorded their activities and observations day by day, but he was in no writing mood. Jefferson, who was so tolerant of persons he trusted, may have erred on the side of patience, but he himself had a great many things to do. Ten months after he last saw Lewis he chided his former secretary for not communicating with him or the Secretary of War, speaking particularly of their desire to receive the Governor's counsel regarding the long-delayed return of Chief Sheheke to the Mandan country. The good faith of the nation was pledged to this, he said, and something must be done about it. At the same time the President reported a bit of news which should have gratified the leader of the expedition to Oregon: a powerful company was being formed to engage in Indian commerce on a large scale. This was under the direction of "a most excellent man," Mr. Astor, a merchant of New York. Regarding the publishing project, Jefferson said only this: "We have no tidings yet of the forwardness of your printer. I hope the first part will not be

<hr>

[33] Lewis to the Public, Mar. 14, 1807, first printed in *National Intelligencer*, Mar. 17 (Jackson, pp. 385–386 with note); John Conrad's estimate and prospectus of c. Apr. 1, 1807 (*ibid.*, pp. 392–397); rival projects of Robert Frazer and Patrick Gass (*ibid.*, pp. 345–346; 399–408). TJ, back in Washington after his visit home, wrote TMR Mar. 24, 1807 (MHS) that Lewis was expected to return from Philadelphia about July 1.

delayed much longer." Had he known the actual situation he might have said of these publishing matters, as he did of the country's foreign affairs, that they did not seem to clear up at all.[34]

He could have made precisely the same observation in the letter he wrote Lewis more than a year later, when he was no longer President. After introducing an Englishman who was on a botanizing tour and might be a good man for Lewis to consult regarding his own botanical observations, Jefferson said: "I am very often applied to know when your work will begin to appear; and I have so long promised copies to my literary correspondents in France, that I am almost bankrupt in their eyes. I shall be very happy to receive from yourself information of your expectations on this subject. Everybody is impatient for it."[35] He received no such information, and in the first summer of his retirement he learned that virtually all of the Indian vocabularies he had been collecting for thirty years, and to which the explorers had made additions, had been lost on their way from Washington. Writing Dr. Benjamin S. Barton about this "irreparable misfortune," he said he still had one morsel he had received from Captain Lewis.[36] But in more than two years he had received no literary or scientific fruits from the explorer he loved and honored most.

Toward the end of November, 1809, when he had been nearly nine months out of office, he learned of the death of Lewis on his way east, from bullet wounds presumed to have been self-inflicted. At the same time Jefferson was informed that one of Lewis's bills had been protested by the Secretary of War, and he probably surmised that the main purpose of the trip was to straighten out his accounts. Yet the former President could not have been fully aware of the financial tangle in which the Governor had become involved in connection with the return of Chief Sheheke to his own country. About ten days before his patron retired from office, Lewis signed an agreement with the St. Louis Fur Company whereby Sheheke and his entourage were to journey homeward under the guardianship of 125 militiamen. These were to be recruited by the company, which was to enjoy certain trading opportunities and receive $7000. Lewis's drafts up to that amount were honored by Madison's Secretary of War, William Eustis, but that official showed annoyance at his failure to consult the Depart-

[34] TJ to Lewis, July 17, 1808 (Ford, IX, 199–200; Jackson, pp. 444–446, with good notes); TJ to John Jacob Astor, Apr. 13, 1808 (L. & B., XII, 28). He did not establish his post Astoria until 1811.

[35] TJ to Lewis, Aug. 16, 1809 (Jackson, pp. 458–459).

[36] TJ to B. S. Barton, Sept. 21, 1809 (*ibid.*, p. 465). The trunk containing the vocabularies was stolen and the contents scattered by the disappointed thief. Only a few pages were recovered.

ment and declined to honor a further draft. (The additional expenses of this operation bring the estimated total to some $10,000.) That Lewis deserved so sharp a rebuke is highly questionable, but the facts are that, at long last and apparently in a mood of desperation, he carried out the instructions of Jefferson at an embarrassing cost and began his journey eastward in a distressed state of mind.[37]

Added to Lewis's frustrations arising from the fantastic episode of the Mandan chief were those connected with his own failure to proceed with the writing project he had announced more than two years before. Whether or not this troubled man would ever have completed it if his journey had not been so abruptly terminated, no one can know. We do know that among his effects that were sent to Jefferson were the notebooks containing most of the journals of the expedition to the Pacific.[38] The ex-President had no reason to anticipate that these would remain unpublished until the twentieth century, or even that he would have to wait five more years for a reliable published account of the expedition. But he had the satisfaction of knowing that his instructions had been followed — that invaluable source materials had been assembled and preserved.[39]

These later events, and his own subsequent efforts to disseminate knowledge of the most successful expedition he had fathered, do not belong in the story of his presidency. While still in office he must have realized that in important respects it had not fulfilled his hopes. It had caused the courses of the Missouri and the Columbia to be charted but had also disclosed the extent of the mountain barrier that blocked the way to the Pacific. Though the explorers had been notably skillful in their dealings with the Indians, hostile nations continued to threaten prospective traders, and the friendly Mandan chief who had been induced to visit the Great White Father was confronted with almost insuperable obstacles on his way home. No doubt the relative position of Americans vis-à-vis their British commercial rivals in the Northwest had been improved, but there was little reason to believe that the

[37] The estimate of the total cost of the "reconveyance" of the Mandan chief is that of Jackson, p. 431n. The pertinent documents, including the agreement of Feb. 24, 1809, with the St. Louis Fur Co.; Eustis to Lewis, July 15, 1809, and Lewis to Eustis, Aug. 18, 1809; James Neelly to TJ, Oct. 18, 1809 (received Nov. 21), announcing Lewis's death; and Chouteau to the Secretary of War, Dec. 14, 1809, describing the successful expedition to the Mandan country, are in Jackson, pp. 446-461, 467-468, 479-484.

[38] Item in "Memorandum of Lewis's Personal Effects" (ibid., p. 471).

[39] The Original Journals, ed. by R. G. Thwaites, were published in 8 vols. in 1904-1905 (their history is told in vol. I, xxxiv-lx). The History of the Expedition, by Nicholas Biddle, prepared for the press by Paul Allen, appeared in 1814 (2 vols.).

preachments of the President and his emissaries would deter the Indian nations from warring among themselves. The explorers had provided a fresh body of information about the tribes east of the Rockies, but their detailed observations on those of the transmontane country and the Pacific coast, which were to be so greatly prized by the anthropologists and ethnologists of a later time, remained locked in their journals — along with their comments on the flora and fauna of the region, which latter-day botanists and zoologists were to seize upon.[40]

While the actual achievements of this expedition were not and would not soon be fully known, the lack of success in the Southwest was immediately apparent. The peaceful exploration of the region below the Missouri had been blocked by hostile Indians and Spaniards. There the great arteries had not been delineated as Jefferson had planned. He had reason to be disappointed that achievement was so limited, that so many hopes had failed.

But his vision extended farther and comprehended more than that of anybody else in public life, and, thinking of himself as working for posterity, he was more concerned that things should be well started than that they be quickly finished. In his mid-sixties, when discussing gardening, he once said that men of his age should really confine themselves to annuals. Nevertheless, he continued to plant trees whose full growth he could not hope to see. In few things that he did as President was he more in character than as a patron of exploration, and he could well afford to leave his performance in that role to the judgment of posterity. One may doubt if any successor of his ever approached it.

[40] The scientific contributions of the expedition are described and assessed in the Lewis and Clark Anniversary number, *Journal of the Washington Academy of Sciences* (Nov., 1954). The articles deal at some length with the contributions to geography, botany, and ethnography, but the one on zoology is brief, since the contributions in this field were regarded by the author as slight in comparison with those in the others. They are described in considerable detail, however, in R. D. Burroughs, ed., *Natural History of the Lewis and Clark Expedition* (1961).

Conspiracy and Domestic Security

[XIII]

Enter General Wilkinson

JEFFERSON said afterwards that he did not learn of the conspiracy of Aaron Burr until September, 1806, which was just about the time that Lewis and Clark returned, and did not get a specific view of its objects until a month after that.[1] Not even yet are scholars fully agreed as to what these objects were, but, having access to once-secret documents, they know more about the inception of the conspiracy than he did. Accordingly, it may now be dated back to meetings between Vice President Burr and General James Wilkinson in Philadelphia shortly after Hamilton's fatal "interview" with the former at Weehawken in the summer of 1804, or even to a visit the General made Burr in New York before the duel, on his own return from New Orleans after the delivery of the province of Louisiana to the United States.[2] Scholars can only speculate about what was said at these meetings, and Jefferson may be presumed to have known nothing about them. Nor was he in position to read Anthony Merry's dispatches to his home government, which show that Burr was weaving a web of intrigue by the time he relinquished the vice-presidential office in March, 1805. He then broached a plan to separate the western states from the Union with British aid — aid which, as afterwards appeared, was not forthcoming.[3] Meanwhile, Jefferson had made certain territorial appointments by means of which he may seem to have played unwittingly into Burr's hands.

In the summer of 1804 he appointed James Brown as secretary and J. B. Prevost, Burr's stepson, as one of the judges of the newly created

---

[1] TJ to Gideon Granger, Mar. 9, 1814 (Ford, IX, 456).

[2] T. P. Abernethy, *The Burr Conspiracy* (1954), pp. 14–15; Nathan Schachner, *Aaron Burr* (1937), p. 282. Each of these books is referred to hereafter merely by the author's name.

[3] Merry to Harrowby, Mar. 29, 1805, No. 15, Most Secret (FO, 5:45).

Territory of Orleans (Lower Louisiana). But, however welcome these appointments may have been to Burr, they can be easily explained without reference to his personal influence. James Brown was a brother of Senator John Brown of Kentucky, who was close to Burr, but the Senator had been a friend of Jefferson's since his days as a law student in Virginia and was a loyal supporter of the President. Furthermore, James Brown was an able lawyer, whose appointment was strongly approved of by Claiborne. Actually, he served only a few months, to the Governor's great regret. As for Prevost, he had been called to Jefferson's attention in 1801 by James Monroe and had himself applied for the post of judge in 1803. It would appear that these particular appointments had no appreciable conspiratorial significance when the President made them.[4]

More attention must be given the appointments to the Louisiana Territory (Upper Louisiana) in March, 1805. These were necessitated by an act passed by Congress at the very end of the session. Burr's brother-in-law, Joseph Browne, was named secretary of the new territory, seemingly on his sole recommendation, and General James Wilkinson was appointed governor.[5] Writing his daughter Theodosia, the former Vice President said: "Wilkinson and Browne will suit most admirably as eaters and laughers, and, I believe, in all other particulars."[6] While his final phrase was ambiguous, he was undoubtedly pleased with the prospect. But there was no apparent reason why, at this particular time, Jefferson should either have suspected Burr of ulterior motives in seeking for his brother-in-law a minor post in a remote place or should have wanted to gratify him by making the appointment. Now out of office, Burr had no political power base, and as yet there was no sufficient reason for Jefferson to suppose that he hoped to establish one beyond the mountains. Offices in the territories were hard to fill, and the appointment of Browne probably seemed inconsequential.

That of Wilkinson as governor was another matter and we may properly ask why Jefferson made it. He had inherited from the previ-

[4] See TJ to James Brown, July 20, 1804, and J. B. Prevost to TJ, July 26, 1804 (Carter, IX, 269–270, with notes). Also, TJ to Claiborne, Aug. 30, 1804 (*ibid.*, IX, 282); Claiborne to TJ, Oct. 5, 1804, and Jan. 10, 1805 (*ibid.*, IX, 307, 366). Schachner (p. 263) and Adams (*History*, III, 219–220) refer to these two appointments along with those to the Louisiana Territory, making too much of the former if not of the latter, in my opinion.

[5] Act for the Government of Louisiana Territory, Mar. 3, 1805; Burr to TJ, Mar. 10, 1805; the President to the Secretary of State, Mar. 11, 1805; commissions dated Mar. 11, 1805 (Carter, XIII, 92–100, with notes).

[6] Mar. 10, 1805 (Mark Van Doren, ed., *Correspondence of Aaron Burr and His Daughter Theodosia* [1929], p. 204).

GENERAL JAMES WILKINSON
Portrait by Charles Willson Peale

ous administration this flamboyant officer, who, throughout a fantastic career, aroused suspicions in the minds of many of his contemporaries while casting a spell on others. In our own time he has been described on high scholarly authority as "the most skillful and unscrupulous plotter this country has ever produced," but the extent of his villainy and double-dealing was not unmistakably revealed until after scholars had explored the Spanish archives, where for generations proof of major machinations of his lay hidden.[7] Rumors that the Commanding General of the United States Army was in the pay of Spain were widely circulated during the presidency of John Adams. Wilkinson, a native of Maryland who was an officer during the American Revolution, moved to Kentucky afterwards and engaged in commerce and land speculation. How much George Washington knew about his involvement in the "Spanish Conspiracy," which was designed to effect the separation of remote Kentucky from the Union, would be difficult to ascertain, but the first President commissioned him a lieutenant colonel on his return to the army in 1791 and promoted him to brigadier general after about a year. He became the ranking officer on the death of Anthony Wayne late in 1796. While well aware of the value of his knowledge of the frontier and of his skill as a wilderness diplomat, Washington was also aware of discreditable rumors about him and, toward the end of his administration, made private inquiry with respect to these. As a result, charges that the General was a pensioner of Spain were in the files of Adams's Secretary of State.[8]

It was probably because of the belief that these charges could not be substantiated without Spanish corroboration, which was not to be expected, that nothing was done about them. The second President quieted Wilkinson's apprehensions. Writing him early in 1798, John Adams said that scarcely anybody arrived from the Mississippi region without bringing the rumor that he was in the pay of Spain. "They seem to be in such a temper, that nobody escapes accusation," he observed. After stating that these rumors had made no impression on him, Adams thus expressed his confidence in the Commanding General: "I esteem your talents, I respect your services, and feel an attachment to your person, as I do to every man whose name and

[7] Abernethy, p. 15; for a summary of Wilkinson's earlier career, see pp. 4–5.
[8] Andrew Ellicott to Timothy Pickering, Nov. 14, 1798 (C. V. Mathews, *Andrew Ellicott: His Life and Letters* [1908], pp. 161–163). See also Ellicott's deposition of May 22, 1808, in Wilkinson's *Memoirs of Our Own Times* (1816), II, App. XXVIII.

character I have so long known in the service of our country, whose behavior has been consistent."[9]

In these years of national beginnings and localized patriotism, intrigue with officials of other nations was much more common than afterwards, and reports of it were rife. But, during the interim between the assumption of American sovereignty at Natchez in 1798, when the Spanish finally recognized the thirty-first parallel as the boundary line, and the transfer of Louisiana to the United States, even the Spanish seem to have regarded Wilkinson as loyal to his own government. It was in 1804, when he was in New Orleans to receive, with Acting Governor Claiborne, the newly acquired province, that his secret intrigue with the Spaniards was resumed.[10] We now know that he requested the arrears on his pension and that he actually got 12,000 pesos. This was in return for his "Reflections" on boundaries and the military situation and his promise to ascertain and report on the plans of his own government.[11]

We may doubt if the Spanish got their money's worth: he seems to have told them little they did not know already or could not have easily ascertained, and he may have suggested little or nothing they would not have thought of anyway. But he unquestionably sank to dark depths of treachery in pursuit of personal gain. This transaction was to be a closely guarded secret, Wilkinson being referred to as Number 13. He purchased a cargo of sugar with his Mexican dollars, and, when rumors arose about his newly acquired wealth, claimed that he had realized on an old tobacco contract with the Spanish. No legal proof to the contrary was available to his critics. It was characteristic procedure for the General to attribute to his enemies, who were numerous, reports unfavorable to himself; and, at a time of rancorous politics and wild rumors, his loyal friends were disposed to accept his ingenious explanations.

Of him a modern scholar has said: "He was a consummate liar and endowed with a genius for imposing on abler men, as for example Aaron Burr and Thomas Jefferson. He seemed to compel them to do

[9] Adams to Wilkinson, Feb. 4, 1798 (*Works*, VIII, 563–564). Wilkinson included this letter in his *Memoirs*, II, 154–156, effectively italicizing some of its expressions.
[10] I. J. Cox, "General Wilkinson and His Later Intrigues with the Spaniards" (*A.H.R.*, July, 1914, pp. 794–812).
[11] "Reflections on Louisiana by Vincente Folch" in J. A. Robertson, ed. and trans., *Louisiana under the Rule of Spain, France, and the United States, 1785–1807*, II (1911), 325–347. The signature of the Governor of West Florida, one of the principals in the negotiation, was used in order to protect Wilkinson.

his bidding through some form of hypnosis."[12] We may report at this point his claim to the Spanish that he knew "what was concealed in the heart of the President."[13] This sounds like an idle boast. Although he had gratified Jefferson in times past by sending him curiosities from the frontier, no intimacy between them had been established. There are clear signs, however, of Wilkinson's intimacy with influential men who could reach the ear of the President, whether or not they could read his heart. Among these was Samuel Smith from Wilkinson's native state of Maryland, who as a member of Congress played a significant part in the electoral contest between Jefferson and Burr, and who afterwards as a senator was a political power to be reckoned with. His brother Robert was secretary of the navy. Throughout this administration, also, Wilkinson was befriended by his immediate civil superior, Secretary of War Dearborn, in whose integrity Jefferson had full confidence and whose loyalty to him and to the country, in fact, cannot be seriously doubted.

About three years before Wilkinson renewed his Spanish connections, Jefferson received from Samuel Smith the suggestion that he appoint the General governor of Mississippi Territory. This the President declined to do on the ground that the civil and military authority should not be combined, and on the further ground that residence at Natchez would interfere with Wilkinson's "superintendence of the military posts" as Commanding General of the Army.[14] Since Jefferson would have liked to gratify Smith at this time, he may have overstated his regret, but he gave no sign that he disapproved of Wilkinson. He said he sincerely wished that the General could receive this appointment and that they must help him in some other way. Wilkinson, who set a high value on his own services, was extraordinarily successful in convincing his influential friends, like Samuel Smith and Dearborn, that he needed and deserved more money. His salary as a brigadier general was $225 a month, which would not carry a free spender very far even in that day. His private operations had not been profitable, and he was getting nothing from the Spanish at this time.

Means were found to supplement his inadequate army pay. Before the Louisiana Purchase he was for several years an Indian commissioner, receiving special compensation for this according to accepted practice. He rendered services that the government valued, and, although certain critical congressmen who afterwards examined his

---

[12] W. F. McCaleb, *New Light on Aaron Burr* (1963), p. 18. While this author's view of Burr is questioned by Abernethy and others, there is little disposition among scholars to defend Wilkinson.

[13] Cox, "General Wilkinson and His Later Intrigues," p. 797.

[14] TJ to Samuel Smith, Mar. 24, 1801 (Ford, VIII, 28–29).

accounts regarded these services as disproportionately expensive, he endured considerable hardship. According to his own account he traveled, in the years 1802–1803, more than sixteen thousand miles on public business through forests and on inland waterways.[15] The cost of his hospitality in New Orleans, when he represented his government there in 1803–1804, was unquestionably excessive according to the standards of the day. At public expense he celebrated the acquisition of Louisiana to the tune of more than $6,600, which no doubt he thought the country could well afford since it had made such a wonderful bargain. It was at just this time that, to meet his incessant demands, the Spaniards made a financial deal with him. Jefferson was unaware of it, to be sure, and not until the end of the administration was there a full revelation of how much Wilkinson had cost the government in dollars and cents. It finally came out that extra allowances had been made him for rations and quarters — in violation of the law in the opinion of many, although the Attorney General gave an opinion to the contrary. The extent of Jefferson's permissiveness in these matters seems impossible to determine, but we may perhaps assume that he was imperfectly aware of what was going on until he felt himself committed by the course of events to defend Wilkinson against his critics. There seems little doubt that Dearborn, besides granting the General special favors such as permitting him to receive advance payments on his salary, shielded his friend. Jefferson tended to err on the side of trustfulness in dealing with officials whom he regarded as personally loyal, and complaints against the Commanding General were based chiefly on hearsay. Like Washington and Adams before him, Jefferson started out by regarding Wilkinson as a useful man on the frontier, and thus he long continued to regard him.[16]

The recess appointment as governor of the Louisiana Territory that Jefferson gave Wilkinson, a week after Congress had adjourned and he himself had entered on his second term, can be more naturally attributed to the General's representations to his friends Samuel Smith and Dearborn and their representations to the President than to direct effort on the part of Burr, even though the former Vice President was

[15] *Memoirs* (1816), I, vii; see also J. R. Jacobs, *Tarnished Warrior* (1938), pp. 195–199.

[16] A committee of the House of Representatives, after an investigation, made a detailed report on Wilkinson's financial relations with the government, Feb. 22, 1809 (National Archives). Mary P. Adams, in her useful dissertation, "Jefferson's Military Policy" (UVA, 1958), has drawn extensively on this (especially pp. 91–117). I have greatly benefited from her study. For a comment on the value of Wilkinson's services as Commanding General, see Jackson, *Pike Journals*, II, 102–103n.

222 JEFFERSON THE PRESIDENT: SECOND TERM

responsible for the appointment of his own brother-in-law as territorial secretary. Wilkinson was in town during the congressional session and it would have been like him to expatiate upon the inadequacy of his salary as an officer and the value of his services to the country. As governor he would receive each year $2000 in addition to his $2700 as a brigadier general. Besides the secretary, Jefferson appointed at this time three judges. In this stage of territorial government they shared legislative powers with the governor.[17] Burr promptly commended Wilkinson to one of them, as also did Postmaster General Granger, who had this to say of him: "He is one of the most agreeable, best informed, most genteel, moderate and sensible republicans in the nation."[18] But in the fierce quarrels that ensued in Upper Louisiana in the next few months all three of these men were antagonistic to Wilkinson, and a major line of division was that between the party of the judges and that of the Governor.[19] A conflict of authority also arose between Wilkinson and the previously appointed commandants of districts, who had brevet military rank and both military and civil functions. Wittingly or unwittingly, Jefferson had created a sort of balance of forces, although he certainly did not thereby attain equilibrium.

Reports of fierce dissension in the territory, coupled with conflicting explanations of its causes, reached the high officials of the government during the late summer and fall of 1805.[20] The local alignment was reflected in the Senate when that body got around to voting on the nominations. There was strong opposition to both Wilkinson and Judge J. B. C. Lucas, and with few exceptions those who opposed the one favored the other. In the case of the latter, who was confirmed by the margin of only one vote, Wilkinson's particular friends, Samuel Smith of Maryland and John Smith of Ohio, were in opposition along with the Federalists, who were said to have objected to the part Lucas

17 Act of Mar. 3, 1805, Sections 3, 4 (Carter, XIII, 93).

18 Burr to Rufus Easton, Mar. 18, 1805; Gideon Granger to Easton, Mar. 16, 1805 (W. V. N. Bay, *Reminiscences of the Bench and Bar of Missouri* [1878], pp. 81, 598).

19 The commission of Wilkinson was dated Mar. 11, 1805, as were those of Joseph Browne as secretary, and Return J. Meigs, Jr., as judge. John B. C. Lucas was commissioned as judge, Mar. 12, and Rufus Easton as judge, Mar. 13, 1805. The latter, a friend of Gideon Granger's whom Burr sought unsuccessfully to cultivate, was not renominated in December (Carter, XIII, 98–101, 105).

20 The confusion and dissension in Louisiana Territory is abundantly documented in Carter, vol. XIII. Wilkinson's cause was presented by him in such letters as those he wrote the secretaries of War and State (*ibid.*, pp. 164–172, 189–191, 302–306). Among letters criticizing him are several to the Attorney General and the Secretary of the Treasury (pp. 270–276, 286–289, 319–324).

had played in the impeachment and conviction of Judge Addison of Pennsylvania. The vote on Wilkinson was not quite so close (17 to 14), but the pattern was essentially the same in reverse, since the Federalists and the two friendly Smiths voted for him while nearly all the other Republicans opposed. The ostensible ground for the objection of the latter to his appointment was the union of civil and military authority in one person, which they regarded as unrepublican.[21] Discreditable reports about Wilkinson's actions in St. Louis were afloat, but there was no apparent reason to give these a conspiratorial interpretation.

By this time Jefferson had received a warning against the "intrigues" of Colonel Burr. This came in an anonymous hand-printed letter, mailed in Philadelphia, which reached him on December 1, 1805, and was followed a few days later by another from the same "Friend."[22] In these communications Burr was charged with being a *British* pensioner and Wilkinson's name did not appear. About two weeks after the General's confirmation as governor, however, a charge that he was a pensioner of Spain reached Jefferson in Washington. This came from Joseph H. Daveiss, United States attorney for Kentucky, in a confidential letter warning the President of a widespread western plot against the Union but not mentioning Burr.[23] Thoroughly convinced that Wilkinson was in Spanish pay, Daveiss mentioned Andrew Ellicott's early report of it (to Adams's Secretary of State) and said that a hint to the wise was sufficient. The President was enjoined to maintain secrecy, although he might show the letter to Madison and Gallatin. Besides them, Jefferson consulted Dearborn, who may be presumed to have reassured him. The comments of the Secretary of the Treasury are of special significance because the most damaging recent reports on the Governor's conduct had been made to him. Said Gallatin:

[21] TJ sent the nominations to the Senate, Dec. 20, 1805, and consent was given Jan. 27, 1806 (*Senate Exec. Procs.*, II, 8, 18). Plumer commented on the vote Jan. 27, saying regretfully that nearly three days had been spent on the nominations of Wilkinson and Lucas (*Memorandum*, pp. 392-393). He did not express his personal distrust of Wilkinson until later.

[22] Letters received Dec. 1 and 5, 1805 (LC, 26942, 26967). See pp. 234-235, below.

[23] J. H. Daveiss to TJ, Jan. 10, 1806; received Feb. 8 (LC, 27210-27212). This was printed in Daveiss, *A View of the President's Conduct, Concerning the Conspiracy of 1806* (1807); reference here (pp. 69-71) and hereafter to pamphlet reprinted in Apr.-June and July-Sept., 1917, issues of *Quarterly Publication of the Historical and Philosophical Society of Ohio*, IX. Cited hereafter as Daveiss, *View*.

Of the General I have no very exalted opinion; he is extravagant and needy, and would not, I think, feel much delicacy in speculating on public money or public land. In both these respects he must be closely watched; and he has now united himself with every man in Louisiana who had received or claims large grants under the Spanish government (Gratiot, the Chouteaus, Soulard, &c.). But, though not perhaps very scrupulous in that respect, and although I fear that he may sacrifice to a certain degree the interests of the United States to his desire of being popular in his government [that is, with the former subjects of Spain in Louisiana], he is honorable in his private dealings, and of betraying his to a foreign country I believe him to be altogether incapable. Yet Ellicott's information, together with this hint, may induce caution; and if anything can be done which may lead to discoveries either in respect to him or others, it would seem proper; but how to proceed I do not know.[24]

The letter of Daveiss on which the Secretary of the Treasury made these comments had been nearly a month in transit. Since Jefferson replied to it two or three days after he heard from Gallatin, he had acted with reasonable celerity, considering the slowness of all movement in those days.[25] Giving no sign of panic but recognizing the importance of the allegations of Daveiss, he asked that official to communicate all he knew or had heard about the plot, especially the names of persons involved in it. This letter was nearly six weeks in reaching the District Attorney, partly because of his own movements; and, in his impatience, he addressed several communications to the President before he got it. In the first of these, besides recurring to earlier reports of Wilkinson's relations with Spain, he expressed deep suspicions of Burr's recent journey to the West. A little later he sent Jefferson a list of ten suspects that must have staggered the President when he looked at it in early March. Starting with his attorney general, John Breckinridge, and ending with Governor William Henry Harrison of Indiana Territory, it included two judges, two western senators, and Henry Clay. The order may have had no significance, but, while Wilkinson was near the top, Burr was almost at the bottom.[26] Jefferson was not ready to believe that all of these men were

[24] Gallatin to TJ, Feb. 12, 1806 (*Writings*, I, 290).

[25] TJ to Daveiss, Feb. 15, 1806 (LC, 27416; Daveiss, *View*, p. 77). The recipient said he got this Mar. 27.

[26] List of Feb. 13, 1806 (LC, 27395a; printed in footnote of 1917 edn. of Daveiss, *View*, p. 75). It came after Daveiss's letter of Feb. 10, 1806 (*ibid.*, pp. 72–74; LC, 27393–27394), received Mar. 8, and was as follows: "Breckenridge, Fowler,

conspirators, and he could not have failed to note that this was a list of Republicans. The compiler of it was a Federalist and a brother-in-law of John Marshall who had been appointed to his present position by John Adams. As we now know, a number of these men were in fact very close to Burr, and Daveiss afterwards removed Breckinridge and Henry Clay from his list while adding others to it, but by overreaching himself he had fatally damaged his credibility with Jefferson, who thought of him as a purveyor of rumors and a partisan troublemaker. The head of the Republican party was not disposed to borrow trouble at a time when John Randolph was threatening the unity he sought so persistently to preserve. He saw no need to reply to later letters until, pressed by Daveiss, he formally acknowledged them in September.[27] In the light of later events it may appear that he brushed off his informant too quickly, but in the spring of 1806 he was honoring the judgment of Gallatin and Dearborn regarding Wilkinson's loyalty rather than that of the Federalist attorney and was unwilling to recognize the latter as an investigating agent.

Meanwhile, the General's appointment as governor had been attacked in the House on the same grounds as in the Senate — that it joined the civil and military authority in one person. Jefferson himself had raised precisely the same objection against the appointment of Wilkinson as governor of the Mississippi Territory at the beginning of his administration. It was revived in the House of Representatives by John Randolph, who so often deplored inconsistency and clamored for unadulterated republicanism, and who was on the verge of his break with the administration over the conduct of foreign policy. Late in February he introduced three resolutions bearing on the question of plurality of offices. The last of these, providing that no officer of the army or navy should hold civil office, was adopted by a decisive vote and a bill to that effect was passed on April 11. This was admittedly aimed at Wilkinson, but, in comparison with John Randolph's diatribe against the government with respect to negotiations with Spain, his references to the administration were notably restrained. While he did not hesitate to express the judgment that the President should not have appointed the General as governor, he said that he regarded the persons making the appointment as less reprehensible than those at whose "importunate solicitation" it was made.[28] Also notable is the fact

---

Wilkinson, Adair, senator; Smith do. [i.e. ditto — presumably of Ohio], Sebastian, the judge Ct. of Appeals; Innes, the judge District court; Clay, the lawyer; Burr; Harrison, Govr."

[27] TJ to Daveiss, Sept. 12, 1806 (Daveiss, *View*, pp. 95–96). The intervening letters can be readily seen in the same collection.

[28] *Annals*, 9 Cong., 1 sess., p. 928.

that the resolution and bill were strongly supported on the floor by John W. Eppes and that Jefferson's other son-in-law, Thomas Mann Randolph, voted for them. This was clearly a vote for pure republicanism and against Wilkinson, but it was only a muted attack on the President.[29]

News of John Randolph's resolutions was promptly transmitted to Wilkinson by his friend Samuel Smith, but it was a month in reaching him and the letters he himself promptly wrote the Senator and the President, taking an equal time in transit, did not arrive until after the House had voted.[30] At the time Smith was still smarting over the nomination of William Pinkney as commissioner to Great Britain and his own failure to prevent the confirmation of John Armstrong as commissioner to treat with Spain.[31] Sending Wilkinson's letter to Jefferson, the Senator strongly urged that there be no change in the governorship until Wilkinson had had time to justify his appointment by his conduct, saying that a resignation now would be a triumph for his and the President's enemies. Smith sought to give the impression that these were one and the same.[32] Wilkinson himself took the line that his troubles in the territory (the extent and nature of which can be little more than suggested here) were attributable to the jealousies and designs of local enemies; among these he made special reference to Judge Lucas, whom he described as a devil. As for the opposition to him in Washington, he claimed that this arose from enmities not merely to him but also to the President — to whom he himself was prepared to give his last breath and last drop of blood. He spoke particularly of the "mad career" of John Randolph, whose course threatened to "spread the poison of disaffection everywhere." This was in the letter to Smith, who passed it on. In writing Jefferson, Wilkinson was less denunciatory and somewhat less effusive. Avowing loyalty

[29] Resolutions introduced Feb. 24, 1806; bill passed Apr. 11, 1806, by a vote of 64 to 34. The most important references to the debates and votes are in *Annals*, 9 Cong., 1 sess., pp. 923–931, 935–936, 1005–1015. Barnabas Bidwell and Joseph B. Varnum, loyal New England supporters of TJ, voted in the negative; and in certain respects the vote suggests the old alignment on the Yazoo lands. The Senate voted 17 to 10 on Apr. 12, to postpone this House bill to the next session (*ibid.*, p. 235).

[30] Wilkinson to Smith, Mar. 29, 1806, enclosed in Smith to TJ, Apr. 28; Wilkinson to TJ, Mar. 29, received Apr. 25, 1806 (Carter, XIII, 466–467, 502). Wilkinson burned Smith's letter to him.

[31] See above, p. 114.

[32] Among them he named Samuel Hammond, a district commandant whose nomination to be a lieutenant colonel in the regular army was defeated by a combination of Federalist senators and Republican friends similar to the one that had supported Wilkinson (*Senate Exec. Procs.*, II, 24, 30). Smith now described him as a snake in the grass.

and declaring his willingness to be disposed of in any way the President might see fit, he asseverated on his honor that he had conformed his conduct to Jefferson's desire by avoiding "every species of interested pursuit" since his arrival in St. Louis. That is, he set himself up as a devoted public servant who had been subjected to undeserved persecution. Most particularly, he sought to disclaim any involvement in land speculation, but it would appear from the congressional votes that he was supported in the East by persons interested in one way or another in western lands, and that John Randolph had marshaled against him essentially the same group that had opposed the Yazoo claims.

Jefferson was inclined to attribute Wilkinson's troubles in Upper Louisiana to representations of his enemies. Such, presumably, was Dearborn's opinion. At this time of dissension in the party, also, Jefferson appears to have been concerned not to alienate Samuel Smith. Writing that aggressive senator, he over-stated the case. After declaring that he had repented of but one appointment in the territory, that of Judge Lucas, whose temper overruled all that appointee's good qualities, he said: "Not a single fact has appeared which occasions me to doubt that I could have made a fitter appointment than General Wilkinson."[33] As to his alleged departure from principle in joining the civil to the military authority, he claimed that he did not consider Upper Louisiana as a government (such as the Mississippi Territory), but as merely a military station. At this stage, indeed, it may have been no more than that, and there was need to unify its administration. Also, his range of choice was limited. But, in his effort to put the best face on things and to assuage Samuel Smith, he was unwisely reassuring. He said that nothing was contemplated with respect to Wilkinson at the time, adding that they would have to see what turn things would take at home and abroad during the summer. The Senator, highly gratified, responded by saying that he still thought, as he always had, that the General was "precisely the man best fitted for the appointment in every point of view."[34] He had reason to be surprised when he learned that, two days after Jefferson wrote him, the Secretary of War dispatched to Wilkinson in the President's name orders to leave the Territory of Louisiana as quickly as practicable and proceed to Orleans Territory, to assume command of the forces in that quarter.[35]

At first glance it would appear that Jefferson did not let his right hand know what his left hand was doing — that, in the effort to be

[33] TJ to Samuel Smith, May 4, 1806 (Carter, XIII, 504).
[34] Smith to TJ, May 5, 1806 (LC, 27781); received May 10 at Monticello.
[35] Dearborn to Wilkinson, May 6, 1806 (Carter, XIII, 505–507).

conciliatory, he was disingenuous. Perhaps he was, but there is ground for the opinion that within two days he actually changed his mind — not because of anything further he had learned of the schemes of Burr or of Wilkinson's connection with them, but because of fresh information from the southern border. The reason assigned by Dearborn for the orders to Wilkinson was the receipt of information of Spanish threats. He instructed the General to repel any invasion of the regions east of the Sabine and on the American side of what was called West Florida. The day before the Secretary of War sent these unexpected instructions, and the day after the President wrote the Senator so reassuringly, the former received a letter from Claiborne. In this the Governor of the Orleans Territory expressed the fear that the Freeman expedition up the Red River would be interrupted by their "jealous and ill-disposed Spanish neighbors" and reported Spanish military activities at Mobile.[36] Jefferson, who was about to set out for Monticello after the congressional session ended, did not have time for much deliberation on these warnings and may have acted more hastily than he would have normally. He may have concluded that the opportunity now afforded to relieve Upper Louisiana of its most controversial official was not to be missed. A few months later he was to say that the discord at St. Louis was so inveterate that he would have liked to remove every appointed official if that action had been feasible.[37] But, regardless of the situation there, the circumstances on the southern border would have readily suggested the desirability of the presence of the Commanding Officer of the Army. The General was recognized as a self-seeker who was hard to handle, but his loyalty was not mistrusted by the government. A word of explanation to Smith, which would surely have been relayed to Wilkinson, would appear to have been in order, but neither during his brief visit to Monticello nor after his return to Washington did Jefferson send one.

Since the administration made no effort to dissociate the orders to Wilkinson and the local quarrels in which he was embroiled, both he and Smith interpreted the action of the government as a victory for his enemies. The fact (as alleged by him) that some of them had predicted his removal several weeks earlier on the basis of inside information from Washington (as alleged by them) contributed to his discomfiture. His immediate response was to bring fresh charges against his local foes; and he soon showed that he had no intention of heeding the

[36] Claiborne to TJ, Mar. 26, 1806; received May 5 (Carter, IX, 615–616). See p. 196, above.
[37] TJ to Samuel Smith, Oct. 15, 1806 (LC, 28352).

injunction to proceed quickly on his journey southward. To the Secretary of War, who had allowed him some leeway and of whom he stood in no awe, he gave no date for his departure, but he told his friend Samuel Smith that he would leave in about two weeks.[38] In fact he remained in Upper Louisiana nearly all summer, for reasons best known to himself. The dangerous illness of his wife was one he mentioned — she died a few months later. The explanation he finally gave Dearborn was that, having received later information from the Orleans Territory than that on which the government had acted, he concluded that the situation there was no longer perilous and that he should remain long enough to adjust his public accounts and attend to civil concerns and Indian affairs. He set his judgment against that of his civil superiors and was clearly insubordinate in spirit, but there was one matter of real concern to his government that he attended to. He sent back to their own country a large body of Osage Indians under the guardianship of Lieutenant Zebulon M. Pike.[39]

The expedition that was dispatched in midsummer actually took Pike as far into Spanish territory as Santa Fe. In connection with it ulterior motives have been attributed to Wilkinson, who was undoubtedly interested in determining a route to New Mexico, whether for purposes of trade or connivance with the Spanish. From the point of view of the administration, however, this was a legitimate expedition since its chief ostensible purpose was to convey home a body of Indians to whose safety the government was committed. Wilkinson's written instructions to Pike were such as Jefferson would have approved.[40] Besides conveying the Osages, the Lieutenant was to treat with other Indian nations, and in so doing he was expected to reach the headwaters of the Arkansas and Red rivers, thus gaining geographical information greatly desired by the President. Since he might find himself near the Spanish settlements of New Mexico, the explorer was warned to move with great circumspection and avoid offense. The Lieutenant (who became a captain while on this journey) was instructed to make scientific observations, although less stress was laid on them than in Jefferson's directions to Meriwether Lewis.

Among historians there has been considerable discussion of secret

[38] Wilkinson to the Secretary of War, and to Samuel Smith, June 17, 1806 (Carter, XIII, 520–522). Smith gave his interpretation of events in a letter of Aug. 8, 1806, to TJ (LC, 28158–28160). In this he said that the conduct of the "Cabal" had been insulting to TJ, and urged that no one of them be appointed to succeed Wilkinson. He took it for granted that the General had been ordered "down the river . . . with a view of ultimately dropping him as Governor."

[39] Wilkinson to Dearborn from Cantonment, Mo., Aug. 2, 1806 (Jackson, *Pike Journals*, II, 128–133).

[40] Wilkinson to Pike, June 24, 1806 (*ibid.*, I, 285–288).

purposes that Wilkinson may have had for this expedition. He may have intended Pike to enter Spanish territory; and Dr. John H. Robinson, who was attached to the expedition at a late stage in the preparations, may have gone along as a courier to assure Captain-General Salcedo that Wilkinson would maintain peace.[41] But Jefferson appears to have had no suspicions of him in this connection, and Pike seems to have shared no dark secrets and actually to have lost his way. This was because he was deceived by the manuscript map which Baron Alexander von Humboldt brought to Washington in 1804 and of which Burr surreptitiously procured a copy. It got to Pike through Wilkinson and led him to suppose that the Red River rose east of Taos. The use that Pike afterwards made of this map, in preparing his own for publication, occasioned the Baron to protest to Jefferson, but the recipient of the grizzly cubs seems always to have regarded the explorer who sent them as an honest and generous man.[42] The fact that Wilkinson had dispatched him marred Pike's fame in later years, but he received assurance that the President approved his conduct and set high value on the geographical knowledge he acquired.[43]

Pike's expedition was delayed because of illness among the Indians and did not set out until July 15. (He fell into Spanish hands in February, 1807, and arrived in Natchitoches in July.) Wilkinson may have remained in Upper Louisiana that long in order to dispatch it. But the explanation of his long delay that has carried greatest weight with historians is that he was timing his movements with those of Burr. He himself got to Natchez on September 7, 1806. There we shall leave him while recurring to the man whom he may have already decided to betray.

[41] Abernethy, pp. 119–121. See comment of Jackson, *Pike Journals*, II, 132.

[42] On the Humboldt map, and Pike's use of it, see Jackson, *Pike Journals*, I, 455–457; II, 368–369; also I, 384. For the correspondence between Humboldt and TJ, in 1811 and 1813, see II, 377, 387–388. For the episode of the grizzly cubs, see p. 208, above.

[43] Dearborn to Pike, Feb. 24, 1808 (*ibid.*, II, 300–301); see also TJ to Dearborn, June 22, 1807 (Ford, IX, 85–86).

[XIV]

Colonel Burr Excites Alarms

1805–1806

JEFFERSON could not have been unaware of the rumors to which
Aaron Burr's western tour in the late spring and summer of 1805
gave rise; and, like many other people, he must have wondered what
the former Vice President was up to.[1] In midsummer a startling series
of "Queries" appeared in a Federalist paper in Philadelphia and these
were copied throughout the country.[2] The rhetorical questions in this
unsigned communication suggested a number of possibilities that Burr
might have in mind: a revolutionary movement in the West, leading to
the formation of a separate government; the seizure and distribution of
the public lands there; the reduction and despoiling of Mexico.

The editor of the Philadelphia *Aurora*, whose Republican partisanship was intense, promptly gave attention to the extraordinary anonymous article in a rival paper. William Duane, regarding most of the
questions as fantastic, was disposed to attribute them to some wicked
and desperate man or to a wicked faction (Federalist) seeking to
promote divisiveness, but he did not rule out the possibility that they
emanated from a representative of a foreign country.[3] In his opinion,
the reason for associating these perfidious designs with Burr was that

---

[1] This tour is described in W. F. McCaleb, *The Aaron Burr Conspiracy* (1936),
ch. II; T. P. Abernethy, *Burr Conspiracy*, ch. III; N. Schachner, *Burr*, ch. XX;
and elsewhere. Beginning in April, it took Burr as far south as New Orleans and as
far west as St. Louis. On it he visited and conferred with important men at many
points.

[2] Quoted in McCaleb, *Burr Conspiracy*, p. 38, apparently from a Kentucky
paper. They originally appeared in Philadelphia *Gazette of the U.S.*, a Federalist
paper, and were discussed query by query in *Aurora*, July 30, 1805. This discussion was copied in Richmond *Enquirer*, Aug. 9, 1805.

[3] In his statement of Jan. 26, 1807, to TJ (LC, 28875–28883), Erick Bollman said
Burr knew they were written by Yrujo.

he was "exactly such a character as would be open to the suspicion of all parties," and that his low state might be presumed "to render him fit for any enterprise, however desperate." Duane observed that the supposed project was akin to the Blount conspiracy of the previous decade and might be linked with the Yazoo claims, which had been so bitterly debated during the recent session of Congress. He had been told at that time, he said, that "if the Yazoo speculators did not obtain their claims from Congress, they would march a force into that country."[4] This discerning observer provided a clue to the later support of Burr: in the East, Federalists and land speculators tended to be sympathetic to him.

Jefferson could hardly have missed the "Queries" and Duane's comment on them, for if he did not receive the *Aurora* while enjoying bucolic bliss at Monticello in the late summer, he saw Ritchie's Richmond *Enquirer* in which they were copied. Like other eastern papers, however, this one was devoting far more space to belated reports of the trial of Justice Chase than to the actual or imagined doings of Aaron Burr, and the President probably dismissed these from his mind. He fully shared Duane's confidence in the loyalty of the vast majority of Westerners to the Union and to his own government. That confidence was to remain unshaken, but before he got back to Washington in October the administration was informed that Burr, on his visit to New Orleans, had associated intimately with conspicuous critics of the territorial government. It was reported at the same time that he had been markedly attentive to Morales, the former Spanish Intendant, who was still there.[5] Collusion with the Spanish in a secessionist move might have been suspected. We now know that Burr also conferred with persons in the Mexican Association, whose desires to "liberate" that province could not have met with Spanish approval. At this stage, however, Yrujo regarded that supposed project as absurd.

After Burr had finished the journey that occasioned such confused reports and speculations, the adventurer told Anthony Merry in Washington that he had been received in the West with even greater favor than he had expected.[6] No doubt he had found many a receptive ear for anti-Spanish talk; and, on his visit to St. Louis in September, he and Wilkinson may have worked out a plan for the invasion of Mexico. The General is said to have believed that war with Spain was

[4] On the so-called Blount conspiracy, looking to the seizure of West Florida and Louisiana in conjunction with the British, see T. P. Abernethy, *The South in the New Nation* (1961), ch. VII; for the Yazoo debate, see *Jefferson the President: First Term*, ch. XXIV.

[5] Clairborne to Madison, Aug. 6, 1805 (Carter, IX, 489).

[6] Merry to Mulgrave, Nov. 25, 1805 (FO, 5:45, p. 164).

AARON BURR
Portrait by John Vanderlyn, 1809

likely, and about this time it was recognized within the government that one was possible.[7] But, disquieted by the "Queries" and by the news that "absurd and wild reports" representing Burr's projects were circulating in New Orleans, he may have begun to waver in his support of Burr after that traveler left St. Louis.[8] He afterwards claimed that on this visit he said to Burr: "The Western people disaffected to the Government! They are bigoted to Jefferson and democracy."[9] Presumably, Burr was quite unaware of the General's misgivings, but he had other grounds for discouragement. On his visit to Washington in November, 1805, when he gave Merry such an optimistic report of his western journey, he learned from that minister that the British government had made no response to his advances.

Continuing to observe the forms of politeness, the President had the former Vice President to dinner. Writing Wilkinson a little later, Burr said that his reception in Washington was as usual. Besides talking with Jefferson on one or more occasions, and also with the Secretary of War, he interested himself in Wilkinson's confirmation as governor of Louisiana Territory, apparently exciting no suspicions by so doing. Early in the new year he wrote the General: "You will know, long before this can reach you, that we are to have no Spanish war, except in ink and words."[10] He was reflecting the current mood of the government, no doubt, but the Spanish were actually strengthening their forces on the frontier at just this time. Troops from Havana arrived in Pensacola before he reached Washington, and the likelihood of border conflicts increased during the spring and summer.

It was after Jefferson had Burr to dinner and gave him a long private conference that the President received in succession two anonymous letters with a Philadelphia postmark that warned him against the intrigues of this "new Catiline." The writer described himself as a personal friend as well as a lover of his country but sought to disguise his identity by printing his warnings in capitals.[11] He charged Colonel Burr not only with meditating the overthrow of the administration but of conspiring against the state and he referred in unmistakable language to Burr's connection with Anthony Merry. The second letter, which was primarily a warning against Miranda, asserted that that adventurer and Burr were working toward the same end. While their plans were ostensibly directed against a foreign power, their true

---

[7] See ch. IV, above.

[8] Abernethy, *Burr Conspiracy*, pp. 31–35.

[9] McCaleb, *Burr Conspiracy*, pp. 36–37, quoting testimony at the Burr trial.

[10] Burr to Wilkinson, Dec. 12, 1805, and Jan. 6, 1806 (Wilkinson, *Memoirs*, II, Apps. LXXXIV, LXXXVI, quotation from the latter).

[11] Undated letters, received Dec. 1, 5, 1805 (LC, 26942, 26967).

object was the destruction of Jefferson's government, his ruin, and "the material injury of the Atlantic states."

Although Jefferson may have given no more thought to these anonymous letters than he customarily did to others of a crackpot variety, he was aware by this time at least that Burr was conniving with Merry about something. Certain Federalist senators and congressmen had not been above doing so at one time or another, as he must have known. Afterwards he expressed the opinion that Yrujo was involved in Burr's schemes, and he may have suspected that Burr and his emissaries were intriguing with the Spaniard in Philadelphia that winter, as in fact they were. If he had been in position to read the dispatches Yrujo sent home he would have inevitably concluded that a conspiracy was brewing to separate the western states from the Union, for that was the purpose Burr announced to Yrujo as well as to Merry. Through former Senator Jonathan Dayton he even broached a plan to overthrow the government in Washington by a coup d'état. Whether or not he was seriously considering this is a matter of speculation. In behalf of the contention that his purposes were not really treasonable, it has been asserted by a modern defender that his intrigue with Merry and Yrujo was only "a consummate piece of imposture," designed to extract money from them while masking his real purpose to attack Mexico.[12] Like Wilkinson, he was entirely capable of double talk and may well have had dual purposes — supplementary or alternative, and contingent on circumstances. At any rate, having procured no money from the British and little from the Spanish, he was back in Washington toward the end of the winter; and there, besides dining again with the President, he offered himself for appointment to a public position. Regardless of his clandestine negotiations with foreigners and with prospective American abettors of his schemes, this was a surprising action. It demonstrates the effrontery of the man — unless it was a mark of his extreme desperation.

There had been a good deal of newspaper talk, inspired no doubt by Burr himself, that he was to be appointed minister to Great Britain.[13]

---

[12] McCaleb, *Burr Conspiracy*, pp. xiii–xiv, from preface of 1st edn. of that work. This scholar, who describes the intrigue in ch. III, giving numerous extracts from the correspondence, does not believe that Burr could have seriously considered "so utterly a harebrained enterprise" as the overthrow of the government in Washington (p. 57). Abernethy, who deals with these matters in *Burr Conspiracy*, pp. 38–40 and ch. IV, finds support for the opinion that he did (p. 42) and does not doubt Burr's disunionist intentions, though recognizing that these changed in form and came to center on New Orleans.

[13] This was before the nomination of William Pinkney on Apr. 19, 1806. Plumer noted on Feb. 22 that Burr dined with TJ that day. He commented on the newspaper reports and the man himself Mar. 2 (*Memorandum*, pp. 436, 440–442).

Giving no credit to the report, Senator William Plumer said: "Mr. Jefferson has no confidence in him. He knows him to be capable of the darkest measures — a designing dangerous man." William Eaton, the frustrated captor of Derne in Tripoli to whom Burr made advances that winter, afterwards said he warned the President about this time that Burr was dangerous. Also, Eaton said he suggested that Burr should be given a diplomatic post to get him out of the country.[14]

As Jefferson recalled their conversation and recorded it in a private memorandum, Burr said to him:

> that I had always used him with politeness, but nothing more: that he aided in bringing on the present order of things, that he had supported the admn, & that he could do me much harm: he wished however to be on differt. ground: he was now disengaged from all particular business, willing to engage in something, should be in town some days, if I should have anything to propose to him.[15]

It was characteristic of Jefferson to try to take the sting off a necessary rebuff or other unpleasant action. In this case he erred on the side of polite dissimulation in asserting his own recognition of Burr's talents and his continued confidence that, if opportunity were afforded, they would be usefully employed for the public good. But, he said, he could not be unaware that Burr had lost the confidence of the public — not because of what certain newspapers had said, but because, in the late congressional caucus (1804), Burr had not received a single vote for continuance in the vice presidency. More recently, in fact, he had received a sharp rebuff from members of his former party in New York, where at a meeting of a Republican group it had been unanimously resolved that he did not and *ought not* possess the confidence of the party.[16] While Jefferson did not refer to this action, he made it abundantly clear that he saw no place for Burr in public life. Politically, the former Vice President was an outcast. As for Burr's statement that he could do him much harm, Jefferson said that, while he saw no reason why Burr should want to harm him, he had no fear on

[14] L. B. Wright and J. H. Macleod, "William Eaton's Relations with Aaron Burr" (*Miss. Valley Hist. Rev.*, XXXI, 527).

[15] Memo. of Apr. 15, 1806, reporting a conference of about a month before (Ford, I, 311).

[16] Report of a meeting of Feb. 18, 1806, by Plumer (*Memorandum*, p. 441). Without entering into a consideration of the factionalism that may have been involved, we are warranted in assuming that the effort to rehabilitate Burr in New York politics was unsuccessful.

that ground. Verging on self-righteousness or bravado, he asserted that
he had never done anything that he was unwilling to have revealed —
that he had done nothing for his own interest or that of a friend but
had always acted in the public interest. This sweeping claim suggests
that he was more perturbed than he would admit.

He succeeded in maintaining the outward forms of personal good
will, at any rate. He had Burr to dinner again and received from him a
parting call that turned out to be final. Meanwhile, in connection with
a pending lawsuit between Burr and one of his bitterest critics, the
charge had been made that Jefferson had entered into a deal with
Federalist James A. Bayard to break the electoral deadlock of 1801.[17]
Jefferson believed that the action had no other purpose than to
calumniate him; and he may have supposed that Burr was carrying out
the implied threat to harm him. Perhaps this minor episode served to
distract attention from a much greater danger, and it may have been
calculated to do just that.

Though he kept his eyes on the border, Jefferson does not appear to
have been concerned at this stage about any brewing domestic conspiracy. John Randolph had recently revolted in the House, and for a
time a duel between him and Thomas Mann Randolph was a dire
possibility. It will be recalled, also, that George Wythe died in
Richmond during the summer of 1806. Both as the highest public
official and as a kindly human being Jefferson had much to occupy his
mind, and he was never one to borrow trouble.

Letters of warning continued to arrive from Joseph H. Daveiss in
Kentucky. He said afterwards that he sent Jefferson eight altogether
and that, in order to avoid public notice, he put most of them under
cover to Gallatin, with whom he had official correspondence. Therefore, the sagacious Secretary of the Treasury was undoubtedly aware
of these letters and may be presumed to have been consulted about
them. As we have previously observed, the Federalist attorney's sweeping accusations of complicity in a conspiracy extended to so many
persons and to such persons that they seemed incredible to Jefferson,
who had lost none of his confidence in the loyalty of Westerners,
especially western Republicans, to his government. "Mr. Burr's connections are more extensive than any man supposes," said Daveiss in a
letter that reached the President in March, 1806.[18] But, even if this
should be true, were these relations conspiratorial? In midsummer
Daveiss gave his fullest account of the "present project," describing it

[17] See *Jefferson the President: First Term*, App. I, pp. 487–488.
[18] Daveiss to TJ, Feb. 10, 1806; received Mar. 8 (*View*, p. 74).

as a new scheme grafted on the original one and stating its objects as follows:

> To cause a revolt of the Spanish provinces, and a severance of all the western states and territories from the Union — to coalesce and form one government — to purchase great quantities of land in the Spanish settlements, to ensure the desired influence when the crisis comes.[19]

With this scheme as now described he associated all the persons he had previously named. Burr and Wilkinson were included though they were not especially emphasized in this particular letter. With only one of these men, John Brown, actually a recent addition to his list of suspects, did Daveiss admit that he was on bad personal terms.

About the same time, in August, Jefferson got from Brown, a former senator and supposedly loyal supporter, a letter which strengthened his own opinion that the accusations of the Kentucky Federalist were political in motivation.[20] After reporting that the revolt of John Randolph had had no unfavorable effect in the state, Brown said that a newspaper recently established in Frankfort, the *Western World*, had disturbed the citizenry greatly.[21] The editor, John Wood, was said to have been sent to Kentucky by John Marshall and to number among his particular patrons the Chief Justice's brothers-in-law, Humphrey Marshall (also his cousin) and Joseph H. Daveiss. His declared object, according to John Brown, was to prove that virtually all the influential Republicans in the state had been or were engaged in conspiracies against the Union and that many influential characters in the Atlantic states were connected with them. Brown charged Wood with the publication of "malignant and unblushing falsehoods" worthy of James Thomson Callender or William Cobbett and said that the patrons of this journalist cherished family resentments against him and Wilkinson and sought private revenge. Daveiss himself soon denied that he had had any hand whatever in the *Western World*, but even now his protests are unconvincing.[22] And it is easy to see why, in those days of slow communication, intense partisanship, and wild rumors, Jefferson continued to disregard one whom he considered

---

19 Daveiss to TJ, July 14, 1806 (*ibid.,* pp. 90–92).

20 John Brown to TJ, July 25, 1806; received Aug. 14 (LC, 28096).

21 This paper was frequently quoted in Richmond *Virginia Gazette* (Federalist), though not in Richmond *Enquirer*.

22 Daveiss to Madison, Aug. 14, 1806 (*View,* p. 94). That he and Humphrey Marshall controlled the *Western World* is explicitly stated by Beveridge (*Marshall,* III, 315).

a political enemy. He paid little heed to warnings issued by persons whom he himself suspected.

Ignoring Daveiss, he said afterwards that he got the "very first intimation of the plot" in a letter from Colonel George Morgan, received at Monticello on September 15, 1806. On his way west Burr visited Morgan at his farm, Morganza, about fifteen miles from Pittsburgh, and sought to enlist the old man's sons in a military expedition. Also, he engaged in loose talk about the future independence of the West and spoke contemptuously of the federal government. Jefferson said that Morgan's letter and one he got a few days later from John Nicholson, who lived in Herkimer, New York, suggested Burr's maneuvers "in a general way," and that he urged them as good citizens to transmit all the information they could procure, assuring them that he would not commit them personally beyond their own desires. He told Morgan he was anxious to learn the names of those who might reject as well as those who might accept "parricide propositions."[23]

About a month later the Secretary of State got from General Presley Neville and Judge Samuel Roberts of Pittsburgh a secondhand report of Burr's conversations with an unnamed "gentleman of high respectability" who was readily identifiable as George Morgan.[24] These two prominent men, along with Chief Justice Tilghman of Pennsylvania, had listened to Morgan and his sons at his urgent request and they made their rather detailed report with admitted reluctance. Colonel Burr was said to have predicted the separation of the western country from the pusillanimous Atlantic states within a very few years, and to have pointed to himself as the strong leader who could carry an insurrection to success. He was said to have stated that a wide field was to be opened for men of talent and enterprise and to have inquired particularly about the militia and the military characters of the district. "In short the whole tenor of his conversation was such as to leave a strong impression on the minds of those gentlemen with whom these conversations were held [the Morgans] that a plan was arranging or arranged for effecting the separation of the Union, in which Colonel

[23] TJ to George Morgan, Mar. 26, 1807 (L. & B., XI, 173–174); TJ to Gideon Granger, Mar. 9, 1814 (Ford, IX, 456). Morgan's letter was dated Aug. 29, 1806, and Nicholson's Sept. 6. I have found neither. TJ replied to both Sept. 19, 1806 (LC, 28286, 28288). It has been said that TJ previously received and laid aside a plan of Aug. 10, 1806, from Commodore Thomas Truxtun to counteract Burr's plot (Abernethy, p. 84); but this plan (LC, 28169), though dated Aug. 10, was sent Dec. 4 and received Dec. 6 (LC, 28526).

[24] Neville and Roberts to Madison, Oct. 7, 1806; endorsed by TJ without date but seen by him by Oct. 22 (Letters in Relation to Burr's Conspiracy, LC). Abernethy, pp. 63–65, gives a fuller account of this episode than we have space for here.

Burr seemed to have no ordinary interest." The writers of the letter hoped that these alarms were not well founded. While ostensibly making a faithful report of Morgan's representations, they were not reinforcing his judgment of Burr's purposes. The patriotic old man afterwards wrote Jefferson that he had been deceived in his confidence in Neville, whose house had become the rendezvous of "all the genteely disaffected" — presumably all Federalists.[25] Also, we now know that Chief Justice Tilghman attributed Morgan's fears to senility, even to delirium, and that Governor Thomas McKean, whom he soon consulted, saw no need to warn the government against Burr. Thus the force of the allegations against him that issued from western Pennsylvania was weakened.

Shortly after Madison got the letter from Pittsburgh, Jefferson received one from John Nicholson in Herkimer, New York, describing the activities of Comfort Tyler, who was seeking to assemble recruits and collect supplies for Burr.[26] Besides reinforcing the opinion that the Colonel was planning an expedition, this correspondent expressed his own opinion that there was disunionist sentiment in many Westerners. According to Jefferson's later statement, however, it was a communication from Gideon Granger, received October 20, 1806, that crystallized things by conveying something more than suspicions of Aaron Burr.[27] This contained revelations by General William Eaton, who had gone to see Jefferson in the spring, meaning to say more than he did, and who was destined to be the first witness for the prosecution in Burr's famous trial in Richmond.[28] Eaton's brilliant feat in the Tripolitan War and his subsequent disappointments induced in him a spirit of discontent to which Burr sought to appeal. The disgruntled captor of Derne listened at first but afterwards spurned Burr; and, according to his own statement, he communicated all the information he had to a senator and two congressmen. Later in the summer, when he was at home in Brimfield, Massachusetts, his stepson received a letter reporting that Burr, passing through Marietta, Ohio, had contracted for the building of a number of river boats there and had

25 Morgan to TJ, Jan. 19, 1807 (LC, 28827–28828). Neville's son enlisted with Burr.
26 John Nicholson to TJ, Oct. 14, 1806; received Oct. 24 (Bixby, pp. 134–136).
27 Dated Oct. 16, 1806; in "Burr-Blennerhassett Documents," *Quarterly Publication of the Historical and Philosophical Society of Ohio*, IX (1914), 10–13.
28 Wright and Macleod, in their excellent article in *Miss. Valley Hist. Rev.*, XXXI, 523–536, restore Eaton to a proper place in the history of the Burr conspiracy and, in my opinion, confirm his testimony. For his services in the Tripolitan War, see pp. 40–41, above.

offered commissions to several young men for a private expedition.[29]
Eaton, whose fears were revived by this information from the West,
now unbosomed himself to Congressman William Ely of Massachusetts. He said that in the previous winter Burr had offered him the
second command, under Wilkinson, of an expedition that was designed
to effect the separation of the western states from the Union. Convers-
ing with Ely in Springfield one evening in October, Gideon Granger
received this startling report secondhand; and, after getting a confirmation of it from Eaton in person along with additional details, he
promptly transmitted it to the President in Washington. Eaton was an
intemperate and vainglorious man whose credibility as a witness was to
be undermined by Burr's clever lawyers in the trial which took place
months later. They then created the impression that his testimony was
in return for the settlement of his claims against the government for
expenses incurred in the Tripolitan War. But he talked with Congressman Ely and Gideon Granger months before the settlement, and
Jefferson, who had previously discounted his extravagance of speech,
received his testimony through a member of his own political circle
whom he had shown no disposition to distrust.[30]

ii

During the week after the President learned of Eaton's disclosures
through his Postmaster General, he held three meetings of his department heads, who had not been previously called together since his
return from Monticello.[31] Judging from his account of the earliest of
these meetings, first consideration was not given the Burr conspiracy
but the defense of the southern border. In this account, furthermore,
there is scarcely a hint that external and internal dangers were related.

The situation in the Southwest had become more alarming since
General Wilkinson had been ordered to proceed from St. Louis to
Orleans Territory and to prevent any Spanish advance across the

[29] On Oct. 27, 1806, Eaton sent Madison an extract from a letter of Morris B.
Belknap of Marietta to his stepson, Timothy Danielson, dated Oct. 11, 1806
(Letters in Relation to Burr's Conspiracy, LC). The one referred to in the present
connection was said to have been dated in September.

[30] Because of Granger's association with the claimants of Yazoo lands, he was
suspected by many of being involved with Burr (see Abernethy, pp. 85-86, and
Jefferson the President: First Term, pp. 453-455). There is no reason to suppose
that Jefferson harbored such a suspicion, but it might have been expected to make
Granger's action in this instance more rather than less impressive.

[31] Oct. 22, 24, 25, 1806 (Ford, I, 317-320). If there had been any other meeting
of the Council since summer TJ left no record of it.

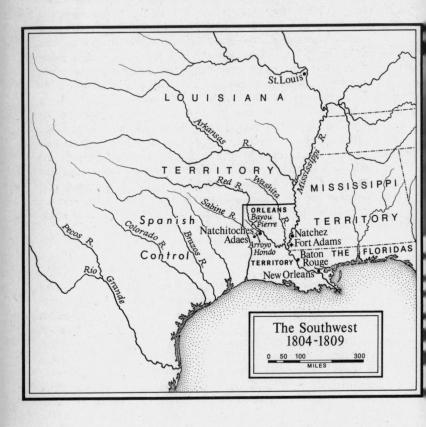

The Southwest
1804-1809

0   50   100   300
MILES

Sabine. In July the Spanish flag had been raised at Bayou Pierre, to the east of the river, and Colonel Herrera had arrived there with cavalrymen in August. Patrols penetrated as far as the Arroyo Hondo, which the Spaniards claimed was the border, about seven miles from the American post at Natchitoches. Jefferson had not given up hope of settling boundary questions with the Spanish amicably, but he had made it abundantly clear that he regarded the American title as far as the Sabine (the western boundary of the present state of Louisiana) as indisputable, and the Secretary of War had given orders that it must be defended. Colonel Thomas H. Cushing, in command at Natchitoches, had protested against the movement of Spanish troops; and Governor Claiborne, who joined him there, had done so at greater length, referring also to the turning back of the Freeman expedition on the Red River and other Spanish "outrages."[32] The administration, whose information lagged weeks behind the course of actual events on the distant frontier, had copies of these letters, and it was also aware that Wilkinson, who was under specific orders to maintain the Sabine boundary, had at length reached Natchez.[33]

The President and his advisers now reviewed the military situation with particular regard to the disposition of troops in the Southwest and of gunboats at or near New Orleans. The decisions they reached regarding the movement of regulars from that city to Natchitoches and the raising of a volunteer force in the territories of Orleans and Mississippi need not concern us here since they did not affect the outcome of this particular confrontation. In view of the actions already taken by Claiborne to mobilize the militia, and the enthusiasm manifested by Americans on the frontier, it appears, however, that sufficient force was available to expel the invaders, whose strength had in fact been greatly overestimated.

If there was any reference at this first meeting to the danger that Burr would launch an expedition against Mexico, Jefferson left no record of it. The "scheme" specifically mentioned by him was that of separating the western states from the rest of the Union, and he thought it likely that, if attempted, it would be in collusion with the

[32] Letters exchanged in August between Cushing and Claiborne on the one hand and Herrera on the other were communicated to Congress by TJ on Dec. 2, 1806 (*Annals*, 9 Cong., 2 sess., pp. 916–921). Developments on the frontier in this period are described in Abernethy, ch. X, and in greater detail in McCaleb, *Burr Conspiracy*, ch. V.

[33] TJ's memo of Oct. 22 contained references that show his familiarity with Wilkinson's letter of Sept. 8 to the Secretary of War. By this time, in fact, the General was at Natchitoches, and there had been highly important developments of which the government was yet unaware.

Spanish. He and his advisers unanimously agreed that confidential letters be written governors and district attorneys in the West to have Burr "strictly watched and on his committing any overt act unequivocally, to have him tried for treason, misdemeanor, or whatever other offence" his act might amount to. The same instructions applied to his followers, but no specific suspects were named.

A major one, second in importance only to Burr, had been named by Eaton; and Jefferson himself said that General Wilkinson was now under "very general suspicion of infidelity." Furthermore, he had disobeyed orders to proceed from St. Louis to the southern frontier with "all practicable dispatch." What should be done about him? Consideration of this question was postponed for reasons the President did not record, but presumably because of the difficulties involved in it.

At the meeting next day further actions with respect to Burr were unanimously agreed to. Captains Preble and Decatur were to be ordered to New Orleans and the former, in consultation with Claiborne, was to be given great discretionary powers. Additional gunboats were to be dispatched thither if it should be found that the appropriations would permit.[34] Furthermore, John Graham, secretary of the Orleans Territory, who was in Washington, was to be sent on Burr's trail with discretionary powers to consult confidentially with the governors and to arrest him if he had made himself liable. Graham was to be commissioned as governor of Louisiana Territory, succeeding Wilkinson, and Burr's brother-in-law was to be removed from his post there.[35] The governors of Orleans and Mississippi territories and Colonel Freeman were to be warned. The decision about General Wilkinson was again postponed "for further information."

At the next meeting, all these decisions with respect to Burr were rescinded except those regarding the warnings to officials on the lower Mississippi and the mission of Graham, who was now clothed with confidential authority to act as might seem necessary. The reason assigned by Jefferson for this apparent retreat was that in the mail just received from the West no word was heard from any quarter of any movement by Burr, who might thus be assumed to have committed no overt act. It afterwards came out that available funds were insufficient to dispatch the gunboats. Furthermore, on second thought the Presi-

[34] This seems a surprising proviso if the country was facing such a crisis as the actions respecting the high naval officers implied; but, as the Secretary of the Navy afterwards complained, the government was unable to take this step because of the limitations imposed upon it by congressional action. Robert Smith to TJ, Dec. 22, 1806 (LC, 28620–28621).

[35] Graham afterwards declined this appointment.

dent and his advisers may have concluded that they did not have much to go on beyond previous reports, and that it would be unwise to raise premature alarms. Meanwhile, Graham could accomplish discreetly by word of mouth what the President had thought to do by writing. The confusion in the counsels of the government at this stage was unrevealed to the public, and might be unknown even now if Jefferson had not left a private record of it. Ten days after the third of these Cabinet meetings he told his son-in-law, on the strength of what the government had learned about the boat-building on the Ohio, that Burr was "unquestionably very actively engaged" in preparations for the severance of the Union. He was convinced of this purpose by that time, if he had not been sooner, but he had not yet changed his mind about the necessary limitation of governmental action. "We give him all the attention our situation admits," he said; "as yet we have no legal proof of any overt act which the law can lay hold of."[36]

He remained confident of the loyalty of the Westerners, and strong influences were probably exerted in Wilkinson's behalf. He had influential friends at court who may be supposed to have argued that he was trustworthy — the Secretary of War and presumably the Secretary of the Navy, brother of his staunch supporter Senator Samuel Smith of Maryland. The President and his chief advisers may have decided that, at this stage and at this distance from the scene of operations, they had no choice but to rely on him despite his past record of intrigue with the Spanish and his recent insubordination. To have taken any sort of disciplinary action against him when he was in command on the threatened border would have been hazardous, and to have questioned his loyalty might have driven him irretrievably into the arms of Burr.

In reality, events on the remote southwestern frontier so far outran decision making in Washington as to cause this to seem inconsequential. Before the President and his ministers entered into this series of deliberations Wilkinson had decided to abandon Burr and in his own egocentric way to stand by the government. He had acted on this decision before these meetings ended, although the relevant communications to his government did not arrive until another month and they told only part of his story even then.

About two weeks after the meeting of the Cabinet at which judgment on him was deferred, fresh instructions were sent him. Besides showing that the administration was sticking by him, these reflected a

[36] TJ to TMR, Nov. 3, 1806 (*Papers, M.H.S.,* p. 118).

change in its mood.[37] Ostensibly because of the "great probability" of
an early settlement of differences with Spain by negotiation at Paris (a
probability that Jefferson did not report to Congress in his annual
message three weeks later), and the desire to avoid needless bloodshed,
the Executive was now "extremely desirous" of avoiding a clash on the
border. Previously, Wilkinson had been directed to employ force to
maintain the line of the Sabine, and the government had not conceded
American claims west of that stream. The Executive had now determined "to assume the Sabine as the temporary line between the troops
of the two nations." The Spaniards should hold no place east of it
except Bayou Pierre, where, since the cession of Louisiana to the
United States, they had actually had a small post, unobserved at first
by the Americans. The President was conceding that they should not
be expelled by force from that place. He left no doubt that Wilkinson's main objectives must be the maintenance of the peace and the
attainment of a compromise which would enable him to return with
his troops as quickly as possible to Fort Adams, on the Mississippi
below Natchez.

If these instructions had been made public they would undoubtedly
have been seized upon as a sign of the ambivalence of the administration in times of crisis. The alleged reason for them would probably
have been dismissed as another example of unwarranted reliance on
diplomacy. But, since the instructions turned out to be unnecessary,
these reflections are largely academic. Three days before Jefferson
recorded them Wilkinson signed (November 5, 1806) an agreement
with Herrera, who had withdrawn behind the Sabine on his own voli-
tion several weeks earlier. According to this agreement, the Americans
were to remain behind the Arroyo Hondo and the Spanish behind the
Sabine, the intervening territory being recognized as neutral ground
until the boundaries should be determined by diplomacy.[38] Acting on
his own judgment before he got his fresh instructions, the General

37 Memo of TJ, Nov. 8, 1806, including suggestions from Gallatin and Madison
(LC, 28422-28427). McCaleb gives extracts (*Burr Conspiracy*, pp. 132-133), including "Notes" which I do not find in precisely that form but which, in my opinion,
correctly reflect the dominant sentiment of the group.

38 Wilkinson's negotiations with the Spanish are admirably described by Abernethy, in ch. X; on the Neutral Ground Agreement, see especially, pp. 154-155.
He believes that Herrera, fearing an American attack on Mexico which would be
followed by a revolution there to the advantage of Napoleon, was more responsible for the maintenance of peace on the frontier than Wilkinson. McCaleb, *Burr
Conspiracy*, pp. 131-135, charges Wilkinson with compromising American claims
east of the Sabine and rendering ridiculous American "pretensions" to the Rio
Grande boundary.

removed the threat of immediate conflict on the border, as his government wanted him to do.

Several weeks before Jefferson got the welcome news of the Neutral
Ground Agreement, he received from Wilkinson at Natchitoches
dispatches bearing on the conspiracy. These dispatches, which arrived
on November 25, a week before the President sent his annual message
to Congress, were borne for reasons of secrecy and security by Lieutenant Thomas A. Smith, who was journeying to Washington on the
pretext of resigning his commission. Wilkinson, describing him as an
admirable young officer, asked the President to see that the resignation
was not accepted. The communications included two letters to Jefferson, dated October 21, 1806, one of which was marked "Confidential,"
and a paper dated the previous day. This was unsigned but Wilkinson
afterwards acknowledged it by publishing it in his *Memoirs* over his
own name.[39] No more in it than in the confidential letter of the next
day did he mention any conspirator by name, but it purported to be a
revelation of a conspiracy, rather than of the state of Wilkinson's
mind, and as such it should concern us first.

In this ostensibly anonymous communication, which was calculated
to create a horrendous impression, the reporter claimed to be presenting information he had received from such direct and confidential
channels that he could not doubt its authenticity. He stated that a
numerous and powerful association, extending from New York to the
western territories, had been formed to rendezvous eight to ten thousand men in New Orleans, whence an expedition would proceed with
naval support to Vera Cruz about February 1. An uprising against the
existing government of Mexico was expected. A body of associates
would descend the Allegheny River, and the first general rendezvous
would be near the rapids of the Ohio on or before November 20.
Proceeding thence by lightboats, the expedition would be joined by
auxiliaries from Tennessee and other quarters. The van was expected
to reach New Orleans in December. After painting the prospect in
such startling colors, the reporter said that the authority under which
the enterprise was projected was unknown to him. Nor did he know
how it was supported. But he said that influential characters had been
engaged in it for six months, and that British maritime co-operation
was expected.

In this report of an alleged enterprise there was no reference to the

[39] *Memoirs*, II, App. XCV. In its unsigned form it is in Letters in Relation to
Burr's Conspiracy, LC, as are the two letters of Oct. 21, 1806, to TJ.

separation of the western states from the rest of the Union or to known designs on the Territory of Orleans or the city of New Orleans. In his confidential letter to Jefferson, however, Wilkinson expressed this opinion:

> But should this association be formed, in opposition to the Laws & in defiance of Government, then I have no doubt the revolt of this Territory will be made an auxiliary step to the main design of attacking Mexico, to give it a new master in the place of promised Liberty. . . .

In view of this danger, he was disposed to hazard his discretion, to make the best possible compromise with the Spaniards about the boundary, and to throw himself into New Orleans with his little band "to be ready to defend that capital against usurpation and violence." This, indeed, is what he did. In a postscript to his confidential letter to the President, however, he suggested that, if the Spanish should be seriously disposed to war, the "delirium of the associates" might be corrected by "a suitable appeal to their patriotism to engage them in the service of their country." As an "expedient to prevent the horrors of a civil conflict" he was obviously not averse to a foreign war, and ostensibly he was still attracted by the idea of attacking Mexico.[40]

If the timetable Wilkinson communicated to the President had been correct (in fact, it was not), his warnings could not have been expected to reach Washington soon enough to do much good. He was implying that everything depended on what he himself might do on the frontier and in New Orleans. He had already informed the Secretary of War of the withdrawal of Herrera across the Sabine, but he had also reported that higher Spanish officials declined to accept this as the boundary. On the same day that he dispatched his communications to Jefferson he wrote Dearborn from Natchitoches that he would march to the Sabine, but that he intended to propose the arrangement he had previously described and which, as we have seen, he actually effected. Thus he hoped to appear in New Orleans as its savior. In his own opinion, no doubt, the strength of his personal position lay in the indispensability he implied, but unquestionably he recognized the importance of establishing himself in the minds of his civil superiors as a national patriot and loyal public servant. In one of the letters he wrote Jefferson on October 21, obviously seeking to dissociate his

[40] Wilkinson to TJ, Confidential, Oct. 21, 1806 (Letters in Relation to Burr's Conspiracy, LC). He omitted the postscript when publishing this letter in his *Memoirs*, II, App. XCV.

name from that of Burr and the latter's associates, he vigorously defended himself against the charges that had been made against him by John Wood's *Western World* in Kentucky. He claimed that he had been "bespattered with obloquy and slandered with a degree of virulence and indecency surpassing all example, and this merely to gratify the envy, hatred and malice of the Marshall family." It need not be supposed that by this assertion he acquitted himself of the charges of past collusion with the Spanish, but the line he took could have been expected to be effective with Jefferson, who believed that loyal followers of his in Kentucky had been attacked by Daveiss and other Federalists for political reasons.

In the verbose confidential letter which accompanied his allegedly anonymous revelations Wilkinson claimed to be staggered by "the magnitude of the enterprise, the desperation of the plan, and the stupendous consequences" with which it was pregnant. Assuming a pose of ignorance and bewildered innocence, he wrote: "I have never in my whole life found myself in such circumstances of perplexity and embarrassment as at present; for I am not only uninformed of the prime mover and ultimate objects of this daring enterprise, but am ignorant of the foundation on which it rests, of the means by which it is to be supported, and whether any immediate or collateral *protection,* internal or external, is expected." It need not be supposed that the President was convinced by this mendacious disclaimer. Jefferson and his advisers could easily have thought up reasons why Wilkinson, because of past associations, might have been reluctant to name Aaron Burr. But they themselves had no difficulty in identifying the prime mover. Because of previous rumors and warnings, Burr might have been expected to come at once to mind. Furthermore, Lieutenant Smith was not sworn to secrecy. From him and others Jefferson learned that Samuel Swartwout, brother of Burr's henchman, John Swartwout, recently removed by the President from the post of United States marshal in New York, had been visiting Wilkinson. The purpose of this visit was suggested by something else the General said: "Among other allurements proposed to me, I am informed you connive at the combination, and that our country will justify it, but when I examine my orders of the 6th of May, I am obliged to discredit these imputations." If Jefferson did not already know that Burr had assured many people in the West that he would condone an attack on Spanish possessions, he could learn from this statement that such was in fact the case. What was of more immediate importance was the conclusion to which Wilkinson's revelation pointed — that overtures had been made to him and that these had been rejected.

Nearly two months were to pass before Jefferson saw a decoded copy of the letter of Burr to the General, written in the previous summer, which Swartwout had delivered on October 8 and which was more like a summons than an overture.[41] If he had seen this on November 25 along with the other communications he could hardly have failed to suspect strongly that, whatever the General might think now, *he had been* much more deeply implicated than he would admit. It now appears that Wilkinson faced a real dilemma after he heard from Burr and before he wrote Jefferson. The result of Herrera's withdrawal across the Sabine, beyond which he himself had no authority to go, had been to stalemate him.[42] Uncertainties about Spanish purposes remained, but there was little likelihood of an immediate clash on the border such as Burr and his associates had been counting on. Wilkinson had little choice but to proceed to the river he had been instructed to guard, and the way would thus be opened for Burr to proceed to New Orleans with neither opposition nor support from Wilkinson. Furthermore, along with the letter from Burr, he had received from the hand of Samuel Swartwout an alarming note from Jonathan Dayton, indubitably regarded by him as an "associate." This said: "It is now well ascertained that you are to be displaced in the next session. Jefferson will affect to yield reluctantly to the public sentiment, but yield he will. Prepare yourself therefore for it: you know the rest."[43] This unauthorized prediction, which was not to become part of the public record for many months, was followed by an exhortation: "You are not a man to despair or even despond, especially when such prospects offer in another quarter. Are you ready? Are your numerous associates ready? wealth and glory, Louisiana and Mexico."

Pressure was being brought to bear on Wilkinson, and the exaggerated report of prospects and preparations he had received from Swartwout may be regarded as deliberate deception. The result of these representations was to force his hand. Apparently he had been dubious of the enterprise for some time, believing that too much talk had imperiled it. Faced under these particular military circumstances with a choice between the Enterprise and the Administration, he

41 Burr's letter of July 29, 1806, of which Wilkinson received a duplicate from Burr's agent Erick Bollman early in November, was included by TJ in the documents he submitted to Congress on Jan. 22, 28, 1807; and appears to have been first seen by him on Jan. 18. See below, p. 263.

42 Abernethy, p. 148.

43 Dayton to Wilkinson, July 24, 1806, in cipher (*Trial of Col. Aaron Burr . . . taken in short-hand by T. Carpenter*, III [1808], App. L). The copy in Letters in Relation to Burr's Conspiracy, LC, differs slightly from this printed version.

decided for the latter. And the compromise with the Spaniards that freed his own hands while preserving the peace was compatible with his role as their pensioner. The Burrites afterwards contended that he effected it for precisely that reason. His motives were probably mixed, but we cannot now doubt that he was an unconscionable double-dealer.

When Jefferson received Wilkinson's communications in Washington he naturally focused his attention on the immediate threat disclosed by them. He was convinced that Burr's claim of forthcoming naval support from the British was unwarranted, and he probably believed the size of the projected expedition down the western waterways to be greatly exaggerated, as in fact it was. He was not as alarmed as Wilkinson seemed to be, and, although he did not say so, he may have regarded some of the General's explanations and expostulations as disingenuous. But Wilkinson had given convincing evidence that he was now on the side of the government. Furthermore, there was no escape from the consideration that in the existing situation in the Southwest he was virtually indispensable. It would seem that the government *had* to trust him while heeding his warnings. Under these circumstances Jefferson called together his ministers and reached various decisions with their counsel. Then, by issuing a proclamation, he took public notice of the conspiracy without as yet naming Aaron Burr.

[XV]

Thwarting an Unlawful Enterprise

1806-1807

THE proclamation Jefferson issued a couple of days after he received Wilkinson's horrendous warnings was ostensibly designed to forestall a military expedition or enterprise against the dominions of Spain.[1] He sought to make only such charges as could be proved and to refer to no actions that were not demonstrably illegal. Therefore, he made no mention in public of any design to separate the western states from the Union, although he had said privately that he believed this to be Burr's purpose. Since the United States was not at war with Spain, a private expedition against her dominions would have been in direct violation of a statute of 1794. There was no such law on the books when Jefferson, as secretary of state, was so embarrassed by the scheming French minister, Citizen Genet. This law, enacted soon after his retirement from George Washington's official family, was occasioned by Genet's anti-Spanish projects and the efforts to enlist Americans in these — including certain Kentuckians now reported as sympathetic to Burr.[2] That adventurer was seeking to exploit the strong anti-Spanish feeling still existing in the West, but the government now had an effective legal weapon with which to oppose him.

On the other hand, Jefferson was uncertain about the means he could employ under existing law to prevent an enterprise that was directed, not against a foreign country, but against the United States. At this juncture he had no attorney general to consult with, for John

---

[1] The Proclamation of Nov. 27, 1806, can be readily seen in Ford, VIII, 481–482, and *Annals*, 9 Cong., 2 sess., pp. 686–687.

[2] The particular reference is to the Michaux episode. See *Jefferson and the Ordeal of Liberty*, pp. 104–108. The law was approved June 5, 1794 (*Annals*, 3 Cong., pp. 1461–1464).

Breckinridge was detained in Kentucky by illness and died there in December. Therefore, he had Madison look into the laws bearing on the use of the military in cases of insurrection and received from him an opinion. The conclusion of this was as follows: "Thus it does not appear that regular troops [as distinguished from militia] can be employed under any legal provision against insurrections — but only against expeditions having foreign countries as the object."[3] No doubt a liberal constructionist of the Constitution and apostle of national power like Alexander Hamilton would have asserted that a sovereign government needs no specific authorization to employ its own troops to prevent its dissolution; but the authority of the President to call out the militia to suppress domestic insurrections had been questioned at the time of the Whiskey Rebellion, and the Act of 1795, which was designed to remedy this difficulty, referred only to the militia.[4] Jefferson was sufficiently disturbed over the inadequacy of the means that were legally employable against internal dangers to mention it in his annual message to Congress, a few days after he issued his proclamation.[5] Furthermore, a week before Christmas, he sent a congressman from Virginia the draft of a measure extending to the President the same authority to call out the land and naval forces to suppress domestic insurrections or enforce the laws that he already had to call out the militia. A bill couched in language almost identical with this was duly passed by Congress and became law at the very end of the session.[6] If Jefferson had employed regular troops for such purposes prior to this extension of his authority he might have been supported by most of his countrymen, but almost certainly he would have been censured by some of them.[7] Thus there were advantages in saying that the expedition was directed against a foreign nation.

In his proclamation, Jefferson lumped together the "sundry persons" believed to be "conspiring and confederating." He said he had been informed that they were fitting out and arming vessels; that they were collecting military equipment and provisions; that they were "deceiv-

[3] Madison to TJ, received Oct. 30, 1806 (LC, 28393).
[4] Act approved Feb. 28, 1795 (*Annals*, 3 Cong., pp. 1508–1510). See D. H. Pollitt, "Presidential Use of Troops to Execute the Laws," in *N.C. Law Review* (Feb., 1958), XXXVI, especially pp. 122–129.
[5] See Ford, VIII, 491.
[6] TJ to John Dawson, Dec. 19, 1806 (LC, 28595); Act approved Mar. 3, 1807 (*Annals*, 9 Cong., 2 sess., p. 1286).
[7] An example of the sort of criticism that might have been expected is afforded by remarks of G. W. Campbell in the House, Jan. 16, 1807: "If the militia are incompetent to maintain the peace, it is full time to acknowledge the futility of our political principles" (*Annals*, 9 Cong., 2 sess., p. 346).

ing and seducing honest and well-meaning citizens, under various pretences, to engage in their criminal enterprises"; and that they were organizing themselves for these, contrary to the law. He warned all citizens against participation, under penalty of prosecution; and he enjoined all officials — civil and military, federal, state, and territorial — to prevent by all lawful means the carrying out of such enterprises. He authorized and requested them to seize vessels, supplies, and arms and to bring participants to punishment. John Graham was already on his way west, and warnings had previously been sent to officials in the territories of Orleans and Mississippi. Warnings were now sent to major points along the Ohio and Mississippi at which the expedition might be stopped.[8]

If, as Wilkinson had reported in his anonymous communication, the expedition was expected to reach a total of from eight to ten thousand men, the actions of the government, besides being slow, were disproportionate to the magnitude of the enterprise. There is no way of determining how many persons were recruited, but, from the number of boats and the quantity of supplies arranged for, it has been estimated that some fifteen hundred were actually expected to go down the rivers.[9] A few weeks later Jefferson said he did not believe there were ever as many as five hundred men engaged for the expedition.[10] He does not appear to have taken Wilkinson's figures seriously. Relying as he did on the loyalty of Westerners, he was confident that the enterprise would lose most of its adherents as soon as they learned that, contrary to Burr's representations, the government was not supporting it or conniving in it. Writing Governor Claiborne about three weeks after the proclamation, he said he trusted that Burr would be stopped on the Ohio.[11] If not, he would rendezvous at Natchez, and was to be opposed at the best point below that place, probably near Fort Adams, by the troops there, along with the militiamen who had been assembled from the contiguous territories and the gunboats that had come up the river. The supposition was that these forces would be sufficient even if Wilkinson was still on the Sabine, but if he and his troops were available that would be all the better.[12]

The possibility remained that Burr might surmount all these obstacles and reach New Orleans, where the danger of disaffection was greatest and whence the expedition for Vera Cruz was supposed to

[8] Memo. of Cabinet meeting, Nov. 25, 1806 (Ford, I, 320–321).
[9] T. P. Abernethy, *Burr Conspiracy*, pp. 102–103.
[10] TJ to Wilkinson, Jan. 3, 1807 (Ford, IX, 2).
[11] TJ to Claiborne, Dec. 20, 1806, a letter he did not send but retained as a record (Ford, VIII, 501–502).
[12] They were actually in New Orleans before this letter was written.

sail.[13] The President told the troubled Secretary of the Navy that if Burr should not be stopped on the Ohio or at Fort Adams, he would ask Congress for an immediate naval appropriation and would dispatch a large military force to "retake" New Orleans.[14] Read in print and taken by itself, this promise gives a false impression, for he never expected Burr to get there. And the day after he sought to reassure his Secretary of the Navy, he got convincing news that New Orleans was in no real danger.[15]

This was on Christmas Eve, nearly a month after the presidential proclamation, and there had been no great excitement in the capital meanwhile. Jefferson's proclamation contained strong words but gave a general impression of restraint. In his annual address to Congress the following week his only direct reference to the enterprise was brief; and he neither used the word "conspiracy" nor named supposed conspirators. It was after reporting on Spanish affairs that he spoke of the expedition and the measures taken against it.[16] Stressing the necessity of suppressing "the criminal attempts of private individuals to decide for their country the question of peace or war," he left no doubt that the government itself was seeking to maintain peace. The documents communicated with the message bore on the troubled situation on the Spanish border.[17] Since the latest of these was an extract of a letter of October 21 from Wilkinson, the information conveyed was six weeks old. The startling communications from that officer that had occasioned the proclamation remained in Jefferson's confidential files. It was later in the message, after he had said that domestic insurrection should not really be expected in such a self-governing society as Americans enjoyed, that he raised the question whether or not further powers of prevention should be given the government.[18]

Judging from the report of the British Minister to his home office, the belief was "universally prevalent" that there were conspiracies for

[13] It now appears that the conspirators, counting on the disaffection, hoped to gain control of New Orleans by a coup d'état (Abernethy, p. 165).

[14] Robert Smith to TJ, Nov. 11 and Dec. 22, 1806 (LC, 28437; 28620–28621); TJ to Smith, Dec. 23, 1806 (Ford, VIII, 504).

[15] See below, pp. 257–259. Mary P. Adams, in her dissertation, "Jefferson's Military Policy," p. 40, takes the position that he postponed the orders for the apprehension of Burr so long that it was doubtful that they could have reached their destination in time to be of any value. She says he was evidently waiting for Burr to commit an overt act and was then planning to retake the territory. But the orders that led to the apprehension of Burr actually reached their destination in sufficient time. Furthermore, I can see no reason for doubting that TJ wanted the expedition stopped as soon as possible.

[16] In his message of Dec. 2, 1806 (Ford, VIII, 489–490).

[17] Annals, 9 Cong., 2 sess., pp. 915–925.

[18] See p. 253, above.

the separation of the western states and that Burr was involved in these. David Erskine, who had just succeeded Anthony Merry, had picked up from that minister and his Federalist friends the idea that, except against the British, Jefferson had always pursued a "temporizing line." Therefore, Erskine could not believe that he would have adopted "such strong measures" in the absence of convincing information; and, considering the circumstances, he was surprised that there was so little alarm.[19]

After the issuance of the proclamation, William Plumer, besides noting that reports of Burr's activities had circulated from one end of the country to the other for some time, stated that he contemplated the inclusion of the western states in the new empire he intended to form. The Senator himself was unwilling to believe, however, that Burr had spoken as foolishly as Eaton said he had. From his own observation Plumer testified to the elusiveness of this cunning man, to whose language he had been particularly attentive: "I found he possessed the talent of making an impression of an opinion upon the subject, on the person with whom he conversed, without explicitly stating or necessarily giving his sentiments thereon. In every thing he said or did, he had a design — and perhaps no man's language was ever so apparently explicit, and at the same time so covert and indefinite."[20]

The difficulty of discerning, and even more of demonstrating, Burr's real objectives was increased in the fall by certain actions of his which Jefferson became aware of but which he regarded as no more than a cover for other designs. From Charles Lynch of Kentucky the adventurer purchased a claim to some 350,000 acres of land on the Washita (Ouachita) River — a stream that had been recently explored by William Dunbar and was known to lie wholly within the United States. The claim acquired by Burr, however, went back to a grant made a decade earlier by the Spanish Governor to the Baron de Bastrop. The conditions of this grant had been met on neither side, and no Spanish patent had been issued. The validity of Burr's title, in the eyes of American authorities, was questionable to say the least. It is possible that he seriously planned to establish a settlement or a military outpost at a later time when, as he hoped, this region would be under other jurisdiction. In view of the late date of the purchase, it may be presumed to have been an afterthought and not to have entered into his original plan. Land could be promised recruits, and they could be

[19] Erskine to Fox, Dec. 4, 1806, No. 2 (FO, 5:52 [1], pp. 59–63). He reported on the proclamation and the annual message, commenting on the favorable financial situation of the government.
[20] Nov. 29, 1806; see also Nov. 28 (*Memorandum*, pp. 515–518).

led to believe that this was to be an agricultural enterprise, although it was not even secondarily that at this stage. Tools for clearing roads were provided, but there appear to have been no seeds or agricultural implements.[21]

Jefferson afterwards said that, about the time he issued his proclamation, he interpreted Burr's plans as follows:

> It appeared that he contemplated two distinct objects, which might be carried on either jointly or separately, and either one or the other first, as circumstances should direct. One of these was the severance of the union of these States by the Allegany mountains; the other an attack on Mexico. A third object was provided, merely ostensible, to wit the settlement of a pretended purchase of a tract of country on the Washita, claimed by a Baron Bastrop. This was to serve as the pretext for all his preparations, an allurement for such followers as really wished to acquire settlements in that country, and a cover under which to retreat in the event of a final discomfiture of both branches of his real design.[22]

The attachment of Westerners to the Union and to the administration, on which Jefferson counted so strongly, was strikingly demonstrated by actions on the Ohio River of which he was informed the day before Christmas. He preferred that western officials should stop the expedition by their own power without federal interposition, and in fact local authority was effectually invoked at the most crucial spot after the receipt of his warning. The expedition was so weakened before it got started that it was never again a real menace and the man most responsible for this lethal blow was the Governor of the newest state, Ohio. The wisdom of sending John Graham west as Jefferson's emissary was unmistakably demonstrated. Reaching Marietta before Wilkinson's revelations got to Washington, he picked up information to pretty much the same effect from Burr's gullible supporter Harman Blennerhassett, on whose island the expedition was to assemble, and from others. He also learned that across the river in Wood County, Virginia, within the jurisdiction of which lay Blennerhassett's Island, a committee had been organized against any illegal scheme.[23] Proceed-

---

[21] The treatment of the episode of the Bastrop lands by Abernethy, pp. 73-77, seems to me convincing. See, however, the account by N. Schachner (*Burr*, pp. 317, 329-330).

[22] In message of Jan. 22, 1807, to Congress (*Annals*, 9 Cong., 2 sess., pp. 39-43; *A.S.P., Misc.*, I, 468).

[23] James Wilson to Madison, Nov. 21, 1806 (Letters in Relation to Burr's Conspiracy, LC). These events on the Ohio are well described by Abernethy, pp. 104-109.

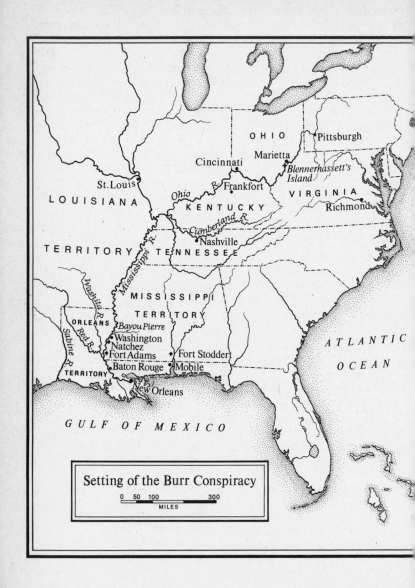

Setting of the Burr Conspiracy

0 50 100   300
MILES

ing to Chillicothe, Graham saw Governor Edward Tiffin before that official received Dearborn's instructions to seize any boats that were being built for Burr near Marietta. Tiffin promptly sought and received from the Ohio legislature authority to seize the stores and boats on the Muskingum River and to arrest Burr's agents. The supposition among the legislators was that he planned to take New Orleans and set up an independent government which the western states were expected ultimately to join.

On orders from the Governor ten boats were intercepted on the river on December 9 and others, some of them unfinished, were seized in the boatyard. Some two hundred barrels of supplies were confiscated.[24] A few boats escaped from Blennerhassett's Island, carrying the owner and Comfort Tyler among others. They implied by their flight that they harbored no illusions regarding the legality of their enterprise. They eluded the watch that was set at Cincinnati and were ultimately joined by Burr at the mouth of the Cumberland. Other boats outran Graham's warnings, and when Burr himself joined the flotilla at almost the end of the year it consisted altogether of ten boats, carrying at a maximum about one hundred men, along with another loaded with supplies.[25] As Jefferson was to tell Congress, this expedition constituted no grave threat to New Orleans.

During the fall, while Burr's henchmen were making preparations on the Ohio River, he had been busily engaged in Kentucky and Tennessee, especially in the former. There he had a number of friends who were prominent Republicans and some of whom were believed to have been involved in past separatist plots. The reports reaching Washington from Kentucky in November and December were most confusing. As we have seen, the lead against Burr in that locality was taken by Federalists, especially United States Attorney Daveiss. Burr had given his old friends to understand that the administration approved his projected expedition, and they were disposed to rally to his defense against a political enemy. Not until John Graham's arrival in mid-December did these Republican leaders become aware of the attitude of Jefferson, and this was too late to cause Burr to be apprehended in Kentucky.

Previous to this, efforts on the part of Daveiss to bring him to justice, efforts with which the administration had nothing whatever to do, had proved abortive. The climax was reached on December 5,

---

[24] In his entry of Dec. 24, 1806, Plumer says information about this action reached Washington that day (*Memorandum*, p. 539). See TJ's comments on it in his letter to Gov. Tiffin, Feb. 2, 1807 (Ford, IX, 21–22).

[25] Abernethy, p. 113.

when, after examining the testimony that was presented, a federal grand jury declined to return a true bill either against him or former Senator John Adair, who was deeply implicated in his schemes.[26] The result was advantageous to him in the court of local public opinion, and this episode was to prove prophetic. It was going to be difficult to establish the illegality of his actions even when far more testimony was available, and there was danger of a revulsion of feeling in his favor as an alleged victim of injustice.[27] By the end of the year, however, the letters and proffers of assistance received by the President, including one from General Andrew Jackson in Nashville, confirmed his judgment that the men of the western waters would strongly support the government against internal danger as soon as they became aware of it.[28]

On the very day toward the end of December that Burr joined the little flotilla of Blennerhassett and Comfort Tyler at the mouth of the Cumberland (which happened to be the day before Captain Meriwether Lewis arrived in Washington) Jefferson told his dinner guest, Senator William Plumer, that he had no doubt the conspiracy would be put down without much trouble or expense despite its extensiveness.[29] Writing Wilkinson early in the new year, he expressed the belief that the enterprise was already crushed.[30] He believed that the "fugitives from justice" would be apprehended long before they could reach New Orleans, and he assured the General that there was no danger of a fleet from the West Indies. He did not want him to relax his preparations to defend the city until they had received further information, but in this reassuring letter he sought to cut down to size an enterprise which Wilkinson had exaggerated.

The British Minister, reporting to his government early in January, likewise took an optimistic view of the situation. There seemed to be no doubt, he said, that an "illicit enterprise" had been contemplated,

[26] Developments in Kentucky are described by Abernethy, pp. 95–100, 110–113. The negative action of the grand jury was known in Washington by Dec. 24 (Plumer, *Memorandum*, p. 540).

[27] A characteristic assertion of innocence is contained in his letter of Nov. 27, 1806, to Gov. William Henry Harrison, an attested copy of which was sent TJ (LC, 30498–30499).

[28] Jackson to TJ, Nov. 24, 1806 (LC, 28504; TJ to Jackson, Dec. 3, 1806 (L. & B., XIX 156–157). Among other letters of reassurance received about this time was one of Dec. 4 from Thomas Truxtun, to whom Burr is supposed to have made advances. Enclosed with this was Truxtun's plan of Aug. 10 "to counteract Col. Burr's schemes" (LC, 28169, 28526).

[29] Dec. 27, 1806 (Plumer, *Memorandum*, p. 544). The entry for this day reports many other interesting comments by TJ on the conspiracy.

[30] TJ to Wilkinson, Jan. 3, 1807 (Ford, IX, 1–3).

the most suspicious circumstance being that a very large sum of money had been collected for it, but he believed that the "prompt means" adopted by the Executive would most probably stop it.[31] Senator Samuel Latham Mitchill of New York, writing his wife about the middle of the month, said that the western people had come out in favor of the government and predicted that Burr would be disappointed. "By what means he will get out of the scrape I do not know," Mitchill added, "but he is full of cunning and subterfuge, and will reserve for himself a hole to creep out at." This senator approved of Wilkinson, saying that, after getting all the information he could out of the emissary sent to tempt him, he forwarded this to the President "like a faithful officer." And, within a week, Mitchill expressed the opinion that the conspiracy was "fully detected and frustrated."[32] This seems to have been a common opinion by that time, but there were many people in Congress who were deeply suspicious of Wilkinson; and, in view of what had happened in Kentucky, many must have wondered just how much could really be pinned on Burr. It would appear that the resolution calling on the President for information which the House of Representatives adopted on January 16 was more indicative of impatience than alarm.

This was introduced by John Randolph, who admitted that he could no longer "rest satisfied in that state of supineness and apathy" in which the House had remained for the past six or seven weeks.[33] His performance in this connection affords another example of his assertiveness in his own behalf and in behalf of the legislative branch vis-à-vis the executive, but the natural desire to have authoritative information regarding this important matter, rather than mere newspaper reports, was expressed by many.

As introduced, the resolution consisted of two members, and in the end these were voted on separately. The first called upon the President to lay before the House any information in his possession, except such as he might believe that the public welfare required him to withhold, bearing on any illegal combination of individuals against the peace and safety of the Union, or any expedition planned against the territories of any power at peace with the United States. The second member of the resolution requested the President to let the House know what

[31] Erskine to Howick, Jan. 6, 1807 (FO, 5:52 [2], pp. 81–88).
[32] Jan. 16, 22, 1807 (*Harper's New Monthly Mag.*, LVIII [April, 1879], 751). The latter letter was written before TJ's message of the same date had been transmitted to Congress.
[33] *Annals*, 9 Cong., 2 sess., p. 334; resolution as introduced, p. 336; speeches and votes, pp. 334–359.

measures he had pursued and proposed to take against such a combination or expedition. Randolph left no doubt that he was much more
concerned about a conspiracy against the Union than an attack on
Spanish territories. Highly suspicious of Spain, he thought it more
likely that she was the aggressor than the defendant. He also made it
clear that he cultivated a degree of skepticism in politics and that his
confidence in the Executive depended on the latter's conduct. The
main objection to the requests to the President, as voiced in the debate,
was that they reflected a lack of confidence in him. Only a small
number of Republican stalwarts, like Barnabas Bidwell and Joseph B.
Varnum, opposed the first member of the resolution when the test
came. Jefferson's former secretary, William A. Burwell, and his son-in-
law, John W. Eppes, spoke in favor of it and it carried by a vote of 109
to 14. Objection to the second member was much stronger, and only
after the reference to the measures the President *proposed* to take had
been stricken out of John Randolph's motion was it adopted by a vote
of 67 to 52. Thus Jefferson was not asked to show his full hand before
the game was over.

If the issue of confidence had been unmistakably raised, there is little
reason to doubt that, at a time when Jefferson was being deluged with
petitions to consent to a third term, the Republican majority would
have rallied round him. The action of the House was not taken by him
as a rebuke, though he doubtless regarded it as unnecessary and if it
had come much earlier he would almost certainly have thought it ill-
timed. There were a number of reasons why he had not communicated
with Congress regarding the conspiracy during the five or six weeks of
legislative "supineness and apathy" which John Randolph deplored.
Reports of the arrival of General Wilkinson in New Orleans and of
the seizure of Burr's boats and supplies on the upper Ohio, reached the
legislators through the newspapers. He saw no need to call upon them
for action, and they could not have done anything soon enough to
affect the immediate situation anyway. He told Senator Plumer privately that he believed there was now sufficient proof of the guilt of
Blennerhassett but was not sure of this in the case of Burr, whom he
regarded as the archtraitor but who had emerged triumphant from the
abortive judicial proceedings in Kentucky — as the senators and representatives now knew.[34] In a private letter written less than a week
before he received from the hands of John Randolph the request of the
House for information about the conspiracy, he expressed himself on
this subject with a frankness he had not yet permitted himself in
public:

[34] Entry of Dec. 27, 1806 (Plumer, *Memorandum*, p. 543).

Burr's enterprise is the most extraordinary since the days of Don Quixot. It is so extravagant that those who know his understanding would not believe it if the proofs admitted doubt. He has meant to place himself on the throne of Montezuma, and extend his empire to the Allegany seizing on N Orleans as the instrument of compulsion for our Western States. I think his undertaking effectually crippled by the activity of Ohio. Whether Kentucky will give him the coup de grace is doubtful; but if he is able to descend the river with any means we are sufficiently prepared at New Orleans. I hope however Kentucky will do its duty & finish the matter for the honour of popular govmt and the discouragement of all arguments for standing armies.[35]

From these judgments he did not afterwards deviate, but, insofar as they related to Burr's objectives, they were based on statements which had not been given under oath and many of which had been made in confidence. He recognized the need for some testimony that was unquestionably incriminating and could be communicated to Congress with propriety. A document received from Wilkinson on January 18 seemed to meet both requirements. In New Orleans it had already been made part of the public record by the General himself in support of his charges against Burr's messengers. This was Burr's letter of July 29, 1806, which Wilkinson had received in cipher from Samuel Swartwout on October 8; he got Erick Bollman's duplicate a few weeks later. Retaining the original, he gave out, in mid-December, "as fair an interpretation" of it as he had been able to make thus far.[36] On reading this for the first time, Jefferson may have wondered about the General's past relations with Burr, but Wilkinson's actions clearly demonstrated that he was against Burr *now*, and upon its face the letter offered convincing evidence of that adventurous gentleman's conspiratorial purposes and activities.

The first part of this startling communication, as Jefferson first saw it, reads as follows:

I, Aaron Burr, have obtained funds, and have actually commenced the enterprise. Detachments from different points, and under different pretences, will rendezvous on the Ohio 1st November.

[35] TJ to Rev. Charles Clay, Jan. 11, 1807 (Ford, IX, 7).
[36] See p. 250 and note 41 above. It was Wilkinson's version of the duplicate entrusted to Bollman and received by him Nov. 6, 1806, that TJ got first. (I am following the capitalization and punctuation of this.) He transmitted it to Congress in his message of Jan. 22, 1807, and, receiving the Swartwout duplicate on Jan. 23, TJ transmitted that on Jan. 26 (*Annals,* 9 Cong., 2 sess., pp. 39–43; 1008–1012).

Everything internal and external favors views. Protection of
England is secured T[ruxtun] is going to Jamaica to arrange
with the Admiral on that station, and will meet on the Mississippi
— England — navy of the United States are ready to join, and
final orders are given to my friends and followers. It will be a
host of choice spirits. Wilkinson shall be second to Burr only.
Wilkinson shall dictate the rank and promotion of his officers.
Burr will proceed westward, 1st August, never to return; with
him goes his daughter: the husband will follow in October, with
a corps of worthies.

Time was to show that Wilkinson modified this letter upon occasion
to suit his own purposes. In the copy he sent Jefferson the name of
Burr appears in the first line, which is not the case in the version he
himself afterwards quoted.[37] Wilkinson also omitted the acknowledgment of a letter from him to Burr, dated May 13, which showed that
the two men had been in previous communication. He sought to give
the impression that he had received a fresh proposal. Such was not the
implication of the instructions to him in the body of the letter, but
here the ingenious General made a significant alteration. Burr had said:
"Our object, my dear friend, is brought to a point so long desired." In
the version now submitted this sentence reads: "The project is brought
to the point so long desired."

The plan of operations as described here by Burr called for the
descent of the rivers by "the first five hundred or one thousand men in
light boats, now constructing for that purpose" (a much less impressive movement than the one predicted in Wilkinson's own earlier
report), and for the meeting of Burr and the General at Natchez,
where they would decide whether or not to take Baton Rouge from
the Spanish before proceeding to New Orleans. The objective of the
mission was clearly shown to be Mexico, where it was claimed the
people were prepared to receive them. Said Burr: "The gods invite to
glory and fortune: it remains to be seen whether we deserve the boon."

This sensational letter was included among the documents that
Jefferson communicated to Congress with his special message of January 22, 1807. Since his information from the inland waterways lagged a
month behind events, he had heard by that date only that Burr was
descending the Cumberland with two boats. His doubts that the boats
assembling at the river's mouth would be arrested before reaching the

[37] Burr's letter appears in its generally accepted form in W. F. McCaleb, pp.
68–69, and elsewhere. A facsimile of the cipher letter is in "Burr-Blennerhasset
Documents," *Quarterly Publication of the Historical and Philosophical Society of
Ohio,* IX (1914).

Mississippi had increased rather than diminished, but, in view of the small size of the expedition and the preparations made to intercept it, he rightly judged that the termination of the enterprise was approaching and that a disclosure of information such as the House had requested could now be safely made. His communication was not confidential. The senators ordered five hundred copies of it printed for their own use; it appeared in the *National Intelligencer* the next day; and its contents quickly became a matter of public knowledge.[38]

He did not believe that the present state of the evidence warranted him in exposing the names of alleged conspirators (referred to by Burr as "choice spirits") except that of the "principal actor," whose guilt was "placed beyond question." For this unqualified assertion, which was held by defenders of Burr to be a prejudgment of the case, he was afterwards severely criticized; and, with the benefit of hindsight, we may now conclude that it was most unfortunate. The most damning document (Burr's letter to Wilkinson) spoke for itself, and Jefferson might have adopted a more tentative tone in his own message. Thus he might have reduced the danger, though he could hardly have obviated it, that his own political enemies and those of Wilkinson would make a martyr out of Burr, claiming that he was the victim of persecution. The charge, often made by hostile contemporaries of Jefferson and taken up subsequently by some historians, that, ever since the electoral tie of 1800, he had been vindictive toward his accidental rival, is not borne out by Jefferson's own words and actions prior to the beginning of what he was sure was a conspiracy against the government and the country. His attitude in the present connection can be best explained in terms of the developing circumstances, and it is not hard to see how he reached the conclusion that Burr's guilt was indubitable. The testimony against him probably seemed more rather than less credible because it came from one who had been intimately associated with him.

In his message to Congress Jefferson gave an admirable statement of developments as he had become aware of them, along with an impressive account of the measures he had taken. He praised Governor Tiffin and the legislature of Ohio for their prompt, energetic, and patriotic action, which so materially disabled Burr's enterprise at the outset. He dismissed the surmises that foreign powers were engaged in it and, in general, was reassuring rather than alarming. Speaking of Wilkinson's conduct in dispatching from Natchitoches in October the information that occasioned the presidential proclamation of November 27, he said that the General acted "with the honor of a soldier and fidelity of a

[38] Erskine sent a copy to his government, Feb. 1, 1807 (FO, 5:52 [2], pp. 91–96).

good citizen." This now seems an over-statement, but he was not aware of the surrounding circumstances as modern scholars are.

The references to Wilkinson in the final paragraph raise a more difficult question. That his sworn statements were submitted to Congress by Jefferson without critical comment is not surprising. If the President had any doubts of the credibility of the Commanding General he would have been unwise to voice them publicly. But he had to report that Wilkinson, who was in fact acting on his own authority, had caused Burr's emissaries to be arrested and to be embarked for eastern ports, although they were entitled to trial in the Territory of Orleans. Furthermore, by his own admission, Wilkinson had circumvented the local judicial authorities who had ordered their release on writs of habeas corpus. Jefferson glossed over the legal difficulties, saying that these men were probably transported because an impartial trial could not be expected at the time in New Orleans and because they could not be safely confined there as yet. Putting the best face he could on the matter, he suggested that justice was more likely of attainment in Washington.

Without entering at this point into the complicated question of the legal proceedings against Swartwout and Bollman, we can say here that Wilkinson's conduct in New Orleans was admittedly high-handed and that Jefferson was being placed in a position where he must either palliate his actions or repudiate them. Furthermore, since Wilkinson had declared under oath that Bollman had committed misprision of treason against the United States, no lesser charge than treason was now to be expected in Burr's case, although it would have been much easier to prove that he had tried to launch an illegal expedition against Mexico. Jefferson undoubtedly believed that Burr's *purposes* were treasonable, but in the matter of punitive procedure Wilkinson forced his hand and limited his freedom of action. Whatever the General's motives may have been, up to a point he had served his country well, in Jefferson's judgment. His support was not as crucial now as it had been earlier, but there was reason to believe that a strong hand was still needed in remote and distracted New Orleans. Furthermore, it was he who had provided the testimony which, in Jefferson's opinion, clinched the argument against the chief conspirator. As an instrument of justice, however, this equivocal character was miscast, and from this time on he was to prove a grave embarrassment to the administration.

[XVI]

Uncertain Verdict in Washington

WHEN the President, in response to the resolution that impatient John Randolph had caused the House to adopt, sent Congress his special message on the conspiracy, nobody in Washington yet knew that Burr had surrendered to the civil authorities in the Territory of Mississippi. Not until a month later was that event officially reported to the legislators.[1] This was not the end of the journey for the "principal actor." He was released, took flight while still on bond, and was not captured until another month had passed. To all practical purposes, however, his enterprise was terminated, and its failure was anticipated by many people in the capital from the time of the presidential message in late January.

The *National Intelligencer*, which made space for the entire message and the papers accompanying it, observed that it might perhaps be read with greater interest than any document heretofore presented to the American public. Commenting on the enterprise that was disclosed, this journal said: "Indignation and abhorrence towards the traitors can only be exceeded by exultation at the issue — an issue which entitles our republican system, and those who administer it, to a distinction that does not fade before the lustre of ancient times."[2] Jefferson himself regarded the outcome as a vindication of a system which relied on the citizenry rather than on military might; and he believed that the easy suppression of this movement had increased public confidence in the government.[3] But his administration would have faced less embarrassment and fewer problems after the event if the expedition of Aaron Burr had been dispersed less easily.

[1] It occurred on Jan. 18, 1807, a few days before TJ's message of Jan. 22, and was communicated to Congress by him on Feb. 19 (*Annals,* 9 Cong., 2 sess., p. 72; *A.S.P., Misc.,* I, 478).

[2] *National Intelligencer,* Jan. 23, 1807.

[3] TJ to Claiborne, Feb. 3, 1807 (L. & B., XI, 151).

The day before the congressional session ended on March 3, the British Minister reported to his government that the administration was generally believed to have created a greater alarm than the nature and extent of the supposed conspiracy could justify.[4] Erskine himself was persuaded that there might have been great difficulty in suppressing it if "prompt and strong measures" had not been adopted when it was first discovered. He believed, however, that public opinion condemned the conduct of Wilkinson in New Orleans as arbitrary and tyrannical. He wrote from the capital of the country, where, far from the scene of danger, critics of the administration found it easy to deny that the public safety had been at stake.

Historians still differ about the gravity of the situation the government had faced, but until this time Jefferson himself had gone to great pains not to exaggerate it. He rejoiced that he himself had been spared the necessity of crushing Burr's unlawful enterprise by force. Unlike Alexander Hamilton in the Whiskey Rebellion in the previous decade, he did not seize upon it as a welcome opportunity to display military might and thereby enhance federal authority. When congratulating the Governor and legislature of Ohio on the efficacious actions in the neighborhood of Marietta, he said: "The hand of the people has given the mortal blow to a conspiracy which, in other countries would have called for an appeal to armies, and has proved that government to be the strongest of which every man feels himself a part. It is a happy illustration, too, of the importance of preserving to the State authorities all that vigor which the Constitution foresaw would be necessary, not only for their own safety, but for that of the whole."[5] Granting the officials and citizens of Ohio major credit for the thwarting of the conspirators, he claimed for his own government only that it had given timely warning. And, far from showing any jealousy or regret, he regarded himself as fortunate in having been able to remain true to the principle of a limited and moderate government despite the crisis.

Opponents and critics of the administration were disposed to minimize its services in securing the country against danger, but otherwise the happenings in Ohio offered little grist for their mill. Their attention and that of others in Washington was focused on New Orleans and on actions reported by Wilkinson in documents that Jefferson had submitted to Congress — actions which, as the General acknowledged, went beyond and even against the law. He claimed justification on the ground of dangers which were now known in Washington to be

---

[4] Erskine to Howick, Mar. 2, 1807 (FO, 5:52 [2], pp. 117-121).
[5] TJ to Gov. Edward Tiffin, Feb. 2, 1807 (Ford, IX, 21-22, where the Governor is given the wrong initials).

greatly reduced and which that flamboyant officer could now be charged with having exaggerated in the first place. Jefferson's political enemies seized upon the opportunity to castigate the arbitrary actions of Wilkinson and to stigmatize the administration for condoning them and thereby imperiling both the rule of law and the freedom of the individual. Jefferson attributed the outcry against Wilkinson to the Federalists and John Randolph's little band of dissident Republicans, and he had good reason to suppose that he himself was their major target, but there were many other people who distrusted the General, deplored illegality, and feared military authority.[6] Thus Jefferson, who had felt compelled to depend on him, was in an embarrassing situation, and the success of the government in attaining the end it sought, the freeing of the country from what he regarded as a dangerous threat, was obscured and belittled while indignation was vented on the means that had been employed by one of its agents.

Bollman and Swartwout, who had been apprehended by Wilkinson, arrived in Washington in military custody the day after Jefferson sent his message to Congress.[7] From Wilkinson's correspondence already communicated to that body it was known that writs of habeas corpus had been issued in behalf of both of these men and that he had prevented their delivery. He had also caused the arrest of James Alexander and Peter V. Ogden, the latter of whom was released from prison on such a writ. The General charged that Judge James Workman, who issued it, was sympathetic to Burr. Writing Wilkinson on February 3, Jefferson said that Alexander had arrived in Washington and that Ogden was expected. He did not believe that the evidence was sufficient to commit them. The warning he sent Wilkinson at that time not to deport persons on mere suspicion came too late to do much good.[8] What he thought of the legal evidence against Bollman and Swartwout, the emissaries who had carried Burr's incriminating letter, he did not say. He reported to Congress that he had promptly delivered to the district attorney the evidence Wilkinson had sent, "with instructions to lay the same before the judges, and apply for their process to bring the accused to justice."

He soon had an opportunity to form a judgment on the more intelligent and better informed of these two men, for Dr. Bollman promptly

---

[6] Doubts and suspicions were voiced in loyal Republican papers, as in Richmond *Enquirer* and *Virginia Argus*, Mar. 3, 1807.

[7] As TJ reported in a message of Jan. 26, 1807, with which he sent Wilkinson's affidavit of Dec. 26, 1806, including Swartwout's duplicate of Burr's letter as decoded (*A.S.P., Misc.*, I, 471–473; *Annals*, 9 Cong., 2 sess., pp. 45, 1012–1016).

[8] TJ to Wilkinson, Feb. 3, 1807 (L. & B., XI, 149).

sought and was immediately granted an interview with him. Madison, who was present at Jefferson's request, made notes on it.[9] Having been assured that nothing he said would be used against him, Bollman talked at length. His denials need not be taken at face value, for he was not under oath and was naturally trying to make out as good a case as possible.[10] On the other hand, since he obviously remained loyal to Burr, credence can be given such admissions of his as bore out the charge that the purposes and actions of his leader were illegal. He left no possible doubt of Burr's plan to invade Mexico, although he seemed in no sense disturbed by the illegality of a project whose success, in his opinion, would be to the ultimate advantage of the United States. He flatly denied any intention on Burr's part to effect a separation of the American Union, claiming that talk of his to that effect was merely designed to deceive the Spanish Minister. Jefferson himself was convinced that Yrujo had been deliberately kept in the dark about the designs against Mexico, but there is no reason to suppose that Bollman's testimony caused the President to alter his opinion that Burr would have separated the Union if he could have. While Bollman denied that there was any intention to revolutionize Louisiana, he admitted that Burr planned to seize the French artillery in New Orleans and to requisition the shipping he needed to transport his troops to Vera Cruz. These purposes implied a disregard not only of private rights but also of international obligations and the sovereignty of the Territory of Orleans.

Bollman's description of the enterprise as a whole made it seem no less extraordinary than it had appeared in Wilkinson's first revelation of it. His account was calculated to weaken Jefferson's confidence in the General, against whom Bollman showed "the strongest resentment" and gave very damaging testimony. He represented Wilkinson as a party to Burr's plans who had been expected to resign his commission in the United States Army and serve as second in command but who had acted "contrary to all Burr's calculations" and had thus upset them. Jefferson may be presumed either to have discounted this part of the testimony or to have continued to disregard Wilkinson's dubious past because of his supposed present loyalty.

Shortly after Bollman made these oral communications, Jefferson asked him to commit them to writing, giving his own word of honor

[9] Printed in *Letters and Other Writings of James Madison* (1865), II, 393–401; MS in LC, 28865–28870. Bollman was a German, fluent in French as well as English, who had an adventurous career in Europe and had been taken up by Burr after his failure in business in America (see Abernethy, *Burr Conspiracy*, p. 57).

[10] For his purposes as viewed by his interlocutors, see Madison's *Letters*, as cited above, II, 401.

that they would never be used against Bollman himself, and that the papers would never go out of his (Jefferson's) hands. As a result, he received a lengthy written communication which differed from the one recorded by Madison chiefly in that Bollman had more to say about Wilkinson and his own conversations with him in New Orleans and about the desirability of the "emancipation" of Spanish America.[11] Though not yet aware that Burr had surrendered in Mississippi, Bollman recognized that, because of Wilkinson's unexpected conduct, the position of his own chief had become desperate. He therefore expressed the hope that the United States government, "seizing with a great mind the great features of his enterprise," would stop the hostilities between him and Wilkinson, declare war on Spain, allow Burr to proceed, and render his success indubitable by loaning him money and providing naval cooperation. While admitting the unlikelihood that such a line of conduct would be adopted, he said that perhaps no sovereign ever had a "more glorious opportunity" than the President of the United States had at that moment "to take a most important and most beneficent part in the affairs of the world at large." Obviously unrepentant about his own part in Burr's enterprise, he offered various practical suggestions if the United States should participate in it.

ii

The fact that Bollman had had an interview with the President became known quickly, but what had occurred in it was confidential. Meanwhile, the Senate in secret session took hasty and unprecedented action by passing a bill suspending the privilege of the writ of habeas corpus for three months in certain cases. No proof has been adduced for the claim of some of Jefferson's political enemies, a claim which has been repeated in modern historical works, that he requested this. The man who introduced the original resolution was William Branch Giles of Virginia, who has been improperly described as Jefferson's personal representative in the Senate. In fact, though highly partisan, he was a man of pronounced independence who took orders from no one. A clue to his motives may be found in the hostility to the federal judiciary that he had strongly expressed on many occasions. Presumably he was resentful of the conduct of the judges in New Orleans and Kentucky and fearful of what those in Washington might do to embarrass

[11] TJ to Bollman, Jan. 25, 1807 (LC, 28864); Bollman to TJ, Jan. 26, 1807, with enclosure (LC, 28875-28883). TJ afterwards sent the document to George Hay, Burr's prosecutor, instructing him to show it to no one except his associate counsel. TJ to George Hay, May 20, 1807 (Ford, IX, 52); see below, pp. 307-308.

the administration. With him on the committee which reported this bill was Samuel Smith of Maryland, Wilkinson's devoted friend. In the course of the debate he read portions of a letter from the General in which suspicion was cast on one of the judges in New Orleans (Workman) who had granted an alleged conspirator (Ogden) a writ of habeas corpus and released him. The admitted purpose of the bill was to keep Bollman, Swartwout, and other supposed conspirators in confinement; and its wording was such that it amounted to a legalization of the arrests that had been ordered by Wilkinson. Not only did Senator Smith display much anxiety that it be passed; he took it to the House, seeking the speedy concurrence of that body. The third member of the committee could not be justly charged with hostility to the judiciary or with a desire to shield Wilkinson, but, according to William Plumer, Senator John Quincy Adams was *passionately zealous* for the passage of the bill. The only serious critic of it was James A. Bayard, and hardly anybody voted against it. A single senator could have prevented the suspension of the rules whereby the bill was introduced and passed on the same day, but nobody objected. Plumer, whose account of the proceedings is the fullest we have, himself favored the measure, thinking that little evil would result from it and that the state of things required it. While anticipating that ultimately Wilkinson's duplicity would be punished, he believed that military commanders must be supported in time of rebellion and public danger. This moderate Federalist said: "A mistaken zeal for liberty — for theoretic liberty — has often endangered the security of nations."[12]

Viewing the political scene from New York, Rufus King, one of the most distinguished of the Federalists in retirement, privately stated that this measure would have put in the power of the Chief Executive and his minions every man in the country who was not prepared "to fall

[12] Quotation, with punctuation slightly modified, from Plumer, *Memorandum*, p. 592; for his account of the proceedings of Jan. 23, 1807, and comments of the next few days, see pp. 585–592. He said only three or four voted against the bill. J. Q. Adams describes the episode more briefly in his *Memoirs*, I, 445–446, saying that only Bayard voted in the negative. Only the barest facts are in *Annals*, 9 Cong., 2 sess., p. 44. Charles Warren (*Supreme Court*, I, 302) says TJ requested the action. Beveridge (*Marshall*, III, 346) incorrectly describes Giles as TJ's "personal representative." He says nothing of the presence of J. Q. Adams on the committee, but cites J. Q. to John Adams, Jan. 27, 1807 (*Writings*, III, 158). The reference there to "the papers from the President on which the Senate acted" may have conveyed the false impression that this action was recommended in TJ's message. D. R. Anderson, *William Branch Giles* (1914), pp. 106–107, describes Giles's actions, intimating in no way that TJ prompted them. The statement of Marshall Smelser in *The Democratic Republic, 1801–1815* (1968), p. 119, that TJ "asked for *ex post facto* suspension of the writ for three months" shows the persistence of this unsupported claim.

down and worship the Idol of Democracy." The effort to suspend habeas corpus, he said, was "religiously believed" to have been made at the instigation of the President.[13] In the debate on the measure in the House, however, the assertion was made that Jefferson had *not* recommended it and there is no reason to suppose he had.[14] The bill provided that in *all* cases where "any person or persons, charged on oath [as in Wilkinson's affidavits] with treason, misprision of treason, or other high crime or misdemeanor, endangering the peace, safety, or neutrality of the United States" *had been* or should be arrested or imprisoned by warrant or authority of the President, or the chief executive of any state or territory, or any person acting under presidential authority, the privilege of the writ of habeas corpus should be suspended for three months.[15]

In the House, where the bill was discussed in open session, Jefferson's son-in-law, John W. Eppes, moved its rejection, and his former secretary, William A. Burwell, made the first recorded speech against it. Eppes spoke at considerable length a little later.[16] There may have been a purposeful sting in John Randolph's declaration that he was extremely happy to observe the quarter from which opposition to the bill originated, but in this debate the issue was not between the administration and its critics. It was a Federalist, James Elliott of Vermont, who described the bill as the "most extraordinary proposition" ever presented to them for consideration; but most of the speeches against it were made by Republicans, and the supreme importance of habeas corpus as a safeguard of human liberty against arbitrary governmental action was recognized by virtually everybody. The compelling argument was that the danger facing the country was not grave enough to warrant its suspension. The various speakers made more of the potential tyranny of lesser officials than that of the Presi-

[13] His comments are in an unpublished "article" found in his papers (King, IV, 543–549; quotations from p. 547). He gave the House credit for checking this "act of tyranny."

[14] For a particular reference to the legislative origins of the measure, see *Annals*, 9 Cong., 2 sess., p. 423. In his entry for Jan. 23, 1807, Plumer says (*Memorandum*, p. 590) that TJ, presuming that the bill would be passed into law that day, instructed the district attorney to seek from the court a warrant against Bollman and Swartwout. TJ afterwards reported to Congress that he did this on that day, but there is no evidence known to me that his action was based on the expectation of the concurrence of the House in the Senate bill. Nor does it seem likely that he or anybody else could have expected that body to suspend its rules and take immediate action. In fact, the House adjourned on Friday, Jan. 23, before Senator Smith could get there, and he did not deliver the message until Monday.

[15] Text of the Senate bill as delivered to the House in *Annals*, 9 Cong., 2 sess., p. 402, italics added; debate and actions there, pp. 402–425.

[16] *Ibid.*, pp. 403–406, 409–411, for their speeches.

dent. Jefferson's supporters appear to have succeeded in dissociating him from this odious measure. John Randolph asserted that the military had not only usurped the civil authority but had assumed omnipotent authority, and he raised the question whether the United States was under a military government. Such was certainly not the case anywhere outside of New Orleans.

The net result of these proceedings was that the Senate bill was rejected on the day the House received it. The vote, 113 to 19, represented an overwhelming victory for the freedom of the individual. In the course of the debate there were a number of references (by Republicans) to the blessings previously and presently enjoyed by Americans under the existing government. Thus Varnum of Massachusetts said: "While the nation, from one extreme to the other, enjoys a degree of prosperity and happiness unparalleled in any other nation, and not a single individual within our limits has any reason to complain of oppression, an insurrection is fomented, subversive of the Government and destructive of the rights of the people."[17] But the discussion as a whole tended to minimize the dangers that had been escaped and to distract attention not only from the security that had been maintained but also from the moderation that had so generally attended the conduct of the administration. The senators had appeared to be still alarmed about Burr and greatly concerned lest he and his accomplices escape punishment. In the more representative House, on the other hand, the members seemed more fearful and resentful of Wilkinson, who in the eyes of many now appeared as the major villain. Besides his dubious reputation, there were tangible reasons for this. Two of the men arrested and transported by him were in Washington under military guard and they appealed to human sympathy, as Burr himself was to do after his lonely flight and final apprehension.

A few days after the House rejected the bill calling for the suspension of the privilege of the writ of habeas corpus, Bollman and Swartwout were committed for treason, without bail, by the circuit court of the District of Columbia. The government was inevitably cast in the role of prosecutor and had to bear whatever odium might be attached to this action. Jefferson now had an attorney general, for he had appointed Caesar A. Rodney to the vacant post, and he may be presumed to have taken counsel with that official. He may also be presumed to have expected the proceedings to follow an orderly legal course. But, unhappily this case assumed a political complexion from the start, since his two appointees to this court favored the commit-

17 *Ibid.*, p. 412.

ment of the two emissaries of Burr while the Federalist, Judge William Cranch, nephew of Abigail Adams, dissented.

Despite the fact that Cranch was one of John Adams's "midnight judges," Jefferson had reappointed him and named him chief justice of this court. If, however, he could have read a letter the young judge wrote his father at this juncture, no doubt the President would have regarded it as another example of Federalist self-righteousness and of the proneness of Federalist judges to view the conduct of his administration through the eyes of political partisanship. In his private letter Cranch said: "I have dared to set the law and the Constitution in opposition to the arm of Executive power, supported by popular clamor. . . . I felt that the public interest might be benefitted by committing those gentlemen for trial, yet I could not consent to sacrifice the most important constitutional provision in favor of individual liberty, to reasons of State."[18] He did little more than hint at the perennial problem of reconciling individual liberty with the interests and necessities of state. Instead of recognizing that Jefferson as a champion of personal freedom who was also the responsible head of a nation was confronted with a dilemma, the Judge attributed his actions to a craving for power and popularity. The conflict between the Jeffersonian Republicans and the Federalist judiciary was entering upon a new phase which, like the previous ones, was to be marked by mutual distrust. The President may have exaggerated the political motivation of his foes, as they did his, but he undoubtedly believed that partisan judges would thwart his government if they could.

The Supreme Court had not yet acted on the application of Bollman and Swartwout for a writ of habeas corpus when, early in February, Jefferson expressed himself about the General's conduct in private letters to him and Governor Claiborne in New Orleans.[19] Though agreeing that the public safety must be the first concern, Jefferson clearly implied that, in the light of the information available to him, the danger had not been great enough to warrant all that Wilkinson admittedly had done. The President's statement that the evidence against two of the deported men was insufficient and his warning to the General not to deport persons on grounds of suspicion alone now seem much too mild. His position in history as a champion of human

---

[18] Warren, *Supreme Court*, I, 303–304, describes this episode, giving a long extract from Judge Cranch's letter of Feb. 2, 1807. Though terming the opinion "noble," this judicious historian recognizes that Cranch's Federalism colored his language.

[19] TJ to Wilkinson and to Claiborne, Feb. 3, 1807 (L. & B., XI, 147–151). With these letters he sent a copy of his message of Jan. 22 to Congress.

rights and an upholder of the rule of law would have been strengthened if he had issued a stern rebuke. But his knowledge of developments in New Orleans lagged a month and more behind events. He did
not know that, in the middle of January, Wilkinson had made one of
his most sensational arrests, that of John Adair, former senator from
Kentucky, who had just arrived in New Orleans. Shortly afterwards he
shipped this former friend to Baltimore, where in due course he was
released for lack of evidence.[20] Since the excited General claimed that,
if left at large, Adair would have fomented an insurrection, he might
not have stayed his hand even if he had received Jefferson's mild words
of warning, but the fact is that he did not get them until after Congress
had adjourned.[21] Those who conducted public affairs in that era continued to be plagued by the difficulties of communication. On the
periphery of the Republic the Commanding General was virtually
beyond control and in Washington the President learned of one *fait
accompli* after another.

While Jefferson cannot escape the charge of gullibility in his relations with Wilkinson, the simplest explanation of his course is that one
seemingly necessary step followed another until he had reached a
position from which it would have been extremely difficult to withdraw. Having decided in November not only that the General was
now loyal to him and the government, but also that he must rely on
the tattered warrior as a major agent in checking Burr, and having
concluded by January if not earlier that he was of prime importance in
the exposure of the conspiracy and the punishment of the conspirators,
the President saw no choice at this stage but to support him. He
himself did not yet know that the enterprise was terminated, though
he had no doubt it soon would be, and he was necessarily uncertain of
the situation in distant New Orleans. Furthermore, he recognized that
Wilkinson's information about the actual course and prospects of
Burr's expedition had been incomplete.

The General may not really have estimated the likely number of
Burr's supporters to be as great as he originally reported, but, when he
ordered these arrests and deportations (except for that of Adair), he
had not learned of the crippling blow that had been struck against the
expedition in Ohio, and he said he was expecting it to receive strong

---

[20] Wilkinson arrested Adair on Jan. 14. On this action and other developments
in New Orleans, see Abernethy, pp. 180–182.

[21] He acknowledged TJ's letter of Feb. 3 on Mar. 20, saying he received it Mar.
15.

support from the sea. Jefferson was giving him the full benefit of the doubt when he said: "In approving, therefore, as we do approve, of the defensive operations for New Orleans, we are obliged to estimate them, not according to our own view of the danger, but to place ourselves in your situation, and only with your information."

His power of projection, his ability to put himself in another person's place, was one of the reasons for his harmonious relations with his civil lieutenants, and in his dealings at this time with his chief military officer he gave a conspicuous example of sympathetic understanding. This was more than Wilkinson deserved, as he might have suspected, but he was in character when he said: "I am thoroughly sensible of the painful difficulties of your situation, expecting an attack from an overwhelming force, unversed in law, surrounded by suspected persons, and in a nation tender as to everything infringing liberty, and especially from the military." Recognizing these circumstances, he condoned the General's past actions in New Orleans. He issued a warning about future conduct, however, and he did not pronounce to Wilkinson, who was prone to over-reach himself, the principle he laid down at this time in his private letter to Claiborne, who was much less self-assertive. To the Governor he said: "On great occasions every good officer must be ready to risk himself in going beyond the strict line of law, when the public preservation requires it."

Far from repudiating this principle in later years, he elaborated upon it on one occasion after his retirement from the presidency. This was in a private response to an inquiry from an admirer of his statesmanship who had agreed to furnish Wilkinson some assistance in the preparation of his memoirs. We may be disposed to dismiss this reply as a rationalization of his own defense of Wilkinson's conduct in New Orleans, but it was a reasoned statement based on reflection. It suggests that he was more of a relativist at the end of his public career than at its beginning. From his sanctuary at Monticello he wrote:

The question you propose, whether circumstances do not sometimes occur which make it a duty in officers of high trust to assume authorities beyond the law, is easy of solution in principle, but sometimes embarrassing in practice: a strict observance of the written laws is doubtless *one* of the high duties of a good citizen: but it is not the *highest*. The laws of necessity, of self-preservation, of saving our country when in danger, are of higher obligation. To lose our country by a scrupulous adherence to written law, would be to lose the law itself, with life, liberty, property &

all those who are enjoying them with us; thus absurdly sacrificing the end to the means.[22]

After giving examples from the history of the American Revolution
and his own administration (suggesting that he now felt that occasionally he himself had been too scrupulous), he commented on Wilkinson's situation in New Orleans much as he had done to that officer at
the time. He believed that no honest man could deny that the General,
under the circumstances as he understood them, was warranted in
seizing "notorious conspirators." In justification of his sending them to
Washington on his own responsibility, in disregard if not in defiance
of local judicial authority, Jefferson had this to say:

> The danger of their rescue, of their continuing their machina-
> tions, the tardiness and weakness of the law, apathy of the judges,
> active patronage of the whole tribe of lawyers, unknown dis-
> position of the juries, an hourly expectation of the enemy, salva-
> tion of the city, and of the Union itself, which would have been
> convulsed to its centre had that conspiracy succeeded; all these
> constituted a law of necessity and self-preservation and rendered
> the *salus populi* supreme over the written law. The officer who is
> called to act on this superior ground does indeed risk himself on
> the justice of the controlling powers of the constitution and his
> station makes it his duty to incur that risk. But those controlling
> powers, and his fellow citizens generally, are bound to judge
> [him] according to the circumstances under which he acted.

These principles and examples, he said, did not relate to petty cases;
it was "incumbent on those only who accept of great charges to risk
themselves on great occasions," when the nation's safety or highest
interests are at stake. While recognizing that the line of discrimination
between cases might be difficult to draw, he said that the good officer
was bound to draw it "at his own peril, and throw himself on the
justice of the country and the rectitude of his motives." That was
precisely what Wilkinson had done, but in many minds there were
serious doubts of his wisdom and patriotic purpose.

Even in retrospect, Jefferson accepted as essentially correct Wilkinson's interpretation of the necessities under which he labored. In one

---

[22] To J. B. Colvin, Sept. 20, 1810 (L. & B., XII, 418–422; LC, 33964–33965, which
is quoted here), replying to Colvin's letter of Sept. 14 (LC, 33952). Burr's modern
champion, W. F. McCaleb, has described TJ's letter as reprehensible, showing him
at his worst (*New Light*, p. 128).

of the lengthy private letters he wrote the President while still there the General said he had been forced to take strong-handed measures "to destroy the concert and co-operation of the conspirators, to stem the torrent of disaffection, and to save the city from the horrors of civil commotion."[23] Also, he said repeatedly that he was buffeting a combination of influential enemies, having only Governor Claiborne and a few other officials on his side. But anyone familiar with his past might have suspected that he fomented hostility while ostensibly seeking to compose civil strife, and that he confused enmity to himself with hostility to the government. Into the details of the local situation we cannot enter here, but from the point of view of the administration it was significant, no doubt, that Claiborne approved of his conduct on the whole. The force of the Governor's approbation is weakened by the fact that, although a modifying influence, he was identified with Wilkinson's conduct in the public mind and was also an object of local censure. On the other hand, it is strengthened by the consideration that he was originally suspicious of the General and did not share the full confidence of that egotistical commander.

Regarding him the Governor wrote the Secretary of War: "*he has deserved well of the United States.*" While recognizing that exception might be taken to some of his measures, Claiborne was decidedly of the opinion that "the general policy he pursued was the best that could (under all circumstances) have been resorted to, and that to him this City and Territory are in a great measure indebted for their present safety."[24] He said the same thing to Jefferson a couple of months later, adding that as an eyewitness of Wilkinson's conduct who was familiar with his correspondence he himself verily believed that "he opposed Burr from principle and that his acts were directed by the purest motives of honest patriotism." While not pretending that the General had done no wrong, he believed that Wilkinson had been "an honest, zealous, and active agent in the suppression of a conspiracy which had for its objects the subversion of our Government, and the dismemberment of the Union."[25]

Judging from his letters to Wilkinson and Claiborne, Jefferson believed that the court of public opinion would approve the conduct of the former with respect to Swartwout and Bollman, whom he had sent to Washington, and also with respect to Burr, Blennerhassett, and

[23] Wilkinson to TJ, Feb. 13, 1807 (Letters in Relation to Burr's Conspiracy, LC).
[24] Claiborne to Dearborn, Mar. 3, 1807; received Apr. 27 (Carter, IX, 712).
[25] Claiborne to TJ, May 3, 1807; received June 15 (*ibid.*, 729–731).

Comfort Tyler, if they should fall into his hands and be arrested.[26] In Jefferson's eyes these were "notorious conspirators." In one of his letters to Jefferson, Wilkinson said: "For the justice you have done me, I can only say command my life, and if I had fortune I would add that also."[27] At this stage he may have been as loyal to the President and the government as he could be to anybody or anything, but he was highly suspect as an instrument of retributive justice.

Jefferson's opinion that the evidence against Peter V. Ogden was insufficient to warrant his commitment was confirmed when, on his arrival in Baltimore, he was discharged on a writ of habeas corpus by Judge Joseph H. Nicholson. It will be recalled that Nicholson had left the House of Representatives to assume a post in the judiciary of Maryland. The former Congressman also discharged former Senator John Adair, and, when reporting his actions, asked the President if he had any affidavits against the two men. In reply Jefferson said that he had no evidence against Adair, though he had been informed that the officer in charge of these prisoners had brought a packet from Wilkinson to be delivered to him. If this should be found to contain conclusive evidence, they could be arrested again, if that action should seem worth while. "Their crimes are defeated," he added, "and whether they shall be punished or not belongs to another department, and is not the subject of even a wish on my part."[28] Judge Nicholson had recently received from his intimate friend John Randolph, ruthless critic of Wilkinson and major gadfly of the administration, a letter saying that "whenever government comes into court demanding justice to be done upon an individual, it should come with clean hands; at least, that they should be unstained with oppression, committed upon the person of him whom they have dragged to the bar of criminal justice."[29] There is no evidence that Jefferson knew about this private letter, but he

[26] In *Aurora*, Feb. 26, 1807, William Duane said that if Wilkinson had *not* made the arrests, "he would have been stigmatized as a perfidious traitor, perhaps by the general sentiment of the country"; and on Mar. 11 this journalist said that if the country should not "justify and indemnify" Wilkinson they would deserve "to be betrayed by some new Arnold." On Feb. 27, in a rather extensive discussion which he himself regarded as dispassionate, he justified Wilkinson by arguments not unlike those of Jefferson himself.

[27] Wilkinson to TJ, Mar. 3, 1807; received May 4 (Letters in Relation to Burr's Conspiracy, LC). This was before he got TJ's letter of Feb. 3. He expressed his great appreciation of that in his letter of Mar. 20 (same collection).

[28] TJ to J. H. Nicholson, Feb. 20, 1807 (Ford, IX, 31–32), replying to Nicholson's letter of Feb. 18 (LC, 29020). On Feb. 20, Nathaniel Macon reported that TJ thought Nicholson could not have acted otherwise (Nicholson Papers, 3:1383).

[29] Quoted from Nicholson Papers in Warren, I, 305n.

could not have helped knowing that his government was being identified with Wilkinson's highhandedness. His reply to Nicholson suggests
his annoyance and his desire to dissociate himself from it. But in declaring his indifference to the outcome of the legal proceedings against
suspects, while affirming his adherence to the doctrine of the separation of powers, he was disingenuous. His strong desire to punish men
whom he regarded as traitors may be assumed. On the other hand, his
enemies and critics were certainly not warranted in identifying him
with all the actions against the men Wilkinson had caused to be
arrested. Precisely what he himself did at this stage is extremely difficult to determine, but the available records do not show that in his
conduct towards them he over-stepped the bounds of official propriety.

He regretted the action of Wilkinson against Ogden, and his warning to that imperious officer that the public would turn against him if
he deported persons without sufficient proof of guilt was borne out in
the case of Adair. In the court of public opinion that former friend of
the General who now proceeded to Washington was a damaging
witness against him as a Spanish intriguer. Adair also poured into
receptive senatorial ears reports of inhumane treatment he had received and of discomforts he had suffered on his enforced voyage from
New Orleans. Considering these, along with what he had learned of
the treatment of others, Senator William Plumer was led to observe
that "this vain, intriguing, haughty, infamous Wilkinson" had deprived
prisoners of rights guaranteed by the laws even to "common *convicted*
malefactors."[30] Shortly before Plumer penned these words, the public
had learned from a presidential message that Burr had surrendered to
the civil authorities in Mississippi Territory, and nobody in Washington yet knew that he afterwards got away.[31] Jefferson had told
Wilkinson that "seeing no danger here, violations of law are felt with
strength." He could have underlined this observation when the
Supreme Court discharged Bollman and Swartwout, two days after the
presidential message.

iii

In the opinion he delivered on February 21, ten days before the
congressional session ended, Chief Justice John Marshall spoke for a

[30] Feb. 21, 1807 (Plumer, *Memorandum*, pp. 618–619); see also entry of Feb. 20
(p. 614).

[31] By striking coincidence, he was apprehended for a second time on the very
day that his first apprehension was reported to Congress by Jefferson.

majority of the Supreme Court in ruling that the evidence submitted was not sufficient to hold Burr's emissaries for trial on the charge of treason in levying war against the United States. He spoke for all the justices in holding that these men could not be tried in the District of Columbia because their alleged crimes had not been committed there.[32] Since the prisoners could have been discharged on the latter ground alone, the Chief Justice said more than he needed to, as he did in the case of Marbury vs. Madison. He and certain lawyers for the defense took this occasion to reflect on the conduct of the executive branch and to renew the conflict between it and the judiciary. His lengthy discussion of treason can be more appropriately referred to hereafter in connection with the trial of Burr, where it occasioned him considerable embarrassment. Though analysis of Wilkinson's vague affidavits could not have failed to discomfit those who had given them credence, they need not otherwise concern us here. But, since these proceedings occurred in no vacuum, something should be said about the political implications of the case.

The Supreme Court was no longer an exclusive Federalist preserve. In April, 1804, more than three years after his first inauguration, Jefferson made his first appointment to the Court in the person of Judge William Johnson of South Carolina. This he did after assuring himself not only of the nominee's legal abilities but also of his loyalty to the Republican party.[53] In the autumn of 1806 he made his second appointment, that of Henry Brockholst Livingston of New York, but this Justice was absent during the proceedings we are now considering. On this occasion, therefore, Johnson, considerably the youngest Justice, was the only Republican member of a court that Marshall had habituated to unanimous decisions and to opinions delivered by himself.

After application had been made in behalf of Bollman and Swartwout for a writ of habeas corpus, the first question to be decided was whether the Supreme Court had the right to issue it. When this was first argued (February 11), Attorney General Rodney, after stating that he would make no remarks at this stage, said that if the Court should determine to issue a writ he would "cheerfully submit to it."[34] On the following day, however, a strong note of partisanship was

[32] 4 Cranch, 125–137; described and discussed by Beveridge (Marshall, III, 349–357).

[33] D. G. Morgan, Justice William Johnson (1954), ch. III, especially pp. 49–52. This author gives an admirable brief account of the Supreme Court to this time and of its domination by Marshall.

[34] National Intelligencer, Feb. 11, 1807.

imparted to the proceedings when Robert Goodloe Harper and Luther Martin of Maryland voluntarily entered into them in behalf of the prisoners. Both were intolerant Federalists and the latter had made bitter personal attacks on Jefferson before now.[35] A couple of days later Marshall delivered the opinion of the majority of the Court upholding its power to issue the writ. In his dissenting opinion Johnson objected to Harper's language without mentioning him by name. He saw no place, he said, for "popular observations on the necessity of protecting the citizen from executive oppression" or for "animated addresses calculated to enlist the passions of prejudices of an audience."[36] He himself argued that the Court had no right to exercise appellate jurisdiction, as it was doing in this case, without express authorization by act of Congress. Republicans often charged that it seized upon every opportunity to enlarge its jurisdiction.

A week before the delivery of these opinions a resolution bearing on the rights of individuals vis-à-vis the executive branch of the government had been introduced in the House of Representatives by a Federalist, James M. Broom of Delaware. It read as follows:

> *Resolved,* That it is expedient to make further provision for securing the privilege of the writ of habeas corpus to persons in custody under or by color of the authority of the United States.

The spirited and highly interesting debate on this did not begin until after John Marshall had asserted his authority and it ended on the very day he exercised this by releasing the two men who had been imprisoned by Wilkinson.[37] Republicans claimed that the resolution, which was admittedly occasioned by the actions of the General in New Orleans, was unnecessary and inappropriate. On the other hand, Federalists asserted that their concern was to safeguard individuals against arbitrary and tyrannical actions in the future. Devotion to sacred human rights was avowed by all, and words of abiding worth were spoken, but this was primarily a partisan debate.

In his strong opening speech, Broom said that the Commanding General had avowed his disobedience to the laws, claiming only that he was justified by the conspiracy. But that was at an end, and human liberties should not be subject to the forbearance of military power.[38]

[35] In particular, see *Jefferson and the Ordeal of Liberty*, pp. 346–350.
[36] Morgan, p. 56, quoting from 4 Cranch, 107.
[37] Introduced Feb. 7, 1807; debated Feb. 17–19 (*Annals,* 9 Cong., 2 sess., pp. 472, 502–590).
[38] *Ibid.,* p. 506.

William A. Burwell, the first Republican to speak, said that everybody recognized that Wilkinson had acted illegally. He himself anticipated that the General would soon be prosecuted, apparently meaning that he would be sued for damages, as he actually was afterwards by John Adair.[39] Congressman Eppes, while saying much the same thing, recognized that allowance should be made for the dangers confronted by Wilkinson in New Orleans. The Republicans as a group showed little disposition to defend Wilkinson, though several argued that judgment on him should be suspended. One of them, Sloan of New Jersey, believed that, in view of the perils of the conspiracy, his conduct was "not only justifiable but highly commendable."[40] Another, while recognizing that there might be differences of opinion about the degree of guilt of Bollman and Swartwout, ventured to say that nobody believed them innocent.[41] Even the Federalist leader, Josiah Quincy, who claimed to have eschewed partisanship in this debate, was unwilling to say that no case could ever justify illegal and unconstitutional action.[42] It was left to John Randolph to reject relativism utterly. With characteristic vividness he said that if a military man should transport a member of the House or any one of the miserable citizens of Washington to New Orleans he should be "precipitated from the top of the Capitol." The impassioned orator asserted that if military men should "undertake to violate the civil institutions of their country, they should pay the penalty of their lives." For this outburst more than one congressman chided him, and, in response to his belittlement of the conspiracy, passages from his own speeches were quoted to show that he himself had voiced extravagant fears at other times. He denied any sympathy for Burr, but he left no doubt that he regarded Wilkinson as equally a traitor.[43]

Republicans claimed that the real purpose of the resolution was to embarrass the administration. Broom said that the offenses had been committed "in full view of the highest authorities of the Union," and Burwell charged him with giving the impression that arrests had been extended through the whole nation and that "no man was safe from persecution." Eppes pressed the political charges more vigorously, saying that the Federalists had assumed new principles "like a Sunday vest" and that the true purpose of the resolution was "to afford an

39 *Ibid.*, p. 510.
40 *Ibid.*, p. 534.
41 *Ibid.*, p. 546.
42 *Ibid.*, p. 566.
43 *Ibid.*, pp. 551, 576, and elsewhere.

opportunity to gentlemen who care not much about personal rights to make some noise about them." But he was wielding a two-edged sword, for past defenders of personal rights could be charged with having abandoned them; and John Randolph warned that if the juggling of positions continued the people would be apt to conclude that Federalism or Republicanism depended on being in or out of the government.[44] According to Eppes, the termination of the affair in the West did not suit the Federalist palate. "To reduce an insurrection without an army or navy is a very anti-federal thing," he said. "They do not understand and cannot admire that kind of energy in government which derives its force from confidence and attachment on the part of the people."[45] There was a good deal of truth in what he said, and, while he was no spokesman for his father-in-law, that eminent gentleman was saying much the same thing.

The contradictions of the position into which Jefferson, as the responsible head of the government, had been driven by the excesses of his Commanding General were not lost upon his contemporary critics. In this political skirmish, however, he received few wounds. The attack on him was not direct. In alleging indifference to the Constitution, John Randolph hurled his darts at the Republican party, not at its head, though no doubt his reasons were tactical. There was not much generosity in politics in this era, but one Federalist, James Elliott, though vigorously supporting the resolution, flatly denied that any dissatisfaction with the Executive was implied by it. If he had known what Jefferson had written Wilkinson a couple of weeks earlier, he might not have asked the rhetorical question: "Has the Government avowed its approbation of its military chief?" Said this Vermont Federalist: "For me, I acquit the Administration. The General has taken upon himself the responsibility attached to his conduct, and upon his shoulders let it rest." Though tired of hearing about the infallibility of the administration, he credited it with "integrity and general ability."[46]

Quite obviously, however, the resolution put Jefferson's partisans on the defensive. On the third day of the debate his former secretary caused it to change direction. Burwell, taking his cue from the dissent of Justice Johnson in the Supreme Court, moved that the following words be added to the original resolution:

[44] *Ibid.*, p. 550. He made other comments on Republican inconsistency which are highly quotable though often unfair.
[45] *Ibid.*, pp. 512–513.
[46] *Ibid.*, p. 532.

286 JEFFERSON THE PRESIDENT: SECOND TERM

and the necessity of defining the power of the Supreme Court of the United States in issuing the writ of habeas corpus.[47]

Declaring himself in favor of full inquiry, Burwell said that he believed the Court lacked the power to issue the writ in the present instance and that if its power was not narrowed to particular cases it might "interfere with the whole criminal jurisdiction of the United States." Surprisingly, this amendment was adopted without opposition, and the Broom resolution offered little partisan advantage after that. Even if it had been adopted there was little likelihood that anything conclusive would have come of it during the few remaining days of the session, and after three days of debate it was indefinitely postponed. The vote was very close and the Republicans as a group were probably more relieved than the Federalists by this action, but John Marshall should also have been relieved. Burwell and Thomas Mann Randolph were among the Republicans voting against postponement, and it is hard to believe they would have done this if they regarded the resolution as a rebuke to Jefferson or would have thought its passage a humiliation.[48]

The man whose reputation suffered most was Wilkinson. The report that Burr had surrendered to the civil authorities in Mississippi, as given in a message from the President which was received in the midst of the last day's debate, was creditable to Jefferson in showing that his proclamation and instructions had been received in the territory in ample time. But he communicated the news in a letter from the Acting Governor which read: "Thus, sir, this mighty alarm, with all its exaggerations, has eventuated in nine boats and one hundred men, and the major part of these are boys, or young men just from school. . . . I believe them really ignorant and deluded. I believe that they are the dupes of stratagem, if the asseverations of Generals Eaton and Wilkinson are to be believed."[49] More than one person said at the time that the mountain had brought forth a mouse. The credibility of Wilkinson had become exceedingly dubious, and the discharge of Bollman and

[47] *Ibid.*, p. 557. J. Q. Adams in his *Memoirs*, I, 459, reported that Giles, exasperated by the action of the Court, threatened to introduce in the Senate a motion for a "declaratory amendment of the Constitution, taking from the Court *all* jurisdiction in criminal cases."

[48] Final vote, 60 to 58 (*Annals*, 9 Cong., 2 sess., pp. 589–590). Overlooking the amendment, Beveridge says: "Only by the most desperate efforts was Jefferson saved from the rebuke and humiliation of the passage of the resolution" (*Marshall*, III, 360). McCaleb, who describes this as "truly a crisis in Jefferson's career," also gives an incorrect impression of the debate (*Burr Conspiracy*, pp. 247–248).

[49] *Annals*, 9 Cong., 2 sess., pp. 72, 1018–1019; *A.S.P., Misc.*, I, 478.

Swartwout by the Supreme Court could hardly have failed to shake public confidence in him further.

On that same day, Senator Plumer privately recorded his judgment that the President ought instantly to remove the General from the two offices he still held, that of commander of the army and that of governor of Upper Louisiana, adding that otherwise he would damn Jefferson and the administration. Also, the Senator reported that Thomas Mann Randolph, who had left the President's House in a state of jealousy against Eppes and was temporarily a fellow lodger of Plumer's, had expressed the same opinion.[50] A week later the Senator noted that the President had nominated Captain Meriwether Lewis to be governor of the Upper Louisiana Territory and rejoiced that this meant the removal of Wilkinson from that post.[51] With the confirmation of Lewis, which quickly followed, the General ceased to draw the governor's salary, as he had continued to do during his absence from the Territory.[52]

Apparently Jefferson did not seriously consider removing him from the command of the army, although the crisis in the West had passed. About this time the Cabinet agreed to certain measures for liquidating the temporary military establishment that had been designed to cope with the conspiracy. It was decided to discharge the militia from the stations on the Ohio as far down the river as the mouth of the Cumberland. Also, it was agreed that the boats that had been seized, except for those of Blennerhassett, were to be returned or paid for. Furthermore, an inquiry into Burr's activities was to be instituted, the Attorney General being instructed to prepare "interrogatories."[53] Though the conspiracy had ended in an anticlimax, Jefferson, who had been so careful not to alarm the country unduly at the outset, had not ceased to believe that it had had very dangerous potentialities and that Wilkinson had been indispensable in foiling it.[54] Yet, as Plumer had

[50] Feb. 21, 1807 (*Memorandum*, pp. 618-619). See account of TMR's withdrawal on pp. 141-143, above. It is possible that his opinion that TJ preferred Eppes to him was connected with the respective attitudes of the two sons-in-law to Wilkinson at this time, but it is hard to believe that this lessened TJ's devotion to TMR. Plumer was of the opinion that this was entirely unaffected, and it was abundantly demonstrated in the next few days.

[51] Entry of Feb. 28, 1807 (*Memorandum*, p. 633), the day TJ sent the nomination to the Senate (see p. 205, above).

[52] Wilkinson was paid through Mar. 2, 1807. Lewis's salary began Mar. 3, though he did not actually assume his duties for another year (Carter, XIV, 107, n. 33).

[53] TJ's memo. of Feb. 27, 1807. This inquiry was not begun until after a meeting on Apr. 3, when it was agreed that it should be begun immediately (Ford, I, 323-324).

[54] This is also the judgment of Abernethy, pp. 274-275.

observed, public indignation seemed to be transferred to him from
Burr. The Senator expected to hear that the latter had been tried in the
Mississippi Territory and acquitted. Jefferson himself anticipated the
same thing, although he expected him to be subsequently arrested.
Both prophecies were fulfilled. The President also told the Senator that
he feared Burr would be discharged again, "the Courts being inclined
to construe the law too favorably for the accused and too rigidly
against the Government."[55] Later events were to strengthen this
opinion.

[55] Entries of Feb. 21 and Mar. 4, 1807 (*Memorandum*, pp. 619, 641).

The Administration
and the Courts

[XVII]

The President and Burr's Prosecution

JEFFERSON had expected to leave Washington for Monticello
about a week after the adjournment of Congress on March 3, but
was unable to do so for more than a month. The delay was owing in
the first place to the desperate illness of his son-in-law, Thomas Mann
Randolph, and the slow recovery of that hypersensitive young congressman in the President's House, to which he had been induced to
return after his brief and painful stay in a boarding-house.[1] Jefferson's
own physical ills provided a further reason for the delay of their departure. After picking up a cold he suffered one of his periodic headaches. Though somewhat less severe than others he had endured, this
lasted about three weeks, keeping him in a darkened room nearly all
day when at its worst and, as he complained, leaving him only an hour
or two for work. On the last day of the congressional session, when he
was still well, he received a copy of the treaty that James Monroe and
William Pinkney had negotiated with the British. The formal document did not arrive until March 15, however, and he was so displeased
with it that he did not call a special session of the Senate to consider
it.[2] Thus it was at a time of disappointment about the state of foreign
affairs, as well as one of physical incapacity, that he was apprised of
developments relating to Aaron Burr since the adventurer's first apprehension in the Territory of Mississippi. That was the latest event he
had been in a position to report to Congress.

Accounts of further happenings in the little town of Washington,
the territorial capital, got into the eastern newspapers in the month of
March.[3] During this period of his own relative inactivity Jefferson

[1] For this episode and further personal details see above, pp. 141–143.
[2] He did not submit it at the regular session in the fall; see below, ch. XXII.
[3] For a full story with ample references, see Abernethy, *Burr Conspiracy*, ch.
XIII. For the events of particular concern to us here, the most important newspaper references are *National Intelligencer*, Mar. 11, 18, 1807; Richmond *Enquirer*,
Mar. 17, 24.

appears to have made no written comment on these events, but the reports themselves left little doubt that matters had been botched at the territorial capital and none whatever that Burr was again at large.

Some two weeks after his apprehension, during which he has ingratiated himself with leading inhabitants of a district permeated with anti-Spanish spirit and had received many favors at their hands, Burr was brought before the territorial supreme court during the first week in February. One of the two presiding judges was Peter B. Bruin, who was said to have always been drunk when he could get anything to drink and who subsequently resigned from office under threat of impeachment on charges of neglect of duty and intoxication on the bench. This notoriously bibulous official, who had been appointed in the Federalist era, was Burr's first host on his arrival at Bayou Pierre. The other judge was Thomas Rodney, a Jefferson appointee and the father of Caesar A. Rodney, Attorney General of the United States. News of the appointment of his son could not yet have reached the elder Rodney, however, and the officials in the national capital had no part in these proceedings. Though certainly not sympathetic to Burr, Judge Rodney did not want him to fall into the hands of Wilkinson, whose arbitrary actions he himself had denounced.[4] The attorney general of the territory, an appointee of former Governor Claiborne, was George Poindexter, soon to become delegate of the territory to Congress. He showed good sense in declining to press for an indictment.

After the grand jury had been impaneled, Poindexter moved to discharge it on the ground that this court lacked jurisdiction. In his opinion the wisest course for the territorial judges would be to convey the accused immediately to a competent tribunal, and thereby "effectually prevent the contemplated military expedition against Mexico, and maintain inviolate the constitution of the United States." Burr opposed this motion, holding that the court had jurisdiction and apparently believing that if tried here he would be acquitted. Considering the weakness of the available depositions, which Poindexter had deemed insufficient ground for a true bill, and in view of the local sentiment against Spain and against Wilkinson, such might indeed have been the case. Burr's alcoholic friend Judge Bruin opposed the discharge of the grand jury unless Burr should be discharged from his recognizance at the same time. Neither he nor Judge Rodney doubted that their court had jurisdiction. Accordingly, despite Poindexter, the grand jury heard the testimony and brought in a presentment. It was

---

[4] In a letter of Feb., 1807, to his son, describing these proceedings and events through Feb. 12. (*Pa. Mag. Hist. & Biog.*, XLIV [1920], 299–302).

afterwards asserted that this body was packed with Federalists; but whether it was or not, the document might just as well have been written by Burr himself.[5]

On the basis of the evidence presented, it said, the grand jury were of the opinion that he had been guilty of no illegal act or given "any just occasion for alarm or inequietude" to the people of the territory. Besides giving Burr a clean bill of health, the grand jury condemned the past conduct of the Acting Governor and the various military actions and arrests in this district that had been occasioned by his expedition. Also, striking a blow at Wilkinson, they expressed regret at the adoption in a neighboring territory of similar measures, "as if sanctioned by the Executive of our Country," adding that these "must sap the vitals of our political existence, and crumple the glorious fabric in the dust."

After they had voiced these sentiments the grand jurors were discharged, but since the court was divided on the motion of Burr's attorney that he be discharged from his recognizance (Bruin favoring, Rodney opposing), this was denied. When Burr disappeared, Governor Williams, who had recently returned to the territory, held that he had jumped his bail and offered a reward of $2000 for his arrest. Fearing that he would fall into the hands of Wilkinson, he fled to the Southeast, and about two weeks later he was a military prisoner at Fort Stoddert (February 19, 1807). News of his capture and confinement reached the town of Washington, Mississippi Territory, before it got to Washington, D.C. Judge Rodney wrote his son, the Attorney General, that he was glad Burr would have to answer for his misdeeds at a time when perhaps they would be better known than when he was before the grand jury in the territorial court. Previously the Judge had been in a rather uncertain state of mind about the man whom the President regarded as the chief conspirator. Now, on the strength of what he had read in recent newspapers, he went so far as to say that Burr's object was "the most diabolical treason," — in which only "the most wicked adversaries and traitors to Republican Government could combine." He trusted, however, that the vigilance already manifested by the President would "convince all such that they presume too much on his peaceable and unsuspecting mind."[6] In fact Jefferson was over-trustful of persons he regarded as loyal, such as Wilkinson, whom

[5] Printed in McCaleb, *Burr Conspiracy*, p. 228, and in *National Intelligencer*, Mar. 18, 1807, with minor variations; also Richmond *Enquirer*, Mar. 24. An attested copy, enclosed in a letter of Governor Williams to Madison, Feb. 23, 1807, is in Burr Papers, LC. My quotations are from this.

[6] Thomas to C. A. Rodney, Mar. 1, 1807 (*Pa. Mag. Hist. & Biog.*, XLIV [1920], 302–303).

Judge Rodney strongly suspected; but this was by no means true of his attitude toward his political enemies, and he was convinced that the Federalists were now making common cause with Burr.[7] He was soon to say that, far from crediting him with vigilance, his partisan critics had made the first ground of their complaint "the supine inattention of the administration to a treason stalking through the land in open day."[8] Later, they charged him with entering improperly into the prosecution. We should inquire, therefore, just what the administration did to bring Burr to justice.

Two days after the congressional session ended, Lieutenant Edmund Pendleton Gaines, who was in command at Fort Stoddert, rid himself of the danger of Burr's escape by dispatching his prisoner to the national capital under military guard. At that time Jefferson was not even aware that Burr had been recaptured, and apparently he knew nothing of the circumstances until the end of March, when he was informed of reports that had been picked up in Fredericksburg, Virginia. He learned of the approach of the little party soon enough to cause it to be deflected at that point and directed to Richmond, where it arrived on March 26.

Burr's expedition had been fitted out on Blennerhassett's Island, which was in the Ohio River but lay within the bounds of Wood County, Virginia (now West Virginia). Thus it was within the jurisdiction of the United States Court for the Fifth Circuit and of the District of Virginia. Chief Justice Marshall presided over this circuit, under the system of that time, and made his home in Richmond. As a person he was exceedingly popular there and Jefferson probably had more political enemies in the capital than almost anywhere else in his native state. If there was to be a confrontation between the administration and the judiciary no doubt he would have preferred another setting and a somewhat different cast of characters.

He had no Department of Justice to call on, for there was none. There was only the Attorney General, who was the legal consultant of the government on part time and did not have to live in Washington. Fortunately, Caesar A. Rodney was on hand when news of the movements of Burr and his military escort reached the capital, and during March and early April he gave close attention to the prosecution of the notorious prisoner. Precisely what instructions the ailing President gave him at this stage we do not know, but Rodney hastily proceeded

[7] TJ to Gallatin, Mar. 13, 1807 (LC, 29147).
[8] TJ to W. B. Giles, Apr. 20, 1807 (Ford, IX, 42–43).

CHIEF JUSTICE JOHN MARSHALL
Silhouette drawn from life by William Henry Brown
From W. H. Brown, *Portrait Gallery of Distinguished Americans* (1846)

to Fredericksburg.[9] Arriving there after an all-night ride on horseback over intolerable roads, he learned that Dearborn's orders had been duly received and that Burr had already been taken to Richmond. Since he himself was too late to catch the stage to that place, he dispatched to the District Attorney, George Hay, a special messenger with duplicates of the depositions on the strength of which the commitment of Burr was to be sought. Rodney himself managed to hire a carriage and, despite his fatigue, proceeded to Richmond a little later. He arrived in time to appear in court on March 31 and to share in the proceedings that eventuated in the commitment of Burr the next day.

Meanwhile, he had relayed to Jefferson in Washington reports about the second apprehension of Burr. Fuller details became public afterwards, but these seem to have been the first that came to Jefferson's attention. It appeared that the famous fugitive had been captured in disguise fifteen or twenty miles from the southern border, in a region where anti-Spanish sentiment was strong. Thus it could be surmised that when leaving the Natchez district he had in mind some sort of attack on Mobile. His clothing was like that of almost any countryman, including trousers of Virginia homespun and an old cloth coat. He wore old leggings and an old white hat. The fact that he was in precisely the same costume on his journey northward was attributed to his design to arouse sympathy. He had surrendered peaceably in Mississippi Territory, but in a South Carolina village he leaped from his horse and appealed to the crowd of bystanders as a man who had been previously freed by the courts and was now being persecuted by the military.[10]

Along with the duplicates of the depositions, Rodney sent Hay a letter in which he instructed the District Attorney to employ two of the ablest available counsel. One of the men he named was John Wickham, but his fears that Burr might have already retained this recognized leader of the Richmond bar were borne out. On his arrival he learned that Edmund Randolph had likewise been employed by the prisoner, whose negotiations had been unhampered by his military escort and who was obviously trying to get the cream of the local legal talent. Rodney reported to Jefferson that Burr had written Philip Norborne Nicholas, who refused to see him, and wanted to retain William Wirt, who was then out of town.[11] Hay caused that eloquent young man to be forewarned and gained his services for the prosecu-

9 C. A. Rodney to TJ, Mar. 26, 27, 1807 (LC, 29220, 29229–29230).

10 Fragmentary items appeared in a letter from William Tatham to TJ, Mar. 27, 1807 (LC, 29222) as well as in the letters from Rodney.

11 Rodney to TJ from Richmond, Mar. 30, 1807 (LC, 29243).

tion. Failing Wickham, Hay added Alexander MacRae. Neither he nor Wirt was at the hearings on Burr's commitment, but Edmund Randolph and Wickham participated in these. With Hay, a vigorous Republican, Rodney represented the government. This was the only time the Attorney General appeared personally in the case.

In Washington, the President, who had been advised of developments up to this point by Rodney, was less dependent on him for information about the examination of Burr before Chief Justice Marshall, since these proceedings quickly assumed the character of a public spectacle and were promptly reported in the newspapers.[12] The first hearing on March 30 was in a retired room in the Eagle Tavern, but this was adjourned to the courtroom in the capitol the next day. It was then adjourned to the hall of the House of Delegates to accommodate the spectators. On April 1 Marshall committed Burr on the charge of misdemeanor but not on that of treason also, as desired by the prosecution.

We may ask here why the government pressed the graver charge. Judging from the newspapers, the difficulty of establishing it, which was to be so amply demonstrated by later events, was recognized even in Republican circles at this time. On the other hand, one of the most conspicuous scholarly defenders of Burr against the charge of treason says there seems to be "not the slightest doubt" that he and his followers were "guilty of high misdemeanor."[13] It may be assumed, however, that from the time of the communication of Jefferson to Congress (January 22, 1807), in which he unwisely said that Burr's guilt was beyond question, the ultimate prosecution of the "principal actor" on grounds of treason as well as misdemeanor was taken for granted within the inner circle of the government. Jefferson spoke then of "an illegal combination of private individuals against the peace and safety of the Union," as well as of an unauthorized expedition against the territories of Spain; and he was convinced that these purposes were conjoined in Burr's mind.

In the light of present knowledge it is not hard to believe that both of them were in fact conjoined at one time or another, but certain of Jefferson's words may seem to lend color to the charge of some of Burr's present-day defenders that, by the time of the examination in Richmond, the President himself had come to recognize that the dis-

[12] References are given here, however, to the most authoritative account, that of W. W. Hening and William Munford *Examination of Col. Aaron Burr before the Chief Justice of the U.S. . . . together with the Arguments of Counsel and Opinion of the Judge* (Richmond, 1807), rather than to the newspaper stories which appeared a little earlier. It is referred to hereafter as *Examination*.

[13] McCaleb, *Burr Conspiracy*, p. 299.

unionist purpose had been abandoned by force of necessity. Writing the American Minister to Spain about this time, he said that Burr soon saw that the fidelity of the western country was not to be shaken and "turned himself wholly toward Mexico."[14] In this private letter Jefferson was emphasizing the good faith manifested by the American government towards Spain in suppressing this revolt and telling his representative how these events should be described to the Spanish and French. He was anxious to remain on amicable terms with both of them now that relations with the British had worsened. But this statement, made in these circumstances, was not an expression of his full opinion. He had not ceased to believe that Burr had intended to seize New Orleans before proceeding to Mexico.[15] While recognizing that the suppression of the conspiracy before it was ripe had increased the difficulty of proving it treasonable, he was convinced it was that in intention and believed that overt acts could be proved. Such doubts as he had expressed bore chiefly on the attitude of the judiciary, which he expected to be hostile to the prosecution because of its hostility to his government. The crucial questions, as became increasingly evident, were what treason really consisted of and how it must be proved, and the decisive judgment was to be that of John Marshall.

The Chief Justice had spoken to these points in the cases of Swartwout and Bollman, when he discharged these two emissaries of Burr from confinement. The constitutional definition of treason, which he read aloud, was undoubtedly familiar to the Attorney General and the President: "Treason against the United States, shall consist only in levying War against them, or in adhering to their Enemies, giving them Aid and Comfort." Anyone who heard these words afresh could not have failed to be reminded that in American law the crime of treason was sharply limited; and the intended prosecutors of Burr must have wondered just how he could be proved to have levied war against his country. He had not been physically present at Blennerhassett's Island when the expedition set out from that place. But the Chief Justice had stated in his opinion that anyone who played a part in a treasonable conspiracy was a traitor, no matter how remote from the scene of action he may have been.[16] Upon its face this opinion seemed to warrant the government's preferring a charge of treason against Aaron Burr; and just before the examination in

[14] TJ to James Bowdoin, Apr. 2, 1807 (Ford, IX, 41). See comments on this in McCaleb, *Burr Conspiracy*, pp. 262–263.
[15] TJ to Lafayette, July 14, 1807 (Ford, IX, 114).
[16] 4 Cranch, 126.

Richmond, both Rodney and Hay expressed confidence that Marshall would commit him on that charge.

Burr himself participated in these proceedings, as he was to do in those that followed, thereby strongly reinforcing his counsel. Denying that his flight was an evidence of guilt, he claimed that he was trying to escape the "arm of military power," that he was not fleeing from investigation but from military despotism.[17] He was reflecting on the character and motives of Wilkinson, as he and his counsel were to continue to do with good effect throughout this case. Also, they were to claim repeatedly that he was the object of persecution by the executive. Little countenance for it could have been afforded by the first and only speech of the Attorney General. In this Rodney said:

> For my part, I wish for nothing but that justice may be done, and not to avail myself of any testimony but such as is perfectly correct. I do not desire to take advantage of the reports which have resounded thro' the newspapers so long, and so strongly have agitated the public mind. However the tempest may rage without these walls, I am satisfied there is not a swell which will roll a wave to your feet. I rejoice that, on this occasion, men of talents and liberality have been found of sufficient independence of mind to come forward to defend the prisoner, notwithstanding the general opinion of his guilt. — And I wish it were possible that the walls of this room could expand, and that, not only those who now hear me, but all the people of America were present, and could hear this discussion. — They would then be convinced that there is no disposition in the government or in myself, to persecute Col. Burr.[18]

Apart from the unfortunate reference to the "general opinion" of Burr's guilt, this statement, if taken at face value, gives an impression of fair-mindedness on the part of the ranking representative of the government. At almost the same time a note of moderation was sounded in the paper that was supposed to reflect best the views of the administration. Addressing itself particularly to the press of the country, the *National Intelligencer* said:

> Let Aaron Burr have a fair, an impartial trial! Our constitution, our laws, and our political principles all guarantee it. And that this guarantee may be solid and availing, let the federal

[17] *Examination*, pp. 22–23.
[18] *Ibid.*, p. 26.

[Federalist] prints abstain from their violence, and let them not by an unjust and impolitic attack on the administration, compel its friends, who are, in other words, the people of the United States, to a retaliation which, however justly it may react on them, may likewise unjustly affect the accused.[19]

Short of a detailed investigation of both the Federalist and Republican papers in this period, one could not safely aver that either the pot or the kettle was the blacker. But there can be no possible doubt that the partisan defenders of Burr, in and out of court, charged the administration with persecution and the President with vindictiveness. These charges have persisted for more than a century and a half. One modern writer asserts that when Jefferson heard of the capture of Burr in old clothes he was "exultant" and says that his attitude toward this captive was "sadistic."[20] In the absence of reliable testimony one cannot speak with confidence about anybody's state of mind at a particular moment. In view of Burr's past actions, Jefferson might have been expected to be vindictive toward him, but it would be difficult to prove that he was. Shortly after the examination before John Marshall he said: "Against Burr, personally, I never had one hostile sentiment."[21] This assertion may be questioned as being too much to be believed, but there is abundant evidence that, previously, he had been notably tolerant of one he had good reason to regard as a troublemaker. Irrespective of personal feelings that we are in no position to gauge, he himself was the major guardian of the peace and security of the country and as such could hardly have failed to be indignant against one he believed to have endangered them. He had unwisely stated in public that Burr's guilt was unquestionable, but the government was duty-bound to prosecute him if there was any likelihood of it at all.

In support of the motion of the District Attorney to commit Burr on both charges, Rodney cited Blackstone's judgment that "probable cause" was enough for commitment. Speaking to this point, the Chief Justice said: "I do not understand him [Blackstone] as meaning to say that the hand of malignity may grasp any individual against whom its hate may be directed, or whom it may capriciously seize, charge with some secret crime, and put on him the proof of his innocence." Marshall "explicitly stated" to reporters afterwards that he was not alluding to the conduct of the government in the present case, but his

19 *National Intelligencer*, Apr. 1, 1807, in the editorial introduction to an item from Richmond *Enquirer* of Mar. 27.

20 McCaleb, *New Light*, p. 110. This writer throws adjectives around with reckless abandon.

21 TJ to W. B. Giles, Apr. 20, 1807 (Ford, IX, 46).

observations could hardly have been interpreted other than as a reflection on the Chief Executive, and we may seriously doubt that his subsequent denial erased the impression created by this injudicious observation from the bench.[22] Again and again defenders of Burr were to condemn Jefferson for having prejudged him; and in turn partisans of the President were to claim that, as in the case of Marbury vs. Madison, the Chief Justice went out of his way to lecture the executive branch of the government. A conspicuous example was provided by some of the things he said in the opinion with which these proceedings closed.

The evidence presented by the prosecution at this time consisted of the affidavits and depositions of Eaton, Wilkinson, and others that had been introduced in the cases of Swartwout and Bollman, along with the oral testimony of Major Nicholas Perkins, bearing on Burr's apprehension and later conduct. When Marshall released the two emissaries he had emphasized the necessity of procuring evidence of an overt act, and he now chided the executive branch of the government, to which the important power of prosecution was entrusted, for not having obtained affidavits establishing the fact that Burr had assembled troops as alleged. He claimed that there had been ample time to do this, and, although he did not insist on such proof as was necessary in a trial, he regarded the evidence as insufficient to warrant his inserting the charge of treason in the indictment. This omission was relatively unimportant, he said, since the prosecution could still seek an indictment for high treason, assuming they had the necessary testimony.[23]

One result of Burr's commitment on the charge of misdemeanor only was that he could be released on bail. After Marshall said he regarded $10,000 as about right, Hay expressed the opinion that this was not enough and that Burr could raise $100,000 if necessary. Wickham for the defense described it as too much, and the prisoner himself expressed doubt of his ability to raise it. After a few hours, however, he appeared with five securities and entered into a recognizance for appearance at the next circuit court on May 22. Marshall had stuck to the figure he originally suggested, but he received some criti-

---

[22] *Examination*, pp. 30-31. Beveridge, in his highly colored account of this episode (*Marshall*, III, 376-377), says that the Chief Justice intended his statements to reflect on Jefferson and disclaimed his intention in order "to forestall the use he knew Jefferson would make" of the impression Marshall had created. With complete partisanship this biographer says that his hero's words "accurately described the conduct of the Administration" and he himself describes these words as "statesmanlike." Actually, his interpretation amounts to a serious reflection on Marshall and belies the claim of "patience, consideration, and prudence" he makes for him (p. 375).

[23] *Examination*, pp. 35-36.

cism in Republican papers for permitting so many securities, no one of whom would have lost much if Burr had failed to appear on the designated date. Rodney believed that he would run away, while others predicted that his actions would depend on whether or not he thought he would be convicted.

Shortly after his release on bail he dined at John Wickham's and the fact that the Chief Justice was a fellow guest occasioned considerable comment in the Republican press.[24] Giving Marshall the benefit of the doubt, we shall assume that he did not know in advance that the man who had just appeared before him in court, and was to do so again, would be there and that he himself remained out of politeness. But there can be no doubt that Burr's counselor had committed a grave indiscretion in issuing his invitations. Nor can there be any doubt that the chief reason for Federalist attachment to Burr, despite the fact that he had killed Hamilton, was antipathy to Jefferson. Politics makes strange loyalties and antipathies, as is instanced by the statement in the local Federalist paper that the trial would give the government "full time to defend itself against the high charge of persecution and tyranny."[25] One would suppose from this that the administration rather than Burr was on trial. His release on bail gave this astute man seven weeks to prepare his defense. Rodney reported to Jefferson early in May that he was in Philadelphia with Bollman and others.[26]

Responsibility for the prosecution, as Marshall stated emphatically in court, lay with the executive. Jefferson was well aware of that before the Chief Justice charged his branch of the government with culpable tardiness in the collection of evidence. Before Congress rose and about a week after Marshall released Swartwout and Bollman, the President and his high executive officers had decided to institute a far-reaching inquiry into the actions of Burr and his adherents. Little or nothing may have been done to further this during the last busy days of the congressional session, and Jefferson himself fell ill soon thereafter. Despite the headache which left him so little time for business, he met with his executive council in the middle of March. Persons were then named to conduct this inquiry at particular places. At a meeting on April 3, by which time Jefferson was largely restored to his customary good health, he and his department heads agreed that it should be

---

[24] *Virginia Argus*, Apr. 7, 1807; communication in Richmond *Enquirer*, Apr. 10, from "A Stranger from the Country." Describing this episode, Beveridge (*Marshall*, III, 394-396) castigates Marshall's critics as passionate partisans.

[25] *Virginia Gazette*, Apr. 4, 1807.

[26] Rodney to TJ from Wilmington, Del., May 6, 1807 (LC, 29375). Beveridge says Burr had only three weeks (*Marshall*, III, 380).

begun by the Attorney General immediately.[27] That official had not yet returned from Richmond and presumably the President had not yet learned that a couple of days earlier the executive branch had been chided by the Chief Justice. He could hardly have expected the reproof, for he had requested Rodney to inform Marshall unofficially that there would be unavoidable delays in the collection of evidence from distant places. Following the arrival of Rodney in Washington, Jefferson conferred with him during the days before his own departure for Monticello with his son-in-law on April 7. He may have gone over the "interrogatories" (questionnaires, we would say) that Rodney had been instructed to send out.[28] Before the Attorney General himself left Washington about a week later, he informed the President at Monticello that he had taken steps to summon the important witnesses; and within a month, writing from his home in Wilmington, Delaware, he reported that all the interrogatories had been dispatched.[29]

Meanwhile, during Jefferson's stay at Monticello, his chief lieutenants at his request looked into the question of meeting any extraordinary expenses which might be incurred in connection with the prosecution. Secretary Gallatin, citing as a precedent certain actions of George Washington with regard to the Whiskey Rebellion, ruled that, in the absence of a special appropriation, extraordinary expenses should be met from the general contingency fund on the President's order. Such an order was issued by Jefferson soon thereafter on Rodney's behalf.[30] Thus it appears that, during the interval between the commitment of Burr and the meeting of the Court on May 22, the executive government proceeded promptly, and with careful regard for legality, to perform the duty that the Chief Justice had so sharply called to its attention. Jefferson, ensconced at Monticello during most of this period of weeks, kept in close touch with developments, but if he superintended the collection of testimony, as was to be indignantly alleged afterwards, he did so in only a general way. His actions were those that might have reasonably been expected of a responsible executive charged with the enforcement of the laws.

At first some of his own supporters were fearful that he was doing too little. Such was the impression conveyed by a letter he received

[27] Memos. of meetings of Feb. 27, Mar. 17, Apr. 3, 1807 (Ford, I, 323–324).
[28] Printed copy with printed covering letter, both undated, in Letters in Relation to Burr's Conspiracy, LC.
[29] Rodney to TJ, Apr. 10, 1807 (LC, 29280; May 6 (LC, 29374–29375).
[30] TJ to Madison, Apr. 14, 1807 (Ford, IX, 42); Gallatin to TJ, Apr. 18, 1807 (LC, 29320); Rodney to TJ, May 6, 1807, as cited above. TJ reported on expenditures from the contingent fund, Jan. 8, 1808, and Jan. 31, 1809 (Annals, 10 Cong., 1 sess., I, 78; 2 sess., p. 321).

shortly after his arrival at Monticello and before he had received much more than a preliminary report from the Attorney General. This letter, from William Branch Giles, was unquestionably anxious and may be described as needling.[31] The Senator, writing from Southside Virginia soon after he learned of the hearings in Richmond, reported that they had excited "a very great degree of sensibility" in his quarter. He claimed that all the real friends of the administration wanted a "fair and full" investigation of Burr's conduct to be made, and he laid special emphasis on the desirability of calling Wilkinson as a witness. He implied that Republicans shared the doubts of Federalists about the case, and by urging that the President give personal attention to these matters he suggested that Jefferson had not done so sufficiently before now. (He may have been uninformed of Jefferson's illness.) Thus the pressure of John Marshall on the one hand was reinforced by that of a bitter critic of the judiciary on the other, and the Chief Executive was called on to justify his conduct in order to retain the full confidence of his own supporters.

Strongly partisan expressions are rare in Jefferson's public utterances, which were characteristically measured and restrained. When he used extreme language it was nearly always in a private communication to someone of whose loyalty to the party or to him personally he had no doubt. His reply to Giles, who was more partisan and violent than he, is a case in point.[32] The distinction between public utterances and private letters — which are more numerous in the case of a man who carefully preserves them than of one who does not — is often ignored or blurred by historical writers. Apparently there is little surviving record of what Marshall said to his friends and political supporters at this time. Jefferson was warranted in saying in private that the Federalists had made Burr's cause their own. But he went on to make the extreme assertion that they were "mortified only that he [Burr] did not separate the Union or overturn the government," and that if there had been hope of success they would have joined him to overthrow the Republic and set up a monarchy. His comments on what he called "the tricks of the judges" may have been less than judicious but they were germane. He would have had difficulty in proving that Marshall was trying to force a trial before evidence could be collected, but in view of the enormous difficulty of communication in those days he could demonstrate convincingly that the Chief Justice's rebuke was unwarranted. Assuming that probability of guilt was all that need be estab-

---

[31] Giles to TJ, Apr. 6, 1807; received Apr. 16 (LC, 29264-29265; printed in D. R. Anderson, *William Branch Giles* [1914], p. 110).
[32] TJ to Giles, Apr. 20, 1807 (Ford, IX, 42-46).

lished to commit a suspect, he claimed that sufficient evidence had been presented, saying that the judge himself recognized the probability of Burr's guilty intentions. While admitting that the government did not yet know what could be established, he drew up a tentative list of overt acts which he supposed provable and some if not all of which, in his opinion, were doubted by no candid man in the entire country.

Upon this letter, chiefly, later critics of Jefferson's conduct have based their assertions about his reaction to the opinion of the Chief Justice in the examination in Richmond. If he was not "enraged" by this, he was unquestionably indignant at Marshall's rebuke, and at this time he expressed himself strongly regarding the past performance of the judiciary. "If," he said, "there ever had been an instance in this or the preceding administrations, of federal [Federalist] judges so applying principles of law as to condemn a federal [Federalist] or acquit a republican offender, I should have judged them in the present case with more charity." In this letter, which he intended to be reassuring, he went on to say that the country would reach its own judgment and apply the necessary correctives. "If a member of the Executive or Legislature does wrong, the day is never far distant when the people will remove him. They will see then and amend the error in our Constitution, which makes any branch independent of the nation. They will see that one of the great co-ordinate branches of the government, setting itself in opposition to the other two, and to the common sense of the nation, proclaims immunity to that class of offenders which endeavors to overturn the Constitution, and are themselves protected in it by the Constitution itself; for impeachment is a farce which will not be tried again. If their protection of Burr produced this amendment, it will do more good than his condemnation would have done."

This private statement has been interpreted by certain historians as a threat that if the Chief Justice should allow Burr to escape he himself would be removed.[33] But Jefferson was making a generalized comment and he explicitly stated that the impeachment process could not be relied upon. He was expressing here his concern over the irresponsibility of the judiciary, except to the Constitution as interpreted by them, and from other sayings of his it is clear what sort of amendment to the Constitution he had in mind. While recognizing that the judiciary should not be dependent on executive authority, as it had formerly been in England, he believed that its complete independence was an anomaly in a self-governing society and that somebody should

[33] Adams, History, III, 447.

have authority to determine the question of judges' good behavior. In his old age he expressed regret that the Constitution did not vest this in a majority of the legislature, the branch of the government most representative of the public will.[34] In this statement he left out the executive. Early in his first term he was reported to have favored the grant of authority to the President to remove a federal judge on the recommendation of Congress.[35] Such a constitutional provision had been recommended by Judge Edmund Pendleton of Virginia and was in accord with the procedure in some of the states. It was no such novel idea as it would seem today, but it would have been bitterly contested then by all those who distrusted popular government. The statement of Jefferson to Giles, whose antipathy to the judiciary was notorious, is insufficient ground for supposing that an amendment was in contemplation now. The immediate task of the responsible officials was to proceed with the prosecution of Burr.

In one of his letters from Wilmington, Rodney said: "I flatter myself we shall have ample evidence at the Court to induce a grand jury who are impartial & intelligent, to find a bill for treason, after which I hope he will no longer be permitted to roam at large." He expressed similar optimism in a letter he wrote in Wilmington the day the Court opened in Richmond.[36] This part-time official had directed the summoning of witnesses and the procuring of depositions, performing in this limited period, and to some extent later in the summer, the sort of task which might have been expected to fall to the Attorney General of the United States. The most natural explanation of his virtual withdrawal from the case at this point is that he had already done all that could have been reasonably expected of him under the terms of his employment and that at this juncture he had to devote himself to his own affairs. He wrote Jefferson that he had no doubt Hay and his colleague would "conduct the business in the most correct, prudent, and efficient manner." One result of his own withdrawal, however, was that, except for such direction as Jefferson might give them, they were left to their own devices.

Toward the end of the trial one of the lawyers for the defense, in the course of an interminable and intemperate speech, said: "I insist that the president's interference with the prosecution is improper, illegal, and unconstitutional. From the very moment that a case enters into the pale of the judiciary, he ought to avoid all interference with

34 In his autobiography, begun at the age of seventy-seven (Ford, I, 111–112).
35 See *Jefferson the President: First Term*, p. 462.
36 Rodney to TJ, May 6, 22, 1807 (LC, 29374–29375, 29468).

it."[37] There is a question, of course, as to the precise meaning of "interference," as there is as to the exact moment when the "pale of the judiciary" is entered; but, while no government could have been expected to let a case of this importance go by default, the fact is that after this one was brought before the Chief Justice on May 22, 1807, the President did very little about it except in response to actions of the court itself.

A couple of days before the session began in Richmond, Jefferson sent District Attorney Hay, for the information of the prosecution, the signed statement he had previously procured from Dr. Erick Bollman. Actually, this added little to Madison's report of the interview of Burr's messenger with the President, and the promise that it would not be used against him was scrupulously kept. Along with the statement, Jefferson sent a pardon which was subsequently interpreted by the government as irrevocable and which, in effect, granted Bollman immunity for turning state's evidence, which he actually did only in private. His attitude was equivocal at first, but he soon rejected the pardon; and, when Hay proffered it to him in court, he rejected it again with high indignation.[38] The matter did not end there, however, for his relations with Jefferson were considerably publicized during the summer.

Seeking to correct an account of proceedings with respect to him in court, Bollman wrote a letter to the editor of the *Aurora*. In this, besides denying that he had made his statement to Jefferson on the promise of a pardon, he said, as Luther Martin had proudly asserted in court, that his only reason for not rejecting the pardon when it was first offered him by the District Attorney in private was his desire to do so publicly. Commenting on this, Duane's paper said: "It is really amusing, tho' painful, to see men who could embark in the most atrocious treasons . . . assuming airs and the *tones* of virtue and honor."[39] About a week later the *Aurora* printed a long article in which Bollman described his dealings with Jefferson and charged the President with breaking his promise not to let his (Bollman's) written

[37] Benjamin Botts, Aug. 26, 1807 (*Report of the Trials of Colonel Aaron Burr*, II [1875 ed.], reported by David Robertson, p. 208. Referred to hereafter as Robertson).

[38] Early letters bearing on the Bollman statement are TJ to Hay, May 20, 28, 1807 (Ford, IX, 52–58, 52–53n.); Hay to TJ, May 25, 31, 1807 (LC, 29452, 29482–29483). For previous events, see above, pp. 269–271. The matter came up in court June 13 (Robertson, I, 188–195).

[39] *Aurora*, July 8, 1807; dispatch dated Richmond, June 27.

statement get out of his hands.[40] In an editorial the next day the *Aurora* said that Bollman, like Burr, instead of proving his own innocence, sought to heap odium on public officials. His sense of honor, said Duane, was that among thieves. As for the President, he could not have been expected to keep treason unrevealed; and the only limitation on his action was the promise that Bollman's statement was not to be used against him.[41] The *Virginia Argus*, which reprinted Bollman's letter, took stronger ground. Said this Republican paper: "His charge then against the President for a breach of honor in betraying his confidential communication, is the most groundless and imprudent charge that ever was brought against any one since the creation of Man!"[42] While such partisan extravagance must of course be discounted, Bollman was obviously trying to reinforce the contention that Jefferson was a persecutor who would stick at nothing. He himself might have been accused of breaking faith with Burr by conferring with the President in the first place.

Jefferson's reasons for breaking his promise can only be surmised. No doubt it appeared to him much less important than the promise not to use these revelations against Bollman himself, and no doubt he afterwards regretted having ever made it to a man whom he regarded as untrustworthy. There would have been no point in procuring this testimony in the first place merely for his personal information and he might have charged himself with dereliction of duty in not making it available to the prosecution. If he let the paper get out of his own hands he did not let it get out of the hands of men he trusted.

Whether he deserved blame on ethical grounds for sending Bollman's paper, or would deserve blame on patriotic grounds if he had not sent it, the fact is that he did little else at this stage. Writing Hay on June 2, he said: "While Burr's case is depending before the court, I will trouble you, from time to time, with what occurs to me."[43] What occurred to him at that time was that, if and when opportunity should be afforded, it should be seized to deny that the "extrajudicial opinion" in Marbury *vs.* Madison constituted authority. He took this occasion to outline anew his conception of the mutual independence of the three co-ordinate branches of the federal government.[44] The District

---

[40] *Ibid.*, July 16, 1807. This is largely reprinted in Davis, *Memoirs of Aaron Burr* (1837), II, 387–391. Among the deleted passages was one in which Bollman said, perhaps sarcastically, that despite his ill treatment by the President, he was "inclined" to believe that TJ was not motivated by ill will toward him.

[41] *Aurora*, July 17, 1807.

[42] *Virginia Argus*, Aug. 1, 1807; letter reprinted July 25.

[43] TJ to Hay, June 2, 1807 (Ford, IX, 53–54n.).

[44] See *Jefferson the President: First Term*, pp. 154–156.

Attorney did not believe that Marbury *vs.* Madison could be "brought to bear on any point worth notice in Burr's case," but the latter may be regarded as the last major episode in the conflict between the executive and judicial branches during Jefferson's presidency. The degree to which political partisanship and personal animosities entered into it can best be perceived from the unfolding story. Suffice it to say here that the Burrites seized and retained the initiative while the Chief Justice set the rules, and the President, offstage, was in no position to do much about it.

[XVIII]

The Defense *vs.* the Executive

THE prosecution of Burr began "under very inauspicious circumstances" — so Jefferson observed to the District Attorney on the
strength of the first report he received of proceedings in the court in
Richmond.[1] He took occasion to enjoin Hay to procure a full record
of all testimony, saying that this must be afterwards laid before the
Legislature and, through them, before the public. Although appre-
hensive of the rulings of the judge from the outset, he gave no sign of
doubt that the case of the government would be ably presented. But
if he had been present on May 22, 1807, in the chamber in the state
capitol where the sessions were held, and had surveyed the opposing
counsel, he could hardly have failed to perceive that the odds were
against the prosecution. George Hay, now forty-one years old, who
was to marry James Monroe's daughter as his second wife before the
end of Jefferson's presidency and was to be appointed a district judge
by President John Quincy Adams, was able, diligent, and loyal; his
colleague Alexander MacRae, Lieutenant Governor of the state, was a
man of force, regarded by some as untactful; and William Wirt at
thirty-four was an orator of great promise. But, even before the arrival
of the redoubtable Luther Martin, the prosecutors were outnumbered
and outweighed by John Wickham, Benjamin Botts, Edmund Randolph, and John Baker.[2] Furthermore, Burr acted vigorously in his own
behalf, setting a tone of aggressiveness at the very beginning and putting the prosecution on the defensive.

[1] TJ to George Hay, May 26, 1807. Most of his letters to Hay, May 20–Sept. 7,
1807, have been conveniently assembled in Ford, IX, 52–64. These may also be
seen, with a few additional letters, in L. & B., XI. References to Hay's letters to
him, from LC, are made at appropriate points hereafter.

[2] Comments on these men are made in Samuel Mordecai, *Richmond in By-Gone
Days* (1860), especially ch. VII; in Charles Warren, *History of the American Bar*
(1913), pp. 267–268; in Beveridge, III, ch. VIII; and elsewhere. Charles Lee joined
the counsel for the defense Aug. 17.

His first move was to question certain actions of the United States Marshal in assembling a panel of grand jurymen. Authorized by law to summon twenty-four, that official had accepted excuses from two and called two others. While this appears to have been a common practice in the state courts, the Chief Justice ruled that the Marshal had exceeded his discretion.[3] More importance was attached to Burr's claim that he had the right to challenge grand jurymen "for favor," as in the case of a petit jury. To this procedure Virginians, including Jefferson, were unaccustomed. The persons Burr objected to were William Branch Giles and Wilson Cary Nicholas; and, at the suggestion of Hay, who was not disposed to quibble in this matter, they were given the opportunity to withdraw voluntarily and both did so. Attorney General Rodney, while describing the exclusions from the grand jury by Burr as a novel thing, admitted that the latter's lawyers had discovered precedents which he regarded as applicable.[4] Speaking for the defense, Wickham said that "in the present case, where such important interests are at stake, and where *such unjustifiable means have been used to prejudice the public mind against Colonel Burr*, it is his right to take every advantage which the law gives him."[5] Writing Jefferson after he had observed Burr in further action, Hay said: "He takes every advantage, denies every position advanced in the prosecution, acquiesces in no decision, however solemnly made, or frequently repeated and while he boldly asserts his innocence, adopts every measure within his power to bar the door to an inquiry." Discouraged and already overworked, the District Attorney expressed surprise at the extent of Burr's support. "There is among mankind," he observed, "a sympathy for villainy which sometimes shows itself in defiance of every principle of patriotism and truth."[6]

The prosecution having yielded to all of Burr's objections, the grand jury was formed and sworn the first day. The Chief Justice named as its foreman John Randolph, who held no brief for Burr but was at odds with the administration and utterly distrustful of Wilkinson.[7] For upwards of three weeks the grand jury could do nothing. The District Attorney, following the advice of Rodney as well as his own judgment, delayed presenting his bills, which called for the indictment of Burr on charges of both treason and misdemeanor, until he could present the full evidence. Specifically, he was awaiting the arrival of

[3] The Proceedings of May 22, which we deal with here, are in *Trial of Aaron Burr for Treason*, from the report of David Robertson, I, 1-15.
[4] Rodney to Madison, May 31, 1807 (MP, 32:46).
[5] Robertson, I, 4. Italics inserted.
[6] Hay to TJ, May 31, 1807 (LC, 29482-29483); May 25 (LC, 29452-29453).
[7] List in Robertson, I, 13.

his most important witness, James Wilkinson. Whether or not the tardiness of the General was justifiable on the ground of duties in New Orleans that he could not quickly lay aside, or of the bad weather he encountered at sea, it was a grave embarrassment to the prosecution. Partisans of Burr asserted that he was afraid to come, and counsel for the defense intimated that the fault lay with the administration since he was under military orders.

While unwilling to go before the grand jury as yet, Hay believed that the depositions now in hand warranted his asking the court to commit Burr on the charge of treason. He did not want the accused man to remain loose on bail. Days of wrangling ensued, in the course of which the defense raised charges of persecution and the prosecution described these as an attempted diversion. Marshall agreed to hear evidence in support of Hay's motion, but some of his rulings perturbed the District Attorney. He rejected an affidavit which Jefferson had sent Hay from Washington (that of Jacob Denbaugh) on the ground that it was improperly certified and did not appear to be on oath; and he did not permit the introduction of Wilkinson's affidavit because it offered no proof of an overt act. Reporting these rebuffs to Jefferson, Hay observed: "I do not believe that the C. Justice does wrong with his eyes open, but that his eyes are almost closed, is a position of which no man can doubt who has observed his conduct before and since the examination."[8] Burr had not been committed for treason by Marshall, but Hay gained further assurance that he would not escape trial. The lawyers for the defense would not agree to an increase in bail, but Burr himself consented to it, saying he wished to spare the court embarrassment. Accordingly, he himself was bound in the sum of $10,000 and four securities in the sum of $2500 each. Among the latter was Luther Martin, who had arrived from Baltimore and joined the counsel for the defense that very day.[9]

The participation of the former Attorney General of Maryland in the trial was regarded by many in Richmond as unnecessary in view of the local talent on which Burr had drawn so heavily. One observer remarked, however, that Martin had qualities not attributable to the members of the Richmond bar: he could be counted on to "brow-beat his opponents" and abuse the government.[10] He is said to have become attached to Burr when acting as counsel for the defense in the impeachment trial of Justice Chase, and there could be no possible doubt

---

[8] Hay to TJ, May 31, 1807; for details, see Robertson, I, 62–81.

[9] May 28, 1807 (ibid., I, 86).

[10] Extract of a letter in Richmond *Enquirer*, June 20, 1807. The Republican press was distinctly unfriendly to Martin.

Courtesy of the Philadelphia City Archives

LUTHER MARTIN
Portrait by William S. Tiffany
in the National Park Collection, Independence Hall, Philadelphia

of his hatred of Jefferson. His virulent attack on the latter, while Vice President, because of references to Captain Michael Cresap in the *Notes on Virginia*, was sufficient proof of that. While ostensibly seeking to clear the name of his long-dead father-in-law, whom he claimed that Jefferson had calumniated in his uncritical report of the oration of the Indian chief Logan, he was obviously seeking to blacken Jefferson's reputation, and in this episode he showed himself to be a master of invective and innuendo.[11] During his service of more than half a century as attorney general of Maryland this slovenly and excessively bibulous man, whose domestic life had been stormy and tragic, had come to be regarded as a fabulous lawyer. To be sure, not everybody agreed that he deserved his fame. One contemporary, observing that he neither looked nor acted like a great man, said that he was a "singular compound of strange qualities."[12] Opinions of him differed according to the side one was on, but he could be expected to add a strong note of personal and partisan bitterness to the proceedings. For nearly two weeks, however, there was little he could do but provide security for Burr to the amount of $2500 — a very considerable sum for a man of his notorious improvidence. The grand jury was summoned a couple of times, only to be adjourned when Hay in obvious embarrassment announced that Wilkinson had not come and that the date of his arrival was still problematical.

Into this vacuum Burr injected a motion that a subpoena *duces tecum* be issued to the President of the United States, requiring the delivery of the letter and other papers he had received from Wilkinson under the date of October 21 last, together with copies of his reply and of orders respecting Burr that had been issued to officers at Natchez, New Orleans, and other places by the departments of War and the Navy. Reporting this motion to Jefferson before it was argued, the District Attorney, who had stated that the government was "perfectly disposed" to supply Burr with any evidence that was proper to communicate, described it as a mere maneuver. He believed that Burr and his counsel really hoped the papers would not be sent and that their detention would "afford some pretext for clamor." To Jefferson he also said: "L. Martin has been here a long time, perfectly inactive. He wants an opportunity of saying something about the administration and the subject is selected to furnish a topic. If this be not a correct supposition, how comes it that the materiality of these papers has

11 See *Jefferson and the Ordeal of Liberty*, pp. 346–356.
12 Matthew Bramble to S. P. P. Fay in W. W. Story, *Life and Letters of Joseph Story* (1851), I, 163–164.

escaped notice until this moment?"[13] Burr had timed his action well, and the motion gave Martin an admirable opportunity to castigate the administration. Another purpose of this diversionary maneuver was surmised by Jefferson himself — that of precipitating a contest between the judiciary and the executive authorities.

The motion for a subpoena represented a direct attempt to involve the President personally in the case. Thus this episode warrants considerably more detailed consideration than do the proceedings as a whole, an adequate account of which would in fact require another book. In viewing it we must never lose sight of chronology or be unaware of the slowness of communication. On the very day that Jefferson learned of the motion for a subpoena through a letter from Hay, the arguments of counsel ended, and his reply to it was not read to the court until three days after the Chief Justice delivered his opinion.[14] If Jefferson's conciliatory response had become known earlier it should have strengthened the contention of Hay that the desired documents could have been procured as readily on personal request as on public demand.

Early in the three-day debate on Burr's motion the District Attorney expressed the hope that it was not intended to show off the talents of counsel; and, after the debate was over, he told Jefferson that two-thirds of the speeches were addressed to the people.[15] It was an unedifying performance, marred by incessant squabbling and an excessive degree of irrelevance. The personal attendance of the President was not required; Burr and his counsel said that they wanted only the papers. The lawyers for the prosecution, who were obviously caught off guard by the motion, avoided a challenge of the authority of the court, and argued against this particular subpoena — chiefly on the grounds that it was premature and that the materiality of the papers was not established. Viewed as a legal contest this one seems unsubstantial, but its political implications are inescapable. The proceedings frequently threatened to degenerate into a partisan brawl.

The palm for intemperance, exaggeration, and misrepresentation unquestionably went to Luther Martin. Describing as tyrannical the orders from the departments of War and the Navy that were now demanded, he said that "the life and property of an innocent man were

[13] Hay to TJ, June 9, 1807, received June 12 (LC, 29510–29511). Burr gave notice of the motion that day and it was argued June 10–12 (Robertson, I, 94–186).

[14] TJ to Hay, June 12, 1807 (Ford, IX, 55–56n.), read in court June 16 (Robertson, I, 211–212). Marshall delivered his opinion June 13 (ibid., 172–186).

[15] Ibid., I, 101; Hay to TJ, June 14, 1807 (LC, 29533–29535). The debate of June 10–12 is reported in Robertson, I, 94–165.

to be exposed to destruction" by them and that Burr was entitled to resist them.[16] If it was his purpose to goad his opponents, he succeeded with Hay, who described this doctrine as monstrous and said sarcastically that, considering that Martin had come all the way from Maryland to enlighten the Virginia bar "by his great talents and erudition," something less abhorrent had been expected of him."[17] In his first long speech the lawyer from Maryland made the irresponsible and unwarranted charge that copies of these illegal and tyrannical orders had been refused under presidential influence. Accordingly, he claimed that direct application for them must be made to the President himself. He wholly ignored the fact that such application had already been made by Hay. Addressing the Chief Justice, he made remarks that were destined to gain fame of a sort:

This is a peculiar case, sir. The president has undertaken to prejudge my client by declaring that "Of his guilt there can be no doubt." He has assumed to himself the knowledge of the Supreme Being himself, and pretended to search the heart of my highly respected friend. He has proclaimed him a traitor in the face of that country which has rewarded him. He has let slip the dogs of war, the hell-hounds of persecution, to hunt down my friend. And would this president of the United States, who has raised all this absurd clamor, pretend to keep back the papers which are wanted for this trial, where life itself is at stake?

After delivering a tirade against the Commander-in-Chief such as has been rarely heard from a reputable lawyer in a federal court, he turned his guns on the Commanding General of the Army. Wilkinson might have "instilled as much poison into the ear of the president, as Satan himself breathed into the ear of Eve," he said; and he reminded the court that the General had "already ground down the civil authorities into dust, and subjected all around him to a military despotism."

At this juncture nobody assumed the unenviable task of defending Wilkinson, but blunt-spoken Alexander MacRae promptly protested against the blast against the President. Addressing the Chief Justice, who had remained silent, he said:

I could have wished, sir, that instead of talking about shadows; instead of complaining against certain pretended persecutions attributed to the government of the United States; instead of in-

[16] Martin's speech of June 10, 1807, to which we are referring here, is in *ibid.*, I, 109-113.
[17] This was the next day, June 11 (*ibid.*, p. 139).

dulging in defamation and abuse against the officers of government, which can neither be justified nor excused, they had confined their observations to the single and simple question now presented to your consideration, Whether this court had the right to issue a *subpoena duces tecum*, addressed to the president of the United States.[18]

This counselor was of the opinion that, according to precedent, a subpoena should not go against the President. Nonetheless, the prosecution conceded that, when life was in jeopardy, that illustrious personage might be summoned like anybody else, if he could disclose important facts and if national interests would permit him to attend. Why, then, this invidious comparison with the irresponsible British monarch, as though he had set himself above the law? Only time would show whether MacRae's prediction was correct that, when all the facts were known and when truth rather than passion should guide understanding, the "bolt" against Jefferson's reputation would vanish in thin air. Beyond any doubt, however, the instant rebuke of Luther Martin by this speaker was amply warranted.

William Wirt also protested strongly against the "invective against the administration." He did not attribute this merely to Martin, but claimed that it was the settled policy of the defense from the beginning. After reminding the Chief Justice of the first speeches of Botts and Wickham, members of the gentlemanly Richmond bar, he asked if they had not repeatedly "flown off at a tangent from the subject to launch into declamations against the government." Continually they had exhibited the prisoner "as a persecuted patriot: a Russell or a Sidney, bleeding under the scourge of a despot, and dying for virtue's sake!" He asked what was intended, expected, or hoped from "these perpetual philippics against the government." He thought such conduct disrespectful of the court itself, and wondered what a foreigner would think if he heard "the federal administration thus reviled to the federal judiciary."[19]

Wickham took up the challenge, denying that the counsel for the defense had begun the attack, and, while displaying no such ferocity as Martin, he charged the prosecution with speaking improperly of Burr. The Chief Justice finally broke silence, stating that, while the court did not approve of many observations that had been made in the heat of debate, it had hitherto avoided interfering. Now he "thought it proper to declare that the gentlemen on both sides had acted improperly in the

[18] This part of MacRae's speech is in *ibid.*, I, 113–114.
[19] *Ibid.*, pp. 130–132.

style and spirit of their remarks" and expressed the wish that henceforth they should confine themselves to the point really at issue. It seems that the defense counsel had offended the more, but in any case Marshall should certainly have spoken sooner.[20]

He delivered his opinion on Burr's motion after two more days of indecorous debate.[21] The Chief Justice conceded less to presidential convenience than Burr had done. Addressing himself directly to the theoretical question, which had actually been waived by the prosecution, he held that either a general subpoena or a subpoena *duces tecum* could be issued to the President just as to anybody else. In his eyes the only ground for exemption would be that the President's time was wholly demanded for national objects. "But," continued the Chief Justice, "it is apparent that this demand is not unremitting, and if it should exist at the time when his attendance on a court is required, it would be sworn on the return of the subpoena, and would rather constitute a reason for not obeying the process of the court, than a reason against its being issued."[22] What he said, in effect, was that the burden of proof would be on the President, who would have to justify his non-attendance on oath. The Chief Justice, who had previously pointed out unnecessarily that an American President was not a king, called attention to the liability of English executive officers to subpoena, but the parallel between England and the United States was certainly imperfect as regarded the distances to be covered.

That Marshall recognized some difficulties was shown by his statement that "whatever difference may exist with respect to the power to compel the same obedience to the process, as if it had been directed to a private citizen, there exists no difference with respect to the right to obtain it."[23] In fact he was claiming a theoretical "right" that he was wholly powerless to enforce. The safeguard of the President against unnecessary subpoenas, he said, "is to be looked for in the conduct of the court after the subpoenas have been issued." That is, he held that the court, not the President, must be the final judge.

Having established to his own satisfaction the right of his court to issue to the President a subpoena *duces tecum* requiring him to bring a paper or papers with him, Marshall turned to the question of issuing one in this particular case. Since this had been the real point at issue in the debate, he addressed himself chiefly to the arguments of the prosecution, virtually all of which he brushed away. Of particular concern

[20] *Ibid.*, pp. 135–136.
[21] Marshall's opinion of June 13, 1807, is in *ibid.*, I, 172–186.
[22] *Ibid.*, p. 177.
[23] *Ibid.*, p. 178.

to us here are his comments on the claim that, in the public interest, certain papers should not be disclosed. He attributed to the District Attorney and his colleagues more reluctance than was borne out by their own words. At the most they had manifested uncertainty and their main argument had been directed to the question of materiality. Concerning the public interest, Marshall had this to say: "If it [Wilkinson's letter to Jefferson] does not contain any matter, which it would be imprudent to disclose, which it is not the wish of the executive to disclose; such matter, if it be not immediately and essentially applicable to the point, will, of course, be suppressed. . . . Everything of this kind, however, will have its due consideration on the return of the subpoena."[24] Presumably he meant that the decision whether to disclose or withhold lay with the court, which would take the wishes of the executive into account but might overrule them.

More than once in the course of his opinion Marshall denied that he intended any disrespect of the President, but at several points he implied that the government was undisposed to give fair treatment to the accused, and one unguarded expression of his amounted to the assertion that it "wished" the conviction of Burr. This elicited immediate protest from Alexander MacRae and, according to George Hay, created a general sensation.[25] After expressing the hope that the expression had accidentally fallen from the Chief Justice's pen and did not represent his deliberate opinion, MacRae declared: "We wish for nothing, sir, but a fair and competent investigation of this case. It is far from our wishes that Aaron Burr should be convicted but upon the most satisfactory evidence." The District Attorney informed Jefferson that on hearing this "mild but determined" demand for an explanation, Marshall "actually blushed." In reply he denied any intention to insinuate that either the counsel for the prosecution or the administration wished Burr convicted, whether innocent or guilty. He said, however, that their frequent assertions of Burr's guilt made it seem probable "that they were not indifferent on the subject." MacRae then said that, from the testimony they had examined, they thought it very

---

24 *Ibid.*, p. 184.
25 *Ibid.*, pp. 185–188; Hay to TJ, June 14, 1807 (LC, 29533–29535), received June 17. Both MacRae in his protest and Marshall in his reply used the word "wished." Hay told Jefferson that Marshall had said "wished and expected," and had afterwards erased the objectionable expression. Presumably he erased the word "wished" and either inserted or left the word "expected." In Robertson's report the passage reads: "Should it [the present prosecution] terminate as is expected on the part of the United States, all those concerned in it should certainly regret that a paper which the accused believed to be essential to his defense . . . had been withheld from him."

probable that Burr was really guilty, but that was a very different thing from wanting to find him guilty or to convict him willy-nilly. Hay reported to Jefferson that later in the day, "when the crowd was thinned, the Judge acknowledged the impropriety of the expression objected to, and informed us from the bench that he had erased it." Following the adjournment of the court, he told Hay that "he regretted the remark, and then by way of apology said that he had been so pressed for time, that he had never read the opinion, after he had written it." The District Attorney was not mollified.

ii

Jefferson learned of these developments three days after the events themselves. Hay wrote him about the motion for a subpoena shortly after it was made and he replied immediately. (Without having been either authorized or forbidden to do so, Hay produced and read Jefferson's letter in court, but this was too late to affect the proceedings there.) Though the District Attorney questioned the materiality of the papers, he contended from the first that they could be procured on request and he urged Jefferson to send them. Also, he reported at the outset that the personal attendance of the President would not be required. Without mentioning the subpoena, which obviously he sought to forestall, Jefferson said in his prompt reply:

> Reserving the necessary right of the President of the U.S. to decide, independently of all other authority, what papers, coming to him as President, the public interests permit to be communicated, & to whom, I assure you of my readiness under that restriction, voluntarily to furnish on all occasions, whatever the purposes of justice may require.[26]

Though he asserted that he alone must decide what could be safely communicated, he gave no sign that he regarded the document most wanted by Burr as one that the public interest required him to withhold. He said, however, that it was not now in his possession. He had turned Wilkinson's letter over to the Attorney General, along with other papers relating to Burr, when Rodney went to Richmond in March, and had supposed it was in the hands of the District Attorney. He was asking Rodney to send it but feared there might be some delay since the whereabouts of that peripatetic official were uncertain.

[26] TJ to Hay, June 12, 1807 (Ford, IX, 55–56n., replying to Hay's letter of June 9. Hay read it in court June 16.

Jefferson did not remember everything that was in the letter and accordingly instructed the District Attorney to use his own judgment in withholding such parts of it as were not "directly material for the purposes of justice." Grounds of disagreement on the limits of executive and judicial authority could have been perceived in Jefferson's reservations and instructions, but the outstanding fact was that he was willing to meet the desires of the defense insofar as he properly could. The request for copies of orders issued by the executive departments presented some difficulties, since it was general rather than specific. But he was asking Dearborn to examine his official communications, and on that same day he sent copies of a couple of orders from the War Department. Hay already had one from the Department of the Navy.

Three days after Jefferson wrote this conciliatory letter, and the day before it was read by Hay in court, the subpoena which had been speeded to Washington by Burr's special messenger was served on the President, as one was also served on Robert Smith and on Dearborn. The document had on it an endorsement signed by Burr, saying that the transmission of the specified papers to the clerk of the court would be "admitted as sufficient observance of the process, without the personal attendance of any or either of the persons therein named."[27] Burr reported to the court four days later that the only reply to the subpoena received from Jefferson was a verbal one, that no papers would be sent by the messenger. He then said that unless he received satisfactory intimation that they would be sent some other way he would move next day that the court "enforce its process."[28] Actually there was intimation enough in Jefferson's letter that had already been read in court; and on the next day another and longer letter was communicated by Hay at the President's request.[29] This was addressed to the District Attorney, not the court, but, more than anything else Jefferson wrote, it constituted his public reply to the court's order.

After summarizing the actions he had taken, he stated his belief that he had anticipated and "substantially fulfilled" the object of the subpoena. Furthermore, he offered to make available, in the form of depositions, anything else within the knowledge of the heads of departments that might be useful to the defense. Though his attendance in Richmond was not required by Burr, apparently he wanted to

[27] File of the Clerk's Office, U.S. District Court for the Eastern District of Virginia, Richmond (photostat, UVA). Less reasonably, the endorsement required certificates from "all the persons named in the process" that no other orders had been given military and naval officers respecting Burr and his party.

[28] June 19, 1807 (Robertson, I, 259).

[29] TJ to Hay, June 17, 1807 (Ford, IX, 56–57n.); read June 20 (Robertson, I, 265–267).

make his position on this question unmistakable. If he had read Marshall's opinion, no doubt he would have been even more disposed to do so. For the record he wrote:

> As to our personal attendance in Richmond, I am persuaded the Court is sensible that paramount duties of the nation at large control the obligation of compliance with their summons in this case; as they would, should we receive a similar one, to attend the trials of Blennerhassett & others, in the Mississippi territory, those instituted at St. Louis and other places on the western waters, or at any place, other than the seat of government. To comply with such calls would leave the nation without an executive branch, whose agency, nevertheless, is understood to be so constantly necessary, that it is the sole branch which the constitution requires to be always in function. It could not mean that it should be withdrawn from it's station by any co-ordinate authority.

By this calm statement he made it clear that he was not going to abandon his post in Washington and go to Richmond no matter what John Marshall might say. And if anyone could have seriously doubted the soundness of his position, events demonstrated it within a week, when the *Leopard* fired on the *Chesapeake*, creating a crisis in Anglo-American relations.

Having disposed of the question of personal appearance, he took up that of papers. Observing that there was both a public and private side to the operations of government, he assigned mere executive proceedings to the latter. "All nations have found it necessary," he said, "that for the advantageous conduct of their affairs, some of these proceedings, at least, should remain known to their executive functionary only. He, of course, must be the sole judge of which of them the public interests will permit publication." He then referred to the express recognition of this by Congress when requesting papers of the President. He enclosed the congressional resolution which led to his message of January 22 respecting Burr.

Largely confining himself to practicalities, he indulged in no extended theoretical discussion; and it is clear that this advocate of harmony and a viable government was seeking to avoid a confrontation with the judiciary without yielding his executive prerogatives. His steps to make the desired papers available were taken *before* he was actually served with the subpoena; and, ostensibly, he had responded to a private request of the District Attorney in a spirit of fairness to the accused. Having sought to fulfill the *objects* of the subpoena, he gave the least possible notice to the summons itself. Unquestionably he regarded it as both unnecessary and improper. He did not say that publicly in so many words, but at the end of this letter he said this: "The respect mutually due between the constituted authorities, in their official intercourse, as well as sincere dispositions to do for every man what is just, will always insure from the executive, in exercising the discrimination confided to him, the same candor and integrity to which the nation has in like manner trusted in the disposal of its judiciary authorities." No doubt he intended this as both a plea for intra-governmental harmony and a polite rebuke of judicial self-righteousness.

In a private letter he sent Hay along with the one he asked the District Attorney to communicate, he said that the latter was written "in a spirit of conciliation and with the desire to avoid conflicts of authority between the high branches of the government which would discredit it at home and abroad."[30] While saying that the attempt of Burr and his counsel to convert the trial into "a contest between the judiciary and executive authorities was to be expected," he expressed surprise that the Chief Justice "should lend himself to it, and take the first step to bring it on." He doubted if Marshall's good sense would permit him to press the contest, but just in case he should issue some process calling for forceful action against the President or department heads, Jefferson asked that he be notified by the quickest possible method. Also, he asked Hay to instruct the United States Marshal to have no part in any such action. The constitutional powers of the Executive were sufficient, he said, to protect the other branches from "usurpation of pre-eminence" by the judiciary, and to guard individuals, including the Marshal, against "judiciary vengeance." He hoped the Chief Justice would allow the question to lie over for the present, and that before long legislative means would be provided for "giving to individuals the benefit of the testimony of the executive functionaries, *without breaking up the government*."[31] He did not specify what sort of legislative action he had in mind, but he clearly perceived the duality of this problem. As a humane man who was also a practical administrator he recognized that the rights of individuals and the necessities of government must somehow be reconciled.

Two days after he thus expressed himself he saw the opinion of the

[30] Draft of undated letter in LC, 28710 and Ford, IX, 62n. Ford assigns this to a later date and says it may never have been sent. Beveridge (III, 518–520) assigns this to the misdemeanor trial, without giving his reason. It can be better regarded as an accompaniment of TJ's letter of June 17; and since TJ did not indicate that it was *not* sent, as he customarily did in such cases, I think we may assume it was. It clearly shows his attitude, at all events.

[31] Italics added.

Chief Justice. To this he made no public reply, but in a letter to Hay he commented on it with the freedom he allowed himself in private.[32] He said that he had not read the argument with much attention, since he considered the question as *coram non judice* (that is, outside the jurisdiction of the court). He observed, however, that Marshall spent much time on smaller objections to the position he was determined to support and passed over more important ones. "Laying down the position generally, that all persons owe obedience to subpoenas," said the President, "he admits no exception unless it can be produced in his law books. But if the Constitution enjoins on a particular officer to be always engaged in a particular set of duties imposed on him, does not this supersede the general law, subjecting him to minor duties inconsistent with these? The Constitution enjoins his constant agency in the concerns of 6 millions of people. Is the law paramount to this, which calls on him on behalf of a single one?" According to this reasoning, he said, the Chief Justice might be summoned from the bench to serve on the posse of the sheriff of his county to quell a riot. On practical grounds he regarded the summons to himself as an absurdity, and he believed it to be incompatible with the leading principle of the Constitution — the independence of its three branches of each other. After saying that the judiciary were especially jealous of this, he asked: "But would the executive be independent of the judiciary, if he were subject to the *commands* of the latter, and to imprisonment for disobedience; if the several courts could bandy him from pillar to post, keep him constantly trudging from north to south and east to west, and withdraw him entirely from his constitutional duties?" He obviously regarded Marshall's opinion as an empty gesture, but the remark that the President's duties were not unremitting got under his skin. Suspecting that the Chief Justice may have been alluding to his annual long visit to Monticello, he pointed out that he carried on the public business there as continuously as when he was in Washington, and even more laboriously because communications must be in writing. However, everybody knew where he was, as they would not if he were perpetually on the road under the orders of the judiciary.

No doubt Jefferson expected the District Attorney to bear in mind the sentiments he now expressed, and even to voice them upon occasion, but he did not ask Hay to communicate them to the court. He continued to avoid open conflict with the Chief Justice, and it now appears not only that he had much the better of the argument, but also that he was more punctilious in maintaining the outward forms of

[32] TJ to Hay, June 20, 1807 (Ford, IX, 59–60*n*.).

respect that were due the head of one branch of the government from the head of another.

When Hay read Jefferson's letter of June 17 in court he stated that he had received and would deposit with the clerk the various departmental orders, and that when Wilkinson's letter of October 21, 1806, had been received the return would be complete.[33] Burr and his counsel had little choice but to accept this announcement at the moment as a compliance with the subpoena, and there were other reasons why he did not carry out his threat of the previous day to call upon the court to enforce its process against the President. He and his lawyers were focusing attention on Wilkinson at the time, and, following his indictment, they gave major attention to his own physical well-being.

Meanwhile in Washington, besides facing the international crisis occasioned by the *Leopard-Chesapeake* incident, Jefferson was meeting with difficulty in his effort to fulfill the object of the court. Burr had demanded Wilkinson's letter of October 21, 1806, because Jefferson referred to it in the special message to Congress in which he first informed that body of the revelations of the conspiracy that had been made to him.[34] Though Burr asked for such documents as accompanied this letter, he did not know there were two letters of that date — a fact which Jefferson said he himself had forgotten. On receiving from the Attorney General a letter of October 21, he quickly perceived that it was the wrong one since it was unrelated to the facts stated in the presidential message. Soon thereafter, on a visit to Washington, Rodney informed the President that he could not find the other one. The court was still in session but this matter was quiescent when Jefferson told Hay that he was instituting further inquiries, that the missing letter would be forwarded as soon as found, and that in the meantime a copy could probably be procured from Wilkinson.[35]

[33] June 20, 1807 (Robertson, I, 267).

[34] Jan. 22, 1807 (Ford, IX, 16). The most important document submitted by TJ and made public at this time was the deciphered letter of Burr to Wilkinson, July 29, 1806.

[35] TJ to Rodney, June 19, 1807 (LC, 29546); to Hay, June 23 (Ford, IX, 60–61*n*.). See above, pp. 247–249, for an account of the several communications received by TJ from Wilkinson on Nov. 21, 1806, including two letters dated Oct. 21. The one that "had no relation to the facts" stated in the presidential message must have been the one in which Wilkinson defended his patriotism against charges recently made in the press. The one relating to the conspiracy was marked "confidential" and contained a postscript on a separate sheet, which Wilkinson omitted when he published this letter in his *Memoirs*. This could have been interpreted as indicating that the General himself was not averse to an attack on Mexico. It was not

The General had finally arrived in Richmond, to the great relief of the District Attorney. Although Hay had sought to explain Wilkinson's non-appearance, he had made no effort up to this time to defend him against current charges, aspersions, and rumors; in fact, he was somewhat uncertain about the General. After an interview with that resplendent officer, however, he underwent a change of heart. Writing the President, he said: "His erect attitude, the serenity of his countenance, the composure of his manners, the mild but determined expression of his eye, all conspired to make me think that he has been most grossly calumniated." In a postscript, written after another interview during which he read many of Wilkinson's papers, he said he was now convinced that Burr "for the vilest purposes" had caused the General's name to be constantly associated with his own. Also, Hay was convinced that Wilkinson could not have acted better than he did toward the conspirators.[36]

No doubt the District Attorney was aware that his comments would be welcome to Jefferson, but abler men than he had been fooled by Wilkinson, and he appears to have been dazzled. In court the next day, after referring to his reassuring conversation with the General, he stated that he now felt it his duty to defend him, being well satisfied that he was a patriot and an honest man. "All my suspicions, imbibed from the mysterious circumstances in the case, have completely vanished," said Hay, "and being convinced of his unsullied integrity, I shall defend him with the most perfect sincerity."[37] Without anticipating the speaker's final judgment of Wilkinson, one can safely remark that he said more than was necessary at this stage and overcommitted himself.

In his message of January 22 to Congress, Jefferson had contented himself with praising Wilkinson's patriotism in revealing the conspiracy; he had not claimed in public that the General had manifested "unsullied integrity" in his career as a whole. His opinion that in this particular matter Wilkinson had served his country well was reinforced, no doubt, by that of Hay. We should also note that, two days before he got Hay's letter, he received one from Claiborne in New

---

TJ's custom to disclose confidential letters, but his instructions to Hay to withhold anything not "directly material for the purposes of justice" probably seemed to him a sufficient safeguard. Actually, the "facts" stated in TJ's message of Jan. 22, 1807, were not drawn from this letter to the extent implied; some were in the anonymous communication that accompanied it, and information was gained from Wilkinson's messenger.

[36] Hay to TJ, June 14, 1807; received June 17 (LC, 29533-29535).
[37] June 15, 1807 (Robertson, I, 199).

Orleans, approving the conduct of Wilkinson there. In this the Governor said that the General "deserved well of his country" and expressed the belief that he opposed Burr from principle and was motivated by pure and honest patriotism.[38] Thus the judgment of men who were trusted by him supported Jefferson's opinion (or rationalization) that the accusations against Wilkinson were blamable on Burr and the latter's suporters. Keeping his reservations to himself if he had any, he over-committed himself in private.

Replying to a letter from the General, he warmly congratulated him upon his arrival, "against the impudent surmises and hopes of the band of conspirators" who were attempting "to cover their crimes under noise and insolence."[39] By referring to Wilkinson's "fiery trial at New Orleans" and attributing the clamors against him wholly to criminals who were seeking to distract attention from themselves and their leader, he seemed to give his entire sanction to conduct which was regarded by many as arbitrary and tyrannical. Previously he himself had expressed disapproval of some of it in private.

No one who had observed Burr and his counsel in action and was aware of the attitude of John Randolph, foreman of the grand jury, could have doubted that Wilkinson faced a severe ordeal in Richmond. If he needed reassurance he got it in full measure in the final paragraph of the President's letter:

> Your enemies have filled the public ear with slanders, & your mind with trouble on that account. The establishment of their guilt will let the world see what they ought to think of their clamors; it will dissipate the doubts of those who doubted for want of knolege, and will place you on the higher ground in the public estimate and public confidence. No one is more sensible than myself of the injustice which has been aimed at you.

In this private letter Jefferson gave a brief account of his own actions in response to the subpoena. Some explanation was natural and proper since a confidential communication from Wilkinson had been specifically demanded. Referring to the letter of October 21, 1806, he said: "If you have a copy of it, and chuse to give it in, it will, I think, have a good effect; for it was my intention, if I should receive it from

---

[38] Claiborne to TJ, May 3, 1807; received June 15 (Carter, IX, 729). Claiborne said much the same thing in a letter of Mar. 3 to Dearborn; received Apr. 27 (*ibid.*, IX, 712). For a previous reference to these letters, see above, p. 279.

[39] TJ to Wilkinson, June 21, 1807 (Ford, IX, 5–6*n.*). Though he said he was replying to Wilkinson's of the 16th, presumably it was of the 17th (Letters Relating to Burr's Conspiracy, LC).

Mr. Rodney, not to communicate it without your consent, after I learnt of your arrival." He had not told Hay, and through him informed the court, that the production of the original of this letter was contingent on Wilkinson's approval. The writer could hardly have wanted to expose the postscript to public view. This could have been withheld by Hay under the authority Jefferson gave him (it was on a separate page from the body of the letter); but it is very likely that Wilkinson preferred to exhibit a copy rather than an original, and this may help explain certain later developments.[40] Jefferson further limited his own freedom of action out of consideration for the man whom he credited with exposing the conspiracy and regarded as the most important witness for the prosecution.

Before Wilkinson arrived at Richmond, John Randolph privately remarked that it had once been a matter of astonishment to him that the administration should "choose to embark its reputation in the same bottom" with such a man, but that now nothing surprised him.[41] He added that he could not see how Wilkinson's guilt implied the innocence of Burr. "My inference," he said, "would have been quite opposite." By the same token, the guilt of Burr need not imply the innocence of Wilkinson. If Jefferson did not disbelieve in the General's complicity in the conspiracy prior to his exposure of it, he had, in effect, pardoned Wilkinson for turning state's evidence, and he was now in the unfortunate position of seeming to approve of him wholly. John Randolph was not noted for objectivity, but it would be hard for any chronicler of these events to refrain from quoting his description of Wilkinson as "the most finished scoundrel that ever lived" and his further reference to him as "the man whom the king delighteth to honor."[42] This particular king was not at his best in dealing with scoundrels, especially this one.

Jefferson was in no position to observe the impression the star witness for the prosecution made on the grand jury when he appeared before it in closed session.[43] "Perhaps you never saw human nature in so degraded a situation," wrote John Randolph to his friend Nicholson afterwards.[44] Like Randolph's statement that nobody pretended to think Wilkinson innocent, this may be regarded as an exaggeration, but the General was forced to make damaging admissions — including that

[40] See above, note 35; and page 343.

[41] Randolph to J. H. Nicholson, May 31, 1807 (Nicholson Papers, 3:13945).

[42] Randolph to Nicholson, June 28, 1807 (ibid., 3:1398C).

[43] Wilkinson was sworn and sent to the grand jury June 15. Hay said that Burr was better informed of what went on there than he was.

[44] June 25, 1807 (Nicholson Papers, 3:1398A).

of having deleted from the ciphered letter (before he sent it to Jefferson) passages implying previous knowledge of the conspiracy and earlier collaboration with Burr.[45] After the grand jury had made its presentments, the news leaked out that it had almost indicted Wilkinson. Reports of this near-action varied in detail and led to assertions, denials, and corrections in the Richmond press which in general followed party lines. The Federalist *Virginia Gazette* and a grand juror sympathetic to Burr claimed that the vote was on a motion to present Wilkinson for treason, while the Republican *Virginia Argus* and a couple of other jurymen said that the charge was misprision of treason, as Wilkinson himself reported to Jefferson. There was agreement that the motion to indict him was defeated by the close vote of nine to seven.[46] Wilkinson claimed that the ground for the attempt to present him was his failure to report Dayton to Jefferson, saying that he felt himself to be between Scylla and Charybdis: "The jury would dishonor me for failing of my duty, and Burr and his conspirators for performing it."[47] The man whom John Randolph termed "the mammoth of iniquity" and described as a villain "from the bark to the very core" had a narrow escape from indictment. It has been averred that he owed this wholly to politics, and the case was unquestionably shot through with politics, on both sides, from beginning to end. But, in view of Marshall's emphasis on overt acts, there was ground for honest doubt of Wilkinson's probable complicity in the conspiracy.[48]

Clearly recognizing that the psychological effect of discrediting him would be to the advantage of Burr, the defense introduced a motion for an attachment to him for "attempting to obstruct the free administration of justice." Specifically, he was charged with the coercion of a witness.[49] The wrangling over this motion, which was eventually denied, was interrupted on June 24 by the report of John Randolph that the grand jury had agreed on indictments against Burr and Blennerhassett for both treason and misdemeanor. A day later he re-

[45] Abernethy, p. 239, note 43, referring to a copy of the letter (in Cabell Papers, UVA), showing Wilkinson's omissions.

[46] The chief newspaper references are: *Virginia Gazette*, July 4, 11, 15, and Aug. 12, 1807; *Virginia Argus*, July 1, 29. At least three grand jurymen were involved in the newspaper discussion: Munford Beverly, John Brockenborough, and William Daniel.

[47] Wilkinson to TJ, June 29, 1807 (LC, 29614–29615).

[48] Beveridge, *Marshall*, III, 464, note 2. For John Randolph's later explanation of the failure to indict Wilkinson, which may have been an afterthought, see below, ch. XX.

[49] Motion made June 20 (Robertson, I, 268). It occupied most of the time of the court until June 27, when Marshall denied it (*ibid.*, I, 390–393).

ported presentments against five others, for treason in levying war
against the United States at Blennerhassett's Island.[50]

Immediately following his indictment, Burr raised the question of
the power of the court to grant him bail at its discretion. Considerable
argument ensued, but, since the defense could not produce precedents
satisfactory to the Chief Justice, he committed Burr to the custody of
the United States Marshal, who conducted him to the public (that is,
the county and city) jail.[51] A couple of days later three members of
Burr's counsel (Randolph, Wickham, and Botts, all of whom were
Virginians), having noted the "miserable state" of the prison where he
was confined and the virtual impossibility of consulting with him since
he did not have a room to himself, sought to have him removed to
more comfortable and convenient quarters. The counselors for the
prosecution were silent on this motion. After long and desultory
arguments by the defense, the court determined that he should be
removed to his former lodgings near the capitol, provided these could
be made sufficiently strong. Benjamin H. Latrobe, who was there as a
witness, was requested to inspect them. On his report the court
ordered that the front room in the house now occupied by Luther
Martin be prepared by securing the windows with bars and the door
with a padlock, and that a guard of seven men be placed in the adjoining unfinished house on the same story.[52] Since there was no provision
in Richmond for federal prisoners at the time, the arrangement was not
as extraordinary as it would now appear, but the prosecutors were not
satisfied with it. They soon got the executive council of the state to
offer quarters on the third floor of the penitentiary; and, on the last
day of the session (June 30), the court ordered that Burr be transferred to these as soon as they were made fit. In the meantime, he had
pleaded not guilty and the trial had been postponed to August 3.[53] By
July 3 he was in his new quarters, which, as described by him to his
daughter Theodosia, were more commodious than the barred room he
had occupied for a few days in the house with Luther Martin. Furthermore, he could see his friends and lawyers at any time he liked.

Martin assumed the painful task of informing Burr's son-in-law of
the indictment and imprisonment of his "much esteemed friend." To
Joseph Alston he wrote: "Never, I believe, did any government thirst

---

[50] *Ibid.,* I, 329–330, 359–360. The five were Jonathan Dayton, Senator John Smith
of Ohio, Comfort Tyler, Israel Smith, and Davis Floyd.

[51] *Ibid.,* I, 330–338.

[52] *Ibid.,* I, 385–386.

[53] *Ibid.,* I, 393–396.

more for the blood of a victim than our enlightened, philosophic, mild, philanthropic government for the blood of my friend."[54] Speaking of the counsel for the prosecution, which he thought could be truly described as the persecution, he said that the savage and unfeeling manner adopted by all three of them "would dishonor any beings but demons from Hell." In his opinion Colonel Burr was as innocent of anything treasonable as an unborn child, and would surely triumph over the "malignant jealousy and inveterate hatred" by which he was being persecuted. He had no doubt that the government would feel no more compunction in taking Burr's life than that with which a philosopher views a rat expiring with convulsions. He was confident, he said, that the government did not believe Burr "to have been guilty of a treasonable act or design." This passionate counselor saw, or claimed to see, nothing but vindictiveness in the minds of the President and his associates. Into the mind of the President this utterly hostile commentator read what he wanted to, but, judging from other accounts, he was realistic in his assessment of local public opinion. He said that the prisoner had many warm friends in Richmond who were standing by him in adversity, that the "popular odium" (which he himself attributed to the base and artful excitation of the government) had greatly decreased and was still decreasing, and that Wilkinson was regarded by many as "the basest of villains."

Before Alston and Theodosia got there, Burr described his situation in several cheerful letters to his beloved daughter.[55] He had three rooms on the third floor and a polite jailer, who let him keep his light on when everybody else's was off. Here he received messages and gifts — "oranges, lemons, pineapples, raspberries, apricots, cream, butter, ice, and some ordinary articles." Friends and acquaintances were permitted to visit him until ten at night and he was never spied on. During the month of his confinement before his trial he appears to have suffered neither discomfort nor boredom in what he called his "mansion," and not without warrant did William Duane refer to him as the "emperor of the penitentiary."

[54] Martin to Alston, June 26, 1807 (*Amer. Antiq. Soc. Procs.*, XXIX, 123–124).
[55] July 3, 6, 24, 30, 1807 (Mark Van Doren, ed., *Correspondence of Aaron Burr and His Daughter Theodosia* [1929], pp. 222–224).

[XIX]

Futile Proceedings in Richmond

TWO days before the indictment of Burr for treason, the British
frigate *Leopard* made an outrageous attack on the hapless American
frigate *Chesapeake* off the Virginia Capes. Since Jefferson's major attention was necessarily given to the crisis precipitated by that startling
event, he had little time during the month of July to think of the
"emperor of the penitentiary."[1] The defenders of Burr had asserted,
and were never to cease asserting, that his prosecution was actually
persecution by the administration, but all they really had to go on, up
to this point, was the fact that the President had originally set the
wheels in motion and had publicly expressed his confidence of Burr's
guilt. Except for his response to the subpoena, his personal activities in
connection with the legal proceedings had been virtually limited to the
effort to procure witnesses, which the Chief Justice had declared to be
the inescapable obligation of the government. Jefferson's part in this
was generally indirect. Insofar as he could, he acted through his agents,
including the Attorney General when that part-time official was available. He had made a direct personal effort, however, to procure the
testimony of Dr. Erick Bollman, and, as we have seen, this episode was
publicized in the summer. While the President was absorbed in the
problem of Anglo-American relations, his past relations with Burr's
emissary were aired.[2] Into the partisan controversy that ensued he did
not enter, though he was staunchly defended by his journalistic friends.

The treason trial proper occurred in the month of August, when
Jefferson was at Monticello. International affairs must have still been
uppermost in his mind, and he said that he gained his information
about happenings in Richmond from newspapers. He had a couple of
letters from Hay, however, and an occasional communication from

[1] See below, page 425.
[2] See above, pp. 307–308.

Rodney in Delaware. The case was now unquestionably in the "pale of the judiciary," and one gains the distinct impression that he had no more to do with it than he could help. He was perceptibly annoyed when the question of the subpoena came up again. On the first day of the session Burr reminded the court that the subpoena *duces tecum*, addressed to the President, had been only partly complied with. Thereupon Hay said that he now had the letter not previously furnished — that is, Wilkinson's of October 21, 1806 — and was ready to produce it. Burr then stated that he was also applying for a communication from General Eaton to the President and that if this was not produced by the District Attorney he would move for another subpoena to Jefferson.[3]

That gentleman learned of this fresh threat from the newspapers. In the brief letter he promptly wrote Hay he disposed of the question of his personal attendance by saying that higher duties kept him where he was. Still resentful, it seems, of the assertion of John Marshall that his presidential duties were not unremitting, he reminded Hay that he kept out of Washington during the late summer for reasons of health and transacted public business day by day at Monticello. As for the communication from Eaton, he stated that it had been delivered to the Attorney General with all the others relating to Burr, and that if Hay did not have it Rodney was the person to whom a subpoena should be directed.[4] Without raising questions of legality or propriety, he continued to confine himself to practicalities. He need not have troubled himself, however, for Burr did not make the threatened motion. Presumably Hay had the document from Eaton and produced it well in advance of Eaton's appearance as the first witness for the prosecution.

The letter from Wilkinson was another matter. Hay's statement on August 3 left the impression that he had the original, but when Burr again demanded it on the day the jury was sworn (August 15), the District Attorney said that he had not yet found it, although he had a copy of it from Wilkinson. This Burr would not accept and he may be presumed to have recognized that he did not need the document at this stage.[5] At any rate he did not carry out his threat to move for a subpoena to the Attorney General if the original letter was not found and made available at the next meeting of the court. This particular matter seems to have remained in abeyance until the trial for misde-

---

[3] Aug. 3, 1807 (Robertson, *Trial of Aaron Burr for Treason*, I, 400-401).

[4] TJ to Hay, Aug. 7, 1807 (Ford, IX, 61-62n.).

[5] Robertson, I, 480.

meanor, when it came up again.[6] Responsibility for the document rested with the District Attorney and the Attorney General and it played no further part in the trial for treason.

In the middle of July, writing his friend Du Pont de Nemours, Jefferson said: "Burr's conspiracy has been one of the most flagitious of which history will ever furnish an example. . . . Yet altho' there is not a man in the U. S. who is not satisfied of the depth of his guilt, such are the jealous provisions of our laws in favor of the accused, and against the accuser, that I question if he can be convicted."[7] The provisons to which he specifically referred were those applying to ordinary criminal cases: the right of the accused to challenge prospective jurors and the requirement of unanimity for conviction. Of these provisions he expressed no disapproval, and he stated here as he did many times elsewhere that the entire affair confirmed the "innate strength" of the American form of government. He made no reference whatever to judicial partisanship. His judgment of American opinion about Burr's guilt was over-stated in this private letter, but the preponderant opinion was clearly shown by the difficulty in impaneling a jury. Nearly everybody who was summoned admitted that he had formed an adverse opinion, and ninety-six men were called before twelve were chosen. Some of these had expressed an unfavorable opinion about Burr's intentions. His willingness to let that pass and to co-operate at this stage may have arisen from his expectation that the case would really be decided by the court rather than the jury, as to all practical purposes it was.

The form of the indictment (afterwards criticized by Marshall) and the procedure of the prosecution were determined by his statements about treason in his opinion in the case of Bollman and Swartwout.[8] In this the Chief Justice said:

> It is not the intention of the court to say, that no individual can be guilty of this crime, who has not appeared in arms against his country. On the contrary, if war be actually levied, that is, if a body of men be actually assembled, for the purpose of effecting by force a treasonable purpose, all those who perform any part, however minute, or however remote from the scene of action, and who are actually leagued in the general conspiracy are to be considered as traitors.

[6] Sept. 3–5, 1807; see below, pp. 342–345.
[7] TJ to Du Pont, July 14, 1807 (Ford, IX, 111).
[8] 4 Cranch, 125–136, especially 126–127; discussed by Beveridge, III, 349–357; see also Abernethy, *The Burr Conspiracy*, p. 244.

On this ground the grand jury indicted participants in the events on Blennerhassett's Island on December 11, 1806, along with Burr, who was obviously not present but whose part in bringing these events about was believed to have been far more than minute. To prove the "treasonable purpose" of the assemblage and the involvement of the man regarded as the prime mover, the government collected some 140 witnesses, and the officials most directly concerned believed the evidence to be overwhelming. Before any testimony had been presented, however, the District Attorney made this prophetic statement to Jefferson: "There is but one chance for the accused, and that is a good one because it rests with the Chief Justice. It is already hinted, but not by himself [that] the decision of the Supreme Court will not [be] deemed binding." Earlier in the letter the District Attorney had said of Marshall: "He seems to think that his reputation is irretrievably gone, and that he now has nothing to lose by doing as he pleases. His concern for Mr. Burr is wonderful." Years before, when Burr was rising in the esteem of Republicans, Marshall had described him as profligate and desperate. "Yet," said Hay, "when the Gr. Jury brought in their bill, the Chief Justice gazed at him, for a long time, without appearing conscious that he was doing so, with an expression of sympathy & sorrow, as strong as the human countenance can exhibit without *palpable* emotion." Hay's impression may have been heightened by his imagination, but this report could hardly have failed to deepen Jefferson's distrust of Marshall. In his reply he said: "Before an impartial jury, Burr's conduct would convict himself, were not one word of testimony to be offered against him. But to what a state will our law be reduced by party feelings in those who administer it?"[9]

We can only speculate about Marshall's sympathies, but there is evidence that around the time of Burr's indictment he was harboring doubts about some of the things he had said in his opinion in the case of Bollman and Swartwout. He expressed them in a letter to one of the Justices and in private conversation. Members of the grand jury and the District Judge, Cyrus Griffin, who was sitting with Marshall and played a negligible part in the proceedings, appear to have had no doubts that the ruling in that case applied to this one.[10] In his opening argument, Hay quoted Marshall's words with confidence. A few days later, however, Jefferson, who had been reading about the trial in the newspapers, commented to the Attorney General that these exhibited

[9] Hay to TJ, Aug. 11, 1807 (LC, 29916–29917); TJ, to Hay, Aug. 20 (Ford, IX, 62–63n.).
[10] Marshall to William Cushing, June 29, 1807 (R.T. Paine Papers, MHS); J. C. Cabell to Thos. Ritchie, Sept. 10, 1807 (Cabell papers, UVA), letter not sent.

"strange scenes indeed." To Gallatin he wrote: "Burr's trial goes on to the astonishment of all, as to the manner of conducting it." By this time he must have been informed of the squabble over the order of examining witnesses and may have known of Marshall's opinion on this question.[11] After General William Eaton had been sworn as the first witness, Burr objected on the ground that presumably his testimony would relate to alleged conversations at Washington — not to anything that happened on Blennerhassett's Island. Burr and his counsel claimed that an overt act must be proved before any other testimony could be admitted. After the lawyers for the defense had presented arguments on which they were soon to elaborate, and William Wirt had stoutly claimed for the prosecution the right to display the evidence in its own way, Marshall delivered an opinion which has been described by a distinguished constitutional scholar as "a model of ambiguous and equivocal statement."[12] He permitted the examination of Eaton and a few others (not including Wilkinson) whose testimony bore chiefly on Burr's intentions, but after eleven of the 140 witnesses had been examined, the defense sought to sever the slender thread by which the "Damocles sword of irrelevancy" was suspended over the heads of the prosecution.

This was on August 20, the third day after the examination began, by which time the testimony regarding events on Blennerhassett's Island had been presented. The prosecution was on the point of presenting other testimony which Burr and his counsel described as collateral and beyond the jurisdiction of the court, since he was in Kentucky on the date given in the indictment. In an elaborate speech Wickham objected to the admission of any evidence not relating directly to the overt act. A couple of minor witnesses were examined thereafter, but otherwise the time of the court was occupied over a period of ten days with the argument of counsel.[13] Local interest in the trial continued to be very great, despite the intense August heat and the excessively long speeches. That of Luther Martin lasted fourteen hours but is reported to have exhausted him not at all. In sheer wordage the counsel for the defense, which was now reinforced by former Attorney General Charles Lee, a Federalist stalwart, had much the better of it, but the most memorable passage was in a speech by Wirt — the passage in which he vividly described what Burr had done

[11] TJ to Rodney, Aug. 19, 1807 (LC, 29985); TJ to Gallatin, Aug. 20 (L. & B., XI, 338); dispute on Aug. 17, Marshall's opinion, Aug. 18 (Robertson, I, 508-535).
[12] E. S. Corwin, *John Marshall and the Constitution* (1921), p. 102.
[13] Wickham began speaking Aug. 20, and the debate was concluded Aug. 29 (Robertson, I, 596-677; II, 1-494).

to Blennerhassett and characterized as a monstrous perversion the designation of the latter as the principal offender and the former as a mere accessory.[14]

Burr's defenders not only rejected the common law doctrine that in treason all are principals; also, they designated as an *obiter dictum* or *gratis dictum* the statement about the nature of treason in Marshall's opinion in the case of Bollman and Swartwout. Of this William Wirt said: "A plain man would imagine that, when the Supreme Court had taken up and decided the case, its decision would form a precedent on the subject."[15] On the other hand, Luther Martin dismissed it summarily. As a binding judicial decision, he said, "it ought to have no more weight than the ballad or song of Chevy Chase."[16] One wonders what the effect on American constitutional law would have been if all of Marshall's opinions had been shorn of their *obiter dicta!* Of the lengthy one he rendered on August 31, granting the motion of Burr's counsel, the frustrated District Attorney wrote the President: "The opinion of the C. Justice is too voluminous to be generally read, and on the great question about the overt act of levying war too obscure and perplexed to be understood. The *explanation* of the opinion of the S[upreme] Court in the Case of Bollman and Swartwout renders it very difficult to apprehend what was before perfectly intelligible."[17]

In court a couple of days later, William Wirt said:

> We were governed by our construction of the opinion of the supreme court. If we were mistaken, it was an error common to those enlightened men who were on the grand jury, and whose minds are as much illuminated as those of any men in this state; and an error which I believe most men of intelligence might commit. The court however has said that the opinion of the supreme court has been misconceived; but no blame ought to be attached to us for that, as the misconception was general and common to the ablest men in this country.[18]

To a plain historian, unversed in legal subtleties and technicalities, the subject remains obscure, while the attempt of Marshall to reconcile his two opinions seems labored and unconvincing.

According to his biographer, the one that terminated the treason trial of Burr is among the longest he ever rendered and contains more

---

[14] *Ibid.*, II, 118–120.
[15] *Ibid.*, II, 77.
[16] *Ibid.*, II, 410; see also 412.
[17] Hay to TJ, Sept. 1, 1807 (LC, 30067).
[18] Robertson (1808 edn.), II, 499.

references to decisions and authorities than all the rest of his major constitutional opinions combined.[19] He had much to explain and his virtual pronouncement of Burr's innocence had to be justified. As Attorney General Rodney said, "C. Justice Marshall has it seems acquitted Burr."[20] Not only so. As Hay immediately perceived, he acquitted the whole party at Blennerhassett's Island by his interpretation of the expression "levying war." He now treated this as a technical term, saying that it involved an assemblage in force, in condition to make war, and employing some degree of violence. He said that the decision in the case of Bollman and Swartwout could not have meant that the Supreme Court considered as an actual levying of war "a secret unarmed meeting, although that meeting be of conspirators, and although it met with treasonable intent."[21] That is, regardless of the purpose of the particular meeting on which the case of the government rested, this was *not* an overt act such as was referred to in the definition of treason in the Constitution. From Marshall's statement one might have concluded that, in his judgment, Burr would not have been guilty of treason even if he had been at Blennerhassett's in person, whatever his plans were. The indictment charged him with committing treason at that particular place on a specific date. The Chief Justice held that this indictment could be supported only by testimony that he was physically present, as admittedly he was not; or constructively present, which Marshall denied; or by the admission of the doctrine that the procurer of an act could be considered as having performed it.[22] His expressions of doubt about that doctrine, and other references by him to Burr as an accessory, could be interpreted as identifying him with the position which William Wirt regarded as monstrous — namely, that the instigator of a crime is a lesser offender than his agents. Leaving the question of procurement open while giving the impression that he opposed the doctrine, Marshall held that in any case procurement would have to be established by two witnesses, just as the overt act must be — a contention which has been denied by certain later commentators.[23] At the time, the prosecution contended that this could be proved by the chain of events that would be revealed by the testimony as a whole, including earlier statements and later actions of Burr. It may be noted also that, whatever may be

[19] Beveridge, II, 504; opinion sympathetically described, 504–513. It may be seen in Robertson, II, 495–550 (references are to 1875 edition unless indicated otherwise); 4 Cranch, 470–506.

[20] Rodney to Madison, Sept. 18, 1807 (MP, 33:16).

[21] Robertson, II, 519.

[22] *Ibid.*, II, 542.

[23] Notably by Corwin, *John Marshall and the Constitution*, p. 107.

said of legal proof, his responsibility for the assemblage has been generally assumed by modern students of these events, including his ardent defenders. The only real question has been that of his purposes.

Holding that no overt act at Blennerhassett's Island had been proved and that testimony regarding actions in other places and other jurisdictions was not competent to prove it, Marshall ruled that this testimony was irrelevant and inadmissible. Granting the motion of the defense, he submitted the case to the jury. That body quickly reached a verdict on September 1, but couched this in unusual language: "We of the jury say that Aaron Burr is not proved to be guilty under this indictment by any evidence submitted to us. We therefore find him not guilty." The defense protested, but Marshall let this stand, while saying that an entry of "not guilty" would be made in the record. Actually, the jury's exact wording deserves to stand, as a fair judgment.[24]

Jefferson appears never to have discussed Marshall's opinion in strict legal terms. One wonders when he read with care the lengthy document, if indeed he ever did. Unquestionably he viewed this as a political decision. On learning of it he wrote promptly to Hay: "The event has been what was evidently intended from the beginning of the trial, that is to say, not only to clear Burr, but to prevent the evidence from ever going before the world."[25] As expressed to the District Attorney, his immediate concern was that the evidence be "committed to writing, either as delivered in court, or as taken by yourself in the presence of any of Burr's counsel who may choose to attend to cross examine." He was naïve if he believed that any of the lawyers for the defense would thus co-operate, but he was undoubtedly serious in his desire to lay everything he could before Congress, that they might decide whether the "defect" had been "in the evidence of guilt, or in the law, or in the application of the law," and that they might "provide a proper remedy for the past and future." There can be no doubt of his conviction that something was wrong, since one whom he regarded as a notorious traitor had escaped punishment.

His statement that he was entirely satisfied with the conduct of the case by Hay and his colleagues may perhaps be attributed in part to his recognition of their need of sympathy and encouragement. Hay had reported that Wirt was sick and that he himself was exhausted: he said

---

[24] Robertson, II, 550–552. According to Bradley Chapin, in *The American Law of Treason: Revolutionary and Early National Origins* (1964), p. 105, the fundamental fact about the case was that the indictment was faulty.

[25] TJ to Hay, Sept. 4, 1807 (LC, 30084). Part of this sentence is omitted in L. & B., XI, 360.

that the Judge, by cutting off all the treason trials, had saved his life. But neither at this nor at any other time did Jefferson intimate that they were blamable for the outcome. In his mind, therefore, whatever fault there was must have lain in the law itself or the application of it by the Chief Justice, and we can safely assume that he was thinking chiefly of the latter. His reference here to the past as well as the future may suggest that he was in a punitive mood; but it does not follow that, after having stated in another connection that impeachment was a farce, he was disposed to invoke such procedure against John Marshall. Since the signal failure to convict a much more vulnerable judge, Samuel Chase, the only remedy against judicial irresponsibility that he had expressly favored was removal on joint address of Congress. To James Wilkinson, who deserved sympathy far less than Hay but whose personality evoked stronger language, he said that the recent scenes in Richmond were "equivalent to a proclamation of impunity to every traitorous combination which may be formed to destroy the Union." Then he made a prediction: "However, they will produce an amendment to the Constitution which, keeping the judges independent of the Executive, will not leave them so, of the nation."[26] Apparently this was the strongest expression of his hopes at this juncture.

Like the claim that the prosecution of Burr was really persecution, the charge that the threat of impeachment hung over Marshall was voiced by defense counsel. In fact, throughout the controversy between the Republicans and the judiciary it was a stock Federalist contention. They and certain later historians with them followed the party line. Charles Lee seizing upon a statement by Hay, charged him with saying that there was no difference between the opinion the defense counsel wanted Marshall to give and that for which Chase was impeached. In response the District Attorney denied that any threat or disrespect was involved, and Marshall himself said that he did not consider that anything personal was intended.[27] But Marshall's biographer perceived sinister implications and magnified the threat. "Time and again," says Albert J. Beveridge, "the District Attorney insinuated that impeachment would be Marshall's fate if he did not permit the jury to hear all the testimony."[28] Furthermore, this writer interprets Marshall's much-quoted closing words as an answer to threats of impeachment by Wirt and Hay. In these, besides announcing in a characteristic tone of imperturbable impartiality that his court dared

[26] TJ to Wilkinson, Sept. 20, 1807 (Ford, IX, 142). This letter was written after Burr's acquittal of misdemeanor.
[27] Robertson, II, 237–239, 293–294.
[28] Beveridge, III, 500.

neither usurp power nor shrink from its duty, he said: "No man is desirous of becoming the peculiar subject of calumny."[29] He had abundant reason to believe that his opinion would be unpopular with Republicans, but he could count on its being highly popular in anti-administration circles; and, as the presiding officer in this case, he had permitted attacks on the President of the United States that approached calumny if they did not reach it. His manner was not arrogant and he was an amiable man, but he assumed the mantle of self-righteousness.

While intimating that Marshall's interpretation of the law made the conviction of procurers of treason virtually impossible, Jefferson entered into no discussion of it as such. Therefore, we are fortunately spared the necessity of doing so here.[30] In his next annual message to Congress he spoke of the necessity of guarding against *both* the destruction of the government by treason and the oppression of the citizens under pretense of it.[31] There is no sufficient reason to suppose that, under pretense of domestic danger, he had sought to oppress Burr or anybody else. The attempt of the counsel for the defense and his political foes to cast him in the role of persecutor and to attribute his actions to personal vindictiveness was destined to leave its mark on subsequent accounts and interpretations of these events, but these partisan claims and charges now appear to have been grossly exaggerated if not wholly unwarranted. It would have been strange indeed if he had not been deeply resentful of Burr, but there is no sufficient reason to doubt that, throughout this affair, his primary concern was for domestic security against present and future danger. The persistence of the Union was far from assured during his presidency and he was determined to preserve it. At times — as in his condonation of Wilkinson's conduct in New Orleans — the vision of individual liberty by which his steps had so long been guided may have been partially obscured by the vision of Union. (One is reminded of Abraham Lincoln.) At times he may have appeared to shift his priorities — as, indeed, any responsible statesman must sometimes do. Unfortunately, his public position was weakened by the very fact that the acute danger had been averted, and that, long before this treason trial ended, it had come to seem unreal. Although his public statement that he was

[29] *Ibid.*, III, 512; Robertson, II, 549.

[30] Without attempting even to summarize the literature on this subject, I will refer here only to the critical treatment by E. S. Corwin in *John Marshall and the Constitution*, ch. IV, and the favorable recent treatment by Bradley Chapin in *American Law of Treason* (1964), ch. VII, and R. K. Faulkner, *Jurisprudence of John Marshall* (1968), App. II.

[31] Ford, IX, 164. Further reference to this message is made in the next chapter.

convinced of Burr's guilt may be attributed to his desire to justify the alarm he had sounded, it was not unnaturally regarded by many as improper. After that irretrievable blunder, he does not appear to have overstepped the bounds of official propriety or to have done any more in behalf of the prosecution than was to be expected of a responsible executive. It certainly need not be supposed that he had ceased to be concerned for the protection of individual rights against the claims of government. By force of the circumstances of this famous case, however, he was inevitably identified with the latter, while John Marshall assumed the role of protector of the former. This apparent reversal of his position was indeed ironical.

Later developments with regard to Burr were anticlimactic and verged on the farcical. The alleged conspirator was still under indictment for misdemeanor — that is, for launching an expedition against the possessions of Spain. But Blennerhassett's Island, where Burr was not physically present, was specifically referred to in the indictment; and the District Attorney preferred to seek Burr's commitment for trial for treason in another district, such as that of Kentucky, where he had undoubtedly joined the expedition at the mouth of the Cumberland. Counsel for the defense strongly combatted this, and Marshall held that the charge of misdemeanor under the existing indictment would have to be disposed of first. Hay, weary and ill, informed Jefferson that he was disposed to dismiss this; but the President, who had the counsel of Madison, then visiting him at Monticello, advised that the prosecution proceed with the misdemeanor trial in Richmond. Actually, this was just what the defense wanted. Jefferson doubted if Marshall would impose a long sentence if Burr were convicted but had not quite given up hope that this man, whom he regarded as still extremely dangerous, would be kept out of circulation for a time. If the prosecution should be defeated, he said, it would "heap coals of fire on the Judge"; if it should succeed, it would give them time to consider whether a prosecution for treason should be instituted against Burr in some other court.[32]

He appears to have given no further suggestions or instructions regarding the conduct of this trial, and his further involvement in it was owing to the actions of Burr himself. Shortly before the prisoner was discharged from the indictment for treason and released on bail of

[32] TJ to Hay, Sept. 7, 1807 (Ford, IX, 63n., replying to Hay's letter of Sept. 5 (LC, 30088–30089); also TJ to Hay, Sept. 4 (L. & B., XI, 360–361). The proceedings of the court, Sept. 1–2, 1807, may be seen in Robertson (1808 edn.), II, 446–481.

$5000 (over which there was much argument) to appear on the lesser charge, he again raised the question of the subpoena to the President. For a period of three days the court was occupied with this, and Jefferson's correspondence with Hay at this stage related to little else.[33] On September 3, seizing the opportunity to create a diversion, Burr stated that a letter previously demanded of the President had been often promised but not yet produced. Thereupon, Hay again reported that he could not find it, though he had a copy of it, verified on oath.[34] Burr asserted that Jefferson was in contempt of court, but, recognizing that resort to a process would be unpleasant and would occasion delay, he said that perhaps an authenticated copy of the letter of October 21 would suffice. There was extended argument on this point, and it is not clear just what happened, since attention shifted to a letter of November 12, 1806, from Wilkinson to the President. This was covered by the subpoena according to Burr. The District Attorney had this letter in his possession but stubbornly refused to produce it in its entirety.[35] He said that certain passages in it contained confidential comments on various persons which in his opinion were immaterial to the defense and could not be properly revealed. Everybody believed that these would embarrass the General. Hay justified his stand on the authority given him by the President, and there was much argument about that in the unseemly squabble that ensued. At length one of the defense counsel moved that the trial be postponed until this letter was produced. Marshall took an equivocal position, saying in his opinion that he could not go the whole way with either side, but the net result of these deliberations was the issuance of another subpoena *duces tecum* to the President, who was still at Monticello.[36]

It was not brought by a special messenger of Burr's this time; it was sent by Hay, along with the letter from Wilkinson, with the request that Jefferson return such parts of this as he thought proper to communicate. In his own letter, Hay had this to say of the Chief Justice and his opinion:

> He stated very distinctly that whatever right the P[resident] U.S. might have to withhold parts of the letter, that right could not be delegated; and seemed to think that any return from the

[33] This account of events in court, Sept. 3–5, 1807, is based on the latter work, II, 481–485, 501–502, 504–537.
[34] See above, pp. 333–334.
[35] Wilkinson published it in his *Memoirs*, II, App. C.
[36] See note 45 below for comments on this episode in the light of developments since the first printing of this account.

P[resident] himself would be sufficient. But on this point he was far from being explicit, and it is impossible to foresee what will be the state of his nerves. Wirt, who has hitherto advocated the *integrity* of the Chief Justice, now abandons him. This last opinion has opened his eyes, and he speaks in the strongest terms of reprobation.[37]

Late in August, in another connection, Jefferson had requested Rodney to give him a formal opinion "on the question whether the court of one district could have an attachment executed in another to compel the attendance of a witness."[38] Shortly before he got Hay's letter and the second subpoena he received an informal opinion from the Attorney General. Rodney said he did not believe the court would, by attachment, enforce obedience to subpoenas served on persons who had duties paramount to the obligations of a witness.[39] In his reply to Hay's letter, Jefferson said: "As I do not believe that the district courts have a power of commanding the executive government to abandon superior duties & attend on them, at whatever distance, I am unwilling, by any notice of the subpoena, to set a precedent which might sanction a proceeding so preposterous." Accordingly, he returned the subpoena and sent at the same time a letter for the court that covered "substantially all they ought to desire." He provided a copy of all the parts of Wilkinson's letter that he thought proper to make public, leaving out wholly confidential passages, given for his information in the discharge of his executive functions, and assuring the court that these were in nowise material to this case. His certificate to that effect was duly read to the court by Hay and was received without comment.[40] Although

[37] Hay to TJ, Sept. 5, 1807 (LC, 30088-30089).

[38] TJ to Rodney, Aug. 26, 1807 (courtesy of William Andrews Clark Memorial Library, UCLA). See ch. XXI below for the connection of this request with the Connecticut libel cases.

[39] Rodney to TJ, Aug. 31, 1807, received Sept. 5 (LC, 30057-30058). His lengthy formal opinion, dated Sept. 15, was not sent until Oct. 1; received Oct. 3 (LC, 30148-30165). In this Rodney held that a court *could not* issue an attachment against any person "bound by obligations superior to those of a witness, who has public duties to perform imposed by the Constitution or laws of the U.S. which his attendance as a witness would prevent him from executing with punctuality & Fidelity."

[40] TJ to Hay, Sept. 7, 1807, with certificate (Ford, IX, 63-64n.); report of proceedings of Sept. 5, 9 in T. Carpenter, *Trial of Col. Aaron Burr* (1808), III, 38, 45-46. At this point Beveridge (III, 518-520) refers to the draft of the letter from TJ to Hay (Ford, IX, 62n.) which I have connected with his letter of June 17, 1807 (see p. 323 and note 30). Since the draft is undated the matter is debatable, but Beveridge's interpretation of TJ's state of mind is supported by no evidence. His desire to avoid "a direct encounter" with the chief officer of another co-

the record is somewhat confused, the honors were clearly his. Without opposing the course of justice or directly confronting the judiciary he had declined to recognize the rightfulness of a subpoena to himself and had upheld his own right to withhold what he believed the public interest did not permit him to disclose.

His actions had no perceptible effect on the misdemeanor trial, the outcome of which was a foregone conclusion. The jury was impaneled on the day his certificate was read, and some testimony was heard beyond what had been admitted at the treason trial. After five days, however, Marshall's opinion on a motion of the defense for the exclusion of testimony brought the proceedings to an abrupt close for essentially the same reasons that had been assigned in the previous trial.[41] On the next day, after Hay's move for a *nolle prosequi* had been denied, the jury brought in a verdict of not guilty. They did not qualify this as the jury had done in the treason trial, but they would have been warranted in using similar language. Burr could not be convicted in this district, on this testimony, on this indictment.

The possibility remained that he might be convicted elsewhere. Accordingly, Hay moved his commitment for trial in Ohio or Kentucky on charges of treason and misdemeanor. The hearings on his motion lasted more than a month, and in this connection the prosecution was able to present many and important witnesses who had been hitherto unheard. According to Burr, the Chief Justice, having relaxed from previous rules of evidence, was now willing to hear anything "without regard to distance of time and place." He also told his beloved daughter Theodosia that the outcome was "a sort of drawn battle" and attributed it to a desire to conciliate public opinion. According to other reports he was exasperated; Hay told Jefferson that he was rude and insulting to the Chief Justice.[42] On October 20, Marshall committed him and Blennerhassett "for preparing and providing the means for a military expedition against the territories of a foreign Prince, with whom the United States were at peace."[43] That

---

ordinate branch of the government had been manifested from the time that he first learned of the subpoena and certainly need not be attributed to fear. I can see no justification whatever for the contrast this biographer draws between the President as a frightened man and "the obstinate and fearless, if gentle-mannered, Marshall."

[41] Sept. 14, 1807 (*A.S.P., Misc.,* I, 637–641).

[42] Burr to Theodosia, Sept. 28; Oct. 23, 1807 (*Correspondence,* pp. 224, 225); Hay to TJ, Oct. 21, 1807 (LC, 30325–30326).

[43] Opinion of Oct. 20, 1807 (*A.S.P., Misc.,* I, 641–645).

is, he committed them for misdemeanor, and his opinion as a whole shows that he was dubious of their guilt of that. They had to provide bail before being released; and, when Congress convened a few days later, it was not known that they would never come up for trial.[44] But to all practical purposes the case was closed.[45]

[44] They gave bail to appear at Chillicothe, Ohio, in January, 1808, but the administration made no effort to press the case.

[45] Since this account of the Burr trial was written, the question of executive privilege, as raised by President Richard M. Nixon, has attracted much attention, and what I have designated as the second subpoena to TJ has been frequently referred to in that connection. In his review of this book, Garry Wills argued that no second subpoena was issued to TJ, though one was issued to the District Attorney and sent by him to the President at Monticello (*N.Y. Review of Books*, May 2, 1974). In this contention the reviewer may be right, although nobody has seen the document he refers to and, as I have stated elsewhere, I regard the distinction he makes as unimportant since it was a letter to TJ that was demanded (Ibid., July 18, 1974). My statement (*N.Y. Times*, Nov. 26, 1973) that the acceptance by the court of this letter as edited by TJ was a recognition of "a degree of executive privilege" has been questioned by Raoul Berger in the epilogue of his book *Executive Privilege: A Constitutional Myth* (Cambridge, 1974), pp. 358–360, and in *Am. Bar Assn. Journal*, June 1974, p. 705. Without emphasizing the expression "executive privilege," I hold to the view that Marshall recognized the President's position in this particular matter and that both he and Jefferson sought to avoid a confrontation. I am now more disposed than I was originally to say that, as between the President and Chief Justice, the honors were even rather than that they lay with Jefferson. And I have nothing but admiration for the treatment of this episode in the historic opinion of Chief Justice Warren E. Burger on the question of subpoena and executive privilege (*United States* vs. *Richard M. Nixon*, July 24, 1974).

[XX]

Aftermath of Conspiracy

1807-1808

CRITICISM of the Chief Justice in the Republican papers, especially those in Richmond, appears to have been much more pronounced after the legal proceedings had ended than while they were going on. Throughout the course of these, on the other hand, there were harsh Federalist attacks on the President, who was charged with improper involvement in the case.[1] One writer in the Federalist *Virginia Gazette* said, toward the end of the final hearings on Burr's commitment, that the piece which had been so long acting in Richmond should be called "King Tom's Puppet Show" or "Much Ado about Nothing." A more sweeping assertion was made in that paper a little earlier: "History will hardly furnish an example of such oppressive tyranny as has been practised under the administration of Mr. Jefferson."[2]

This may be regarded as no more than an example of the rhetorical extremism that partisanship assumed in that era, but a presidential action which was partially revealed and vigorously exploited at this time has been cited by unfriendly later commentators as an example of Jefferson's vindictiveness, the object of his wrath in this instance being Luther Martin. The story begins in the summer of 1807, when Jefferson was participating in the task of collecting testimony and assembling witnesses; and it leaves no doubt whatever that, while his public response to the subpoena was decorous and his recorded private comments on it were generally restrained, he was angered by the man he called the "federal bulldog" and would have liked to punish him.

---

[1] I make no reference here to what was said about Burr. A full study of the attitude of the press to the conspiracy and trial would be welcome.

[2] *Virginia Gazette*, Oct. 17; Sept. 30, 1807.

About a week after he was charged by Martin with loosing the "hell-hounds of war" against the Marylander's "honorable friend," he received from Baltimore a letter which, as he told Hay, conveyed "singular information."[3] This reported the statement of an old Revolutionary officer named Philip Graybell, now a flour merchant, that Luther Martin in conversation had shown that he had long been familiar with Burr's conspiratorial plans. Jefferson promptly requested Rodney to interview Graybell and told Hay that a subpoena should immediately be dispatched for him.[4] Meanwhile, the District Attorney could be considering just what use to make of the evidence. "Shall we move to commit L. M. as *particeps criminis* with Burr?" asked Jefferson. "Graybell will fix upon him misprision of treason at least. And at any rate, his evidence will put down this unprincipled & impudent federal bull-dog, and add another proof that the most clamorous defenders of Burr are all his accomplices. It will explain why L. M. flew so hastily to the aid of his 'honorable friend,' abandoning his clients & their property during the session of a principal court in Maryland, now filled, as I am told, with the clamors & ruin of his clients."

After this spiteful though not unnatural outburst the busy President appears to have done nothing more in this matter, but during the summer depositions were procured from three persons, presumably by Rodney, and these were duly deposited with the clerk of the court. Martin stated afterwards that Hay informed him of these, and also that one witness arrived. No legal action followed — because the grand jury had been dismissed, according to Martin — and the documents were not publicly displayed until fall. Then General William Eaton, whom the defense counsel had humiliated when he appeared as a witness for the government and who was smarting under recent newspaper attacks that he attributed to Martin, got copies from the clerk's office and gave them to the press. According to these, Luther Martin, several times in the previous year, had predicted that the separation of the western states from the Union would be shortly effected under the leadership of Burr, whom he referred to as the future emperor of Louisiana.[5]

[3] TJ to Hay, June 19, 1807 (Ford, IX, 58*n*.), sending a copy of a letter of June 17 from John Gordon (Letters Relating to Burr's Conspiracy, LC; copy through courtesy of Julian P. Boyd).

[4] TJ to Rodney, June 19, 1807 (LC, 29546), sending Gordon's letter. At the same time he asked for the missing letter of Oct. 21, 1806, from Wilkinson.

[5] In certain articles in a forceful series by INVESTIGATOR in the Federalist *Virginia Gazette*, especially Aug. 15 and Sept. 19, 1807, Eaton was made to appear a fool. Replying in the issue of Sept. 23, he named Martin as INVESTIGATOR. Ridiculed

Eaton was no match for Luther Martin in disputation, if indeed anybody was. In his lengthy reply the legal warrior claimed that he had purposed to publish these affidavits on his own account, but preferred that the public should learn of the "kind intentions" of the administration from a person (Eaton) who appeared to have recently become one of its favorites.[6] He referred to the government as "enraged" by his interposition between it and its intended victim, his friend Burr, and spoke of the sycophancy of informers. He interpreted the summoning of witnesses against him as an unsuccessful attempt to intimidate him from returning to Richmond for the trial in August. Though he regarded the depositions as "miserable," he sought to explain them out of respect for his fellow citizens. He admitted that he wholly disapproved of the purchase of Louisiana, which could not be settled in fifty or a hundred years, and, while denying that he had predicted the dismemberment of the Union in twelve months, he stated that he regarded this as inevitable. (Actually, many other Federalists, especially in New England, thought the same.) He had made no secret of these sentiments and opinions, he said; and, after the conduct of Burr began to be discussed, he had amused himself by observing in jocular fashion that the Colonel would be the beneficiary of the purchase and become the emperor of Louisiana. He denied, however, that he had any correspondence with Burr from the time that gentleman first went west until he was "wantonly and unconstitutionally deprived of his liberty" by the military authority. Also, he categorically denied that he knew anything of Burr's plans.

In the final paragraph of a paper that was calculated to throw the onus on his detractors and that mingled innuendo with humor, the adventurer's loquacious friend made particular reference to Jefferson. "From the information the public have now obtained, thro' General Eaton and myself," he said, "it must be pretty evident that my friend the President would hang me if he could . . . but if he found that not in his power, he would deprive me of my liberty. Now to the public I solemnly declare that if the President was entirely and absolutely at my mercy, I would neither hang, nor imprison him, nor would I hurt one precious hair of his head; I would do nothing worse with him, than to send him to Monticello, there to employ himself, in peace and tranquility, in his favorite pursuits of economizing and philosophizing."[7]

---

further by PHILO INVESTIGATOR on Sept. 26, he published the affidavits Oct. 7. Dated in July and August, they were from John Campbell White, Edward Hall, and Philip Graybell.

[6] *Ibid.*, Oct. 10, 1807.

[7] Punctuation slightly modified.

No doubt political supporters as well as enemies of the President chuckled over this, while conceding Martin's prowess both at the bar and in public controversy. But he had unmistakably revealed that a major animating purpose of his was to relegate Jefferson to obscurity.

This indomitable warrior continued to take shots at the administration and its head after his "honorable friend" had been committed for future trial and released on bail. According to Harman Blennerhassett, who traveled with him northward, he never lacked for ammunition, always kept his gun primed and loaded, and fired it indiscriminately — as he did in Washington in a hotel frequented by members of Congress.[8] He created more excitement in his own Baltimore a few days later. Burr and several of his coadjutors had just arrived and on November 2 were Martin's guests at dinner. According to the Democratic-Republicans, who were strong and active in Baltimore though they did not control the city government, very few others would have been willing to entertain "Aaron the First" and his minions.[9] The fact that, shortly after Burr passed through Washington, the *National Intelligencer* congratulated the city on his not remaining in it is further evidence of the dislike and distrust with which he was still regarded by supporters of the government.[10] But, as a near-outcast, he might have been expected to arouse some compassion, and at this stage a policy of silence would have been to his advantage. On the day after his arrival Luther Martin published an inflammatory statement in the local Federalist paper. This led an opposing paper to observe that his dislike of the administration exceeded his zeal for Burr — actually, they both appear to have been immeasurable — and that the less he said the better it would be for the public peace.[11] However the responsibility for ensuing events may be distributed, the latter observation seems incontestable.

In his communication he boastfully asserted that he and his colleagues had saved seven worthy men from the "ignominious death" to which they had been destined by the administration. He referred proudly to lawyers who could not be intimidated by presidential vengeance or popular frenzy, and he said that the administration should be grateful for having been saved from "*staining* their *souls*

[8] Oct. 27, 1807 (W. H. Safford, *Blennerhassett Papers* [1861], p. 464).

[9] TJ himself rarely if ever designated the members of his party as Democratic-Republicans, but they themselves did so here and elsewhere in the Middle Atlantic states.

[10] *National Intelligencer*, Nov. 4, 1807.

[11] Comment in Baltimore *American*, Nov. 4.

with the *blood of innocence*."[12] He then described Burr's innocent intentions to found a settlement, claiming that he planned a military expedition against Mexico *only* in the case of war. This was precisely the contention of the defense counsel in the most recent proceedings in Richmond; and it remains until this day the most charitable interpretation of Burr's enterprise that has been seriously advanced.[13] In pressing it at that time, however, Martin showed no sign of charity toward the government, not even suggesting that it could have made an honest mistake. Therefore, he made it more difficult for those of uncertain mind and generous spirit to give his client the benefit of the doubt and tended to polarize opinion further on strict party lines.

We can give here only a scanty account of the exciting events in Baltimore on the day of and the day following Burr's arrival.[14] Martin and his dinner guests were serenaded with the rogue's march by a group of militiamen who happened to muster that evening; and there were rumors then and next day that tar and feathers would be conferred on the "illustrious strangers." They were not thus honored; and Burr and Swartwout, escorted to the stage-office by a guard provided by the mayor, left town before the unfriendly proceedings of November 3. These consisted of a procession in the afternoon and the hanging of four effigies. The civil authorities ordered out two troops of cavalry to preserve order, and friends of Martin mounted guard with him at his house. Blennerhassett, after dining at his hotel, went first to the garret and then to the roof, whence he viewed the procession. Though politically hostile commentators described it as riotous and turbulent, it appears to have been peaceful. What was designated on the one side as a mob was described on the other as a legitimate assemblage, designed to expose "obnoxious characters" and to express "abhorrence of treason."[15] The effigies were of Martin and Blennerhassett, who were

[12] Quotes from communication as reprinted in Baltimore *American*, Nov. 19, 1807.

[13] We do not pause here to inquire whether this interpretation can be reconciled with considerations of chronology and land titles, and with facts and contemporary opinions that are now known, but the difficulties should have appeared at various points in this narrative.

[14] There is a full, documented report after the event in Baltimore *American*, Nov. 19, 1807. See also the account of Nov. 3 in *Blennerhassett Papers*, pp. 478–481. Federalist reaction is suggested by extracts from Baltimore in Richmond *Virginia Gazette*, Nov. 10, 13, 1807.

[15] Blennerhassett believed that it was incited by the "Democratic printers," but after the event it was strongly supported by a party meeting at which the action of the civil authorities in calling out the military was condemned (Baltimore *American*, Nov. 7, 1807).

in town; of Burr, who had left; and of John Marshall, who was then enjoying a much-needed rest in the Blue Ridge. A little later the Chief Justice wrote Judge Richard Peters that he had been occupied with the "most unpleasant case" ever brought before a judge in a country "affected to be governed by laws." He also said he had been so engaged in circuit court duties after his vacation that he had given little thought to the attentions paid him in Baltimore and elsewhere.[16] No doubt he was referring to Washington, where the congressional session had begun a few days after the judicial proceedings in Richmond ended.

ii

Congress had been called to meet earlier than usual because of the critical international situation, and in his annual message the President gave major attention to that. The first draft of this message, including the section toward the end that bore on the conspiracy, was written before he learned of final developments in the court at Richmond. According to his custom, he submitted this rough draft to his ministers for comments and suggestions; and those of the Attorney General were made after Marshall's action of October 20 had become known.[17] In view of Burr's commitment for further trial, Rodney suggested the omission of a considerable portion of the passage relating to him. For this or some other reason, Jefferson left out several sentences that were critical of the courts or might have been so interpreted.

In his tentative draft he had observed that "whenever the laws were appealed to in aid of the public safety" — that is, in the various legal proceedings against Burr and his associates — the courts had always operated in favor of those who were endangering it. In fairness he should have allowed for the inadequacy of testimony in the hearings in Kentucky and Mississippi Territory, where there was much tolerance of adventurers of this sort anyway, and even for shortage of evidence in the early proceedings in Richmond. He might have acknowledged some degree of miscalculation on the part of the prosecution and the government, explicable though this might be. But in his own mind he seems unquestionably to have blamed the courts for what he regarded as a miscarriage of justice. In earlier private correspondence his Attorney General had taken essentially the same position. After Burr had been acquitted of misdemeanor as well as treason Rodney wrote:

16 Extract from letter quoted by Beveridge, III, 529.
17 The first and second drafts of the message of Oct. 27, 1807, are in Ford, IX, 145–166, comments from Gallatin and Rodney being given in the notes; the latter, which were received Oct. 23, are on p. 151.

"Our counsel at Richmond have acted like men & have acquitted themselves with honor. But it is in vain to struggle against wind & tide. The current on the bench was irresistible."[18] In the same letter he expressed the belief that the whole country was convinced of Burr's guilt, stating that people voiced their convictions as freely as if he had been found guilty by the jury. "A few of the Federal leaders may feign a contrary opinion," he said, "but it is all affectation."

Rodney thought that something more — that is, another trial — was due the country and believed that the judicial climate would be more favorable in Kentucky. It seems impossible to determine whether or not Jefferson viewed the prospect with any real hope, but, after he learned that Burr had been committed and heard from Rodney, he must have concluded that public censure of the judiciary would be premature. In the message he sent Congress he referred to the happy defeat of the enterprises of Burr and his associates "against the public peace," attributing this, as previously, to "the patriotic exertions of the militia, . . . the fidelity of the army, and energy of the Commander in chief" — that is, Wilkinson. His view of the treasonable nature of these enterprises was unchanged, and the failure "to bring the offenders to justice" undoubtedly called for some sort of report. The one he now promised to make was an account of the proceedings of the court in Richmond, with the testimony presented there and some other evidence. Addressing the Great Council of the nation, and using much the same language he had used to the District Attorney, he said: "From the whole you will be enabled to judge whether the defect was in the testimony, in the law, or in the administration of the law; and wherever it shall be found, the legislature alone can apply or originate the remedy."

After Burr's second acquittal in Richmond the Attorney General had written the President: "The judiciary have been so much elevated above every other department of the government, by the fashion & I may add the folly of the times, that it seems dangerous to question their omnipotence. But the period has arrived when this colossal power, which bestrides the Legislative & Executive authorities, should be reduced to its proper limits."[19] Jefferson had thought that for some time, as his private utterances show, but he appears never to have said so publicly. Rodney did not "pretend to say" what was the best remedy for existing ills. Jefferson was not saying what he thought it was, but, as we have remarked several times already, he was certainly

18 Rodney to TJ, Oct. 1, 1807 (LC, 30236–30237).
19 *Ibid.*

not recommending impeachment proceedings that would surely fail. In a frustrated state of mind, at a time when circumstances compelled him to give major attention to foreign matters, he was reminding the Great Council of the nation of domestic problems that were to prove perennial in a self-governing society. This was not merely a question of maintaining a proper balance between co-ordinate departments; it was also that of maintaining a proper balance between individual liberty and national security. Without pointing to any particular solution he posed the problem by saying that the framers of the Constitution undoubtedly supposed they had guarded the government against "destruction by treason," as well as the citizens against "oppression under pretense of it"; and that if these ends were not obtained, it was of importance to inquire by what more effectual means they might be secured.

His opinion that these ends had not been attained was stated more expressly in private several weeks before Congress convened. This was in a letter, written after Burr's second acquittal, in response to one enclosing a partial "view" of the trial. To William Thomson, who was clearly on his side, he wrote:

> The scenes which have been acting at Richmond are sufficient to fill us with alarm. We had supposed we possessed fixed laws to guard us equally against treason & oppression. But it now appears we have no law but the will of the judge. Never will chicanery have a more difficult task than has been now accomplished to warp the text of the law to the will of him who is to construe it. Our case too is the more desperate as to attempt to make the law plainer by amendment is only throwing out new materials for sophistry.[20]

He expressed great satisfaction with the paper sent him (though we may doubt if he read all of its seventy-two pages) and said he would be "happy to see the whole subject as well digested." About three weeks after he gave this person this encouragement he received from him what was described as a "little work" but may be presumed to have represented Thomson's attempt to meet the full prescription.[21] The

[20] TJ to William Thomson, Sept. 26, 1807 (Ford, IX, 143–144), replying to a letter dated July 10 but not received until Sept. 23 (Bixby, pp. 145–147). Presumably, Thomson held up his letter, much of which concerned writing on the West he hoped to do, until he could send a fuller "view" of Burr's trial, only the preliminaries of which had taken place by July 10.

[21] Thomson to TJ, Oct. 17, 1807; received Oct. 19 (Bixby, p. 147). I have found no reply from TJ, who may have returned the paper without comment.

author admitted that it was somewhat acrimonious and, while Jefferson appears to have expressed no opinion of the piece in this form, he did not call off this particular bloodhound. The paper may be identified as one that afterwards appeared seriatim in leading Republican papers and that constitutes a castigation of the Chief Justice.[22] That Jefferson directly instigated the journalistic attacks on Marshall at this stage cannot be proved, and in view of his customary procedure we may assume that he did not tell anybody what to say, as we also may that he maintained the proprieties in public. That he welcomed public criticism of the Chief Justice's conduct of this case, however, cannot be doubted. He wanted him condemned in the court of public opinion. Until this time, though, he had given surprisingly little sign of personal resentment; even in private he spoke in behalf of the public interest.

While the temptation to over-personalize the conflict between the President and the Chief Justice must be resisted, we should note certain publications of this year which might have been expected to exacerbate the feelings of the former towards the latter. One of these was a pamphlet by Joseph H. Daveiss, former district attorney of Kentucky and brother-in-law of Marshall, in which he published his correspondence with Jefferson and severely censured the President's handling of the conspiracy from the start.[23] The animus of Daveiss against Jefferson can be readily attributed to his removal from office, and John Marshall need not have been connected in any way with his actions, but inevitably the two men were associated in the mind of anybody who was aware of their relationship. In this pamphlet Blennerhassett saw "indiscriminate censure" not only of Jefferson and Wilkinson, but also of Burr, and he went so far as to say that Marshall would really have liked to ruin them all — as, in this view, his conduct of the final hearings showed.[24] This interpretation may be discounted as extreme, but the comment shows that this observer believed the Chief Justice to be anti-Jefferson rather than pro-Burr. The President had a copy of the Daveiss pamphlet, whether or not he read it. Blennerhassett, who did not see it until mid-November, described it as "a hasty, passionate performance . . . bearing hard upon Jefferson's

---

[22] "Letters to John Marshall" by Lucius. These appeared in *Aurora*, Nov. 21, 25, 28, and Dec. 1, 1807; and in Richmond *Enquirer* soon thereafter. See Beveridge, III, 525–526, 533–535.

[23] J. H. Daveiss, *A View of the President's Conduct, concerning the Conspiracy of 1806* (Frankfort, Ky., 1807). For previous references to Daveiss and this correspondence see above, pp. 223–225, 237–239.

[24] *Blennerhassett Papers*, pp. 465–467; comment of Oct. 27, 1807.

hypocricy and neglect of the author, and the early information he gave him of Burr's designs and first movements." In the opinion of one who had come to realize that he had been duped by Burr, the publication, defective though it was, would mortify Jefferson by revealing his unwillingness to open his eyes to the intrigues of Wilkinson with Spain.[25] Near the end of the pamphlet appeared a profile of the third President. In this, after admitting that Jefferson had been a friend to his country prior to the adoption of the Constitution, Daveiss said:

> But he has long since made his judgment play the whore to his ambition; for I have no doubt he has been intriguing through the instrumentality of the vilest printers and tools for the place he now fills almost ever since the constitution was adopted; and that the character given me of him by the ever to be lamented Hamilton, is that which the historian of the next age will give him — "that he was a man as fond of place and power, and as great a hypocrite as ever lived."[26]

Blennerhassett did not mention this Hamiltonian echo, but in referring to the publication he made an observation that deserves attention: "This performance, together with Judge Marshall's last volume of the *Life of Washington*, exposing the origin and views of the present Democratic party in power, have by this time, I have no doubt, inspired Jefferson with a more deadly hatred of the Marshall faction than he has ever conceived of all the Burrites he ever heard of." It is likely that Jefferson brushed off Daveiss, but he undoubtedly resented Marshall's *Life of Washington* until his dying day. Actually, the most severe of his recorded comments on it were made in the last decade of his life, when, reflecting on the distant past as old men do, he was straightening out his own records for the benefit of posterity.[27] These comments did not relate to the conduct of Burr's trial by the Chief Justice, but the last volume of the biography came out shortly before that trial and the work was unquestionably viewed by Jefferson then, as it was later, as a "party diatribe."[28]

All five of the volumes were published during his presidency and he was well aware that the work was in process before any part of it appeared in print. When he said in advance that the life of Washington was being written principally for electioneering purposes he was farther from the truth than John Adams, who observed in the next

[25] Comment of Nov. 18, 1807 (*ibid.*, pp. 501–502).
[26] Daveiss, *View*, p. 143.
[27] In the introduction to the "Anas," signed Feb. 4, 1818 (Ford, I, 155–156).
[28] TJ to John Adams, Aug. 10, 1815 (*A.-J. Letters*, II, 453).

decade that its main purpose was to make money. Marshall was burdened with debt and had high hopes of a profitable return from this venture — much higher than events were to justify. Jefferson was entirely warranted, however, in his expectation that this would be history from the Federalist point of view; and, in the hope of offsetting it, he tried to induce Joel Barlow to write a history of the United States from the Revolution downward.[29] It need not be supposed that, if Barlow had produced such a work, scholars of our time would have regarded it as objective. Jefferson undoubtedly expected it to be written from the point of view of republicanism as this was understood by him, and to be sympathetic to the Republican party. But if we may judge from the documents and other sources that he mentioned in this and other letters and offered to make available to Barlow, he would have set history on a broader base than Marshall did. And, judging from the standards he set for himself in scholarly matters, he would have urged a higher degree of accuracy. As Marshall himself recognized, his own work, hurried into the world too precipitately, was full of errors. Jefferson expressed entire confidence that the materials made available to Barlow would be put into "the most judicious form to convey useful information to the nation & to posterity."[30] This was said before the appearance of the final volume of Marshall's series, the one he regarded as most injudicious and misrepresentative.

He bought the successive volumes as they came out in boards, paying three dollars for each, and had the entire set bound in calf at the additional expense of a dollar per volume. By the early spring of 1807 he may have had a copy of the last one, dealing with Washington's presidency and extending to the General's death late in the Adams administration, and he may be assumed to have had it by summer.[31] No contemporary comment of his on the volume bearing most on his own career seems to have been recorded, but in the autumn after his retirement from the presidency he took it up seriously and began to make notes on it.[32] He admitted that he was proceeding very slowly, however, and not until the last decade of his life did he record his measured judgment of the work. (He bought

[29] TJ to Barlow, then in Paris, May 3, 1802 (Ford, VIII, 151), associating Madison with the proposal; Adams to TJ, July 3, 1813 (*A.-J. Letters*, II, 349). Beveridge (III, ch. V) gives an excellent account of "the least satisfactory of all the labors of Marshall's life"; this leaves no doubt of his financial motives.

[30] TJ to Barlow, July 9, 1806 (LC, 28020).

[31] Details from E. M. Sowerby, *Catalogue of the Library of Thomas Jefferson*, I (1952), 241–243. He was billed for Vol. V on Mar. 30, 1807; and for the binding of the set in calf on June 30.

[32] TJ to Barlow, Oct. 8, 1809 (Ford, IX, 262, with notes from LC, 41764–41765).

another copy of it in 1815.) In this he showed no concern to reply to such aspersions as Marshall may have made on him personally but excoriated that historic adversary for indifference to the values most cherished by himself. He deplored the biographer's failure to reflect the spirit of the American Revolution as he himself understood it and was convinced that Washington did — Marshall's cold indifference to "the holy cause which inspired the bosom, & nerved the arm of the patriot warrior." This holy purpose was to change the conditions of men, to vindicate the rights of humanity, and the passion he breathed into these words may be said to measure the difference between him, a humanist and basic libertarian, and Marshall, a man of lesser democratic faith who laid major stress on law, order, and property.[33]

While Jefferson believed that Marshall had abused his materials in depicting the American Revolution, he was convinced that he had done so even more in his account of the period following the adoption of the Constitution, especially in his account of party differences. Judging from this, the republican party (significantly, Jefferson himself did not capitalize the word) were "a mere set of grumblers, and disorganizers, satisfied with no government, without fixed principles of any, . . . gaping after loaves and fishes, and ready to change principles, as well as position, at any time, with their adversaries." Instead, as he himself asserted, they were trying "to keep the government within the line of the Constitution, and prevent its being monarchised in practice."[34]

In his old age he was writing for the future, seeking to defend at the bar of history the party of opposition that the biographer had belittled. He did not enter into the events of his own administration when his party was in the majority, for Marshall did not deal with these. From the references to Jefferson himself, which that gentleman ignored and were actually not numerous, one may assume that the Chief Justice, like his brother-in-law Daveiss, followed the line that Hamilton had laid down, regarding him as a man of inordinate ambition who courted popularity without scruple.[35] One bit of descriptive comment is of

[33] For an illuminating discussion of their differences, see J. P. Boyd, "The Chasm That Separated Thomas Jefferson and John Marshall," in Gottfried Dietze, ed., *Essays on the American Constitution* (1964).

[34] Comment in 1818 (Ford, I, 156).

[35] In Note VI at the end of Vol. V, Marshall summarizes the charges made against Hamilton and Jefferson when they were in office together, the implication being that those against Hamilton were unwarranted. Most if not quite all of those against Jefferson were made by Hamilton. The outline of the arguments of the two men on the constitutionality of the Bank of the United States in Note III seems to be the first account of them to appear in print (see *Jefferson and the Rights of Man*, p. 348).

particular interest in connection with the events of the Burr conspiracy and trial. After stating that Jefferson's observations of the
abuses of the monarchy in France might have been expected to lead to
the belief that liberty could be endangered only by executive power,
he said:

> Mr. Jefferson therefore seems to have entertained no appre-
> hensions from the debility of the government; no jealousy of the
> state sovereignties; and no suspicion of their encroachments. His
> fears took a different direction, and all his precautions were used
> to check and limit the exercise of the authorities claimed by the
> government of the United States. Neither could he perceive
> danger to liberty except from the constituted authorities, and
> *especially from the executive.*[36]

This was not the line his critics were taking in 1807, when they
charged him as an executive with tyranny, though they continued to
claim, as the Chief Justice and his brother-in-law did, that the President was primarily interested in maintaining his popularity.

It does not appear that Marshall's ponderous work had any noteworthy effect on public opinion at this time. As a Republican paper
observed, the great body of the people who had expressed dissatisfaction at the Chief Justice's conduct had never read his voluminous
production and never would.[37] Such influence as it exerted was on
posterity.

iii

Nearly a month passed before Jefferson was able to fulfill the
promise in his annual message to transmit to Congress a copy of the
proceedings and evidence in the court in Richmond.[38] The interminable speeches of counsel were not included, though their examination and cross-examination of witnesses were. The testimony was that
of the witnesses in the various trials and hearings, along with some
additional depositions and documents, all duly attested.[39] The opinions
of the Chief Justice were taken from a newspaper to which he himself

---

[36] *Life of Washington*, V (1807), 354. Italics added.

[37] Baltimore *American*, Nov. 19, 1807.

[38] Nov. 23, 1807 (*A.S.P., Misc.*, I, 486–645; *Annals*, 10 Cong., 1 sess., I, 386–778).

[39] The testimony was edited to some degree, with the approval of the witnesses.
The work of taking and transcribing it was done by two men who were destined
to distinction as legal reporters, William W. Hening and William Munford. Hay
described procedure in his letter of Oct. 15, 1807, to TJ (LC, 30287–30288).

had delivered them and were vouched for by the editor. No one could justly claim that there was any shortage of reliable information.

Following the submission of this documentary record there were certain developments in this session of Congress that were closely related to it. The Senate inquired into the conduct of one of its members, John Smith of Ohio, whose indictment for misdemeanor had been quashed when Burr was acquitted; the House sought to institute an inquiry into the conduct of General Wilkinson; proposals were made but not pressed to render federal judges removable on joint address; and a futile attempt was made, chiefly in the Senate, to define the crime of treason more precisely. With these actions and near-actions the governmental proceedings incident to the conspiracy petered out.

The movement to expel Senator Smith began four days after the President sent the documents. A committee, headed by John Quincy Adams, was appointed to conduct an investigation.[40] It met almost every day, including Christmas, until on the last day of the year it made a report which was almost wholly the work of Adams.[41] This called for the expulsion of Smith because of his participation in a conspiracy "against the *peace, union,* and *liberties,* of the people of the United States." Final action was not taken until more than three months later, when the vote was 19 to 10 for expulsion. This was one less than the necessary two-thirds, but Smith resigned soon thereafter.[42] The political position of Adams was now anomalous, for he generally supported the policies of the administration and was to be read out of the Federalist party a few months later, but his attitude in this matter was owing to no partisan considerations. Several Republicans, notably William Branch Giles, who regarded the evidence against Smith as insufficient, opposed the resolution.[43] But those favoring it were overwhelmingly Republican, and the opposition had a pronounced Federalist coloration. Smith had as counsel two Federalist lawyers, Francis Scott Key, who had not yet written "The Star-Spangled Banner," and Robert Goodloe Harper, who had been a conspicuous partisan for a decade and more. Adams claimed that the Senate could expel a member on grounds that would be insufficient to convict him

40 Nov. 27, 1807 (*Annals*, 10 Cong., 1 sess., I, 39–42). The timing of the action may be attributed to the fact that Smith attended that day, for the first time in the session.

41 Dec. 31, 1807 (*ibid.*, I, 56–63); J. Q. Adams, *Wrtings*, III, 173–184, and final note.

42 Apr. 9, 1808 (*Annals*, 10 Cong., 1 sess., I, 324); also, see discussion on Apr. 1, 5, 6, 8 and entries for those days in *Memoirs* of J. Q. Adams, esp. I, 527–529.

43 Anderson, *Giles*, pp. 120–121.

in a court, while Federalists disputed this contention and charged
Adams with reflecting on the judiciary. While denying any disposition
at this time to question Marshall's decisions, Adams made an observation which could not have failed to annoy Burr's champions:

> But whether the transactions proved against Aaron Burr did or
> did not amount, in technical language, to an overt act of levying
> war, your committee have not a scruple of doubt upon their
> minds that, but for the vigilance and energy of the government,
> and of faithful citizens under its directions, in arresting their
> program and in crushing his designs, they would, in a very short
> lapse of time, have terminated not only in war, but in a war of the
> most horrible description, in a war at once foreign and do-
> mestic.[44]

The administration could have desired no stronger statement. A
milder but significant one was made by James A. Bayard, a Federalist
who took sharp issue with Adams on matters of procedure and voted
against Smith's expulsion. He said: "I do not consider the question to
be, whether there was a conspiracy of which Burr was the author.
That such a conspiracy did exist I firmly believe; and I further believe
that scarcely a man in the United States doubts it."[45]

A report circulated in Federalist circles that Smith had something on
the President and that the failure to expel him was owing to fear of his
revealing this. The story was said to have been started by Adams, but
he cited only an intimation from Smith himself in support of it.[46]
Furthermore, Adams, having done his duty as he saw it and being
concerned for Smith and his family, thought that he had been "sufficiently reprobated" by the vote.[47] Though Jefferson as a humane man
may have felt the same way, there is no evidence that he exerted any
influence on the Senate's action in this case. In the summer, however,
while the treason trial was still going on, he had received a letter from
John Smith, the publication of which would have undoubtedly embarrassed him. From New Orleans the Senator wrote:

> Although I am the friend of Gen. Wilkinson, I think it my duty
> to inform you, that it has been confidently asserted to me by one
> of your friends & mine, since I arrived in this city & only two or

[44] J. Q. Adams, *Writings*, III, 182–183.
[45] Jan. 7, 1808 (*Annals*, 10 Cong., 1 sess., p. 71).
[46] Adams, *Memoirs*, Jan. 2, 1808 (I, 499); Pickering to Rufus King, Jan. 21, 1809;
King to Pickering, Jan. 31, 1809 (King, V, 129, 132).
[47] *Memoirs*, I, 529 (entry of Apr. 9, 1808).

three days ago, that Gen. Wilkinson has been in Spanish pay for
many years, & that the most unequivocal proofs of it are in the
hands of a few designing Federalists, who are waiting with
anxious hope for the time when you may have committed your
reputation with the General's and then publish the evidence of
his guilt.[48]

He added that some believed that a "collusion" with Governor Folch
of West Florida would be attempted. Thus the Senator brought down
to date the charge that Wilkinson was a pensioner of Spain.

If this letter made any impression on Jefferson he gave no sign of it.
Writing him in seeming bewilderment after Burr's second acquittal,
Wilkinson said that the conduct of the Chief Justice almost warranted
the suspicion that he had been a party to the conspiracy. The President
never said anything like that, but in his reply he voiced his own indignation at the action of the court more strongly perhaps than in any
other letter he wrote in this interval, and he again outdid himself in
expressing his confidence in the General. "It is with pleasure," he said,
"that I perceive from all the expressions of public sentiment, that the
virulence of those whose treasons you have defeated only place you on
higher ground in the opinion of the nation."[49] To justify this exaggerated statement in the light of present knowledge would be quite
impossible. It should be noted, however, that when this was made
Wilkinson had testified only in the closed session of the grand jury,
and that the Burrites had manifested extreme virulence toward him. By
now Jefferson may be presumed to have identified Senator John Smith
with them. The same could certainly not be said of his attitude toward
George Hay, who had previously expressed entire confidence in
Wilkinson, but whose faith was shaken as the hearings on Burr's
commitment proceeded and the General himself appeared as a witness.
Toward the end of that hearing the District Attorney revealed to the
President that he had changed his mind. Rather reluctantly and somewhat apologetically he wrote:

Gen. Wilkinson said to me the other day that as soon as he got to
Washington, he should solicit an inquiry before a court martial
into his conduct. I hope he will do so, and whether he does or not,
I hope the inquiry will be instituted. The declaration which I
made in Court in his favor some time ago was precipitate and
tho' I have not retracted it, everybody sees that I have not at-

48 Smith to TJ, July 6, 1807; received Aug. 15 (LC, 29657).
49 TJ to Wilkinson, Sept. 20, 1807 (Ford, IX, 142), replying to Wilkinson's
letter of Sept. 15 (LC, 30145–30146).

tempted the task which I, in fact, promised to perform. My confidence in him is shaken, if not destroyed. I am sorry for it, on his own account and because you have expressed opinions in his favor. But you did not know then what you will soon know, and what I did not learn until after, long after my declaration above mentioned.[50]

Presumably he was referring to a fresh, and to his mind credible, report of Wilkinson's collusion with the Spanish. And, in any case, the extreme vulnerability of the General and his unreliability as a witness were unmistakably revealed in the testimony Hay soon sent Jefferson and Jefferson duly transmitted to Congress. No one reading this testimony and the pitiless cross-examination could doubt that Wilkinson had taken liberties with the cipher letter from Burr which Jefferson had presented to Congress as a revelation of the conspiracy; and anyone could see here the letter from Dayton to Wilkinson, asserting that he was to be displaced by Jefferson, which appears to have precipitated the General's action in betraying the conspiracy.[51] In combatting the charge of treason, Burr and his counsel had to admit a projected expedition against Mexico, but they claimed that this was contingent on war with Spain. Not only did they seek to associate Wilkinson with it; they claimed that he caused war to be averted in the interest of the Spanish court, of which he was a hireling, and that he raised the charge of treason as a cover. Thus Wickham said:

Our ground of defence is, that Colonel Burr's expedition was in concurrence with General Wilkinson against the dominions of the King of Spain, in case of a war. If we prove, that, at the time Wilkinson was pretending to favor Burr's expedition, and secretly determined to defeat it, he was receiving a Spanish pension, this will explain his conduct. He defeated the enterprise of Burr by hatching a charge of treason against the United States, on purpose to serve the King, whose money he was receiving.[52]

Modern scholars with access to Spanish archives now know that Wilkinson was, in fact, receiving money from Spain at the time the conspiracy was brewing, his pension having been recently renewed.[53]

[50] George Hay to TJ, Oct. 15, 1807; received Oct. 18 (LC, 30287–30288). See above, p. 326.

[51] See above, pp. 264, 250.

[52] Oct. 17, 1806, in connection with the examination of Thomas Power (*A.S.P., Misc.*, I, 608; see Abernethy, p. 250, and his discussion of the Wilkinson case in ch. XV).

[53] See above, p. 219.

Documentary proof of this was not forthcoming in that century and the charges of his collusion with the Spanish with which Jefferson and his two predecessors were familiar related to transactions in an earlier decade. Furthermore, in the eyes of the administration, these had not been proved. From the court proceedings, however, it could have been believed that, despite his denial, Wilkinson had been in correspondence with Spanish officials when the province of Louisiana was still in their country's possession; and, after the hearings ended, evidence came to light that he had received a considerable payment from their hands. This evidence was passed on to John Randolph by Daniel Clark, delegate from Orleans Territory, a former associate of Wilkinson who had turned against him.[54]

The General may have suspected this transaction when, on the day before Christmas, he challenged the Congressman to a duel for remarks the latter was reported to have made about him. Randolph, interpreting the reference as being to what he had said in the grand jury in Richmond, and recognizing no right on the part of the General to hold him accountable for his opinion, declined the challenge. With finality he said, "I cannot descend to your level."[55] Wilkinson, who had denied a challenge from young Swartwout in Richmond, now said that only respect for Randolph's position had deterred him from chastising his critic with his cane. He scattered handbills through the District of Columbia in which he denounced the Congressman as a "prevaricating, base, calumniating scoundrel, poltroon and coward." It is not surprising that John Randolph's verbal ferocity should have been answered in kind, but he was not proved by these words to have been cowardly, and the documents he shortly displayed in the House seemed clearly to reveal the General as a peculating scoundrel. They showed not merely that he had been in affectionate correspondence with Spanish officials a decade before now, but also that he had received from them $9640 — delivered to him in the year 1796 in barrels of sugar and tobacco. After reading to the House a series of incriminating letters, Randolph moved that the President be requested to institute an inquiry into the conduct of the General with relation to his having "corruptly received money from the Government of Spain or its agents" at any time while in the service of the United States.[56]

This resolution was adopted by a substantial majority after two weeks, during which the House concerned itself with little else. The

54 Clark received the papers from Thomas Power, a Spanish citizen who had served as go-between (Abernethy, pp. 264–265).
55 Bruce, I, 313–314, quoting from both letters.
56 Dec. 31, 1807 (Annals, 10 Cong., 1 sess., I, 1257–1261).

propriety of such a request to the President was questioned by a number of speakers, and a motion that the House itself should set up a special committee to conduct an inquiry was defeated. During the week following the introduction of the original resolution, the fact became known that a court of inquiry into Wilkinson's conduct had already been instituted at his request, although Congress had not been officially informed of this. Ostensibly the adoption of the resolution implied no lack of confidence in the President. His former secretary, William A. Burwell, strongly supported it; and his son-in-law, John W. Eppes, introduced a further resolution calling on him for all available information bearing on combinations between foreign agents and American citizens, or tending to show that any officer of the United States had corruptly received money from a foreign government. This was adopted unanimously.[57]

In response to the Randolph resolution, Jefferson informed the House that a court of inquiry had already been set up by the Secretary of War at Wilkinson's request and had commenced its proceedings. In partial compliance with the Eppes resolution, he communicated half a dozen documents deposited in the government offices during previous administrations and stated that certain papers sent the Secretary of State by Daniel Clark during his own administration were being looked for.[58] He said that he had received letters in connection with the Burr conspiracy in which suspicions were voiced and insinuations made against Wilkinson, but that the information communicated by the House was "the first direct testimony" ever made known to him that charged Wilkinson with "a corrupt receipt of money." This assertion seems equivocal, for he had unquestionably heard charges to that effect, but he regarded these as vague and unattested. A couple of weeks later, when communicating pertinent extracts from papers from Daniel Clark that had now been found, he said that in none of these had they discerned "any information of the corrupt receipt of money by any officer of the United States from any foreign agent."[59] No doubt Jefferson was believing what he wanted to, but it would appear that, for all Daniel Clark's efforts at this and later times to incriminate Wilkinson, he himself had been so involved in Mexican matters that he never revealed his full hand.

[57] The discussions of Dec. 31, 1807, and Jan. 5-13, 1808, can be followed in *Annals*, 10 Cong., 1 sess. For the final actions, see pp. 1445, 1458-1461.
[58] Message of Jan. 20, 1808, with documents (*A.S.P., Misc.*, I, 705-712).
[59] Message of Feb. 4, 1808, with documents (*ibid.*, I, 712-713). Documents afterwards communicated to the House by Daniel Clark were printed and transmitted to the President (*Annals*, 10 Cong., 1 sess., II, 2275-2276; 2794-2802).

The military tribunal which Dearborn ordered on January 2 and which set to work on January 11, consisted of three military officers, all of lower rank than the Commanding General. The judge advocate to whom Jefferson delivered the documents received by him from Congress was the district attorney of the District of Columbia.[60] Not unnaturally this court was regarded by John Randolph and others as incapable of conducting the sort of inquiry he desired. But the House had disapproved the idea of a committee of its own; and even if it had appointed one we may doubt if the ultimate outcome would have been very different. The negative results attained in Madison's administration by a congressional committee which turned up considerably more testimony would suggest this. The proceedings in Jefferson's administration dragged on for nearly six months and Wilkinson conducted his own defense as Burr had done with comparable success.

The Governor of Spanish West Florida, Vizente Folch, believed that he was Wilkinson's savior and he undoubtedly rendered the General signal service. For one thing he got rid of the incriminating evidence in his files by sending all that pertained to the "old story" to the archives in Havana (whence it was subsequently transferred to Spain), correctly predicting that no American then living would be able to recover it. Also, in a public statement, he attested to Wilkinson's loyalty to his own government, and he helped him procure an affidavit supporting his claim about the circumstances under which he had received money from Spanish coffers.[61] The court of inquiry accepted as highly probable his statement that such money as he had received was owed him on an old tobacco contract, and was of the opinion that there was no evidence of his ever having received a pension from Spain for "corrupt purposes."[62] In the light of present knowledge the official statement that he appeared "to have discharged the duties of his station with honor to himself and fidelity to his country" is indeed ironical. Jefferson seems never to have doubted his loyalty from the time of his break with Burr, however; and, although he never went so far as to absolve the General from all previous misdeeds, the findings of the military court may be safely presumed to have been welcome to him. He countenanced what has been described in our day as a whitewash; but, in view of the actions of Governor

[60] Walter Jones. The officers were Col. Henry Burbeck, president; Col. Thos. H. Cushing, and Lieut. Col. Jonathan Williams.
[61] The intrigue with Folch is described by I. J. Cox in *A.H.R.*, XIX, 807–809, with pertinent quotations from documents. See also Abernethy, pp. 272–273, and deposition of Joseph Collins, Apr. 25, 1808, in Wilkinson's *Memoirs*, II, App. XXII.
[62] Report of the Court, approved by TJ, July 2, 1808 (*ibid.*, II, 12–13).

Folch, we may doubt if it could have been proved to the satisfaction of any court at that time that Wilkinson was a Spanish pensioner. In view of the suspicions that remained it may appear that Jefferson would have been wise to ease him out of his high position after this formal vindication; but there was no obvious way to "kick him upstairs" or otherwise provide for him, and Jefferson continued to manifest toward him a loyalty far beyond his deserts. Whether this should be attributed to temperamental weakness or foolish consistency or political expediency remains until this day a matter of opinion, but it appears to have done Jefferson more political harm than good.

The outcome of the official inquiry into the conduct of Wilkinson was not known until some weeks after the adjournment of Congress. Meanwhile, the charges against him in the House had served to distract the attention of that body from the conduct of the courts in the Burr trials and the place of the judiciary in the American system. Such consideration as these matters received in this busy congressional session was largely confined to the Senate. An amendment to the Constitution such as Jefferson might have been expected to welcome, but which he appears to have done nothing to advance, was introduced very early in the session by Senator Tiffin of Ohio. This called for the appointment of federal judges for terms of years and their removal on address of two-thirds of both houses of Congress. Resolutions to the same effect were presented soon thereafter in behalf of the legislature of Vermont, and more drastic ones at the instance of the legislature of Pennsylvania. The latter, which lacked the approval of the Governor, called for removal on the address of a majority of the members of the House and Senate present and voting, and also for conviction by a mere majority in impeachment trials. Toward the end of the session resolutions were presented by Senator John Quincy Adams from the legislature of Massachusetts, which was under Republican control at the time, asking for removal on address by a majority of the House and two-thirds of the Senate. These resolutions were repealed by the next legislature, however, nothing having happened with respect to any of these proposals in this session of Congress. All were buried in committee, and specific disapproval of such proposals was expressed by some of the other state legislatures.[63] This was no concerted movement with

[63] For a summarized account, with references, see H. V. Ames, *Proposed Amendments to the Constitution* (*Annual Report A.H.A., 1896*, II [1897], 150, 328). Tiffin's proposed amendment was introduced Nov. 5, 1807; and the various resolutions were presented to the Senate on Jan. 25, Feb. 22, and Apr. 12, 1808, respectively. The Pennsylvania resolutions were introduced and discussed briefly in the House on Feb. 24, 1808.

party backing. Many Republicans continued to be dissatisfied with the "irresponsibility" of the judiciary, but the psychological moment for the adoption of an amendment of this sort had passed, if it ever existed. The opportunity afforded by the case of Judge Pickering had not been seized; and there was no such ground for action against John Marshall as there had been against Samuel Chase.[64] Thus the situation was unchanged: a judge could be removed only by conviction on impeachment.

Equally futile was the attempt to redefine the crime of treason, which Marshall's critics believed he had made so restrictive that it was virtually impossible to prove. Lacking a specific recommendation from Jefferson, we can best judge of the attitude of the administration in this matter from a letter of Rodney's, written on request to John Randolph. In this the Attorney General called attention to the need to punish combinations and conspiracies "for the purpose of committing treason." That is, he would not limit treason to the actual levying of war and to persons involved in that overt act. A bill, apparently designed to broaden the definition of treason according to this suggestion, was introduced in the House by Randolph late in the session, but it was not debated or brought to a vote.[65] The House was much more concerned with other matters.

In the Senate, William Branch Giles, as chairman of a committee appointed to consider the part of the President's message dealing with the evidence in the Burr trial, reported on February 11, 1808, a bill that went much further. The fact that Timothy Pickering described this as a presidential measure is not proof that it was. While Jefferson probably approved of the purpose of the proposal, there is no evidence that he had any responsibility for its details.[66] This effort to define "levying war" against the United States exemplifies the difficulties and dangers of specification. Enough was included here to provide grounds for legalized tyranny. Under this definition not only would the Southern secessionists of 1861 have been guilty of treason on several counts, but so would have been the participants in the Whiskey Rebellion and anybody else who forcibly resisted the general execution of any public law. The penalties prescribed in the measure would have been extended to anyone traitorously aiding or assisting in the per-

---

[64] See *Jefferson the President: First Term*, ch. XXV.

[65] Text of bill of Mar. 2, 1808, with Rodney's letter of Dec. 2, 1807, is in *Annals*, 10 Cong., 1 sess., II, 1717–1719.

[66] Anderson, *Giles*, pp. 116–121; Pickering to R. King, Feb. 24, 1808, cited by Warren, I, 314*n*. The text of the first and pertinent section, which is too long to be quoted here, can be seen in *Annals*, 10 Cong., 1 sess., I, 108–109.

formance of any of the specified actions, "although not personally present" when the action was committed. This provision, with which Jefferson's general sympathy may be presumed, was obviously designed to take care of such a case as that of Burr, who was not present at Blennerhassett's Island. According to Giles, the doctrine of treason was written on the minds of the judges, and he compared these minds to changeable silk, which might vary its complexion "when held up to political sunshine." In this passage, said Joseph Story who was in Washington at the time, he attacked the Chief Justice "with insidious warmth," and on the strength of private utterances we may be sure that Jefferson agreed with him. The same may be said of Giles's reference to a judge, obviously Marshall, who, "forgetting the nature of his office, is perpetually aspiring not only to render his department absolutely independent, but to render it supreme over all the other departments of the Government."[67]

The chief critics of Giles's proposals whose speeches are recorded were Republicans who agreed with much he said. Thus Pope of Kentucky regarded the Constitution as defective in not providing for the removal of judges on joint address, and Mitchill of New York admitted that the doctrine of treason was clouded with great uncertainty.[68] But that Senator questioned the authority of Congress to go beyond the constitutional definition, and the wisdom of this redefinition was doubted by others besides Federalists. The precise form it had assumed by the time it was finally voted on is far from clear in the surviving record. What was originally called a treason bill, was recommitted, several times amended, and changed into a bill for the punishment of certain crimes. As such it was passed toward the end of the session by a vote of 18 to 10, the Federalists being in opposition.[69] No action was taken on it in the House. Actually, the Senate gave less attention to this question than to that of expelling John Smith of Ohio, and during this session it was much more concerned with commercial questions than with those that were carried over from the Burr trials. Redefinition of treason was proved impracticable if not impossible. Even to many who regarded the Marshall interpretation as too restrictive this seemed better than one that was too broad.

[67] Ibid., I, 125, 126; Story is quoted by Anderson, p. 119; Warren, I, 314-315.
[68] Annals, 10 Cong., 1 sess., I, 136, 110.
[69] Apr. 6, 1808 (ibid., p. 207); see also App., pp. 108-127, 135-149, 159-160; J. Q. Adams, Memoirs, I, 527. Pope was added to the committee, and Mitchill, who originally opposed the section dealing with treason, finally voted for the bill. Presumably the amendments modified it.

It would appear that after this minor skirmish the judges remained in possession of the field, but if the struggle during Jefferson's presidency between the judiciary on the one hand and the executive and legislative branches on the other is viewed as a whole, it may be described not inaccurately as a sort of drawn battle.

[XXI]

Liberty and Libel

1806–1809

IN the spring of 1806, more than a year before Burr was indicted in
Richmond, a Republican judge in Connecticut, recently appointed
by Jefferson, drew attention to a danger that he regarded as more
menacing than treason. District Judge Pierpont Edwards, charging a
federal grand jury in New Haven, stated that a licentious press, un-
restrained and unpunished, could eventually destroy the strongest
government.[1] This was the sort of language that the Federalists had
employed in defense of the Sedition Act when they were in control of
the national government and that the Republican opposition had then
decried. Furthermore, indictments of half a dozen persons for libel
issued from this court at this and a later session. These proved abortive,
but by means of them Jefferson's party laid itself open to the charge of
grave inconsistency. At a time when, in the country as a whole, public
attention was focused on other dangers, domestic and foreign, only
Connecticut Federalists appear to have made much of these actions and
threats against critics of the government and the President. Quite
clearly, they did not originate with him, and he appears to have been
unaware of them until some months after they started, but the charge
that he condoned them for a time is inescapable.

About a month after the session of the circuit court in New Haven,
he received from an association of Baptists in North Carolina an
address voicing gratitude for the civil and religious liberty they were
enjoying. Under his government and patronage, they said, *"there is
none that shall make us afraid."* Such expressions of confidence can be

---

[1] Litchfield (Conn.) *Witness,* Apr. 30, 1806, reporting a session of the circuit
court that ended about ten days earlier; Hartford *American Mercury,* May 1. The
charge was delivered Apr. 14.

matched many times over, and his record as a champion of religious freedom was in fact unquestionable. A broader claim was made for him by a Franco-American bookseller in Baltimore who addressed him as "Unique fidel conservateur des droits de l'homme."[2] With respect to *civil* liberties, especially freedom of speech and the press, the Connecticut libel cases, more perhaps than anything else that happened during his presidency, would appear to cast a shadow on his title as a conservator of human rights. To be more precise, they appear to have been signally inconsistent with the avowed principles of Jefferson and his party, for these actions and threats emanated from a federal court, and while the Republicans never supposed that freedom of speech and the press should be unlimited, they had denied the federal government any constitutional powers of restriction. But, whether the prosecutions were legitimate or not, they cannot be understood apart from the existing situation in Connecticut. There the Federalists were in full control of the state government and there, more than anywhere else, the local Republicans were subject to persecution in state courts and the President to denunciation in pulpits. The Federalist establishment provided extreme provocation, and the Connecticut Republicans undoubtedly believed that they were more sinned against than sinning.[3]

Nowhere else did Jefferson's supporters operate under such difficulties or have so little success as in Connecticut. It was one of the two states he did not carry in the election of 1804. In the Land of Steady Habits, where the Congregational clergy and the magistrates were still two sides of the same shield, his party was anti-clerical from the outset, and as elsewhere in New England it had the support of the "dissenting" sects, especially the Baptists. The state had no constitution other than the charter of 1662, and the Republicans made a political issue of this lack. At a historic meeting in New Haven on August 29, 1804, they urged the calling of a convention to draft a constitution. Among the signers of an address to the freemen were five justices of the peace. As a consequence these men were removed by the General Court (Assembly) in November — an action which Senator Plumer of New Hampshire described as impolitic.[4]

---

[2] Chowan Association of Baptists to TJ, May 20, 1806 (LC, 27827); J. P. Reibelt to TJ, Aug. 24, 1806 (LC, 28212).

[3] These libel cases are treated by Leonard W. Levy in *Jefferson and Civil Liberties* (1963), pp. 61–66, but in my opinion this author does not allow sufficiently for the local situation and its effect on imperfect human beings.

[4] Plumer gives a rather full account in an entry of Dec. 6, 1804 (*Memorandum*, pp. 213–215). There is a good account of the Republican party during TJ's administration in R. J. Purcell, *Connecticut in Transition, 1775–1818* (1963 edn.), ch. VI.

His belief that appearances augured a change in the government of Connecticut was not borne out, but in 1805 the Republicans set up a more effective organization than hitherto under a state manager, Alexander D. Wolcott, whom Jefferson had appointed collector at Middletown early in his administration.[5] And in the elections in the spring of 1806 they made their best showing to date. Shortly before these were held, Jefferson appointed as United States district judge Pierpont Edwards, son of Jonathan Edwards, who was well qualified for the post on professional grounds and had been one of the chief party leaders from the start. Since the President had recently reappointed Joseph Willcox as marshal and named Hezekiah Huntington as district attorney, the Republicans were now in full control of this United States court.[6]

The state courts still were wholly in Federalist hands, and from them the members of the minority expected nothing but persecution. "We live in a conquered country," said the leading Republican paper, asserting that the lawyers, supported by the clergy, had absolute dominion.[7] According to the Hartford *American Mercury*, whose editor was fined $1000 for an alleged libel, Republicans from the President down could be slandered with impunity year after year; they could be called "knaves, liars, atheists, swindlers, thieves, adulterers and murderers" without having any court to which they could resort for vindication. This editor may be charged with partisan bias, but Senator William Plumer, a Federalist New Englander, confided to his diary his judgment that the people of Connecticut had "more cunning, more art, hypocrisy and meanness than those of any other State." He based this opinion, he said, on much information, including knowledge of the Connecticut members of Congress, all of whom boarded at the same place as he. "In Connecticut," he said, "in almost every town, there are meeting houses, stocks and whipping posts. Articles for which they find much use."[8]

Federalists in that state defined the issue as being between "Religion and Infidelity, Morality and Debauchery, legal Government and total Disorganization."[9] An editor on the other side viewed things differently. "In the present day," said he, "it is more honorable to be called a republican felon than a Connecticut Saint; but it is not comfortable to

5 Cunningham, pp. 128–132.
6 TJ appointed Edwards in February, 1806; in the previous December he reappointed Willcox, whom he had appointed four years before, and appointed Huntington.
7 Hartford *American Mercury*, Apr. 3, 1806.
8 Mar. 4, 1806 (*Memorandum*, pp. 442–443).
9 Quoted by Purcell, pp. 152–153.

be dragged from your families and business, and to be shut up in jail."[10] He was referring specifically to Selleck Osborne, the Republican editor of the Litchfield *Witness*, who was confined at the time with two felons and had himself been described as a criminal by the sheriff. In the eyes of his sympathizers he was merely a debtor; he had declined to pay his fine after one of his convictions for libel. His offense consisted of the statement in his paper, for which the printer was also punished, that a Federalist gentleman reminded a Republican of the latter's indebtedness to him and thus sought to influence that man's vote.[11] Litchfield, justly renowned in later generations for serenity and charm, was a Federalist stronghold which Selleck Osborne had the temerity to invade; and there can be no doubt of the determined effort of the local establishment to crush his paper. Thomas Collier's *Litchfield Monitor* represented the dominant group and to it Judge Tapping Reeve, chiefly noted in history for his pioneer law school, made frequent contributions of a strongly partisan nature. When the circuit court was held in New Haven in April, Osborne was in prison and an object of Republican commiseration.

Owing to the absence of Justice Paterson, who was ill, District Judge Edwards presided over the court. Critics of its actions pointed out that Alexander Wolcott, the Republican state manager, attended the sessions faithfully and consulted with the District Attorney frequently.[12] Federalists rejoiced that his designs to "revolutionize" the state had been exposed when one of his circulars fell into their hands, and claimed that he and his fellows anticipated a "banquet of revenge." It was alleged by them that the Marshal packed the jury. In view of Federalist comments on the incompetence of the District Attorney, Hezekiah Huntington, they could hardly have credited him with being the prime mover in these libel cases; they may have assigned that role to Wolcott. They were relatively respectful of Judge Edwards before this business ended, but it was started by his charge to the grand jury.

Toward the end of this charge he said:

> While an examination of the measures of Government is conducted with decency and evidently has for its object the public good, it can never be hostile to the well-being of society; but

[10] Hartford *American Mercury*, July 24, 1806.

[11] *Ibid.*, Apr. 10, 1806.

[12] *Connecticut Courant*, Apr. 23, 1806; HAMPDEN, *A Letter to the President of the United States, touching the Prosecutions, under his Patronage, before the Circuit Court of the District of Connecticut* (1808), p. 8. The latter, a pamphlet of 28 pp., cited hereafter as HAMPDEN, is a contemporary Federalist account.

when publications . . . are the offspring of revenge for disappointment, as to party views, unfounded in truth, or principle, are
calculated to create distrust and jealousy, to excite hatred against
the government, and those who are intrusted with the management of it, and to bring any or all of them into contempt, . . .
the authors of them become just objects of detestation and de-
merit exemplary punishment. . . .

Such publications, if the authors of them may not be restrained,
but are permitted to continue them with impunity, will more
effectually undermine and sap the foundation of our Constitution,
and Government, than any kind of treason that can be named.
Treason, in its technical sense, has rarely overturned any government, but a licentious press, regardless of decency or truth, under
the conduct of daring men, stimulated by a spirit of revenge and
unchecked in its career, will eventually destroy any government,
the wisest and strongest that can be imagined.[13]

He charged the grand jurors, therefore, to regard authors and publishers of such "libels" as offenders against the law. Justice Samuel
Chase might have said that this was precisely his position. In fact,
Judge Edwards declared that he was voicing the sentiments of the
great majority of the Supreme Court. These sentiments, however, had
historically been opposed by the Republican party, which claimed that
the authority of the federal courts was limited to what was expressly
granted in the Constitution. Accordingly, they denied these courts any
jurisdiction over common-law offenses such as libel. Furthermore, they
argued that the First Amendment prohibited a statutory restriction of
free speech and had thus considered the Sedition Act to be unconstitutional. Edwards avoided being bound by Republican theory by saying
that whatever his own opinion might be, he was declaring the law as
established by precedent. By making this equivocal statement he left
himself a door of escape; he seems to have been saying in effect that he
was merely administering to the Federalists a dose of their own
medicine according to the highest judicial prescription. One may
suspect that he had his tongue in his cheek throughout these proceedings.

Another question, much agitated in this period, was whether "truth"
could be given in evidence by the defense in libel cases. The Republican position on this had not been wholly consistent, but Jefferson
himself was on record as upholding the right of the defendant to prove

[13] Litchfield *Witness*, Apr. 30, 1806; Hartford *American Mercury*, May 1.

his case.[14] Judge Edwards relieved the minds of the Federalists by saying he would be governed by the state law that allowed such evidence to be given.[15]

At the April session of the court the grand jury returned three bills of indictment.[16] One of these was against Judge Tapping Reeve, for an expressed opinion that a certain expenditure of public money by the federal government was unconstitutional, but the statute of limitations applied in this case and Judge Edwards refused to issue a warrant against this kinsman of his. Another was against Thomas Collier, editor of the *Litchfield Monitor*, for a publication castigating Jefferson's official conduct in extravagant language and accusing him of subverting the Constitution. A third was against Thaddeus Osgood, a ministerial candidate, for alleged utterances in a sermon at Branford on the previous Thanksgiving Day. He was charged with having described Jefferson as "a base, traitorous infidel, debaucher and liar." The Reverend William Bentley of Salem, Massachusetts, a Jeffersonian, seems to have been referring to this intemperate sermon when he confided the following observation to his diary: "The political conduct of the clergy is nowhere so insolent as in Connecticut."[17] The cases of Osgood and Collier were both continued to the next session. The former defendant is said to have been imprisoned for two days before he could procure bail. A couple of prominent Federalists (Elias Shipman and David Daggett) promptly provided it for the Litchfield journalist.

In the interim between the April and September sessions of the court, the Republican press rang the changes on the charge that Selleck Osborne was a victim of party vengeance, and his plight as a prisoner in Litchfield seems to have attracted much wider attention than the punitive actions that had been initiated against Collier and Osgood. The treatment of Osborne afforded Republicans an example of one-sided justice which could be vividly portrayed and by means of which they could put their local foes on the defensive. One of them said that the Federalists seemed determined to crush Osborne "by fists, whips,

[14] See comments on the Croswell case in *Jefferson the President: First Term*, pp. 232–233.

[15] HAMPDEN, p. 9.

[16] Copies of these and others referred to hereafter, from the U.S. Circuit Court Records in the Federal Records Center, Boston, have been made available to me through the courtesy of Pierce Gaines, Esq., of Fairfield, Conn.

[17] Entry of Dec. 29, 1805 (*Diary*, III, 208). I do not enter further into this case because that of Azel Backus, which came up at the next session, is even more lurid and, for the purposes of this study, more important.

cudgels, actions, prosecutions, fines, imprisonment and close confinement in a dark, damp, noisome dungeon, with maniacs and felons, to the certain injury of his health, and the probable risk of his life."[18] Federalists, including the sheriff, denied that he was mistreated and pointed out that his martyrdom was self-imposed.[19] His sympathizers made the most of it. At a party festival the Republicans defiantly held in Litchfield in August they marched in solemn procession by the window (so-called) of his cell — some saluting and others uncovering their heads as they passed.[20] Apparently he continued to wield his trenchant pen while incarcerated. In September an effective item from his paper was copied in Hartford, under the heading "Federal Dictionary":

SLANDER — Whatever is said truly or falsely, against Federalists.
TRUTH — *Whatever* is said against democrats. . . .
GOSPEL PREACHING — Calling Mr. Jefferson, in the pulpit, an *infidel*, a *debaucher* and a *liar*. . . .
IMPARTIAL JUDGE — One who extols the men of one party — and denounces those of the other as "a stench in the nostrils of a holy God."
CHARITY — (obsolete).[21]

The September session of the circuit court was held in Hartford, after the elections in the middle of the month. Federalists resented the publicity that had been given Selleck Osborne's case by Republican newspapers throughout the country. They charged that contributions had been received from a number of other states in support of a wretch whose object was the revolutionary one of overthrowing the government of Connecticut. But no success was gained by the Republicans in Litchfield, where they appear to have over-reached themselves. That town elected a solid slate of Federalist representatives in the legislature.[22] In the elections as a whole the Republicans lost some ground.

Judge Edwards again sat alone in court, and the Federalists again accused Marshal Willcox of packing the grand jury, but they seem to

---

[18] Hartford *American Mercury*, Aug. 14, 1806.

[19] The sheriff's explanation is in *Connecticut Courant*, July 30, 1806; see also Aug. 7 and Sept. 5, 10.

[20] Hartford *American Mercury*, Aug. 21, 1806, reporting events of Aug. 6.

[21] *Ibid.*, Sept. 11, 1806.

[22] Purcell, pp. 175–176. The charge, which appears to have been exaggerated, that the Republicans had mistreated an aged clergyman may have contributed to their overwhelming defeat in Litchfield. Examples of Federalist denunciation can be seen in *Connecticut Courant*, Sept. 10, 1806. See also Sept. 5, 1806.

have found no fault with the Judge's charge to it. According to one report, this was "calculated rather to soothe than to agitate the public mind."[23] Edwards declined for the second time to issue a warrant against Tapping Reeve, and the case of Collier was continued. So was that of Osgood, on the basis of a fresh indictment in place of a faulty one drawn by District Attorney Huntington, whose ineptitude the Federalists made so much of. Osgood was released on his own bond. Chief interest attaches to two fresh indictments that were approved by the grand jury. One was against the publishers of the *Connecticut Courant*, Hudson and Goodwin, for printing a severe criticism of the secret appropriation of two million dollars which was designed to further the negotiations for West Florida. Since John Randolph had vehemently assailed the same measure in Congress, this was not a novel attack.[24] It related to an official action, while the other indictment, against the Reverend Azel Backus, bore more directly on the President's personal conduct.

The clergyman was described as "a wicked and evilly disposed person," seeking to incite "hatred, contempt, and indignation" against the government and its head. The same had been said of Thaddeus Osgood, but Backus was charged with having used more abusive language. It was alleged that, in a sermon delivered in Bethlehem, Litchfield County, shortly before the presidential election of 1804, he described Jefferson as "a liar, whoremaster, debaucher, drunkard, gambler," and also an infidel who appointed only infidels to office. Backus was said to have anticipated martyrdom if the President should be re-elected, and to have predicted that all the meeting-houses and Bibles in the land would be burned. He was alleged to have repeated these dire predictions in a sermon about a year and a half later and to have adverted to the likelihood or at least the possibility that his own head would be severed from his body by guillotine. Reportedly he added to his charges of presidential immorality by asserting that Jefferson "keeps a wench as his whore, and brings up in his family black females for that purpose."[25]

According to Federalist report, the deputy marshal sent to arrest Backus had himself been fined five or six hundred dollars for a "foul

23 HAMPDEN, p. 10. Approbation was expressed in *Connecticut Courant*, Sept. 31, 1806. My account of the proceedings is largely based on these two contemporary sources and on the transcripts from the U.S. Circuit Court Records in the Federal Records Center, Boston.
24 See above, ch. V, especially p. 75.
25 U.S. Circuit Court Records (Boston), Law, III, 218–223; session of April, 1807, quoting indictment of 1806.

slander" against another clergyman, and he was declared to have been discourteous and inconsiderate in handling this man of God. No charges to that effect were either proved or disproved, however. The case was continued, and Backus was released on bail. Apparently the prosecution was in no hurry, and obviously both sides were maneuvering for political advantage.

ii

During the session of the court the local Republican paper printed a toast that had been given by a supporter of the administration in Massachusetts:

> Thomas Jefferson, President of the United States, who levels his breastwork, spikes his cannon, bares his bosom to the shafts of his enemies, and gives the deepest wound by a dignified silence.[26]

Intended as an answer to those who asked why he did not vindicate himself, this was a metaphorical description of the policy he had nearly always followed when personally attacked. Some Federalists asserted at the time that he instigated the counterattacks by his partisans in Connecticut, but the claim seems to be wholly without factual foundation, and he undoubtedly sought to follow a hands-off policy with respect to the actions of his local supporters everywhere. Up to this time he seems to have had little or no information about doings in Connecticut that he regarded as reliable. In the middle of October, however, he received from the Postmaster General, Gideon Granger, whose services as a sentinel he generally valued, a report which he might have been expected to trust. As an account of events this was not detailed, but Granger's comments were pertinent and challenging.[27]

To the prosecution of these critics of the government and its head Granger was opposed, on the grounds of both Republican principles and political expediency. He said that every one of the indicted men was a bitter enemy of his, and that his passions might be gratified by their punishment. But he asked: "Where will be the liberty of future generations if the dreadful doctrines maintained by Federalists on this point are to be sanctioned by precedents given by the republican administration?" His apprehension was increased by his belief that

[26] Hartford *American Mercury*, Sept. 25, 1806.

[27] Granger to TJ, from Suffield, Conn., Oct. 9, 1806 (LC, 28332–28334); received Oct. 15. In the first part of this letter, he referred to attacks on him in the *Aurora* and expressed his willingness to retire.

there was a sympathetic reaction in favor of any victim of prosecution. Indeed, he attributed Republican losses in the last election to these libel suits. Also, he pointed out that in any case in which Jefferson's private character was involved, the talent and wealth of the Federalists would be employed against him and his local defenders would be at a disadvantage.

If, at this stage, Jefferson had dropped a hint to the District Attorney that these threatened prosecutions were unwelcome to him, he would have avoided subsequent embarrassment while guarding against a blemish on his own record as a friend of civil liberties. What he said to Granger when next he saw the Postmaster General in Washington we do not know, and there appears to be no record of any reply to this letter. He was confronted with pressing problems of national concern at the time; he had recently received reports of Burr's conspiracy to which he gave credence; and by comparison, the controversy in little Connecticut may have seemed but a teapot tempest which would, or at least might, subside. At all events, at this time the President made no known effort to still it.

A few days after he got Granger's letter, no doubt he read in the Richmond *Enquirer* a reassuring expression of Republican opinion on this question. That generally moderate paper asserted that Connecticut was the *only* state where presentments against libelers of the President had been made by Republican juries, and challenged the Federalists to say as much of their record. This *tu quoque* argument was followed by an explanation: "But why *this* prosecution in Connecticut? Seek for the *reason* in Selleck Osborne's gaol. . . . Seek for it in the prosecutions, that have been instituted in almost every *state* court in Connecticut. Is it surprising that the republican party should attempt to *counteract* such federal [Federalist] inquisition? . . . And that in return for state prosecutions, the republican party should retaliate in the federal courts?"[28]

On the last day of the year Jefferson received a communication from a group of Republican citizens of Hartford who argued to the same effect.[29] While avowing devotion to liberty of the press, and asserting the right of everyone to examine the measures of government, they denied the right of anyone to charge the authors of policy with subversive motives. Also, they drew a distinction between scrutiny of the official conduct of the Chief Magistrate and attacks on him

[28] Richmond *Enquirer*, Oct. 17, 1806.
[29] Thomas Seymour and six others to TJ, Dec. 20, 1806 (Bixby, pp. 137–140).

as a man. They were little concerned with theory, however; they sought to describe the actual situation in Connecticut, letting Jefferson know just what they were up against:

> The opponents of the General Government in this State, under the mask of superior virtue, religion and patriotism, have commenced and persevered in a systematic plan for the ruin of every Individual, who holds an Office, or advocates the Government of the United States. . . . Not contented with this systematic attack on character; unsatisfied by the general wreck of reputation which has marked its progress, they are determined that the bare means of subsistence shall not be left to the victims of their intolerance. With these objects in view, not only Suits at Law to rob us of our property, but criminal prosecutions have commenced. While on the other hand the Characters, and not the Characters alone, but the opinions and conduct of the Federalists, from the highest Judge to the most obscure Justice of the Peace, are not only protected, but vindicated.

We may safely assume that the validity of these charges was not questioned by Jefferson. Furthermore, the assertion that his political foes had been emboldened in their course because of their confidence that no United States court would take cognizance of their calumnies against him and his administration was calculated to impress him. So also were the comments on attitudes toward the recent actions in Judge Edwards's court against "political priests" and Federalist printers. "Public opinion has decided on the correctness of the procedure," said these citizens of Hartford; "moderate Federalists approve it; the violent are silent; and the Republicans, with a few solitary exceptions, applaud it." Not only so. The effects of these actions had been good. The public presses, while still free to examine the measures of the government, had already become less personal in their abuse. The intolerant majority had already softened its asperity, and the minority, despairing of justice in state courts, could anticipate "exact justice" to its enemies in the courts of the United States. If this view of things was correct, Gideon Granger was one of the rare exceptions among Connecticut Republicans, and his dire predictions of public reaction against the prosecutions were unwarranted. Actually, they were only indictments as yet and not even in Connecticut do the Federalists appear to have made much noise about them. Congressman Samuel W. Dana said as much on several occasions, but early in the new year he himself brought them up in Congress.

This representative from Connecticut does not appear to have mentioned his state by name, and he may have been seeking to avoid discussion of past Federalist actions there. The four prosecutions to which he referred as pending in the courts of the United States were unmistakably those in Connecticut, but his emphasis was on the fact that they had not arisen from any existing federal statute but were sustained at common law. He offered a resolution calling for the appointment of a committee to inquire whether prosecutions at common law for libelous publications or defamatory words against persons holding office or places of trust under the United States should be sustained in federal courts; and to inquire whether truth might be given in evidence if such prosecutions should be sustained. Thus he raised the fundamental questions of theory, or principle, obviously hoping to cast doubt on Republican consistency. Much of the relatively brief discussion that followed bore on the question of procedure — whether to set up a special committee or refer the matter to the Committee of the Whole. The latter course was followed and nothing came of Dana's move. Representative John W. Eppes addressed himself vigorously to the basic questions, however, taking a thoroughly consistent Republican position.[30]

Jefferson's son-in-law suggested more positive resolutions without formally offering them. These explicitly asserted that the common law of England was *not* a part of the law of the United States or a state except when specifically adopted, and that federal prosecution for libel at common law was a violation of freedom of the press and contrary to the Constitution. Also, they stated that in all prosecutions a citizen had the natural right to give the truth as evidence. Dana was unwilling to accept these resolutions as a substitute for his own, since that would imply his agreement with every word of them. He may have been unwilling to go as far as Eppes with respect to judges, being aware of the past conduct of certain Federalist Justices of the Supreme Court. Eppes said he would favor impeachment of any judge who dared to institute such proceedings and would vote for his conviction. One would suppose him to have been as unsympathetic to Judge Pierpont Edwards as to Justice Samuel Chase.

There is no reason to believe that the President of the United States had shown Representative Eppes the letter from Republicans of "high respectability" at Hartford in which Edwards was described as "a judge eminent for his talents and attached to the administration of his country," who had been called by "an unexpected order of provi-

[30] For proceedings, Jan. 2, 1807, see *Annals*, 9 Cong., 2 sess., pp. 247–252.

dence" to a position in which he could restore the balance of justice in Connecticut. And when Jefferson finally got around to answering this letter, some six weeks after the congressional discussion of basic principles, he addressed himself chiefly to the actualities of the local situation.[31] "I have seen with deep concern the afflicting oppression under which the republican citizens of Connecticut suffer from an unjust majority," he said. He claimed that he had previously heard little of the "countervailing prosecutions" in the federal court and believed that he had expressed no opinion on them. But what he said now was clearly not in condemnation of those who supported them: "That a spirit of indignation and retaliation should arise when opportunity should present itself, was too much within the human constitution to excite either surprise or censure, and confined to an appeal to truth only, it cannot lessen the useful freedom of the press."

This statement was consistent with the position he had previously taken that defendants in libel cases should be given the opportunity to prove their charges, but he made no reference to the Republican "principle" that federal courts did not have common-law jurisdiction. From libel actions against his personal critics, however, he sought to dissociate himself, saying that he had made no effort to contradict the "thousands of calumnies" propagated against him. In this respect, in fact, his record withstands critical scrutiny. He continued to regard freedom of the press as compatible with orderly government, he said. He also believed that the press was impotent when abandoned to falsehood, but he left to others the task of restoring it "by recalling it within the pale of truth." He hoped that such restoration could be effected in Connecticut and believed that, if it were, "republican principles" would prevail. These expressions might have been readily interpreted in terms of party, and he did not intimate that his supporters were using improper means. Undoubtedly he was encouraging them to persist in their arduous struggle against "an interested aristocracy of priests and lawyers," who had resorted to abhorrent "falsehoods and artifices." Always disposed to accept the judgment of local leaders in local matters, he probably believed that the large majority of his beleaguered partisans in this state strongly approved of the "countervailing prosecutions." On the strength of this sympathetic private letter they could hardly have failed to believe that he himself did so tacitly, while desiring to have no personal part in them. Besides being reluctant to chide his loyal supporters, he may have been hesitant

31 TJ to Thomas Seymour, Feb. 11, 1807 (Ford, IX, 28–31).

to intervene in judicial matters, especially since these proceedings might not come to anything.

Nothing decisive happened at the next session of the circuit court (April, 1807), and in the interim between this and the September session the treason trial of Aaron Burr took place in Richmond. This had passed through the first of its several frustrating phases when, in June, Jefferson penned the bitterest comments he ever made on the abuses of the freedom of the press. If the letter he wrote John Norvell, a youthful Kentuckian who asked his opinion about the proper conduct of a newspaper, may be regarded as indicative of his state of mind, this was the period of his darkest disillusionment with the press.[32] It was a dark era in the history of American journalism, and in rhetorical violence the Federalist papers appear to have surpassed the Republican.[33] His grievances against the former were cumulative, but he now drew a blanket indictment and pronounced a plague on both houses.

The young Kentuckian must have been surprised to learn from the President of the United States that a paper restrained to true facts and sound principles could not be expected to find many subscribers. "It is a melancholy truth," wrote Jefferson, "that a suppression of the press could not more completely deprive the nation of its benefits, than is done by its abandoned prostitution to falsehood. Nothing can now be believed which is seen in a newspaper. Truth itself becomes suspicious by being put into that polluted vessel." This was strong and bitter medicine from one who, a score of years earlier, had stated extravagantly that if he had to choose between a government without newspapers and newspapers without a government he would choose the latter.[34] To be sure, he was again indulging in hyperbole. He could not have believed such evil of the *National Intelligencer* and the Richmond *Enquirer*, but he was abundantly warranted in saying that the press was sharply limiting its usefulness by its own excess, that it was much more disposed to claim freedom than to recognize its own responsibilities. He suggested that an editor should divide his paper into four parts, labeling them successively as Truths, Probabilities,

---

[32] TJ to John Norvell, June 11, 1807 (LC, 29519–29520). The texts in L. & B., XI, 222–226; and in Ford, IX, 71–75 (with the wrong date) differ from the original only in minor respects. In *Jefferson and the Press* (1943), pp. 54–58, F. L. Mott quotes and discusses the pertinent passages.

[33] See comment of J. M. Banner, Jr., *To the Hartford Convention* (1970), p. 23.

[34] TJ to Edward Carrington, Jan. 16, 1787 (Boyd, XI, 49).

Possibilities, and Lies. The first two would be necessarily short, he said, while the latter would gratify the public.

One paragraph in this uncharacteristically cynical letter, though couched in general terms, may have reflected a resentment of personal attacks, which normally he kept to himself:

> Such an editor, too, would have to set his face against the demoralizing practice of feeding the public mind habitually on slander, and the depravity of taste which this nauseous ailment induces. Defamation is becoming a necessary of life; insomuch, that a dish of tea in the morning or evening cannot be digested without this stimulant. Even those who do not believe these abominations, still read them with complaisance to their auditors, and instead of the abhorrence and indignation which should fill a virtuous mind, betray a secret pleasure in the possibility that some may believe them, though they do not themselves. It seems to escape them, that it is not he who prints, but he who pays for printing a slander, who is its real author.

This man of notably sanguine temperament and inveterate optimism had certainly not lost his faith in the generality of human beings, and it was fortunate that this cynical letter was not published in his lifetime. When its recipient finally gave it to the world, he stated that there had been a manifest improvement in the character and conduct of American newspapers; and, although Jefferson continued to be highly dubious of their trustworthiness, he had said by this time that these formidable censors performed a necessary service in arraigning officials at the bar of public opinion and were the best instrument for enlightening the mind of man.[35] At the present moment, however, he was in a mood of extreme disillusionment.

There is no reason to suppose that, during the weeks immediately following the dispatch of his querulous letter to young Norvell, Jefferson's feelings about those whom he regarded as purveyors of falsehood and slander were moderated. No doubt he continued to regard the offensive journalists and clergymen in Connecticut as richly deserving of prosecution, or at least of the threat of it. At some time during the summer, however, he reached the conclusion that the punitive actions

---

[35] TJ to A. Coray, Oct. 31, 1823 (L. & B., XV, 489). Norvell printed the letter in the Philadelphia *Aurora and Franklin Gazette*, Sept. 5, 1826; and it was reluctantly reprinted in *Niles Register*, Sept. 30. This version varies in some details from the original.

in the federal court in that state must be stopped. We cannot be sure of the precise form in which he expressed his desire, since the two letters he wrote Gideon Granger, his agent in this matter, have not been discovered.[36] Following his receipt of these, Granger made successive trips to Hartford, where he consulted with the District Attorney and others. In his representations to them Granger emphasized the inconsistency of the prosecutions with the principles of their party, and he now spoke in the President's name. He said afterwards that Jefferson intervened when he perceived that there was a determination to press the prosecutions, and the records leave no doubt that he specially objected to that of the Reverend Azel Backus. This bore directly on his own moral character, which he rarely if ever sought to defend. Furthermore, he became aware by the late summer of 1807 that, in support of the clergyman's charges of immorality, witnesses had been summoned from Virginia — James Madison, John Walker, General Henry Lee, John Nicholas, and David M. Randolph. The utterances alleged in the indictment of Backus did not point to the Walker affair specifically, but Jefferson was now left in no doubt that his foes purposed again to expose to view the one unquestionable scandal of his life. Though he had acknowledged his fault privately, he had abundant reason not to want this episode exhumed and exploited further for political purposes.[37] By this time he had made what he regarded as sufficient amends for a grave mistake of his young manhood, and, according to his statement to Madison, those interested in the matter "had agreed mutually to endeavor that it should be for ever buried in oblivion."[38] His own desire to keep it there may serve to explain the absence from his papers of the copies of the letters to Granger in which he may be presumed to have mentioned it.

He spoke advisedly when he said that the dragging of it into court would be harrowing to all who were directly concerned with it, for General Light-Horse Harry Lee had written him to that effect, as John Nicholas had written Madison. Speaking for John Walker as well as himself, Nicholas (a political foe) had urged Madison to devise some way of getting out of this disagreeable situation.[39] And Jefferson wrote Madison: "I had not supposed there was a being in human shape such a savage as to have summoned Mr. W. in such a case. On account of the feelings of that family I shall spare nothing to have this article

[36] TJ to Granger, Aug. 24, 26, 1807, listed in Index of Correspondence and referred to in Granger's reply of Sept. 8 (LC, 30116–30117).
[37] See above, pp. 14–15, and *Jefferson the President: First Term*, pp. 216–223.
[38] TJ to Madison, Aug. 25, 1807 (MP, 32:118).
[39] John Nicholas to Madison, Aug. 22, 1807 (MP, 33:116).

withdrawn." Henry Lee had good reason not to go, said Jefferson, since he was detained in Richmond as a witness in the Burr trial; and, on advice from Rodney, Jefferson believed that the other witnesses could not be made to do so from their distant district.[40] No one of these witnesses made the long journey, and their failure to appear led to some talk of contempt of court, but defenders of Backus were more disposed to attribute it to the interference of the President. They were correct in that supposition. Madison reassured Nicholas before the session began; and, before it ended, Jefferson asked his Secretary of State to pass the word along that the Backus case would be dropped at that session, on the ground that it was "not cognisable" by a court of the United States.[41]

Jefferson was proved overly optimistic, for the prosecutions were not dismissed at this session. Granger informed him, however, that they eventually would be on grounds of general principles of law and policy.[42] The President's agent had to cope with objectors. From the beginning it seemed necessary to lump the prosecutions together; and among the faithful he found those who, while disbelieving in their legality, thought them necessary as policy because of the "severe persecutions under which they labored." But for the emphasis on the Backus case, they might not have concurred. Also, there were serious questions about the time and manner of killing the prosecutions. The net result was that everything was continued until the April term (1808).

During the intervening months, the President's attention was necessarily focused on foreign affairs rather than on those of Connecticut, but at some time he discussed the latter with Gideon Granger and he received from the Postmaster General certain oral declarations from Parson Backus. According to Granger's later report the clergyman denied having used the expressions against the President with which he was charged in the indictment and sent assurances that, while he did not admire Jefferson as a politician, "he held his character in high respect as a person who had rendered many important services to his country, as the friend of science and as a man." Whether or not the clergyman said precisely that, he was obviously trying to be concilia-tory at this critical state of national affairs. Early in the new year, Granger, at the end of a letter from New York in which he appraised

[40] On Rodney's formal opinion of a slightly later date, see above, p. 344. Presumably, TJ had received the same opinion informally.
[41] John Nicholas to Madison, Sept. 7, 8, 1807 (MP, 33:6, 7); TJ to Madison, Sept. 18, 1807 (Ford, IX, 139).
[42] Granger to TJ, Sept. 8, 1807; received Sept. 18 (LC, 30116–30117).

public reaction to the embargo, asked Jefferson if he should seek to put
an end to the prosecutions in Connecticut, whither he was going. In
reply Jefferson said he certainly wished he would, for the reasons
assigned in past letters. He added that these had been strengthened by
the verbal declarations from defendant Backus, and, not to be outdone,
he declared in turn that he bore the clergyman no ill will.[43]

At the session of the circuit court in April, 1808, the District
Attorney entered a *nolle prosequi* on all the libel indictments except
that against Hudson and Goodwin of the *Connecticut Courant*, which
was referred to the Supreme Court as a test case. The counsel for the
defense, Federalists though they were, had taken the position more
characteristic of Republicans that the court had no jurisdiction of
offenses at common law. Judge Edwards had not made his position
clear, but he had several times said that there was no point in proceeding with any of the cases until the question of jurisdiction was settled.
Justice Livingston appeared at this session, and the report got out that
he and Edwards were in disagreement. The latter had said that the
matter must be referred to the Supreme Court anyway. That august
tribunal did not act on it until nearly four years had passed. Then
Justice William Johnson delivered for the majority a notable opinion,
holding that the courts of the United States had no common-law jurisdiction in cases of libel against the government. This appointee of
Jefferson said that he considered the question "as having been long
since settled in public opinion."[44]

No doubt he spoke truly of the preponderant opinion by that time,
when Jefferson had been nearly three years out of office. But, a few
weeks after his retirement, John Randolph expressed surprise that the
Connecticut libel cases had failed to create a sensation. This political
purist attributed the failure to "the difference between men in power
and men out of power . . . between profession and practice." Early in
a special session of Congress he introduced a resolution calling for the
appointment of a committee to inquire whether any and what prosecutions for libel had been initiated in the federal courts and to report
provisions for securing the freedom of speech and the press. After a
minor verbal change this was unanimously adopted. Nothing beyond
the appointment of a committee appears ever to have come of this

[43] Granger to TJ, Jan. 19, 1808, from New York (LC, 30808); TJ to Granger,
Jan. 22, 1808 (LC, 30814); details regarding the declarations of Backus from
Granger's communication in *National Intelligencer*, July 21, 1809.

[44] United States *vs.* Hudson and Goodwin, Feb. 13, 1812 (7 Cranch, 32–33). The
dissenters were not listed. D. G. Morgan discusses the opinion in *Justice William
Johnson* (1954), pp. 77–79, saying that Justice Story remained unconvinced.

action, but something can be learned from the discussion.[45] John Randolph was vehement, as might have been expected, while Congressman Dana, spokesman for Connecticut Federalism, was surprisingly mild. He appears to have been content with the protection provided the defendants by state law, which permitted the giving of truth in evidence, and he stated that nobody had actually suffered except in inconvenience and expense. While recognizing that many Federalists in the state believed that the administration had instigated the indictments, he expressed his own disbelief in this and claimed that his party had made little noise about them. The reasons for this may have been that the Federalists were not yet willing to concede that there could be no actions against libel at common law, and that at least some of them conceded that their own persecution of their political foes had invited retribution. Regardless of theoretical consistency, it did appear that the defendants were getting no more than they deserved. No one of them fitted the role of martyr as well as Selleck Osborne at any rate.

Some months before Jefferson's retirement a Federalist account of the abortive prosecutions in Connecticut appeared in a pamphlet that was printed in New Haven, and in this he was designated as their patron.[46] Though this was in the form of a letter to him, he may never have seen it; and, if he did, no doubt he brushed it off as a partisan effusion. But he was disturbed by the report of Randolph's resolution and the discussion of it in Congress, which reached him in retirement at Monticello. In his opinion the resolution created the impression that he had instituted the proceedings, or at least acquiesced in them. It occasioned a letter to his friend Wilson Cary Nicholas, a member of the House of Representatives, in which he gave his remembrance of his connection with the prosecutions.[47] He recognized that he spoke from imperfect memory and presumably did not search in his voluminous correspondence for the letters bearing on the episode. At all events, he gave an incorrect impression with regard to both emphasis and timing. The unreliability of the memories of elderly men is a matter of common observation, but his forgetfulness of his reply to the group of Hartford Republicans was distinctly convenient. He can be readily excused for not mentioning the Walker affair, which he and the other principals had agreed to relegate to oblivion, but he is not known to have objected to the assumption of common-law jurisdiction by the

[45] May 25, 1809 (*Annals*, 11 Cong., 1 sess., I, 75-89).
[46] *Letter to the President* by HAMPDEN (New Haven, 1808). This account, on which we have already drawn, has been attributed to David Daggett.
[47] TJ to W. C. Nicholas, June 13, 1809 (Ford, IX, 253-255).

federal court in Connecticut until threatened with the resurrection of that old scandal.

Recognizing that he might be in error about details, he referred his friend Nicholas to Gideon Granger for confirmation of the substantial facts. The Congressman reported to the former President, however, that Granger's recollection of the circumstances did not precisely correspond with his, especially as to the time of his interposition.[48] Also, Granger was under an impression that some of the backers of the prosecutions believed that, while the President did not direct the commencement of these, he had no objection to their being carried on. The Postmaster General promised to draft and publish under a pseudonym a statement which, he believed, would satisfy the public and be acceptable in Connecticut. The statement appeared in the *National Intelligencer* a few days later over the name VERITAS.[49] Designed as it was to be satisfactory everywhere, it could not have been expected to set forth the whole truth. Its chronology was vague, but it said that the prosecutions were first reported to Jefferson by the author. It asserted as a fact that he openly disapproved of the prosecutions from the beginning but was reluctant to interfere in judicial matters. This may have been the impression Granger gained from private conversation. He properly avoided giving further publicity to the Walker affair and made no reference to Jefferson's sympathy for his persecuted followers in Connecticut, but otherwise the statement was substantially correct with respect to the President's actions and presumable motives. Some months later, Jefferson thanked the author for "setting the public judgment to rights."[50]

This was not quite his last reference to this confused episode, for he was reminded of it four years later by Granger, who was charged at the time with having been a Burrite and was accused of having sided with the Federalists because of the part he had played in silencing the prosecutions in Connecticut. Our concern here is with only the latter charge, though Jefferson actually devoted more attention to the former in his reply.[51] Stating that he had been useful in a case "peculiarly interesting" to Jefferson's feelings, Granger now asked for a *quid pro quo*. There was a threatening note in his letter: he stated that he had full evidence which he could publish in his own defense, though he would very reluctantly do so. To make such action unnecessary he

[48] W. C. Nicholas to TJ, July 18, 1809 (LC, 33386–33387).
[49] *National Intelligencer*, July 21, 1809.
[50] TJ to Granger, Jan. 24, 1810 (LC, 33653–33654).
[51] Granger to TJ, Feb. 22, 1814 (LC, 35679–35680); TJ to Granger, Mar. 9, 1814 (Ford, IX, 454–458).

asked for a letter from Jefferson which would "forever silence calumny" against him and demonstrate his past usefulness.

The threat was wholly unnecessary as well as improper, for Jefferson, whose loyalty to his friends and followers bordered on the
excessive, could have been expected to support one who, as he believed, had served him and his party well. Painfully aware of the decay
of his memory, he examined his voluminous papers with care this time
and gave, he said, the best account of the facts that he could. Going
through his correspondence with Granger was task enough, for it had
been very extensive. Perhaps we may assume that copies of his two
letters of August, 1807, in which presumably he had mentioned the
Walker affair, were not in his papers; he had probably destroyed them
long before now and had tried to forget them. The reasons for the
dismissal of the prosecutions that he assigned were those that had been
advanced by Granger in the first place: namely, that they were inconsistent with Republican principles. Furthermore, he said, they were
chiefly for charges against himself, and he had made it a rule to notice
nothing of the kind. Such was in fact the case, but his condonation of
them for a time remains to be explained.

Nearly seven years after he intervened, he said that the prosecutions
had to be dismissed as a matter of duty. Making no reference to the
chronology of events, he added this statement: "But I wished it to be
done with all possible respect to the worthy citizens who had advised
them, and in such way as to spare their feelings which had been justly
irritated by the intemperance of their adversaries." This seems to be
the nearest he ever came to an explanation of his conduct, and it shows
him in character as a sympathetic party chieftain who was loath to
intervene in local matters. He was undisposed to discredit loyal local
leaders and to appear to be letting his persecuted followers down. In
the episode as a whole this champion of free speech, who had previously disapproved of federal action against libel, was more inconsistent
than he could bring himself to admit, but his actions are explicable in
human as well as political terms and they should certainly be viewed in
their full setting of vexatious circumstance.

The Dilemmas of Neutrality

[XXII]

The Monroe-Pinkney Treaty
and the Impressment Question

LIKE most Presidents of the United States who have been subjected to the ordeal of a second term, Jefferson did not fare as well in this as in his first; and, as has so often happened, his troubles multiplied in his last two years. The fortunes of an administration cannot be charted with mathematical precision, but, viewed in perspective, his second appears to have reached its apogee before it was half over. The major cause of his declining fortunes is clear: his chief difficulties were owing, directly or indirectly, to the course of foreign affairs. These we have long left in abeyance while carrying the domestic story well beyond them in point of time. We return to them in the midst of the congressional session of 1806–1807, when the President got bad news from James Monroe and William Pinkney, his representatives in England. Since he was apprised, about the same time, of the stalemate of the negotiations for West Florida that he had launched with such difficulty, the foreign affairs of the country had unquestionably taken a turn for the worse.[1] Both in Paris and London Jefferson's hopes were blasted.

Ironically, he could have viewed the domestic scene with genuine satisfaction at just this time. The Federalist opposition in the country as a whole was feeble, and, while dissension in his own party was by no means resolved, the revolt of John Randolph had been contained and his own position as party leader seemed virtually impregnable. The appeals with which his mail was flooded, that he consent to a third term, gave him abundant ground to believe that he had been highly successful as President. One of the many addresses spoke of the "unexampled felicity" with which his "benign administration" had con-

---

[1] On the failure of the mission of Armstrong and Bowdoin, see above, pp. 91–94.

ducted the affairs of the country.[2] To another group it seemed that he had translated the theory of representative government into fact. The unity of the country had been threatened by the Burr conspiracy, but that had been thwarted by the actions of patriotic citizens in Ohio, and he was soon to learn that the adventurer had surrendered to the authorities in Mississippi Territory. The frustrations and vexations incident to Burr's trial came months later. About this time a friend and admirer predicted that many dynasties would pass before the presidential office would again be filled by one who united as he did "attachment to liberty and the capacity to govern."[3] But subsequent events were to cause both to be questioned. Doubts regarding his attachment to liberty were to arise from the proceedings against Burr, his support of James Wilkinson, and the prosecutions for libel in Connecticut — all of which have already been considered in this book. Questions regarding his capacity to govern were to arise chiefly from his conduct of foreign affairs and from the domestic implications and consequences of his foreign policy. He was to meet his most severe test in the field of Anglo-American relations.[4]

Jefferson's original hopes for the negotiations of Monroe and Pinkney with the British now appear to have been much too sanguine; he did not allow sufficiently for the psychology of the British at a time when they were engaged in a death struggle with Napoleon, and he over-valued the Non-Importation Act as a threat. This war was more ruthless than the one in which the same major powers had engaged when he was secretary of state, and no neutral country could expect benevolence or even decent consideration from them. But the accentuation of American grievances could be attributed to the policies of a previous British ministry, and, in view of the friendliness of the present foreign secretary, Charles James Fox, the timing of American actions had seemed good. Actually, the slowness of transportation and communication continued to place the Americans at a great disadvantage in the matter of timing; and if there ever was an opportune moment this was lost. Apart from considerations of domestic sentiment, it might have been wiser to leave matters wholly in Monroe's hands, for the appointment of Pinkney provided the British with an occasion for delay, and in the meantime Fox fell ill. On July 8, 1806, in a letter to Jefferson, Monroe said that, while this was most unfortunate, hopes were entertained of the speedy recovery of the Foreign

[2] Columbia County, N.Y., Republicans to TJ, Dec. 12, 1806 (LC, 28570–28571). For other comments referred to here, see above, pp. 167–170.

[3] W. C. Nicholas to TJ, Jan. 20, 1807 (LC, 28832–28835).

[4] For developments in the spring of 1806, see ch. VII, above.

Secretary. Fox died on the very day this letter was received in Washington more than two months later.[5] Meanwhile, Lord Henry Holland, nephew of Fox, and Baron Auckland (William Eden), president of the Board of Trade, had been appointed British commissioners. Jefferson was doubtful if anything could be expected of the latter, whom he described as "too much wedded to the ancient maritime code and navigation principles of England, too much practiced in the tactics of diplomacy."[6] Auckland was very close to Lord Grenville, whose power in the ministry inevitably increased with the illness and death of Fox. Jefferson, who had not forgotten the part played by Grenville in the negotiation of Jay's treaty, thought it most unfortunate that they would have to deal with him. Actually the President was less than fair to Grenville; and, although Lord Howick, Fox's successor in the Foreign Office, was less friendly than he had been, this short-lived ministry was more conciliatory to the United States than the previous one had been and the next one was to be.

Shortly before Congress convened, Jefferson learned from Monroe and Pinkney that negotiations were proceeding in a friendly spirit and that the Americans had high hopes of attaining the "great objects" entrusted to them.[7] In fact, their letter, which was addressed to Madison, spelled out grave difficulties before arriving at an optimistic conclusion. In Jefferson's papers there is a brief report on the progress of the negotiation, presumably drafted by the clerk of the Department of State, which gives a more favorable impression than does the letter as a whole, and the President probably saw this before examining the official communication in detail.[8] With this report went a request that the effective date of the Non-Importation Act be further postponed so as to afford sufficient time to complete the negotiations. Accordingly, Jefferson sent Congress a recommendation to that effect in a brief but optimistic message. Congress promptly agreed, designating July 1, 1807, as the effective date and authorizing the President to suspend the operations further if he should see fit, although not beyond the second Monday in December next, when Congress would again be in session.[9]

Before the end of the year there was excitement over the entrance into Chesapeake Bay of the *Cambrian*, one of the three British armed vessels that had been ordered away after the episode of the *Leander* six

[5] Monroe to TJ, July 8, 1806; received Sept. 13 (LC, 28017).
[6] TJ to Monroe, Oct. 26, 1806 (Ford, VIII, 477).
[7] Monroe and Pinkney to Madison, Sept. 11, 1806; postscript, Sept. 12 (*A.S.P.F.R.*, III, 133–135).
[8] Nov. 27, 1806 (LC, 28491).
[9] Message of Dec. 3, 1806; action of Dec. 19 (*Annals*, 9 Cong., 2 sess., pp. 16, 1250; message also in Ford, VIII, 496–497).

months earlier. Jefferson drafted a proclamation forbidding all inter-course with her or any other armed British vessel in American waters, but did not need to issue this since the *Cambrian* departed of her own accord.[10] At this stage, affairs on the Spanish-American front were more alarming than on the Anglo-American. Shortly before the con-gressional session began, Jefferson had issued the proclamation in which, without yet naming Burr, he warned against an unlawful expedition against Spanish possessions. He had not then learned that this had been dealt a fatal blow on the Ohio River. Reports of develop-ments in Europe were even more belated. When the President received his guests on New Year's Day, 1807, he had not yet heard of Napo-leon's Berlin decree, issued in November, which had lacked little of paralyzing the negotiations in London between the British and Ameri-can commissioners. More than two months were to pass before he became fully aware of the terms of the treaty that Monroe and Pinkney signed on the last day of the year. By February 1 he learned that the British commissioners had declined to include in this any reference to the impressment of seamen, which they claimed as a right and practiced, they said, as a national necessity. In the hope of prevent-ing a complete breakdown in the negotiations, however, they offered "the most positive assurances" that caution and restraint would be observed, and, on the strength of this written promise, Monroe and Pinkney decided to continue the negotiations.[11]

Whether or not they were wise is still a matter of scholarly dispute, but they had unquestionably departed from the letter of their instruc-tions; and, in the minds of the President and Secretary of State, they had yielded on the most important issue. The immediate occasion for setting up their mission had been the imposition of fresh restrictions on American commerce, but the humiliating British practice of impress-ment was coupled with these by Jefferson from the outset; and effectual relief from it was given first place in their instructions. Madison, speaking in Jefferson's name, described this as a necessary preliminary to the repeal of the Non-Importation Act. A satisfactory provision with respect to the re-export trade was also a necessary preliminary, but impressment was made the matter of first impor-tance.[12] At this point, therefore, it seems desirable to take a closer look at what has been described as "the most corrosive issue" in the entire

---

[10] Proclamation dated Dec. 20, 1806 (Ford, VIII, 499–501). On the *Leander* incident, see above, pp. 115–116.

[11] Monroe and Pinkney to Madison, Nov. 11, 1806, enclosing the British note of Nov. 8 (*A.S.P.F.R.*, III, 137–140).

[12] Madison to Monroe and Pinkney, May 17, 1806 (*ibid.*, 120–121).

IMPRESSMENT OF AN AMERICAN SEAMAN
From a drawing by Stanley M. Arthurs,
reproduced from the frontispiece of A. T. Mahan's
Sea Power in Its Relation to the War of 1812, Volume I (1905)

history of Anglo-American relations, and at the position this administration took with respect to it.[13]

"On the impressment of our seamen our remonstrances have never
been intermitted," said Jefferson in his special message on neutral commerce early in 1806. The memorials that he had received by the dozen
in recent weeks and many of which he communicated to Congress related to the unprecedented seizure of American ships and cargoes. They
bore on rights of property. He was by no means indifferent to these,
but it is significant that he took this occasion to remind the legislators
of long-continued and recently increased infringements on the rights
of men as men. In order to make the attitude of the government clear,
he submitted with this message a long extract from a letter of the
Secretary of State to James Monroe in England. Written a couple of
years earlier, this was an exposition of the subject of impressment from
the American point of view, and along with the official instructions to
Monroe and Pinkney, which argued to the same effect, it constituted
an authoritative statement of the position to which the administration
adhered.[14]

This adherence was too rigid, in the opinion of certain later
commentators and some of the President's contemporaries, but not in
that of ex-President John Adams, who several years later said that "in
his zeal for the liberty of American seamen" Jefferson had fallen
behind neither of his predecessors. Adams might have added that
Jefferson faced this problem in more acute form than he and George
Washington did, but no doubt he believed that he had paid his successor compliment enough. Speaking of the position of his own
administration on the British impressment of seamen, he said: "The
practice was asserted to be not only incompatible with every principle
of justice and every feeling of humanity, but wholly irreconcilable
with all thoughts of a continuance of peace and friendship between the
two nations."[15] This unequivocal statement may be set alongside the
one in Madison's instructions to Monroe and Pinkney that an effectual
remedy for the practice of impressment was indispensable.

There was no need for John Yankee to describe the horrors and
indignities of a practice which Americans, and especially seagoing
New Englanders, had become increasingly aware of, but his son John

[13] S. F. Bemis, *Diplomatic History of the U.S.* (1950), p. 144.
[14] Message of Jan. 17, 1806, with extract from Madison's letter of Jan. 6, 1804
(*A.S.P.F.R.*, II, 727, 730–734).
[15] Jan. 9, 1809. In "The Inadmissible Principles of the King of England's Proclamation of October 16, 1807, Considered" (*Works*, IX, 327).

Quincy thought it desirable to do so a score of years later, when the memory of them had dimmed. His description of impressment is more vivid than anything in the disquisitions of Madison, and it leaves no room to doubt the inhumanity of the practice:

> This authorized system of kidnapping upon the ocean was prac-
> tised under the odious pretence of a *right* in the King of Great
> Britain to force his own subjects into his naval service in time of
> war. To the execution of this law no judge, no jury, no writ of
> *habeas corpus,* affords to the British seaman the protection of
> liberty or of life. Its execution is on the desert of the ocean; its
> executors armed men, — every lieutenant or midshipman in the
> navy, under no control but his will, under no responsibility but
> his discretion, interested to seize the men whose service he wants
> in his own ship, and sure of impunity for the outrage, even if the
> man should ultimately be discharged and restored to his liberty.
> The *pretence* was the right of the king to take his own subjects
> only; the practice was to presume every man a British subject who
> was wanted. The burden of proof that he was not a British sub-
> ject was put upon the seaman himself; and a native American
> could not embark upon the ocean, without an authenticated docu-
> ment certifying his name, his age, his stature, and describing his
> eyes and nose and mouth and chin, the color of his hair and com-
> plexion, and the marks and scars about his person, — like the ad-
> vertisement for a runaway negro. Whenever an American mer-
> chant ship met a British armed vessel at sea, she was visited by a
> midshipman or lieutenant from the man-of-war, at whose com-
> mand her whole crew was summoned upon her deck; and there
> every man of them passed in review before this often beardless
> boy, who compared their persons with their protections [certifi-
> cates], and finished by taking or leaving the man, just as his
> temper or fancy decided his choice.[16]

John Quincy Adams, who had been a transatlantic voyager before he became a senator from Massachusetts, spoke of ills such as he had seen with his own eyes as a passenger on a merchant vessel. James Madison, who had never been on the high seas, tended to bookishness in his discussions of impressment; he made frequent and extended reference to the law of nations and tenor of treaties — in which he found no sanction for British claims. Irrespective of theory, he re-garded their practice as "peculiarly indefensible" when tested by

[16] Dec. 30, 1828, in his "Reply to the Letter of Massachusetts Federalists" (Henry Adams, *Documents Relating to New England Federalism* [1877], pp. 178–179).

reason and justice, because it deprived an individual seaman of his dearest rights. Denying him any appeal or trial, it left his destiny to the arbitrary will of an officer. It was an offense against persons such as was not committed against property, for, as Madison pointed out, even the least considerable seizure of property on the seas was subject to later trial before a regular tribunal. In setting human rights above those of property the Secretary of State reflected unmistakably the spirit of the President in whose name he spoke. A major reason for Jefferson's persistent protest against impressment was his revulsion against its cruelty and injustice. This was not the only reason. National pride was also at stake, and the issue of sovereignty was crucial. In the view of the administration, the sovereignty of the Republic extended to all the ships that flew its flag on the high seas, and that emblem provided sufficient legal protection to their crews. Disregard of the flag constituted an affront and a humiliation.

Officers of the Royal Navy were contemptuous of such claims, and officials in England would not concede them in theory for the sufficient reason that they did not have to.[17] They brushed aside arguments from books, refusing to concede the illegality of a practice the British had engaged in from the time of Queen Anne, and knowing that the "law of nations" of which Madison made so much was in fact unenforceable. They did not question the King's *right* to force his subjects into his naval service in time of war (which John Quincy Adams described as odious); and, irrespective of the means employed, they regarded impressment as an absolute necessity if the navy was to be manned. Conditions in it were bad on any reckoning, and, with the great expansion of the American merchant marine in recent years, the Mistress of the Seas was faced with a grave problem of desertion. Life on American ships, while scarcely blissful, was perceptibly less hellish and the pay was better. No one could deny that, in the search for deserters, native Americans might be seized as Britishers; mistakes were easy because of the similarity in looks and language — which may be safely presumed to have been greater at that time than it was later. Furthermore, the British did not recognize the validity of American naturalization, which had been liberalized in Jefferson's administration, and they had good ground for claiming that certificates of American citizenship could be obtained with ridiculous ease. Wittingly or unwittingly, Madison minimized the number of British deserters in

[17] There are illuminating discussions of the British attitude toward impressment in A. L. Burt, *The United States, Great Britain, and British North America* (1961 edn.), especially pp. 211–228; and Bradford Perkins, *Prologue to War* (1963), pp. 84–95, referred to hereafter as Perkins.

American service and magnified the number of impressed Americans, but it now appears that in this exchange his country was actually the gainer.[18]

For all these reasons it is now easy to see why the British authorities were undisposed to make any concessions which might weaken their naval power while their country was engaged in what they properly regarded as a death struggle with Napoleon. And in retrospect it seems that the problem of impressment was virtually insoluble as long as the struggle lasted. By the same token Jefferson and his government may seem to have been unrealistic in making a settlement of this problem a *sine qua non* at this time. No doubt he believed that his feeling about this "authorized system of kidnapping on the ocean" was or should have been shared by reasonable and humane men everywhere. The practice of impressment, like the slave trade, should have been a burden on the conscience of mankind, and it could have been properly condemned *in toto* on moral grounds. But, viewing the existing international situation, one is impelled to ask if Jefferson was sufficiently aware that diplomacy, like domestic politics, is the art of the possible.

Allowance must be made for the fact that he could not feel the pulse of the Atlantic world as he could that of his own country. Being insufficiently informed of opinion elsewhere, this inveterate optimist and passionate patriot was disposed to believe it to be what he wanted it to be. But misjudgment was to be found in official circles on both sides of the Atlantic, and if the President of the United States cherished exaggerated expectations, these did not extend to the entire cessation of impressment. The specific modifications in practice that the administration insisted on were limited to merchant vessels on the high seas, and the principle to be recognized was that, on the desert of the ocean, American sovereignty accompanied its flag. In his elaborate letters of instruction Madison no more challenged British rights in their own territorial waters than he surrendered American rights in theirs. He strongly contested Great Britain's authority over the "narrow seas" (including the Channel and other waters surrounding the British Isles), insistence on which had wrecked the nearly successful negotiations of Rufus King early in Jefferson's first term.[19] But, if necessary, he was willing to concede that British jurisdiction extended four leagues, or roughly twelve miles, from their shore line. In view of the fact that most American ships visited British harbors at one time or another, the cessation of impressment on the high seas might not have

---

[18] Perkins (pp. 90-93) gives various estimates.
[19] In 1803. The episode is well described by Perkins in *First Rapprochement* (1955), pp. 154-157. It was referred to in Madison's instructions.

reduced the total greatly in the long run. Specifically, the American government sought only a partial solution of this problem and it recognized that some sort of action should be taken on its own part against the desertion of British seamen.

Conceivably the British could have yielded impressment on the high seas without grave risk, but they regarded this as an opening wedge, no doubt, and were disposed to yield no legal claim whatsoever. Their commissioners appeared friendly during the negotiations, but when the cards were down their government forbade the making of any reference to impressment in the treaty.[20] Even so, they claimed a desire to remove, in practice, all causes of American dissatisfaction. In a formal note, signed by the commissioners and sanctioned by the Cabinet, Monroe and Pinkney were assured that instructions had been given and would be repeated and enforced "for the observance of the greatest caution in the impressing of British seamen"; that the "strictest care" would be taken to safeguard citizens of the United States, and that "immediate and prompt redress" would be afforded when any injury was represented.

In the long letter to their government in which they enclosed this communication, the American commissioners described the cruel dilemma with which they were faced.[21] If they had explicitly followed the instructions they had, they would have broken off negotiations at this point, although, as they believed, they could reasonably expect to make satisfactory arrangements about matters of trade. In deciding to proceed on their own responsibility to the "other objects of negotiation," they reversed the order of priorities that had been laid down, but they were persuaded that the British note placed impressment on almost as good a footing as it would have been by treaty. They believed it to be as obligatory on the British government as a treaty, and that it expressed all the American desires "except the relinquishment of the principle." In their expressed opinion the British, while declining to give up or modify time-honored claims that were strongly supported by national feeling, had granted the substance of what the United States government was seeking.

The sincerity and patriotism of the American commissioners are open to no doubt, and their predicament evokes much sympathy, but it is still a question whether they were more realistic than gullible. Things looked very different on the two sides of the Atlantic. Pinkney

[20] The story of the negotiations in England is told more fully in Harry Ammon's *James Monroe*, ch. XIV, and Perkins's *Prologue*, ch. IV.

[21] Monroe and Pinkney to Madison, Nov. 11, 1806, enclosing the note from the British commissioners dated Nov. 8 (*A.S.P.F.R.*, III, 137–140).

had not conferred in person with Madison or Jefferson before he sailed, and in his previous participation in the Anglo-American controversy he had been concerned with matters of commerce. Monroe had been more than three years abroad, and during recent months in England he had seen more evidence of the seizure of American vessels than of the impressment of American seamen. The fact that his personal relations with his own government were clouded may possibly have affected his judgment, but we have no sure evidence that it did. There seems little doubt that he and Pinkney were motivated by a growing fear of Napoleon, and that they were more deeply concerned for a rapprochement with Great Britain than were Jefferson and Madison, who were striving to keep their country unentangled. At all events, the envoys greatly underestimated the convictions and emotions of their distant superiors about impressment.

According to the President, who was the more disturbed by their communication the more he considered it, they also greatly misjudged the temper of the American people, who, in his opinion, would rather go without a treaty than with one that did not settle the question of impressment. That was also the opinion of David M. Erskine, the young British minister who had replaced Anthony Merry in the autumn. Writing the Foreign Secretary after an interview with Madison, he said: "I think it my duty to observe to your lordship that all the parties in this country take a warm interest on the point of the non-impressment of sailors (claimed as British) out of American ships on the high seas, and . . . I am persuaded that no cordiality can be expected from this country whilst it is deemed necessary by His Majesty to enforce that right."[22]

Jefferson wondered if, in this dilemma, he should not consult the Senate; but, at a meeting of the Cabinet that he promptly called, it was decided not to do so, since it was also unanimously decided to continue on the course already charted and announced.[23] For a treaty not securing the country against impressment they would not give up the principle of the Non-Importation Act, and thus yield "the only peaceful instrument" (economic coercion) for gaining American rights of all sorts. Furthermore, if they should do this they would weaken the position of the United States vis-à-vis Napoleon. This may be regarded

[22] Erskine to Howick, Feb. 2, 1807 (FO, 5:52 [2], pp. 111–114). According to Perkins (p. 104), Erskine "did not challenge American positions." It was to his credit as a reporter, however, that he did not over-emphasize Federalist opinion as Merry had done.

[23] TJ to Madison, Feb. 1, 1807 (L. & B., XI, 146; memo. of Cabinet meeting of Feb. 2 (Ford, I, 322–323).

as another way of saying that complete American independence and neutrality must be maintained. According to Jefferson's own record, he and his advisers believed that the moment was favorable for taking a stand, that the British would probably yield the right of impressment in this hour of need, except in their own ports. They had come close to doing that in their earlier negotiations with Rufus King, and even in the present negotiations, before the British commissioners referred the matter to higher authority. He was over-estimating their desire to conciliate the United States and thus strengthen their position against Napoleon. He stood on firmer ground when he said that a bad treaty, far from restoring friendship, would result in constant irritation. Madison thought that something more might be done to prevent the desertion of British seamen — that the right to employ them in American vessels might be renounced — but otherwise there seems to have been no divergence of opinion at this meeting.

Writing Monroe and Pinkney promptly thereafter, Madison stated that if they had concluded a treaty omitting all reference to the vital question of impressment — as in fact they already had — the President could not accept it, and they must so inform the British commissioners.[24] They were not asked to terminate their negotiations, and the position of the government as described in these further instructions was in certain respects less rigid than it had been hitherto. The President was unwilling to accept a *formal* agreement covering the other points of negotiation while the major point of impressment was left to an *informal* agreement. However, he would accept an informal understanding, covering *all* points, if satisfactory in substance. He would "earnestly, and probably successfully," recommend that the Non-Importation Act be inoperative as long as such an agreement, especially the parts relating to neutral trade and impressment, should be respected in practice by the British. Conceivably this sort of approach, with its emphasis on practice rather than theory and its assumption of good will, might have appealed to the pragmatic Britishers if it had been suggested to them when the negotiations reached an impasse in the previous autumn. But, as Madison's incisive comments showed, a different agreement about impressment was required than the informal one that Monroe and Pinkney had acceded to. He left no doubt that the administration regarded as virtually meaningless the remedy the British had proposed. Naval officers could not be trusted in this business, and there could be no adequate remedy for the ills incident to impressment until they were deprived of all discretionary authority

[24] Madison to Monroe and Pinkney, Feb. 3, 1807 (*A.S.P.F.R.*, III, 153–156), replying to their letter of Nov. 11, 1806.

with respect to it. That Americans needed "peremptory security against the propensities of British commanders" could not be doubted, and American engagement to facilitate the return of deserters was in Madison's eyes adequate as a *quid pro quo*. He was wholly right in saying that to yield to British claims would be to deny the sovereignty of the United States under its flag; and he voiced abundant American experience when he said that if the British expected to meet this problem by instructions, these would have to be very different from those of the past.

Some three weeks after Jefferson got the message about impressment that he and Madison found so unsatisfactory they received a brief but cheerful letter from Monroe and Pinkney. Written a couple of days after Christmas, this reported that the commissioners were about to conclude a treaty on "all the points" which had been the object of their negotiation, and on terms which they trusted their government would approve. In view of recent developments in London, it is hard to justify this tone of unqualified optimism; but, following Napoleon's Berlin decree, negotiations nearly broke down, and apparently their satisfaction in having worked out a settlement under these difficulties blinded them to imperfections in it which were considerably greater than they had anticipated. A couple of weeks before the end of the session, Jefferson sent this letter without comment to Congress.[25] Perhaps he concluded that he had to send the legislators something to curb their impatience, but by so doing he could not have failed to arouse false hopes. He had been wise in withholding the earlier letter, for that would have been prematurely disquieting, but some intimation of possible disappointment would have been in order. This would have taken some of the onus off the commissioners when disappointment was afterwards revealed, and perhaps would have tended to silence those who claimed that Monroe was being denigrated to the advantage of Madison. But nothing appears to have been done to cushion the shock before the treaty came.

It reached the President in the form of a copy, which Erskine speeded to the Secretary of State hours before the adjournment of Congress. The official document, which Monroe and Pinkney transmitted by a special messenger, along with a long letter of explanation, did not arrive until twelve days later. The caution of the envoys worked to their disadvantage. This was the time that Thomas Mann Randolph fell ill after leaving the President's House in a mood of

[25] Monroe and Pinkney to Madison, Dec. 27, 1806; sent to Congress, Feb. 19, 1807 (*A.S.P.F.R.*, III, 141; *Annals*, 9 Cong., 2 sess., p. 925).

jealousy and the perturbed President fell ill in turn.[26] Because of his indisposition, he was not at the Capitol in the last hours of the session to sign bills, according to his custom, and a joint committee brought him a batch of them.[27] Report of the receipt of a copy of the treaty by Erskine having reached the Senate, certain members of that body had asked that inquiry be made whether they would be shortly called to consider it; if so, some of them would remain in Washington. "Certainly not," was Jefferson's reply as recorded by Senator John Quincy Adams, one of the committeemen. The President may not have read the treaty with care as yet, but if he did not know that it omitted all reference to impressment, Madison could have told him so.

Attached to it was a note signed by the two British commissioners which attracted immediate attention. In this, after expostulating against Napoleon's Berlin decree, which declared Great Britain blockaded and forbade the landing of British products in his ports, they voiced certain reservations in behalf of their King. He would not agree to ratify the treaty or be precluded by its terms from adopting counteracting measures unless assured that the government of the United States would not submit to the French "innovations."[28] That is, American resistance to the enforcement of Napoleon's edict was required. This would involve the United States in the war on the side of the British, said the President. Since the explanatory letter from Monroe and Pinkney had not yet arrived, he did not know that only with great difficulty had they prevented the inclusion of a similar statement in the treaty itself, and that they did not sanction the one the British commissioners made. He saw no way to account for their having signed such a treaty with such a proviso except to suppose that, sharing the panic created by Napoleon's decree, they had concluded that the United States could not avoid involvement in the war and that the wise course was to make common cause with the British. (He was not informed of the full circumstances, but his supposition was not far from true.) To his mind this note, along with the absence from the treaty of any reference to impressment, provided a sufficient reason for his not troubling the Senate. Elsewhere he said that acceptance of the treaty, subject to this British qualification, would mean that they would not be bound by its terms, while the United States would be.

Madison had promptly informed Erskine that the note in itself was

[26] See above, pp. 141–143.
[27] These events are described in an entry of Mar. 3, 1807, in J. Q. Adams's *Memoirs*, I, 465–466; and in Erskine's letter of Mar. 6, 1807, to Howick (FO, 5:52 [2], pp. 127–135).
[28] The note is in *A.S.P.F.R.*, III, 151–152, following the text of the treaty.

sufficient ground for rejection of the treaty, even if every article in that document had been satisfactory. Because of Jefferson's illness, the British Minister did not see him until a couple of days later. Erskine then heard the same two objections. The President referred to impressment first, but these further comments of his were reported to the Foreign Secretary in London:

> He said that the Note delivered by Lords Holland and Auckland to their Commissioners previous to the Signature of the Treaty would render it impossible for the most popular Administration to make the People satisfied with the Ratification of any Treaty so explained, and that the influence of Washington himself would not have been sufficient to restrain the Impatience of the People of the United States at the Idea of being called upon for Assurance of what they would do in the Event of a grave Insult and Injury being offered to their Country by any Power.[29]

Jefferson believed that British contemptuousness of American sovereignty was intolerable to his countrymen, as it was to him. Erskine could not have been expected to put it just that way, but he wrote his home office a week later: "I think the public opinion will support the President in his objections to the Treaty."[30]

A similar opinion was strongly expressed by a Republican senator who wrote Monroe while Jefferson and Madison were awaiting the arrival of an official communication from the two American commissioners. William Branch Giles, who was not a member of the congressional committee that waited on the President on March 3 but was well informed about the meeting, gave a report of it which was presumably the first that Monroe received.[31] "The obvious tendency of the explanatory note, and the silence respecting seamen, have excited universal disappointment and astonishment," said the Senator. While expressing high confidence in the commissioners, he implied that they had not acted in accord with dominant American opinion. He described this as follows: "The only party here in favor of making a common cause with G.B. or taking any part whatever in the war, until absolutely forced to it, is the mere Anglican party, accompanied by a few wildly eccentric men, who have no influence whatever, and are considered generally as men of disordered imaginations. They are

[29] Erskine to Howick, Mar. 6, 1807 (FO, 5:52 [2], pp. 127–135, Dispatch No. 8).
[30] Erskine to Howick, Mar. 10, 1807 (FO, 5:52 [2], pp. 135–137).
[31] Giles to Monroe, Mar. 4, 1807 (D. R. Anderson, *William Branch Giles*, p. 108).

totally destitute of influence, and destroy every person or object they endeavor to support. It is feared that some of the wild effusions of some of these men, have been mistaken by our commissioners for indications of the public sentiment." His reference was obviously to John Randolph and his little band. Jefferson himself, while well aware of that erratic statesman's intense hostility to Madison, never went so far as to suggest that he influenced Monroe's official conduct.

Before the President heard from the American commissioners, he received evidence that the threat in the British note was not an empty one. Erskine announced to Madison that his government, in retaliation against Napoleon's Berlin decree, had issued an order prohibiting commerce between his ports. This action imperiled a major part of American commerce. Respecting it the government took the position that the extent to which the French decree would be enforced was uncertain, and that presumptively it would not affect the commerce of the United States in violation of its treaty with France. (The French did not begin to enforce it against American shipping until the following September.) According to the announcement, the British order was to become effective at once. Thus the peril to American commerce from the British was immediate, while that from the French was or seemed remote.[32] This reminder of the indifference of the British government to neutral rights and interests and of their ruthless exercise of naval power cast fresh doubt on the expressions of good will that Monroe and Pinkney reported.

Jefferson believed that his government had manifested its good will by his proclamation postponing the effective date of the Non-Importation Act. He said in private that he was holding the treaty in suspense pending further negotiation, and that his decision whether or not to call the Senate was dependent on the outcome of these. Reiterating that the absence of reference to impressment and the attached British note were sufficient in themselves to make the treaty unacceptable, he avoided comment on its other terms. Some persons outside the administration were aware of certain of its commercial provisions, but he did not lay it before Congress until another year and then only for purposes of information. Perhaps he himself was delayed in examining it closely by the periodic headache which, for several weeks, allowed him only an hour or two for work each day, but before this spell of physical illness was over he perceived in the treaty other grounds for dissatisfaction besides those already mentioned. Writing Monroe, he

[32] Erskine to Madison, Mar. 12, 1807; Madison to Erskine, Mar. 20, 29 (*A.S.P.F.R.*, III, 158–159); Armstrong to Madison, Dec. 24, 1806, with enclosures (*Annals*, 9 Cong., 2 sess., pp. 925–928).

said that it would be considered a "hard treaty" when its terms became known.[33] To him the British appeared "to have screwed every article as far as it would bear, to have taken everything, and yielded nothing." In his opinion the evil outweighed the good except in the article dealing with the re-export trade, which modified the rigid requirements of a broken voyage as stated in the *Essex* case and promised to be advantageous to the American carrying trade.[34] But that article was limited to the duration of the present hostilities, and a stipulation had been inserted that bound the United States to pass no non-importation or non-exportation laws for a period of ten years. Since a similar provision in Jay's treaty had aroused violent protests from Republicans, Jefferson must have been amazed that Monroe should have acceded to the surrender of what he himself regarded as the country's most effective peaceful weapon.

Viewed in retrospect from the American angle, the treaty does appear to have been a hard one. It was marked by fewer gains in the realm of trade than the American commissioners expected when they retreated from their position on impressment. It can be defended only on the grounds that they could have procured no better under increasingly difficult circumstances, and that the United States should have begun to make common cause with Great Britain at this point. Jefferson's rejection of the document his representatives signed is wholly understandable; indeed, that he should have accepted it in this form is unthinkable. There were entirely too many things wrong with it. Much more surprising is the hope he continued to express that a satisfactory understanding could be reached by negotiation. Allowance must always be made for his congenital optimism, but he was still counting on his ability to play one contending power against the other, and he believed that, in their hour of need, the British could not afford to alienate the United States.

The faults of the treaty, including those relating to commerce, were promptly exposed at a Cabinet meeting, and were elaborated upon by Madison in a lengthy letter of instruction he dispatched two months later.[35] The delay in dispatching this was owing in part to the diffi-

[33] TJ to Monroe, Mar. 21, 1807 (Ford, IX, 35–37). His letters of Mar. 24 to R. R. Livingston, and of Mar. 25 to Levi Lincoln (*ibid.*, IX, 37–38n.) show how he presented the case at home.
[34] Article 11. Perkins (pp. 136–139 and elsewhere in ch. IV) points out the disadvantages of the treaty even in the realm of trade, but thinks nonetheless that Monroe and Pinkney did well.
[35] Memo. of Cabinet meeting of Mar. 17, 1807 (Ford, I, 323–324); Madison to Monroe and Pinkney, May 20, 1807 (*A.S.P.F.R.*, III, 166–173). Madison wrote Monroe privately Mar. 20, expressing sympathy along with dissatisfaction and saying he would send fresh instructions (MP, 31:118).

JEFFERSON THE PRESIDENT: SECOND TERM

culty of conveyance, but much time must have been required to compose such a disquisition. Madison's paper attests his great ability as a dialectician but it asked for more than he should have expected. We concern ourselves here with its bearing on the crucial and continuing problem of impressment. On the principle at issue the administration stood fast. The President could not recognize "even constructively" the one for which the British contended. But he and his advisers were well aware of the serious practical problem of British deserters, and in seeking the relinquishment of impressment on the high seas were disposed to offer a *quid pro quo*.

At a meeting a month after the adjournment of Congress and shortly before Jefferson, recuperating from his illness, set out for a month's visit home, the Cabinet agreed to a renewed proposal of Madison's. This was that they should offer not to employ any of Britain's seamen in return for her agreement not to make impressments from American ships on the high seas.[36] On inquiring into the number of British seamen actually serving on American vessels, however, Gallatin found that this was considerably greater than they had supposed. The eminently practical Secretary of the Treasury concluded that an engagement to employ *no* British seamen would injure American navigation far more than any restrictions that were likely to be laid on American commerce. His judgment was that the economic sacrifice was too great for the object.[37] Faced with these disturbing figures, Madison modified his proposal so as to apply to British sailors who had not been in American employ as long as two years. Estimating that, even in this form, it might deprive the United States of five thousand seamen, Gallatin reported to Jefferson that he was agreeable to it nonetheless, if thereby they could get rid of impressment and gain some reasonable modifications in certain commercial articles.[38] Accordingly, in his instructions to Monroe and Pinkney, Madison proposed an agreement between the two countries, to be effective when either of them was at war, that neither would employ any citizen or subject of the other who had been for at least two years continuously and voluntarily engaged in its service or been within its jurisdiction. This proposal was deliberately drawn so as to exclude naturalized Americans, and the British might have been expected to question the validity of the citizenship of many of them. Other difficulties of enforcement could easily have been anticipated, but this proposal reflected a genuine recognition of the British as well as the American dilemma. Its force

---

[36] Memo. of meeting of Apr. 3, 1807 (Ford, I, 324).
[37] Gallatin to TJ, Apr. 13, 1807 (*Writings*, I, 332–333).
[38] Gallatin to TJ, Apr. 16, 1807 (*ibid.*, I, 335–336).

was weakened by its enmeshment in over-elaborate instructions which, viewed as a whole, could have been readily regarded as intransigent. Furthermore, a month before Madison dispatched them, a political change of which the American government was yet uninformed occurred in England. The Portland ministry assumed authority. The most influential member of this, Stephen Perceval, regarding Jefferson's government as pro-French, was more disposed to tighten than to relax British policy with respect to both commerce and impressment. And, at the very beginning of the summer, British naval officers, exercising naked power, brought Anglo-American relations almost to the breaking point.

The inaction of the President with respect to the treaty during the spring of 1807 occasioned some unfavorable comments by Federalists and dissident Republicans, but Jefferson does not appear to have said very much about them while he was ill in Washington and recuperating at Monticello. He had little difficulty in brushing off complaints about his failure to call the Senate, being entirely convinced that there would have been no point whatever in his doing so and being confident that public sentiment would support him in his basic objection to the treaty.[39] He was more troubled by the allegation that the administration was belittling the work of Monroe in the interest of Madison's nomination for the presidency, and in writing the former he went to more pains to avow his own neutrality in an infra-party contest he deplored than to salve Monroe's wounds as a diplomat. He did not realize how badly hurt this long-time friend was by what appeared to be the summary rejection of his work. Jefferson did not allow sufficiently for Monroe's sensitivity and not until another year was their old understanding restored.[40] In his limited communication with the distant envoy after the receipt of the treaty, Jefferson showed less than his customary perceptiveness and finesse; and Madison, to whom matters were largely left during the next few weeks, while certainly not unsympathetic in his private letters to Monroe, sounded didactic in his formal instructions.[41]

[39] A good letter bearing on these points that found its way into Madison's papers (MP, 32:110) was written by Jacob Crowninshield, presumably to Dearborn (1807).

[40] In his letter of Apr. 30, 1807, to Giles (S.M.H., V, 4–5), Monroe admitted his surprise and disappointment at the reception of the treaty, and his pain increased as he brooded over his relations with the administration since his return from Spain. The treatment of his mood in the last pages of ch. XIV of Ammon's *Monroe* is sympathetic but judicious.

[41] The private letters I have in mind are TJ's of Mar. 21, 1807 (Ford, IX, 35–37), and Madison's of Mar. 20 and May 25 (MP, 31:118; 32:42).

The President and his Secretary of State might have gone to greater pains to guard the reputation as well as to spare the feelings of their representative and friend in England. In his remarks to the congressional committee on March 3, Jefferson undoubtedly gave the impression that fault lay with the commissioners rather than with the administration, and he was not reported to have manifested any appreciation of their difficulties. At the time he was only partially informed of these, and he was painfully aware that the commissioners had violated their instructions. But, while he did not extenuate the actions of Monroe, he did not recall him; instead, he showed his confidence in him by continuing him as a negotiator. Though he undoubtedly wanted to keep the administration free of blame for what he regarded as a bad treaty and expected to be an unpopular one, he reflected in no way on the honesty and patriotism of the commissioners.

John Randolph would have had Monroe believe that there was a deliberate attempt and continued campaign on the part of the administration to injure his public standing in behalf of Madison's candidacy for the presidency.[42] "Hypocrisy and treachery have reached their acme amongst us," he said with characteristic extremism. He named certain unshaken friends of Monroe, however, among whom was Joseph H. Nicholson of Maryland. As it happened, Monroe had recently received a letter from Randolph's former congressional lieutenant. This was essentially factual, and, while showing an appreciation of Monroe's difficulties in England, it suggested no sinister plot against him at home.[43] Nicholson had this to say about public sentiment:

The President's Popularity is unbounded, and his will is that of the nation. His approbation seems to be the Criterion by which the correctness of all public Events is tested. Any treaty therefore which he sanctions will be approved of by a very large Proportion of the People.

In view, however, of political events that had already occurred in England, and of a naval event which was to occur off the Virginia Capes on the longest day of the year, there was not much prospect of any sort of treaty.

42 Randolph to Monroe, May 30, 1807 (Monroe Papers, LC).
43 J. H. Nicholson to Monroe, Apr. 22, 1807 (ibid.).

[XXIII]

The *Chesapeake* Affair

THE hospitality that the United States as a neutral nation accorded the warships of belligerent powers in this era may be surprising to moderns, but it was compatible with international law and usage as then understood, as it was with humane considerations in a slow-moving age of sail. The British enjoyed the larger share of this hospitality because of their naval preponderance, and by the same token they abused it more. In American ports and harbors their ships of war could be refitted, provisioned, and supplied with water; their sick and wounded could receive such succor as facilities afforded. Local cordiality was hardly to be expected, however, for circumstances were not conducive to good will. Too many guests were on hand or in the offing and their manners were often bad. The British Minister, whose perceptiveness of American sentiment did not always redound to his credit in the Foreign Office, believed that more ill will had been excited by "a few trifling illegal captures" immediately off the coast and by instances of "insulting behavior" by some of His Majesty's naval commanders in the harbors and waters of the United States than by the most rigorous enforcement of British maritime rights elsewhere. Erskine readily recognized that it was "highly grating to the feelings of an independent nation" to observe that their entire coast was "watched as closely as if it was blockaded, and every ship coming in or going out of their harbors examined in sight of the shore by British squadrons stationed within their waters."[1]

Jefferson said publicly that abuses of the laws of hospitality had, with few exceptions, "become habitual to the commanders of the British armed vessels hovering on our coasts and frequenting our

[1] Erskine to Canning, Oct. 5, 1807, No. 25 (FO, 5:52). These comments were made some months after the *Chesapeake* affair but are applicable to an earlier period.

harbors."[2] He had not forgotten that a cannon shot from H.M.S. *Leander* had killed an innocent American; that he had then ordered her, along with her fellow ships, the *Cambrian* and the *Driver*, out of American waters; that the *Cambrian* had briefly but defiantly returned; that, despite American representations, Captain Whitby of the *Leander* had been acquitted. Captain William Love of the sloop of war *Driver* had recently disregarded this order by entering Charleston harbor, where he complained that he had difficulty in getting water and threatened to use force. When the Captain Commandant of Fort Johnson protested his presence, he stated that he expected to sail anyway but delivered a tirade against the proclamation that had been invoked against him. He said that this would have "disgraced the sanguinary pen of Robespierre, or the most miserable and petty state of Barbary."[3]

This singularly insulting outburst, which was duly protested through regular diplomatic channels, could not have failed to exacerbate the feelings of the Americans who were aware of it. The whole country knew about an incident that occurred off the Virginia Capes a few weeks later. This was occasioned by events in Norfolk and nearby waters, where a British squadron was seeking, among other things, to intercept a couple of armed French vessels that had been driven by the weather into Chesapeake Bay and were undergoing repairs.[4] While lying at anchor in Hampton Roads or Lynnhaven Bay they were faced not only with the necessity of procuring water and fresh provisions but also with the problem of desertion, which was accentuated by the propinquity of the American shore. To tough-minded British commanders the reception of runaways was an extremely offensive form of hospitality, but restive seamen daringly sought to avail themselves of it as they had opportunity. That these rough fellows could have been welcomed by the citizenry as residents need not be supposed, but they had their uses as seamen. Some of them — the number is disputed — enlisted for service on the American frigate *Chesapeake*, then being outfitted at Norfolk for a voyage to the Mediterranean, where vigilance was still required against the Barbary pirates.

[2] In his proclamation of July 2, 1807, following the attack on the *Chesapeake* (Ford, IX, 93).
[3] Capt. Love to Capt. Commandant Michael Kalteisen, May 3, 1807 (*A.S.P.F.R.*, III, 8).
[4] The size of the British squadron varied. It consisted of two or three seventy-fours and a number of smaller vessels. The chief primary sources for the *Leopard-Chesapeake* affair and its preliminaries are the documents in *A.S.P.F.R.*, III, 6–23, and the dispatches of Erskine, to which specific reference is made at various places hereafter.

As we have seen, Jefferson's administration was not oblivious of the problem of desertion. Madison in particular was disturbed by the presence of British seamen in the American merchant marine; and in his instructions to Monroe and Pinkney after the rejection of their treaty he presented a definite plan to reduce the number of these. But his instructions were too late to play any part in events in Virginia waters during the late winter and early spring of 1807; and at all times the administration linked the problems of desertion and impressment. Until the British should do something effectual about the one, the United States would do no more than the law required about the other. And the Secretary of State made it clear to Erskine early in the year that, in the absence of specific treaty stipulations, the law required nothing.[5] The case in question was one of desertion from a merchant ship, but if Erskine had any doubts he soon learned that the United States government recognized no obligation to return deserters from any sort of British vessel.[6]

It was in connection with deserters from the British navy that trouble arose in Norfolk. In February a little group of seamen escaped from H.M.S. *Melampus*, then anchored in Hampton Roads. At the time there was an entertainment on board and all the ship's boats were hoisted up except the captain's gig. In this the fleeing sailors reached the shore, although fired upon. After giving three cheers they hastened inland, and three of them enlisted for service in the United States frigate *Chesapeake*. Learning of this, the British Consul at Norfolk asked that the seamen be returned to duty on H.M.S. *Melampus*. He addressed himself to Captain Stephen Decatur, noted for his heroism in the Tripolitan War, who was now commander of the Norfolk Navy Yard. Decatur referred the request to the recruiting officer, who denied it.[7] Toward the end of March, Erskine took up the matter with Madison and, according to his own report, "demanded" the surrender of these seamen. Thereupon the Secretary of State, denying that the demand rested on any legal grounds that the United States recognized, flatly rejected it.[8]

According to Erskine, Madison made no reference at this time to the nationality of the deserters and would have taken this legal position in any case. Within a few days, however, he stated that he believed these particular seamen to be American citizens. At the request of the Secre-

---

[5] Madison to Erskine, Jan. 7, 1807, replying to Erskine's letter of Jan. 4; copies enclosed in Erskine's dispatch No. 4 of Feb. 1 to Howick (FO, 5:52).

[6] See comments of Brant in *Madison*, IV, 378.

[7] John Hamilton to Capt. Decatur, Mar. 6, 1807; A. Sinclair to Hamilton, Mar. 8; Hamilton to Sinclair, Mar. 9 (*A.S.P.F.R.*, III, 16–17).

[8] Erskine to Canning, July 17, 1807, No. 21 (FO, 5:52).

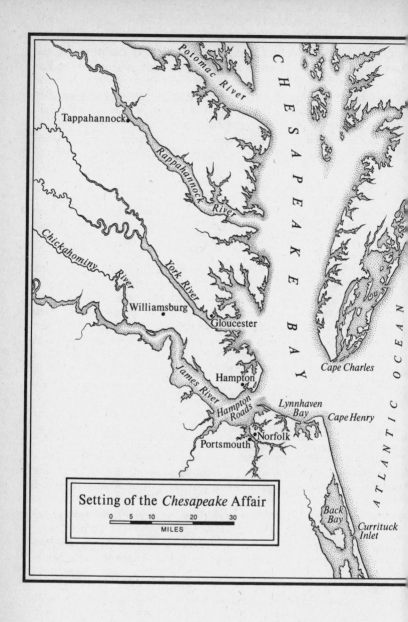

Setting of the *Chesapeake* Affair

0 5 10 20 30
MILES

tary of the Navy, Captain James Barron inquired into the matter and reported that all three of them were natives. Affidavits that were obtained later left no doubt that William Ware and John Strahan (or Strachan) were born in Maryland. Daniel Martin had been brought to Massachusetts, presumably from South America, as a boy of six and had been an indentured servant. Both he and Ware were described as mulattos. Barron reported that all three of these seamen had been impressed. Seemingly the Captain took the position that they did not belong in the category of deserters. From British accounts and records it appears not only that they were unsavory characters, but also that they had enlisted in the Royal Navy. Had Jefferson and Madison known or believed this in the spring of 1807, as they seem to have by the end of the summer, they might have recognized that it weakened their case on the side of psychology, but it would not have affected their legal position. Madison informed Erskine that the law forbade the enlistment of Americans in the service of a belligerent power when their own country was neutral. Accordingly, the enlistment of these men was a legal nullity.

British naval officers may have been unaware of this nice point of law, and there was no doubt whatsoever in their minds that the men were deserters. Nor did they doubt that there were others on the roster of the *Chesapeake*. Certain British writers have called attention to a group of five deserters from H.M. Sloop *Halifax* who were alleged to have enlisted on the *Chesapeake* and to have scoffed at their former officers on the streets of Norfolk.[9] It seems that they enlisted under assumed names and therefore were unidentifiable. The name of one member of this group, Jenkin Ratford, alias John Wilson, an unquestionable Britisher who was said to have been particularly insulting to one of his former officers, will come up again.

Reports of the frustration of the British captains were duly made to the Commander-in-Chief of His Majesty's ships and vessels on the North American Station. Whereupon Vice Admiral George Cranfield Berkeley dispatched from his headquarters at Halifax an order to the respective captains and commanders subject to his authority. Berkeley, who owed his appointment chiefly to political influence, was highhanded toward his civil superiors at home and contemptuous of Americans, believing that they would always yield under the threat of force.[10] He asserted as a fact that *many* British subjects had deserted

[9] Anthony Steel, "More Light on the Chesapeake" (*Mariner's Mirror*, XXXIX [1953], 247). This article is valuable in describing the provocation of the naval officers and their state of mind. It is not so good on the American state of mind, however, and in my opinion is unfair to Madison.
[10] See the comments of Perkins, p. 140.

and entered service on the *Chesapeake* under official American protection. Since they could be recovered in no other way, he directed that any of his captains who should meet the *Chesapeake* at sea should show her captain his order and require that she be searched for deserters. Oddly enough, he did not list the *Melampus* among the British ships from which desertion was alleged. It may also be noted that, in his final sentence, he said that if the Americans should demand it, they might make a similar search of British vessels for their deserters.[11] That a mutual search was offered may have seemed to him a good talking point, but in view of the relatively small number of American deserters this ostensible reciprocity would have been too one-sided to be appealing, and fair play was not to be expected of hard-boiled British officers conscious of their overwhelming strength. However, Captain S. P. Humphreys of H.M.S. *Leopard*, who bore the order from Halifax to the squadron that was availing itself of American hospitality off Norfolk and to whose lot the execution of it fell, is said to have questioned its wisdom. It arrived on June 21, 1807, and on the next day the frigate *Chesapeake* set sail.

About five weeks before this, Captain James Barron, who had gained an excellent reputation in operations in the Mediterranean was appointed commodore of the ships destined for service there. He hoisted his broad pennant when he came aboard on June 21. It afterwards came out that he had been aboard only twice before and had not particularly concerned himself with the state and condition of the ship. He anticipated no trouble on this side of the Atlantic, though well aware that the three alleged deserters from H.M.S. *Melampus* were in the crew. There was a rumor on board that the captain of that ship had threatened to take these men from the *Chesapeake*, but if Barron heard this he did not heed it.

The frigate, with more than 370 men aboard, weighed anchor the morning of June 22 and made sail with a pleasant breeze from the south southwest.[12] About nine o'clock they passed the *Melampus*, anchored with the *Bellona* in Lynnhaven Bay. Soon after midday, according to the logbook, they sighted another ship, which turned out to be H.M.S. *Leopard* of fifty guns. According to the report of a

[11] Berkeley's order of June 1, 1807, can be seen in *A.S.P.F.R.*, III, 12. A copy was enclosed in the letter of Capt. Douglas to Erskine, June 24, 1807 (FO, 5:52 [3], pp. 203–209).
[12] This account of the events of the day is largely based on Barron's letter of June 23, 1807, to the Secretary of the Navy; the logbook of the *Chesapeake;* the report of a committee of inquiry, Oct. 5–Nov. 4, 1807 (*A.S.P.F.R.*, III, 18–23); and Humphreys's letter to Capt. Douglas, June 22. Copy enclosed in Douglas to Erskine, June 24 (FO, 5:52 [3], pp. 203–209).

board of inquiry some months later, the maneuvers of this ship should have aroused Barron's suspicions. She hauled by the wind close around Cape Henry, got the weather gauge when the wind shifted, tacked in shore on the same tack as the *Chesapeake* when the frigate got off her pilot, and gave the appearance of readiness for action. In midafternoon, some three leagues off Cape Henry, the *Chesapeake* was hailed by her; and Barron, learning that her captain desired to send a messenger aboard, caused his ship to heave to. The officer presented to him Berkeley's letter ordering that the ship be searched for British deserters.

In his reply, which was transmitted to Captain Humphreys in about three-quarters of an hour, Barron said that he knew of no such men as were described, that he had particularly instructed the recruiting officer not to enlist British deserters, and that he knew of none on board his ship. He may be adjudged to have been technically correct, for the deserters from the *Melampus* were not British subjects; and others, like those from the *Halifax*, had enlisted under second names. He was entirely correct in declining to permit his crew to be mustered by anybody except their own officers. His peers and superiors afterwards agreed that he gave the proper answer. They severely criticized him, however, for not having recognized sooner the purpose of Humphreys to carry out Berkeley's order by force, and for making tardy and inadequate provision for resistance. Perhaps his tardiness and indecisiveness should be attributed to incredulity. Following the receipt of Barron's letter Captain Humphreys, by his own account, repeatedly hailed and remonstrated with him, but Barron stated that he could not understand what was said, and Humphreys described his answers as evasive. At length, after a warning shot, the *Leopard* fired into the unprepared *Chesapeake*, and in ten or twenty minutes the flags of the frigate were lowered. A British officer then came aboard, demanded and received the muster book, examined the crew, and took off the three deserters from the *Melampus*, along with John Wilson, alias Jenkin Ratford, who was undoubtedly both a deserter and a British subject. Captain Humphreys said there were several other British subjects in the crew but that these did not claim the protection of his flag and did not fall within the limit of his orders.

After the four men had been removed, Barron sent Humphreys a message saying that he considered the *Chesapeake* to be the British Commander's prize and was ready to deliver her. Humphreys declined this offer, but in carrying out orders which, as he believed, permitted no deviation he had in effect committed an act of war. And his immediate return to Lynnhaven Bay, where the squadron was defiantly anchored in Virginia waters, seemed to Americans a striking example

of British insolence. In the operation whereby he had recovered four
deserters, only one of whom was a subject of the King, his guns had
killed three American seamen, seriously wounded eight others, and
slightly wounded ten, including Barron. As the hapless frigate passed
the British squadron in Lynnhaven Bay on her way back to port,
Captain Douglas observed that her hull, masts, and sails had suffered
material injury. And the American officers who reported on the
damage referred to her as "the *late* United States frigate *Chesapeake*."[13]
Altogether this was one of the most humiliating episodes in American naval history. There was uncertainty whether the *Chesapeake* had
fired no shots or one, or was about to fire when the order came to
lower the colors. Although she was no match for the more powerful
Leopard, it afterwards appeared that she was gravely unprepared. But,
regardless of the responsibility for her condition, and regardless of any
provocation of the British by the reception of deserters, it was an
incontestable fact that they had violated American sovereignty, fired
on the flag, and destroyed American life and property. Wars have
often been occasioned by lesser incidents.

The *Chesapeake* made sail shortly after 8 P.M. on that fateful Monday with three and a half feet of water in her hold, and soon after
midday on Tuesday she came to in Hampton Roads. Word of her fate
did not reach Washington until two days later, and did not get to
London until a month after that, but there was immediate excitement
in the maritime district whose inhabitants learned of it first. The fierce
indignation that was aroused by the sight of dead and wounded seamen
being unloaded from the crippled frigate was strikingly manifest at
Hampton, where angry men destroyed two hundred water casks
aboard a schooner that was ready to take them to the thirsty squadron
anchored in Lynnhaven Bay. The loss of these casks infuriated Commodore Douglas and his fellows, as was intended. A few days later it
was rumored that he would invade Hampton to procure water; and, to
prevent a landing, Captain Decatur hastily assembled such gunboats as
were available. No invasion was attempted, but this episode continued
to rankle in the minds of the British officers. In due course Vice
Admiral Berkeley complained of it bitterly to Erskine, urging the
restoration of the casks or their equivalent and the punishment of the
"aggressors."[14]

The punitive action of these incensed inhabitants of Hampton was

[13] *A.S.P.F.R.*, III, 19, italics added.
[14] See especially Erskine to Canning, Dispatch No. 24, Sept. 1, 1807, enclosing a
copy of his letter of Aug. 28 to Berkeley (FO, 5:52). Information about his
actions and those of the British squadron are given in communications of Decatur
to the Secretary of the Navy (Extracts in *A.S.P.F.R.*, III, 20–21).

THE "LEOPARD" AND THE "CHESAPEAKE"

Watercolor drawing of the *Leopard* firing on the *Chesapeake* (at right),
attributed to Charles T. Warren and/or his son Alfred William Warren

strongly commended at a meeting of citizens of Norfolk and Portsmouth on Wednesday, June 24, when a number of resolutions were unanimously adopted. Sending Canning a copy of these about a week later, Erskine said that they had already been adopted in substance in Philadelphia and would be throughout the nation.[15] Similar expressions of violent indignation and patriotic determination to maintain historic rights and liberties were indeed to be quickly voiced in all parts of the country, but besides having a just claim to priority, these resolutions were significant because of the specific actions they approved. Until the national government should be informed of the "unwarranted and unprovoked" attack on the *Chesapeake* and the "inhuman murder" of their fellow citizens, and until the decision of that government should be made known, the citizens unanimously agreed to meet this "awful crisis" with measures of their own. The most important of these was the complete cessation of communication with the British warships and their agents on shore, and the denial to them of all provisions and supplies. Not only did the citizens bind themselves to this suspension of hospitality; they left no doubt of their determination to require it of others, and they extended it to such British warships as should subsequently appear. They also requested the pilots of the district to discontinue their services to the armed visitors. Other resolutions called for defense measures, subscription lists for the relief of the wounded and the families of the slain, the setting up of an executive committee (headed by Brigadier General Thomas Matthews of the Virginia militia), and the publicizing of their resolves. Their words and actions were in the spirit of 1776, which was frequently referred to that summer.

Commodore Douglas and his fellow officers were alleged to have made other threats besides the one against Hampton. One was that they would retake the *Chesapeake* if not supplied with the articles they wanted; another was that if the President should issue a proclamation similar to the one regarding the *Leander* (as in fact he did) they would regard this as a hostile act and immediately begin hostile operations. Captain Decatur reported that, after the attack on the *Chesapeake*, they caused all the vessels passing in or out of the Capes to come to, by firing on them. One of these was a revenue cutter carrying Vice President Clinton and his sick daughter home to New York, though this craft was not fired at thirty-five times as was rumored. They did not detain any vessels, however, and for a few days they remained in

[15] Clipping enclosed in Dispatch No. 18 of July 2, 1807 (FO, 5:52 [3], pp. 190–191).

Lynnhaven Bay. Meanwhile, this "awful crisis" was receiving the concentrated attention of Jefferson and his advisers in Washington.

ii

Commodore Barron's report to the Secretary of the Navy, which
reached the capital on June 25, was borne by Captain Charles Gordon,
who had served under him on the unfortunate *Chesapeake* and was
therefore in position to provide further testimony. So was his companion, Dr. Bullus, who had also been on board, expecting to proceed
to the Mediterranean and assume a consulate. The account of events
which appeared in the *National Intelligencer* the next day and was
widely reprinted was based on the information thus made available.[16]
This account was headed "British Outrage," and the letters and resolutions that reached Jefferson in the next few days left no doubt that the
attack on the frigate was so regarded by all varieties of Americans.
Transmitting resolutions from Richmond, Alexander MacRae, who as
a member of the counsel for the prosecution of Aaron Burr was
acutely aware of the partisanship that had been manifested in his case,
reported that there was no party spirit at the recent meeting in the
Virginia capital: "All appeared zealously to vie who should be fore-
most in manifesting a patriotic indignation at the insult offered, and an
invincible determination to avenge the wrong done to the government
and to the people of our country." Writing of a meeting of citizens in
Baltimore, Senator Samuel Smith said: "There appeared but one opinion — War — in case that satisfaction is not given."[17]

Sentiments of this sort were to be voiced again and again during the
next few weeks. Commenting on the unanimity, Erskine soon wrote
Canning that, although he believed it would be difficult to induce the
country to go to war with Great Britain on commercial grounds, or
even to secure redress for supposed grievances, "the passions of the
people might be worked upon to any extent by an appeal to them on
the ground of national insult."[18] About the same time Jefferson himself said: "They [the British] have often enough, God knows, given us
cause of war before; but it has been on points which would not have
united the nation. But now they have touched a chord which vibrates

[16] TJ commended this to TMR, July 5, 1807, as the truest account that had yet
appeared (LC, 29649). On July 2, Erskine sent a clipping of it to Canning.
[17] Alexander MacRae to TJ, June 27, 1807 (LC, 29600) received July 1; Samuel
Smith to TJ, June 30, 1807 (LC, 29619).
[18] Erskine to Canning, July 17, 1807, No. 20 (FO, 5:52 [3], pp. 198–203). He
expressed the same opinion in other letters.

in every heart."[19] More than once during the summer he expressed the opinion that there had been no such exasperation since the battle of Lexington, and the belief that not even then had there been such unanimity. At no time during his presidency, certainly, had his countrymen been in an equally belligerent mood. Very frequently in the course of tragic human history demagogues and tyrants have exploited such moods to gain power or to aggrandize it. No ulterior motives of this sort can be properly deduced from the words or actions of Jefferson, but as a patriot he was pleased by the ardor displayed in all quarters, and he hoped that it would last until a redress of grievances could be had. Also, as one who had recently protested in private (in his letter to John Norvell) against venomous personal attacks on public men, and whom the defenders of Burr had already made a target of, he could not have failed to enjoy the expressions of loyalty and support he was now receiving by every mail. He should have known, to be sure, that they were addressed to him because he symbolized the nation.

His hopes and fears alternated during these hot summer weeks, and he by no means dismissed the possibility of war. But he did not have the authority to declare it; and, regarding the constitutional separation of powers as seriously as he did, he was disposed to do nothing that would commit Congress in advance. Furthermore, as he and his advisers agreed, international usage and common justice required that an opportunity be given any government to disavow and atone for the actions of its agents. This consideration was inescapable, but American protests and demands would have to be made through diplomatic channels, and, under the best of circumstances, the British response would be long in coming. This delay was actually welcome to the administration, since it would permit American ships and sailors to get home before fighting should begin. But promptitude on the part of the government as well as patience and foresight was imperative at this juncture. Not only had the sovereignty of the United States been flaunted and its flag insulted; there was acute danger of further incidents in the district centering on Norfolk.

Confronted with this dilemma, Jefferson's government acted as quickly as could have been properly expected and with what appeared to be essential wisdom. Some delay was caused by the absence of two of his department heads from Washington. The Secretary of War was on his way to Maine, and the Secretary of the Treasury was in New York with his family. Jefferson summoned them both, by letter, at 5:30 P.M. on the day that Captain Gordon and Dr. Bullus arrived in

19 TJ to Wm. Duane, July 20, 1807 (Ford, IX, 120).

Washington. Dearborn returned promptly from Philadelphia, which was as far as he had gone, but Gallatin, whose counsel was specially important, did not get back to the capital until July 1. Presumably he came immediately to the President's House as requested, and he may have been in time to accept Jefferson's invitation to dinner. At the meeting of the Cabinet next day unanimous approval was given a proclamation ordering British warships out of American waters which Jefferson had drafted with Madison's aid. He and his counselors decided to send to England a small armed vessel, the *Revenge*, with dispatches for Monroe, instructing him to demand satisfaction for the attack on the *Chesapeake*. Specifically, this was to include disavowal of the action and of the right to search a neutral armed vessel, the restoration of the seamen who had been forcibly removed, and the recall of Admiral Berkeley (whose name Jefferson spelled "Barclay.")[20] A court of inquiry on the conduct of Commodore James Barron had already been ordered (though this did not sit until fall), and it was now agreed that all American armed vessels should be recalled from the Mediterranean and await orders at Boston.

There were three other meetings in the next five days. At the first of these the important question of calling Congress was considered. Jefferson wanted the Legislature to meet on October 26, which was several weeks earlier than usual and would be time enough to consider a reply from England. This date was tentatively agreed to, although Robert Smith and Gallatin, who certainly did not see eye to eye in all things, preferred an earlier one. No call was to be issued for some weeks. At the other meetings decisions were reached regarding military and naval matters. These looked to the defense of coastal districts, especially that of Norfolk, but there was also talk of a winter invasion of Canada.[21] The memoranda in which Jefferson recorded these decisions were not open to view then as they are now; and, although he summarized his policies and gave reasons for them in private letters in the next few weeks, he made no comprehensive public statement about the way he proposed to meet this crisis. He did not gratify his excited countrymen by announcing that he would send the *Revenge* to England with demands for satisfaction, nor did he reassure the timorous by declaring publicly his inflexible determination to defend them. He would not endanger diplomacy by publicizing its processes, but he announced an order that was designed to free his country from the

---

[20] Memo. of meeting of July 2, 1807 (*ibid.*, I, 324-325). Actually, the recall of the Admiral was not included in the demands made later.

[21] Memos. of meetings of July 4, 5, 7, 1807 (*ibid.*, I, 325); Gallatin to his wife, July 10 (Henry Adams, *Life of Albert Gallatin* [1879], p. 358).

dangers created by the presence of British warships in American waters. The proclamation issued by him on July 2 was addressed to the most immediate problem.[22]

It was neither inflammatory nor hortatory in tone, but in considerable part it was explanatory. After asserting anew the policy of neutrality, describing the hospitality that had been afforded the warships of belligerents, and stating that it had been habitually abused by British commanders who had gone unpunished, he said: "At length a deed, transcending all we have hitherto seen or suffered, brings the public sensibility to a serious crisis, and our forbearance to a necessary pause." In his terse but graphic account of the attack on the *Chesapeake* he gave official sanction to the interpretation of it as having been wholly unprovoked, and he stressed the enormity of the offense of the British commander in forcibly taking from an American warship seamen who, as he had been apprised, were native Americans. He did not refer to these men as deserters, actual or alleged; nor did he claim that they had previously been impressed by the British. These matters were irrelevant anyway; the essential fact was that the sovereignty of the Republic had been flaunted near its own shores and its hospitality gravely abused in its own waters. He and Madison were disposed to lay the blame for the latest outrage chiefly on Admiral Berkeley, and he referred here to "assurances of the most friendly dispositions on the part of the British government." These were to be reinforced by Erskine in the next few days if they had not been already. Jefferson publicly used the words, "honorable reparation," thus leaving the door to negotiation open. He referred to "uncontrolled abuses" which imperiled the peace, and by inescapable implication blamed the British government for ineffectual control of its naval commanders. But he declined to interpret the attack on the *Chesapeake* as an act of war and refrained from issuing an ultimatum. He merely announced a discontinuance of hospitality, as he had a perfect legal right to do. He regarded this as a precautionary rather than a punitive measure, but it was a challenge to power-conscious naval commanders who were capable of reprisals.

[22] The proclamation as reported to Congress is in *A.S.P.F.R.*, III, 23–24. Drafts by TJ are in LC, 29629 (incomplete but apparently the final draft as far as it goes) and 29630–29631 (printed in Ford, IX, 89–99). A draft of the middle portion by Madison, received June 29, is in LC, 29612–29613 (printed in Ford, IX, 99n.). Since there seems to be no clear first draft, it is difficult to determine the precise responsibility for the changes in phraseology. In general the proclamation appears to have been strengthened in the course of revision, probably at the suggestion of Madison (see Brant, IV, 381–382), but some needlessly offensive expressions were modified or omitted. Obviously it was prepared with great care and in its final form reflected TJ's considered judgment.

Following the killing of an innocent American by a shot from the *Leander*, the President had ordered from American waters that warship and two others that were then in the vicinity of New York. He now ordered away *all* British armed vessels (except those bearing official dispatches and those regularly engaged in carrying mail), and he forbade the entrance of others in the future. Recognizing the possibility, even the likelihood, that this order would not be obeyed, he forbade all communication with or assistance to such vessels as might remain. He imposed virtually the same restrictions as those already prescribed by the citizens of Norfolk and Portsmouth. In the sense that he recognized certain exceptions of an official or humane sort he modified their policy somewhat, but in all essential points he gave legal sanction to what had been extra-legal procedure, declaring that anyone affording aid to British armed vessels contrary to his prohibition would, if convicted, suffer all the pains and penalties provided by the laws.

"I imagine the ardor of our fellow citizens is scarcely satisfied by our proclamation," wrote Jefferson to John Page a week after he issued it; and that old friend promptly informed him that his supposition was correct.[23] Meanwhile, a Federalist paper in a maritime district to the southward had commented rather dourly on the prospect. Said the Charleston *Courier:* "The outrage will determine how far the patience and proclamation system of Mr. Jefferson will extend. O! for a Washington or an Adams to wield the sword of state!" But this paper, reporting a public meeting in this city a few days later, said that personal feelings and party prejudices were wholly yielded to love of country.[24] Toward the end of July the *National Intelligencer* observed that never, perhaps, had there been "so memorable an example of unanimity, as that evinced in the United States at this interesting crisis." The character of this virtual unanimity was suggested by a comment in the same paper a few days later that all the prints in the country except for two or three in Boston had taken "*American* ground in relation to the late outrageous conduct of Britain."[25] The response was spontaneously and overwhelmingly patriotic. Gallatin, an intensely practical man, told his wife that, while glad to see the spirit of the country, he placed "but a moderate degree of confidence on

23 TJ to John Page, July 9, 1807; Page to TJ, July 12 (LC, 29684, 29715).
24 Charleston *Courier*, July 3, 9, 1807. News of TJ's proclamation of July 2 could not have reached Charleston by July 3, but something of the sort appears to have been anticipated.
25 *National Intelligencer*, July 24, 27, 1807.

those first declarations in which many act from the first impulse of their feelings, more from sympathy or fear, and only a few from a calm view of the subject."[26] His own calm view at this stage was that, while war was probably inevitable, observance of international propriety was necessary and procrastination desirable. John Quincy Adams of Massachusetts could be counted on to take an "American" position, regardless of any pro-British sentiments that might be voiced in his state and party, but he sought to guide his steps by the light of reason. It is therefore worthy of note that, in a set of resolutions he drafted for a town meeting in Boston, besides condemning the British and praising the spirited actions of the citizens of Norfolk and Portsmouth, he expressed sincere approval of the proclamation and "the firm and dispassionate course of policy pursued by the President."[27]

A firm policy was dreaded by pacifists, from some of whom Jefferson heard, and a dispassionate policy could not have been expected to satisfy patriotic activists in that or any other age. Jefferson's long-suffering patience was a trial to contemporaries of his as it has been to many later critics. Judge Joseph H. Nicholson, former congressional lieutenant of John Randolph and a cousin of Gallatin's wife, saw no justification for diplomacy until the American seamen were returned by the British, and he expressed the hope that the *Revenge* would bring Monroe and Pinkney back from England.[28] A more characteristic attitude was one of loyalty to the President in a time of crisis, combined with uncertainty respecting his full policy and a willingness to wait and see. That, in fact, was what he himself was doing; and in the meantime he was keeping national defense as well as diplomacy in his own hands without recourse to Congress. He believed that he had sufficient means and authority to cope with immediate dangers. Fresh ones soon appeared in the Norfolk maritime district.

On July 3 the British squadron under Commodore Douglas sailed from Lynnhaven Bay to Hampton Roads and set up what amounted to a blockade of Norfolk. The action was unconnected with Jefferson's proclamation of the day before, since Douglas and his fellow officers had not yet learned of this. They made their move in response to a resolution of the citizens' committee calling for the prohibition of communication between them and the British Consul. Seeing this in

[26] Gallatin to his wife, July 10, 1807 (Adams, *Gallatin*, p. 358).
[27] July 16, 1807 (J. Q. Adams, *Writings*, III, 161, with account of this nonpartisan meeting in footnote).
[28] J. H. Nicholson to Gallatin, July 14, 1807, followed by Gallatin's reply of July 17 (Adams, *Gallatin*, pp. 360–362).

the newspapers, the Commodore wrote a letter of protest to the Mayor of Norfolk. That official must be perfectly aware, he said, that the British flag never had been and never would be insulted with impunity. He claimed that, while he obviously had the power to obstruct all the trade of Chesapeake Bay, he had forborne to do so in the hope that "general unanimity would be restored." In referring to the "late circumstance" he spoke of the removal of British deserters from the *Chesapeake* without mentioning that the frigate had been fired on. Decisions on this incident must be left to the respective governments, he said. Meanwhile, he was determined to shut up the port of Norfolk if the infringement on British rights was not annulled. According to him, the question of peace or war therefore rested with the inhabitants of Norfolk. This menacing letter was printed and circulated as a broadside, along with the Mayor's spirited reply.[29] Writing on July 4, Mayor Lee said that the unintimidated citizens were prepared for the worst the British might attempt. If, without waiting for the decision of the two governments, Douglas should commence hostilities, the inhabitants of Norfolk would conform to his example. They left to him, therefore, the decision between war and peace.

Jefferson's knowledge of developments in the Norfolk district inevitably lagged two or three days behind events, but he kept in close personal touch with the situation. Besides Decatur's letters to the Secretary of the Navy, he had reports almost every day from Colonel William Tatham, whose offer to serve as a lookout on Lynnhaven Bay he speedily and gladly accepted.[30] The news of the movement of the squadron into Hampton Roads and of its threatening posture there led him to say that the British commanders had their feet "on the threshold of war," and that there might be blows any hour. This was in a letter to the Secretary of War, then on the road to New York. He now requested Dearborn to return as soon as he had settled on a plan for the defense of that port and witnessed an experiment of Robert Fulton's in which a vessel was to be destroyed by torpedoes.[31] Jefferson feared that, if the present state of affairs continued, Congress might have to be called sooner than expected, and the executive officers might have to remain in the hot and sticky capital all summer.

[29] J. E. Douglas to Mayor Richard E. Lee, July 3, 1807; Lee to Douglas, July 4. Circulars enclosed in Erskine's Dispatch No. 20, July 17, 1807 (FO, 5:52). Movements of ships reported by Decatur to the Secretary of the Navy, July 4 (*A.S.P.F.R.*, III, 21).

[30] TJ to Tatham, July 6, 1807 (L. & B., XI, 259). Tatham, who had been surveying the coast, had what TJ called a "proper vessel" and some men. He received an allowance from the government for his services.

[31] TJ to Dearborn, July 7, 1807 (Ford, IX, 101).

(This was bad news to one who had expected to go to Maine.) In the absence of the Secretary of War the President assumed that official's functions. On a single day (July 8) he wrote a dozen letters dealing with military matters and problems of defense. Among them was one to the masters and other officers of the ports of Norfolk and Portsmouth, accepting their tender of services in repairing and erecting military works and, to his particular satisfaction, in manning gunboats. Also, he wrote to the Commandant of Fort Nelson, and to General Thomas Matthews of the militia, but greatest interest attaches to his letter to Governor William H. Cabell of Virginia. Just before his departure, Dearborn, by direction of the President, had addressed a letter to all the governors, calling upon them to organize, arm, and equip their respective portions of 100,000 militia as provided by law. These state troops were not actually called out as yet, but were subject to future requisition. In Virginia, circumstances required speedy action. Because of the grave situation at Norfolk, the President authorized and requested the Governor to order into immediate duty at federal expense such portions of the militia as he should judge necessary.[32]

The period of grave and immediate danger at the mouth of Chesapeake Bay lasted about two weeks. A day or two after the heated verbal exchange between Commodore Douglas and the Mayor of Norfolk, the former sent word to the latter that his letter contained no menace and that he had no hostile designs against Norfolk. Captain Decatur was dubious, however, and continued his preparations to repel a landing, which he was confident would be very costly to those attempting it. A few days later (July 12) he reported that the squadron lying in Hampton Roads had brought to every passing vessel but had detained none. By that time only the *Bellona* and the *Leopard* were still there, the *Triumph* and *Melampus* having returned to Lynnhaven Bay.[33] Because of the obstacles to his communication with the shore, Douglas may not have seen Jefferson's proclamation when it appeared in printed form in Norfolk on July 7, but a copy of it was transmitted to him by General Matthews three days later. Erskine also sent him one under cover of a flag of truce. He may have been impressed by the letter in which Erskine politely pointed out the desirability of avoiding

[32] These letters of July 8, 1807, are in L. & B., XI, 261–265. The one to Cabell is also in Ford, IX, 88. Dearborn's letter to the governors, dated July 6, is quoted in part from the records of the War Department, by Mary P. Adams in her dissertation, "Jefferson's Military Policy," p. 137. Legal authorization was provided by the Act of Apr. 18, 1806.

[33] Extracts from letters of Decatur to the Secretary of the Navy, July 8, 12, 1807 (*A.S.P.F.R.*, III, 21).

all hostile measures until His Majesty's commands should be known.[34] Gallatin, who was certain that Douglas had acted on his own authority since the attack on the *Chesapeake*, did not believe that a land attack was to be expected of the British naval commanders. Writing his wife, he said: "They will not venture on any hostilities on shore until they receive orders from Great Britain; for their naval arrogance induces them to make unfounded distinctions between what is legal on land or on water even within our jurisdiction, and they have not really sense or knowledge enough to feel that their present conduct within the Chesapeake is as much an actual invasion as if an army was actually landed."[35]

No advantage appears to have been taken of a humane offer of Jefferson's: namely, that on assurance of the immediate departure of any British armed vessel, water and supplies sufficient to carry her to Halifax or the West Indies might be provided.[36] The British commanders were not disposed to leave American waters, especially since the French ships they were stalking had not yet emerged. On July 17, however, Jefferson learned that the last of the British vessels had vacated the Roads for Lynnhaven Bay.[37] This they may have done for practical rather than political reasons: they were still within American jurisdiction but in a better position to secure supplies of water. Landing parties were dispatched with that purpose; and a couple of midshipmen, along with three seamen, were captured by patrolling militiamen. They were detained by order of General Matthews until the pleasure of the government should be known, and the Virginia Council of State took the position that they were properly held. Governor Cabell believed that while force might be used, under authority of the President's proclamation, to prevent the British from obtaining supplies, authority did not extend to the detention of persons. Accordingly, he wrote Jefferson in great anxiety and asked for a ruling.[38]

In his reply to the Governor, Jefferson recognized that the situation created by the presence of the British naval force within American waters was so novel that differences of opinion regarding the status of

---

[34] Erskine to Douglas, July 8, 1807 (copy enclosed in Dispatch No. 20 to Canning).
[35] Gallatin to his wife, July 14, 1807 (Adams, *Gallatin*, p. 359).
[36] TJ to Cabell, July 16, 1807 (L. & B., XI, 280–281).
[37] TJ to Dearborn, July 17, 1807 (*ibid.*, XI, 284–285).
[38] Cabell to TJ, July 20, 1807 (LC, 29778), describing the circumstances. Before getting this letter on July 22, TJ wrote TMR that the British landed frequently, procured water, and even got provisions from "secret customers," July 20, 1807 (LC, 29773).

the captured men was to be expected. Taking his stand on the act of Congress for the preservation of peace in American harbors, which authorized a "qualified war" against such persons, he held that the captives could be held as prisoners of war.[39] Their restoration, therefore, would be an act of favor. But, until response should be given by the British government to the demand for "reparation for the past and security for the future," he believed it advisable to avoid every act which might precipitate general war. Accordingly, the captives should be permitted to return to their ships with their boat and arms. Whether this should be done a second, third, or fourth time would depend on circumstances, he said, and in the meantime the proclamation must be strictly adhered to. He commended the military for their vigilance and enjoined them to maintain it, authorizing them to use force without hesitation to intercept communication with the British vessels and to prevent their procuring supplies of any sort.

Shortly after taking this moderate but firm position, Jefferson consulted with Dearborn, now returned from New York, about the situation at the point of most immediate danger. He concluded — correctly, as events were to prove — that until they received orders from England the British commanders would commit no acts of hostility other than those of defiantly remaining in American waters and bringing to vessels within American jurisdiction. He believed that Norfolk was now sufficiently secured anyway — by the repaired *Chesapeake* and the French frigate *Cybele* (which presumably would participate in the defense), by the twelve gunboats now in the harbor and four more that were expected, and by the works at Fort Nelson. A company of artillery should be retained, as should a company of cavalry to patrol the shore of Lynnhaven Bay, but otherwise, as he informed Governor Cabell, he saw no need to hold the militia. This resource should be husbanded for possible later use, and in the meantime there was no point in endangering the health of the men by keeping them in tidewater during the sickly season. For the same reason, at a time of anticipated tranquillity, he himself was planning to leave Washington for Monticello, according to his custom. On the day after he wrote the Governor he informed Colonel Tatham of the termination of his special assignment as lookout.[40] He had given the Governor explicit instructions to report to him regularly, and while at

[39] TJ to Cabell, July 24, 1807 (Ford, IX, 89–90n.), referring to Act of Mar. 3, 1805 (*Annals*, 8 Cong., 2 sess., pp. 1694–1698; *Jefferson the President: First Term*, pp. 443–444).
[40] TJ to Cabell, July 27, 1807 (*ibid.*, IX, 90–92n.); TJ to Col. William Tatham, July 28, 1807 (L. & B., XI, 299–300).

Monticello he was to hear from that official by almost every mail. Not until after his return to Washington in the autumn was he to learn that the British squadron had at last left American waters, and even then British armed ships continued to hover off the coast.

The stabilization of the situation in the Norfolk district confirmed Jefferson in the view that there was no need for him to call Congress to meet at an earlier date than the one tentatively decided on. Throughout July he had been pressed by some of his most loyal supporters to issue an immediate call. His intimate friend, Senator Wilson Cary Nicholas of Virginia, urged it, and John Page wrote him late in the month that sentiment for such a call was growing in Virginia. Secretary Robert Smith and Senator Samuel Smith, brothers-in-law of Nicholas, strongly supported his plea, and in this matter if not in others Gallatin agreed with the Smith brothers. Jefferson explained his position to the Senator from Maryland the day before he issued, on July 31, a proclamation summoning Congress to meet on October 26.[41] Besides saying that, until a response had been received from the British government, Congress would have no ground "sufficiently certain" on which to decide between peace and war, he claimed that in the meantime the executive officers were making every preparation that could be made if Congress were in session. By this time, in fact, they had weathered the immediate dangers without legislative help. Also, the Cabinet had made provision, on paper, not only for measures of general defense but also for offensive action against Canada.[42] Congress *might* authorize additional gunboats, Jefferson wrote Senator Smith, but it had declined to do so at its recent session and, though needed, they could wait until winter. What, besides fervid rhetoric, he could have got out of Congress at this stage cannot be ascertained, but he did not seize upon the opportunity afforded by the patriotic ardor of these weeks to mobilize the legislators in support of a more extensive military and naval establishment.[43] His Secretary of the Treasury believed that four months of peace would be invaluable in enabling the country to get its ships and seamen home and to prepare for the war he regarded as inevitable. Except that he was generally more hopeful of the outcome of negotiation, Jefferson said much the same thing in a number of private letters. It remained to be seen what precisely would

---

[41] TJ to Samuel Smith, July 30, 1807 (L. & B., XI, 301). Among other letters that may be cited in this connection are W. C. Nicholas to TJ, July 7, 1807 (LC, 29669–29670); Robert Smith to TJ, July 17 (LC, 29755–29759); John Page to TJ, July 25 (LC, 29806–29807); Gallatin to his wife, July 10 (Adams, *Gallatin*, p. 358).

[42] Memos. of meetings of July 26, 27, 28 (Ford, I, 325–330).

[43] His defense policy is discussed in chs. XXVII, XXVIII, below.

be done on the home front during the remainder of the congressional recess. Meanwhile, as Titans dueled on the world stage, indifferent to those they trod on, he and his representatives would be seeking to maintain the honor and safeguard the peace of their young country by wielding the weapon of diplomacy.

Madison's letter to Monroe, informing him officially of the *Chesapeake* affair and giving him instructions, was dated July 6, but the *Revenge* did not set sail until after the middle of the month. Along with a letter of July 17, describing the actions of the British squadron in Hampton Roads, it was borne on the *Revenge* by Dr. Bullus, and it reached Monroe the last day in August.[44] Not until the last day of November, which was more than five months after the attack on the *Chesapeake*, did the President and the Secretary of State learn what response the British had made to the American demands. Our concern here is with the latter, not with the response that was to be so long in coming.

"Reparation for the past, and security for the future" — this joint objective was stated by Jefferson again and again in private letters. Madison spelled it out in his official instructions. The latest enormity was not subject to discussion, he said, since the immunity of ships of war from any kind of search had never been contested by any nation. He added that the offense was the greater in this particular case because the seamen who were removed were American citizens and were believed to have been previously impressed. The demand for reparation was independent of these facts and suppositions, however, and as Madison rightly said, it required no arguing. But precisely what form should this reparation take? In the first place, there must be a formal disavowal of the action, made with becoming solemnity. Judging from instances of past apologies made by one nation to another that Madison cited, he was calling for the sending of a special emissary to the United States to make amends. In the second place, the four seamen must be restored to the ships from which they were taken. This demand, while proper in the abstract, was sure to occasion difficulty in the case of Jenkin Ratford, about whom at this time Madison appears to have been imperfectly informed. He and Jefferson were well informed, however, about the attitude of the British government to impressment, and for that reason the most surprising requirement now set forth was the entire abolition of this practice from American merchant vessels on the high seas. In previous instructions Madison had offered as a *quid pro*

44 Madison to Monroe, July 6, 1807 (Hunt, VII, 454-460; *A.S.P.F.R.*, III, 183-185); Madison to Monroe, July 17, 1807 (Hunt, VII, 463-464).

quo an American agreement designed to reduce the number of British seamen in American service. He now sought to withhold this proposal as long as possible and to use it as a bargaining weapon. Since the crucial problem with the British was the recovery of deserters, one might argue that this was the time to emphasize the proposal. And, from the American point of view, the main issue in the present case was *not* impressment. In reiterating demands which had previously been rejected, Jefferson and Madison probably thought they had fresh leverage, and undoubtedly they could count on more support at home. Also, they may have concluded that reparation without provision for future security would be meaningless, and that while they were about it they might as well keep the record straight. Whether or not they were wise in coupling these two questions remained to be seen, but they might have anticipated that this demand would provide the British officials with an excuse for equivocation and procrastination. Another difficulty they did foresee — namely, the claim that the President, by means of his proclamation, had taken reparation into his own hands. Their response was that this was a necessary precautionary measure, well within the authority of the President, and that no restraint on his power to take action of this sort could be countenanced. The assumption was that similar action would have been taken against the French in comparable circumstances, but, since the proclamation spoke only of the British, the latter might have been expected to charge the United States with a departure from neutrality.

The *Revenge* also carried official dispatches from Madison and private letters from Jefferson to representatives and friends in France. It was at this point that Armstrong and Bowdoin were ordered to suspend negotiations for the purchase of West Florida — negotiations which in fact had never got started.[45] The ostensible reason was financial: the money might be needed for purposes of war. But hope of the eventual acquisition of this region, and more immediately of gaining provision for the use of Mobile, was not dead. Madison anticipated that if the United States should become engaged in a contest with Great Britain, the Spanish would be more amenable. Writing Bowdoin, Jefferson said: "In this state of things, cordial friendship with France, and peace at least with Spain, become more interesting."[46] Several times within the next few weeks, he said that he was mortified at having to wish success to Napoleon, and in spirit he was clearly not pro-French, but he became increasingly anti-British as the summer

[45] Madison to Armstrong and Bowdoin, July 15, 1807 (Hunt, VII, 460–462); see above, p. 93.
[46] TJ to Bowdoin, July 10, 1807 (L. & B., XI, 269).

wore on. At the outset he cherished the hope that the chief offenders against American interests, recognizing the danger that the weight of the United States might be thrown in the scale against them, would be more disposed to yield to American representations than hitherto. Such might conceivably have been the case, but desperate circumstances induced in the British government, not a more conciliatory, but a more ruthless policy toward neutrals.

[XXIV]

Entr'acte: President and Tsar

THE synchronization of historic events in the summer of 1807 is a fascinating exercise and a very necessary one if their interrelation is to be understood. About two weeks after the *Leopard* fired on the *Chesapeake* off the Virginia Capes, and nearly a month before news of this action reached London, Napoleon and Tsar Alexander I of Russia had a momentous meeting on a raft in the Niemen River; and the day after Madison drafted Monroe's instructions, the two emperors and the hapless King of Prussia signed the treaties of Tilsit (July 7, 1807). These events in eastern Europe signalized the demise of the Third Coalition against the French conqueror and the resolution of the war into a duel to the death between him and the British.[1] The news that Napoleon's most formidable antagonist on the Continent had come to terms with him did not reach America until September, while Jefferson was still at Monticello, and not until he was back in Washington in October was he in position to perceive that the net result of the change in the character of the war was to increase the plight of the few remaining neutrals. The British official mind had hardened before Monroe learned of the outrage on the *Chesapeake*. Another result of the agreement of the two emperors at Tilsit, although a minor one, was to render meaningless and ironical a paragraph in Monroe's instructions which must have been inserted at Jefferson's request. At this point, therefore, we pause for a few moments, in a sort of entr'acte, to consider the relations between the President of the United States and the most charming and most hope-inspiring of the Romanoffs.

In a paragraph towards the end of the letter he received at the end of August, Monroe was instructed to explain matters to the Russian

---

[1] The Third Coalition of 1805 included Great Britain, Sweden, Russia, and Austria. The latter country was detached at the end of the year, following the battle of Austerlitz, and Prussia was added afterwards.

440 JEFFERSON THE PRESIDENT: SECOND TERM

Minister in case of an express or probable rejection of American demands by the British.[2] The President wanted it to be made known that he regretted a rupture with a country the Russian Emperor was allied with. Unaware, at the very time he was writing these words, that the subsisting Anglo-Russian relations were in the process of being reversed, the Secretary of State spoke of the good will and respect for the United States and for the President personally that had been manifested by the Tsar, and emphasized the desirability of cultivating the friendship of a power which had principles and interests so much in common with those of the United States. There was certainly no similarity between the two forms of government, but Alexander, while ostensibly a complete autocrat, was said to have imbibed the principles of republicanism from his Swiss tutor, Frédéric César de La Harpe, and was regarded by heirs of the Enlightenment as the most liberal-minded monarch in Europe. What was more immediately to the point, he was believed to be a friend of small countries and a staunch supporter of neutral rights at sea.

Such was Jefferson's opinion of him, as is clearly shown by a private letter the President wrote a week or two later to William Duane of he *Aurora*, whom he believed to be insufficiently aware of the Emperor's character and potential value to the United States.[3] "A more virtuous man, I believe, does not exist," said Jefferson, "nor one who is more enthusiastically devoted to better the condition of mankind." He fully recognized that such a spirit did not suit the Russian noblesse and expressed doubts elsewhere of the ability of the liberal and humane Tsar to accomplish much in the way of domestic reform — which, in fact, turned out to be sharply limited. In this particular context there was more significance in the reference to the "peculiar affection" for the United States and its government of which he had given proof. "Our nation being, like his, habitually neutral," said Jefferson, "our interests as to neutral rights, and our sentiments agree. And whenever conferences for peace shall take place, we are assured of a friend in him. . . . I am confident that Russia (while her present monarch lives) is the most cordially friendly to us of any power on earth, will go furthest to serve us, and is most worthy of conciliation." If the head of the American Republic anticipated an early peace conference, time was to show that he was much too sanguine; there was not to be one until long after he had left office. And he considerably over-estimated

[2] Madison to Monroe, July 6, 1807 (Hunt, VII, 459–460). This paragraph does not appear in the letter as submitted to Congress months later with other documents (*A.S.P.F.R.*, III, 183–185).
[3] TJ to Duane, July 20, 1807 (Ford, IX, 120–121).

the efficacy of good will in the power politics of the age. But, characteristically, he was taking the long look, and he based his hopes on
personal correspondence with the Tsar. Ignoring the obvious differences and defying the vast distance between their countries, the two
men had exchanged letters which are of abiding interest even though
they were without effect on the inexorable course of events at the
time.

The letters that actually passed between the President and the Tsar
numbered only four, two on each side, beginning with one that Jefferson wrote about three years before the attack on the *Chesapeake.*[4] He
had considered entering into correspondence with the young Emperor
considerably before that. The first suggestion that he do so appears to
have been made to him in the autumn of his second year as President,
when he received letters from Joseph Priestley and Thomas Cooper. It
will be recalled that both of these learned men were English refugees
and were regarded as radicals. The older man had recently received
from a former parishioner of his, J. H. Stone, long a refugee in Paris, a
letter containing "particulars" about Alexander. Priestley had Cooper
copy these and sent them to Jefferson, believing they would bring him
pleasure. In Cooper's letter, which was filled with extravagant praise of
Jefferson, he said that he was sufficiently impressed with Stone's
presentation of Alexander to wish that Jefferson were his correspondent, but that he did not consider either Stone or La Harpe a suitable
intermediary.[5]

To Cooper, who regarded Alexander with "fearful hope," Jefferson
wrote that the information about the young ruler kindled "a great deal
of interest in his existence, and strong spasms of the heart in his favor."
Correspondence with him would be very interesting to those who
were "sincerely anxious to see mankind raised from their present
abject condition." Writing Priestley the same day, he observed that
the appearance of such a man on a throne was a remarkable phenome-
non, but that Alexander faced a "herculean task" in seeking to bring

---

[4] These and extracts from several related letters were published by N. Hans
under the heading "Tsar Alexander I and Jefferson: Unpublished Correspondence," in *Slavonic and East European Review,* XXXII, 215–225 (Dec. 1953).
There is an excellent fresh account of the Tsar and his foreign policy in ch. II of
The Foreign Ministers of Alexander I (1969) by Patricia K. Grimsted.

[5] Cooper to TJ, Oct. 25, 1802 (LC, 21873–21874); Priestley to TJ, Oct. 29, 1802
(LC, 21911); both received Nov. 6. See also Dumas Malone, *The Public Life of
Thomas Cooper* (1926), pp. 166–167. The undated document from LC, 146:25396,
in *Slavonic and East European Review,* XXXII, 216, is there designated as the
enclosure mentioned by Priestley. Since it is in TJ's handwriting, it appears to be
a copy made by him of part of the extract or of some other letter. At all events,
the general nature of the information sent him is clear.

freedom and happiness to an unprepared people. In response to Priestley's suggestion that a brief account of the American Constitution be sent the Tsar, he expressed doubts that anything adapted to the English or American mind would serve a very practical purpose in Russia. He expected to give thought to the matter, but obviously he was disposed to make no move until he was convinced that a communication from him would be welcome to Alexander and until a suitable occasion was afforded.[6]

Slightly more than a year after this exchange of letters, Jefferson wrote one to Monroe, still in France, in which he informed that minister of the extent of his "literary correspondence" with foreigners.[7] The persons he named were nearly all men of learning, though some of them were in a position to pass on his ideas to their governments. He believed that he could "make private friendships instrumental to the public good by inspiring a confidence which is denied to public, and official communications." He had engaged in considerable private correspondence with his own representatives abroad, but not with any foreign head of state as yet. He told Monroe that an opening had been given him of "making a communication" which would be acceptable to the Emperor Alexander, "either directly or indirectly, and as from one private individual to another," but that he had not yet decided whether or not to do it. He did not know that an action of the Emperor himself that very month was to offer him a suitable occasion.

Toward the end of January, 1804, the Tsar interceded in behalf of the Americans who had been captured when the frigate *Philadelphia* ran aground (October 31, 1803) and were imprisoned in Tripoli. On hearing of the capture of the unfortunate vessel, the enterprising American Consul General at St. Petersburg, Levett Harris, wrote the Grand Chancellor and asked that the Russian government intercede with that of Turkey, which in turn could make demands of Tripoli. The Grand Chancellor promptly replied as follows:

It is with great pleasure I announce to you that His Imperial Majesty, guided by the most favorable dispositions for your Government, has given me orders to direct the Minister at Constantinople to make the strongest representations to the Turkish Court, in order that a Firman [royal order] be dispatched to the Bey of Tripoli to liberate not only the crew but the Vessel itself.[8]

[6] TJ to Cooper, Nov. 29, 1802, and to Priestley, same date (Ford, VIII, 176–181).
[7] TJ to Monroe, Jan. 8, 1804 (Ford, VIII, 286–287).
[8] Count de Worontzoff to Levett Harris, Jan. 25, 1804 (translated from the French), replying to Harris's letter to him of Jan. 20 (D. W. Knox, ed., *Naval Documents Related to the United States Wars with the Barbary Powers* [1941], III, 358).

The *Philadelphia* was destroyed a few weeks later by the heroic action of Stephen Decatur and his men, and the prisoners were not released until the Tripolitan War was ended months later by a treaty that provided for their ransom.[9] Judged by its tangible results, the action of the Emperor was an empty gesture, but in American circles at the time it was regarded as momentous. Informing Captain Edward Preble of it, the Consul General said he "must be convinced of the importance of an intercession so ascendant as that of the Monarch of Russia." Levett Harris was under the spell of the young Emperor's charisma and well aware of his commanding stature on the continental scene.[10] Preble subsequently released a Russian ship that had been captured as a violator of the American blockade of Tripoli, telling the Russian Ambassador at Constantinople that he did so because of the impression made on him by the "generous interposition of His Russian Majesty." More realistically, he informed the Secretary of the Navy that, regarding the ship as of little value, he availed himself of the opportunity to pay a compliment to the Russian flag.[11]

The generous action of the Emperor was referred to by James Monroe in a letter to the Russian Ambassador to England; and it occasioned an official letter from the Secretary of State which may have been the most effusive Madison ever wrote.[12] Referring to the friendly interposition of the Tsar, he said: "The President sees in it a ray of that luminous benevolence which shines in the character of his Imperial Majesty, and which emanating from the best feelings of the heart gives the brightest ornament to the attributes of his high station." He spoke of the President's "exalted esteem" for the Emperor, and of his disposition to cultivate good will and to exchange good offices with a country whose sovereign so merited them by his "honorable and beneficent example."

The official expression of appreciation of the Tsar's act of benevolence and friendly disposition toward the American Republic was accompanied by a personal letter from Jefferson in which he greeted that far-distant ruler as "Great and good friend."[13] Though a rela-

[9] See above, pp. 37–41; and, for the plight of the prisoners, G. W. Allen, *Our Navy and the Barbary Corsairs* (1905), pp. 153–157.

[10] Levett Harris to Capt. Edward Preble, Jan. 26–Feb. 7, 1804 (*Naval Documents . . . Barbary Powers*, III, 397).

[11] Preble to the Russian Ambassador at Constantinople, June 6, 1804; Preble to the Secretary of the Navy, June 14–July 5, 1804 (*ibid.*, IV, 158–159, 190). See also Levett Harris to Capt. Samuel Barron, March 8/20, 1805 (*ibid.*, V, 428–430).

[12] Monroe to the Russian Ambassador, Mar. 27, 1804 (*ibid.*, III, 534); Madison to the Lord Chancellor of the Empire of Russia, June 10, 1804 (*ibid.*, IV, 176–177).

[13] TJ to Alexander, Emperor of Russia, June 15, 1804 (LC, 24458); *Slavonic and East European Review*, XXXII, 221.

tively restrained letter, largely confined to generalities, it breathed good will. On the practical side, the President spoke with pleasure of the rising commerce between the two countries, assuring the Emperor that his flag would find in American harbors "hospitality, freedom and protection," and that his subjects would enjoy there "all the privileges of the most favored nation." His main concern, however, was with personal rather than commercial relations, and he did not speak as yet of neutral rights and the freedom of the seas. He was seeking to encourage the European ruler whose great potentialities he recognized and whose immense difficulties he perceived. In his final paragraph, he said:

I avail myself of this occasion of expressing the exalted pleasure I have felt in observing the various acts of your administration, during the short time you have yet been on the throne of your country, & seeing in them manifestations of the virtue & wisdom from which they flow. What has not your country to hope from a career which has begun from such auspicious developments! Sound principles, pursued with a steady step, dealing out good progressively as your people are prepared to receive & to hold it fast, cannot fail to carry them & yourself far in the improvement of their condition, during the course of your life. I pray to God that it may long continue for their happiness & your glory, and that he may always have you in his safe and holy keeping.

No doubt it seemed to Jefferson that the Tsar was embarked on a holy mission. If he had any reservations about him, or any doubts of the propriety of corresponding with him, these must have been dispelled by a belated communication from Paris that he received early in July. It consisted of a long letter from Joel Barlow, written five months earlier, together with a brief one from the Tsar's former tutor, La Harpe, written four months before that. This was addressed to Priestley's friend Stone, who had sent it to Barlow with the suggestion that he transmit it to the President. It showed that Alexander was in a receptive mood long before Jefferson found occasion to address him and it is fascinating in itself.[14]

The President could not have failed to be gratified by La Harpe's expression of high respect for him as a member of the noble society of friends of man who sought light and liberty for all. Coupled with this was the reminder that, at the eastern extremity of Europe, there was

[14] La Harpe to Stone, Oct. 20, 1803, in French (*ibid.*, 218); Stone to Barlow on back; Barlow to TJ, Feb. 11, 1804 (long extract, *ibid.*, pp. 218–220; full letter [LC, 23901–23904]; received by TJ July 8, 1804).

another chief of a powerful nation, who, born to a throne, bore in his heart "tous les sentiments qui constituent le Citoyen et le Philanthrope par excellence." The young ruler was reported to have read and admired writings of Jefferson that had been made available to him by his tutor and to have expressed the desire to become more intimately acquainted with their author. A rapprochement between two men who were in position to influence the destinies of "a considerable portion of humanity" was highly desirable, in La Harpe's opinion, and with these sentiments Stone and Barlow heartily agreed.

Alexander's confidential letters to La Harpe were circulated among kindred spirits of the latter and in several of these, according to Barlow, the Tsar had spoken of Jefferson with particular respect. Quoted words of his in La Harpe's letters were interpreted as an overture to a correspondence into which the Tsar, because of his veneration for Jefferson's character, was unwilling to enter before first ascertaining that it would be agreeable to him. Barlow believed that such correspondence would be of immense value to Alexander and, through him, to the world. To Jefferson the poet wrote:

> You have been nourished in the purest political region of our globe. Your genius has added to the general stock of knowledge; your reputation, experience and the station you fill command respect; and your principles and opinions will be contemplated, weighted and digested with more attention than those of any other man perhaps now alive, — more than even yours would be were you in another situation. We are always anxious to read and consider the opinions of chiefs of nations believing them to be in some measure those of the people they govern. Hence it is from those high stations that useful principles can be delivered to the world to the greatest advantage.

Barlow took the liberty of suggesting specific topics with which Jefferson might usefully deal in this projected correspondence; but, recognizing the delicacy of the Tsar's position, he thought that care should be taken not to recommend too much. Jefferson needed no such warning, but he may well have been influenced by Barlow's comments on the common interests of Russia and the United States in foreign affairs.[15] According to Barlow, the question of the freedom of the seas was of particular interest to Alexander, and he was in special need of information and evidence of support in this connection. After pointing

[15] This part of Barlow's letter is not printed in *Slavonic and East European Review*.

out that Russia and the United States had no overseas possessions to protect and that their exports were necessities to the manufacturing nations, he expressed the belief that they were in a position to "come forward with a plan for the liberty of the seas that could not be resisted," and that the adoption of this would have incalculable effects on humanity. This, in his opinion, was a necessary step toward permanent peace. Foreseeing a time when Russia would have as preponderant a population in one hemisphere as the United States would have in the other, Barlow said: "This makes it still more important that all good principles should be cultivated by them both with particular zeal; and this not only for the benefit of the vast numbers which will compose their own nations, but because it will give them a vogue, and command their reception with all their neighbors, even to the greatest part of the world."

These prognostications reflected the optimism and grandiosity of the author of *The Vision of Columbus*, and we need not suppose that Jefferson, who had suffered so many rebuffs as a diplomat, ever set his hopes that high. It is a fact, however, that when he next wrote the Tsar he stressed the common interests of the two countries and spoke particularly of the rights of neutrals on the seas. Meanwhile, he had to wait a year and a half for a reply to his first letter. Such, indeed, were the delays in communication between their two ends of the earth that effective cooperation of the sort envisaged by Barlow would have been exceedingly difficult if not quite impracticable.

Alexander's first letter to Jefferson was written toward the end of the summer of 1805 and was received by him the day after the battle of Austerlitz more than three months later.[16] The fact that he was addressed as "Monsieur" rather than as "Monsieur le Président" could hardly have distressed one so indifferent to protocol. In other respects the imperial letter left nothing to be desired on the score of politeness and it could not have failed to convey an impression of sincere good will. Furthermore, this absolutist ruler expressed his admiration for the American Republic, its Constitution, and its President, whom he described as equally virtuous and enlightened. These expressions might have been dismissed as idle compliments, but Jefferson, who had received nothing of the sort from Napoleon or George III, viewed them with great satisfaction. He had reason to believe that by this exchange of civilities the foundation had been laid for a high-level friendship.

He did not press matters, but waited more than four months before

[16] Alexander to TJ, Aug. 20, 1805, in French (*Slavonic and East European Review*, XXXII, 221–222; LC, 26550; received Dec. 3).

writing the Tsar again. He had become aware of the defeat of Austerlitz by that time, but he made no mention of this important event in
Russian history. He had just received from the Consul General in St.
Petersburg as a gift a bust of the Emperor. His self-imposed rule was
to accept no present of more than minor value while in office. "But,"
he said, "my particular esteem for the character of the Emperor places
his image in my mind above the scope of law. I receive it, therefore,
and shall cherish it with affection. It nourishes the contemplation of all
the good placed in his power, and of his disposition to do it." He also
said it would constitute "one of the most valued ornaments" of the
retreat he was preparing for himself at home.[17] In due course he
placed it in the parlor at Monticello, opposite Napoleon toward whom
his feelings were quite different, and there visitors can still see them
both.

In the letter he wrote Alexander in the spring of 1806, shortly after
his own sixty-third birthday, Jefferson made no mention of the bust he
had so recently acquired, but at this time he sent certain works on the
Constitution of the United States, which, as he afterwards learned,
were received by the Tsar as fresh tokens of friendship. Also, he
embraced the opportunity to express his "sincere respect and veneration" for the character of a sovereign whose ruling passion was "the
advancement and happiness of his people; and not of his own people
only, but who can extend his eye and his good will to a distant and
infant nation unoffending in its course, unambitious in its views."[18] He
was now in hopes, however, that this correspondence would amount to
more than an exchange of compliments. Telling Madison that, since his
letters might lead to something of importance, he wanted the "gentlemen of the administration" to read it, and he asked the Secretary of
State to correct it severely. Madison had previously expressed some
doubt of the complete disinterestedness of the friendly Tsar and had
stressed the necessity of avoiding any sort of commitment to Russia.[19]
In his letter Jefferson stated explicitly that his country had no part in
the troubles of Europe, but he claimed that it shared with the northern
countries that were headed by Russia an attachment to peace and an
interest in neutral rights. Looking forward to the settlement which
would bring peace to Europe some day, he said that two personages, of
whom Alexander was one (and Napoleon obviously the other) had it

[17] TJ to Levett Harris, Apr. 18, 1806 (L. & B., XI, 101). It was a plaster cast of a
marble bust by Fedot Schubin (c. 1801), and the bust now at Monticello may be
presumed to be just like it.
[18] TJ to Alexander, Apr. 19, 1806 (Ford, VIII, 439–441).
[19] TJ to Madison, Apr. 11, 1806 (MP, Rives Coll., 3:698), a letter to which I
have not found Madison's reply; Madison to TJ, Sept. 22, 1804 (LC, 24897).

TWO EMPERORS AT MONTICELLO
Busts of Tsar Alexander I and Napoleon in the parlor

in their power "to render eminent service to nations in general, by incorporating into the act of pacification, a correct definition of the rights of neutrals on the high seas." Recognizing that the United States could have no share in the pacification, he described the Tsar as a broad-minded umpire who would take under his protection the rights of unrepresented countries. "It is only by a happy concurrence of good characters and good occasions, that a step can now and then be taken to advance the well-being of nations," he said, adding that if the occasion should prove to be good, he was sure that Alexander's character would "not be wanting to avail the world of it." His prayer was that the life of his imperial correspondent would be "an epoch in the history of the condition of man."

Judging from the reply he promptly made, Alexander was touched by Jefferson's words.[20] While reaffirming the intentions with which the President had credited him, he said he was aware that there were vast obstacles to the attainment of such an order of things as he desired — an order conforming to "the common interest of all civilized nations, and solidly guaranteed against the efforts of ambition and greed." But the goal was too beautiful and too dear to his heart for him to let himself be cast down. From Jefferson's words he had received powerful encouragement and he manifested the pleasure with which he had received Jefferson's precious letters by asking a continuation of them.

The recipient of this letter did not reply to it, presumably because no suitable occasion was afforded. But the instructions to Monroe and his letter to William Duane in the summer of 1807 are clear evidence that his admiration for the Tsar and his confidence in him had not declined. What he thought of Alexander's actions at Tilsit, when he learned of them in the fall, we do not know. These actions could hardly have suggested disinterested concern for the well-being of small countries, and they might have been regarded as signs of the Tsar's ambivalence. But they reflected feelings about that monarch's former ally which the President of the United States might certainly have been expected to share. While the later story that Alexander greeted Napoleon with the declaration, "I hate the British as much as you do," has been discredited, there can be no doubt of his bitterness at their failure to support him.[21] Furthermore, he resented their maritime aggressions and committed himself anew to the doctrine of the free-

[20] Alexander to TJ, Aug. 10, 1806, in French, said to be in his handwriting (*Slavonic and East European Review*, XXXII, 223–224; LC, 28175–28176; received Nov. 19, 1806).
[21] See J. H. Rose, *Life of Napoleon I* (1924), II, 117–118.

dom of the seas. Napoleon, for reasons of his own, was still giving lip service to this doctrine, and the immediate effect of these developments may have been to soften Jefferson's feelings about that ruthless conqueror. At this time his own country was much less troubled by the tyrant of the land than by the tyrant of the sea. It was not directly affected by the autocracy of the Tsar, whose good intentions Jefferson did not doubt. Accordingly, he continued to be pro-Russian.

Since he was taking the long view while cultivating the friendship of Alexander, it seems fitting to make brief reference here to an episode in his last year in office which will receive attention later in this narrative. He tried to send to the Russian court a full-fledged minister in the person of his former secretary, William Short, and drafted a letter for him to present to the Tsar.[22] Unhappily, however, the Senate defeated this nomination, chiefly on the ground that such a mission was not needed. The senators were of the same opinion when, at the outset of Madison's administration, they defeated his nomination of John Quincy Adams to the same post, but they changed their minds a few weeks later and in due course Adams received a most cordial reception in St. Petersburg. The warmth of his welcome and the strong expressions of friendship for the United States that he received from Tsar and Chancellor have seemed surprising to certain later commentators in view of the sharp contrast between the governments of the two countries, but they can hardly be dissociated from the correspondence between a President and an Emperor who regarded themselves as kindred spirits. It may also be noted in passing that the suspicious New Englander was as captivated by the Tsar close at hand as the more gullible Virginian had been at a distance.[23]

[22] TJ to Alexander, Aug. 29, 1808 (Ford, IX, 206-207); see below, pp. 661-664.
[23] See J. Q. Adams's *Memoirs*, II, 51-55.

[XXV]

Between Peace and War

1807

JAMES MONROE, in London, learned about the *Chesapeake* affair and the settlement between Alexander and Napoleon several weeks before he received his instructions; and on August 4, 1807, he wrote Madison a letter which, with its enclosures, constituted a preliminary report on developments in the British capital.[1] This happened to be the day that Jefferson arrived at Monticello for his two months' stay in the hills during the sickly season, but Monroe's communication was almost that long on the road. Meanwhile, the President again parried a subpoena from the court in Richmond and Aaron Burr was acquitted of misdemeanor as well as treason.[2] At Monticello Jefferson attended to more matters of personal business than we shall take space to mention, and he spent eight days on a trip to Poplar Forest in September. Madison visited him for a couple of days before that, and during most of this period there were daily mails between Monticello and Montpelier. He remained in close touch with Governor Cabell, who kept him informed about the movements of the British squadron off the Virginia Capes; and, having learned of threats from the Indians in the Northwest (instigated, as he believed, by the British in Canada), he instructed the Secretary of War to see that the militia of Michigan, Ohio, and Indiana, were put in readiness for service at a moment's notice.[3] No doubt he was heartened by the patriotic resolutions, addresses, and offers of service with which his mail was flooded and to which he made fitting acknowledgment with his own pen. But the

---

[1] Monroe to Madison, Aug. 4, 1807, with copies of his letters to and from Canning, July 25–Aug. 3 (*A.S.P.F.R.*, III, 186–188).

[2] See ch. XIX, above.

[3] TJ to Dearborn, Aug. 28, 1807 (Ford, IX, 131–134).

report from Monroe, together with the news of the court-martial proceedings in Halifax (August 26) and the execution of one of the seamen who had been forcibly removed from the *Chesapeake*, could not have failed to dampen his hopes of a satisfactory settlement with the British.

He and Madison learned from Monroe's communication that the American Minister received his first report of the *Leopard-Chesapeake* affair in a letter from George Canning.[4] In this the names of the two vessels and details of the "transaction" were not given, but it was stated that American lives had been lost. The Foreign Secretary expressed "the deepest regret" and promised that if the British officers "should prove to have been culpable, the most prompt and effectual reparation" would be afforded. The inescapable implication was that such proof had not been received. Monroe interpreted this note as an assurance that the act was not authorized by the British government, but when he read the account of the affair in the newspapers and understood, from what he regarded as good authority, that the official account corresponded with this, he was immediately convinced that the British were the aggressors. He concluded, therefore, that what Canning was waiting for was information about the nationality of the alleged deserters on whose account the attack was made — information that Monroe regarded as irrelevant since the question at issue was the inviolability of an American naval vessel. In an interview with him soon thereafter Canning specifically inquired about the citizenship of the seamen. Though Monroe held that this question had no bearing on the principle he was contending for, Canning seemed undisposed to drop it and did not yet concede the principle. Monroe regarded Canning's remarks as generally conciliatory, however. He took occasion to mention earlier grievances over the conduct of British naval officers, to which he would have given particular attention had not more serious matters intervened. Regarding the latter, it was understood that he would write a formal note, and on that same day he did so.

While such promptness and diligence would normally be commendable, the abruptness and ineptness of the note suggest that it was written too hastily. Monroe exposed the weakness of his own position at the start by admitting that he was acting without instructions from his government, on the basis of accounts which he described as reliable but which were obviously unofficial. In his indignation, furthermore, he over-stated his case. Thus he stated unequivocally that the *Leopard* attacked the *Chesapeake* "to assert and enforce the unfounded and most unjustifiable pretensions to search for deserters." The claim that

[4] Canning to Monroe, July 25, 1807 (*A.S.P.F.R.*, III, 187).

these pretensions lacked legal foundation was warranted, but the British government, informed by Admiral Berkeley of what he regarded as the flagrant enlistment of British deserters for service on an American ship of war, could not have been expected to agree that the effort to recover them was wholly unjustifiable. Monroe's designation of the action off the Virginia Capes as one of "complete hostility" was abrasive; and his reference to earlier instances of "great indignity and outrage" was unfortunate, since he himself had said that they should not enter into the discussion of a much more serious action. Claiming full confidence that the British government would regard this as "a flagrant abuse of its own authority," he asked for a frank and speedy disavowal of it, along with assurance that the responsible officer would suffer punishment befitting "so unexampled an aggression on the sovereignty of a neutral nation."

In his reply to this undiplomatic letter, Canning administered what amounted to a rebuke to Monroe for speaking without instructions from home or precise information, and chided him for referring to lesser grievances, which, as he himself had said, should not enter into the present discussion. The Foreign Secretary expressed surprise that Monroe should have questioned the disposition of the government to make such amends as should prove to be warranted. Nonetheless, in order to evince devotion to the principles of justice and moderation, he said: "His Majesty neither does nor has at any time maintained the pretension of a right to search ships of war, in the national service of any State, for deserters." Sending this letter to his own government, Monroe stated that it might be "considered as conceding essentially the point desired," but when he said that its tone was rather harsh he was indulging in no exaggeration. Having been worsted in this encounter with a better-informed and more skillful diplomat, armed with power, he resolved to say nothing more to him until he heard from his own government, and in the meantime to be as conciliatory as circumstances would permit.

The fears reflected in his communication at this time were in marked contrast to the hopefulness he had manifested during his negotiations of the past year. Reporting that there was a strong party favoring the extension of the war to the United States, he said: "This party is composed of the ship owners, the navy, the East and West India merchants, and certain political characters of great consideration in the state. So powerful is this combination, that it is most certain that nothing can be obtained of the Government on any point but what may be extorted by necessity. The disasters to the north ought to inspire moderation, but, with respect to the northern Powers, it seems to have produced directly the opposite effect."

The disasters he referred to were the defeats of the coalition that preceded and led to the settlement at Tilsit, whereby Russia withdrew from the war and left the Continent at the mercy of Napoleon. Monroe could not have been expected to be fully informed of all the provisions agreed to by the conqueror and the Tsar Alexander, of whom Jefferson was hoping so much. Some of these were unannounced, though Canning had quickly found out about them.[5] Without mentioning the territorial settlement, Monroe referred to a supposed agreement to force on the British "a maritime code more favorable to neutral nations." While this was quite in the character of the Tsar as Jefferson understood him, Napoleon could hardly have been credited with benevolence toward the remaining neutrals. The wary British had good reason to fear that he would extend his power to Denmark, seeking to make the Baltic a closed sea and to challenge British naval supremacy by availing himself of the Danish and Russian fleets. The British response to this ominous threat had been decided on a couple of weeks before Canning heard of the *Chesapeake* affair in remote waters. Monroe wrote Madison that a powerful fleet had been dispatched with the purpose of seizing that of little Denmark, a country with which Great Britain was at peace, and possibly that of Russia, a recent British ally. To him this probably seemed but another example of British ruthlessness, as it unquestionably did to Jefferson and Madison when they learned of it. And it should have been obvious that His Majesty's government was in no mood to yield to the claims of any weak neutral.

Monroe's report on developments in London came to the attention of the Secretary of State and the President shortly after the latter returned from his brief visit to Poplar Forest in September. The circumstances of its transmission and receipt provide a minor illustration of the vicissitudes of communication in that era. After it had crossed the Atlantic in the care of the traveler to whom Monroe had entrusted it and had reached Washington, it got into the hands of a post rider who passed by Montpelier without delivering it. Finding Madison's mail in the rider's valise when he reached Monticello, Jefferson, after administering a rebuke to him, sent it back to Montpelier unopened. On returning the communication from London for Jefferson's perusal, Madison suggested that he should not have been so

[5] On the treaties and Canning's knowledge, see J. H. Rose, *Life of Napoleon I,* II, ch. XXVII; G. C. Brodrick and J. K. Frothingham in *Political History of England,* ed. by Wm. Hunt and R. L. Poole, XI (1919), 52–56.

scrupulous. Only two days were lost by the mishap, however, and at this stage they were in no position to do anything anyway.

Madison wrote Jefferson: "You will find that the British Government renounces the pretension to search ships of war for deserters; but employs words which may possibly be meant to qualify the renunciation, or at least to quibble away the promised atonement."[6] His apprehension was increased by the irritation he perceived in Canning's note, but he was most disturbed at this time by the recent trials of the four deserters at Halifax. The actions of Berkeley, who had not waited on the slow processes of diplomacy, suggested that the Admiral had little fear of the civil authorities in England, where in fact powerful influence was being exerted in his behalf. One of the seamen, Jenkin Ratford, whom Madison now described as probably a British subject, had been executed, and the embarrassment of having to return him had thus been avoided by the British. The annoyance of the Secretary of State over the proceedings at Halifax, which he described as insulting, was strongly expressed in a letter he wrote Monroe. Besides insisting that the "severest example" must be made of the person or persons responsible for this offense against American honor (presumably Berkeley), he protested vigorously against the trials of the three Americans.[7] This outburst may be regarded as a futile protest against a *fait accompli* which is chiefly significant as revealing his state of mind. Before he and Jefferson got back to Washington they had reason to believe that their specific demands would not be — in fact could not be — wholly granted. The particular actions that incensed Madison most were those of the British naval officers and he told Jefferson that he was more convinced than ever of "the absolute necessity of a radical cure for the ills inflicted by British ships of war frequenting our waters." Jefferson was in full agreement with this judgment, no doubt, but both he and the Secretary of State seem to have been more disposed to quiet public fear than to excite it.

He went along with Madison's suggestion that the assurances given by Canning be publicized unofficially. Accordingly, the part of the letter to Monroe in which the Foreign Secretary disavowed the pretension to search warships and promised satisfaction if the attack on the *Chesapeake* rested on no other grounds was published in the *National Intelligencer*. Canning's actual words were given without quotation

[6] Madison to TJ, Sept. 20, 1807 (LC, 30188–30189). The mishap about the mails is referred to in this letter and in TJ's of the same date (LC, 30183).
[7] Madison to Monroe, Oct. 21, 1807 (Hunt, VII, 466–468). He wrote a letter of protest to Erskine, Oct. 9 (FO, 5:52 [5], pp. 282–283). Anthony Steel (in *Mariner's Mirror*, XXXIX, 252) says that Madison disregarded the relative lightness of the punishment of the three Americans.

marks and without any indication of the source of the information.[8]
The purpose of this handout to Samuel Harrison Smith's paper, as
stated by Madison, was to enable the public to judge of the chances of
peace for itself. The significance of the qualification attached to
Canning's promise probably escaped many readers, and other items in
the newspapers created the impression that the civil authorities in
England were peaceably disposed, whatever might be said of naval
commanders in American waters. It was reported that Canning had
expressed in the House of Commons "the most unequivocal desire and
wish" to maintain with the United States "the relations of peace and
amity," and had said that no new instructions respecting that country
had been issued by the present ministry. Erskine believed that this
intelligence encouraged the hope that Berkeley's orders would not be
justified and that honorable reparation would be offered.[9] Gazettes
reporting Canning's communication to the House of Commons were
received by Madison from Monroe about this time, along with a letter
in which the latter said that no step unfriendly to the United States
had yet been taken by the government.[10] He reported, however, that
Canning had inquired about Jefferson's proclamation (of which Monroe himself had not yet been officially informed), and he stated that,
since the war party was strong and active, he could not anticipate the
probable course of events. That was not the worst of it. On the day
that Jefferson reached Washington he received a private report on the
prevalent mood of the British which in its pessimism went beyond any
as yet made by Monroe.

Immediately on arriving in New York after a visit to England, David
Humphreys communicated to the President his observations on the
state of opinion there.[11] This former aide to George Washington,
whom Jefferson had replaced as minister to Spain with a Republican
appointee in 1801, wrote as a patriotic American, not as a Federalist. He
reported that several pamphlets that appeared in London some weeks
earlier were "calculated to prepare the public mind for a rupture with
America," and said he was inclined to believe that a war with the
Republic would be more popular than the one against the revolting

[8] Madison to TJ, Sept. 21, 1807; and Madison to TJ, Sept. 22 (LC, 30198–30200);
National Intelligencer, Sept. 28.

[9] *National Intelligencer*, Oct. 2, 1807; Erskine to Canning, Oct. 5, No. 25 (FO,
5:52). On the same date, in Dispatch No. 26, Erskine acknowledged Canning's
note of Aug. 3, accompanying copies of Monroe's letter and his reply, and
instructing Erskine to make his own language conformable to the sentiments
Canning had expressed.

[10] Monroe to Madison, Aug. 14, 1807 (*A.S.P.F.R.*, III, 188).

[11] Humphreys to TJ, Sept. 25, 1807 (LC, 30219–30221), received Oct. 3.

colonies had been. Not only did naval officers, shipowners, and ancient enemies of American independence favor war with the United States; old friends looked forward to it as "an almost inevitable event, and not very much to be deprecated — at best, much less so than the loss of the smallest of their naval rights." They attributed American prosperity to British indulgence, which had been abused and could not be safely continued. "To maintain the naval superiority or perish as a nation, is the prevalent doctrine of the day," he said. He believed that the abstract question of searching ships of war, if considered alone, would be decided to American satisfaction with little hesitation.[12] In his opinion, however, such would not be the case if it should be insisted that the American flag protected persons in merchant as well as naval vessels. But that was just what Monroe had been instructed to insist upon. Toward the end of his letter Humphreys said that he saw slight chance of Americans' enjoying permanent safety except by "becoming in a great degree an armed and united people." Jefferson appears to have made no reply, but he could hardly have dismissed these observations from mind while preparing his annual message to Congress.

The expedition against Denmark occasioned heated references in the newspapers during the weeks immediately preceding the congressional session, arousing the indignation of William Duane in particular. Jefferson always respected the publisher of the *Aurora*, while recognizing that he often let his passions run away with him. Less friendly observers charged him with inveterate Anglophobia. Commenting on the declarations of the minister who has gone down in history as Copenhagen Jackson, Duane said these meant that the British no longer distinguished between a neutral and an enemy, that ordinary covenants such as treaties would no longer stand in the way of their policy, that in their view no neutral would be secure except under their protection.[13] About ten days before Congress convened, in an editorial that was republished after the fall of Copenhagen had been reported, Duane drew an explicit parallel between the situation of Denmark and that of his own country, saying that if Americans had twenty-four sail of the line as the Danes had, they might well be asked to deposit them in some British port. Making no allowance for the threat the British themselves faced from Napoleon, Duane thus addressed his countrymen:

> *People of America!* Do you expect anything more of justice
> from the *amicable* dispositions of the British than the *Danes?*

[12] After studying comments in the newspapers in this period, Perkins concludes that even this went beyond popular opinion (*Prologue to War*, pp. 191–192).

[13] *Aurora*, Oct. 2, 1807, under the heading, "No Neutrals — But Allies or Enemies."

Do you think that those who invade Zealand, would hesitate to invade Long Island, or Rhode Island, or Sullivan's Island?[14]

The geographical analogy that this fiery journalist presented was imperfect, but there could be little doubt that the beleaguered British had arrived at the point where necessity overrode law; and Duane had correctly concluded that in their eyes there could be no real neutrals. To be sure, the same could have been said of Napoleon — a fact of which Americans were soon to become more aware than they were now. Meanwhile, it appeared that, in the face of overwhelming British sea power, Denmark, far from being protected by her navy, was all the more endangered because of its existence. This small country had found no safety in a policy of armed neutrality.

ii

During his presidency Jefferson's attitude toward Great Britain and France varied directly with his hopes and fears, especially his fears, for the security and well-being of his own country. For a time in his first term, before the acquisition of Louisiana, he believed that the future of the United States was most endangered by imperial France. In this period he flirted briefly with the idea of an alliance with Great Britain, and, early in the summer of 1803, he spoke of that country as a bulwark against the Napoleonic torrent which threatened to engulf the world. Of this bulwark, he said, mankind should not be deprived.[15] In fact, the torrent was being deflected from his own shores by that time, and he had more freedom than hitherto to voice sentiments of universal benevolence. Unlike certain New England Federalists, however, he did not recognize the British as the ordained custodians of human liberties. He assigned that role to his own countrymen; and, during the summer of 1807, he was in no doubt as to which power most endangered them. In a private letter to a friend and supporter he expressed himself on this point without reserve:

I never expected to be under the necessity of wishing success to Buonaparte. But the English being equally tyrannical at sea as he is on land, & that tyranny bearing on us in every point of either honor or interest, I say, 'down with England' and as for what Buonaparte is then to do to us, let us trust to the chapter of acci-

14 *Ibid.*, Oct. 17, 1807. See also Oct. 4, Nov. 3.
15 TJ to Sir John Sinclair, June 30, 1803 (L. & B., X, 397).

dents. I cannot, with the Anglomen, prefer a certain present evil to a future hypothetical one.[16]

He was still indifferent to Napoleon and down on England when preparing his message to Congress in October, and the early drafts of that message reflected a more belligerent spirit than he had revealed to the public. Two of his ministers who did not always agree, the Secretary of the Treasury and the Secretary of the Navy, said in almost the same words that the message sounded like a manifesto designed to prepare the minds of their countrymen for war.[17] They both regarded certain representations and expressions of his as ill-timed. Robert Smith suggested that these be saved until circumstances might necessitate them. Peace was their favorite object, he said, not the excitation of Congress while negotiations with the British were still going on. At this juncture the Secretary of the Navy was clearly a counselor of delay and moderation.

The specific alterations proposed by Gallatin pointed in the same direction and he wrote at greater length about the existing situation. They were in a state of indecision, he said, and must remain so until after they received a reply from England. In his opinion this would probably be determinative, but he stated explicitly what Madison had hinted at — namely, that it might be equivocal. The British government might take "some new and admissible ground" and delay settlement while this was being considered. Meanwhile, as long as there was any hope at all of an honorable settlement, Gallatin believed that nothing should be done to widen the breach or injure British pride unnecessarily. The President should not bring up old grievances that were already well known.

Shortly after the attack on the *Chesapeake*, Gallatin had said privately that he regarded war as unavoidable and that he was devoting his attention to the necessary preparation for it. At that time he also said that, although "not very sanguine as to the brilliancy of our exploits, the field where we can act without a navy being very limited, and perfectly aware that a war in a great degree passive and consisting

[16] TJ to Thomas Leiper, Aug. 21, 1807 (Ford, IX, 130).

[17] Three drafts of TJ's message are in LC, 30360–30371. The two first but not the last are printed in parallel columns in Ford, IX, 145–166. In the notes are extensive comments by Gallatin (from LC, 30327–30330; 30334–30335) and brief ones by Rodney (from LC, 30344). Ford does not give the comments of Dearborn (LC, 30278), who also thought the early wording too strong, or of Robert Smith (LC, 30300–30302) and seems to have regarded the second draft as the final one. In printed form, it is in *Annals*, 10 Cong., 1 sess., I, 14–18 (Oct. 27, 1807). TJ may be presumed to have discussed the message with Madison in person.

of privations will become very irksome to the people," he felt no apprehension of the final result.[18] When counseling the President in the autumn he did not say that he had changed his mind, but his emphasis was certainly not on belligerency. Regarding the support of public opinion as valuable abroad and indispensable at home, he said: "We will be universally justified in the eyes of the world, and unanimously supported by the nation, if the ground of war be England's refusal to disavow or to make satisfaction for the outrage on the *Chesapeake*. But I am confident that we will meet with a most formidable opposition should England do that and we should still declare war because she refuses to make the proposed arrangement regarding seamen." Accordingly, he suggested that some course short of war might be proper, the odium of declaring war being left to England. The tone he was recommending to the President contrasted with the sharp one assumed by the Secretary of State that very day in his letter to Monroe regarding the proceedings of the court-martial at Halifax. It would seem that at this stage Madison was the more doctrinaire and legalistic of the two, while Gallatin was more realistic and flexible.

To this practical man delay seemed desirable for many reasons. Even if Canada should be invaded this could be better done in winter, when reinforcements from England could not be brought in. Furthermore, American ships in the Far East had not reached home, and the necessary steps for defense had been taken in only small part. Viewing the subject from all angles, he was convinced that the proper course would be to prepare "to the utmost" for war and to pursue it with vigor if it should prove unavoidable, but in the meantime to be cautious in both word and deed, hoping to preserve peace. He wrote his wife a little later that he had succeeded in neutralizing Jefferson's unnecessarily warlike message and regarded this as fortunate, since the inclinations of the public were unquestionably peaceful.[19] Others had played a part in moderating the message, but, since Jefferson accepted virtually all of Gallatin's specific suggestions, the influence of the sagacious Secretary of the Treasury is indubitable and may have been preponderant. Unfortunately we do not know just what advice was given by Madison.

In the message the President sent Congress he clearly and succinctly described American grievances not previously reported to that body, and the continuing efforts of the government to remedy these peaceably, but he made no direct reference to the likelihood of war. He

[18] Gallatin to J. H. Nicholson, July 17, 1807 (*Writings*, I, 339).
[19] Gallatin to his wife, Oct. 30, 1807 (Adams, *Life*, pp. 363-364).

recognized the possibility of a change in international relations. These, he said, were "now awaiting the determination of others"; and as far as this message went the "others" were the British. He referred to a Spanish decree, conformable to Napoleon's Berlin decree, but thought it probable that, like the latter, it was not being applied to the United States.[20] He still cherished the hope that old differences with Spain might be brought to an issue of some sort; and he said that with other European nations harmony had been uninterrupted. That is, there were no particular grievances against France at the moment. His tone was unmistakably anti-British, but apart from the tentatively projected invasion of Canada, which could not be properly discussed in public, the role he foresaw for his country was wholly defensive, and the posture his government had assumed was one of watchful waiting. In the summer, when he believed that the public mind was made up for war, he had stated in private that he hoped it would continue so.[21] It would be nearer the truth to say that he hoped for the continuance of public indignation against the British in support of his efforts to gain satisfaction from them. But it was not to be expected that public indignation would continue at fever pitch in the absence of further provocation; and, in the weeks following his *Chesapeake* proclamation, he had done more to allay than to heighten it. In his message to Congress he managed, with the help of his advisers, to avoid impaling himself on either horn of his dilemma. While stating grievances impressively he eschewed incendiarism; and, in a time of necessary indecision, he reflected not only the judgment of the administration as a whole but also, it seems, the preponderant opinion of his countrymen. His report on the efforts of the government to prepare for possible hostilities was couched in such general terms that his auditors could have gained the impression that it had done considerably less than it actually did. He had said privately that, while he and his associates would need the confidence of their friends that everything was being done that could be, they would like to appear to be doing nothing.[22] The reasons for this cryptic statement appear to have been that, on the one hand, he did not want to forewarn the British before the ships could get home, and that, on the other, he did not want to commit Congress or seem to encroach in any way on the prerogatives of that body. The wisdom of this degree of secrecy may be questioned, but Gallatin was deeply concerned for those ships and all of the

[20] A translation of the Spanish decree of Feb. 19, 1807, was transmitted with the message (*A.S.P.F.R.*, III, 6).
[21] TJ to William Duane, July 20, 1807 (Ford, IX, 120).
[22] *Ibid.*

high officials of the executive branch were well aware that their actions would be subjected to sharp legislative scrutiny.

Until Congress should meet and act, the President and his lieutenants had to work within the limits of existing laws and appropriations. The provisions for national defense made during the two last congressional sessions were somewhat larger than hitherto but, far from reflecting the purpose to pursue warlike preparations "to the utmost," they were based on the expectation that peace would continue.[23] In his efforts to meet the exigencies of the situation during the summer and early autumn of 1807, Jefferson admitted that in one respect he had stretched his authority. In his message to Congress he said that engagements had been entered into for military and naval stores beyond existing authorization and that expenses, also unprovided for, had been incurred in putting gunboats into service. Pointed inquiries were made by the Federalist leader, Congressman Josiah Quincy, and others. John Randolph brought up the question of the application of money to one object when it had been appropriated for another and drew an analogy with Republican criticisms of Hamilton in the Giles resolutions. He quoted and chided his old friend Gallatin and charged the Republicans with abjuring past principles without admitting it. Both he and Quincy voted for the appropriations, however, and only two members of the House voted against them.[24]

Jefferson had promptly availed himself of the discretionary authority granted him by law to require the governors of the states to organize and put in readiness for immediate service their respective quotas of 100,000 militia.[25] Companies of militia were activated in Virginia to protect the port of Norfolk, and in Michigan to meet the threat from the Indians. In the most recent congressional session a bill to increase the regular army that had passed the Senate was lost in the House, and a bill was then passed authorizing the President to accept companies of volunteers which would be credited to particular states towards their quotas of militia.[26] Jefferson received numerous offers of service by

[23] These provisions, and the actions of the executive under them, are described in detail by Mary P. Adams in her dissertation, "Jefferson's Military Policy," pp. 124–170, and by R. A. Erney in his dissertation, "The Public Life of Henry Dearborn," pp. 152–184. I describe them only briefly here, reserving comments on military and naval policy as a whole to chs. XXVII, XXVIII.

[24] Nov. 9, 10, 1807 (*Annals*, 10 Cong., 1 sess., pp. 818–853). For an account of the Giles resolutions, see *Jefferson and the Ordeal of Liberty*, ch. II.

[25] See above, p. 432.

[26] Feb. 24, 1807 (*Annals*, 9 Cong., 2 sess., pp. 1259–1260). The total was limited to 30,000.

mail which he referred to the various governors; and, toward the end of the summer, he had Dearborn write the governors, urging them to form companies of volunteers. These were preferable to the regular militia in that they were more likely to be young and eager. The measures of this period were subjected to no severe test, but he could report that danger had been averted both at Norfolk and in the Northwest. After the British had been heard from, he said, Congress could consider the question of the regular army.

During the two preceding years Congress had appropriated $300,000 for fortifications, which was a pitiably small sum for a country with so many exposed harbors. At Jefferson's request, Gallatin drew up a list of these, showing their relative need of protection.[27] Limited as it was in funds, the government had concentrated on New York, Charleston, and New Orleans, but had run into difficulties and made little progress anywhere.[28] Without entering into further consideration of this difficult problem at this point, suffice it to say that Jefferson, in his message, referred to the defense of the exposed points of the country as one of the first objects entitled to attention, and suggested that some of the surplus funds in the Treasury (on which he made a highly favorable report) might be applied to it.

At the session of 1805–1806, Congress had appropriated $250,000 for gunboats but, to Jefferson's regret, had failed to make a further appropriation in 1806–1807. He now said that he left to the wisdom of the Legislature the question whether the "movable force on the water, so material in aid of the defensive works on the land, should be augmented in this or any other form." That he sought augmentation in this form was clearly shown by later events, and in connection with these we shall describe and discuss his naval policy more fully.[29] In his message he stated that the existing gunboats had been assigned chiefly to the Chesapeake Bay, New York, and New Orleans. Besides the task of getting them ready for service, the administration had faced that of manning them; and he suggested the formation of a special body of naval militia for that purpose.

In what was in effect an interim report he made few specific suggestions. He had other ways of making them, and bills privately approved by him could be introduced by his supporters, as some were before he learned of developments in England. But there was an unmistakably tentative quality in the document that he had prepared while awaiting

[27] In Gallatin's memo. of preparatory measures (*Writings*, I, 342–344).

[28] The activities and frustrations of the Secretary of War in connection with fortification are described in detail by Erney, pp. 173–180.

[29] See below, ch. XXVII.

news from abroad. It was fortunate, he said, that this would arrive when the Supreme Council of the nation was assembled and ready to aid him by its wisdom and authority. His deferential expressions may be attributed to his characteristic politeness, but he had a clear recognition of the limitations imposed on his own authority by the constitutional system as he interpreted it. He jealously guarded his prerogatives in the conduct of foreign affairs; he had not yet revealed to the legislators precisely what he had asked of the British. Questions of peace and war, however, had to be referred to Congress and considered in the light of public opinion. His attitude at this juncture may perhaps be described as fatalistic. It reminds one of the reflections of Prince Andrey on Marshal Kutusov in Tolstoy's *War and Peace:* "He knows that there is something stronger and more important than his will — that is, the inevitable march of events, . . . and, seeing their significance, can abstain from meddling, from following his own will, and aiming at something else."[30] The analogy between the situation of the President of the United States at this time and that of the Russian general who, after the pact between his Emperor and Napoleon had been broken, foiled that conqueror by retreating, is imperfect, but Jefferson was in no egotistical or imperious mood while waiting to learn just how the course of international affairs had been determined by others.

iii

Not until the end of November, more than a month after he sent his annual message to Congress, did he learn of the outcome of the negotiations over the *Chesapeake* affair in London. Erskine, who received his official dispatches before Jefferson and Madison got theirs, showed them copies of the letters that ended the discussion.[31] Writing his son-in-law about Canning's letter, Jefferson described it as "unfriendly, proud, and harsh." With respect to the attack on the *Chesapeake*, it seemed to offer little more than "the disavowal of having ordered the act," and in his opinion it showed slight concern to avoid war.[32] He was entirely correct about its tone and essentially so about its purport. The Foreign Secretary admitted that British naval officers had committed, without authorization, a hostile act and that the injured coun-

---

[30] *War and Peace*, Modern Library edn., n.d., p. 697.
[31] Canning to Monroe, Sept. 23, 1807; Monroe to Canning, Sept. 29 (*A.S.P.F.R.*, III, 199–202). Presumably TJ also saw at this time Monroe's letter of Sept. 7 (*ibid.*, 189–191), to which Canning was replying.
[32] TJ to TMR, Nov. 30, 1807 (LC, 30506).

try was entitled to reparation. Claiming, however, that the United States was also guilty of hostile acts, he argued that these must be considered before the precise nature of the reparation could be determined. He implied that the enlistment of British deserters was one of them and specifically mentioned the President's proclamation. While expressing entire willingness to give further consideration to matters relating to the *Chesapeake,* affair, he categorically denied that impressment was one of these. Thus he effectually terminated the current negotiations, for Monroe had to state that he was explicitly instructed *not* to separate the two questions. That hapless minister, acting on Madison's instruction, had suggested that a special envoy carry to America the message of apology and reparation. The idea was to make the amends impressive. Seizing upon this suggestion, Canning stated that a special envoy would be sent to enter into negotiations about the *Chesapeake* which Monroe, because of his instructions, could not carry on.

In this situation Monroe appeals to human sympathy, and his superiors at home invite criticism for having granted him no leeway. Speaking of the procedure of the Americans in this negotiation, Canning said to one of his own countrymen: "If they had taken our atonement by itself, as we offered it, they would have appeared to gain something. But they have so managed matters that we shall now appear to bully them even in making reparation. Nothing could be more advantageous for us than the course which they have taken."[33] One may question if what they offered in the first place really amounted to atonement. Canning qualified his assurances, and he never sounded apologetic. No doubt he was convinced that public sentiment in England would not have supported a formal apology. Procrastination was his policy and Monroe's rigid instructions made this easier to pursue, but it need not be supposed that he would have made atonement that the American government would have regarded as sufficient if the impressment question had not come up. Nor does he appear to have assumed the role of bully with reluctance.

Shortly after Jefferson and Madison saw Erskine's copy of Canning's letter to Monroe, somebody in the government prepared a brief summary of it for publication in the *National Intelligencer.* The paragraph that appeared in print was introduced by the statement (which may have been written in the office of the newspaper) that it was derived from public rumor, but we may be sure that its authenticity was recognized by others besides Erskine, who promptly sent a copy

[33] Canning to Lord Boringdon, Sept. 30, 1807 (quoted by Perkins, pp. 195-196).

of it to his own government.[34] Jefferson revealed his state of mind more fully in a longer statement which has been preserved through the years in his papers. Presumably it was a tentative draft of which he thought better and made no use.[35] Some things in it probably seemed too strong even for anonymous publication. In it he suggested that the dispatching of a special British negotiator might prove to be "a mere maneuver to avoid settlement"; and he stated that, in the meantime, the peace of the United States was at the mercy of British officers, "whose interest and wish is war with all mankind." He asserted that the British, claiming the right to take their seamen (and Americans with them) wherever they found them, were doing so not only on the high seas, but in foreign ports and that, according to their principle, they might send their press gangs into the streets of New York and Norfolk. The two questions which Canning had sought to separate were to his mind inseparable; and he stated that there could be no hope of friendship or even of the continuance of peace between the two countries so long as Americans who left their own shores were in danger of seizure by the first British officer they chanced to meet and of consignment to service in the Royal Navy.

The shorter statement which was released for anonymous publication contained no reference to the likelihood of eventual war or to the horrors of impressment. Within its limits it was a faithful report of the position Canning had taken, though it did not reflect the forcefulness of his presentation of his country's case. Nor could it have been expected to do so since he argued from a premise the American government was unable to accept — namely, what John Quincy Adams called "the odious pretence of a *right* in the King of Great Britain to force his own subjects into his naval service in time of war."[36] Jefferson could accept no argument in extenuation of the press gang. The final sentence of the paragraph that was prepared by the administration reflected a judgment so similar to his private comment to his son-in-law that he may be presumed to have written it. It said: "The letter is in a style more haughty than conciliatory, and calculated rather to increase than lessen the sentiment of indignation so generally excited by the unprincipled conduct of G.B. towards neutrals generally, and particularly towards the United States."

---

[34] TJ sent an advance copy of it to TMR with his letter of Nov. 30, 1807 (LC, 30506). It appeared in the *National Intelligencer* on Dec. 2, 1807, and Erskine sent a clipping of it with his letter of that date to Canning, No. 29 (FO, 5:52).

[35] LC, 169:29583. The date and designation of this on the index card are wholly conjectural. From internal evidence the statement appears to have been prepared for newspaper publication.

[36] See above, p. 401.

In his annual message to Congress, Jefferson had avoided such language; and during recent weeks he had been disturbed when highly pessimistic rumors about the negotiations in London were circulated.[37] He had blown both hot and cold during the long period of uncertainty. Until this time, though, he had been notably restrained in public, guarding against any utterance that might imperil the negotiations. Also, he had shown genuine concern for the accurate reporting of events. Ostensibly, the purpose of the thinly disguised statement in the *National Intelligencer* was to provide the public with correct information that he was not yet in position to communicate officially. At this moment, however, he was not at all averse to a rekindling of the spirit of indignation against the British. At the opening of Congress he had judged the members to be "extremely disposed for peace."[38] Since that time their dander had risen, as was shown by the report of a committee of the House. This asserted that the outrage on the *Chesapeake* was "stamped with circumstances of indignity and insult, of which there is scarcely to be found a parallel in the history of civilized nations"; and that, if sanctioned by the British government, it provided just cause for "instant and severe retaliation."[39] Sending a copy of this to his own government, along with the statement about Canning's letter in the *National Intelligencer*, Erskine reported that the question of peace or war was still being debated throughout the country. While he still believed that cordiality toward the British was not to be expected while the practice of impressment was continued, he clung to the opinion that war would be prevented by a "fair reparation" for the attack on the *Chesapeake*.[40] The legislators were in better position to consider the prospects of that a few days later, when the President, having heard from Monroe, sent them copies of that minister's correspondence with Canning.

In his very brief message Jefferson stated that the discussion of the *Chesapeake* affair was to be transferred to Washington by a special minister and requested that, since the negotiation was still pending, the documents be considered as confidential.[41] In view of the fact that he

[37] TJ to TMR, Nov. 16, 1807 (LC, 30466).
[38] TJ to TMR, Oct. 26, 1807 (LC, 30353).
[39] The report of Nov. 17, 1807, with accompanying documents including the findings of the court of inquiry held on board the *Chesapeake* (Oct. 5–Nov. 4) is in *Annals*, 10 Cong., 2 sess., II, 2287–2326, and in *A.S.P.F.R.*, III, 6–23. Court-martial proceedings against Barron began Jan. 4, 1808. These resulted in his suspension for five years without pay (*Proceedings of the General Court Martial convened for the Trial of Commodore James Barron*, published by Navy Dept., 1822).
[40] Erskine to Canning, Dec. 2, 1807, No. 29 (FO, 5:52).
[41] Communicated Dec. 8, 1807, in a message dated Dec. 7 (*A.S.P.F.R.*, III, 24). The letters were not made public until Mar. 22, 1808, after the negotiations with

had caused a summary of one of these to be promptly printed in a newspaper, this request seems highly inconsistent and it may be cited as an example of his devious procedure. But he did not ask that the documents be returned to him, as he customarily did when seeking to maintain secrecy in a delicate diplomatic situation. The present situation was one of frustration rather than delicacy, and what he appears to have meant was that the forms of official propriety should be observed. While he employed indirect means to let his opinion of Canning's attitude become known, he refrained from official comment on the correspondence. The legislators could now perceive for themselves the harshness of the Foreign Minister's tone and the arrogance of his manner. Canning had left little ground for an immediate rejoinder, however. By causing the question of reparation to be deferred that astute diplomat, showing himself to be also an adroit parliamentarian, had postponed debate on that issue by moving an adjournment. But George H. Rose, who had received the assignment as special British envoy, was still a long way from Washington when fresh reports from overseas heightened the crisis in the international affairs of the neutral Republic and precipitated a fateful action.

Rose in Washington had ended. At that time TJ transmitted also the documents bearing on the Monroe-Pinkney treaty. Not till then did he send Congress Monroe's instructions regarding the *Chesapeake,* and this appears to have been the case with Monroe's letter of Oct. 10, 1807, to Madison about the negotiations.

[XXVI]

The Lesser Evil: The Embargo

JUST after he learned of the disappointing outcome of Monroe's negotiations regarding the *Chesapeake*, Jefferson observed to his son-in-law that, on receiving the official papers, Congress would take up the question whether "War, Embargo or Nothing" should be the nation's course. He was of the opinion that the legislators would be disposed to take the middle way while adopting certain measures of defense.[1] The particular defense measures he mentioned in this connection conformed closely to previous recommendations of his, but he gave the impression that he had nothing to do with them. In deference to the doctrine of the separation of powers he customarily expressed himself this way regarding legislative matters. Judging from the results thus far his avoidance of any appearance of dictation was wise, and his extraordinary success in dealing with Congress had been due, in part at least, to his sensitivity to and respect for congressional opinion — or, to be more precise, for the opinion of the Republican majority. By this time he was paying little attention to Federalists in Congress or anywhere else, and the fulminations of Burr's lawyers and the rulings of Chief Justice Marshall appear to have strengthened his conviction that his political foes were intransigent and irreconcilable. His personal popularity at this stage cannot be measured with precision, but one might assume that the loyalty of his countrymen to him as their chief of state was enhanced in a time of danger from abroad, and there is much evidence that it was. Furthermore, the Federalists were weaker than ever in Congress, and the revolt of John Randolph, far from dividing the Republicans seriously, had caused all but a fragment of them to rally even more closely around Jefferson as their leader. Randolph could never be silenced, but staunch friends of the administration took control in this congressional session.

[1] TJ to TMR, Nov. 30, 1807 (LC, 30506).

Avoiding a contest he could not win, Nathaniel Macon absented himself at the beginning of the session, and his name was not even presented for the speakership of the House. To that post Joseph B. Varnum of Massachusetts was elected, and he appointed George W. Campbell of Tennessee chairman of the Ways and Means Committee. Gallatin, who doubted if anybody could handle its business as well as John Randolph, regretted his replacement at the time, but as floor leader during this session Campbell matched Randolph at his best.[2] It would have been unlike Jefferson to play an overt part in such an internal matter as the organization of the House of Representatives, but he had regretted the retirement of Barnabas Bidwell and had encouraged Wilson Cary Nicholas to stand for Thomas Mann Randolph's old seat, expecting this friend and neighbor to play a more important legislative role than in fact he did.[3] In Campbell the President found both a loyal supporter and an eloquent champion. Less than two weeks after he wrote his son-in-law, in the course of a debate during which he was charged on the one hand with seeking to impose his will on Congress, and on the other with not making proposals that were sufficiently specific, Campbell paid him effusive tribute. After declaring that the President's past record constituted all the defense he needed, the new floor leader said:

So long as virtue, wisdom and patriotism continue to be revered in the world, so long will his character remain a distinguished monument of the triumph of liberty and the rights of man over despotism and aristocracy, around which the sons of freedom will rejoice to rally; when the memory of those who attempt to defame him, will have been forgotten, having vanished and become obscured by the superior lustre of his well-earned fame, like the feeble gleam of the glow-worm before the splendid glory of the mid-day sun.[4]

Besides being eloquent and responsive, Campbell could deliver the votes — as Jefferson must have quickly perceived.

[2] The organization of the House and the leadership of Campbell are well described and discussed by A. B. Lacy in his dissertation, "Jefferson and Congress," pp. 184–201. At the end of the previous session the regulars, hoping to displace Randolph, who was Macon's appointee, had favored the election of committee chairmen. Now, with Varnum in the chair, they reversed their position and defeated a move to effect this change.

[3] TJ to Bidwell, July 11, 1807 (Ford, IX, 106–107); TJ to Nicholas, Feb. 28, 1807 (ibid., pp. 32–33).

[4] Dec. 11, 1807, in a debate on an appropriation for gunboats (Annals, 10 Cong., 1 sess., p. 1165; quoted by Lacy, p. 192).

There was no such party discipline in the Senate, but the Republican majority there was even larger than in the House — 22 to 7. Furthermore, the ablest as well as the most independent of the Federalists gave clear sign early in the session that he would support the national interest, as he perceived it, regardless of the sentiment of his party and constituents. The private correspondence of John Quincy Adams shows as unmistakably that he had reservations about Jefferson's policy as his diary does that he enjoyed the conversation at that gentleman's dinner table, but in this critical time he was one of the most consistent supporters of the administration. As chairman of the committee to which was referred the part of the President's message dealing with the outrages by British warships in American waters, he presented early in the session a bill that specifically authorized such action as Jefferson had taken. In fact, what was commonly known as the aggression bill went a good deal further. It provided that no British armed vessel should enter American waters unless reparation for the attack on the *Chesapeake* had been made to the President's satisfaction. Not only so. It forbade entrance to any vessel that had committed trespass or spoliation on any American merchant ship. Senator Adams told his father that he was personally responsible for few of the provisions of this measure and that it might be too high-toned, but that he strongly supported its principles and believed it to be indicative of senatorial sentiment with regard to the *Chesapeake* affair and "the support of our own authority within our own jurisdiction." Actually, only three die-hard Federalists voted against it. The aggression bill was indefinitely postponed in the House, where it was regarded as unnecessary and even as going too far, but the all-but-unanimous action of the Senate, in advance of the report on Monroe's negotiations, could not have failed to be reassuring to Jefferson.[5] Two days later Adams introduced a resolution calling upon the President for a report on seamen who had been impressed by the British. This action, manifesting an interest in the subject which was to endure, led to a lengthy report, prepared by the Department of State, which was submitted several months later.[6]

Jefferson talked as though he were leaving the decision between peace and war wholly to the body that was authorized by the Constitution to make it. But he had shown no reluctance in assuming responsibility in the conduct of foreign affairs, and he could have been

---

[5] The aggression bill was introduced Nov. 23, 1807, and passed Dec. 2 by a vote of 26 to 3 (*Annals*, 10 Cong., 1 sess., pp. 33-38, 40). In the House on Dec. 29, TJ's old secretary, W. A. Burwell, implied that it granted too much power to the President (*ibid.*, pp. 1243-1245). J. Q. Adams wrote his father about it Dec. 27 (*Writings*, III, 167).

[6] Adams, *Writings*, III, 167; *A.S.P.F.R.*, III, 36-79.

charged with the abdication of leadership if he had made no recommendation in this crisis.[7] His indignation against the "tyrants of the sea" had been fired anew, and it may have been greater than that of most of the members of Congress. He undoubtedly believed that war was justifiable and for a time seems to have regarded it as inevitable. His unwillingness to recommend it now cannot be properly attributed to pacifism on his part. We may doubt if any statesman of his age perceived more clearly the ills of war; but his actions against the Barbary pirates, and those he authorized in connection with the acquisition of Louisiana, showed that he was by no means averse to the use of force when in his judgment circumstances required it.[8] As a pragmatic statesman, however, he had to ask another question: Did circumstances *permit* recourse to force? That public opinion would have supported war more generally and more ardently in July than in December seems a safe speculation, and Jefferson may have been disappointed that public indignation against the British did not revive in its earlier intensity. This is not to say that he now *wanted* war and did not ask for it merely because he could not get it.[9] He had probably been relieved by Gallatin's suggestion that something less would be desirable, and, besides congressional opinion and the unpreparedness of the country, there were other compelling reasons why an immediate recommendation of war against Great Britain was not a viable option. For the time at least it had been removed from the list of alternatives by the course of events.

At this stage the President could not well invoke the outrage on the *Chesapeake* as a *casus belli*. What Gallatin had recognized as a possibility had turned out to be a reality: the British reply to American representations was *not* determinative. The deferment of the negotiations might be only a maneuver and nothing whatsoever might come of them — in fact, nothing did — but they could not be summarily rejected. And, although as indignant as ever about impressment, Jefferson seems to have been convinced by his Secretary of the Treasury and others that war on that issue would neither have been recognized

[7] Henry Adams (*History*, IV, 145–151) gives a grossly exaggerated account of this situation, saying that at this stage TJ's authority approached the absolute and that "his power found no restraint."

[8] The references to his "pacifism" in L. M. Sears, *Jefferson and the Embargo* (1927), ch. I and elsewhere, reflect the anti-military spirit of the decade in which that book was written.

[9] In *Prologue to War*, p. 149, Bradford Perkins says: "In July Jefferson could have had war but did not want it; now he probably wanted it but could not hope to get it." This single quotation does not do justice to the author's able treatment of this matter, but he credits TJ with more calculation than I perceive and is more confident than I am in his assessment of public opinion.

abroad as justifiable nor sanctioned by public opinion at home. Commercial difficulties with the British had not been resolved and there was little likelihood that they would be, but as far as Jefferson's knowledge went there had been no fresh provocation sufficient to arouse the country. War with the British on any account would have amounted to taking the side of France, but the French Minister had reported a few weeks earlier that he was shocked by the aversion of Americans to his country and saw no hope of an alliance.[10] War with the British, which had not seemed a wise and proper course in the summer, seemed even less so now. It might be inevitable in the long run — sagacious Gallatin believed it was but that the British should be left to declare it. The course he had suggested a month earlier — that they wait and prepare — still had much to commend it, and it was thoroughly compatible with Jefferson's temperament and basic policy.

Writing his father the very day that Jefferson learned of the outcome of Monroe's negotiations, John Quincy Adams said: "I remain of my first opinion on arrival here. The President's policy is *procrastination*, and if Great Britain does not wage *complete* war upon us, we shall end with doing nothing this session."[11] This was a discerning comment on Jefferson's policy. One is reminded again of the philosophy of Kutusov, as reported by Tolstoy. After quoting the French proverb "Dans le doute abstiens-toi" [When in doubt, don't], the General observed: "The strongest of all warriors are these two — time and patience."[12] The American President was a man of unusual patience who never doubted that time was on the side of his young country. The designation of him as a prophet of pacifism is unwarranted, but he was unquestionably a major prophet of non-involvement in world affairs. For his own time and generation it was basically a wise policy.

One of the options he mentioned to his son-in-law was to do nothing. In view of what actually happened to neutral nations during the Napoleonic wars, and also during the world wars of the twentieth century, it might be contended that the only thing a neutral can really do in such a power struggle is to grin and bear it. When physical resistance amounts to self-destruction and diplomacy brings no relief, it may appear that there is no feasible alternative to acquiescence. The government might limit itself to protestation, in the hope of redress after the hostilities are over, and leave defiance to individuals who are

[10] Turreau to Talleyrand, Sept. 4, 1807, quoted by Adams, *History*, IV, 141–142, from A.E.C.P.E.U., vol. 60.
[11] J. Q. to John Adams, Nov. 30, 1807 (*Writings*, III, 164).
[12] *War and Peace*, Mod. Lib. edn., p. 696.

willing to take risks — such as shipowners and sea captains, hoping that the gains from occasional success will overbalance many losses. There was highly profitable blockade-running in the Napoleonic Wars, as in the American Civil War, and Thomas Jefferson's government might have smiled on it as that of Jefferson Davis did. But deliberate governmental passivity, however acceptable it might be to those daring individuals who profited under it, could hardly have been an avowed policy that could be commended to the country as a whole, or that would have satisfied a proud people. And, although he mentioned to his son-in-law the possibility that Congress might decide to do nothing, he did not think this likely. Feeling the congressional pulse, he doubtless recognized that a policy of "nothingness" would be chiefly advocated by his political enemies. The Federalists as a group were not negative with respect to such measures of national defense as the upbuilding of the navy and the fortification of the harbors; but, as became increasingly clear, some of them would go to almost any length to avoid a rupture with Great Britain, not unnaturally believing that this would play into the hands of Napoleon.[13] Though Jefferson showed no disposition to listen to his political enemies he was very sensitive to Republican opinion, which he regarded as that of the overwhelming majority of his countrymen. His partisans in Congress were of uncertain mind as to the means to be employed in this crisis, but they were less tolerant of British offenses than the die-hard Federalists and, in view of the policy of their party in times past, they might have been expected to believe in the efficacy of economic measures of retaliation against their historic enemy. The Republicans could have been taunted if, when in overwhelming majority, they had renounced policies they had advocated when in opposition; and Erskine predicted, before the session started, that commercial restrictions on British trade would be adopted.[14]

As Jefferson well remembered, the weapon of economic pressure against the British was employed by the Patriot party before the Declaration of Independence. He was still in France when Madison invoked it without success in the first Congress under the Constitution. The little representative from Virginia then proposed discrimination in the tariff and tonnage laws against countries that did not have commercial treaties with the United States. He was aiming particularly at

[13] For a good statement of the attitude of the Essex Junto, see S. F. Bemis, *John Quincy Adams and the Foundations of American Foreign Policy* (1949), pp. 139-140.
[14] Comment from *N.Y. Evening Post* quoted without date in Brant, IV, 399; Erskine to Canning, Oct. 5, 1807, No. 29 (FO, 5:52).

the British and their trade practices, but the policy advocated by him then and by Jefferson as secretary of state soon thereafter could have been properly designated as one of reciprocity.[15] The question of primacy is of no particular importance, for the two men saw eye to eye. They were in no sense enemies of American commerce. Jefferson was seeking to advance it by helping his country break through the closed commercial systems of the time, and he was convinced that discrimination, or the threat of it, was the most powerful instrument the Republic had. The issue was joined in 1791, when reports of his, condemning British restrictions, were followed by a movement in Congress under Madison's leadership to effect retaliatory measures such as he favored. This movement was blocked by Hamilton, but British dread of this sort of retaliation was shown by the instructions to Hammond, their first minister to the United States. From these it appears that the defeat of such legislation was the chief immediate purpose of his mission.[16] The issue was joined again in 1793–1794. At the very end of his secretaryship of state Jefferson made a report on commerce in which he described and condemned British restrictions, as in fairness he could hardly have escaped doing. He continued to advocate a commercial treaty, but failing this he recommended counter-prohibitions, duties, and regulations. Shortly thereafter, in a time of fresh grievances against Britain, Madison introduced resolutions in Congress which called for retaliatory action and so alarmed Hamilton that he recommended the mission of John Jay to England.[17] The resulting treaty was far from satisfactory to the Republican party, but obviously the threat of economic retaliation had not been wholly without effect. That Jefferson and Madison retained their faith in it as a weapon should not be surprising. We should note, however, that the specific measures they had proposed thus far were relatively mild, and that Jefferson, who was so eager for a favorable treaty with Great Britain, laid special emphasis on the value of economic threats in negotiation. Circumstances had not occasioned him to advocate economic reprisals as an alternative to war.

Unfortunately, the extant records of the deliberations of the high executive officials regarding the international problems they faced in the critical month of December are very scanty. Jefferson and Madison do not appear to have communicated with each other by letters or

[15] See *Jefferson and the Rights of Man*, pp. 308–309.
[16] *Ibid.*, pp. 333–336.
[17] For TJ's Report, see *Jefferson and the Ordeal of Liberty*, pp. 154–161; for Madison's Resolutions, see Brant, III, ch. XXX.

memoranda at this time or to have reduced their conversations to writing. There was some correspondence between the President and the Secretary of the Treasury and upon this we must largely depend.[18] Several days before he sent copies of the Canning-Monroe correspondence to Congress, he said to Gallatin: "What is *good* in this case cannot be effected; we have, therefore, only to find out what will be *least bad*."[19] These words aptly describe the situation as a whole: there was no *good* way out of it, and the country was faced with a choice of evils.

At the moment he and Gallatin were talking in particular about the Non-Importation Act, already on the statute books, which, in the absence of further legislative action, would become effective in about ten days. Enacted in the spring of 1806, this measure, which forbade the importation of designated British goods, was not to become effective until the fall of that year, the idea being that as a threat it would be helpful to Monroe and Pinkney in their negotiations during the summer. "A milk and water bill, a dose of chicken broth to be taken nine months hence," said John Randolph. His words had seemed too contemptuous at the time, but events had borne out his prediction that this measure would not greatly alarm the British government.[20] In its weakness it reflected the difficulties that generally attend the enactment of restrictive economic measures, which are so often watered down on the protests of affected interests, but the administration had not favored the Gregg resolution, calling for the exclusion of *all* British imports until satisfactory arrangements had been made regarding impressment and commerce. Federalists interpreted this resolution as a virtual declaration of war that was clearly not warranted while negotiations were in prospect. Furthermore, Gallatin recognized the effect such drastic action would have on the government's revenue, which was chiefly derived from import duties. Looking backward, we may conclude that the situation really required a much stronger measure than the one adopted and a greater threat. That a bill calling for *complete* non-importation could have been passed, however, even if backed by the administration, is highly questionable. John Randolph, who appears here as an advocate of inaction, would have liked it even less than the one he derided.

---

[18] Jefferson and Madison rarely if ever wrote each other when in Washington together, but he and Gallatin did so frequently. He appears to have left no memorandum of any discussion of this situation in the Cabinet as a whole.

[19] Dec. 3, 1807, replying to a letter of the day before (Gallatin, *Writings*, I, 367).

[20] For the act, approved Apr. 18, 1806, to become effective Nov. 15, see *Annals*, 9 Cong., 1 sess., pp. 1259–1262; for the debate, see ch. VII above.

The law went into effect as scheduled on November 15, 1806, and, remaining in operation for about five weeks, it led to a number of prosecutions, seizures, and penalties.[21] For reasons that were primarily diplomatic but may have been to some extent administrative, Jefferson recommended the suspension of the law. Congress suspended it until the summer of 1807, causing the penalties to be remitted, and authorized him to suspend it further but not to a date later than December 14, when that body would again be in session. This he duly did, and the question he faced as that date approached was whether or not he should do anything about it. What had hitherto been, except for a few weeks, merely a threat could now be regarded as an anti-British measure of reprisal or economic coercion. Though not a powerful weapon, it was two-edged, and Americans as well as English could expect financial injury from it.

Toward the end of November, when Jefferson was still waiting to find out what had happened in London, a debate was precipitated in the House of Representatives by a memorial from "sundry merchants and traders" of Philadelphia, praying for the repeal of the Non-Importation Act. This culminated in the defeat of a resolution to refer the memorial to the Committee of Commerce and Manufactures.[22] The debate was not on the merits of the measure. John Randolph continued to ridicule it, and others described it as irritating and futile, but most of the argument of the supporters of the resolution bore on the right of petition. Their opponents, on the other hand, made no special point of defending the act — one of them even admitted that he disliked it. But it represented the approved policy of the government, they said, and this was no time for conciliation or wavering or retreat. They held that even the reference of the memorial to a committee would be a degradation of their dignity. This was a delaying action on the part of the majority, who were undoubtedly waiting not only for news from England but also for a recommendation or intimation from the President. Presumably they were disposed to follow his lead in almost anything, but we can hardly doubt that most of them would have regarded the repeal of the Non-Importation Act as an ignoble action.

Other memorials against it were received by the House in the next

---

[21] An excellent account of this act, which has received slight attention in most treatments of the embargo, is given by Herbert Heaton in "Non-Importation, 1806–1812" (*Journal of Economic Hist.*, I [1941], 178–198). The experiences of Peter A. Schenk, surveyor of customs in New York, to which he gives particular attention and some of which are distinctly amusing, illustrate the confusion caused by the successive suspensions of the law.

[22] Nov. 27, 1807 (*Annals*, 10 Cong., 1 sess., pp. 961–981). The vote was 79 to 50.

few weeks. Federalist Congressman Josiah Quincy presented twenty-two, signed by nine hundred merchants and others in Boston. These prayed for the modification, suspension, or repeal of the measure and occasioned a similar though briefer debate. Unlike the Philadelphia memorial, these memorials were not rejected; they were referred to the Committee of the Whole, which was considering a modification of the law by that time.[23] Senator John Quincy Adams, who had supported the measure in the first place as a presumable aid to diplomacy and who was being pressed by his constituents, had himself lost faith in it by now. He did not think that its opponents should strive for its repeal so long as the executive department continued to regard it as useful, but was of the opinion that the administration should give it up. "It is too much, or too little, for the present state of things," he said, "and its effects will distress our own people, without producing the purpose for which it was intended beyond the Atlantic."[24] He thought that the memorials from New England might possibly provide the high officials of the government with an excuse for abandoning something in which they had little confidence. On the very day that Adams thus expressed himself, a letter from the Secretary of the Treasury, relating to this law, was communicated to the House of Representatives.

Gallatin was fully aware of the difficulty of administering the existing law, not only because of the imprecision of its language, but also because it was a limited law which required constant interpretation and invited claims of exception. He may have had these considerations in mind when, addressing the President, he threw out the following suggestion: "To repeal the present Non-Importation Act, and in lieu thereof to pass a general non-importation Act (from Great Britain), to take place, say on 1st February next." Apparently he believed that there should be a prohibitive measure or none at all.[25] Reporting that Madison objected to the proposition without saying why, Jefferson himself suggested the possibility of suspending the present law, by act of Congress, until the end of the session.[26] Such action would undoubtedly have been regarded as a retreat and he may have flirted with this idea only momentarily, but he clearly implied that he did not have a high opinion of the law in its present form.

[23] Dec. 14, 1807 (*Annals*, 10 Cong., 1 sess., pp. 1172–1177). The reference to the "modification" of the act was held to differentiate the Boston memorials from the Philadelphia memorial, which was again presented the next day but was not referred (*ibid.*, pp. 1178–1188).

[24] J. Q. Adams to Joseph Hall, Dec. 11, 1807 (*Writings*, III, 165).

[25] Gallatin to TJ, Dec. 2, 1807 (*Writings*, I, 367).

[26] TJ to Gallatin, Dec. 3, 1807 (*ibid.*); also, Gallatin to TJ, Dec. 5, 1807 (LC, 30550).

Speculation about what might have been is hazardous, but it seems safe to say that the best way to strike at the British was through their exports. (Napoleon was trying to do that with his Continental System.) Accordingly, it would appear that Gallatin suggested the most effective means of procuring from them a redress of grievances. But the more effective such a law was, the more it would have played into the hands of France and the less compatible it would have been with a policy of neutrality. If the members of the triumvirate were not fully aware of this before they learned in mid-December that Napoleon's Berlin decree would be applied to their country, they were well aware of it thereafter. If neutrality was to be maintained, a general non-importation act, directed against the British alone, was not a viable option.

In strict logic the pallid measure already on the statute books was unneutral, but it was relatively unprovocative and Gallatin regarded it as unenforceable. Accordingly, he would have preferred that it remain inoperative until modified, and he so stated with Jefferson's presumable approval. This was when he was making suggestions to the committee of the House to which this matter had been referred.[27] Since the House took no action before December 14, the law went into effect automatically, and it was more than two months before Congress passed a supplementary measure which made it more precise and enforceable. While the list of permitted articles was lengthened, previous penalties were remitted, and a provision allowing ships that had sailed before December 14, 1807, to bring back any cargo they liked within six months amounted to a virtual suspension of the measure until June.[28] To all practical purposes the Non-Importation Act had given way to the embargo, which was directed against American exports and which, in form at least, was compatible with the policy of neutrality.

ii

On the very day the unamended Non-Importation Act went into effect, dispatches reached Washington from Armstrong in Paris. Also, about that time, Jefferson and Madison learned of certain pronouncements in London. Accordingly, on December 18, which was only ten days after the President had submitted to Congress, virtually without comment, the correspondence bearing on the *Chesapeake* affair, he sent

[27] Gallatin to Chairman Thomas Newton, Dec. 5, 1807; communicated Dec. 11 (*A.S.P., Commerce and Manufactures,* I [1832], 699).

[28] Act of Feb. 27, 1808 (*Annals,* 10 Cong., 1 sess., pp. 2834–2835).

HOLDUP ON THE HIGHWAY OF NATIONS

Jefferson is victimized by King George and Napoleon
in "Intercourse or Impartial Dealings," a political cartoon by "Peter Pencil"
from *A History of American Graphic Humor* by William Murrell, Volume I

that body an equally brief but more startling message, along with more alarming documents. These showed unmistakably the great and increasing dangers with which American ships, seamen, and merchandise were threatened by *both* of the belligerent powers.[29]

One of the documents contained an official ruling that Napoleon's Berlin decree, by which he sought to close the Continent to all British products, applied to the vessels of all nations. There was to be no exception henceforth in favor of the United States. It was to become increasingly clear that, in the eyes of the French no less than the English, there were no more neutrals. Jefferson had already been informed that Portugal was in danger, but probably had not heard as yet that French troops had invaded that neutral country, whose fleet was coveted by Napoleon jut as that of the Danes had been by the British. Americans had not yet learned that the endangered Portuguese King had foiled the conqueror by setting sail for Brazil, but they were now sharply reminded that the Continental System imposed a threat to their commerce and that they were confronted with a dilemma. The government had not yet received official notice of the latest Orders in Council with which the British had retaliated against the Napoleonic decree, but the President and Secretary of State were aware of them and could not have failed to perceive the impossibility of conforming to both sets of regulations.[30]

From another document submitted by Jefferson, a proclamation of King George, the legislators now learned that, far from relaxing the hated practice of impressment, the British were going to engage in it even more vigorously. Not only was the "right" to remove British seamen from neutral merchant vessels reasserted; it was claimed that they could be demanded from war vessels. Procedure was regularized in cases of refusal, the question of redress being left to higher authority than ship captains, but in this provision there was little comfort for weak neutrals. The validity of papers of naturalization, on which

[29] Message of Dec. 18, 1807, with Extract of a Letter from the Grand Judge, Minister of Justice, to the Imperial Attorney General for the Council of Prizes, dated Paris, Sept. 18, 1807; and, from the *London Gazette*, A Proclamation by King George, Oct. 16, 1807, "for recalling and prohibiting British seamen from serving foreign Princes and States" (*A.S.P.F.R.*, III, 25–26). Included with these were letters between Armstrong and Champagny, the return of which TJ requested (*ibid.*, 243–244; communicated Nov. 8, 1808).

[30] The Orders in Council of Nov. 11, 1807, were not communicated to Congress by TJ until Feb. 4, 1808, but reports of them appeared in several American papers and probably reached him by Dec. 17, 1807. There was a report in the *Aurora* that day. J. Q. Adams believed the orders were the principal cause of the recommendation of an embargo (H. Adams, *Documents Relating to New England Federalism*, p. 189).

Americans had so long relied, was denied. By this proclamation the sanction of the highest British authority was given to policies and practices which were regarded by Jefferson and Madison, along with John and John Quincy Adams, as infringements on American sovereignty and a denial of basic human rights.

Recognizing the supreme importance of safeguarding the "essential resources" of the country — its ships and goods and sailors — Jefferson said in his brief message: "I deem it my duty to recommend the subject to the consideration of Congress, who will doubtless perceive all the advantages which may be expected from an inhibition of the departure of our vessels." Thus he recommended the immediate adoption of an embargo without entering into any discussion of the merits of such a measure.

In a letter he wrote Jefferson in the morning of that same day, Gallatin said that the decision of the administration had been hastily made "on the first view of our foreign intelligence," and he spoke of the projected measure as one of doubtful policy.[31] It seems clear that the reports from Europe that were received between December 14 and 18 precipitated the action of the latter date, and that the haste of which Gallatin spoke, without saying that it was avoidable, can be explained on grounds of the immediacy of peril. Because of this, no doubt, Gallatin acquiesced in an embargo. Although he did not think it would have any effect on the postponed negotiations about the *Chesapeake* or on British maritime policy, he was deeply concerned to get American ships and sailors home. He believed that the measure should be limited in time and regarded as tentative. He said to the President: "In every point of view, privations, sufferings, revenue, effect on the enemy, politics at home, &c., I prefer war to a permanent embargo." He did not claim that war was a feasible option at the moment, but he made an additional comment that was to prove prophetic and was destined to be quoted through the generations by advocates of *laissez faire:* "Governmental prohibitions do always more mischief than had been calculated; and it is not without much hesitation that a statesman should hazard to regulate the concerns of individuals as if he could do it better than themselves."

Replying immediately, Jefferson asked this trusted counselor to be at the President's House before half past ten so that they might be together before the message got out of their hands. Believing that the circumstances admitted of no delay, he did not allow himself much

[31] Gallatin to TJ, Dec. 18, 1807 (*Writings*, I, 368).

time to consider Gallatin's latest observations.[32] It need not be supposed, however, that he was indifferent to the sound Jeffersonian doctrine Gallatin had pronounced. No doubt the idea of controlling the actions of his fellow countrymen beyond the point of absolute necessity was as abhorrent to him as it had always been. But the intensification of the power struggle in Europe had so narrowed his options that he saw no immediate alternative to an embargo. Gallatin, though normally unrhetorical, was indulging in hyperbole when he spoke of a *permanent* embargo, which was in fact unthinkable. In a private letter toward the end of the winter Jefferson said: "For a certain length of time I think the embargo is a less evil than war. But after a time it will not be so."[33] For reasons he did not assign, he was now calling for an embargo that was indeterminate. Madison was soon to say that it should last long enough to achieve its purpose, but the only purpose mentioned in the presidential message was to safeguard American ships and cargoes and seamen.

That was all Jefferson said in public. He made a somewhat fuller statement within a month in a private letter to John Taylor of Caroline:

> The embargo keeping at home our vessels, cargoes & seamen, saves us the necessity of making their capture the cause of immediate war: for if going to England, France had determined to take them; if to any other place, England was to take them. Till they return to some sense of moral duty therefore, we keep within ourselves. This gives time, time may produce peace in Europe: peace in Europe removes all causes of difference, till another European war: and by that time our debt may be paid, our revenues clear, & our strength increased.[34]

In these terms the embargo was wholly a precautionary measure and a play for time, and as such it was in line with his general policy of calculated procrastination. He kept on believing that something would turn up and that in the long run his country would be the gainer. In the very long run events were to prove him right, but he greatly underestimated the duration of this conflict, as he over-estimated the pa-

[32] TJ to Gallatin, Dec. 18, 1807 (*ibid.*, I, 369). He accepted the recommendation that foreign vessels be excepted, and presumably Gallatin agreed with him that the message should not be held up until the arrival of Monroe a couple of days later.
[33] TJ to Major Joseph Eggleston, Mar. 7, 1808 (LC, 31085). In a letter to Madison, Mar. 11, 1808, he described this as "an universal opinion (Ford, IX, 179).
[34] TJ to John Taylor, Jan. 6, 1808 (LC, 30732).

tience of his own countrymen. At the outset the embargo could be justified as a temporary and tentative protective measure, but as time went on it was viewed increasingly as a form of peaceable coercion, as a positive rather than a negative instrument of national policy. The views of the Secretary of State are of special interest in this connection.

The armed conflict with the British which eventually ensued was called "Mr. Madison's War." A sympathetic biographer of that statesman says that "his too were the policies short of war by which the Jefferson administration sought to avoid it, or to postpone it while the country gathered basic strength." This writer also says that Madison's responsibility for the resulting domestic disunity was greater than Jefferson's, since the policy of "attempted coercion of the European belligerents" was "peculiarly his own."[35] Even if correct, this judgment does not at all relieve Jefferson of the responsibility that was inescapably his as President. Furthermore, he always asserted that there never were any differences of importance between him and his lieutenant, and such was their rapport that any attempt to distinguish between them in matters of foreign policy is attended with almost insuperable difficulty. There is no special significance in the fact that the embargo message was based on a draft by Madison.[36] It is worthy of note, though, that by the time the bill was passed, someone with advance information had in readiness an extended exposition of it as both a defensive and coercive measure. This was published anonymously but seems to have been the work of Madison.[37] It may have had Jefferson's full approval, but it claimed more for the measure than Jefferson himself was doing privately at the time.

Later in the year, when certain Federalists were saying that the Secretary of the Navy had opposed the embargo in the first place, Jefferson said: "The administration was never more unanimous than in the recommendation of the embargo, every member being present & concurring, and no one more cordially than Mr. Smith." Apparently there was a Cabinet meeting on December 17 at which the proposal was approved by everybody. We lack precise information about a conference between the President and the congressional leaders most in his confidence which must have taken place, but we may assume

---

[35] Irving Brant (Madison, IV, 401, 481). I gain the impression that these statements were made in recognition of Madison's influence rather than in dispraise of him.

[36] TJ to Madison, July 14, 1824 (LC, 40509; L. & B., XVI, 69-70; drafts in LC, 30611-30612).

[37] See below, pp. 487-489.

that they were or became convinced that an embargo was the best available alternative to war and that immediate action was necessary.[38] The bill that was quickly passed was unquestionably regarded as a party measure, though the haste of the action seemed justifiable on patriotic and pragmatic grounds.

The Senate acted first. The President's message with accompanying documents was referred to a committee of which Samuel Smith was chairman and John Quincy Adams a member. The latter, who was in trouble with his constituents, expressed doubts about the propriety of an embargo, but eventually agreed to the presentation of a bill. He told his father that he supported this as "merely precautionary and defensive." The rules were suspended and the bill was passed that very day — Friday, December 18, 1807. As one of the committeemen afterwards explained, customary deliberation and delay would have enabled many vessels to go to sea in anticipation of the action and would thus have defeated its purpose. Half a dozen Republicans, along with the Federalists, would have preferred to wait at least one day longer, but they were over-borne, and the final vote, except for Adams, followed party lines.[39]

The bill the Senate had passed so expeditiously was promptly transmitted to the House, where it commanded the full attention of the representatives, behind closed doors, the rest of that day and again on Saturday and Monday. The obvious reason for this secrecy was the same as had impelled the Senate to act with such speed. There was nothing sinister about it; but, unfortunately, no record of the proceedings in the Committee of the Whole is available. We have only a record of the motions and the votes.[40] Shortly before the receipt of the Senate bill, two congressmen vied for the privilege of introducing a resolution calling for an embargo and John Randolph gained it. Nonetheless, he voted against the measure and became one of its bitterest critics. Writing his friend Nicholson, he said: "The circumstances under which it presented itself were peculiar and compelled me to

[38] Reference to Robert Smith in letter of TJ to J. G. Jackson, Oct. 3, 1808 (LC, 32202). Years later J. Q. Adams said that a deputation of congressional leaders waited on TJ and, as Adams was told, overcame his reluctance to assume the responsibility for recommending the embargo. (*Parties in the U.S.*, pp. 77–78; see also *Documents Relating to New-England Federalism*, p. 188.) We shall assume, nevertheless, that he took the initiative — however reluctantly.

[39] The brief account in *Annals*, 10 Cong., 1 sess., pp. 50–51, can be supplemented by the *Memoirs* of J. Q. Adams, I, 491–492, and his letter to his father, Dec. 27, 1807, in his *Writings*, III, 168–169 with footnotes.

[40] Dec. 18–21, 1807 (*Annals*, 10 Cong., 1 sess., pp. 1215–1223).

oppose it; although otherwise a favorite measure with me, as you well know."[41] He had long favored an embargo as a defensive measure but appears to have been perturbed by the thought that this was coercive. Certain of his critics afterwards attributed his *volte face* to his belief that, far from being a neutral action, this was aimed only at the British, that in fact it was dictated by Napoleon.[42] This was a favorite line of Federalist attack on the embargo from the start. The day after the House acted, Congressman Taggart of Massachusetts wrote a friend: "It is said and believed that our Minister has been insulted at Paris, that Bonaparte has declared to him that he will have no neutral, and that the only price of avoiding a war with France is to shut our ports against England, or in other words provoke England to hostility against us, and then the door will be opened for an alliance offensive and defensive with France."[43] This observer did not believe that those voting in the affirmative wanted to throw the country into the arms of France, but regarded them as blind to the implications of their action. As for "Thomas the first" (the last of the kind, he hoped), they had fully adopted the doctrine "that the king can do no wrong."

Federalist papers made much of the fact that Jefferson asked the return of the letters of Armstrong and Champagny and they deplored the secrecy of the congressional proceedings.[44] The secrecy, which undoubtedly added to public bewilderment, may have been maintained to a greater degree than was necessary, but the charge of collusion with the French was wholly without foundation. A more effective charge was that the measure was not adequately debated. It was claimed that advocates of the bill made little effort to defend it — that they left the floor to its opponents and, knowing that they had the votes, kept calling for the question.[45] It was asserted that they did say that the law would not be relinquished until Great Britain and France had given complete satisfaction. According to a pessimistic Federalist estimate this could not possibly take less than three months and might be expected to take a year or more. A motion to limit the law to sixty

[41] Randolph to J. H. Nicholson, Dec. 24, 1807 (quoted by Bruce, *Randolph*, I, 319, with Randolph's italics).
[42] See speech of Congressman Love, Apr. 13, 1808 (*Annals*, 10 Cong., 1 sess., p. 2097).
[43] Samuel Taggart to Rev. John Taylor, Dec. 22, 1807 (*Amer. Antiq. Soc. Procs.*, XXXIII, 224–225). Fear that war with England was intended was expressed on Dec. 26, 1807, in Boston *Columbian Centinel*.
[44] For example, *N.Y. Evening Post*, Dec. 29, 1807.
[45] This claim and others referred to in this paragraph were made in lengthy comments reprinted in *N.Y. Evening Post*, Dec. 29, 1807, from Philadelphia *U.S. Gazette* of Dec. 24.

days was defeated in the House — on the understanding, no doubt, that this was the wish of the executive. The final vote was 82 to 44. Jefferson himself said the opposition consisted of Federalists, members of John Randolph's little band, and "republicans happening to take up mistaken views of the subject."[46]

It is impossible to determine the degree of pressure he and the members of his Cabinet had exerted. No doubt he couched his recommendation in general terms in order to make it more generally acceptable. Nobody knew just what it would lead to — peace or war or a redress of grievances — and anybody was at liberty to see in the measure what he wanted to. But the speedy response of Congress can be better regarded as a tribute of faith in Jefferson's leadership on the part of his political supporters than as a "magnificent feat of legislative dexterity."[47] Nor does it seem just to say that in these circumstances "Jefferson's power found no restraint."[48] If no one in his own circle or party restrained him, a likely explanation is that no one could think of a better course. It is certainly correct to say, however, that, whether in desperation or excessive optimism, he proceeded in a way that was uncharacteristic. Normally, neither he nor the legislative leaders of his party sought to cut off debate, and he customarily sought to give Congress its full share of responsibility. In this instance not only did the course of events give rise to charges of executive dominance; they also served to fix on him most of the responsibility.

In conversation with congressional leaders he and his lieutenants doubtless gave reasons for the choice of this course among their shrunken options, but there had been no public discussion of possible alternatives. The President sounded no clarion call to his countrymen; he issued no proclamation. The nearest thing to an explanation that the government offered the public was contained in certain anonymous contributions to the *National Intelligencer*. The first of these was published the day after Jefferson signed the embargo act, and two others appeared successively a few days later. They looked like editorials, but Madison's authorship was assumed by many and seems most likely.[49] Newspapers on both sides reprinted these pieces. In doing so a leading Federalist organ said that the public, left by the government to "blind conjectures" regarding the embargo, eagerly caught at "every floating

[46] TJ to TMR, Dec. 22, 1807 (LC, 30641).
[47] Perkins, *Prologue*, p. 156, agreeing with Henry Adams (*History*, IV, 176).
[48] H. Adams, IV, 151.
[49] *National Intelligencer*, Dec. 23 (immediately following the text of the act), 25, 28, 1807. From internal evidence, Madison's biographer holds that his authorship is unmistakable (Brant, IV, 402–403).

surmise."[50] Republican papers, as might have been expected, drew on the unnamed spokesman of the administration for arguments.

He described the embargo, not as a lesser evil, but as "of all measures the one peculiarly adapted to the crisis." In view of the uncertainties of this situation superlatives were unwise, and, unless he was referring to a relatively small group, he was unwarranted in claiming that this action reflected unanimity of judgment. After describing the recent actions of the warring powers which had occasioned this measure, he said:

> Thus the ocean presents a field only where no harvest is to be reaped but that of danger, of spoliation and of disgrace.
> Under such circumstances the best to be done is what has been done; a dignified retirement within ourselves; a watchful preservation of our resources; and a demonstration to the world, that we possess a virtue and a patriotism which can take any shape that will best suit the occasion.

In the effort to justify the withdrawal of a non-combatant from the scene of danger, he used many more words than Jefferson had employed in his message to Congress, but up to this point his emphasis was the same. That he regarded the embargo as more than a protective measure, however, is shown in the paragraph that followed:

> It is singularly fortunate that an embargo, whilst it guards our essential resources, will have the collateral effect of making it to the interest of all nations to change the system which has driven our commerce from the ocean.

It would be felt by the warring powers, he said: by the British and the French, especially in the supplies necessary for their colonies, and most of all perhaps by the Spanish, who were dependent on imports for their daily food. Salutary effects on the policies of these countries could be hoped for, but the measure offered them no ground for complaint. "The embargo violates the rights of none," the spokesman said. "Its object is to secure ourselves. It is a measure of precaution, not of aggression." It provided no pretext for war and would be a help, not a hindrance, to negotiation. It was "the best expedient in its best form"; it had been recommended and adopted by those who knew best; and all that remained for a trustful people was to rally round a measure that had been adopted for their good.

[50] *N.Y. Evening Post*, Dec. 28, 1807, reprinting extracts from the first two numbers, and refraining from comment for the time being.

Having described the embargo in his first paper as a virtual panacea, the writer recognized in his second that some ills would be incident to it. He said that there would be occasion for "much fortitude, perhaps for great patience." But, unlike Winston Churchill, who in another century offered his beleaguered countrymen only blood, sweat, and tears, he minimized the necessary sacrifices and described the embargo as, next to war (which the circumstances did not require), the best means of "maintaining the national tone." He did not rule out the possibility of war; at a moment's notice the sword could be drawn from its scabbard. Meanwhile, the embargo would arm the nation. He believed it would be a popular measure and claimed that the necessity for it had been recognized on all hands.

In his final paper, besides arguing that the embargo reduced to nothingness the likelihood that any foreign nation would make war on the United States, the author held that, while the measure would impose privations on Americans, those imposed on the European powers would be far greater. "We shall be deprived of market for our superfluities," he said. "They will feel the want of necessaries." Believing they would suffer most, he assumed that they would tire of the trial first. The position of the United States was unique. "With other injured nations," he said, "there may be no choice, but between disgraceful submission or war. A benignant providence has given to this [nation] a happy resourse for avoiding both." As thus described, the God-given embargo was little short of a flawless weapon.

It seems impossible to determine whether the President fully shared the confidence that was expressed here, presumably by his Secretary of State, in a weapon which was in fact untested. From what little he said at the time and his comments in the next few months, his approach to this problem appears to have been more tentative, as Gallatin's assuredly was. In reality he had faced a choice between evils, and the embargo might have been frankly presented as such to his countrymen. Its critics might have been challenged to propose a less evil alternative. Furthermore, such public representation as was made should have been made by Jefferson himself. We may never know whether his silence at this stage should be attributed to pressure of time, or to his habitual secretiveness with regard to international affairs, or to uncertainties in his own mind. But the fact is that in his stead someone else spoke under a veil of anonymity. If this was Madison, as seems likely, the member of the official family most committed to economic coercion as a positive instrument overstated the case for an untried policy, promising too much for it and grossly underestimating its costs. These claims and arguments undoubtedly brought comfort to many citizens, but they could not have failed to lull many into a state of false security. After commenting on them favorably, a staunch Republican paper observed that the success or failure of the embargo depended on the spirit and patriotism of the American people. If supported by them it would have salutary results.[51] Unhappily, however, they were unprepared for the restrictions and privations which, under unheroic circumstances, they were expected to endure.

[51] Richmond *Enquirer*, Dec. 31, 1807.

[XXVII]

The Problem of National Defense: The Navy

THREE-QUARTERS of a century after these events a distinguished
historian asserted that Jefferson had conducted his government
from the beginning on the theory of peaceable coercion and believed
he had "solved the difficult problem of stopping his enemy, while
running away from him without loss of dignity and without the appearance of flight." Since the British bull, maddened by the Corsican
wolf, was rushing on him, there was no recourse but to flight "if the
President would not stand his ground and stop the animal by skill or
force."[1] This cruel passage implies that Jefferson was pusillanimous, but
does not reveal just how skill or force could and should have been
applied.

It would be nearer the truth to say that, until the ruthless disregard
of his own country by *both* of the great powers became unmistakable,
Jefferson sought to play one against the other. In his first term circumstances had favored him, but in his second they did not. Economic
coercion was a weapon in reserve — a last hope if diplomacy should
fail. It is a question whether he did not set his diplomatic sights too
high, seeking more than he could reasonably have expected, and no
doubt he counted too much and too long on the reasonableness of the
rulers and officials of embattled nations. But his political opponents at
the time do not appear to have suggested a wiser course, and the same
may be said of latter-day critics. The most valid criticism at this stage
and the nearest thing to a constructive suggestion made then or thereafter was that the policy of the government should have been backed
by a greater show of force — that more should have been done to
provide for the physical defense of the country and its interests. When

[1] Henry Adams, *History*, IV, 139–140. This descendent of John and John
Quincy Adams was more censorious than his ancestors, who were much closer to
this scene.

Jefferson, in his embargo message, called to the attention of Congress "the necessity of making every preparation" to meet the needs of the present crisis, he was obviously referring to military and naval provisions. Gallatin had advised him several months earlier that, while waiting, they should "prepare to the utmost for war." What, precisely, did he and his countrymen do in this regard at this time? What can be said of his defense policy as a whole?

The military and naval preparations of a minor power at the beginning of the nineteenth century, when viewed by professionals from the vantage point of the twentieth, cannot fail to seem feeble and amateurish. The unpreparedness of the country for its wars has been the perennial complaint of the professionals, and it is an undeniable fact that, until relatively recent times, Americans have been largely indifferent to the subject while at peace. The French Minister, himself a military man, charged them at this juncture with lack of patriotism and martial zeal, declaring that they viewed insults as merely "unfortunate events, deranging their mercantile interests for a moment."[2] In fact, most of them were farmers, relatively indifferent to mercantile interests, and desiring no part in the world conflict. Most of them thoroughly approved of the policy of non-involvement as expressed in Washington's Farewell Address and Jefferson's first inaugural. There is clear evidence that the latter gentleman was more concerned about both naval and military preparations than most members of Congress, and especially the members of his own party. As the head of a government of divided authority dependent on popular support he had limited powers. He may be blamed for not rearranging his priorities, for not doing more to rouse his countrymen, for deferring too much to his party, but his own ideas were based primarily on pragmatic considerations. He was unquestionably opposed to large permanent establishments, as a potential menace to freedom and an occasion of great expense; and his position is best suggested by his remark to John Adams in extreme old age that the extent of the navy "must be governed by circumstances."[3] The saying covered his attitude toward the army as well as the navy, toward soldiers as well as ships. He may not have judged circumstances correctly, but he tried to be realistic.

In the heyday of imperialism a noted American advocate of sea power asserted that, if the United States in 1800 had had twelve to

---

[2] Turreau to Talleyrand, Sept. 7, 1807 (AECPEU, vol. LX); see the despondent statement of Henry Adams (*History*, IV, 136) that they had discarded "military qualities."

[3] TJ to John Adams, Nov. 1, 1822 (*A.-J. Letters*, II, 585).

twenty ships of the line with a due proportion of frigates and smaller vessels, "we probably should have had no War of 1812; that is, if Jefferson's passion for peace, and abhorrence of navies, could have been left out of the account."[4] John Adams charged his successor with no such abhorrence; and, at a time when such a navy was being talked about, Albert Gallatin took an opposite view of probabilities. In Congress he asserted that if they had had twelve ships of the line in 1793, the country undoubtedly would have been involved in the war, "on one side or the other, according to the fluctuation of public opinion."[5] The reader is at liberty to take his choice between these equally unprovable speculations.

Jefferson, who was Vice President at this time, had long recognized that the country must have *some* naval power. John Adams, who remembered that he had taken the lead in the government in advocating the use of it against the Barbary pirates, credited him with being more of a navy man than Washington or Hamilton.[6] In Adams's own administration, however, during the quasi-war with France, Jefferson had strongly opposed the recommendations of Secretary Benjamin Stoddert. This he did in private letters while Gallatin was leading the opposition in Congress. Deploring the war fever of the hour, and aghast at the extravagance of the government's proposals, he took the position that the country should have no more of a naval force than was necessary to protect its coasts and harbors from depredations. He was opposed to one which, "by its own expenses and the eternal wars in which it will implicate us, will grind us with public burthens, and sink us under them."[7] Stoddert's proposals were whittled down: the naval appropriation as passed (February 25, 1799) called for the construction of six seventy-fours and the building or purchasing of six sloops. Jefferson, Gallatin, and the Republicans of the South and West opposed it even in this form, regarding the action as needlessly expensive and as more likely to lead to war than to prevent it.[8]

[4] A. T. Mahan, *Sea Power in Its Relation to the War of 1812* (1905), I, 74; see also 71–72.

[5] H. H. and M. Sprout, *Rise of American Naval Power* (1967 edn.), p. 45, quoting from *Annals*. For the opposition of Gallatin and the Republicans, in the third session of the Fifth Congress (1798–1799), to the proposals of Secretary Benjamin Stoddert, especially for ships of seventy-four guns, see Julia H. Macleod, "Jefferson and the Navy: A Defense" in *Huntington Library Quarterly*, VIII (1944–1945), 161–163, with references.

[6] Adams to TJ, June 11, 1813; Oct. 15, 1822 (*A.-J. Letters*, II, 328–329, 582–583).

[7] TJ to Elbridge Gerry, Jan. 26, 1799 (Ford, VII, 328).

[8] The latter claim was made by Republicans subsequently. Thus a contributor to the *Aurora*, Jan. 14, 1807, said: "England has always been prepared for war, and very seldom out of one, while Hamburg has been half a century in peace with little or no defense, and enjoying almost half the commerce of the north."

As things turned out, little came of the ambitious program of Stoddert and John Adams. A sharp reduction of the navy was decreed by the Naval Peace Establishment Act, which was approved by Adams the day before he left office. Jefferson's early actions in reducing the effective navy were taken in pursuance of the directives of the Act or in the exercise of the discretion vested in him by it.[9] What with the cessation of the undeclared war with France and the pause in the conflict between that country and Great Britain, extensive and expensive naval developments would hardly have been tolerated by the American public under any administration. Sharp curtailment was to have been expected in any case. Jefferson gladly availed himself of this opportunity, hastening to make hay while the sun was shining — that is, to set about reducing the national debt. Debt reduction was an obsession with him, but, besides being influenced by his personal experiences and observations in debt-ridden Virginia, he had drawn definite conclusions from the experiences of other nations. The thoughts he expressed to Gallatin after his presidency were doubtless in his mind at its beginning: "I consider the fortunes of our republic as depending, in an eminent degree, on the extinguishment of the public debt before we engage in any war," he said, adding that if the debt should reach the point that its discharge was despaired of, they would be "committed to the English career of debt, corruption and rottenness, closing with revolution."[10] He might have said that the troubles of the British government leading to the American Revolution, and those of the French government leading to the French Revolution, both stemmed from financial difficulties.

A country of such enormous potentialities as the United States might have been expected to bear a burden of public debt more readily than Jefferson and Gallatin supposed. But, following the expenditures during the Adams administration, in a time of hysteria, reaction toward economy was natural and salutary; and in the President's opinion the large savings on the navy were effected without injury to essential services. During his first term he perceived no need for capital ships except for service against the Barbary powers, but by dispatching to the Mediterranean frigates that were still in commission he initiated against those piratical states forceful action such as no other country had taken. That this action was not more quickly and more completely successful was owing to many factors, including the ineptitude of naval officers, the grave logistical problems, and the reluctance of

---

[9] See *Jefferson the President: First Term*, pp. 102–103, and references.
[10] TJ to Gallatin, Oct. 11, 1809 (Ford, IX, 264).

Congress to support the operations.[11] It can hardly be attributed to Jefferson's "abhorrence of navies." He was generally well ahead of Congress in his recognition of actual needs — as in his recommendation of a drydock in his second annual message. The proposal was ridiculed at the time by champions of the navy, but he lived long enough to observe that his idea had been accepted.[12]

Considerations of economy bulked larger in his first term than in his second; and, what with the rebuff by the Spanish, the intensification of the war, and the tightening of their commercial policies by the rival powers, the security and interests of the United States were much more gravely imperiled. Under these changed circumstances Jefferson and his chief advisers, beginning with the summer of 1805, gave consideration to the upbuilding of the seagoing navy.[13] Robert Smith, incensed by the supercilious treatment of the American envoys by the Spanish, attributed this to their impression that the country was utterly unprepared for a war and could hardly be provoked to declare one. Accordingly, he believed that the President should recommend to Congress that it provide for the building of additional gunboats, for the putting of all the frigates into commission, for building the six seventy-fours for which most of the materials had been collected, and for the construction of six more warships of that class. With a force of this strength, he said, they would have nothing to fear from such a nation as Spain, but could take a "commanding attitude" with respect to her. That is, if she stood alone. If France were with her, the United States would need an ally. Smith would not have been averse to an alliance with Great Britain, by means of which he believed they could easily take the Floridas and Cuba, but he favored upbuilding the navy in any case.[14]

This appears to have been the strongest position taken by any member of the administration, but, in order to cope with privateers that were infesting the Atlantic coast the Cabinet had already voted, with only Gallatin dissenting, to prepare and put in commission such vessels as had already been authorized by Congress.[15] The question of augmenting the navy further was subsequently under discussion, and Gallatin, while wondering if the remedy would not be worse than the

[11] See Macleod, "Jefferson and the Navy," pp. 166-170, and ch. III, above.
[12] TJ proposed a drydock Dec. 15, 1802; an appropriation for one was made in 1823. He described the original episode to L. M. Wiss, Nov. 27, 1825 (L. & B., XVI, 135-138). It is briefly referred to in *Jefferson the President: First Term*, pp. 263-264; the account by Macleod, pp. 170-173, is fuller and better.
[13] See above, pp. 69-70.
[14] Robert Smith to TJ, Sept. 10, 1805 (LC, 26633-26637), received Sept. 16.
[15] Memo. of the meeting of July 8, 1805 (Ford, I, 307-308).

disease, and saying that he had wanted the measure to be postponed, admitted that for a long time he had had no doubt that "the United States would ultimately have a navy." Without one he was sure that they would "perpetually be liable to injuries and insults" from the belligerent powers. The question was whether it was more to the American interest "to preserve a pacific and temporizing system, and to tolerate those injuries and insults to a great extent, than to be prepared, like the great European nations, to repel every injury by the sword." This question would have to be answered by Congress, he said, and the members of the executive branch could then govern themselves accordingly.[16]

At this juncture and during the months that followed (1805–1806), Jefferson himself showed more concern for the creation of a well-balanced navy than at any other time during his presidency. In his fifth annual message to Congress, besides recommending better fortifications and more gunboats to protect the seaports, he called attention to the materials for the construction of seventy-fours that had been procured under previous authorization and which were subject to the further will of the Legislature.[17] Soon thereafter Congressman Dawson introduced resolutions which, besides providing for fortifications and gunboats, called for an appropriation of $660,000 for six line-of-battle ships. (Actually they would have cost considerably more.) The resolution relating to the latter was soundly defeated when it came up for a vote.[18] That the administration could have brought sufficient pressure to overcome the powerful congressional opposition to this proposal seems most unlikely, and in fact it spent its strength in gaining support for fresh diplomatic ventures.[19] Jefferson still rested his hopes chiefly on negotiation. In the case of the British he believed that the threat of modest economic reprisal would be helpful, but shortly after the congressional session he said that a squadron of ships of the line to guard the ports was indispensable.[20] He did not afterwards recommend one to Congress, however, and his reasons for dropping the idea were presumably those he gave John Adams after his retirement. On

[16] Gallatin to TJ, Sept. 12, 1805 (*Writings*, I, 252–253); see also Gallatin to Madison, Aug. 6, 1805 (*ibid.*, p. 238).

[17] Message of Dec. 3, 1805 (Ford, VIII, 392). See *A.S.P., Naval Affairs*, I, 141, for Smith's report on the materials on hand.

[18] Resolutions introduced Dec. 23, 1805, voted on March 25, 1806 (*Annals*, 9 Cong., 1 sess., pp. 302, 846–848).

[19] Negotiations regarding West Florida and with the British. The revolt of John Randolph occurred in this session. (See chs. V, VII, above.)

[20] TJ to Jacob Crowninshield, May 13, 1806 (Ford, VIII, 453).

full deliberation he concluded that in the situation created by the British triumph at Trafalgar capital ships would be valueless to his country.

Writing his predecessor, he said that if he had differed with Adams regarding the navy, "it was not on the principle but the time." He saw no point in building one that would promptly fall into the same gulf that had "swallowed, not only the minor navies, but even those of the great second rate powers of the sea." That is, any squadron his country could have hoped to build would have met the fate of the little Danish fleet at Copenhagen and the great French and Spanish fleet that Nelson destroyed at Trafalgar. In his judgment the time for the United States to aim at a navy was when these lesser navies were resuscitated to such an extent that an American fleet could turn the scale against the British.[21] If less concerned for a navy than his predecessor, he was more so than his successor, and he pursued a reasoned course.[22] To him sea power was meaningless except as an instrument; and, although the indignities to American ships and seamen might have been reduced somewhat if there had been more frigates on guard at the seaports, any attempt to put a squadron to sea would have been futile and might have been disastrous.[23] It would appear that in contenting himself with a force sufficient to handle the Barbary pirates, and even more in not pressing for ships of the line, he was realistic, but his confidence in gunboats is much more questionable.

That Congress preferred inexpensive gunboats to expensive seventy-fours was clearly manifest in the spring of 1806, when that body authorized the construction of fifty of the former while declining to make an appropriation for the latter.[24] With this action the country took what naval historians have with virtual unanimity regarded as "an unsound line of naval development."[25] Jefferson had not renounced ships of the line at that date; and he never took the position that the navy should consist solely of gunboats.[26] During the following year,

[21] TJ to Adams, May 17, 1813 (*A.-J. Letters*, II, 324–325).
[22] On Madison's indifference, see Macleod, p. 178.
[23] Note the sagacious comments of Marshall Smelser: "Jefferson saw it correctly: when all other navies together equaled the Royal Navy, a new American fleet would tip the balance. After Trafalgar, a lonely, microscopic American fleet would have been gold cast into the sea and might have suffered a Trafalgar-like catastrophe with fatal consequences to morale, even to survival as a republic" (*The Democratic Republic, 1801–1815* [1968], p. 229).
[24] Act of Apr. 21, 1806 (*Annals*, 9 Cong., 1 sess., pp. 1272–1273).
[25] This relatively mild expression is that of Sprout, p. 58.
[26] Theodore Roosevelt so alleged in *The Naval War of 1812* (1882), p. 199.

however, he argued for them strongly in a message to Congress which he communicated with supporting documents.[27]

Gunboats were no novelty. A small number had been authorized, though not built, in the administration of Washington, and they had been seriously proposed in that of John Adams.[28] All the European navies used them, and they had proved helpful in the operations against the Barbary pirates. The first effectual act of Congress (February 28, 1803) relating to them was occasioned by the troubles with Spain at New Orleans and the mouth of the Mississippi, and they were first used in the United States in coast-guard duties. Fifteen were authorized in 1803, and two experimental boats were completed in the summer of 1804.[29] The Department of the Navy then set out to build eight more, and in 1805 Congress provided for an additional twenty-five. Captain Edward Preble, just back from the Barbary wars, shared in the design and construction of a number of them.

To that gallant naval officer General James Wilkinson sent a copy of his "Reflections on the Fortifications and Defence of the Sea Ports of the United States," a paper which was read to the House of Representatives and was a key document in support of the government's position.[30] The ranking officer of the army pointed out the limitations of fixed fortifications. He regarded these as ineffectual except on narrow channels which would bring approaching vessels into point-blank range. Few American ports offered such advantages for defense, he said, and the cost of building adequate fortifications at all of them would be inordinately, even prohibitively, expensive. He reached the conclusion, therefore, that "next to a superior navy," the best protection of the seaports could be provided by "floating batteries" along with some but not extensive fixed fortifications. He was confident that "barges, galleys, or gunboats . . . with the cooperation of heavy movable batteries which may be expeditiously transferred from one part of a town or city to another by men and horses" would provide the "most economical, durable, and effectual means of defense." He supported his position by arguments that bore particularly on the maneuverability of these small vessels.

[27] Feb. 10, 1807 (*A.S.P., Naval Affairs*, I, 163–164).
[28] Marshall Smelser, *The Congress Founds the Navy* (1959), pp. 75–76, 118, 122, 147.
[29] For details of construction and design, see H. I. Chapelle, *History of the American Sailing Navy* (New York, 1949; reprint edn., 1960), ch. IV, "The Gunboat Navy," containing many drawings.
[30] Christopher McKee, in *Edward Preble: A Naval Biography*, pp. 317–319, to which I am much indebted, quotes from the copy in the Preble Papers, LC. The document is mentioned in TJ's message of Feb. 10, 1807, but only its covering letter is in *A.S.P., Naval Affairs*, I, 164.

The crafty General may have been saying what he believed his civil superiors wanted to hear, but he represented the highest military judgment that was available; and Preble, whose patriotism could not be impugned, fully agreed with him. He wrote: "You have taken so clear and correct a view of the subject that I shall only beg leave to observe that my opinion perfectly coincides with your own, and I am convinced, when we have experimentally ascertained the best models for floating batteries destined for the defense or protection of our bays and harbors, that your system will meet with general approbation."[31] Wilkinson's opinions regarding harbor defense, of which Preble expressed such high approval, were known to Jefferson several years before he sent Congress the message in which he made his fullest statement on the subject. Also, he had long known that Horatio Gates was "charmed" with the institution of gunboats. Before his death that General had written: "I believe them to be the most proper defence for large harbors that has hitherto been imagined." More recently, in Washington, the President had consulted Commodore Samuel Barron and Captain Thomas Tingey. The former, who had served in the Mediterranean and observed the use of gunboats there, gave his reasons "for supposing them the proper kind of vessels to afford the most effectual means of defence and annoyance within the bays and rivers" — chiefly because of their maneuverability — and spoke particularly of their suitability to the waters he knew best, within the Virginia Capes and Chesapeake Bay. Captain Tingey added to the weight of the testimony from naval men. He regarded the efficacy of gunboats in defending the coasts, ports, and harbors as "obvious to every person capable of reflection." He laid major emphasis on their celerity of movement.[32] Thus it would appear that "the visionary gunboat theories" of the administration were supported at the time by high military and naval officers whose technical judgment was thought trustworthy. As usual, Jefferson also consulted Gallatin, and from that adviser he learned of the "most splendid achievement" of gunboats — the destruction of a large part of a Turkish fleet by a Russian flotilla in 1788. Jefferson mentioned this in his message.[33]

[31] Quoted by McKee, p. 319. The relationship of Preble to gunboats has been much disputed. Comments range from his brother's assertion that he detested the program to the speculation of Chapelle that his actions were due to his fanatical Republicanism (McKee, p. 317; Chapelle, pp. 207–208). He participated in the building program at any rate.

[32] Letters or extracts from letters of Gates, Barron, and Tingey were sent to Congress with TJ's message of Feb. 10, 1807 (*A.S.P., Naval Affairs*, I, 163–164).

[33] For Gallatin's comments of Feb. 8, 1807, see his *Writings*, I, 329–331. He pointed out that the cost of naval vessels could be expected to exceed the

Speaking specifically to the question of harbor defense and recognizing that the species of naval armament that was proposed would not protect commerce on the high seas or even off the coast, Jefferson recommended a combination of land batteries, movable artillery, floating batteries, and gunboats. Making a distinction between the last two, a distinction which afterwards became blurred, he spoke particularly of gunboats. Some of these should be seagoing, he said, but most of them should be small. He thought that 200 would be required in wartime and suggested their general distribution: 40 should be assigned to the Mississippi and its neighboring waters, and the balance be distributed among the eastern bays and harbors. In peacetime only a small number need be kept afloat. Since 73 were already built or building, only 127 need be authorized and only half of these need be built that year. The estimated total cost, $500,000 to $600,000, was somewhat less than that of the two most expensive frigates and the suggested expenditure during the next year was less than the cost of one.[34]

Jefferson's representations had little effect on the economy-minded legislators. The House agreed to an appropriation of $300,000, half for fortifications and half for gunboats, but the Senate struck out the provision for the latter. The debate bore chiefly on fortifications.[35] The assertion that the sum of $150,000 for these was wholly inadequate was not successfully challenged. Someone said that five millions would be needed to fortify New York alone, and John Randolph voiced the suspicion that the only way to defend that harbor would be to block the channel leading to it. This, he said, would be like curing corns by cutting off one's toes. He considered the total appropriation as a tub thrown to a whale to amuse him, and cynically but astutely observed that it could serve no purpose but to stop clamor, that it was a mere electioneering device. He may have read the minds of the Republican leaders correctly, but the Federalists favored any sort of grant for fortifications as a beginning. They supported this one while voting against the gunboats. Since Jefferson had been reminded by Gallatin of the speed of their construction, he probably saw no grave peril in the

---

estimates both with respect to construction and maintenance and that deterioration was inevitable. In a passage which was reflected years later in TJ's correspondence with John Adams, he said: "It would be an economical measure for every naval nation to burn their navy at the end of a war, and to build a new one when again at war, if it was not that time was necessary to build ships of war." Gunboats, however, could be built in short order and therefore need not all be built at once.

[34] See table in *A.S.P., Naval Affairs*, I, 149.

[35] In the House, Feb. 23, 1807 (*Annals*, 9 Cong., 2 sess., pp. 609–619). There seems to be no record of debate in the Senate.

failure of Congress to follow his recommendations with respect to gunboats at this time, and when, in the next session, he sent Congress more alarming messages he saw no need to repeat his arguments.

The specific recommendation of the administration, as made by the Secretary of the Navy a month before Jefferson sent his embargo message to Congress, was for the construction of 188 additional gunboats at an estimated cost of $852,000. A bill authorizing this expenditure was passed by the Senate with only three negative votes, and, after a debate extending over four days, it was passed in the House by a comparable majority.[36] In this time of crisis most of the Federalists joined the Republicans in supporting the defense policy of which this was a part. A number of them expressed doubts of the efficacy of gunboats, especially in the deep-water harbors of the North. That they would be useful in rivers and shallow waters was generally conceded, and special reference was made to their usefulness at New Orleans. There was a disposition even on the part of the doubters to recognize them as experimental. Leading Federalists like Congressmen Dana of Connecticut and Gardenier of New York, while expressing doubts, supported the measure. Josiah Quincy did not. Taking up the cudgels for a seagoing navy, he said: "I know that, to gentlemen from the South and the West, the very name of a navy is odious. . . . It is a power which, from their local position, they can never wield."[37] There was general agreement, however, that the question at issue was that of harbor defense. Northern representatives, who were less interested in gunboats than in fortifications, were assured that these were included in the defense policy of the administration; and, following the recommendation of $750,000 by the Secretary of War, Congress authorized the expenditure of a million for this purpose.[38] In its effort to protect harbors the government was pursuing what appeared to be a well-balanced policy; and, although the money assigned these complementary purposes may have been misdirected, this was probably as large an amount as could have been effectively utilized in the specified time under existing conditions.

Of the authorized gunboats, 176 were built during Jefferson's administration. These were of such variety that no single description can be given of them. Fitted with both oars and sails and variously rigged,

---

[36] Letter of Robert Smith, Nov. 18, 1807, communicated Nov. 20 A.S.P., Naval Affairs, I, 168; Annals, 10 Cong., 1 sess., pp. 32–33). Bill passed by Senate, Dec. 2, by vote of 26 to 3; debate in House, Dec. 8–11; passed by vote of 111 to 19 (ibid., pp. 44, 1065–1171).
[37] Ibid., p. 1140.
[38] Jan. 8, 1808 (ibid., p. 2815).

they ranged from "small sloops or galleys up to sizable sloops and schooners."[39] Most of them were small, about fifty feet long, but some were more than seventy. Many were built on western rivers, and a few were seagoing. Some were "self-propelled floating batteries," but most of them were unable to carry guns large enough to be effective. The crews consisted of twenty or more, and these boats were generally unpopular with seamen. Federalists were charged with discouraging seamen from serving on them, and from the beginning some ridicule was cast upon them by newspapers identified with the Federalist party. One of these spoke sarcastically of legislators who called "this prodigality, this wasteful imbecility, by the name of economy," and another designated appropriations for gunboats as the "democratic sinking fund."[40] It seems, however, that later naval historians were more contemptuous of the gunboats than their contemporary critics were. The main adverse comment on them at the time was that they were no substitute for a well-balanced navy.

They were subjected to no crucial test during Jefferson's presidency since there was no invasion. Judging from a report made early in Madison's administration by his Secretary of the Navy, the only gunboats then in service were twenty-four at New Orleans. All the others were laid up and were rapidly deteriorating. In reply to a query about the "gunboat system," Secretary of the Navy Hamilton said that under a purely defensive policy no doubt they would be of material aid, but that for any attack on enemy trade or protection of American commerce frigates and smaller cruisers would be not only more effective but, in terms of gunpower and manpower, less expensive.[41] They were never intended for that sort of service, however; and, while the gunboat policy was dropped in Madison's administration, the building of frigates was not resumed until the country was actually at war. Jefferson was clearly less indifferent to the navy than his successor. His judgment that, after Trafalgar, the construction of ships of the line would have been costly folly appears in the perspective of history to have been sound, and we may doubt if the situation would have been materially different if the country had had more frigates in service. Even in purely defensive terms, though, they would probably have

[39] Chapelle, p. 218. None of the numerous designs in this work (ch. IV) seemed suitable for reproduction without redrawing. For a general description, see Sprout, p. 58.
[40] Clippings in LC, 156:27286a and 233:41663; D. H. Fischer, *The Revolution of American Conservatism* (1965), p. 178, note 105, citing *N.Y. Evening Post*.
[41] Secretary Paul Hamilton to the Chairman of the Senate Committee June 6, 1809, with attached table (*A.S.P., Naval Affairs*, I, 194–195). See also Hamilton to the Chairman of the House Committee, June 9, 1809 (*ibid.*, p. 200).

been useful. With respect to them the simplest statement of Jefferson's policy at this stage seems to be that he sought to maintain the *status quo*.[42] Most of the money spent on gunboats now appears to have been wasted, but they appealed to Jefferson and probably even more to Congress on grounds of supposed economy, and in this time of desperation they represented to him a desirable experiment.

This particular experiment yielded no positive results of long-range value, but another that was made in this period pointed to developments of immense significance in naval warfare. As in the matter of drydocks, Jefferson was in advance of the vast body of his American contemporaries in his attitude toward the torpedoes of Robert Fulton. Nowhere else did he reveal more clearly his openmindedness toward methods of defense, and harbor defense in particular, than in his interest in and support of this invention. Early in his first term, Fulton, in Europe at the time, was commended to him by Joel Barlow, who wrote him from Paris that Fulton hoped "very soon to demonstrate the practicality of destroying military navies altogether, and with them the whole system of naval tyranny and civilized piracy."[43] Fulton had just blown up a small vessel in Brest harbor, but despite demonstrations he was unable to arouse the serious interest of the French and British governments. Events were to prove that the perfection of the torpedo lay far in the future and that he was to attain success, not with this, but with the steamboat. Following his return to America toward the end of 1806, however, he resumed experiments with torpedoes. He promptly got in touch with Jefferson and through him with the Secretary of the Navy. In the summer of 1807, about a month after the attack on the *Chesapeake*, the Secretary of War at Jefferson's injunction witnessed the demonstration in New York harbor in which, on his second attempt, Fulton blew up an old brig.[44] Though by no means unsympathetic, Dearborn does not appear to have given serious consideration to this method of harbor defense. Doubtless perceiving that the President was more receptive to novel ideas, Fulton reported the

[42] On the state of the frigates and smaller vessels, exclusive of gunboats, and the estimated cost of repairs, see Robert Smith's communication of Nov. 16, 1807 (*A.S.P., Naval Affairs*, I, 168–169). See also Hamilton's report of June 6, 1809 (*ibid.*, p. 194).

[43] Extracts from this letter of Sept. 15, 1801, and from the correspondence of TJ and Fulton, 1807–1813, are given by Sowerby, I, 525–526, in connection with Fulton's pamphlet, *Torpedo War and Submarine Explosions* (1810), which he sent TJ Feb. 24, 1810.

[44] Fulton to TJ, received Jan. 9, 1807 (LC, 28760); Erney, "The Public Life of Henry Dearborn" (1957), pp. 194–195, describing Dearborn's New York visit.

demonstration to him in detail.[45] Having proved that a ship could be destroyed by an explosion under her bottom, the inventor sought to explain the means of getting the torpedoes (which were what we call mines) into position against ships either at anchor or under sail.[46] He asked Jefferson: "Is there any mode of defence so cheap, so easy of practice, so fitted to common understandings?"

Jefferson was neither averse to economy nor disposed to discourage inventions that might prove useful in either war or peace. Presumably regarding the experiment in New York harbor as a success as far as it went, he wrote the eager inventor: "I consider your torpedoes as very valuable means of defence of harbors, and have no doubt that we should adopt them to a considerable degree."[47] He hastened to add, however, that they could not be relied on solely; the engine had been insufficiently tried and the means of "parrying" the torpedoes had not yet been inquired into. Obviously dubious of some of Fulton's ideas about getting the explosives to their targets, he said that he himself would rather depend on the "submarine boat." Fulton had not mentioned this and with respect to its uses Jefferson appears to have been the more prophetic.

This letter was written the day before Fulton's *Clermont* began her historic voyage up the Hudson. There appears to be no recorded contemporary reference of Jefferson's to that event, but he was well aware of the significance of the development in internal navigation that followed it. Four years after he left office he wrote Fulton: "I rejoice at your success in your steamboats and have no doubt they will be the source of great wealth to yourself and permanent blessing to your country. I hope your torpedoes will equally triumph over doubting friends and presumptuous enemies."[48] No practical use had been made of torpedoes until that time. Early in 1810 Fulton published a pamphlet

[45] Fulton to TJ, July 28, 1807 (LC, 29836–29839). The demonstration took place July 20. According to William Duane, who strongly commended Fulton's project, the "Tories" tried to discredit it, along with all other efforts to provide for the defense of the country (*Aurora*, July 25, 1807).
[46] He described to TJ a floating torpedo or mine, which would drift with the tide across the cable or bow of an anchored vessel, and one attached to a rope and a harpoon, which could be fired from a rowboat against a moving vessel. At a later time he submitted to a congressional committee drawings which make his written explanations understandable though not necessarily credible. See the plates enclosed with the report of a senatorial committee, Feb. 26, 1810 (*A.S.P., Naval Affairs*, I, 211–227).
[47] TJ to Fulton, Aug. 16, 1807 (Ford, IX, 125).
[48] TJ to Fulton, March 8, 1813 (L. & B., XIX, 188). Writing Baron Alexander von Humboldt, June 13, 1817, he said that before long internal navigation by sails and oars would be "looked back to as among the curiosities of antiquity" (L. & B., XV, 128).

ROBERT FULTON
Engraving from an original painting by Alonzo Chappel
From E. A. Duyckinck, *National Portrait Gallery of Eminent Americans* (1862)

entitled *Torpedo War, and Submarine Explosions* and containing
plates that graphically illustrated his invention and "system." A number of copies were made available to the members of Congress and
another was sent Jefferson. On the strength of this representation,
Congress made an appropriation to cover the cost of experiments, and
these were duly made that year in the presence of a congressional
committee.[49] In a letter chiefly devoted to other matters, Jefferson had
said to Fulton: "I sincerely wish the torpedo may go the whole length
you expect of putting down navies. I wish it too much not to become
an easy convert and to give it all my prayers and interest."[50] But the
experiments fell short of the wishes of the inventor and led to the
official conclusion that the practicality of his system had not been
demonstrated. It never was, though the indomitable inventor continued to work on improvements.

In 1813, after the United States had gone to war, he wrote his
admirer at Monticello about a "submarine gun" which Jefferson
promptly commended to the consideration of Madison. In writing
Fulton, he described his own position well when he said that "as we
cannot meet the British with an equality of physical force, we must
supply it by other devices." Nobody was so qualified as Fulton "to
point out to us a mode of salvation"; and he hoped that "either by
subaqueous guns, torpedoes, or diving boats" Fulton would do this
with the aid of the government. He himself had highest hopes of the
"submarine boat."[51] The inventor died a couple of years later without
having contributed as he had hoped to national defense, but that was
not for lack of trying nor for lack of support by Jefferson, in or out of
office.

[49] Macleod says that this appropriation was made largely through TJ's influence
("Jefferson and the Navy," p. 180). It may have been, but I have found no
evidence that it was. The documentary record of the episode, with striking
illustrations, is in *A.S.P., Naval Affairs*, I, 211–227, 234–235.

[50] TJ to Fulton, Apr. 16, 1810 (L. & B., XIX, 173–174).

[51] TJ to Fulton, July 21, 1813 (Sowerby, I, 526).

[XXVIII]

The Military Aspect

JEFFERSON'S personal participation in military affairs was greater than in naval. They were peripheral in his mind during most of his presidency, when he was preoccupied with other matters, but on the strength of his correspondence and the records of the War Department it would be difficult to support the charge that the executive branch of the government was indifferent and inactive in the period of greatest uncertainty and danger — roughly the latter half of his second term.[1] Operating within the limits imposed by existing law and public sentiment, he and Dearborn were commendably diligent and industrious. The limitations under which they labored were very great. Jefferson was a man of his own time and place who viewed the situation as an inveterate civilian and feared the development of a military establishment. But with regard to military needs he was more realistic and forward-looking than most of his American contemporaries, and the country would have been better prepared for war than it actually became if Congress had not delayed to accept some of his recommendations and refused to heed others. After this period of world war was over, an editor observed that there was novelty in the mere fact that American military establishments had not been the creation of royal authority but "the result of popular legislation."[2] As a sincere republican and good

---

[1] Mary P. Adams gives a detailed account of activities during this period in her dissertation, "Jefferson's Military Policy," chs. V, VI; and R. A. Erney covers it in his dissertation on Dearborn, ch. V. These studies supplement each other. Speaking of the former, a modern historian says that the author "has confounded the conventional wisdom on the subject by troubling to read military archives instead of drawing deductions from Jefferson's reputation for military idiocy" (Marshall Smelser, *The Democratic Republic*, p. 161, note 29). The Jeffersonian period is treated by R. F. Weigley in *History of the U.S. Army* (1967), pp. 104-114; and by J. R. Jacobs in *The Beginning of the U.S. Army* (1947), ch. X.

[2] Quoted by L. D. White in *The Jeffersonians* (1951), p. 211, from a discussion of military policy in 1826 in *North American Review*. Administrative problems of the War Department are well discussed by White, pp. 211-216.

democrat, Jefferson was glad that this was so, even under the threat of war, but he did not get all the legislation he asked for and no doubt would have asked for more if he had thought he could get it.

Viewed in retrospect, the organization of the War Department seems rudimentary, and he is open to criticism for not having sought to render it more adequate, as we may suppose Alexander Hamilton would have done. But Jefferson, who was himself a notably systematic and efficient man, was slow to perceive, and probably even slower to admit, the need for more administrative officers in any department, and he feared the development of bureaucracy as well as militarism. He was disposed to work with what he had during his remaining months in office, making no more requests of an economy-minded Congress than he had to. Under these circumstances, in a huge country with primitive means of communication and transportation, and in a highly individualistic and little-organized society, the administration of military affairs on an enlarged scale was attended with staggering difficulties.

Though Henry Dearborn, as secretary of war, showed no such incapacity as he was to show as a military commander in the War of 1812, he himself was well aware of his limitations. Toward the end of 1807, when expressing to Jefferson his desire to retire from his post, he modestly stated that, in the event of the war they were anticipating, the situation would require talents superior to any he had ever claimed. "In time of peace," he said, "a tolerable portion of common understanding with some practical knowledge and pure intentions" might be sufficient for the ordinary duties of his office.[3] During Jefferson's first term, when the army generally consisted of fewer than 3000 men and was expected to do little more than guard the frontier posts, the abilities of this unpretentious and unimaginative official seemed sufficient and his thrift commended him to Congress as well as to the administration. Jefferson never ceased to like and trust him, but in a time of peril the person to whom he turned for a comprehensive view of military needs and for counsel about major policy was the Secretary of the Treasury. The elaborate memorandum, dealing with both defensive and offensive measures, that Gallatin submitted to him in the summer of 1807 contained not only a list of ports to be defended and their respective needs but also a detailed discussion of operations against Canada and an estimate of total military requirements.[4] Gallatin fig-

[3] Dearborn to TJ, Dec. 29, 1807, quoted by Erney, p. 244, from LC, 30676.
[4] Memo. included in letter of Gallatin to TJ, July 25, 1807 (*Writings*, I, 340–353).

ured that 30,000 soldiers would be needed for operations against Upper Canada and the Indians, Lower Canada, and Nova Scotia. The Secretary of War subsequently suggested a somewhat larger force but his task may be described as that of implementing the program that was most fully described by the Secretary of the Treasury.

Jefferson, who erred on the side of praise in dealing with his loyal coadjutors, may have over-stated the case when he wrote Dearborn: "The integrity, attention, skill, and economy with which you have conducted your department, have given me the most compleat and unqualified satisfaction." But he recognized the usefulness and never questioned the fidelity of this public servant. He particularly wanted to avoid the problem of appointing a successor toward the end of his administration, preferring to leave that choice to his own successor. There were personal reasons why Dearborn wanted to return to New England. He had lost a son the year before and his wife had not joined him in Washington this winter. Honoring these personal considerations, Jefferson, at some time during the spring of 1808, assured this loyal Republican of his eventual appointment to the collectorship of customs at Boston, which was to be vacated by Benjamin Lincoln. Meanwhile, he sought to protract Dearborn's stay in his present office as long as possible. The net result was that it lasted until the middle of February, 1809. Thus the service of the Secretary of War was practically co-terminous with that of the President.[5] At the end, political enemies of both men focused attention on the most dubious feature of Dearborn's official conduct — his favoritism to James Wilkinson and his gullibility with respect to that tarnished warrior. But Jefferson himself was embarrassingly committed to the General, and he never doubted that on the whole Dearborn had served the country well.[6]

The greatest difficulty anticipated by Jefferson, if Dearborn should retire from office, was carrying on the fortification of the seaports, which was under the supervision of the Secretary of War as the construction of gunboats was under the supervision of the Secretary of the Navy. The President was more directly concerned with the former than with the latter, but he claimed that he was not familiar with details. The operations extended from Maine to New Orleans and involved the expenditure during 1808 of more than a million dollars. An appropriation of $450,000 for the next year was requested and

[5] TJ's attitude toward Dearborn's retirement and judgment of his services is shown in his letters of Jan. 5 and May 25, 1808 (Ford, IX, 171–172 and note).
[6] See above, ch. XIII. Erney, pp. 245–250, describes the circumstances of Dearborn's confirmation as collector.

promptly granted by Congress.[7] In comparison with the program initiated just after the War of 1812, which involved the ultimate expenditure of upwards of $8,000,000, this one was modest, but it was attended with great difficulties. The winter of 1807–1808 was extremely cold; in his efforts to acquire land sites the thrifty Secretary met with greed on the part of individuals and dilatory action on that of state legislatures; and he was faced with a grave shortage of engineers.

In 1802, under authority of a congressional act of that year, Jefferson had set up a corps of engineers to constitute a military academy at West Point. Thus he became the founder of an institution that was destined to become famous, and the portrait of him by Thomas Sully (1822), now in the library of the Academy, serves as a reminder of his historic role. The contributions by cadets and members of the faculty to the cost of the portrait, a score of years after the founding, attest their appreciation of his services to the institution, but these were rendered under rather ironical circumstances. As secretary of state he had questioned the constitutional authority of Congress to set up a military academy, and prior to his presidency the chief advocates of one were Federalists. In 1800 John Adams had communicated to Congress a report from his Secretary of War, largely reflecting the ideas of Hamilton, which presented a comprehensive plan for a military academy. This was far too much for even a Federalist Congress, and it is not surprising that the measure approved by a Republican Congress was much more limited in scope. Furthermore, it accorded with Jefferson's own current thinking. If little concerned about the professional training of army officers in a time of peace, he fully recognized the usefulness of engineers in peace or war and valued the infant Academy chiefly for its potential scientific contributions. In his presidency it was a military school in little more than name, and the corps of military engineers, headed by Jonathan Williams, nephew of Benjamin Franklin, was limited by law to twenty officers and men.[8]

[7] The progress that had been made was described in detail in a report by Dearborn which TJ communicated to Congress, Jan. 6, 1809 (A.S.P., Mil. Affairs, I, 236–239). Erney, pp. 216–224, gives a full account.

[8] For TJ's position while secretary of state, see his memo. of Nov. 23, 1793 (Ford, I, 269–270). For the report Adams communicated to Congress, Jan. 14, 1800, see A.S.P., Mil. Affairs, I, 133–139. White, who is well aware of the ironies of these historic circumstances, gives a well-documented account of West Point and the army engineers in The Jeffersonians, ch. XVIII. Additional details about the early history of the Academy are in Jacobs, ch. XI, and in S. E. Ambrose, Duty, Honor, Country: A History of West Point (1966), pp. 18–35. S. P. Huntington, in his stimulating book, The Soldier and the State (1957), pp. 198–199, states that the Jeffersonian emphasis as perpetuated at West Point had a profound influence in

At this stage the prime function of the army engineers was to construct fortifications. Under existing conditions a more extensive program of defensive works could not have been wisely undertaken, and this one was not fully carried out. Major works at New Orleans and New York had not been completed when Jefferson's presidency ended. The latter port presented the greatest difficulties: about a third of the appropriation for 1808 was spent on its fortifications, but there were still grave doubts about just what could or should be done. Many of the lesser forts, hastily constructed out of materials available in the localities, lacked durability. Fortifying the harbors may not have been the best way to protect the country, and what was done may be said to have been too little and too late, but under the circumstances the government deserves credit for having done as much as it did, and its diligence seems unquestionable.

The responsiveness of Congress to recommendations of the Executive with respect to harbor defense can be attributed to the ready recognition of the danger to which ports, and local interests with them, would be exposed in case of war. Damaging forays inland might also be expected, and occasional reference was made to the fact that the country now had more centers than it had during the Revolution, when the British were faced with the problem of conquering a map. But neither in legislative nor executive circles does there appear to have been much fear of serious invasion by the Sea Lords, and the contingency plan of an offensive against Canada could hardly have been announced by the President in public. That Congress should have been less responsive to his recommendations regarding military manpower than to those regarding forts was to be expected. As we shall see, it provided for a substantial increase in the regular army, but it had previously foiled the repeated efforts of Jefferson to render the militia a more effective instrument of national defense. The success of these efforts would not have signalized the impending demise of the regular establishment, which Jefferson regarded throughout his presidency as a practical necessity, but it would have been a step in the direction of a genuinely national and more effective people's army. During the War of 1812 he observed to James Monroe, then secretary of war, that American experience had proved "the necessity of obliging every citizen to be a soldier," as had been the case with the Greeks and Romans and

---

furthering "technicism" among army officers and in delaying the development of "military professionalism" in the United States. The question that remains is whether what was bad for the army as an institution was bad for the country in the generation of freedom from foreign danger after 1815.

must be in every free state. The existing militia system, dating back to 1792, was based on the principle of universal obligation to render military service, but he showed himself to be far in advance of predominant American opinion when he said: "We must train and classify the whole of our male citizens, and make military instruction a regular part of collegiate education. We can never be safe till this is done."[9] His ideas may not have crystallized to this degree when he was President, but his later expression of them illuminates the position he took at this time.

His attitude toward the militia was neither contemptuous nor naïve. Not only did he regard a people's army as the only sort that was wholly compatible with republicanism and the maintenance of popular liberties; he valued the services the militia had rendered. Within recent months a body of them in Ohio had delivered a fatal blow to Burr's conspiracy, and companies from his own state had patrolled Lynnhaven Bay after the *Chesapeake* outrage. He had no doubt of the courage of his countrymen or of their willingness to rally to the defense of laws enacted by their representatives and of a country in which they had a stake. The militia, upwards of 600,000 in number, constituted a reservoir on which the government could draw in time of need; and he was not uttering idle words when he expressed in his first inaugural the judgment that, because of the personal participation and interest of its citizens in it, the American government was the strongest on earth. He was well aware, however, of the difficulty that the government faced in attempting to realize on the potentialities that were represented by the militia. Not only did these men lack training, organization, and arms; they were under state control and unresponsive to national, as compared to local, need. The President had constitutional authority to call them into federal service, and by laws passed in Jefferson's administration he was granted wide discretion in so doing, but he was not free to send them anywhere and their service was sharply limited in time.[10]

[9] TJ to Monroe, June 18, 1813 (L. & B., XIII, 261). The basic militia act was that of May 8, 1792 (*Annals*, 2 Cong., pp. 1392–1395).

[10] The laws under which TJ operated in his second term were those of Apr. 18, 1806 (*Annals*, 9 Cong., pp. 1265–1266), and March 30, 1808 (*Annals*, 10 Cong., 1 sess., II, 2846). Both of these set the total number of militia subject to call at 100,000 and limited service to six months. Among public criticisms of the militia system at this stage, special interest attaches to a pamphlet which a former French military officer, Maximilian Godefroy, addressed to the members of Congress in 1807, and to a series of discussions of national defense in William Duane's *Aurora* (especially Nov. 2, 3, 10, 12, 1807) which this occasioned. Godefroy's pamphlet, *Military Reflections on Four Modes of Defense*, a copy of which TJ probably had, dealt with ships of the line, gunboats, and fortifications as well as with the

In his communications to Congress during his first administration, he had referred in only a general way to the need to reform the militia system, but he made a specific recommendation to the legislators in the first congressional session of his second term.[11] This, it should be noted, was well in advance of the troubled events of 1807 that we have been considering. The measure he advocated was called the classification bill. It sought to divide the militiamen into classes on the basis of age, and to apportion services accordingly. Jefferson made frequent reference to Napoleon's creation of a young army, and he believed that most could be expected and should be required of those between twenty-one and twenty-five. The first classification bill specified that militiamen in that age group could be called to service one year out of two in any part of the United States or adjoining countries. Those between twenty-six and thirty-four could be called for three months to serve in their own or an adjacent state, while minors and elders of thirty-five and upwards need serve in only their own state and for not more than three months in a year. At that time the details of the classification led to some objection but the main one was to the lessening of local control.

Though Jefferson emphasized the desirability of local control of local matters throughout his public career, he clearly recognized that the security of the nation was at stake in this instance. He faced a political situation of great difficulty, since opposition to any change in the militia system was strong in his own party. Not only did Barnabas Bidwell and Joseph B. Varnum, stalwart supporters of the administration on other questions, decline to sponsor the classification bill; the latter presented an unfavorable report on it and became its most conspicuous opponent.[12] Jefferson was generally careful not to bring undue pressure to bear on congressional leaders and was specially concerned to retain the loyal support of New Englanders. A bill on the lines of his desire was introduced in the Senate by Samuel Smith, but was defeated by a vote of more than two to one, to the President's great disappointment.[13] Writing Bidwell some weeks later, he said that

---

militia. While Duane did not go along with this author's recommendation of a "free corps," he agreed with him about the ills of the militia. He regarded it as the only safe defense, however, and believed that it could be rendered effective by the legislatures of the country — state and federal. He appears to have been more disturbed by the lack of organization and training than by the local emphasis in the system.

[11] The efforts of TJ and Dearborn toward this end in his second term are described by Erney, pp. 155–159, 231–234.

[12] Jan. 2, 1806 (*Annals*, 9 Cong., 1 sess., pp. 327–330).

[13] *Ibid.*, pp. 69–70, 141.

while this measure might fail for a time, the militia could "never be used for distant service on any other plan," and that Bonaparte would conquer the world if others did not "learn his secret of composing armies of young men only, whose enthusiasm and health enable them to surmount all obstacles."[14]

Jefferson's hopes for the ultimate passage of a classification bill were not borne out. Early in 1808, when military needs were much more imperative than they had been two years earlier, a simpler bill was introduced in the House. Without reference to other age groups, this provided for the creation of a special class of young militiamen, who could be called to serve up to one year in any part of the United States. While this proposal was debated at some length, nothing came of it, the prevailing sentiment being that the existing system was good enough.[15] Apparently the measure did not come up for a vote but was sidetracked when Congress took up the question of increasing the regular army. Senator Samuel Smith told Jefferson that he saw no likelihood that Congress would ever create an effective militia system and such proved to be the case.[16]

During the War of 1812, in a letter to Monroe, the former President said: "I trust it is now seen that the refusal to class [classify] the militia, when proposed years ago, is the real source of all our misfortunes in this war."[17] This was an obvious over-simplification and over-statement. The measure he had favored was not a panacea; at best it was only a beginning. But as a measure of national defense it was sound in principle and deserved adoption. Judging from the slight support it received, we may doubt if he could have exerted enough pressure to secure its passage, and he could hardly have done so without jeopardizing his leadership of his party. He believed that national needs could be reconciled with local and individual interests under his plan, but Congress would have none of it, and that body did nothing to increase the effectiveness of the citizen soldiers except to provide for federal aid in arming and equipping them.[18]

[14] TJ to Bidwell, July 5, 1806 (L. & B., XI, 116). In this letter, more fully and explicitly than anywhere else perhaps, TJ set forth his policy in dealing with party leaders in Congress (see above, pp. 164–166).

[15] For the debate, beginning Jan. 18, 1808, see *Annals*, 10 Cong., 1 sess., pp. 1472–1481, 1484–1486, 1509–1511.

[16] Samuel Smith to TJ, March 11, 1808 (LC, 31118).

[17] TJ to Monroe, Oct. 16, 1814 (Ford, IX, 492).

[18] Congress did nothing about a plan, advanced by TJ early in 1806, whereby fifty acres of land would be granted any able-bodied man who would settle in Orleans Territory and agree to do two years' military service in his first seven years of residence. See E. S. Brown, "Jefferson's Plan for a Military Colony in

Under the original act they were required to arm themselves — the idea being, no doubt, that possession of weapons was general among the citizenry. States had provided arms in varying degree and form, but with few exceptions these troops were inadequately armed. In the spring following the enactment of the embargo, Congress authorized the executive to sell surplus muskets to the states. The state of Georgia bought 4000 a few weeks later, as did Maryland shortly after Jefferson retired from office.[19] But for their great and immediate needs these two states might have been content to avail themselves of the aid offered them by an act that was approved three weeks after the one that authorized purchases. Early in the session John Randolph, who generally deplored all centralizing tendencies, proposed that the federal government arm and equip the whole body of the militia. This proposal was debated intermittently over a period of several months and finally led to the passage of a measure providing for an annual appropriation of $200,000 for this purpose, the quotas of the various states being determined by their proportion of the enrolled militia.[20] Some objected to this measure as carrying a threat to the right of states and individuals to resist encroachments by the federal government, but it also lessened their responsibility and was welcome for that reason. The effects of this legislation during the remaining months of Jefferson's administration are hard to estimate and appear to have been slight, but toward the end of 1812 Madison's Secretary of War reported that 16,000 muskets had been issued under this law that year. By that time if not earlier its practical value had been demonstrated, and the assumption by the federal government of responsibility for arming the militia was an event of more national significance than may have been immediately perceived.[21] Dearborn caused the armories at Springfield

---

Orleans Territory" (Miss. Valley Hist. Rev., VIII (March, 1922), 373–376); discussed by Erney, pp. 159–161. TJ continued to believe that this plan was wise. See his letter of Feb. 26, 1810, to Kosciusko (L. & B., XII, 368).

[19] Act of Apr. 2, 1808; report of sales, dated Feb. 17, 1810 (A.S.P., Mil Affairs, I, 255).

[20] Proposed Dec. 1, 1807 (Annals, 10 Cong., 1 sess., p. 1005); Act approved Apr. 23, 1808 (ibid., p. 2859). Debate in House summarized by Erney, pp. 234–236, with references.

[21] The returns of militia, March 25, 1808, and Feb. 25, 1809 (A.S.P., Mil. Affairs, I, 230–234, 239–243), not all of which were current, show arms, munitions, and accouterments. There appears to have been no notable change in the period between the two returns, but it would seem that there were plenty of muskets, such as they were, for as large a force as the President was authorized to place in federal service (100,000), though not for the entire body of the militia. For the report of the Secretary of War, Dec. 18, 1812, see A.S.P., Mil. Affairs, I, 327, 329.

and Harper's Ferry to increase their output of small arms. They produced only 7000 stands each in 1809 but reached the figure of 10,000 the next year. Dearborn also procured arms on private contract and, judged by contemporary standards, the record of the administration in this area was distinctly creditable.[22]

Late in February, 1808, shortly after the collapse of the negotiations with the special British envoy over the *Chesapeake*, Jefferson recommended to Congress a large increase in the standing army.[23] Because of this action he has been charged with grave inconsistency by critics of an absolutist type of mind, but not even in his first term had he sought to rid the country of the regular military establishment, and he would have been foolish indeed if he had not tried to adjust military policy to the existing situation, irrespective of consistency. An effective citizens' army, adequate to the country's needs as he perceived them, was an unrealized and at the moment an unrealizable ideal. Even if a classification bill had passed he would have been warranted in seeking to increase the regular army, and the demonstrated unwillingness of Congress to permit the reorganization of the traditional militia system left him no choice but to do so.[24]

Since the previous summer he and his advisers had proceeded on the assumption that a total force of 30,000 or more was needed for defense and for offensive operations against Canada, and they could not count on the participation of the militia in the latter. Realizing that a regular army of that size would not be acceptable to Congress and could not be recruited anyway, Dearborn presented a plan for an increase of 6000 regulars and a force of 24,000 volunteers. The latter were to serve in annual stretches over a specified period of years and during this they were to be in training camp for three months each year.[25] The provisions for training and length of service were similar to those Jefferson would have applied to younger militiamen under the classification bill. No draft of a bill embodying these provisions was introduced in this session of Congress, and that body did nothing further about volun-

[22] Erney gives details, pp. 236–239.

[23] Message of Feb. 25, 1808 (*Annals*, 10 Cong., 1 sess., p. 151). For the negotiations with George H. Rose, see below, pp. 566–569.

[24] The modern military historian, R. F. Weigley, approves of TJ's "flexible adjustment to the world as he found it" (*History of the U.S. Army* [1967], pp. 104–105). Henry Adams laid the emphasis on inconsistency when he said of TJ's recommendation: "No such blow had ever been given to the established practices of Republican administration" (*History*, IV, 212).

[25] Details of Dearborn's plan (*A.S.P., Mil. Affairs*, I, 228) and what came of it are given by Erney, pp. 226–231.

teers, but it agreed to the proposal about the regular army, thereby raising the authorized strength of this to approximately 10,000 men. In the course of the lengthy debate in the House of Representatives, fears of a standing army were voiced, and the title that was finally attached to the measure was intended to be reassuring. It read: "An act to raise *for a time* an additional military force."[26] But John Randolph complained that only two others besides himself objected to the bill on principle, and there appears to have been less talk of Republican inconsistency than had been expected.[27]

Jefferson's son-in-law had made himself conspicuously vulnerable. About a week before the President made his recommendation, John W. Eppes, who obviously had not expected it, went so far as to say: "I never yet have voted for a regular army or soldier in time of peace. Whenever an opportunity has offered I have voted them down, and so help me God, I will as long as I live." He now said he was voting for an army, not as a peace establishment, but as part of the "system" designed to meet the deepening crisis of the country's affairs.[28] To John Randolph the "system" was a mass of absurdities and contradictions. He observed that they had just enough navy "to bait the war-trap," that they were building gunboats to protect the harbors, and forts to protect the gunboats. As for the system of embargo, which was one of "withdrawing from every contest, quitting the arena, flying the pit," he asserted that this was antithetical to the system of raising troops and fleets and wholly incompatible with it.[29] To his absolutist mind apparently it was inconceivable that at this stage anyone could regard the two as supplementary. Despite the gibes and the expressions of honest fears, the vote in favor of the bill in the House was overwhelming.[30] If, as has been alleged, the Republican party was now "poorer by the loss of one more traditional principle," the country had gained eight potential regiments.[31]

The military gain was much less in fact than on paper and it was considerably delayed. According to the practice of the time, officers had to be appointed to direct the recruiting before this could begin. The vexatious task of selecting them fell to Dearborn, who was appalled by the lack of qualifications among the applicants and the lack

---

[26] Act of Apr. 12, 1808 (*Annals*, 10 Cong., 1 sess., II, 2849–2852), italics added.

[27] Most of the debate occurred Apr. 4–7, 1808 (*ibid.*, pp. 1901–2061). Randolph's remark is on p. 2061.

[28] Speeches of Feb. 17 and Apr. 7, 1808 (*ibid.*, pp. 1631, 2049).

[29] *Ibid.*, pp. 1960, 1963.

[30] Apr. 7, 1808. On the passage of the bill the vote was 95 to 16. A motion to reconsider was lost, 25 to 60 (*ibid.*, p. 2062).

[31] Quotation from Henry Adams, *History*, IV, 218.

of candor in those who made recommendations. Commissions were regarded as favors granted individuals by the government, he said, and he himself was influenced by political considerations. He declined to name Federalists in Massachusetts, holding that they were disloyal and that there already were a disproportionate number of them in the army.[32] Military service as a serious profession in the United States had little to commend it in this era, and no patriotic call to sacrifice had been sounded. Enlisted men received about five dollars a month, and, while the legislators seem to have regarded this as entirely adequate, the pay was not alluring.

Recruiting was attended with many difficulties, but by the end of 1808 the regular army consisted of some 5700 officers and enlisted men, which was more than twice the number at the end of the previous year. It numbered nearly 7000 in 1809, reaching its highest point before the War of 1812.[33] The recruits were untrained, but this increase represented a genuine achievement, and in the meantime Jefferson gained reassurance from reports of problems faced by the French in Spain. In the fall of 1808, noting that Napoleon, in the effort to subdue a nation of five millions, had to begin with an army of 300,000, the President asked what numbers would be required against eight millions of free Americans spread over their vast country.[34] Long before he arrived at these comforting and possibly transitory reflections, however, his economical Secretary of the Treasury had calculated that in case of war, twice 7000 soldiers would be needed to man the coastal fortifications and guard the northwestern frontier against the Indians and that even more would be required for an invasion of Canada. The regular army did not attain its authorized strength during Jefferson's presidency, and even if it had done so it would have fallen far below what he and his advisers regarded as essential to a wartime posture.

His mature judgment with respect to the means of acquiring military manpower was well expressed during the War of 1812, when needs were undeniable. Writing James Monroe, then secretary of war, he said: "It is nonsense to talk of regulars. They are not to be had among a people so easy and happy at home as ours. We might as well rely on calling down an army of angels from heaven."[35] He did not say that they could be wholly dispensed with and he certainly did not regard them as angelic. In an earlier letter to Monroe, when the situa-

---

[32] His difficulties and state of mind are well described by Erney, pp. 229–230.
[33] Figures from Appendx in Weigley, p. 566.
[34] TJ to James Brown, Oct. 27, 1808 (Ford, IX, 211–212).
[35] TJ to Monroe, Oct. 16, 1814 (*ibid.*, 492).

tion was less desperate, he attributed the tardiness of enlistment to the contentment of the people and saw reason to rejoice that they had "so few of the desperate characters which compose modern regular armies."[36] Viewed out of context his comment might suggest that he regarded all regulars as desperadoes, but no doubt he was thinking of the old world not the new, and his main point was that in America regulars in sufficient number were unobtainable.

Therefore, a people's army was a practical necessity. What he got from Congress did not amount to a good foundation for such an army, but he did get one thing that held future promise. Among the eight regiments recommended by the Secretary of War and authorized by the Act of April 12, 1808, was one of light artillery. Whether the President was as aware of Napoleon's use of mobile artillery as of his employment of young soldiers is uncertain, but he submitted the recommendation and may be assumed to have approved what, in his country, was an innovation. The man who championed Robert Fulton's torpedoes might have been expected to do so. At all events the first American horse-drawn battery was set up in his administration and demonstrated impressively in Washington on July 4, 1808. Mobile artillery had the celerity of movement on land that was attributed to gunboats on water and, unlike the latter, it was to gain later professional approval. As things turned out, however, the life of this particular experiment was short. Dearborn's economical successor, serving under a less imaginative President, concluded that the horses were an extravagance, had them unhitched from the guns, and sold them.[37]

From the modern point of view the activities of this government in what has come to be known as military intelligence seem unorganized and amateurish, but the once-secret records of the War Department show more effort at this time to gain information about the Indians and the situation in Canada than most later historians appear to have been aware of.[38] In the summer of 1807 Dearborn instructed Governor William Hull of Michigan Territory and other officials to make specific inquiry, under conditions of the utmost secrecy, into military dispositions in Canada; and in the autumn he dispatched Peter Sailly, a resident of Plattsburg, New York, to Montreal on a secret mission of inquiry. Sailly sent detailed reports about military posts, armed forces,

[36] TJ to Monroe, June 18, 1813 (L. & B., XIII, 26).
[37] Fairfax Downey, *Sound of the Guns: The Story of American Artillery* (1956), pp. 64–66.
[38] The fullest treatment of these activities that I have seen is that of Mary P. Adams, pp. 185–193, 251–263, 286–287.

and the temper of the people, as did others to a lesser degree.[39] In the winter, the President and the Secretary of War availed themselves of the visit of a couple of Quakers to Indians in the Northwest to inquire into the activities of British agents among them and into the attitude of Tecumseh and the Prophet. The latter was reported to be bitterly hostile to the United States and the general tenor of these various reports was such that they should have discouraged an invasion of Canada. According to information known to have been received by the government, there were as many regulars in the British provinces as in the entire American army. Quebec was known to be strongly fortified and practically invulnerable. In the most favorable report the assertion was made that the country could be taken up to within a few miles of Quebec by 10,000 men, but apart from the militia the United States did not have that many.[40]

Before the end of 1808 it appeared that a considerably larger force would be needed in the far South than had hitherto been supposed. The President heard that an expedition, consisting of 4000 men, was being prepared at Halifax, and that, in case of war or its imminence, this would proceed against New Orleans, Upper Canada being abandoned to the Americans. In response to this reported threat, he and his advisers decided to send to New Orleans all the new recruits from Pennsylvania southward, approximately 2000 in number, along with 1000 of the old troops. Militia from the territories of Orleans and Mississippi were expected to swell the force, but the main point to be emphasized here is that half the regular army was assigned to this locality.[41] It was not anticipated at the time that half of these troops would be lost by disease and desertion within a year. That sad story belongs to the history of the Madison administration, but toward the end of Jefferson's it was clear enough that a little military force had to be stretched a long way.[42]

Before he left Washington to assume command in New Orleans, Wilkinson told the British Minister that many of the new regulars were "such miserable wretches" that he would have "infinite difficulty in bringing them into any state of discipline and order." This indiscreet remark was repeated by Erskine to John Howe, who had been

[39] Sailly to Dearborn, Dec. 30, 1807, and Feb. 18, 1808 (ibid., pp. 253-256, 260).
[40] TJ to Dearborn, Aug. 27, 1808 (L. & B., XII, 152-153).
[41] Memo. of Cabinet meeting, Dec. 1, 1808 (Ford, I, 338). I don't know how TJ learned of this "expedition" or how real the danger was.
[42] For the Terre aux Boeufs tragedy of 1809-1810, which was chiefly due to an unhealthy campsite and is largely blamable on Gen. Wilkinson, see Weigley, pp. 113-114.

sent to the United States on a tour of investigation by Sir George
Prevost, Lieutenant Governor of Nova Scotia, and who duly reported
it to that official. Such was the ease with which the British procured
military intelligence. An earlier traveler, dispatched by Sir George's
predecessor, passed himself off as Swiss, but Howe assumed the role of
visitor and as such received every courtesy. He was even presented to
the President in Washington.[43] Following his detailed instructions, he
reported on politics, governmental policy, and public opinion as well as
on military matters. In fact he had relatively little to say about the
latter, but what he did say must have been reassuring to his superiors in
Halifax and London. In the letter in which he quoted Wilkinson he
observed that the state of American military preparations could excite
no alarm in Nova Scotia that winter (1808–1809) and should interfere
with no plans that Sir George Prevost might have in mind. Though
this observer visited the chief ports as far south as Virginia, he got his
first impressions in New England, and there and elsewhere he con-
sorted chiefly with Federalists, whose opinions he reflected. This could
not be said of David Erskine, but he arrived at essentially the same
conclusion about the military situation.

Writing Canning a few weeks after the beginning of the last legislative session of Jefferson's presidency, he said that if Congress should
decide on war it would have to enter immediately upon preparations of
"a very different nature" from those already taken.[44] Unlike Howe,
he made no invidious comparisons between the British and American
forms of government, and between the talents and character of Federalists and Republicans. Instead, he emphasized economic difficulties,
pointing out the inescapable American dilemma. Even if little or
nothing were done about the navy, the cost of the necessary preparations would be great, while the income of the government, which was
largely derived from duties on imports, would sharply decline in case
of war (as indeed it was already doing under the embargo), and
recourse to excise taxes would be so unpopular as to be virtually
impossible. The prognostications of this fair-minded observer were
calculated to reassure the British authorities about the future, and the
reports of the military measures taken thus far could hardly have
alarmed them about the present.

[43] A report from Lt. William Girod to Sir John Wentworth, and a series of
reports by John Howe to Sir George Prevost, are in *A.H.R.*, XVII, 70–102,
332–364 (Oct., 1911; Jan., 1912), contributed by D. W. Parker. The former traveler
was in the United States in 1807–1808, and the latter made two trips in 1808–1809.
He reported Wilkinson's remark in a letter dated Nov. 27, 1808 (*ibid.*, 343).
[44] Erskine to Canning, Dec. 7, 1808 (FO, 5:58, No. 48).

Jefferson never expected to impress the powers of Europe with armed might. He assumed that the British would be contemptuous of any force his country could possibly display, and he regarded economic reprisal as the most effective American weapon. He was undoubtedly serious and diligent, however, in his efforts to prepare his country for the only sort of war he thought it competent to wage. Writing General Thaddeus Kosciusko less than a year after he left office, he said: "Although we have not made all the provisions which might be necessary for a war in the field of Europe, yet we have not been inattentive to such as would be necessary here. From the moment that the affair of the *Chesapeake* rendered the prospect of war imminent, every faculty was exerted to be prepared for it, and I think I may venture to solace you with the assurance that we are, in a good degree, prepared."[45] For the General's benefit he described the military accomplishments of his administration in considerable detail, over-stating some of them and claiming that as a whole they were greater than was generally believed. But he admitted that the major fortifications were still unfinished and stated that measures bearing on the militia that were specially dear to him had failed to pass. In fact the country had not reached the goal he had set, and events were soon to show that its military preparations were considerably less than good.

Their inadequacy, as demonstrated in the War of 1812, cannot be fairly attributed to him alone. His successor was less concerned about military matters than he, and Madison's first Secretary of War was clearly less competent than Dearborn. Furthermore, if the foundation that was laid in Jefferson's administration was not firm and broad enough, the responsibility was shared by the legislative branch of the government. Jefferson actually got a surprising lot out of Congress. Commenting on the session of 1807–1808, Henry Adams said that the acts passed "made an epoch in the history of the Republican party" and that the "progress toward energy was more rapid than could have been expected from a party like that which Jefferson had educated and which he still controlled."[46] Republican ideology was not created by Jefferson and his control of his party was less than complete. Furthermore, the sentiment of the congressional majority may be presumed to have been essentially that of most of the citizenry. This representative body accepted the President's recommendations and followed his leadership to a notable degree, but it did not give him all he asked for. His failure to ask for more, which might be attributed to his judgment

[45] TJ to Kosciusko, Feb. 26, 1810 (L. & B., XII, 366).
[46] *History*, IV, 223–224.

that he could not get it, has been ascribed by certain latter-day critics to his aversion to war and his expectation that there would be no need to resort to it. There can be no possible doubt that he hoped to maintain peace, but this is not to say that he did not perceive the necessity for contingent plans. It has also been said that both he and Dearborn tended to regard foundations as finished structures.[47] Performance undoubtedly lagged behind authorization, as is often the case in governmental matters, but the records certainly do not show that as commander in chief Jefferson was apathetic.

Another line of criticism is suggested by a comment of the French Minister. "All the political documents issuing from the pen of the President are cold and without color," said Turreau.[48] The words of the militant French representative, who described Great Britain as the enemy of the human race and was vexed because the United States seemed undisposed to take up arms against her, should not be taken at face value. Jefferson need not be supposed to have been feeble and irresolute just because Turreau said so. But he inevitably created an impression of ambivalence while keeping his options open and he did not infuse his countrymen with ardor in his effort to prepare them for a war that he probably regarded as ultimately unavoidable but sought to postpone as long as possible. In view of the uncertainties of this situation and the nature of the government and society over which he presided, it is not surprising that no more was done. A modern historian has said that Jefferson "did about as much as possible to activate what was essentially a friendless third-rate military power in a world at war."[49] This judgment may be too charitable, but, considering the limitations imposed by circumstance, we may doubt if any President could have done much better.

[47] This is the comment of Erney in his excellent critique of defense measures (pp. 240–245). Mary P. Adams sums things up more favorably (pp. 309–313).
[48] Dispatch of May 20, 1808, in AECPEU, LXI, Part II.
[49] Smelser, *Democratic Republic*, p. 161.

An Administration at Ebb Tide

[XXIX]

A More Fitting Habitation

ON New Year's Day, 1808, the President kept open house as was customary, and according to all reports he was visited and congratulated by an unusually large number of persons. John Quincy Adams, who arrived at noon and remained an hour, noted that the company included no Indians and mentioned James Monroe and General Wilkinson as the most prominent "strangers" present.[1] The former, just back from England, faced an uncertain political future, while the latter was soon to figure in court-martial proceedings that were to last beyond the congressional session and result in his dubious vindication. The Senator from Massachusetts was accompanied by his wife, and the assemblage of ladies was said to have been large and brilliant, but few of them could have been connected with the legislative branch of the government. In a recent letter to his daughter Jefferson had reported that the wives of senators and representatives in Washington that winter were fewer in number than the fingers of two hands.[2] Marketing facilities had improved, so that it was no longer necessary to send fifty miles to collect materials for a dinner, as the Marqués de Casa Yrujo said he did when he first came to Washington. But, according to the Secretary of the British legation, the Federal City, while somewhat less discouraging to housekeepers, was still unique, "not possessing a single street or even a single shop." Congressional ladies looked upon it as no Mecca and most legislators, living in boarding-houses, regarded themselves as sojourners. According to this same aristocratic young Britisher, however, Washington was a pleasant place despite its dis-

[1] Adams describes the occasion in *Memoirs*, I, 498; and there is a glowing account in *National Intelligencer*, Jan. 4, 1808.
[2] TJ to Martha, Nov. 23, 1807 (*Family Letters*, p. 315). Various personal items that are mentioned here are drawn from his correspondence with his daughter and grandchildren in this period (*ibid.*, pp. 311–345).

comforts and inconveniences — partly because of the friendliness and hospitality of the President and his ministers.[3]

Before the legislators arrived Jefferson had got through the dining of his friends among the regular residents, so as to be free for what he called his congressional campaign. This consisted of dinners at which, far from being belligerent, he sought to avoid the contention he was so tired of. For a time he had feared that he could not appear at the New Year's reception, when presidential hospitality was offered to all who chose to come. On Christmas Eve he had been taken with an intense toothache — an exceedingly rare experience with him — and, as he told his daughter, he had a swelling on his face as big as a pigeon's egg. Fortunately, this soon subsided. Either Senator Adams did not notice it or thought it not worth mentioning. But, despite the extraction of part of his jawbone, the President did not venture out of doors for a month, and a knot was visible for more than a month after that.[4]

From a personal point of view the year started badly. The news from Albemarle County was disquieting. Thomas Mann Randolph had been trying to straighten out the affairs of his sister, whose husband, David M. Randolph, after sacrificing all his property without being able to pay his debts, had gone to England. She was setting up a boarding-house in Richmond but did not yet have any boarders. Other relatives of Martha's husband, not as close as the one she called Sister Randolph, were in dire straits. "The ruin of the family [that is, of his branch of it] is extending itself daily," she wrote her father. While recognizing with Martha that her husband was under sacred obligation to contribute to his sister's necessities, Jefferson, well aware of that gentleman's liberal disposition, hoped that he would contribute money only when he had it and would avoid future commitments. As for himself he said: "I never in my life have been so disappointed as in my expectations that the office I am in would have enabled me from time to time to assist him in his difficulties. So far otherwise has it turned out that I have now the gloomy prospect of retiring from office loaded with serious debts, which will materially affect the tranquility of my retirement. However, not being apt to deject myself with evils before they happen, I nourish the hope of getting along." He added that he had always hoped and expected that they would all live together at Monticello after he came home to stay, and he believed that with their

lands they would have enough for the style of living they should
follow.

In her response, Martha, saying that she could never be happy if he
were deprived of the comforts to which he had long been accustomed,
reproached herself for the expense to which she and her family had put
him when they lived with him in Washington two years before. He
stoutly denied that they had been a burden and contrasted his happiness during that visit with the "comfortless solitude" of his general
situation.[5] It was not really that bad. John W. Eppes, not yet re-
married, and little Francis were with him. The Congressman was
confined to the house for a month that winter, but the President's
grandson, aged seven, was well and went to school every day. His
secretary, Isaac Coles, who was said to look like him, was there and he
certainly did not lack for company. Also, he received letters regularly
from his granddaughters at Edgehill. His grandson and namesake
appears to have been less literary. He had warned the girls that he
would be an unpunctual correspondent once the congressional season
began. He promised no more than one letter a week and often did not
have time for that, but he always kept his eyes open for bits of poetry
suitable for the scrapbooks they were making. Verse seemed in short
supply, he said; the trumpet of war had frightened the muses. By now
he was somewhat less didactic than he had been with his two daughters
in their childhood and youth, but as a reminder of the importance of
punctuation he sent one of his granddaughters four lines that were
devoid of it, except for the final period, and made no sense without it.
She was to supply the stops, calling on him for aid if need be. Cornelia
must have had to call on somebody, for she was only nine.[6]

Early in the year Joel Barlow, unsilenced by the trumpet of war,
sent him a copy of his ponderous *Columbiad.* The President did not
send that to his granddaughters though he could have spared it. Thanking the poet, he said he would read it after his retirement.[7] The "small
news" with which the little girls provided him brought him the more
pleasure because he had a surfeit of "great news" from other quarters,

[5] Martha to TJ, Jan. 2, 1808; TJ to Martha, Jan. 5; Martha to TJ, Jan. 16; TJ to
Martha, Feb. 6 (*ibid.,* pp. 317–320, 322–323, 327).
[6] To Cornelia Jefferson Randolph, Apr. 3, 1808 (*ibid.,* pp. 339–340, with explanatory note. The lines were as follows:
>I've seen the sea all in a blaze of fire
>I've seen a house high as the moon and higher
>I've seen the sun at twelve oclock at night
>I've seen the man who saw this wondrous sight.
[7] TJ to Barlow, Jan. 24, 1808 (L. & B., XI, 430).

and he responded with unvarying appreciation and characteristic grace. The most diligent of his young correspondents, Ellen Wayles Randolph, aged twelve, in the course of a long letter written at the approach of spring and specially commended by him, inquired about the health of his birds and flowers. In reply he said, "Our birds and flowers are well and send their love to yours."[8]

Though the President's House lacked the atmosphere of domesticity which Jefferson so prized, and the big barnlike structure was by no means a cozy place, it had at length been provided with a good roof. The Surveyor of Public Buildings, Benjamin H. Latrobe, who for the past five years had been in charge of architectural plans and construction under Jefferson's direction, had continued to give most of his time and effort to the Capitol, but had managed to make minor repairs and improvements at the President's House. In his report in the spring of 1808 he stated that half of the enclosing wall and one of its gates had been built and that most of the grounds had been graded.[9] Wings extending from the house toward the departmental buildings on the east and west had been finished earlier. These were of basement height with flat roofs, and on the south side where the ground fell away there was in front of each a covered passageway with columns. The idea was Jefferson's and he drew the first plans. These called for service rooms such as he had at Monticello — including an ice house, a saddle room, servants' quarters, necessaries, and even a hen house.[10] As built, the eastern wing terminated in a fireproof section for the Treasury, taking up five bays of the colonnade.

Besides designing this, Latrobe adjusted the whole of Jefferson's plan to structural requirements and no doubt modified it somewhat in the course of construction. Being in the full sense a professional to whom Jefferson, for all his architectural learning and talent, was but a gentleman amateur, Latrobe suffered many vexations in executing these tasks. He said privately that he was "cramped" in his design by Jefferson's "prejudices in favor of the old French books, out of which he fishes everything." But it was a small sacrifice to humor him, and Latrobe conceded that in style the colonnade was "exactly consistent with

[8] Ellen's letter of March 11, 1808, and his reply of March 14 are in *Family Letters*, pp. 332–334.

[9] Latrobe's report of March 23, 1808, can be conveniently seen in S. K. Padover, ed., *Thomas Jefferson and the National Capital* (1946), pp. 399–413; a brief reference to the President's House is on pp. 408–409. This useful collection of documents is referred to hereafter as Padover.

[10] Fiske Kimball, *Thomas Jefferson, Architect* (1916), p. 66 and Figures 175–177.

Hoban's pile."[11] He disliked the President's House and had a low
opinion of Hoban as an architect, regarding him as little more than a
builder, but his own fruitful collaboration with Jefferson was marked
by sincere appreciation and genuine admiration of his patron. Writing
the President in the late summer of 1807 when he was at Monticello,
Latrobe said: "It is not flattery to say that you have planted the arts in
your country. The works already erected in this city are the monu-
ments of your judgment and of your zeal and of your taste."[12] The
Surveyor of Public Buildings, who was utterly dependent on the
President's favor, could have been charged with exaggeration. There
was little that was monumental in the Federal City as yet, and Jefferson
had inherited both "Hoban's pile" and the unfinished Capitol, which
had been designed by a lesser gentleman amateur, Dr. William
Thornton. His own merit lay in the direction he gave to the continuing building activities in this unprepossessing village. It was indeed
fortunate that at this early stage the most notable American patron of
the arts was in the presidential chair. And by bringing Latrobe into the
service of the government and supporting him against those who resented him as an intruder he rendered much-needed service to an
unartistic community.

After the first two years of his presidency, when the emphasis was
on economy, the congressional appropriations for public buildings,
though sharply contested, were not ungenerous; and, although major
attention had to be given the Capitol, he and Latrobe did something
more for the President's House before he vacated it. The wall was
finished, along with nearly all the grading of the grounds. Midway in
Jefferson's second term Latrobe had drawn new plans for the large and
as yet undistinguished house. Those for the interior were not utilized,
but those for the exterior were eventually carried out. Regarding the
north entrance as unimpressive, Latrobe designed a bold portico with
porte-cochère. For the south front he designed a semi-circular portico
which Jefferson had suggested.[13] By the autumn of 1808 the stone
steps and foundation for the north portico were completed at no inconsiderable cost. Jefferson had urged that this work be given priority
over the planting, doubtless recognizing that its completion would
amount to a committal to the portico. At this time there was only a
rotting wooden platform on the south, but in due course the stone-
work on that side was also finished. On these firm foundations were

[11] Quoted by Talbot Hamlin, in his authoritative work, *Benjamin Henry
Latrobe* (1955), p. 294.
[12] Latrobe to TJ, Aug. 13, 1807 (Padover, p. 395).
[13] Kimball, *Jefferson, Architect*, p. 67.

afterwards erected the stately columns which make the White House, as it came to be known after the War of 1812, a mansion of genuine distinction. The foundations necessitated the porticos and, as things turned out, Hoban directed the construction, largely in accordance with Latrobe's old plans. But since this was not until the 1820's, the columns were seen by him and by Jefferson only in imagination.

The legislators who gathered in Washington in 1807–1808 without their wives were of necessity lodgers and boarders, but at long last the members of the larger branch of Congress had an official home. The south wing of the Capitol was sufficiently complete to be occupied by the House of Representatives in the autumn of 1807. Externally this building matched the north or Senate wing, and the original expectation was that in its interior it would follow the plan of Dr. William Thornton, which had been approved by George Washington. But this was little more than a sketch, and Latrobe, convinced of its impracticality, made a fresh design which Jefferson approved. Thus Latrobe gained the undying enmity of Thornton. Into their enduring feud we need not enter here except to say that Jefferson, while aware of the wastefulness and delay resulting from changes in design, and always mindful of political realities, supported his appointee in all crucial matters. In his mature opinion Latrobe was "the only person in the United States who could have executed the Representative chamber"; and in Latrobe's he was, among his countrymen, "certainly the best judge of the merits of an artist."[14]

Latrobe, who had come to America from England when he was thirty-two and was in his forties during Jefferson's administration, was not only an artist but also an engineer and experienced builder.[15] Recognizing qualifications that were unique at this time in the United States, the President, to whom Congress had granted wide discretion in planning while retaining control of the purse strings, generally gave the Surveyor of Public Buildings a free hand. As a rule he accepted Latrobe's representations, but he did not hesitate to advance his own ideas and at times he could be very stubborn. His insistence on large panel lights in the dome of the House chamber, despite Latrobe's strong preference for a lantern or cupola, is a case in point. Writing the architect-builder when the panels were still unglazed, he said: "It is with real pain I oppose myself to your passion for the lantern, and that in a matter of taste I differ from a professor in his own art. But the

---

[14] Quotations from letters of 1811 and 1814 (Padover, pp. 469, 473).

[15] For details of his earlier life, see Hamlin, Parts I, II. See also the excellent sketch by Fiske Kimball in *D.A.B.*

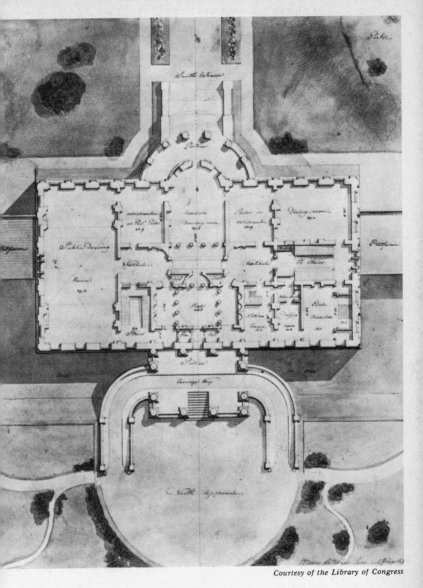

Courtesy of the Library of Congress

PLAN OF THE PRINCIPAL STORY OF THE PRESIDENT'S HOUSE
AS PROPOSED TO BE ALTERED

Original drawing by Benjamin Henry Latrobe, 1807

object of the artist is lost if he fails to please the general eye." After affirming his reverence for the Greek and Roman style, he said he could not remember ever having seen in any of their buildings a lantern, cupola, or belfry. He had supposed the cupola to have been due to the introduction of bells in churches and regarded it as one of the degeneracies of modern architecture. A lantern would offend his eye and he believed it would displease members of Congress.[16]

Without questioning the President's authority, Latrobe stated in his reply that in installing the panel lights he was acting "diametrically contrary" to his own judgment. He claimed, however, that in conceding the point he was moved, not by the desire to retain his post, but by an attachment to Jefferson "arising from gratitude and the highest esteem." He believed that there would be too much light and was certain that cold glass would condense warm vapor. He wondered, therefore, just what he would do when showers fell on the members of Congress from a hundred skylights. As for principles of architectural taste, he said that his were rigidly Grecian and that he was quite willing to be a copyist. But the Roman and Greek buildings that remained were not generally suited to modern public uses and certainly not to the American climate. While unwilling to concede that a cupola could not be beautiful, he wanted one for its usefulness, not its ornamental quality. Good taste, he sagaciously said, "ought never to be at warfare with good sense." As for the legislators, whom he was so concerned to protect from the falling showers, he rashly said that rather than consult them in matters of taste he would dictate to them.[17]

It was fortunate that this statement was made to one who understood the artistic temperament — as he also did the congressional — and was disposed to make the necessary allowances. The President served as a buffer between the person who drew the plans and the men who made the appropriations. This particular issue was compromised to some degree. No lantern was built but smaller panes of glass were used. The results were largely as Latrobe had predicted on the basis of practical experience in building considerably more extensive than that of Jefferson — who carried his passion for light too far at times and was never at his best with roofs.

To the congressmen, crowded and uncomfortable in their temporary quarters in the north or Senate wing of the Capitol, the delays in the completion of the south wing had seemed unconscionable. In the

[16] TJ to Latrobe, Apr. 22, 1807 (Padover, pp. 386–387). This episode is well described by Hamlin, pp. 272–274.

[17] Latrobe to TJ, May 21, 1807 (Padover, pp. 389–392).

spring of 1806 the House, by resolution, had requested the President to cause the building to be ready for occupancy by the opening of the next session in the fall, and a special appropriation was voted to further this purpose. But the building was then far from ready, for reasons that Latrobe went to great pains to set forth and Jefferson duly communicated to the impatient legislators. Latrobe, who was appalled by the shoddy construction of all the major public buildings, had found it necessary to tear down the existing walls of the unfinished south wing and start anew. The exterior work was largely done by the autumn of 1806, but work on the interior had been greatly delayed by the difficulty of getting materials. Except for rough stone, brick, and sand, he said, everything had to be brought from somewhere else to what he called "this infant establishment." Washington was the center of nothing except government and politics. His major difficulties in this instance arose from his inability to get enough suitable freestone for the interior.[18]

Latrobe's major task was to complete the south wing, but his troubles were not confined to that. He was continually repatching the leaky roof of the Senate wing. The leaks had caused ceilings to fall and, as became increasingly evident, had done permanent damage to the timbers supporting the roof and to all the floors. In the late summer of 1807 the roof drove Latrobe to desperation, as he revealed in a letter to Jefferson, then at Monticello awaiting the first word from Monroe about the *Chesapeake*.[19] Before that time he had offered, and Jefferson had approved, a plan calling for extensive changes in the badly constructed interior of this building. More convinced than ever that its reconstruction was imperative, Latrobe made a start that summer, but in the session of 1807–1808 the Senate's sessions were held in a chamber with a floor and ceiling he considered unsafe.

The representatives met in a building that was structurally sound and in a hall that was now finished except for its decoration. The ceiling was unpainted, the woodwork was only primed, the plaster had not dried out, and only a fraction of the sculpture had been completed.[20] Besides the twenty-four capitals in the Corinthian style of the Choragic Monument of Lysicrates in Athens on which Jefferson had insisted, there were to be five panels enriched with foliage, and a colossal eagle was to spread its wings twelve feet and six inches in the

18 Report of the Surveyor of Public Buildings, Nov. 25, 1806, communicated by the President Dec. 15 (*ibid.*, pp. 372–380).
19 Latrobe to TJ, Aug. 13, 1807 (*ibid.*, pp. 394–396).
20 Report of Latrobe, March 23, 1808 (*ibid.*, pp. 400–406).

frieze behind and above the Speaker's chair. Agreeing with Latrobe that no American workman was competent for work of such complexity, Jefferson directed him to apply to Philip Mazzei in Italy and ask him to secure somebody there.[21] As a result two sculptors, Giuseppe Franzoni and Giovanni Andrei, came to Washington early in 1806, to the artistic benefit of the unfinished Capitol and the raw country.[22]

Most of the sculpture was in a crude state when the congressmen took over their new quarters, and many of them may have viewed it as an extravagance. Unquestionably they were agreed that in two respects their hall was highly unsatisfactory. The resounding echoes made it difficult and often quite impossible to hear what anybody said and the heat was intolerable. The architect wryly remarked in his report that these objections had been "forcibly stated and permanently recorded in the speeches of the members." He had foreseen the difficulty of acoustics in this sort of chamber, he said, and had planned to meet it by means of draperies, but had been able to do so to only a limited degree because the appropriations for furnishings ran out. The solution at which he arrived after various conferences was to hang curtains between the columns all round the hall and to have the ceiling painted "in flock." The painting could not be done while the House was in session, but the rich red curtains arrived in February. They had a very favorable effect on the acoustics and were generally admired.[23] So was the painted ceiling when the members reassembled in the fall. During most of the session of 1807–1808, however, if Latrobe's own words may be accepted, the echoes rendered debate "very laborious to the speaker and almost useless to the hearers." Under these circumstances one can but marvel that so much of it was carried on.

Heat was brought into the chamber from stoves in the floor below by means of flues passing through a sort of tunnel beneath the members' seats. Latrobe sought to regulate this and provided better ventilation, but, judging from the comments of the leading Federalist congressman in the middle of March, his efforts were not immediately

[21] Latrobe to Mazzei, March 6, 1805, describing the contemplated work (ibid., pp. 355–358). Mazzei, once a neighbor of TJ's at Colle, is best known in American history as the recipient of a letter in which TJ was alleged to have attacked George Washington. (See Jefferson and the Ordeal of Liberty, pp. 267–268; 302–307.)

[22] See Hamlin, pp. 267–270, for a fuller account of them.

[23] Padover, pp. 403–405; Hamlin, p. 289, gives colorful details.

successful. To his wife Josiah Quincy wrote: "The heat of the Capitol is noxious and insupportable, and it has affected me to fainting. One of the flues of the furnace is behind my chair. I have at length prevailed on the Speaker to forbid our subterranean fires. The effect produced by them is that upon an oyster bake in a Dutch oven."[24]

The climax of Latrobe's troubles came in the spring of 1808, when it became known from the report his presidential patron transmitted to Congress in obvious embarrassment that in the year 1807 he had incurred a deficit of more than $50,000 in his operations. The figure is the more impressive when set against the appropriation of $65,000.[25] Also, it should be remembered that the government was then at greatly increased expense for military preparations and that its income was being adversely affected by the embargo. As Congressman John Randolph put it, this was "no time for a wanton waste of the public money." In the Representatives' Hall, where Latrobe's gorgeous curtains had at length rendered speeches audible, he was subjected to censure which he himself described as copious and coarse. Very harsh things were undoubtedly said, especially by John Randolph, chief emphasis being laid by him and others on the fact that the excess expenditures were unauthorized and illegal.[26] The precedent of making good such a deficit was described as extremely dangerous. John Randolph asserted that "if this were to be permitted, they might as well open the Treasury and dismiss their accounting officers at once." The Federalists did not fail to raise the question of consistency, quoting from Jefferson's first message to Congress a passage in which he called for the strictest fiscal accountability. Latrobe was especially grieved by the attitude of Jefferson's son-in-law. Congressman Eppes, after speaking of a gross abuse of trust, moved a recommittal of the question of an appropriation and an inquiry into the expediency of abolishing the office of Surveyor of the Public Buildings. To cap poor Latrobe's troubles, Dr. William Thornton at this juncture renewed his attack on the architect who had exposed the faults of his design, publishing in the *Washington Federalist* an outrageous letter which occasioned Latrobe to institute a libel suit against him.[27] Despite the furor,

[24] March 15, 1808 (Quincy, *Life,* p. 137).

[25] Report of March 23, 1808, transmitted March 25 (Padover, pp. 398–413).

[26] Latrobe to TJ, May 23, 1808 (*ibid.,* p. 425); *Annals,* 10 Cong., 1 sess., II, 1973–1976, 2276. Considerably more than is recorded here was undoubtedly said in the Committee of the Whole, whose debate was not reported.

[27] Hamlin, pp. 282–286. This dragged on for years until, in 1813, he won a moral victory by gaining a verdict with costs.

an appropriation sufficient to cover the deficit and most of Latrobe's recommendations was eventually approved by an overwhelming vote.[28]

Shortly after the appropriations bill for the public buildings was passed, Jefferson sent Latrobe a stern letter in which he included what amounted to a list of priorities to be followed in the coming year and cautioned him against incurring a single dollar of deficit.[29] "The lesson of the last year has been a serious one," he said. "It has done you great injury, and has been much felt by myself." The deficit was contrary to the principles of the American government, "which make the representatives of the people the sole arbiters of the public expense, and do not permit any work to be forced on them on a larger scale than their judgment deems adapted to the circumstances of the Nation." As a private person he could be and often was extravagant in his pursuit of beauty, but as President he was rigidly insistent on the responsibility of officials, including himself, to keep within the prescribed limits in the expenditure of public funds. Therefore he was rebuking an artist whom he regarded as invaluable but whom he believed to have over-reached himself.

Latrobe never lived down the reputation for extravagance that he gained at this time, and Jefferson's one reservation about him in later years was that in matters of expense he was insufficiently guarded, but there were mitigating circumstances in this particular case. Latrobe described some important ones in a long letter he wrote after Congress had adjourned and the President was at Monticello. The latter, in his reply, did some explaining of his own, and although the old relation of mutual confidence may not have been fully restored they arrived at a better understanding.[30] Latrobe said that the entire blame for the deficiency had been laid on him by the "very words" of the message with which the report was submitted. In this Jefferson said that the existence of the deficit was unknown to him until his arrival in Washington in October, 1808, and that the circumstances under which it arose were given in the report. He now revealed that he had been deeply embarrassed in his effort to find expressions that would not injure Latrobe or hurt his feelings and had engaged in repeated consul-

[28] The key vote on Apr. 25 was 73 to 8, that of Eppes not being recorded (*Annals*, 10 Cong., 1 sess., II, 2277). Latrobe's estimate for 1808, at the end of his report, can be conveniently seen in Padover, pp. 412–413. An item of $15,000 for erecting part of the west front of the House building was rejected.

[29] TJ to Latrobe, Apr. 25, 1808 (Padover, pp. 414–416).

[30] Latrobe to TJ, May 23, 1808 (*ibid.*, pp. 420–427); TJ to Latrobe, June 2, 1808 (*ibid.*, pp. 429–432).

tations with the department heads before deciding on his brief statement. He also said that in his conversations with members of Congress he had reminded them that the cost of buildings nearly always exceeded expectations. Such had certainly been his own experience.

Latrobe had been under great pressure to complete the House wing, and the President had urged him to employ more workmen. While admitting this, Jefferson said he certainly had no thought of exceeding the appropriation. He would probably have advised moderate expenditures beyond this, rather than that the effort to get the Hall of Representatives fit for occupancy should fail, he said, and in that case he would have taken it upon himself to explain matters to Congress and seek their indulgence. Latrobe was generally reluctant to trouble Jefferson and was well aware of the grave problems the President faced in the most difficult year of his presidency, but he stated that in this instance he had not been aware that there was a deficit to report. This surprising state of affairs was attributable to the fact that expenditures were made, not by him, but by Thomas Munroe, the Superintendent of Public Buildings, and that the latter official kept the accounts. Latrobe now strongly protested against this anomalous situation, and Jefferson explained how it had come about. He showed no disposition to alter it materially, doubtless regarding it as desirable to keep this check on the zealous Surveyor of Public Buildings, but he yielded to that gentleman's plea that he be allowed a clerk to keep records for himself. That is, Jefferson agreed that he should call one of his employees by that name and thus avoid the creation of a new office.

Jefferson paid no heed whatsoever to Latrobe's virtual offer to resign, and he believed that by this exchange of explanations he had been saved from the "uneasiness of a silent separation" for unknown causes. He received relatively frequent reports from Latrobe during the rest of the year, and work on the public buildings proceeded according to his list of priorities. It was marred by the collapse of a vault on the ground floor of the Senate wing, which caused the death of Latrobe's able assistant, John Lenthall. This tragic accident, which Latrobe attributed to an unwise change in the construction of an arch in the interest of economy, was explained more fully to the President than to Congress.[31] In this formal report, which the President communicated to that body early in the session of 1808–1809, he stated that

---

[31] Latrobe to TJ, Sept. 23, 1808, with drawings (*ibid.*, pp. 436–439); see also Hamlin, pp. 276–278.

the interior of the Senate wing was being carried up "in solid work" according to the approved plan.[32] This work was not completed while Jefferson was President, however, and he never saw the new Senate chamber with its Doric columns. The elaborate Corinthian capitals in the Hall of Representatives were not all finished by the Italian sculptors until after he had retired, but the ceiling had been painted in a "masterly manner" by George Bridport of Philadelphia and there could be no doubt that Latrobe had created a legislative hall of rare beauty. Also, he claimed in this report that the inconveniences the members had experienced last year had been "obviated by a great variety of improvements." There was still much planting to be done in the grounds of the mansion at the other end of Pennsylvania Avenue, and the Federal City was still a raw as well as an inconvenient place, but a more fitting habitation was being provided for the President and for the Great Council of the nation.

Writing Latrobe in the autumn after his retirement and expressing the hope that Congress would authorize construction of the building between the House and Senate wings, Jefferson said: "I think that the work when finished will be a durable and honorable monument of our infant republic, and will bear favorable comparison with the remains of the same kind of the ancient republics of Greece and Rome."[33] What he wrote a few years later, when the programs of public works had been sharply curtailed with the onset of war, and when Latrobe's spirits were very low, is even more expressive of the hope that had animated them both: "I shall live in the hope that the day will come when an opportunity will be given you of finishing the middle building in a style worthy of the two wings, and worthy of the first temple dedicated to the sovereignty of the people, embellishing with Athenian taste the course of a nation looking far beyond the range of Athenian destinies."[34]

This was not to be. The architect himself sent the former President a detailed description of the destruction by the British of the beautiful Hall of Representatives that Jefferson had regarded as Latrobe's durable monument.[35] Fortunately, however, the aspirations of neither of these artists perished with it.

[32] Report dated Nov. 18, 1808, and transmitted Dec. 1 (Padover, pp. 445-452).
[33] TJ to Latrobe, Oct. 10, 1809 (ibid., p. 462).
[34] TJ to Latrobe, July 12, 1812 (ibid., p. 471).
[35] Latrobe to TJ, after August 1814 (ibid., pp. 473-476).

[XXX]

Unfinished Business

1808

ON New Year's Day, 1808, the following news item appeared in the *Charleston Courier:* "The importation of slaves from Africa ceases this day, according to act of Congress." The announcement had special significance in that particular place, for South Carolina was the only state where such importation was not already illegal. Although the federal government was precluded by a provision of the Constitution from taking action that would be effective before this date, all the states had outlawed the foreign slave trade on their own authority and only South Carolina had reopened it. The bald statement in the Charleston paper was accompanied by statistics of importations during the four years (1804–1807) that the ports of the state had been reopened — 15,676 in the last of these and 39,310 altogether. In the same issue of this paper, there were six notices of the sales of recent cargoes of "Prime Africans."

Jefferson, keeping open house in Washington that day, was in no position to see this paper, and he could have found no reference to the termination of the foreign slave trade in the current issue of the *National Intelligencer.* He himself did not seize upon the occasion to proclaim that a milestone had been passed in the agelong struggle for human freedom, and the attitude of his countrymen appears to have been one of general indifference.[1] No doubt they had got used to the idea since the action of Congress nine months earlier, and even then the desirability of removing the legal sanction from this traffic was gen-

---

[1] On Jan. 1, 1808, there was no reference to the outlawing of the foreign slave trade in either the *National Intelligencer,* the Richmond *Enquirer,* the Philadelphia *Aurora,* or the Boston *Columbian Centinel.* Neither TJ, Madison, nor Gallatin seems to have referred to the matter at this time.

erally taken for granted. The main question was that of the means of enforcement, and the form that the congressional act finally took warranted the supposition that this would not be rigorous. Before considering that measure, however, we should inquire into the attitude of Jefferson, who strongly recommended that Congress act but appears to have done nothing further.

Since the problem of slavery did not now bulk as large in his mind or in that of the public as it did after his retirement, detailed treatment of his relations with it will be deferred until we reach that period.[2] But we should certainly note here that his own ardor had cooled since he had vainly sought to induce the legislature of his state to adopt a very moderate form of gradual emancipation and had excoriated the institution of slavery in his *Notes on Virginia*.[3] Even then he had been inhibited by his doubts of the feasibility of incorporating the freed Negroes in a white society, and had favored emancipation only when coupled with some sort of colonization. He believed that slavery could not last, but to all practical purposes he himself had reached an impasse; and, for all his temperamental optimism, he was convinced that his contemporaries were unwilling as yet to do anything to solve this problem. Toward the end of his first term he wrote his former secretary: "I have long since given up the expectation of any early provision for the extinguishment of slavery among us."[4] To this statement, however, he added the following prognostication:

> But interest is really going over to the side of morality. The value of the slave is every day lessening; his burthen on his master dayly increasing. Interest is therefore preparing the disposition to be just; and this will be goaded from time to time by the insurrectionary spirit of the slaves. This is easily quelled in it's first efforts; but from being local it will become general, and whenever it does it will rise more formidable after every defeat, until we shall be forced, after dreadful scenes & sufferings to release them in their own way, which without such sufferings we might model after our own convenience."[5]

He was speaking from his own observation and experience in Virginia and did not allow for the increased demand for slaves incident to

[2] I expect to treat his relations with slavery more adequately in the final volume of this series.

[3] See *Jefferson the Virginian*, pp. 264–268.

[4] TJ to W. A. Burwell, Jan. 28, 1805 (*Farm Book*, p. 20).

[5] *Ibid.* Capitals inserted at beginning of sentences but spelling and punctuation unchanged.

the rise of cotton culture that was already evident in South Carolina. Nor did he anticipate that his fellow Virginians would ultimately reduce their financial burdens by selling their surplus human stock for labor in distant fields. As for slave revolts, which he regarded as inevitable unless somehow the situation could be peacefully corrected, the ruling group were to prove more successful in suppressing and preventing them than he expected, and the denouement was to be postponed longer than he may have thought possible. But, quite clearly, he perceived no more likelihood of its immediate occurrence than he did of peaceful emancipation. And in view of his inescapable problems, including that of holding the country and his own party together, he avoided being drawn into any controversy over slavery.

Early in his second term, in a letter to a Quaker friend who was an inveterate foe of human bondage, he said: "I have most carefully avoided every public act or manifestation on that subject. Should an occasion ever occur in which I can interpose with decisive effect, I shall certainly know and do my duty with promptitude and zeal."[6] Until its date at least, this quotation bears out the assertion of an able modern critic that "the dominant theme of Jefferson's administration on the subject of slavery was discreet silence."[7] He was certainly in grave doubt as to the means of effecting emancipation and may be said to have both desired and feared it. But we need be in no doubt whatsoever about his attitude toward the foreign slave trade. He had denounced it in a passage which was too much for his colleagues in the Continental Congress and which they deleted from his draft of the Declaration of Independence; and, although his rhetoric may have been more restrained in later life, he was thoroughly consistent on this subject.[8] As a humane man he deplored the barbarities of the traffic, and as a practical man he opposed an increase in the slave population of the country which would add difficulties to what was already an exceedingly difficult situation.[9] By importing nearly forty thousand hapless Africans the South Carolinians may have met their immediate

[6] TJ to George Logan, May 11, 1805 (Ford, VIII, 352).
[7] William Cohen, "Thomas Jefferson and the Problem of Slavery," in *Journal Am. Hist.*, LVI (Dec., 1969), 522.
[8] *Ibid.*, p. 511.
[9] This attitude was reflected in the position he took regarding restrictions on the importation of slaves into the Territory of Orleans. (See *Jefferson the President: First Term*, pp. 358, 360.) The laws prohibiting importations into that territory from abroad were largely nullified by means of the domestic slave trade — a point which I did not make clear in my treatment of that subject. The point I am making here is that TJ's attitude did not change.

need of laborers to till their cotton fields, but they were making the ultimate solution of the slavery question more difficult. The approach of the date when such importation could be forbidden by federal law provided Jefferson with an occasion when he could "interpose with decisive effect." Accordingly, in his message of December 2, 1806, he recommended to Congress that it exercise its constitutional authority "to withdraw the citizens of the United States from all further participation in those violations of human rights which have been so long continued on the unoffending inhabitants of Africa, and which the morality, the reputation, and the best interests of our country have long been eager to proscribe."[10] This eagerness was far from universal among the white citizens, but, judging from the tone of the subsequent debates in Congress, there was general recognition that the time had come when something should be done. The question remained whether the action of the constituted authorities would amount to more than a formal gesture.

Later events were to demonstrate that, while the foreign slave trade might be reduced, it could not be suppressed so long as slavery itself remained a legal institution; and the anomalies of the situation were abundantly revealed in the debates which were carried on intermittently during virtually the whole of this congressional session.[11] Some took the position that, if the penalty were made sufficiently severe, illegal importations would wholly cease, and the Senate favored punishment of traders by death. But representatives from states that had been economic beneficiaries of the traffic in the past (including not only the slaveholding states but also Rhode Island, which had been a nursery of slave traders) were unwilling to designate it as a crime and claimed that a law carrying such a penalty would be unenforceable.[12] Congress was unwilling to go beyond forfeiture, fines, and imprisonment; and in any case some infractions of the law were to be expected.[13] Some Africans would be illegally imported and the question that occupied the legislators most was what to do with them.

[10] Ford, VIII, 492.
[11] The debates in the Senate were not reported. Those in the House are described in considerable detail by W. E. B. Du Bois, *Suppression of the African Slave-Trade* (1896), ch. VIII; U. B. Phillips, *American Negro Slavery* (1918), pp. 139–147; Henry Adams, *History*, III, 356–367. For a diagram, showing the legislative history of the act, and detailed references, see Du Bois, p. 107.
[12] In 1820 the foreign slave trade was designated as piracy by congressional act, but prior to the Civil War, the death penalty seems never to have been invoked by American authority against slave traders.
[13] The Act of March 2, 1807, is in *Annals,* 9 Cong., 2 sess., pp. 1266–1270.

At least a dozen distinct proposals were made which, for one reason or another, were deemed unsatisfactory.[14] The first proposal in the House — that the forfeited blacks should be resold by the government — would have amounted to a contradiction of the purpose of the law and a condonation of the traffic in human beings. To ship them back to Africa was quite impracticable and would have been in fact to return them to bondage there. If set free, where were they to go? As freedmen, subject to no control, they would have been most unwelcome in any slaveholding state; and in a strange society with whose very language they were unfamiliar their mere survival would have been extremely doubtful. The most realistic and humane proposal was that they be conveyed at government expense under direction of the President to some place where slavery was illegal and there be indentured for a term of years. But Congressman Peter Early of Georgia, who was chairman of the committee originally set up to deal with this whole question and was conspicuous in the debates, said that residents of the southern states would resist this provision with their lives.[15] No doubt the assertion was reckless and exaggerated, but the final action was what this representative of the Deep South desired. Illegally imported Africans were to be subject to such regulations as the several legislatures should make.

Along with the principle of state control, which was thus maintained, the chief concern of the representatives from the slaveholding regions was to prevent condemnation of the institution of slavery itself. Early, who stated at the outset that slavery was regretted by everybody, subsequently declared that, far from regarding it as a crime, most Southerners did not regard it as an evil.[16] As for the coastwise slave trade, which was ostensibly domestic, most of the senators and many congressmen wanted to prohibit it altogether. The net result of the discussion was a compromise limiting the trade to larger vessels and requiring the ships' officers to certify that the slaves in their cargoes had not been imported. Saying that the provision impinged on the right of private property, John Randolph stridently voiced the fear that it might become "the pretext of universal emancipation" and declared that it would "blow up the Constitution." If there

---

[14] Du Bois lists twelve (pp. 96–97n.).

[15] *Annals*, 9 Cong., 2 sess., pp. 478–479. Note the comment of Phillips: "This reckless assertion suggests that Early was either set against the framing of an effective law, or that he spoke in mere blind rage" (*American Negro Slavery*, p. 144).

[16] *Ibid.*, p. 142, citing *Annals*, 9 Cong., 2 sess., pp. 174, 238.

ever should be disunion, he said, the line would be drawn between the states that did and those that did not hold slaves.[17]

The threat to the Union arising from this issue was not immediate, but the alignment in Congress tended to be sectional. Jefferson's abstention from this entire dispute can be readily attributed to political prudence and his desire to maintain the unity of his party and the country. Also, he may have been as uncertain about precisely what to recommend to Congress as he was dubious that detailed suggestions from him would be accepted. Since he himself, in 1776, had described the foreign slave trade as piratical, it may be presumed that he would have approved of the death penalty for engaging in it, although in the existing state of public opinion he may well have doubted that this penalty would often be imposed. As for the relatively humane and realistic indenture plan, he would probably have dreaded the presidential responsibility and the likely conflict between federal and state authorities it would have entailed. Being sincerely concerned to stop the importation of slaves, no doubt he would have preferred a stronger measure. Yet, responding to an address from a body of Quakers in the autumn of 1807, he said:

Whatever may have been the circumstances which influenced our forefathers to permit the introduction of personal bondage into any part of these States, and to participate in the wrongs committed on an unoffending quarter of the globe, we may rejoice that such circumstances, and such a sense of them, exist no longer. It is honorable to the nation at large that their legislature availed themselves of the first practicable moment for arresting the progress of this great moral and political error.[18]

In speaking to an anti-slavery group he was putting the best face on the matter. He did not mention it in his annual message to Congress in 1807, at a time when foreign trade of every sort was being curtailed. Congress had set up no mechanism for the enforcement of the act, and, so far as the federal government was concerned, responsibility lay with the Department of the Treasury. Of Gallatin's strong anti-slavery position there can be no possible doubt, but during the last fourteen months of this administration, he was saddled with the almost intolerable task of enforcing the embargo laws. In view of the further fact

[17] *Annals,* 9 Cong., 2 sess., p. 626; see also p. 636.
[18] TJ to Messrs. Thomas, Ellicot, and others, Nov. 13, 1807 (*Works,* Washington edn. [1853], VIII, 119), replying to a communication of Nov. 7.

that the states were slow in passing supplementary legislation, it is not surprising that the record of federal action was essentially negative.[19]

ii

Not only did the Washington political community appear indifferent to the ending of the legalized African slave trade; judging from the actions of the two houses of Congress during the early weeks of 1808, one would have supposed them unaware of the critical situation of their country in a warring world. "The presidential election engrosses the principal attention of the members," wrote Senator John Quincy Adams to his father the ex-President.[20] This was shortly after a Republican congressional caucus had voted overwhelmingly in favor of James Madison for President and the venerable incumbent, George Clinton, for Vice President.[21] While there was no doubt that the Secretary of State was supported by most of the members of his party in Congress, a large number of them did not attend this caucus. Friends of Clinton (who thought himself entitled to a promotion) wanted to leave themselves free to support him for the first office, though hardly anybody believed him likely to gain it or qualified to fill it. John Randolph and his little band of irregulars, who favored James Monroe, were not even invited to attend the meeting. Besides protesting against the proceedings afterwards on constitutional grounds, they formally stated that they believed Madison unfit to fill the presidential office in the present juncture.[22] Reporting the results of the caucus to Thomas Mann Randolph, Jefferson, who did not take the candidacy of Clinton seriously, said that Madison's election was considered "out of all ques-

[19] TJ pardoned a slave-trader, Philip M. Topham, after the Act of March 2, 1807, became effective on Jan. 1, 1808, but this action has no bearing on the enforcement of that law, as the reference to it by Du Bois (p. 128, note 3) would imply. The records in the National Archives show that Topham was convicted under the law of 1794, which prohibited Americans from engaging in slave trade *to* another country (from Africa, possibly to the West Indies, in this instance). The case dragged on for seven years, during half of which Topham, unable to pay his fine of $16,000, was in jail. His release was approved by the New York manumission society which had brought about his original prosecution, and his pardon by TJ amounted to the surrender of the government's claim to a portion of his uncollectable fine (General Records of the Dept. of State: Pardons and Remissions, 1793–1893, I, 146, 148, 149; Petitions for Pardon, 1789–1868, Tray 38, Pardon No. 140).

[20] J. Q. to John Adams, Jan. 27, 1803 (*Writings*, III, 189).

[21] Jan. 23, 1808. There is an excellent account of this caucus and of the maneuvers that preceded and followed it in Cunningham, *Jeffersonian Republicans in Power*, ch. V.

[22] Protest of Feb. 27, 1808, quoted by Cunningham, p. 116, from *National Intelligencer*, Mar. 7.

tion."[23] Nonetheless, he regretted the movement in his own state in behalf of Monroe as a threat to party unity, and on personal grounds he deplored the rivalry between his two long-time friends. This rivalry came into the open when, on the same day in Richmond, one legislative caucus voted to support the Secretary of State and a smaller caucus approved the recent minister to Great Britain.[24] Accordingly, the voters of the state were presented in due course with two rival slates of electors, both claiming to be Republican. While Jefferson unquestionably preferred Madison to anybody else as his successor, he went to great pains never to say so; and this movement in his own state was not directed against him. Apart from John Randolph and a few others, its leaders professed loyalty to him personally, being disposed to blame Madison for what they disliked in the conduct of the government. The situation abounded in ironies and contradictions. The main grievance of the Old Republicans, as they called themselves, was that the administration had been insufficiently loyal to the historic faith of the party. As stated in classic form by the late Edmund Pendleton and perpetuated by his foster son John Taylor of Caroline among others, this emphasized limited government, limited presidential power, increased power on the part of the House of Representatives, and sharp restrictions on financial operations.[25] Gallatin, who approved of the Bank of the United States, might have been blamed for such departures from financial orthodoxy as the administration was charged with, but the effective participation of the executive in legislative matters, which was condemned by Randolph and some other constitutional purists, was owing to the pragmatism of Jefferson, who was as fearful of legislative tyranny as of any other. John Randolph might say that the Republicans in power were just like the Federalists and that the Secretary of State was chiefly responsible, but at just this time a Federalist congressman, describing Madison as "a visionary, theoretic, closet politician," held that Monroe was more practical and less partisan.[26]

The sincerity of this judgment need not be questioned, but the simplest explanation of the relative approval of Monroe by the Fed-

[23] TJ to TMR, Jan. 26, 1808 (LC, 30841).

[24] These caucuses were held on Jan. 21, 1808, but were not reported in Washington until after the caucus of Jan. 23 there. In "James Monroe and the Election of 1808 in Virginia" (*W. & M.*, 3 ser., XX, Jan. 1963), Harry Ammon describes developments in detail, setting this episode on the background of Monroe's frustrating mission to England and the ideological conflict in Virginia. The course of the latter, 1806–1808, is well traced by N. K. Risjord in *The Old Republicans* (1965), ch. IV.

[25] See *Jefferson the President: First Term*, pp. 118–119.

[26] Samuel Taggart in a letter of Jan. 19, 1808 (*Amer. Antiq. Soc. Procs.*, XXXIII, 299).

eralists is that at this stage he was not identifiable with the administration as Madison was and that by building him up at Madison's expense the feeble opposition could hope to accentuate the divisiveness in the dominant party. The charge that he had been victimized was bandied about. George H. Rose, the special British envoy who reached Washington in the middle of January, wrote Canning a couple of weeks later that the general politics of the country had been "bent to the purposes of the election of such a successor to Mr. Jefferson as should be devoted to his views, and subservient to his wishes."[27] To this end, he said, Madison was praised for the wisdom of his instructions while Monroe was blamed for their faulty execution.

As we have already noted, the circumstances of the rejection of the treaty he and William Pinkney negotiated with the British did in fact redound to the discredit of Monroe; and certainly there was no public admission that his instructions had been in any respect unwise. But the President could not have dissociated himself from these, and, while rejecting the treaty, he did not repudiate Monroe.[28] He may have been insufficiently mindful of Monroe's sensibilities, but it is not to be believed that he deliberately sought to depress him at this or any other time. Apparently he and Madison did not ask Monroe's advice about foreign affairs during the latter's visit to the capital in the winter of 1807–1808, and Jefferson was unaware of the extent to which his *amour-propre* was wounded. The movement in support of Monroe's presidential candidacy in his own state, where he was very popular, offered him a prospect of public vindication; and, while he did not encourage his supporters, he did not rebuff them. Jefferson, refusing to recognize this movement as a veiled attack on the administration, sought to maintain an attitude of complete neutrality in what he regarded as an unfortunate, and believed to be an unequal, contest.

Early in the congressional session he had sent a formal reply to the addresses he had received months before from state legislatures, asking his agreement to serve another presidential term.[29] This made official what he had long ago said in private and left the way entirely clear for the congressional caucus. There is nothing in the record to suggest that he sought to influence that body in any way, and he now thought of himself as being more than ever above the battle. Some days before the caucus he wrote a letter which did not bear on the presidential nomination but which he requested his correspondent to keep "sacredly

27 Rose to Canning, Jan. 30, 1808 (FO, 5:56).
28 See above, pp. 407–414.
29 Identical reply to the legislatures of six states, Dec. 10, 1807 (LC, 30574). See pp. 169–170.

secret" lest it be misinterpreted. It was to William Wirt, who, after performing brilliantly in the Burr trial, had manifested a strong desire to render military service. This was in response to the *Chesapeake* outrage, but Jefferson, suspecting that it reflected Wirt's dissatisfaction with the legal profession, suggested that he enter Congress, the "great commanding theatre" of the country.[30] The reference was to the next Congress, when Jefferson would be retired, but in Virginia the election to this would be held in the spring of 1808. On entering the House, Wirt would "at once be placed at the head of the republican body" there, he said, and eventually he would become "the Colossus of the republican government" of the country. Apparently Jefferson had no doubt that the engaging young lawyer would be elected if he wanted to be, and he assumed the inevitability of Wirt's later preferment in what he obviously regarded as an era of political mediocrity. He seemed certain of the victory of his own party in the presidential contest, and, while he named no name, he was wholly confident of the "purity and correctness" of the next executive. The only thing he seemed uncertain about was the propriety of his frank communication. Therefore, somewhat apologetically, he said: "It proceeds from an ardent zeal to see this government (the idol of my soul) continue in good hands, and from a sincere desire to see you whatever you wish to be." He often expressed deep interest in the future of promising young men, but rarely did he use the language of idolatry when speaking of the government from whose toils he was so eager to escape.

Replying to this paternal and patriotic letter, Wirt said that he was inexpressibly grateful for it, but that he had to stick to his profession until he had assured the financial security of his family.[31] In this connection he observed that the grave financial embarrassment of their "amiable and beloved countryman" James Monroe provided "an awful lesson on the subject of devoting one's-self to the country before he shall have secured an independent retreat for old age." While greatly admiring Monroe's public spirit, he feared that the "unfeeling importunity of his creditors" might make that gentleman "almost repent of his patriotism." The subject was of such delicacy, said Wirt, that he mentioned it only to Jefferson, knowing him to be Monroe's discreet and devoted friend.

Wirt himself was much more intimate with the ex-Minister than with the Secretary of State, but in eulogizing the government of

---

[30] TJ to William Wirt, Jan. 10, 1808 (L. & B., XI, 423-424; LC, 30763). For Wirt's project to raise a "legion" of volunteers and its abandonment, see J. P. Kennedy, *Memoirs of the Life of William Wirt*, I (1850), ch. XV.

[31] Wirt to TJ, Jan. 14, 1808 (LC, 30785; largely printed in Kennedy, I, 209-210).

Jefferson he left no doubt that he expected Madison to be the man who would continue it. "The government is most dear to my affections," he said; "its practicability, its energy, its dignity, the protection, prosperity, and happiness which it ensures, are now demonstrated. And after your retirement, the pure and enlightened man to whom we look as your successor will, in my opinion, have no equal on the theatre of public life." A little later, Wirt declined to serve on a committee to promote the candidacy of Monroe, and, after explaining his position to that friend, he actively supported Madison as the unquestionable choice of the party.[32] Jefferson might have taken a similar position for the same reason, but that was something that his sense of presidential propriety and his personal devotion to both men would not let him do.

He said he would not even enter into conversation about this contest, but, after the caucuses were held and the struggle had come into the open, he could not refrain from writing to Monroe.[33] The excuse for his letter was that he wanted to give instructions about some instruments which had been bought for him by Monroe in England and had arrived with the latter's baggage. His insistence on paying for these immediately, despite Monroe's indebtedness to him on other accounts, may be attributed to his awareness of the financial embarrassment of that unfortunate gentleman. Personal generosity and consideration of this sort was habitual to him, and he had made a fine art of friendship throughout his life. At the height of his public career as truly as in his student days in Williamsburg he believed that neither power, nor riches, nor anything else on earth is better than a true friend.[34] Few things pained him more than the alienations that resulted from political differences and rivalries. Thus he was wholly in character when he made this moving statement to Monroe: "I see with infinite grief a contest arising between yourself and another, who have been very dear to each other, and equally so to me." He would remain strictly neutral, he said, though there would probably be reports to the contrary. He had no doubt of the conduct of the principals toward each other but did not expect equal delicacy of their supporters. From experience he knew too well "the progress of political controversy, and the exacerbations of spirit into which it degenerates" not to fear for the mutual esteem of his two old friends. As for himself, he said: "My longings for retirement are so strong that I with difficulty en-

32 For details, see Kennedy, ch. XVI.
33 TJ to Monroe, Feb. 18, 1808 (Ford, IX, 176–178).
34 See *Jefferson the Virginian*, p. 85, and the quotation to this effect that he copied from Euripides.

counter the daily drudgeries of my duty. But my wish for retirement itself is not stronger than that of carrying into it the affections of all my friends. I have ever viewed Mr. Madison and yourself as two principal pillars of my happiness. Were either to be withdrawn, I should consider it as among the greatest calamities which could assail my future peace of mind."

Monroe had difficulty in finding the receipt for the mathematical instruments but was glad to be repaid for them without delay, and, having an excuse for writing, he availed himself of the opportunity to unburden his mind of some of the grievances that had accumulated there during his recent foreign mission. It was unfortunate that he did not do so sooner. He referred specifically to the appointment of William Pinkney as a fellow commissioner, despite his having said that he did not want one, and to the way the treaty negotiated by them was received. At the same time he expressed his undiminished regard for Jefferson, whose kindness to him in his early life he had never forgotten, and whose political and personal fame he had ever sought to promote. He said he would continue to be an inactive spectator of the presidential campaign, and that no one knew the merit of Madison better than he.[35] The old-time intimacy between him and the Secretary of State was not to be restored soon, but the ensuing correspondence between him and the President served at least to remove his fears that he had lost Jefferson's confidence and friendship.[36]

That solicitous gentleman said in one of his letters that explanations between reasonable men could never fail to do good. In this case the explanations he made with such pains showed that many, perhaps most, of the misunderstandings were due to the difficulties and at times complete breakdown of communication. The reasons for the appointment of Pinkney, which Jefferson had given in an undelivered letter and now set forth anew, should have been recognized by Monroe as sufficient; and no doubt he was glad to accept the President's assurance that he had never done or said or thought anything unfriendly to his fame and feeling. Jefferson certainly did not want to hurt Monroe, but it would have been impossible to avoid doing so to some extent when rejecting the treaty he had negotiated. The frustrated diplomat had not forgotten the long and didactic letter Madison had afterwards written him and Pinkney. He now wrote a long reply to this in justification of his own conduct, sending a copy to Jefferson, who included it in the documents relating to the treaty that he communicated to Congress a

---

[35] Monroe to TJ, Feb. 27, 1808 (S.M.H., V, 24–27).
[36] TJ to Monroe on March 10 and April 11, 1808 (Ford, IX, 178–184n.); Monroe wrote TJ on March 22 and April 18 (S.M.H., V, 27–35; 51–52).

little later.[37] One may doubt if the submission of this record was advantageous to Monroe, but at any rate his own representation entered into it.

Regarding the political movement in his behalf as an expression of confidence in him, he made no attempt to stop it. He was well advised, however, to avoid giving the impression that he was hostile to Jefferson. One of his supporters whose loyalty to the President never wavered, John Taylor of Caroline, told him that, in the general opinion of his friends, a difference with Jefferson would destroy his popularity, and that a "multitude" of them would desert him if it was avowed that he would change and Madison would adhere to the "system" of Jefferson's administration. Monroe took the hint and assumed an attitude of reserve toward John Randolph.[38] All this was in the late winter and early spring. In the fall, before the election took place, Monroe asked and received Jefferson's consent to the publication of their correspondence. They agreed to leave out passages and expressions that might needlessly offend others but left enough to show that their friendship was unimpaired.[39]

iii

The congressional session was nearing its end when the President transmitted to the Senate (April 6, 1808) a report on roads and canals, drafted by the Secretary of the Treasury, which comprised the most comprehensive and constructive domestic program that emanated from this administration.[40] If this could have been put into effect it would have constituted a memorable contribution to the physical development of the country, and it could have been expected to contribute greatly to national unity. Circumstances were distinctly unfavorable to its serious consideration at this time, but the report suggests what *might* have been done if the acceleration of the European war had not created a crisis in foreign relations and if the government had been in position to initiate a long-range program of internal improvements.

[37] Monroe to Madison, Feb. 28, 1808 (*A.S.P.F.R.*, III, 173–183), replying to Madison's official letter of May 20, 1807 (*ibid.*, 166–173). See above, pp. 411–412.

[38] Taylor to Monroe, March 20, 1808 (*John P. Branch Historical Papers*, II, Nos. 3, 4; June, 1908); Monroe to John Randolph, March 23, 1808 (S.M.H., V, 35–36).

[39] Richmond *Enquirer*, Nov. 1, 1808, from *Spirit of '76*, Oct. 25, containing portions of six letters, Feb. 18–Apr. 18, 1808. Omissions and other details were discussed in letters of TJ to Monroe, Oct. 12, 13, 1808 (LC, 32192, 32203); Monroe to TJ, Oct. 24 (S.M.H., V, 65–66); Oct. 28, Nov. 1 (LC, 32287, 32329).

[40] Gallatin's report in *A.S.P.*, *Misc.*, I, 724–741, is followed (pp. 742–921) by materials collected by him.

As the term came into general use it referred to improvements in transportation and communication, but Jefferson's own hopes went further. In his second inaugural, anticipating an eventual surplus beyond what was annually set aside to retire the debt, he said that *in time of peace* this could be applied to "rivers, canals, roads, arts, manufactures, education, and other great objects within each state."[41] He believed that, even in time of war, necessary expenses could be met without burdening future generations with debt and that the return of peace would be "a return to the progress of improvement." A few weeks later, after he had received from Gallatin the pleasing news that receipts were exceeding expectations, he said that this hastened the moment when they could begin on "canals, roads, college, &c."[42] He did not refer to these objectives in his next annual message, and at the opening of the congressional session of 1805–1806 his first concern was to secure an appropriation for the purchase of West Florida. Toward the end of that session, however, Congress authorized the beginning of an interstate road across the mountains — from Cumberland, Maryland, to the Ohio River.[43] This enterprise had its genesis in a provision of the Ohio enabling act of four years earlier, following the suggestion of Gallatin, that a portion of the proceeds from the sale of public lands in the new state be applied to such a purpose.[44] But for this financial prospect and this commitment to Ohio a Congress that was representative of local constituencies and responsive to them might have been undisposed to support such an undertaking. Jefferson was soon to become painfully aware of the conflict of local interests that beset it, but he was sufficiently encouraged to devote considerable attention to the subject of internal improvements in his next annual message to Congress.[45] At the time his mind was by no means untroubled. He had recently been apprised of the dangerous doings of Aaron Burr and had issued a proclamation against that mysterious adventurer without as yet charging him with conspiracy by name. But from the Secretary of the Treasury he had learned that before long a surplus was to be expected and he addressed himself to the question of what should be done with it.

[41] Ford, VIII, 343–344.

[42] TJ to Gallatin, May 29, 1805 (Ford, VIII, 357).

[43] March 29, 1806 (*Annals*, 9 Cong., 1 sess., pp. 1236–1238). For a fuller account than can be given here, see J. S. Young, *A Political and Constitutional Study of the Cumberland Road* (1902), chs. I–IV; P. D. Jordan, *The National Road* (1948), ch. IV.

[44] The figures finally arrived at were 2 percent of the net proceeds for roads *to* the state and 3 percent for roads *within* it.

[45] For the portion of his message of Dec. 2, 1806, that bears on this topic, see Ford, VIII, 493–494, or *Annals*, 9 Cong., 2 sess., pp. 14–15.

In presenting his estimates Gallatin was well aware that war might upset all calculations. If the United States should remain at peace, he did not doubt that, by or before the end of Jefferson's term, at least a couple of millions a year would be available for purposes of general improvement. Both he and Jefferson would have liked to anticipate payments on the debt, but they could not do this without the consent of the creditors and a change in the existing contracts.[46] As for internal taxes, he and Jefferson were agreed that these should shortly be relinquished, beginning with the tax on salt. They held that imposts, which were chiefly on luxuries, ought to be generally retained, and Gallatin counted on their continuance at their present rate. In the light of later events, exclusive reliance on duties on imports appears to have been unwise, but the danger that the income from these would be reduced was not immediate.

Looking beyond his own term of office, Jefferson suggested that the surplus expected if peace continued should be applied to great purposes of public improvement. In listing these he now placed education first, thereby differing with Gallatin, on grounds of practicality at least. The Secretary of the Treasury believed that provision for roads would be popular and one for a university unpopular. On his advice Jefferson suggested that a national educational establishment might be endowed by a donation of public lands, which in fact would have been relatively painless. Since the objects he recommended were not among those enumerated in the Constitution, the President supposed that a constitutional amendment would be necessary. He stated elsewhere that several years would be required to secure one, and he wanted to get things started now for just that reason. As a rule, Gallatin was more of a loose constructionist, but he believed that even the broadest possible interpretation of the words "general welfare" would not give the federal government the authority to open roads and canals through the several states without their permission. Therefore, he conceded that a constitutional amendment was needed.

"By these operations," said Jefferson, "new channels of communication will be opened between the States; the lines of separation will disappear, their interests will be identified, and their union cemented by new and indissoluble ties." He was lumping the various improvements together, but, judging from what happened, greatest public interest was manifested in roads and canals, just as Gallatin had expected. At the end of the congressional session the Senate adopted by

[46] See Gallatin's official report communicated Dec. 8, 1806 (*A.S.P.*, *Finance*, II, 204–206); and various comments of his on the draft of TJ's message (*Writings*, I, 319–329, or Ford, VIII, 487–489*n*.).

overwhelming vote the resolution which led to Gallatin's report a year later.[47] By-passing the constitutional problem, the resolution directed the Secretary of the Treasury to prepare a plan for the application, to the opening of canals and the building of roads, of such means as were "within the powers of Congress." He was to state what undertakings required and deserved governmental aid, and also to provide information about works in progress. Thus he was authorized to make a genuinely comprehensive report, and by the same token he needed a long time to prepare it. Meanwhile, he and Jefferson were involved in certain problems and difficulties connected with the Cumberland Road.

Since the cost of the proposed road was soon estimated as $6000 per mile, exclusive of major bridges, little beyond surveying and planning could be done under the original appropriation of $30,000, which was actually the only one made in Jefferson's administration. According to the terms of the Act of March 29, 1806, he appointed three commissioners to lay out the road, subject to his approval. Meanwhile, he was to get the consent of the states through which it would pass. He had no difficulty with Maryland and Virginia, but when he submitted the first report of the commissioners the legislature of Pennsylvania still had the matter under advisement.[48] The commissioners recommended a route from Cumberland to Brownsville in a direct line to a point below Wheeling on the Ohio River. The act whereby the Pennsylvania legislature gave its consent a few weeks later included a resolution that the route be altered so as to pass through Uniontown and Washington if, in the President's judgment, this could be done consistently with the act of Congress, but that, if not, the road could pass over whatever grounds in the state he should deem most advantageous. On the advice of Gallatin, who believed that because of the conflict of local interests and the opposition of Philadelphia nothing better could be expected, Jefferson agreed to a slight deflection of the road to Uniontown, where Gallatin had formerly lived. This was *en route* to Brownsville, and the President would not commit himself beyond the latter point.[49]

Regarding the road across the mountains as an object of great national importance, "particularly as a bond of union," the Secretary

[47] March 2, 1807 (*Annals*, 9 Cong., 2 sess., p. 97; see also p. 95). The resolution was introduced by Worthington of Ohio and the vote was 22 to 3.
[48] Jan. 31, 1807 (*A.S.P., Misc.*, I, 474–477).
[49] Resolution of April 7, 1807 (cited by Young, p. 22); Gallatin to TJ, April 13, 1807 (*Writings*, I, 334); TJ to Congress, Feb. 19, 1808, with the report of the commissioners (*A.S.P., Misc.*, I, 714–715).

of the Treasury was more concerned to remove state and local opposition than to follow a preconceived course, and, being specially aware of the situation in the town of Washington, which had been in his congressional district and had consistently returned a large Republican majority, he urged that Jefferson have a survey made through that place. He thought this should be done out of respect for the Pennsylvania legislature, regardless of Jefferson's final decision, and believed that the deviation from the previously recommended course would be slight anyway.[50] Jefferson did not like the political pressure that was brought to bear on him and believed that the government had erred in the first place by permitting any deviation from the most direct feasible route from Cumberland to the Ohio. He was horrified that certain towns seemed to think the road was undertaken for their particular benefit. One mistake having led to another, however, the government could not now consistently refuse to consider still another. Therefore, he instructed the commissioners to make a survey through the town of Washington and report to him. "The principal object of this road," he said, "is a communication directly westwardly. If, however, inconsiderable deflections from this course will benefit particular places and better accommodate travellers, these are circumstances to be taken into consideration."[51] Two years after his retirement a decision was reached in favor of Washington, and the terminus on the Ohio was afterwards definitely set at Wheeling. Not until 1818, however, did the road reach that place.

In his magnificent report to the Senate, Gallatin described what was being done with respect to roads and canals in various parts of the United States, and by no means did he discourage local projects. What he was advocating, however, was a comprehensive national system which would embrace "all the great interests of the Union" and diffuse and increase national wealth "by opening an intercourse between the remotest extremes" of the country. Such a "system" as he proposed was beyond the scope of individual states, and sufficient private capital for it was not available, but he had no doubt of the ability of the general government to support it in peacetime. A long-range program of debt reduction was being successfully carried out, and the long-range program of internal improvements could be properly regarded as a supplement to and consequence of that.

50 Gallatin to TJ, July 27, 1808 (*Writings*, I, 395). The deviation turned out to be three or four miles.
51 TJ to Commissioners and to Gallatin, Aug. 6, 1808 (L. & B., XII, 117–118). See also the commissioners' report of Aug. 30, submitted Dec. 13 (*A.S.P., Misc.*, I, 940–941).

In his own summary he divided his comprehensive plan into three main parts:[52] (1) From north to south, parallel to the seacoast, he recommended a series of canals to provide internal navigation from Massachusetts to North Carolina, crossing all the principal capes except Cape Fear; and a great turnpike from Maine to Georgia, which was the most expensive single item in his program. (2) From east to west, for communication across and beyond the mountains, he proposed the improvement of four Atlantic rivers (Susquehanna, Potomac, James, and Santee or Savannah), chiefly by canals around their falls; the building of roads from four western rivers (Allegheny, Monongahela, Kanawaha, and Tennessee); a canal around the falls of the Ohio at Louisville; and improvement of the roads to Detroit, St. Louis, and New Orleans. (3) For inland navigation between the seacoast and the Great Lakes and the St. Lawrence he recommended a series of canals, including one around Niagara Falls. Finally, he proposed a generous allowance for unspecified local improvements to benefit districts which would otherwise gain little from the program.

He estimated the cost of this program item by item, arriving at a total figure of $20,000,000 toward which he was confident that in peacetime the Treasury could provide $2,000,000 annually for ten years. While recognizing that in time of war the resources of the country must be first applied to measures of defense, he regarded the predictable surplus as insufficient to maintain a considerably increased land and naval force in peacetime, and he was opposed to such expenditure, believing that it would leave no trace behind it. On the other hand, this great economizer favored expenditures for internal improvements as genuinely productive, and there can be no doubt that Jefferson fully agreed with him.

This report, together with the numerous documents that accompanied it, was referred to a committee of which John Quincy Adams was chairman. On their recommendation, twelve hundred copies were ordered to be printed and the Secretary of the Treasury was requested to send six copies to each member of Congress after the close of the session.[53] To what extent the legislators acquainted themselves with these massive materials during the recess is impossible to determine, but they should have been well informed on this topic when they reassembled in the autumn and received Jefferson's last annual message. Developments in foreign relations received major consideration in that paper, but toward the end of it the President who had freed the

[52] *A.S.P., Misc.*, I, 740.
[53] Resolution of April 12, 1808 (*Annals*, 10 Cong., 1 sess., I, 332).

navigation of the Mississippi and dispatched Lewis and Clark to explore the Missouri and the Columbia, referred to internal improvements.[54]

Despite the embargo and recent expenditures for defense there was still a substantial balance in the Treasury. Jefferson recognized, however, that for a disposable surplus they must look to the time when the freedom and security of commerce had been restored. While he referred the matter to the consideration of Congress with his customary deference, there can be no doubt of his opinion that, when the time should come, as he was sure it would, this surplus ought to be appropriated to purposes of internal improvements and education. This should be done under such powers as Congress might already possess or might acquire by an amendment to the Constitution. During the period of uncertainty about the course of affairs, he said, Congress could employ itself advantageously in obtaining the necessary powers.

In his later years Jefferson spoke more emphatically of the need of an amendment and more dogmatically about its desirable form than he did at this time.[55] When in high office he was more pragmatic than he was in either opposition or retirement. It could have been argued that by signing the Cumberland Road Act he had acceded to the exercise of power not specifically assigned the federal government by the Constitution, but that action could have been regarded as a special case and a minor matter.[56] A nation-wide system of improvements, initiated and supported by the federal government, was a very large matter, and there was really no escape from the judgment that such an undertaking was incompatible with the doctrine of strict construction. Therefore, a constitutional amendment seemed to offer him the only escape from his dilemma.

His suggestion of an anticipatory amendment led to no congressional action, and perhaps it is chiefly significant in that it set an example that his successor James Monroe followed nine years later, after the lapse of a longer period of uncertainty than Jefferson had counted on. Federal action in behalf of internal improvements was then a subject of serious consideration, but Monroe's recommendation of a constitutional amendment was unproductive — partly because the advocates of internal improvements saw no need for it, while their opponents preferred

---

[54] For the part of his message of Nov. 8, 1808, that bears on this topic, see Ford, IX, 224–225. For Gallatin's comments on an earlier draft, see pp. 218–219n.; for his financial report of Dec. 10, 1808, see *A.S.P., Finance,* II, 307–309.

[55] His letter of June 16, 1817, to Gallatin (Ford, X, 91) may be compared with his response to the latter's suggestions regarding his message of Nov. 8, 1808 (Ford, IX, 219n.).

[56] Madison discussed this matter in a letter to Monroe, Dec. 27, 1817 (Hunt, VIII, 404–405).

to leave well enough alone. Jefferson's recommendation might have been equally unproductive, even if the circumstances of the country had been propitious. The most imaginative and constructive domestic program that emanated from his administration would have met with great difficulty in any case, and, as things were, it was inevitably relegated to the category of unfinished business.[57]

[57] Among the items of unfinished business, mention should be made of the highly controversial Batture case, involving alluvial land in New Orleans that was in dispute between Edward Livingston on the one hand and, on the other, officials and citizens who regarded this as public property. On TJ's order of Nov. 30, 1807, Livingston was ejected from this land, and in 1810 he brought suit against the former President. This move came to naught, but eventually, by court order, he was restored to the possession of the property. I do not enter into this case in this volume but defer a consideration of its legal complexities until the time when I shall be dealing with TJ's life in retirement.

[XXXI]

Tightening the Embargo

TOWARD the end of January, Jefferson remarked that the recent British Order in Council (November 11, 1807) had "entirely hushed all opposition to the embargo."[1] He had to wait some days for an official document to submit to Congress, but the order had already appeared in the newspapers and, in fact, had been reported in essence by the time of the embargo message.[2] There was no real surprise in the official communication, but here in cold print was the announcement that any and all vessels trading from or to the ports of France or her allies and their colonies, and all places from which the British flag was excluded, were liable to confiscation. They were "good prize," it was said. Some loopholes were left for trade carried on through British ports, and certain imports were permitted on the payment of specified duties, but, as John Quincy Adams observed, these regulations struck at the root of American independence. "They assume the principle," he said, "that we shall have no commerce in time of war, but with her dominions, and as tributaries to her." Britain needed to take only one more step after this "momentous stride of encroachment" and her former colonists would be back at a stamp act and a tea tax. In his opinion, these orders were "fatal to the liberties for which the sages and heroes of our revolution toiled and bled."[3] The President fully shared these sentiments.

On March 17 he communicated to Congress the Milan decree (December 17, 1807), Napoleon's response which closed the circle of

---

[1] TJ to TMR, Jan. 26, 1808 (LC, 30841).

[2] There were actually three orders dated Nov. 11, 1807. These were communicated to Congress Feb. 4, 1808 (*A.S.P.F.R.*, III, 29–31). They had appeared in *National Intelligencer* Jan. 22, 25. For the report in December, see above, p. 481, note 30.

[3] J. Q. Adams to Harrison Gray Otis, March 31, 1808 (*Writings*, III, 200–201).

maritime infelicities.[4] By this decree all vessels submitting to British regulations, or sailing from or to any port under British control, were declared to have become British property and were therefore "good prize." The Emperor was in no such position as His Britannic Majesty to enforce his similar pretensions on the high seas, but he could easily seize any hapless vessel that came into any of the harbors he controlled.

Before the official communication of these pronouncements, with their dire threats against neutral commerce, George H. Rose finally arrived from England to enter into negotiations regarding the *Chesapeake* affair. Since that affair was neither the cause nor the occasion of the adoption of the embargo, and the outcome of the negotiations could not be reported for some weeks, we need not concern ourselves with them at the moment. We need say here only that, during the winter of 1808, the avowed tightening of commercial restrictions by the tyrants of land and sea served to reinforce the arguments originally advanced in support of the embargo.

Before the opening of spring, Jefferson stated in private that the time would surely come when war would seem preferable to the embargo, but he clung to it as the only alternative to war, and throughout the winter he emphasized its protective value. Delay in learning of its effects abroad was inevitable, and the immediate task of both the legislative and executive branches was to implement a policy that required a great many rules and regulations. The burden of enforcement was promptly assumed by the Secretary of the Treasury, and he immediately recognized that further legislation was needed. During this congressional session three more measures bearing directly on the embargo were passed. These may be designated respectively as the supplementary, the additional, and the enforcement acts.[5]

A week after the embargo went into effect, a committee of the House presented a supplementary measure. While the original act forbade the departure of any American vessel for a foreign port, it prescribed penalties only on registered or sea-letter vessels which might also be engaged in coastwise trade. Specifically, it required the posting of bonds of double the value of the ship and cargo, guaranteeing that goods would be landed only in the United States. Nothing was said about vessels licensed for coastal trade only, and, as one of the collectors promptly observed to Gallatin, there was danger that some of these ships would proceed coastwise and then take off for a foreign

---

[4] *A.S.P.F.R.*, III, 80, 290–291.
[5] Leonard White in *The Jeffersonians*, chs. XXIX, XXX, summarizes all the embargo acts and gives an excellent account of their enforcement.

port.[6] The most significant feature of the supplementary act of January 9, 1808, was the requirement of bonds from vessels in the coastwise trade, and also from those engaged in fishing and whaling.[7] Most of the argument was about fishermen, but there was some objection to the speed with which this measure was being rushed through Congress. Federalist Livermore of Massachusetts said: "The colossal power of a majority had put down the still small voice of reason, and had declared that strength alone should reign." Judging from the overwhelming vote, however, there was general concern to stop the loopholes quickly and play no favorites.[8]

The predominant congressional attitude was manifested in the reception of a memorial from certain merchants of Philadelphia, asking that an exception be made of ships which had already been cleared at the time of the imposition of the embargo but were being detained in the river. After a long debate the committee to which this was referred, while expressing sympathy with the memorialists, denied their right to an exception and went to considerable length in explanation and justification of the embargo.[9] If Congress had permitted the continuance of commerce, said the report, they would have had to provide for its protection, but arming private ships would have been "tantamount to a declaration of war." That the embargo was the best course that Congress could have devised or adopted was "the solemn and profound conviction of the committee, on a review of the whole ground."

After about two months an additional act followed the supplementary act.[10] This tightened the system by requiring bonds of foreign vessels engaged in the coastal trade; and, what was more significant, it forbade the exportation of goods of any sort by land as well as by sea. This provision, which directly affected the northern and southern border states, was violently assailed in the House of Representatives by Barent Gardenier of New York as being totally inconsistent with Jefferson's embargo message, which had merely asked that vessels be forbidden to put to sea. Regarding this as a non-intercourse bill, the irate Congressman was more convinced than ever that the original act was a "sly, cunning measure." They were being led on

[6] Gabriel Christie from Baltimore to Gallatin, Dec. 24, 1807 (Letter Book in Records of Bureau of Customs, National Archives).

[7] Act of Jan. 9, 1808 (*Annals*, 10 Cong., 1 sess., II, 2815–2817).

[8] For proceedings in the House, see *Annals*, 10 Cong., 1 sess., I, 1240–1241, 1244–1257, 1271; Livermore's comment, p. 1250. Final vote in the House, 73 to 22.

[9] Memorial presented and referred Jan. 4, 1808 (*ibid.*, pp. 1272–1277). Report communicated Jan. 11 (*ibid.*, pp. 1384–1387).

[10] Approved March 12, 1808 (*Annals*, 10 Cong., 1 sess., II, 2839–2842).

"step by step," he said, but by an unseen hand and with the real object of fastening them to the car of the "Imperial Conqueror." This bitter speech elicited strong protest from a number of members, including George W. Campbell. The majority leader said that if the maker of these charges could not prove them he should be assigned to infamy and contempt. An intemperate exchange was followed some days later by a duel in which Gardenier, the challenger, was wounded. Jefferson's son-in-law John W. Eppes was Campbell's second.[11]

Gardenier's spectacular opposition to the policy of the government inevitably attracted much attention, but we need not assume that it was typical of the Federalist minority at this stage. In the course of the debate Samuel W. Dana of Connecticut said that he was not partial to an embargo, but that, since one had been laid, he was willing to render it effectual and equalize its operations.[12] He afterwards voted against this bill, as did Josiah Quincy of Massachusetts, but these Federalist leaders were withholding their heavy fire as yet. The measure was adopted by a majority of more than four to one. The Virginian who introduced it said: "If we yield the ground we have taken, our character for stability and firmness will be lost forever."[13] The chief spokesmen for the majority saw no need to yield a policy which was generally approved throughout the country if one could judge from the "unequivocal expressions" of most of the state legislatures. That the original embargo act amounted to a non-exportation measure was now admitted, but one may doubt that those who supported it at the outset expected the policy to apply to land as well as sea. They had been led from one step to another, though not necessarily by an unseen presidential hand. A fairer statement would be that, along with the President, they were driven by the logic of a developing situation. There was ground for the charge that the attempt to remove inequalities amounted to that of making suffering universal, but the framers of this additional measure were concerned to prevent needless harassment and unnecessary hardship. Some of the provisions of the law opened new loopholes and imposed fresh difficulties on those responsible for administration. Exceptions (which proved very short-lived) were made in favor of small vessels engaged wholly in domestic trade,

[11] The debates in the House are in *Annals*, 10 Cong., 1 sess., II, 1649-1675, 1698-1713. Gardenier spoke Feb. 20, 1808 (pp. 1653-1657) and was answered Feb. 22 (Campbell's speech, pp. 1667-1673). Bill passed by the House Feb. 29, by a vote of 97 to 22. Details of the duel of March 2 in *National Intelligencer* March 14.

[12] *Annals*, 10 Cong., 1 sess., II, 1657-1658. For Timothy Pickering's position, see below, pages 570-571.

[13] Thomas Newton, Jr. (*ibid.*, p. 1665).

and by one section of the act the President was vested with authority he neither sought nor wanted. At his discretion and under specified safeguards, he could permit vessels to sail in ballast to bring back to the United States valuable property belonging to American citizens.

From the beginning Jefferson sought to avoid direct involvement in the enforcement of the embargo laws. The statement in the first of these, that no vessel should depart for a foreign port except under the direction of the President, had led some to believe that he could make exceptions. He promptly took and afterwards maintained the position that his authority under this provision extended only to vessels engaged in public matters.[14] While not unsympathetic to the desire of American citizens to bring home valuable property (specie, produce, merchandise) from overseas, he was well aware that he would be besieged with applications, and he did not welcome the discretion Congress had vested in him. He and Gallatin went to great pains to lay down principles, and as things turned out most permits were for the return of property in the West Indies.[15] In minor matters he was disposed to leave decisions to the collectors, but the Secretary of the Treasury issued directives to them in a succession of circulars, and he and the President constantly exchanged notes about the execution of these laws. By and large the collectors were diligent, but more than two months after the passage of the first law Gallatin reported that the collector at New Orleans, claiming that he had no copy of it, had let forty-two vessels depart.[16]

The communications that Jefferson received during the winter and into the spring of 1808 seemed to justify the claim of his followers in Congress that the embargo was generally supported throughout the country. Resolutions of approval from state after state poured across his desk. Early in the year the members of the General Assembly of his own commonwealth unanimously declared that they would "submit with pleasure to the privations arising from the energetic measure recently adopted," and solemnly pledged themselves to support such other measures as might be adopted to produce an honorable peace or avenge the injured honor of the country.[17] To be sure, they did not yet know all they were bargaining for, and the same may be said of

[14] TJ to Gallatin, Jan. 7, 1808 (L. & B., XI, 415); Jan. 14 (Gallatin, *Writings*, I, 369).

[15] Chief references for this period: TJ to Gallatin, Feb. 10, 1808 (L. & B., XI, 439); Gallatin to TJ, March 16, 1808 (*Writings*, I, 377–379); Gallatin to TJ, March 21 (LC, 31177); TJ to Gallatin, March 23 (L. & B., XII, 18–19).

[16] Gallatin to TJ, Feb. 29, 1808 (*Writings*, I, 373–374).

[17] Resolutions of Jan. 13, 1808, with a letter of Jan. 15 from Gov. Cabell (LC, 30781–30782, 30794).

other legislatures which pledged their support, but Jefferson welcomed their concurrence in the embargo and believed that it would have great effect abroad. Most heartening to him, no doubt, were the resolutions of the legislature of Massachusetts, which he received about the middle of February along with assurances from Governor James Sullivan that the electors from that state would support him for a third term if they could.[18] His party was in control of the government of Massachusetts at this time, but he was well aware of opposition to his policies in maritime New England. The Governor had warned him of pro-British sentiments among the High Federalists, and he had already received from certain "Inhabitants of Boston" a petition *against* the embargo, to which, however, he could not reply since it was unsigned. It would appear that the earliest protests tended to be anonymous: he received an anonymous bill for the rent of a store said to belong to an orphan and to have been vacated because of his actions.[19] "All our personal interests are injured by the embargo," he himself said, and quite clearly he expected sporadic mutterings against it; but he remained confident that the vast majority of his countrymen preferred it to war or dishonor.[20]

i i

Winter was giving way to spring, and five days had passed since the President had reported Napoleon's Milan decree to Congress, when he sent that body a special message on negotiations with the British, together with a mass of documents. There was no longer a reason to hold anything back. Canning's special envoy, George H. Rose, bade Jefferson good-bye the day before and had his final audience with Madison that very day (March 22, 1808). Actually, the negotiations about the *Chesapeake* had collapsed a month earlier, and it now appears that there was really no point in starting them in view of Canning's instructions.[21] These were not made known all at once, however.

[18] Resolutions signed by the Governor, Feb. 8, 1808, and received Feb. 17 (LC, 30927); TJ to Sullivan, March 3 (L. & B., XII, 2–3). Among other legislative bodies from which he received resolutions or addresses before the summer of 1808 were those of S.C., N.C., Md., Pa., Ky., N.H., and the Territory of Orleans. He heard from Ga. a little later. Also he had expressions of approval from lesser governmental or political groups in N.Y., Pa., and elsewhere.

[19] LC, 31076; 31208.

[20] TJ to Major Joseph Eggleston, March 7, 1808 (LC, 31085).

[21] *I.B.M.*, pp. 235–242, dated Oct. 24, 1807. Accounts of what happened are based almost entirely on Rose's dispatches to Canning, Dec. 27, 1807–March 28, 1808 (FO, 5:56) and Madison's notes on the negotiations (Hunt, VIII, 1–11). The latter are critically examined by Brant in his account of the episode (*Madison*, IV, ch. XXIX), which supersedes that of Henry Adams (*History*, IV, ch. VIII).

Senator Timothy Pickering, who met Rose in congenial Federalist company soon after his arrival in Washington and judged him to be of a "perfectly conciliatory" disposition, attributed a similar dispositon to the high official who sent him. Jefferson himself soon gained the impression that the British did not want war, but it would seem that Canning, instead of seriously seeking a settlement of this issue, was avoiding the sort of apology that would have been unpopular in England and pursuing a policy of procrastination.[22]

The proclamation that Jefferson issued shortly after the attack on the *Chesapeake*, forbidding the entrance of British ships of war into American waters, was still in effect and at long last had been heeded by His Majesty's naval officers.[23] The administration described this as a preventive rather than a punitive action and claimed that it was abundantly warranted by repeated abuses of American hospitality. Despite the assurances of Monroe that it did not apply to vessels engaged in official business, Canning instructed Rose to seek particular assurances before disembarking; and for this reason the envoy did not reach Washington until nearly three weeks after the *Statira* anchored off Hampton Roads. In mid-January he finally arrived in a launch expressly dispatched by the solicitous Secretary of the Navy and he was treated with every consideration. This episode showed that the Foreign Secretary was requiring his envoy to be a stickler for propriety, and at the very start it called attention to his resentment of the presidential proclamation. His contention, as promptly stated by his emissary, was that the disavowal of the action against the *Chesapeake* and of the right to infringe on American sovereignty by taking deserters from a warship, coupled with the recall of Admiral Berkeley, was sufficient to justify the recall of the proclamation, and that this *must* precede any discussion of reparations. Rose, guided in part by Federalist opinion and indiscreet utterances of the relatively pro-British Secretary of the Navy, explained Madison's unwillingness to yield this point as being due to concern for the President's popularity. American acceptance of what amounted to an ultimatum would unquestionably have been unpopular, but the blow against the *Chesapeake* was only the last of a long series of indignities, and the honor of the country was involved. In view of the relative strength of the two parties Canning's demand was arrogant, and it was unrealistic in view of American sensibilities.[24]

---

[22] Pickering to T. Williams, Jan. 18, 1808 (quoted, *ibid.*, IV, 184); TJ to TMR, Feb. 6, 1808 (LC, 30910); comment of Perkins (*Prologue*, p. 197).

[23] July 2, 1807 (*A.S.P.F.R.*, III, 23–24). See above, pp. 427, 428.

[24] Rose to Canning, Jan. 21, 27, 1808 (FO, 5:56). Though recognizing that Rose's report of what Robert Smith said to him did not necessarily reflect TJ's

After several days of preliminary conference during which the question of precedence was not resolved, Rose, at Madison's suggestion, set forth his position in a letter which was destined to remain the official British statement.[25] In the meantime the personable envoy, presumably on the strength of information received from enemies of the American government, had passed on to his superior in England his first impressions of it. After referring to the "low arts of popularity" and the humble occupations of members of Congress, he said: "It is impossible to calculate how short lived such a system must be. But the excess of the democratic ferment in this people is continuously evinced by the dregs having got up to the top."[26] Apparently he was referring to the legislative rather than the executive branch, but he underestimated both the durability of the Republic and the ability of its spokesmen.

The President and the Secretary of State, though determined to uphold their country's honor, did not want the negotiations to be stalled by a technicality. Furthermore, after Rose learned that Russia had entered the war he became more aware of the value of American neutrality. Accordingly, Madison worked out and finally gained his consent to a plan which required him to depart from the letter of his instructions but not to yield anything of substance. What Madison was trying to do was to make the recall of the proclamation and the agreement to reparations virtually simultaneous. At an informal meeting he read the draft of a message of revocation, and Rose then stated the precise reparations his government would make. Besides disavowing the action of Admiral Berkeley — against whom, however, they declined to do anything further — the British were willing to discharge the men taken by force from the *Chesapeake* (that is, the survivors) and to make pecuniary provision for the widows and orphans of the men killed by the guns of the *Leopard*. Since Canning had stipulated that these men must be shown *not* to have been British subjects or deserters, some difficulty in carrying out these provisions might have been expected, but, everything considered, the reparations would have been acceptable; and, since Rose desired only minor changes in the

---

attitude, Henry Adams proceeds to make the extraordinary statement that "for the first and probably for the last time in history — a President of the United States begged for mercy from a British minister" (*History*, IV, 191). This assertion cannot be justified. We should note, however, that TJ was aware of Robert Smith's informal conference with Rose and himself over-emphasized its importance at a later time. See TJ to William Wirt, May 3, 1811 (L. & B., XIII, 54); also Brant, IV, 408-409.

[25] Jan. 26, 1808 (*A.S.P.F.R.*, III, 213-214).
[26] Rose to Canning, Jan. 17, 1808 (FO, 5:56).

wording of the recall, a settlement could have been effected on these terms.[27] But he had not reached the end of his instructions. He soon produced a demand that the United States disavow the conduct of its agents in encouraging deserters. Madison was wholly unwilling to admit any such conduct. To make matters worse, Rose finally made what Madison regarded as the impossible demand that the United States disavow the conduct of Commodore Barron and thus admit that he had consciously shielded the desired deserters while denying that he had done so.[28]

Thus the negotiators were right back where they had started; and, agreeing to disagree, they left out of the official record everything that had been said since Rose had set forth his position in his letter of January 26.[29] Madison, after a considerable delay because of illness, made formal reply to this, presenting American grievances at length, and Rose duly responded in kind. These three letters constituted the documentary record of the episode as transmitted to Congress.[30] The committee of the Senate to which they were referred, together with other communications, thought them deserving of little comment. It contented itself with saying that the posture of affairs respecting the *Chesapeake* "strengthens the motives for persevering in all the provisional precautionary measures hitherto contemplated."[31] Writing Pinkney in England, Madison said that it remained with the British to resume negotiations regarding the *Chesapeake*, if adjustment was their object. He also stated that, while this insult remained unexpiated, the American government would not commit itself to remove the restrictions on commerce with the British even if the Orders in Council were revoked.[32] Thus there was an obstacle to amicable relations with Canning's country that did not exist in the case of France, and for the failure to remove this he must be chiefly blamed.

One of the noteworthy by-products of Rose's futile mission was the establishment of confidential relations between him and one of the most implacable foes of the government to which he was accredited, Timothy Pickering. The dialogue in which they engaged after diplo-

[27] Rose to Canning, "Secret and Confidential," Feb. 6, 1808 (*ibid.*); Madison's notes on negotiations, Feb. 5 (Hunt, VIII, 3-4).
[28] Madison's notes, Feb. 6–16, 1808 (*ibid.*, 4-8).
[29] Rose to Canning, Feb. 25, 1808 (FO, 5:56).
[30] Rose to Madison, Jan. 26, 1808; Madison to Rose, March 5; Rose to Madison, March 17 (*A.S.P.F.R.*, III, 213-220).
[31] Apr. 16, 1808 (*ibid.*, p. 219*).
[32] Madison to Pinkney, Apr. 4, 1808 (*ibid.*, pp. 221-222). Presumably he was referring particularly to the Non-Importation Act.

macy had failed was marked by considerably more than official impropriety.[33] The Senator from Massachusetts, who had already made known to the envoy his solicitude for peace between their two countries, sent him a letter from Rufus King which could be expected to impress the British government. Pickering was confident that there was no American disposition to commence a war, whatever there might be on the part of the administration to provoke one. Also, he asserted that "our own best citizens consider the interests of the United States to be interwoven with those of Great Britain, and that our safety depends on hers." Rose could have learned more about these enlightened men if only he could have traveled as far as Boston. If their views could prevail, said Pickering, the measures of government would take another direction. To him the prospect seemed encouraging: the embargo would bring an end to the delusions of the people; Jefferson's reign would soon end; Madison could not attain such ascendancy over the public mind; he might not even be elected.

Canning's emissary was little short of effusive in expressing his satisfaction with these comments. In his reply he spoke of the forbearance of his own government and referred to it as the "offended party," who by strange circumstance could "leave his antagonist to his own suicidal devices and self-torment." The "night of delusion" seemed to be vanishing, he said, and Pickering himself had lifted the curtain and let in the light by means of a recently published letter of his which Rose described as a "manly exertion of patriotism." Ostensibly addressed to his constituents, it was a bitter attack on the policies of the administration, especially the embargo, and it evinced full support of the British on the main issues between their government and his own. On the day he left Washington, Rose received from Pickering a copy of this, along with the second of two letters from George Cabot and some information about the Essex Junto — the little group of High Federalist leaders in Massachusetts to which the Senator said he was proud to belong. Rose wrote Pickering the next day from Alexandria before falling down the river, saying that their two countries were "the most naturally allied that exist" and that their interests forced them imperiously together. Such words were music in Pickering's ears, but neither Jefferson nor Madison nor John Quincy Adams had detected any sign that the British would be content with anything less than American subservience. As responsible statesmen they would not have been pleased with an item of news that Rose sent Pickering after his arrival

[33] March 13–May 8, 1808 (Henry Adams, ed., *Documents Relating to New England Federalism*, pp. 366–373).

in England: namely, that the Senator's "manly exertion of patriotism" had created a sensation in that country.[34]

Commenting on Pickering's letter, the *National Intelligencer* said that "almost the exclusive honor of reprobating the embargo" thus far belonged to the Essex Junto. Also, this administration paper described that little group as "the victims of infuriated passion," who were "animated altogether by the hope of embarrassing the measures of government." Jefferson himself, after describing Pickering's paper as a "very malevolent and incendiary denunciation of the administration, bottomed on absolute falsehood," observed to Levi Lincoln, now back in Massachusetts, that the embargo appeared to be approved even by Federalists everywhere except in his former Attorney General's quarter.[35] Whatever the situation may have been elsewhere, the implacable foes of the administration in the commercial center of Boston had unquestionably assumed the offensive. The political implications of Pickering's action were obvious. In the first instance he sent the letter to Governor James Sullivan as "the proper organ of communication" with the legislature of Massachusetts, but that Republican official, denying this, returned it after reading less than a page. He had no intention of letting it become part of the official record and precipitate a debate at the end of the session and on the eve of the spring elections. A copy was also sent George Cabot, however, and he gave this to the press. It was published, along with Sullivan's letter, in a pamphlet which was several times reprinted and was widely copied in newspapers. Describing it as seditious, Levi Lincoln said that in Massachusetts copies of it were sowed much thicker than tares among the wheat.[36]

Senator John Quincy Adams, who had voted for the embargo, who had supported it subsequently as the law of the land, and who still regarded it as the only alternative to war, replied to his colleague's letter.[37] As a fair-minded statesman he regarded Pickering's account of the circumstances attending the adoption of the embargo as erroneous in its most essential points, and by his own report of these he left

34 Rose to Pickering, May 8, 1808 (*ibid.*, p. 371).
35 *National Intelligencer*, March 21, 1808, saying it would print the long letter later and hoped that Republican papers would copy it, since it defeated its own purpose; TJ to Levi Lincoln, March 23, 1808 (L. & B., XII, 20–21).
36 Lincoln to TJ, Apr. 7, 1808 (LC, 38259). In a letter of Apr. 1 he said that 10,000 to 20,000 copies had been printed (LC, 31235–31237). The titles of the editions varied. I used: *Letter from the Hon. Timothy Pickering . . . Exhibiting to His Constituents, A View of the Imminent Danger of an Unnecessary and Ruinous War*, etc. (1 Hartford edn. from 2 Boston edn., 1808). It was dated Feb. 16, 1808; Sullivan replied March 3, and the printer's foreword was dated March 9.
37 J. Q. Adams to H. G. Otis, March 31, 1808 (*Writings*, III, 189–223).

history his debtor. He was amazed that his colleague made no reference to the most important cause of the measure, the British Order in Council of November 11, 1807, and was alarmed that a senator of the United States should have wholly accepted the contentions of another government while labeling those of his own as mere pretenses. Adams denied the desire of their government to go to war, but made a powerful case against the British, revealing at the same time that he had differed little with the administration. He favored a stronger navy and was at least willing to consider the arming of merchant ships; while recognizing that the effects of the embargo could not be ascertained quickly, he would have liked more assurance that it would not be unduly prolonged. This statesmanlike letter was notable not only for its non-partisanship but for its nationalistic spirit, and it was the absence of this from Pickering's partisan appeal that most disturbed him.

That Senator did more than express his lack of confidence in particular measures of the general government; he had none in the government itself and was addressing himself to the legislatures of the states — especially *"those States whose farms are on the ocean, and whose harvests are gathered in every sea."* He claimed that the federal government lacked commercial information and that such information could not be supplied in the desert of Washington. "Nothing but the sense of the commercial States, clearly and emphatically expressed, will save them from ruin," said he in seeming desperation.[38] Adams interpreted this as a call for state interposition, to the divisive effects of which he could see no end.[39]

Levi Lincoln wrote Jefferson that he had expected "everything mean, malignant, and false, at the approaching elections from Pickering and his coadjutors."[40] But he described the letter as pitiful and believed that, despite the noise that was being made by a relatively small number of desperate men, enemies of the government and supporters of the British, the great majority of the people believed in the necessity and utility of the embargo. Governor Sullivan, while professing confidence in his own re-election, declared that the Union itself was at stake. He wrote Jefferson that the Federalist leaders wanted to divide it, leaving the southern states to govern their own Negroes, while they set up in their part of the hemisphere a government under British

[38] *Letter*, p. 10.
[39] He did not mention the Kentucky and Virginia resolutions and was probably unaware of the connection of Jefferson and Madison with these.
[40] Levi Lincoln to TJ, Apr. 1, 1808, received Apr. 8 (LC, 31235-31237).

JOHN QUINCY ADAMS
Portrait by Charles Robert Leslie, 1816

protection.[41] This charge was to be raised again and denied by George Cabot. In spirit Pickering may have been even more of a disunionist than he had been four years earlier, but at this point it is sufficient to say that he and his little coterie, now on the offensive, were unquestionably anti-French and pro-British, and that they had avidly seized on the opportunity to embarrass the administration they hated by championing the immediate economic interests of their own locality, where ships lay idle and sailors were out of work.[42]

The Republican Governor described Pickering's letter as disorganizing and seditious. It was intended to be the one, and whether or not it was the other depends largely on definition. The reply of John Quincy Adams, which Sullivan termed inimitable and sublime, was far more accurate and judicious, and from the national point of view it was in the fullest sense patriotic. But such an appeal to fair-mindedness, such a call for patience, in the general interest, with a policy which was in fact experimental, would have had difficulty in competing with Pickering's localized appeal even if in all other respects the odds had been even. Actually, Pickering had at least a month's start in reaching the public; and, before Adams's letter was published in Boston, the election of the Governor and state senators had already taken place.[43] According to Sullivan, the embargo, under the "exposition" of Pickering, had a "wonderful effect" in Massachusetts. Despite it, he was narrowly re-elected, but Federalist control of the Senate was already assured when Adams's appeal to reason and patriotism arrived. It unquestionably encouraged the loyal Republicans, but it did not prevent the Federalists from gaining control of the lower house of the legislature in early May. These events boded ill for him and for the administration. The worst was not yet known before the congressional session ended, but there could be no doubt that in maritime New England the political tide had turned.

iii

When the President, on March 22, sent Congress the massive documentary record of negotiations with the British, along with communi-

[41] James Sullivan to TJ, Apr. 2, 1808; received Apr. 13 (LC, 31242–31243).
[42] Cabot to Pickering, Oct. 5, 1808 (H. Adams, ed., *New England Federalism*, p. 373). For Pickering's disunionism in 1804, see *Jefferson the President: First Term*, pp. 403–405.
[43] Sullivan to Madison, Apr. 12, 1808, saying that it was published the day before (MP, Rives Coll., 4:859). The governor and senators were elected the first Monday in April; the representatives, the first Monday in May.

cations of the past year with the French government, he had seen Pickering's letter but had received no report as yet on its political effects. The timing of his own action was owing to other considerations, but he believed that, together with his report of Napoleon's Milan decree a few days earlier, it constituted a sufficient answer to the charge of Pickering that the most important concerns of the country were "wrapt up in mystery." He had been much annoyed by earlier complaints to the same effect by Josiah Quincy in the House and linked the two men together.[44] He bombarded the legislators with paper: the documents as printed in a folio volume take up 140 pages, and reading them in the two houses required most of three or four days in each case.[45] Both branches of Congress ordered large printings of nearly all the documents, and to all practical purposes these became accessible to the public generally.[46] Such a mass of material could not be readily digested by anybody, in Congress or elsewhere, but on the face of it no one could justly charge the executive with secretiveness. The papers relating to the British were much the more numerous, but this was inevitable, and there was no real ground for the common Federalist charge of favoritism to Napoleon. In his message Jefferson said: "we find that no conduct on our part, however impartial and friendly, has been sufficient to ensure from either belligerent a just respect for our rights." About a week later, when transmitting in confidence a few recently received letters, including a highly offensive one from the Minister of Foreign Relations of France, he said that the proceedings of both governments indicated "designs of drawing us, if possible, into the vortex of their contests."[47] He told Congress that every bit of fresh information confirmed the prudence of avoiding involvement in the war and of "adhering to the precautionary system hitherto contemplated." In private he said that there was no *immediate* danger of war with France, whatever the future might hold, and that the danger of a rupture with Great Britain had been postponed. For this he credited the embargo, which could be borne until the end of the year in his opinion.[48]

[44] W. C. Nicholas to TJ, March 18, 1808 (LC, 31168), enclosing speech of Quincy, Feb. 19 (*Annals*, 10 Cong., 1 sess., II, 1830–1838); TJ to Nicholas, March 20, and to Levi Lincoln, March 23 (L. & B., XII, 14–15, 20–21).

[45] For the documents submitted on March 22, 1808, see *A.S.P.F.R.*, III, 80–220. The reading of these was spread over March 23, 24, 25, and 28 in both the Senate and the House — if it was finished even then.

[46] The *National Intelligencer* promptly printed the documents relating to the *Chesapeake* affair March 25, 1808, and printed many others thereafter.

[47] Messages of March 22 and 30, 1808 (*A.S.P.F.R.*, III, 80–81); Champagny to Armstrong, Jan. 15 (*ibid.*, pp. 248–249).

[48] TJ to Charles Pinckney, March 30, 1808 (L. & B., XII, 22–24).

Judging from the actions of the present Congress, he had little reason to fear that it would abandon the measure so long as he favored it. Congressman Livermore of Massachusetts had recently moved in the House that the embargo be recalled and that inquiry be made into the feasibility of suspending commercial intercourse with France and countries under her control. Following the defeat of this motion by a vote of more than three to one, that frustrated representative took off for home without informing anybody at his lodgings.[49] A few days later another congressman from that state thus expressed himself in private: "Rarely ever did prince rule more absolutely than T.J. He can manage everything in the national legislature by his rod, and I hesitate not to add that rarely ever was there a man whose popularity has proved and is likely to prove a greater curse to his country."[50] Jefferson's continuing popularity was an important reason for his control over Congress, but he was still avoiding the appearance of infringement on the prerogatives of that body. In none of his messages did he set forth arguments in favor of the embargo. Characteristically, he sought to give the impression that the measure was not imposed from above but represented the judgment of Congress — or at least that of the legislative and executive branches working in full conjunction. Far from seeking to rally his countrymen around his own person, he followed the general policy of keeping as much out of sight as possible. His political foes charged him with hypocrisy, but the wisdom of this policy in the existing governmental situation had been attested, and was to be attested further by the remarkably harmonious relations between him and the congressional majority. The President who had released this mass of diplomatic documents was better aware than most people of the need to enlighten the general public. The fact is, however, that he himself did not make to Congress a summarized statement which could have been copied in newspapers and that he addressed no exhortation to his countrymen.

In view of the distress to which the people were being put and would continue to be put by the embargo, Jefferson's friend Wilson Cary Nicholas told Madison that everything possible should be done to convince them of its necessity, and that he knew no one who could do justice to the subject if the Secretary of State did not. The best chance, as he saw it, would be afforded by the report of the Senate committee

---

[49] *Annals*, 10 Cong., 1 sess., II, 1854; J. Q. Adams, *Memoirs*, I, 522–523. The vote, 82 to 24, was on March 18.

[50] Samuel Taggart to Rev. John Taylor, March 21, 1808 (*Amer. Antiq. Soc. Procs.*, XXXIII, 311).

to which the documents had been referred.[51] As Nicholas may have known, Madison had already been consulted in behalf of that committee, of which Joseph Anderson of Tennessee was chairman and William Branch Giles and John Quincy Adams were members. A few days later Madison presented them with a draft, asking that they revise it so as to make it their own and urging in particular that Adams do so. After the Massachusetts Senator who had recently replied to Pickering made a few changes they accepted and reported it.[52] It amounts to an official statement of the position of the administration and is just the sort of statement Jefferson might have made in his message and which a century and a half later a President might have made on national television. For popular appeal it needed to be enlivened and humanized, but, as the Richmond *Enquirer* observed, it was the clearest and most concise exposition of the foreign relations of the country, of its rights and its situation, that had recently appeared. Calling attention to it by a bold heading — READ! — Thomas Ritchie's paper said that it was "calculated to expose the absurdities and electioneering tricks" of Pickering and his collaborators.[53]

Besides summarizing the actions of the British and the French against American commerce, the report listed and discussed the options of the government in its effort to protect this. As presented in numerical order these options were:

1. Protection by vessels of war. This was impracticable without the passage of considerable time, and the expense of an adequate navy was prohibitive. Furthermore, recourse to this means would inevitably involve collision with one or both of the belligerent powers.

2. Protection by self-armed merchant vessels. This method was open to the same danger of involvement and would have been inadequate anyway.

3. Offensive and defensive war. This should be avoided as long as possible but might be necessary in the end.

4. The general suspension of all foreign commerce. This would be to go beyond the embargo but eventually might have to be a substitute for it.

[51] W. C. Nicholas to Madison, Apr. 11, 1808 (MP, Rives Coll., 4:857).
[52] April 16, 1808 (*A.S.P.F.R.*, III, 220, 219*-220*); *Annals*, 10 Cong., 1 sess., pp. 364–368, without resolutions; Adams, *Memoirs*, I, 531.
[53] Richmond *Enquirer*, April 26, 1808. The *National Intelligencer*, which was so busily engaged in publishing the documents submitted to Congress by TJ, did not publish it until May 4. The extent to which it was publicized elsewhere remains to be ascertained.

5. Embargo. The value of this had already been shown by the number of American vessels that had been captured because of inability to avail themselves of the protection of this measure.

Madison's conclusion, which the committee accepted, was that in the present state of affairs no departure could be recommended "from that policy which withholds our commercial and agricultural property from the licensed depredations of the great maritime belligerent Powers." The emphasis was still on the protective rather than the coercive purposes of the embargo. The report voiced confidence that it would be supported "by all the manly virtue which the good people of the United States have ever discovered on great and patriotic occasions." The committee suggested, however, that juster conduct on the part of the belligerent powers toward neutrals might render the embargo unnecessary, and they recommended that during the recess of Congress the President be given the power to suspend it in such case. Congressional action to that effect was clearly anticipated and this offered a ray of hope. Meanwhile, the logic of events seemed to argue irresistibly for the maintenance of the existing policy. This in turn called for the strengthening of the system, although Madison and this particular committee did not say so. That was left to Gallatin and other committees.

At this time the President was relying more than ever on the Secretary of State and the Secretary of the Treasury, partly for physical reasons. Only a few days after a Federalist congressman had asserted that Jefferson was as absolute a ruler as any prince, the alleged potentate was taken with one of his periodic headaches. This was relatively mild, lasting only ten days, but at its height he told one of his granddaughters that it left him only an hour in any day for writing, and he told Gallatin that there was only one hour during which he was capable of thought. For a week or so after he dispatched the mass of documents to Congress he was in a decided slump, and, after the session ended, he said that it had reduced him to "a state of almost total incapacity for business."[54] The French Minister, reviewing the session, said that feebleness and irresolution had become habitual with the President and that he seemed fatigued with congressional strife.[55] Turreau, who so greatly admired bellicosity, was hardly a judicious commentator, but Jefferson was unquestionably weary and appears to

[54] TJ to Ellen Wayles Randolph, March 29, 1808 (*Family Letters*, p. 338); to Gallatin, March 31 (L. & B., XII, 24); to C. A. Rodney, Apr. 24 (*ibid.*, 36).
[55] Dispatch of May 20, 1808 (AECPEU, LXI, Part II).

have been relatively inactive at this time. While he exchanged ideas with Gallatin about a bill that would make the embargo more effective, he left this matter in the hands of the person who was more aware than anybody else of the loopholes in the existing laws. He accepted without question a draft of Gallatin's which, as we may safely assume, was afterwards made available to the appropriate committees in the Senate and the House and was the basis of what came to be called the Enforcement Act.[56] Thus, while Jefferson's lieutenants were more directly involved than he, it can truly be said with respect to the embargo that the administration got essentially what it wanted from Congress.

Of the two major actions, a tightening of the controls and a grant of authority to suspend them under certain conditions, the latter was taken first — and, oddly enough, it aroused more opposition. The specific conditions were the suspension of hostilities by the warring powers or such changes in their measures affecting neutral commerce as would, in the judgment of the President, leave the country safe. The authorization to suspend these laws was limited to the congressional recess and twenty days thereafter.[57] One would suppose that this would have been regarded by almost everybody as a prudent and unobjectionable measure, but it was opposed by some as giving the President too much discretion and by others as limiting him too much. Furthermore, the debate provided abundant opportunity to attack the embargo itself. There appears to have been virtually no contest in the Senate, but there was a vast amount of talk in the House. John Randolph, one of the most verbose of the objectors, said among other things "An experiment, such is now making, was never before — I will not say tried — it never before entered into the human imagination. There is nothing like it in the narrations of history or in the tales of fiction." Going the whole way, he asserted that both the embargo and the proposed authorization of its suspension were unconstitutional. Both were strongly supported by Campbell and others, however, and the suspension bill was passed in the House by a decisive vote. Opposition in the Senate was trivial.[58]

[56] TJ and Gallatin exchanged letters and ideas, March 30–April 2, 1808 (Gallatin, *Writings*, I, 379–383).
[57] Act approved Apr. 22, 1808 (*Annals*, 10 Cong., 1 sess., II, 2859–2860).
[58] A resolution calling for the authorization of suspension was introduced in the House by G. W. Campbell, Apr. 8, 1808, and extensively debated Apr. 12–14 (*ibid.*, pp. 2083–2171). This resolution was dropped on receipt of a bill that had been introduced in the Senate by Anderson on Apr. 15 and passed by that body Apr. 18 by a vote of 24 to 4 (*Annals*, 10 Cong., 1 sess., I, 360, 368). This bill was debated in the House Apr. 19 and passed at 10:30 P.M. by a vote of 60 to 36 (*Annals*, 10 Cong., 1 sess., II, 2198–2245; quotation from Randolph, p. 2206).

The enforcement bill appears to have aroused less heated discussion and less vigorous opposition than the suspension bill, which is surprising in view of the drastic nature of the measure. It was proposed by Samuel Smith of Maryland in the Senate, where it was readily adopted, and it was made even more rigorous by amendments in the House to which the Senate raised no objection. As recorded, the debate related chiefly to specific provisions, with only slight reference to the policy itself.[59] The most important provisions directly reflected the desires of the administration as manifested in the extant correspondence of Jefferson and Gallatin. The exemptions granted a few weeks earlier to vessels operating in bays, sounds, lakes, and rivers were ended. Each vessel was now required to have clearance papers, to show a manifest of the cargo before departure, and afterwards to produce a certificate proving that it was landed in the United States. Several provisions were designed to overcome difficulties the government had already encountered at Passamaquoddy Bay on the north and St. Mary's River on the south. Departures for ports adjacent to foreign territory were forbidden without express permission from the President. Revenue officers were authorized to take into custody unusual deposits of lumber and provisions in such ports until bonds had been given that they would be landed at a domestic port. This particular section of the bill, which was actually a modification of a suggestion of Jefferson's to Gallatin, received the largest negative vote in the House. American armed vessels were authorized to stop vessels suspected of being engaged in unlawful trade, and customs officials were empowered to detain them in suspicious cases until a presidential decision had been reached. Foreign shipping was excluded from the coastal trade. The requirement that licensed vessels be loaded under the supervision of a revenue officer was added to the bill on motion of a congressman from South Carolina, who based it on his own observation.[60] It did not necessarily reflect the judgment of the Secretary of the Treasury, who may have doubted that he had enough officers to perform such a task. But virtually the entire bill was in accordance with the wishes of the Chief Executive, and, while extending his authority, it greatly increased his responsibility.

Toward the end of the session a Federalist representative from Massachusetts said that the proceedings of Congress had "betrayed

[59] Introduced Apr. 15, 1808, and passed in Senate Apr. 20 by a vote of 21 to 5; debated in the House chiefly on Apr. 22 and passed by a vote of 73 to 26 the next day; approved by TJ on Apr. 25 (ibid., I, 361-363, 372; II, 2259-2262, 2268-2269, 2275, 2870-2874).
[60] Congressman D. R. Williams (ibid., 2259-2260).

nothing but a want of system and imbecility" and blamed this on the President since the majority in the House appeared "to receive impressions from that source with the same facility that the wax receives them from the seal."[61] Whether the legislative actions were wise or foolish was a matter of opinion, but the charge of lack of system seems unwarranted, and Congress was thoroughly consistent in supporting the embargo. The majority were well aware of the wishes of the administration, and, although party lines did not always hold, party discipline was strong. Senator John Quincy Adams was impressed by the absence of the usual differences between the two Houses. He said that this was the first session since the beginning of the government when there had not been a single instance of a conference over disagreeing votes.[62] One would assume that, in a time of recognized crisis, the legislators were rallying around the administration much as they have generally done through the years. For all their emphasis on the separation of powers, they were disposed to accept presidential leadership in foreign affairs, and, having adopted the policy of an embargo and being unable to think of a feasible alternative, they shared his concern to make it effective. One congressman who voted against the enforcement bill did so on the ground that people on the seacoasts, now patiently acquiescing in the embargo as a prudent measure, would become instantly dissatisfied with it when they learned of these precise requirements.[63] That is, what had been approved of in general would be much disliked in particular.

Whether or not this was a true prophecy Jefferson would have abundant opportunity to determine by the time the legislators reassembled in the fall. In the same letter to the Attorney General in which he referred to his physical exhaustion he said: "Congress has just passed an additional embargo law, on which if we act as boldly as I am disposed to do, we can make it effectual."[64] He gave no sign here of the irresolution the French Minister attributed to him, and the next few months were to show that this generally moderate man could be very tough. Turreau, in his review of the recent session, observed that the President's "extreme fear of compromising his authority" with Congress had caused him "to restrict more and more the sphere of his own powers."[65] But, because of the logic of developing circumstances and the sheer momentum of a policy of control once initiated and

---

[61] Samuel Taggart, Apr. 4, 1808 (*Amer. Antiq. Soc. Procs.*, XXXIII, 317).
[62] J. Q. Adams, *Memoirs*, I, 534.
[63] James Sloan of New Jersey (*Annals*, 10 Cong., 1 sess., II, 2268).
[64] TJ to C. A. Rodney, Apr. 24, 1808 (L. & B., XII, 36).
[65] Dispatch of May 20, 1808 (AECPEU, LXI, Part II).

consistently adhered to, the whole trend of the embargo laws was toward the increase of executive authority. A man of Jefferson's temperament could hardly have welcomed the unexampled powers with which he was entrusted by Congress, but as he saw no choice but to seek them he had none but to wield them. Inescapably, the major responsibility was now his.

[XXXII]

The Grievous Task of Enforcement

A FEW days after the recess of Congress a highly optimistic editorial appeared in the Richmond *Enquirer*. That loyal Republican paper thus viewed the prospect: "The people of this country *will* bear with chearfulness any sacrifices or inconveniences which these embargo laws will impose upon them." The writer gave a reason for his confidence: "They know that this is the great crisis, when the leading policy of the U.S. is brought to a decisive experiment."[1] The editorial referred to the embargo several times as an experiment, describing this as unique in American history and implying that it had just begun. It had never been officially presented in such terms, and it had actually assumed its present legal form in response to developing circumstances. Originally recommended as a precautionary measure, it was represented here as one of economic coercion and as a feasible alternative to conventional war. Said this writer: "It is a commercial warfare which is the most suitable to our interest and to our power. . . . It is equally effectual if it be rigidly enforced."

Jefferson seems never to have made such an emphatic declaration of faith in the efficacy of commercial warfare, but his hopes were undoubtedly quickened now that he was provided with what appeared to be adequate weapons with which to wage it. And, about this time, he himself used the term "experiment" in this connection, as he seems not to have done previously. Speaking to Gallatin of the power conferred on the executive by a particular provision of the enforcement law, he said: "I am clear we ought to use it freely that we may, by a fair experiment, know the power of this great weapon, the embargo." A few days later he said: "I place immense value in the experiment being fully made, how far an embargo may be an effectual weapon in future

<hr />

[1] Richmond *Enquirer*, May 3, 1808.

as well as on this occasion."[2] In this experiment he perceived timeless values, and these ennobled it in his own mind. He thought of the embargo as a patriotic enterprise, but as such it had to meet both a domestic and a foreign test. Months earlier John Quincy Adams had described it as "an experiment to see how far the Government might calculate upon the support of the people for the maintenance of their own rights."[3] The decisive test of that support was approaching, but, whatever the outcome of this might be, the ultimate success or failure of what had become an experiment in economic coercion must depend upon its effects abroad.

From certain expressions of Jefferson's one might suppose that he was still pursuing what the British representatives Rose and Erskine described as a Chinese policy. Using identical language in three letters, written on the same day to persons abroad, he said: "During the present paroxysm of the insanity of Europe, we have thought it wisest to break off all intercourse with her."[4] He continued to speak of what the embargo had saved the country from. Writing in midsummer, he said that it gave time "to call home 80 millions of property, 20 or 30,000 seamen, and 2000 vessels."[5] Toward the end of spring, however, he had told Madison what he must have realized from the beginning even though he did not say so — namely, that time would run out, that eventually war would be preferable to the embargo. And he remarked that they should begin to make more use of it as a diplomatic weapon.[6] These observations were made at just the time that the action of Congress forbidding the exportation of goods by land as well as by sea showed unmistakably that governmental policy now extended beyond the safeguarding of ships and seamen. Thus a shift in emphasis, from a predominantly negative and protective policy to one that was more positive and coercive, was indicated. Jefferson made no public statement that implied a change, and he said to Madison in private that they need not assume the air of menace. But they could let the British and French governments know what would happen when the continuance of the embargo would become a greater evil than war itself. At that time, he said, if one of the offending nations had withdrawn its orders or decrees and the other had not, "we must declare war against that other; if neither shall have withdrawn, we must take our choice of

[2] TJ to Gallatin, May 6, 15, 1808 (L. & B., XII, 52, 56).

[3] J. Q. Adams to James Sullivan, Jan. 10, 1808 (*Writings*, III, 186).

[4] To John Armstrong, Thaddeus Kosciusko, and Du Pont de Nemours, May 2, 1808 (L. & B., XII, 43, 45; *J.-D. Correspondence*, p. 101).

[5] TJ to John Langdon, Aug. 2, 1808 (Ford, IX, 201).

[6] TJ to Madison, March 11, 1808 (*ibid.*, 179–184).

enemies between them." Refusing to consider submission to either or both, he was privately voicing his continuing hope that he could play one against the other.

The likelihood of American belligerence in any case except that of actual attack was minimized by both the British and French representatives at this stage; and the threat of it was couched in rather negative terms by Madison. As he put the matter to Pinkney and Armstrong, the failure of either country to withdraw its orders or decrees as applied to the United States, after the other had done so, could be viewed in no other light than that of war. Since each government claimed that its actions were retaliatory against the other, and not directed against neutrals as such, this was a logical deduction, but in this ruthless power struggle the major contestants were indifferent to logic and desperately concerned for advantage. What the only surviving commercial neutral had to offer was the removal of the embargo, which Congress had strengthened and authorized the President to revoke if the measures that had occasioned it were withdrawn. Madison duly sent the American ministers in London and Paris copies of the diplomatic documents Jefferson had communicated to Congress, including his own reply to Erskine with respect to the Orders in Council. Describing this as "unanswerable," Pinkney said it "left nothing to be urged" against them "upon the score of right." After Congress had recessed, the Secretary of State sent both ministers instructions regarding the employment of the embargo as a diplomatic weapon.[7]

Not for many weeks were the President and Secretary of State to learn whether or not their renewed hopes for diplomacy were warranted, but at this time there were some unofficial reports of British opinion that served to raise them. After receiving one of these from the Attorney General, Jefferson wrote that official: "It is very evident that our embargo, added to the exclusion from the Continent, will be most heavily felt in England and Ireland. Liverpool is remonstrating and endeavoring to get the other ports into motion." Recommending the publication of the essential parts of the communication from Rodney, this generally humane man said: "It will show our people that while the embargo gives us double rations, it is starving our enemies."[8] There was cruelty even in commercial warfare. A few days later the National Intelligencer published the texts of petitions of merchants of

[7] The most important letters at this stage were: Madison to Pinkney, Apr. 4, 30, 1808, and Pinkney to Madison, June 5, acknowledging the former (A.S.P.F.R., III, 221–223); Madison to Armstrong, May 2 (ibid., 252–253).

[8] TJ to Rodney, Apr. 24, 1808 (L. & B., XII, 36, slightly corrected).

London and Liverpool to Parliament, along with reports of debates in the Houses of Commons and Lords on policy toward America. Among other items in that paper during the fortnight that Jefferson remained in Washington after the congressional session the one most gratifying to him, no doubt, was an extract of a letter from a gentleman in Liverpool to his brother in Boston:

> The orders of Council touch the very life strings of the commercial interest. Meetings of the merchants are very frequent, both here and in London. The Manufacturing interest in the interior, to the number of upwards of *one hundred thousand*, have petitioned the king for peace. The debates in Parliament are the most lengthy & animated on the side of the opposition, ever known; and if the American government continues the embargo until mid-summer it is the general opinion a relaxation of British commercial restrictions must take place. The voice of the people grows louder and louder every day.[9]

Before the end of the congressional session Jefferson knew that the bill confirming the Orders in Council would surely pass, but, unlike modern scholars, he was not in position to observe how well in hand the British Cabinet had Parliament and how pleased they were with the situation.[10] No doubt he was disposed to magnify the significance of British dissatisfaction. Meanwhile, he himself was beginning to be faced with serious problems of disaffection, despite the overwhelming support of Congress.

About a week before the legislators departed the Washington scene, and about a month after the President learned of Timothy Pickering's verbal assault on the administration in behalf of maritime New England, he received an alarming report of armed resistance to the embargo laws on Lake Champlain. Canada was a natural market for products of this region, as it also was for those of upstate New York, and prior to the passage of the law forbidding exportation by land as well as by sea there was considerable trade in lumber, potash, provisions, and other commodities. From the first that law was disregarded by men who probably did not concede the necessity of its enactment and undoubtedly realized that more than ordinary profit could now be

[9] *National Intelligencer*, May 2, 1808. See also Apr. 29, May 6, and May 18.
[10] British attitudes are well described by Perkins (*Prologue to War*, pp. 203–204).

gained from trade across the border.[11] A letter from the collector on the Vermont side of the lake asking for military aid called particular attention to the use, after the spring thaw, of large rafts bearing armed men. In the season of high water these could ride the rapids and proceed northward by the Richelieu River. Jefferson was informed that in a few weeks the fall of the water would make the rapids impassable to rafts, but, as he told Gallatin, he believed it "important to crush every example of forcible opposition to the law." The Secretary of the Treasury, who had just lost an infant daughter, was unable to attend the Cabinet meeting that was hastily called to consider this matter, but he gave his counsel in writing, and the complicated plan that was worked out was in line with his suggestions. This called for the use, by the collector, of armed vessels manned by volunteers; for the assistance, if need be, of the marshal and a posse raised by him; and finally, if the opposition should require it, for a request to the governor to publish a presidential proclamation that was provided him and to call on the militia. In the proclamation, after stating that information had been received that persons in the Champlain district were combined or combining to form insurrections against the authority and laws of the United States, the President ordered the dispersal of these insurgents and all concerned with such combinations. He commanded all civil and military officers to quell such insurrections by force of arms or otherwise and to seize upon the offenders.[12]

Several weeks later the governors of Vermont and New York issued the proclamation, and each dispatched a small body of militiamen to the Champlain district, but the town of St. Albans, Vermont, afterwards passed resolutions that denied the need for the militia since there was no insurrection. There was nothing more, they claimed, than individual evasions of the embargo.[13] These continued despite the proclamation, however, and Jefferson himself seems to have recognized that it was a mistake. He issued no other of the sort and sought to localize responsibility for enforcement as much as possible. He soon observed to Gallatin that the conduct of some of the military officers and of

[11] There is an excellent treatment of the region in the dissertation of I. I. Rubin, "New York State and the Long Embargo" (New York Univ., 1961), ch. IV, with special reference to the Champlain district at this stage (pp. 112–116).

[12] The proclamation, dated Apr. 19, 1808, is in Richardson, *Messages and Papers of the Presidents* (1907), I, 450–451. The chief letters are two from TJ to Gallatin, Apr. 19 (L. & B., XII, 29–31), and Gallatin to TJ, Apr. 19 (LC, 31316). The episode is described, with references, in B. M. Rich, *The Presidents and Civil Disorders* (1941), pp. 31–32.

[13] Quoted by Rich, p. 32.

ALBERT GALLATIN IN LATER LIFE
Miniature by W. S. Blanchard

some "excellent citizens" in the Champlain district had been "very meritorious" and called for expressions of thanks.[14] But Gallatin was not long in reporting that the attempt to stop trade across the Canadian border in this district was so unpopular that officials and well-intentioned citizens forbore to act against it. Some of the accounts in the newspapers must have been exaggerated — such as one of a raft nearly half a mile long, carrying a veritable fort, five hundred to six hundred armed men, and an enormous cargo.[15] But large rafts were undoubtedly employed, and there were clashes with revenue officers resulting in loss of life. Toward the end of May, by which time the rapids were impassable to rafts, Gallatin expected a considerable decline in illegal trade during the summer, but he believed nonetheless that a regiment of regulars and two armed gunboats were needed on Lake Champlain.[16]

Troubles on the northern border were destined to multiply and in fact to become insurmountable, but at this stage the President was most concerned with the coastal trade, to the regulation of which the recent legislation was specially directed. In a letter he wrote just before setting out for a month at home he described the position he intended to take and which in fact he continued to maintain. To his loyal coadjutor he said: "The great leading object of the Legislature was, and ours in execution of it ought to be, to give complete effect to the embargo laws. They have bidden agriculture, commerce, navigation, to bow before that object, to be nothing in competition with that."[17] Even before the passage of the latest and strongest measure in this series of laws, he had sanctioned the use of force on the Canadian border, and he was now assuming unexampled executive authority in the effort to control the coastal trade. In this position and these actions this generally moderate man was out of his character as an advocate of *laissez faire* who feared the extension of governmental power.

By way of explanation it might be said that his dread of power had declined since he began to wield it, and, human nature being what it is, that should not seem surprising. Also, it certainly can be said that, proceeding from step to step, he went much farther than he originally intended. But few who have exercised great authority ever valued it less for its own sake or have been less tyrannical in person. Perhaps his attitude at this stage may be compared to that of Lincoln, who sub-

14 TJ to Gallatin, May 27, 1808 (L. & B., XII, 66), replying to Gallatin's letter of May 23 with the latest information (*Writings*, I, 390).
15 *National Intelligencer*, May 23, 1808, from *N.Y. Evening Post*.
16 Gallatin to TJ, May 28, 1808 (*Writings*, I, 393).
17 TJ to Gallatin, May 6, 1808 (Gallatin's *Writings*, I, 385-386).

ordinated all else to the cause of saving the Union and, though far from tyrannical in spirit, assumed unexampled powers as commander in chief and infringed on the freedom of individuals in the effort to perform the supreme task that was committed to him. The embargo, which was but a means to an end and proved to be an ineffective one, cannot itself be equated with the Union as a cause, but to Jefferson the support of American rights upon the seas seemed a necessity for the young Republic if it was to maintain its self-respect as an independent nation. This was an objective to which normal individual interests, and even rights, could be justifiably subordinated. The embargo was now the officially approved national instrument for the attainment of this goal. In the effort to enforce it the President exercised control over the economic affairs of individuals that was without precedent in the history of the Republic. But he did not assume these powers; he was granted them by the overwhelming vote of Congress. And the chances are that if this policy had been successful the single-mindedness with which he wielded these powers in the national interest would have gained for him such plaudits as are customarily given effective leaders in historic crises. In connection with this particular crisis, however, it is proper to inquire whether the administration was or could have been effective in the existing circumstances.[18]

Congress had authorized the detention of coastal shipping on suspicion of illegal intent, and Jefferson, who described this power to Gallatin as a panacea, was disposed to use it freely. He regarded as special objects of suspicion shipments of provisions to ports that could be readily supplied with them from the interior. He was chiefly concerned about flour and lumber, but, listing with these a number of other suspicious or dubious commodities, he expressed the opinion that the collectors should detain shipments of them all and refer the cases to Washington. Gallatin thought that this proposal went too far, and Jefferson was not averse to its mitigation so long as this did not defeat the object of the embargo laws. He showed little or no regard for private gain. "I do not wish a single citizen in any of the States to be deprived of a meal of bread," he said, "but I set down the exercise of commerce, merely for profit, as nothing when it carries with it the danger of defeating the objects of the embargo."[19] He had already made specific provision for the shipment of flour to ports and districts that were dependent on imports from elsewhere in the country by

[18] L. M. Sears, in *Jefferson and the Embargo* (1927), ch. IV, gives an excellent account of the administration of these laws between congressional sessions in 1808.

[19] TJ to Gallatin, May 27, 1808 (L. & B., XII, 66).

granting the governors of the states the power to issue certificates in cases of actual need. He dispatched letters to the governors of the chief flour-importing states before going home and addressed the others soon thereafter.[20] Gallatin was dubious of this grant of authority, fearing that the governors would abuse it. As things turned out, only two of them availed themselves of it and only James Sullivan of Massachusetts caused embarrassment. This, however, was very grave. Meanwhile, Gallatin, more aware of the actualities of both the commercial and the administrative situation than Jefferson, worked out a practical plan with respect to foodstuffs. This was that shipments of provisions of no more value than one-eighth of the bond could be made without question.[21]

That Gallatin was as anxious as Jefferson to attain the objectives of the embargo laws may be safely assumed; he was one of the persons most responsible for tightening the restrictions. At the outset of the great experiment, however, the President, while not properly chargeable with lust for power, impresses one as being less pragmatic and more rigid than the Secretary, and he certainly used harsher language regarding those who would circumvent the laws. In writing the governors he left no doubt of his desire to meet the real needs of the citizens, but he said that these must not be made "a cover for the crimes against their country which unprincipled adventurers are in the habit of committing." Long before the term "profiteer" came into common use he spoke of "the unlawful profits of the most worthless part of society"; and quite clearly he believed that this commercial war, waged in the national interest, should evoke sacrificial patriotism. It has been said that his policy, as embodied in the embargo, was "dominated by a problem of theory," and there can be no doubt of his great desire to demonstrate the effectiveness of economic coercion for the future as well as the present.[22] But one gains the impression that he was so obsessed with the immediate problem of making the embargo work as to be unmindful of republican theory and also of certain basic facts of human nature. His faith in the great body of his countrymen was not unwarranted at this stage, but he minimized the impatience of men with hampering restrictions to which they were unaccustomed, and he underrated both the extent and the potency of private greed. He might properly have expected good citizens to deplore forcible resistance to

20 TJ to Governors of New Orleans, Ga., S.C., Mass., and N.H., May 6, 1808 (ibid., 51–52); to the others, May 16 (Gallatin, Writings, I, 389–390).

21 Gallatin to TJ, May 23, 1808 (Writings, I, 390–392). TJ approved this in his letter of May 27 but did not withdraw from the governors the power to issue certificates.

22 White, Jeffersonians, p. 433.

these restrictive laws, but to ask them to regard the evasion of them as criminal was another matter.

He set this experiment on a rigorous course before going home. During the month Jefferson was at Monticello, Gallatin modified the procedure so as to make it more workable and rendered mixed reports on developments. Things had quieted momentarily on the northern border; and, in the matter of coastal commerce, he said they were beginning to do better under the one-eighth rule. The actions of the collectors were not uniform, however, and Governor Sullivan was issuing far too many certificates. Gallatin was troubled about vessels that loaded secretly and sailed without clearance papers, knowing that the British would not require them, but he anticipated no difficulty with the regular traders.[23] From the communications Jefferson received from his own part of the country in this period, he gained the impression that the people still greatly preferred the embargo to war.[24] Viewed from the elevation of Monticello, when he was renewing his strength and faith on a brief visit home, the prospect of the great experiment seemed brighter than it did when he got back to Washington.

ii

Shortly after his return on June 10 he learned from Governor Charles Pinckney of South Carolina that a legal difficulty had appeared in an unexpected place: the federal circuit court that was presided over by Justice William Johnson, Jefferson's only appointee to the Supreme Court and presumably a good Republican. The President was so exercised by this development that he summoned the Attorney General from his home in Delaware for consultation.[25] Several weeks earlier in Charleston, in response to a petition, Johnson had issued a writ of mandamus to compel a collector to issue clearance papers for a coastwise shipment of rice and cotton.[26] At the time the collector had not received Gallatin's instructions applying the one-eighth principle to provisions; and he claimed that the instructions under which he was operating required him to reject the shipment, although he did not

[23] Gallatin to TJ, May 23, 28, 1808 (*Writings*, I, 390–394).
[24] W. A. Burwell to TJ, May 21, 1808 (LC, 31461).
[25] TJ to Rodney, June 20, 1808 (LC, 31578).
[26] D. G. Morgan, in *Justice William Johnson* (1954), ch. IV, gives a full account of the mandamus case with extensive quotations and abundant references. The petition was filed May 25, 1808, and the writ issued three days later. Viewing Johnson's judicial career as a whole, Morgan regards his action in this case as atypical (p. 72).

regard it as suspicious. Johnson believed that even under these early instructions the shipment was permissible, but the ground of his decision was that the congressional Act of April 25, 1808, vested discretion in the collectors and did not authorize the executive to prescribe general rules which might impair this. That is, presidential instructions were mere recommendations. The judgment was promptly hailed by Federalists as a merited rebuke to a power-hungry President and was condemned by loyal Republicans as an example of unwarranted judicial interference in executive matters. Jefferson himself deplored it on the latter ground, and his Attorney General issued an elaborate opinion in which he argued that the circuit court lacked jurisdiction.[27] This question had not been raised in the proceedings, and Johnson afterwards said that he might have acted differently if it had been. He vigorously defended himself against Rodney's widely circulated opinion, however, and obviously regarded the original denial of this particular shipment as an injustice. So it may have been, and Gallatin's later instructions obviated the necessity for such rigidity.

Although not without significance in constitutional history, this case appears to have been something of a tempest in a teapot. From the administrative point of view the denial to the executive of the authority to issue instructions would have been absurd; and, even though discretion was left with the collectors by the letter of the law, the recommendations of the executive could hardly have been disregarded by officials subject to reprimand and removal. Furthermore, Gallatin's practical and effective one-eighth principle would appear to have been as unwarranted an assumption of authority as the unwise absolute requirement it replaced.[28] The effort of the administration to attain uniformity and avoid favoritism was commendable and did not in itself imply the desire to aggrandize executive power. The episode is noteworthy, however, in showing the ever-increasing emphasis on centralized control into which Jefferson was being impelled by the practical requirements of his task, and in disclosing the essential incompatibility of commercial no less than traditional warfare with the individual freedoms he had championed through most of his public life. We may regret that he did not acknowledge this inconsistency and designate it

---

[27] TJ to Gov. Charles Pinckney, July 18, 1808 (L. & B., XII, 102–106); printed copy of Rodney's opinion of July 15 (LC, 31694–31695), quoted and discussed by Morgan (pp. 61–62) with references.

[28] Explicit authority to prescribe general rules was given the President by the Act of Jan. 9, 1809, as a result of Johnson's judgment. Meanwhile, district attorneys were instructed to oppose legal actions like the one at Charleston; and Simeon Theus, the collector there, was reprimanded for having countenanced it (Memo. of Cabinet meeting, June 30, 1808, in Ford, I, 333).

as an inescapable necessity; but, despite this judicial chiding, he appears to have been generally regarded in South Carolina as a patriot and not a tyrant. He received resolutions of approval from the legislature of that state at just this juncture. His worst news did not come from the South and West but from the North, especially from New England, where his bitterest foes had gained control of the most important legislature.

He received a report from Governor James Sullivan shortly after he got back to Washington.[29] Sullivan, who had survived the political upset in Massachusetts, reported that the immediate object of the new Federalist majority was to destroy John Quincy Adams, who had presumed to support the administration and was regarded by the high party leaders as a renegade. He still had a session to serve in the United States Senate, but in the effort to humiliate him his foes precipitated the election for the next term and chose a dependable Federalist, James Lloyd, to succeed him. Also, resolutions critical of national policy were passed with which he could not concur. Accordingly, a few days after Sullivan wrote Jefferson, Adams resigned his seat.[30] He said later that the resolutions, which were drawn by Christopher Gore, were calculated "to sacrifice the best wishes of this nation to the unjust claims and pretensions of a foreign power." To George H. Rose in England these events marked the return of the most important New England state to "sound principles"; and, as he informed Pickering, he could not help being amused at the downfall of Professor Adams.[31] Adams held the chair of rhetoric and oratory at Harvard, and to this he must now devote himself. Sullivan suggested that he be given a diplomatic appointment, as in fact he was by Madison within a year, but his actions and attitude can be attributed to no desire for political preferment. He regarded the High Federalists as submissionists and sectionalists; and never during his long and distinguished career did he manifest more signally his devotion to the principle of national union or demonstrate more strikingly his personal independence.

Though Pickering and Gore suffer by comparison with him in the perspective of history, they had concrete grievances to appeal to and thus gained the immediate political advantage. But neither against Adams nor for the resolutions did the Federalists attain an overwhelming majority such as Jefferson had maintained in Congress, and the

[29] Sullivan to TJ, June 3, 1808; received June 12 (LC, 31525).

[30] To the Honorable Senate and House of Representatives of the Commonwealth of Massachusetts, June 8, 1808 (*Writings*, III, 237-238).

[31] Adams to Orchard Cook, Aug. 22, 1808 (*Writings*, III, 239); Rose to Pickering, Aug. 4, 1808 (H. Adams, ed., *New England Federalism*, p. 372).

Republicans entered a vigorous protest against the resolutions in the journal of the House.[32] Jefferson's party had lost control of the legislature, but the margin was not great and he had not lost control of his party.[33] Even at this center of disaffection its loyal support of him and his policies was still notable, though in many cases it may have been chiefly verbal.

The administration was increasingly troubled by the actions of one of its friends in Massachusetts. Governor Sullivan seemed quite unable to refuse any request for permission to import foodstuffs. Gallatin, who kept a record of the gubernatorial permits, reported in midsummer that Governor Langdon of New Hampshire had issued a small and reasonable number of them and that nobody else besides Sullivan had issued any. In a period of two months that easygoing official, more responsive to local pressure than to national policy, had granted permits for far more barrels of flour than were necessary to meet the normal needs of his commonwealth. He had authorized the importation of corn in roughly comparable amount, along with lesser quantities of rice and rye. Gallatin was convinced that a large proportion of these provisions, especially flour, was getting into eager British hands. Accordingly, at his suggestion, Jefferson politely asked the Governor to cease and desist for a time at least, and also to provide an estimate of the future needs of his state.[34] This was shortly before Jefferson left Washington for his long stay at Monticello, and the ensuing correspondence, which must be described as non-productive, stretched through the summer. In administering to one of his leading supporters what amounted to a rebuke Jefferson was tactful, and he commended the great body of New Englanders as patriotic and law-abiding. His only concern, he said, was to promote the national interest and guard honest citizens against the lawless. Sullivan's letters, on the other hand, revealed his growing doubts of the feasibility of the embargo and his increased fears not only of disunionist sentiment but also of riots and convulsions. With respect to the certificates, he promised discretion which Gallatin did not afterwards perceive, and obviously he regarded

[32] The vote was 248 to 213 against Adams, and 248 to 219 for the resolutions. On the latter, see Helen R. Pinkney, *Christopher Gore, Federalist of Massachusetts* (1969), pp. 106–107, with references.

[33] T. L. Wolford, in "Democratic-Republican Reaction in Massachusetts to the Embargo of 1807" (*New England Quart.*, March, 1942) emphasizes party loyalty and support in this period, holding that the disaffection has been exaggerated.

[34] Gallatin to TJ, July 15, 1808 (*Writings*, I, 394); TJ to Sullivan, July 16 (L. & B., XII, 95–96).

it as politically advantageous in his locality to issue rather than to withhold them.[35]

During the latter half of the summer, when Jefferson was at Monticello, Gallatin was in New York, not only escaping the horrors of the Washington climate but also observing the operation of the embargo laws in the Northeast, where their effectiveness was most uncertain. Had these two high officials not been so widely separated one of the most ludicrous episodes of the season — that of the Chinese merchant — might have been avoided and critcis of the administration deprived of a savory bit of merriment.

It will be recalled that, contrary to his desire, the President had been authorized to permit ships to sail in ballast to bring back property from abroad. Toward the end of June, Gallatin sent him a list of ninety-six applications for these permits that had accumulated in the past two months, and they must have engaged a considerable part of his time before he went home. It is uncertain whether an application from John Jacob Astor and the Boston firm of J. and T. H. Perkins to bring back property from Canton was included, but a request from them was denied some time after June 1 on general grounds. Somewhat arbitrarily, such voyages had been largely restricted to the West Indies.

Under authority of the original embargo law the President from time to time permitted ships to sail to foreign ports for some reason connected with the public interest. Thus, during the summer of 1808, out of courtesy to Turreau's government, he enabled certain French nationals to return home. Receiving at Monticello a request from one Punqua Winchong, allegedly a Chinese merchant and designated by many as a mandarin, Jefferson decided that this fell within the area of international comity. The supposed dignitary was introduced to him by a note from Senator Samuel Lathrop Mitchill of New York, and, judging from the account of him in the *National Intelligencer*, he made quite an impression in Washington — where, however, he missed the President either by accident or design. He wanted to return home in a ship to be engaged by him, with property said to have been worth from forty to fifty thousand dollars. Also, he wanted to attend the obsequies of his grandfather — or, as another account had it, to be in readiness for those of his father, now aged ninety.

Believing that the granting of this petition would amount to a diplomatic act and have favorable results in the mandarin's generally inaccessible country, Jefferson authorized Gallatin in New York to

[35] Sullivan to TJ, July 21, 23, 1808 (LC, 31738–31739, 31751–31753); TJ to Sullivan, Aug. 12 (L. & B., XII, 127–130); Sullivan to TJ, Aug. 24 (LC, 31953).

provide the necessary papers. Gallatin, who scented speculation and disliked any departure from general rules that might be interpreted as favoritism, complied reluctantly. It turned out that the vessel engaged for this long voyage belonged to John Jacob Astor, who was anxious to re-enter the China trade and was hoping for a rich return cargo from Canton. A group of indignant merchants in Philadelphia claimed that Punqua Winchong was neither mandarin nor merchant but a rank imposter, as indeed he was. Unfortunately for the cause of justice, Astor's ship, the *Beaver*, sailed before these charges could be investigated or referred to Jefferson; and months later, after the embargo had been repealed, it returned with a cargo said to have been worth $200,000.[36]

This bizarre episode may be cited as an example of Jefferson's gullibility as well as of Astor's guile. But the President was constantly confronted with what he called "tormenting applications," and, judging from his record as a whole, there can be no real doubt of his persistent effort to avoid any manner of favoritism in the application of the embargo laws.

iii

The dispersal of the high officers of the government at this season according to their custom inevitably slowed the dissemination of information among them. But, since the President and his lieutenants had to communicate in writing, they left to posterity a more revealing record than they might have if they could have engaged in intimate conversation, little of which would probably have been reported. From this high-level correspondence — and especially that between Gallatin and Jefferson — we can gain a sort of bird's-eye view of the operations of the embargo as these appeared to the administration during the latter half of the summer.[37]

The letters that Jefferson read and wrote at Monticello and those from one Cabinet member to another convey one clear though not surprising impression: namely, that there was a direct and vital connection between the enforcement of the embargo in a particular state or district and the political attitude of its officials to the President and his

[36] A detailed account of this affair is given by K. W. Porter in *John Jacob Astor: Business Man*, I (1931), 142–150, with the chief documents, pp. 420–428. Important letters are TJ to Gallatin, July 25, 1808 (L. & B., XII, 106–107); Gallatin to TJ, Aug. 5, 9 (*Writings*, I, 400, 404); TJ to Gallatin, Aug. 15 (L. & B., XII, 134), Aug. 23 (LC, 31948). Account in *National Intelligencer*, July 25.

[37] Gallatin's correspondence from New York, July 29–Sept. 16, 1808 (*Writings*, I, 396–418) is of the first importance in this connection.

party. The attitudes of governors were of paramount importance. The loyalty of Governor Charles Pinckney and the citizenry of South Carolina to the administration, and their acquiescence in these laws, became proverbial in administration circles. Enforcement was more difficult in New York, but Governor Daniel D. Tompkins was highly co-operative and but for him the situation on his state's northern border would have been considerably worse than it was. Enforcement officers met most resistance in New England, where political opposition was greatest. New Hampshire, under Jefferson's old friend and staunch supporter, John Langdon, caused least trouble, while Massachusetts, where Federalists controlled the legislature and James Sullivan clung precariously to the gubernatorial helm, caused most. Though seeking to justify himself, the Governor did not exaggerate the enmity of the High Federalists when he wrote Jefferson: "There is no engine but what is and will be used here against your administration. Truth, justice, and reason are expelled."[38] Gallatin was convinced that foes of the administration in New York and New England were encouraging forcible resistance to the embargo laws and he went so far as to characterize their "party rage" as criminal. Jefferson was never disposed to minimize the political motivation of violent opponents of these laws, but if he was not already aware of other major reasons for the special difficulties of executing them on the northeastern coast he was soon enlightened by his Secretary of the Treasury.

Shortly after he began to observe the problems of enforcement from the vantage point of New York, Gallatin again remarked that the main difficulty was caused by vessels departing without clearance papers in defiance of the law.[39] Once at sea, these ships transferred their cargoes to foreign vessels, mostly British, or sailed to Nova Scotia or the West Indies. From New York northward they could do this much more readily than from the Delaware River, Chesapeake Bay, or the North Carolina coast because of easier access to the sea. The opportunities for evasion were greatest in New England, especially in Massachusetts (then including Maine), which not only had a very extensive coastline but also adjoined Canada. Residents of the Bay State owned more ships than those of any other commonwealth and, with its foreign commerce cut off, its resourceful shippers and daring seamen turned to the coastal trade for recompense. Flour, illegally shipped into Canada, commanded such a price that the temptation to engage in smuggling

---

[38] Sullivan to TJ, Aug. 24, 1808 (LC, 31953).
[39] Gallatin to TJ, July 28, 1808 (*Writings*, I, 396–399). In this letter, more fully than in any other in this period, he discusses the problems of enforcement, especially in the Northeast.

was enormous. And, as in Revolutionary times, there was no stigma attached to getting the better of a distant government that could be designated as tyrannical.[40]

Gallatin had problems with many of the collectors of customs on whom the task of enforcement chiefly fell, but in his reports to Jefferson he laid greater emphasis on the limitations and difficulties under which they labored than upon their incompetence or abuse of their position.[41] Some resigned under criticism or were removed for collusion with violators of the laws. Jefferson made a point of seeing that his removal of the collector at New Bedford was publicized as a warning and he showed no reluctance in accepting Gallatin's disciplinary recommendations, especially in New England.[42] Some of these lesser officials, though loyal and well-meaning, lacked forcefulness and energy, and others were overwhelmed by hostile local sentiment. But Joseph Whipple of Portsmouth, New Hampshire, an ardent Republican who hated Federalists, kept things under excellent control in his port and contributed no little to the high opinion in which his state was held by the President and the Secretary of the Treasury. Gallatin spoke highly of David Gelston in New York, and the deputy collector at the crucial port of Boston, Benjamin Weld, who did most of the work there under General Benjamin Lincoln, was notably conscientious and capable. One gains the impression that on the whole these officials performed their thankless task diligently and with no inconsiderable success. But, except at stations contiguous to foreign territory — such as Passamaquoddy Bay and St. Mary's, Georgia — there was great uncertainty about the right of collectors to seize suspicious property, especially on the water, and in his first extensive report from New York Gallatin said that after making seizures a number of the collectors had been sued. Such a risk they should not be asked to run. He did not believe that the government could expect much support from the courts: juries were unwilling to convict flagrant violators of the laws. He was referring particularly to the Champlain district, but he would have been warranted in saying that there was more human

40 For a general and readable account of trade in this period, see S. E. Morison, *Maritime History of Massachusetts* (1921), ch. XIII. Among the more recent specialized studies are R. D. S. Higham, "The Port of Boston and the Embargo of 1807-1809" (*American Neptune*, July, 1956); J. D. Forbes, "Boston Smuggling, 1807-1815" (*ibid.*, April, 1950).

41 An adequate treatment of Gallatin's relations with the collectors and other minor officials, based on his correspondence with them, would be beyond the scope of this book. See White, *Jeffersonians*, pp. 453-456. I confine myself largely to such things as TJ might have been expected to know.

42 TJ to S. H. Smith of *National Intelligencer*, Aug. 2, 1808, enclosing a notice of this action to be printed (LC, 31808).

sympathy for smugglers almost everywhere than for the government and its representatives.

Appalled by the immensity of the task confronting the government in the northeastern sector, and manifesting rather more pessimism than he was to do at the end of his visit to New York, Gallatin told Jefferson that if the embargo was to be persisted in, two principles must be adopted to make it effective. In the first place, no vessel whatsoever must be permitted to move without special permission from the executive; in the second, the collectors must be given the power to seize property anywhere (including the right to remove rudders from vessels in harbors or otherwise prevent their departure) and these officials must not be liable to personal suits. Then, in words that were destined to be quoted many times in works of history, he set forth the dilemma by which this avowedly liberal and humane administration was confronted. "I am sensible," he said, "that such arbitrary powers are equally dangerous and odious. But a restrictive measure of the nature of the embargo applied to a nation under such circumstances as the United States cannot be enforced without the assistance of means as strong as the measure itself."[43] Also, there must be sufficient physical force to carry the policy into effect. That meant a little army on the Canadian border and a naval patrol off the coast.

This realistic observer did not think they should be greatly surprised at the situation. The powerful British navy could scarcely prevent smuggling, and Napoleon was having great difficulty enforcing his Continental System. Owing in part at least to the Federalists, the embargo was unpopular in certain quarters. The people were confused by the complexity of the orders, decrees, and laws and had no single patriotic object to center on, as they would have had in war. Accordingly, in several districts — especially along the Massachusetts coast and on the Canadian border — selfishness was clearly in the ascendant.

While quicker to acknowledge unpleasant reality than Jefferson and in better position at this time to observe it, Gallatin had a like desire to maintain the peace and still regarded the embargo as the only possible measure by which they could hope to do this. But Congress must either vest the executive with arbitrary power or give up the measure, and in the latter case, unless there should have been a change in the policies of the European powers, he saw no alternative to war. There remained another question: "But with whom?" No encouraging news had come from England, and resentment against the French had increased because of unofficial reports of the Bayonne decree. This was

[43] Gallatin to TJ, July 29, 1808 (*Writings*, I, 398).

an order for the seizure of all American ships in French ports, on the alleged ground that, since they could not sail the seas except in violation of the embargo, they could be assumed to do so on British account or in British connection.[44] Under these doleful circumstances Gallatin saw no choice but for the government to struggle with its difficulties as best it could until the meeting of Congress.

The letter in which he appraised the situation so candidly was nearly two weeks in reaching Jefferson at Monticello. In his prompt reply the President said: "This embargo law is certainly the most embarrassing one we have ever had to execute. I did not expect a crop of so sudden & rank growth of fraud & open opposition by force could have grown up in the U.S."[45] While his lack of reference to any mitigating circumstances suggests that he was rather less tolerant than Gallatin of these manifestations of human self-interest, and he had undoubtedly counted more on patriotic self-sacrifice, he was in full agreement with the Secretary of the Treasury regarding the available alternatives. He had stated in private that the time would come when war would seem preferable to the embargo. In his own region, however, he was sure that this was not yet the case. If the policy should be continued, he agreed that Congress must legalize all the means necessary to attain its purpose. Meanwhile, certain actions had been taken by the executive officers to provide a naval force on the New England coast, where the ships sailing without clearance papers were beyond the control of the collectors.

Before he left Washington, Jefferson had asked the Secretary of the Navy, after consultation with Gallatin, to cause such gunboats as were actually manned and commissioned to be distributed among the bays and ports to aid in the enforcement of the embargo. He named half a dozen places from which complaints of evasion had come, and all of them except Newport were in Massachusetts.[46] Reporting to him about a month later, Gallatin said that only four more gunboats had reached the Massachusetts coast — there were already a couple at Passamaquoddy Bay — and that these had been stationed at Newport,

[44] Madison wrote Armstrong on July 22, 1808, that the Bayonne decree (Apr. 17) had not yet reached the U.S., but that it was "a sweeping stroke at all American vessels on the high seas" (*A.S.P.F.R.*, III, 254–255). No authentic information beyond Armstrong's statements had been received by December, 1808 (*ibid.*, p. 291).

[45] TJ to Gallatin, Aug. 11, 1808 (Ford, IX, 202). He was also replying to Gallatin's letter of Aug. 5 (*Writings*, I, 399–400), received at the same time as that of July 29.

[46] TJ to the Secretary of the Navy, July 16, 1808 (LC, 31698; L. & B., XII, 93, with incorrect designation).

New Bedford, and north and south of the Cape Cod peninsula. But, since they were easily outsailed, he wanted cruising vessels. He acquired larger revenue cutters at Boston, New London, and Portsmouth. Also, he got four cruising vessels from the navy. The smallest of these, the schooner *Revenge*, was set to patrolling the waters around Nantucket and Martha's Vineyard; and the *Chesapeake*, off Block Island, had already done something to redeem her reputation by turning back eight vessels.[47] The sloop *Wasp* and the brig *Argus* were ordered to patrol the coast from Cape Cod to Portland. Before they got to these waters the collector at Gloucester reported forcible opposition to the embargo, and Gallatin had learned of "still more gross proceedings" at Newburyport, a particularly conspicuous center of disaffection and resistance. From there a vessel had sailed "under the protection of a large armed mob assembled on the wharf," which prevented the customs officers from intervening.

At this stage both Gallatin and Jefferson may well have regretted that they did not have more of a navy, though we may doubt if a much larger force could have been effective in view of the opposition to the embargo laws on this coast and the ingenuity of these seafaring people. It would have been impossible, however, for them to engage in exportation under the guise of coastal trade if there had been nothing to export, and, but for the cargoes brought from elsewhere, Massachusetts would have had little or nothing to export but fish. The provisions that finally got into British hands came into the harbors of the state in quantity because of Governor Sullivan's certificates. Shortly before leaving New York for Washington in late September, Gallatin felt compelled to recur to this subject, having been informed, as he wrote Jefferson, that Sullivan continued to issue certificates "pertinaciously."[48] Not only did these create dissatisfaction and operate unfairly; the provisions imported under them were "the foundation of the violations of the embargo" in the state. In a continued effort to meet this problem, Jefferson, despairing of Sullivan, had already turned to Lieutenant Governor Levi Lincoln, whose loyalty to the administration was unquestionable but who gave him little satisfaction in this particular matter. The former Attorney General did not believe that the actual needs of Massachusetts for food could be met under the one-eighth principle, but he was undisposed to assume responsibility for the issuance of certificates.[49] By this time the Governor had become

[47] Gallatin to TJ, Aug. 17, 1808 (*Writings*, I, 406). On the vessels and their disposition see *A.S.P., Naval Affairs*, I, 169.
[48] Gallatin to TJ, Sept. 16, 1808 (*Writings*, I, 418).
[49] TJ to Lincoln, Aug. 22, 1808 (L. & B., XII, 145–147); Lincoln to TJ, Sept. 10 (LC, 32051–32052).

gravely ill, and death wholly removed him from the scene before the end of the year, but on the eve of the congressional session Jefferson and Gallatin were still talking inconclusively about the problems he had created in a region where there were too many of them already.[50] For political, economical, and geographical reasons Massachusetts was a special case. The statement Gallatin made shortly before he left New York may have been too sanguine about the situation elsewhere, but it was significant. Writing Jefferson he said: "With very few exceptions, the embargo is now rigidly enforced in every other port of the sea-border."[51]

Along with the northeastern coast, the Canadian border from Lake Ontario to Lake Champlain and the inefficacy of the embargo there disturbed Gallatin most and argued most strongly against the measure itself. Jefferson said he supposed they could not prevent the things that were happening on the Canada line, but that they must try to "harrass the unprincipled agents" and punish as many as they could.[52] He was referring particularly to armed actions against the collector at the port of Oswego. Both he and Gallatin were disposed to designate them as an insurrection that merited military intervention. The collector, Joel Burt, had confiscated a large shipment of smuggled flour which sixty armed men in ten boats had sought to retrieve. With the aid of the local militia, which he summoned on his own authority, the resolute collector caused them to disperse, but they threatened to return. The situation was called to the attention of Gallatin and Jefferson by the Governor.[53] Tompkins, who was in New York City in August, conferred with Gallatin about the matter, as he also did about delay in the fortification of the harbor, and they both wrote the President.[54] Using language that might have been attributed to Alexander Hamilton, Jefferson wrote the Governor: "I think it so important in example to crush these audacious proceedings, and to make the offenders feel the consequences of individuals daring to oppose a law by force, that no effort should be spared to compass the object." Yet he did not want

---

[50] TJ to Gallatin, Oct. 14, 1808 (L. & B., XII, 169).

[51] Sept. 16, 1808 (*Writings*, I, 418).

[52] TJ to Gallatin, July 29, 1808 (L. & B., XII, 109).

[53] R. W. Irwin, in *Daniel D. Tompkins* (1968), describes the Governor's support of the embargo and the political implications of this (pp. 64–69), and gives an account of the Oswego affair (pp. 70–73). A detailed account of the district in this period is given by I. I. Rubin in his dissertation, "New York State and the Long Embargo" ch. IV; this episode is described on pp. 127–133.

[54] Gallatin to TJ, Aug. 9, 1808 (*Writings*, I, 402–403); Tompkins to TJ, Aug. 9 (LC, 31845–31846).

to issue a proclamation and thus exaggerate the danger; nor did he want the federal government to bear the entire onus of forceful measures. Though clearly influenced by prudential considerations, he was in character in seeking state co-operation. He suggested that the Governor send militia to the troubled area on his own responsibility, and, following Gallatin's recommendation, agreed that the expense of such a detachment should be borne by the federal government. He thought a total of five hundred men would be sufficient.[55] Tompkins, sounding more Jeffersonian than Jefferson, expressed some reluctance at making a display of force, holding that a few convictions would be a more effective deterrent. Apparently he did not realize as fully as Gallatin did how difficult it was to obtain convictions. There were further alarming reports from Oswego, and the Governor did send militia to that point of danger as well as to others.[56] He continued to manifest deep interest in the enforcement of the embargo laws in his state and provided a significant example of co-operation between state and federal governments.

At Gallatin's suggestion, General Wilkinson dispatched regular soldiers, recently recruited in New York, to points of danger in the state. Early in September the Secretary of the Treasury wrote the President that, except at Sackett's Harbor and Oswego, the embargo law was now "carried into effect with as few evasions as could be expected." In the middle of the month, reporting that militia and regulars had either arrived at the Lakes or were on their way there, he expressed the hope that by October everything would be in "tolerable order."[57] Difficulties on the Canadian border were far from over; and recourse to force had been found necessary there, as it had been off the Massachusetts coast, but Gallatin's visit of two months was rather more successful than he expected at its outset. He was troubled, however, by the effects of the embargo on the political fortunes of his party, and at Monticello his chief had been receiving very considerable evidence of unfavorable public opinion.

[55] TJ to Tompkins, Aug. 15, 1808 (L. & B., XII, 131–133).
[56] Tompkins to TJ, Aug. 22, 1808 (LC, 31943).
[57] Gallatin to TJ, Sept. 2, 14, 1808 (*Writings*, I, 414, 417); Gen. Wilkinson to TJ, Sept. 8, 1808 (LC, 32038).

[XXXIII]

Backed to the Wall

ALTHOUGH Jefferson was absorbed in the task of giving complete effect to the embargo laws and insistent on the necessity of subordinating individual interests to the great national objective, it need not be assumed that he had ceased to be sensitive to public opinion. It should be recognized that his means of measuring this were sharply limited during the summer of 1808, when Congress was not in session and, for most of the time, he himself was at Monticello. Latter-day historians, seeking to read the public mind, have had recourse to the newspapers. In that era of political journalism, however, these tended to reflect the respective attitudes of the two contending parties rather than the sentiments of their communities as a whole. Jefferson's opinion of the reliability of the press in matters of fact was never as low as in this period, and he was disposed to minimize the significance of criticism that emanated from his avowed political enemies.

The embargo had been attacked in the opposition press from the beginning and was increasingly an object of ridicule in Federalist circles as the hardships incident to it became more evident. There is no way of knowing whether Jefferson himself read in the *Port Folio* or in a Boston paper the words of a song that was sung on July fourth in New England and was to find its way into later works of history, but it shows the line the Federalists in that region were taking. Of its many stanzas we quote two:

> Our great politicians,
> Those dealers in visions,
>   On *paper*, to all lengths they dare go
> But when call'd to decide,

> Like a *turtle* they hide
>   In their own pretty *shell*, the *Embargo*.
>   . . . .
>
> Our ships, all in motion,
> Once whitened the ocean,
>   They sail'd and returned with a cargo;
> Now doom'd to decay
> They have fallen a prey
>   To Jefferson, worms, and *Embargo*.[1]

Considerable interest still attaches to a satirical poem that appeared in Boston that same summer. This was "The Embargo, or Sketches of Our Times," written by William Cullen Bryant when he was thirteen.[2] This contained an injunction to Jefferson that delighted the young poet's father and was well received in the High Federalist circle in which he moved. After referring to the Chief Executive as a weak and erring ruler who had fled before Tarleton (during the Revolution) and prostrated himself more recently before Napoleon, the precocious boy thus addressed him:

> Go, wretch, resign the presidential chair,
> Disclose thy secret measures foul or fair,
> Go, search, with curious eye, for horned frogs,
> Mongst the wild wastes of Louisianian bogs;
> Or where Ohio rolls his turbid stream,
> Dig for huge bones, thy glory and thy theme;
> Go scan, Philosophist, thy****** charms,
> And sink supinely in her sable arms;
> But quit to abler hands, the helm of state,
> Nor image ruin on thy country's fate.

While this poem reflects an attitude of which Jefferson was doubtless well aware, he is not known ever to have seen it. We must assume that in this period he based his judgment of public opinion on the written communications he is known to have received and must look for clues in his own correspondence. During the first half of the summer these communications seemed to indicate that the embargo continued to be generally approved. From individual sufferers under

---

[1] Quoted in full from *Port Folio*, July 30, 1808, with reference also to Boston *Repertory*, July 15, 1808, in W. W. Jennings, *American Embargo* (1921), pp. 128–129. In ch. V of this work there are numerous quotations from contemporary newspapers. These are not arranged chronologically, however, or according to political alignment.

[2] Editions of 1808 and 1809 are reproduced, with an introduction by T. O. Mabbot, in *Scholars' Facsimiles & Reprints* (Gainesville, Fla., 1955). Account in C. H. Brown, *William Cullen Bryant* (1971), pp. 23–29.

the restrictive laws he received occasional letters of complaint and abuse. Officers of merchant ships in Philadelphia addressed him respectfully and were answered sympathetically, but he made no response to an unemployed seaman in that port who stated that if he should not be driven to cut his own throat he would welcome the opportunity to wring the President's honored neck. Jefferson told Madison that dozens of abusive anonymous messages were to be expected and should be ignored. He may not have kept all of them, but the fact is that there are now relatively few of them in his papers.

The letters he got from his friends and supporters were distinctly encouraging. One of the most heartening was from John Taylor of Caroline, who repeated an anecdote about Nathanael Greene during one of his campaigns in the American Revolution. Touring his camp before dawn one day the General awakened a slumbering officer and asked how he could sleep so peacefully when the army was in such danger. Thereupon the officer replied that it was because he knew General Greene was there. Adopting the same reasoning, John Taylor said that with Jefferson in command he could sleep well.[3] This expression of confidence from his own state was something to cherish, and the harassed President could not have failed to be pleased by the tone and content of the address he received a little earlier from the legislature of distant New Hampshire.[4] Besides a highly complimentary review of his entire administration, this communication contained a pledge of support of the embargo as the law of the land and the "only means that could be devised" to maintain the peace, safety, and honor of the country. Said these memorialists: "We will suffer any privations, rather than submit to degredation and will coöperate with the general government in all its measures." In that New England state the policy of the government was cordially approved by former Senator William Plumer, who had parted company with the High Federalists and who, like Governor Langdon, attributed the clamor in Massachusetts chiefly to the electioneering purposes of designing men.[5]

This was Jefferson's own opinion and he may be blamed for laying too much stress on the political, and too little on the economic, causes of hostility to governmental policy in Massachusetts. Early in the summer, in a letter to an ardent Republican leader in Pennsylvania, he

[3] John Taylor to TJ, July 12, 1808 (LC, 31669).

[4] Dated June 14, 1808 (LC, 31550-31553). TJ acknowledged this Aug. 2, writing both a formal and a private letter to Gov. John Langdon (LC, 31805-31806; Ford, IX, 200-201).

[5] Langdon to TJ, Aug. 13, 1808 (LC, 31877-31879); Plumer to TJ, July 23, 1808 (LC, 31745-31746).

made a distinction between the moderate branch of the opposing party and those whom he called the "federal monarchists." He believed that the latter would welcome any "public calamity," except war with England, which would lessen confidence in the "republican principles and features" of the Constitution.[6] Allowance must be made for the partisan rhetoric into which he was prone to lapse in private correspondence with the faithful, but his judgment that the intransigents would go to almost any length to discredit his conduct of the government was well warranted. Though he did not mention this group by name he must have had them in mind when he said: "They are endeavoring to convince England that we suffer more by the embargo than they do, and that if they will but hold out awhile we must abandon it." These inveterate foes of his were "playing a game of the most mischievous tendency, without perhaps themselves being aware of it," he said, adding that the embargo could be abandoned only for a state of war and that if war with England came these Federalist maneuvers would be responsible for it. He had good reason to suspect some Federalist intrigue with the British and to deplore it on patriotic grounds. But on grounds of principle he could not well object to the flood of addresses and petitions against the embargo that engulfed him at the end of the summer, even though these were instigated by his political enemies, for the right of petition was unquestionable and it was being exercised in a wholly respectful manner by legitimate town meetings.

On August 22, 1808, at Monticello, he received petitions from inhabitants of Boston, Newburyport, and Providence "in legal town meetings assembled." To these he replied four days later.[7] Since he addressed the three town meetings jointly he may be assumed to have recognized that they were acting in concert; and when he received a dozen similar petitions within a week, along with a couple of counter-addresses from his own supporters, it became obvious that a campaign was going on. Writing the publisher of the *National Intelligencer*, he said he was overwhelmed with petitions from Massachusetts. Though he gave the same answers to all of them, they called for more writing than he could get done at Monticello. Therefore, he ordered 150

---

[6] TJ to Michael Leib, June 23, 1808 (Ford, IX, 196–197, where Thomas Leib is incorrectly indicated as the addressee).

[7] These three petitions are in NA, Gen. Record Dept. of State, Misc. Letters, July–Dec., 1808. The one from Boston, dated Aug. 9, was published in the *New England Palladium*, Aug. 12, 1808. TJ's reply of Aug. 26 to the three town meetings is printed in L. & B., XVI, 312–314, and Padover, *Complete Jefferson*, pp. 534–535; original in LC, 31958.

printed copies of a reply to the protesters, and 50 copies of one to the counter-addressers.[8] He made a considerable number of replies before he got these printed ones, and he used up virtually all of the latter. The tide of paper rose rapidly in September, reaching its crest on October 3, when he received 50 protests and 11 counter-addresses. The flow declined thereafter, but by the time Congress convened he had received upwards of 200 of the former and about 50 of the latter. More than ninety percent of them came from Massachusetts.[9]

This campaign started at a town meeting in Boston and the leading Republican paper there attributed it to the Essex Junto.[10] This use of terms was not borne out by the account of the meeting. None of the prominent supporters of the resolutions that were adopted was a member of the Essex Junto and the tone of the address that emanated from this gathering was very different from that of Pickering's letter of the previous spring.[11] This was obviously a Federalist movement, though, and it was clearly expected that the proceedings of this meeting should serve as a model. Copies of them were sent to other towns for concurrence. The resolutions that issued from these differed somewhat. In general they called for the suspension of the embargo as a whole or in part, and some of them asked specifically for the opening of commerce with Spain and Portugal, now in patriotic revolt against Napoleon. The change in the situation in that part of Europe was assigned in the Boston petition as a justification for bringing up the question before the convening of Congress. Some of the petitioners requested the President to call Congress earlier if he himself lacked the authority to suspend or modify the embargo. The preambles varied, but all expressed strong opposition to the existing commercial restrictions as injurious to their particular interests. Christopher Gore was reported to have said in Boston that "we had better be at war with *any power* than in our present situation." But war with Great Britain was not what the Federalist leaders wanted, and these multiplied expressions of discontent, widely publicized in the party press, were unquestionably intended to influence local opinion in the forthcoming

[8] TJ to Samuel Harrison Smith, Sept. 9, 13, 1808 (LC, 32046, 32065).

[9] These figures are largely based on TJ's Index of Correspondence, where he listed, with dates, the protests and counter-addresses and his replies to them. It should be remembered that at this time Maine was part of Massachusetts. Many of these petitions appeared in newspapers.

[10] Boston *Independent Chronicle*, Aug. 11, 1808.

[11] D. H. Fischer, in "The Myth of the Essex Junto" (*W. & M.*, April, 1964, pp. 191–235) does not deal with this particular episode but points out that after 1796 Pickering was one of the few Essexmen not in retirement.

elections. By the same token the addresses from Republican groups were designed to have a counter-effect.[12] In this political struggle the critics of the administration gained a distinct advantage, but the response to their appeal was largely limited to Massachusetts, and it was countered by assurances of support of the administration which, though less numerous, were substantial.

Commenting on Jefferson's reply to the Boston town meeting, the leading Republican paper thanked his political foes for giving him "an opportunity to explain the principles of the embargo."[13] The implication was that he needed a specific occasion. He himself seems to have assumed as much, and, as we have seen, he had left the public defense of the governmental policy to others. He told Madison that he was trying to present "the strongest points in favor of the embargo in a short and clear view."[14] But he had not said that much to Congress as yet or in reply to earlier addresses and resolutions — most of which had been in approval of the policy. Since he made the same response to the other towns that addressed him similarly, this may be regarded as a direct message, and his first one, to the most outspoken opponents of these laws. His response of the same date to the citizens of Boston who had expressed approval of the policy that was being pursued constituted his explanation to his own supporters.[15]

In these communications to foes and friends he took no position that he had not already taken in private letters, but now he belatedly expressed in public his concern at the "inconveniences" to which the whole country was subjected. These he attributed to the circumstances of the times in which they chanced to live — times for which there was no historical parallel. Neither to his critics nor to his supporters did he say that commercial districts were at a special disadvantage, and he reminded the former that the laws of which they complained had been enacted, in response to unrighteous edicts of the chief belligerents, by the persons who had been delegated to exercise legislative powers and whose concern for the common interest could be assumed. That is, these were not *his* laws and they represented *national* policy. Also, he adverted to the difficulty of choosing a course of action. "To

[12] An address from Bostonians who dissented from the opinion of the town meeting appeared in the *Independent Chronicle*, Aug. 15. In that issue and later ones this paper reported refusals to call meetings and meetings that refused to adopt anti-embargo resolutions.

[13] Boston *Independent Chronicle*, Sept. 8, 1808. The specific reference was again to the Junto.

[14] TJ to Madison, Sept. 5, 1808 (L. & B., XII, 156).

[15] TJ to A Portion of the Citizens of Boston, Aug. 26, 1808 (L. & B., XVI, 314-317; Padover, *Complete Jefferson*, pp. 535-536).

have submitted our rightful commerce to prohibitions and tributary exactions from others," he said, "would have been to surrender our independence." The alternative to war that the federal legislature had preferred was to suspend a commerce that was "placed under such unexampled difficulties." Besides saving property and life, this policy had the "peculiar advantage" of giving the belligerents time to revise their conduct.

In his reply to his followers who were supporting this alternative to war he spelled out the disadvantages of the latter to various economic interests and referred, as he was to do increasingly, to the advantages now accruing to manufacturing. He expressed regret that critics of the existing policy were blaming their sufferings, not on the British and French edicts which really caused them, but on laws that had saved them from greater ills. It would be unfortunate, he said, if "their expressions of impatience" should have the effect of prolonging their sufferings by exciting "a fallacious hope" that Americans would ever relinquish their commercial independence. "While these edicts are in force," he asserted confidently, "no American can ever consent to a return of peaceable intercourse with those who maintain them."

The edicts were still in full force and he had no authority to suspend the embargo until they were revoked or modified substantially. Nor would there have been any point in his calling Congress to meet before its appointed date (November 7), since that body could not have been assembled much earlier under existing conditions of communication and transportation. Accordingly, he had no choice but to respond negatively to the petitioners and tell them that existing policy would have to be maintained until those possessing the authority to change it should meet. The promoters of this campaign may have expected a negative reply and have been thinking primarily of influencing public opinion. Gallatin reported at the time that resistance to the embargo in Massachusetts was encouraged by the petitions for its repeal, and these might have been expected to have some effect on the fall elections. Not for some weeks, however, could he and Jefferson hope to learn just what this would be.

During his last days at home before his return to Washington, Jefferson may have had to spend most of his working hours answering petitions from Massachusetts, but he got away from his writing desk long enough to witness the wedding of his eldest grandchild in the parlor at Monticello. Anne Cary Randolph was seventeen and Charles Lewis Bankhead twenty when they were married in mid-September. More than any of the other children she seems to have shared her grandfather's interests in the world of plants. Grandpapa, as they called him, left the flowers to her particular care. He gave no intimation that she herself had been plucked too soon, but as usual he sought to maintain the full family circle as long as possible. The couple spent the winter with the young man's parents at Port Royal, but Jefferson counted on having them back in Albemarle when he himself should return. Writing Anne in November, he said: "I trust it is Mr. Bankhead's intention to join us at Monticello in March and to take his station among my law books in the South pavilion."[16] During the fall he became reasonably assured that such would be the case. Fortunately he did not anticipate that the young husband would not like the law and that because of his intemperance this promising marriage would eventuate in great unhappiness.

Anne's younger brother, Thomas Jefferson Randolph, known in the family as Jefferson and now aged fifteen, accompanied his grandfather to Washington en route to Philadelphia, where he was to take up lodgings for the winter with Charles Willson Peale. This big, good-natured boy had been at the school of James Ogilvie, a competent teacher, at Milton near Monticello. His grandfather did not hope to make a scholar of this outdoor lad, nor did he want him to acquire city habits which would not contribute to his future happiness or usefulness in the country. Therefore, only one season in Philadelphia was being planned for. During this he could attend lectures at the University of Pennsylvania in those branches of science that could not be taught so advantageously elsewhere in America as in Philadelphia. Writing Peale, the grandfather said: "These are Natural history with the advantage of your Museum, Botany aided by Mr. Hamilton's garden, and Anatomy with the benefits of actual dissections."[17] The President had consulted his friends and colleagues in the American Philosophical Society, Doctors Caspar Wistar and Benjamin S. Barton, about the professional aspects of this program, and he believed that in Peale's household the boy would enjoy the same degree of physical and moral safety as in his own home.

Peale gladly agreed to treat Jefferson's grandson and namesake as he would his own sons. His wife, though of a mild and indulgent disposition, would suffer no impropriety of conduct in her household, he said. Presumably without consulting her he added: "She is plain but cheerful, belonging to the Society of the Quakers, without the rigidity of

16 TJ to Anne Cary Bankhead, Nov. 8, 1808 (*Family Letters*, p. 357, with reference to wedding of Sept. 19, 1808, in note).
17 TJ to C. W. Peale, Aug. 24, 1808 (LC, 31952).

some of them."[18] About the middle of October young Randolph set out for Philadelphia, bearing a memorandum from his grandfather and letters to Peale and Caspar Wistar. With the former the President sent an order on the Bank of the United States for $100, as a first installment on the boy's expenses (all of which except those for clothes and pocket money he expected to meet); and in the letter he described rather more fully than elsewhere his purposes in this educational venture. After another year he planned for his grandson to go to the College of William and Mary, where the teaching of mathematics, natural philosophy, and chemistry was good and he could become acquainted with contemporaries from his own state. Dr. Wistar afterwards gained Jefferson's rather reluctant consent to the inclusion of chemical lectures in the Philadelphia program. For a scientific man in a town, said the author of Notes on Virginia, chemistry offered a specially convenient amusement since it could be pursued in one's own cabinet, but for a country gentleman he knew of no source of amusement and health comparable to botany and natural history. The botanical lectures were not to begin until spring, and the course the youth pursued came nearer being premedical than anything else. Actually he matriculated in the medical school, and one gains the impression that he took on more than he could well handle. His grandfather remained in close touch with him, as indeed that gentleman did with the other members of his little family during his last fall and winter in Washington. More than ever before he needed to.[19]

Speaking of this period years later, Jefferson said: "I felt the foundations of the government shaken under my feet by the New England townships."[20] But if he was perturbed to this degree while answering petitions in September, 1808, the political events of the next few weeks should have been reassuring with respect to nearly all the rest of the country and rather less discouraging with respect to New England than he and Gallatin may have expected.

The fact that Madison carried only Vermont of the New England states in the presidential election may be attributed to the embargo and effective campaigning by the Federalists, but wherever there was a

[18] C. W. Peale to TJ, Sept. 1, 1808 (LC, 31995).
[19] Memo of TJ to T. J. Randolph, Oct. 13, 1808 (Family Letters, pp. 350-351); TJ to C. W. Peale and to Caspar Wistar, Oct. 12 (LC, 32193, 32194). TJ to T. M. Randolph, Nov. 22 (LC, 32402). In these and other letters he made many fascinating comments on subjects of study.
[20] TJ to J. C. Cabell, Feb. 2, 1816 (L. & B., XIV, 422).

popular vote the margin was slight.[21] It would appear that the results of the Federalist campaign of protest fell below expectations, and that in the region where opposition to the embargo was most vocal and most vigorous the bulk of the Republicans continued to support the government during the summer and fall. The merchants of Massachusetts themselves were not unanimous in opposing its policy. In the spring the Republicans had suffered a great loss in the death of Jacob Crowninshield while he was attending Congress. This influential merchant of Salem, who emphasized the importance of the Continental market for American exports, did not fit into the pro-British pattern. Neither did William Gray, the largest merchant in the state, who supported the embargo though charged with being a renegade for so doing. Furthermore, there appears to have been more nationalistic spirit in New England than men like Pickering allowed for.[22]

As for the rest of the country, Delaware was Federalist as in 1804, and the presidential candidate of the opposition, Charles C. Pinckney, picked up a few votes in Maryland and North Carolina, but Madison's election by a vote of 122 to 49 could be interpreted as approval of the administration. The extent of this victory was not known when Congress met, but victory was anticipated by then and was authoritatively reported in a couple of weeks. The election was not a referendum on the embargo, but the President had good reason to believe that most of the country was still behind him. The weakness of his position did not lie in the lack of domestic support up to this point; it lay in the failure of his policy to make any significant impression abroad. He erred on the side of understatement when he said, soon after the congressional session began, that the situation was truly difficult. This was partly because of the problem of enforcement, to be sure, but he laid the main emphasis elsewhere. "We have been pressed by the belligerents to the very wall," he said, "and all further retreat [is] impracticable."[23] He had been back in Washington almost a month and the congressional session was about a week away when dispatches from France and England reported official reaction in those countries to the embargo as a diplomatic weapon. Borne from Le Havre and Cowes by the packet schooner *Hope,* they belied that

[21] A convenient account of the elections of 1808, showing the different ways in which presidential electors were then chosen, is in C. O. Paullin, *Atlas of the Historical Geography of the U.S.* (1932), p. 94. In New England electors were chosen by general ticket — i.e., by popular vote — in only New Hampshire and Rhode Island, in both of which the vote was close.

[22] Paul Goodman, in *Democratic-Republicans of Mass.* (1964), ch. VIII, esp. pp. 188–197, admirably describes and discusses political sentiment in this period.

[23] TJ to Levi Lincoln, Nov. 13, 1808 (Ford, IX, 228).

name, being in both cases negative and disappointing.[24] On reading them the President and his advisers learned that American overtures had been completely ignored by one government and flatly rejected by the other.

In its negotiations with the French the government drew a complete blank. Following Madison's instructions, Armstrong protested belatedly but vigorously against Champagny's extraordinary letter of January 15. In this the French Foreign Minister, after arrogantly asserting that the United States must inevitably declare war on Great Britain, stated that American ships in French harbors would be sequestered until the disposition of their country should become known. That is, they were threatened with confiscation if the United States did not declare war. Quite properly the American Minister rejected this blackmail and claimed for his country the right to make its own decisions with respect to peace and war, but Armstrong received no reply to his request for an explanation.[25]

Contemptuousness of this sort injured the French cause in the United States and tended to neutralize anti-British feeling. But, judging from a report to Jefferson by Robert R. Livingston of an interview he had with Napoleon before leaving France, the Emperor had no expectation that the North American Republic would go to war with Great Britain. In the lack of warships that would be quite impracticable, and, according to this report which Jefferson himself found credible, Napoleon regarded the embargo as a wise measure.[26] Jefferson recognized that it was more injurious to the British than to the French, and we may wonder what he thought his government really had to offer Napoleon. One immediate occasion for remonstrance against the French was provided by the capture and burning of four American ships on the high seas by order of Rear Admiral Baudin.[27] The American authorities distinguished between this sort of action, which they described as contrary to international law, and actions in French ports, in accordance with "municipal regulations." The latter could be recognized as being legal, even though unkind, and thus be tolerated.[28]

[24] The *Hope* arrived in New York the morning of Oct. 26, and the bearers of the dispatches reached Washington Oct. 29 (*National Intelligencer*, Oct. 31, 1808).

[25] Armstrong to Champagny, July 4, 1808 (*A.S.P.F.R.*, III, 254), replying to Champagny's letter of Jan. 15 (*ibid.*, 248-249).

[26] R. R. Livingston to TJ, Sept. 22, 1808, received Oct. 3 (LC, 32112-32113); TJ to Livingston, Oct. 15 (Ford, IX, 209-210).

[27] Armstrong to Champagny, July 10, 1808 (*A.S.P.F.R.*, III, 253).

[28] Madison to Armstrong, July 21, 1808; Armstrong to Champagny, Aug. 6 (*ibid.*, 254-255); TJ to Livingston, Sept. 13 (Ford, IX, 210).

The United States was chiefly objecting to what Jefferson called piracy on the high seas. In his opinion this was not much to ask the French to give up, and if the British would make no comparable concession they would have to face the consequences.

Armstrong may have been less diligent than he should have been, but he had little opportunity to pursue this line of reasoning. His protests and representations met with no response whatever, and by the end of the summer he was prepared to give this line up. To Madison he wrote in confidence: "We have somewhat overrated our means of coercing the two great belligerents to a course of justice. The embargo is a measure calculated, above any other, to keep us whole and keep us in peace; but, beyond this, you must not count upon it. Here it is not felt, and in England (in the midst of the more recent and interesting events of the day) it is forgotten." He favored the abandonment of the embargo and the adoption of an armed-ship policy, followed by even stronger measures. He did not describe these beyond saying "we ought not to omit doing all we can, because it is believed here that we cannot do much, and even that we will not do what we have the power of doing."[29]

He was not being very helpful. His superiors in America were convinced that the arming of merchant ships would inevitably lead to collision with one belligerent or the other and thus result in war. No doubt he correctly reported the impression of American pacifism that had been created abroad by what had been said at home, but Madison clearly recognized this particular dilemma. Writing Jefferson about the latter's defense of the embargo in reply to protesters in New England, he sagaciously observed: "It is a nice task to speak of war so as to impress our own people with a dislike to it, and not impress foreign Governments with the idea that they may take advantage of the dislike."[30] Viewed in retrospect this appears to have been in fact a task that bordered on the impossible.

William Pinkney, in England, was under no illusion with respect to British fears of American military and naval might, actual or potential, but he believed that the embargo was hurting Britain economically, and at the end of the summer he saw no reason to change American policy because of anything that had happened in Europe. (His particular reference was to developments in Spain, which Madison among others expected to encourage the British and strengthen their resistance to American pressure.) Furthermore, he continued to believe the

[29] Armstrong to Madison, Aug. 30, 1808 (*A.S.P.F.R.*, III, 256).
[30] Madison to TJ, Sept. 7, 1808 (LC, 32034).

embargo better than any alternative policy.[31] Although he came to believe that Canning had been deliberately procrastinating, he was not ignored by that minister. They had three conferences during the summer and exchanged formal communication in the end.[32] The two men were not in full agreement on what was said at these meetings, as the contentious letters that afterwards passed between them clearly showed. That correspondence illustrates the skill of both men in disputation, but it had no bearing on developments in Washington. Our concern, therefore, is with the official correspondence that reached the American capital shortly before Congress met.

In his written presentation of his country's case Pinkney saw no need to go beyond what Madison had already said in his letter to Erskine about the injustice of the British Orders in Council. This letter had been duly communicated to Canning, who had had plenty of time to read it. What Pinkney did was to offer, in return for the revocation of these Orders insofar as they related to the United States, a suspension of the embargo as it affected Great Britain. In his official letter he referred in general terms to the resulting benefits to the British vis-à-vis the French, claiming that he had illustrated them in their previous conversations. Canning questioned the extent of these illustrations and gave no sign that he was at all impressed by them. He declined to connect the Orders in Council and the embargo in any way. The former, he asserted, were in justifiable retaliation against French action, and if incidental damage was done other parties, it was from the French that they should seek redress. Taking the same line as the High Federalists, he denied that the embargo was occasioned by the British Order of November, 1807, since official notice of it had not been received when the measure was passed. In any case he dismissed the measure as a municipal ordinance to which his government was indifferent, though it would welcome the removal of this inconvenient restriction on Americans themselves. Finally, he observed that no reference had been made to the presidential proclamation excluding British warships from American waters, which he regarded as an unnatural act.

Canning's sarcasm and arrogance of tone were infuriating to Americans and seemed quite unnecessary to some of his own countrymen. In his earlier conversations with Pinkney he had showed no such con-

[31] Pinkney's position was well described in his letter of Sept. 21, 1808, to Madison (*A.S.P.F.R.*, III, 228–230). This was written before he got Canning's of Sept. 23, rejecting his overture, but he indicated no change of opinion when sending all this correspondence to Madison Sept. 24 (*ibid.*, 230–232).

[32] Their interviews were on June 29, July 22, 29. Pinkney wrote Canning Aug. 23, and Canning, returned from a vacation, replied in two letters on Sept. 23.

WILLIAM PINKNEY
Engraving from an original painting by Alonzo Chappel
From E. A. Duyckinck, *National Portrait Gallery of Eminent Americans* (1862)

temptuousness, and there was actually some sentiment within the government to modify the Orders in Council so that they would be less offensive to Americans while accomplishing their intended purpose against the French. But this prestige-conscious government would yield not a whit under pressure. In fact the economic pressure had not been fully felt as yet, and reports of Americans suffering under and in opposition to the embargo had been relayed by Federalist Anglophiles and by the British Minister, who could almost be described as pro-American. Recalcitrance seemed a safe policy since the "Yankees" were expected to cave in first. Under these circumstances, what Canning referred to as Pinkney's overture appears to have been doomed before it was put into writing; and, as things turned out, the power-conscious Foreign Secretary left the feeble American government no way to yield without losing face.[33]

These discouraging dispatches reached Washington while the President was preparing his eighth and last annual message to the Legislature. As usual he consulted Gallatin and Madison about it.[34] The discussion of foreign affairs, which had to be "remodeled" in the light of the latest information, was the most important part of the message. Commenting on an early draft of this, Gallatin observed that the "proposition" to the belligerent powers should be stated more explicitly and more clearly. One may doubt if this fault was overcome in the final draft, but the official documents that accompanied the message fully described the representations of the government, and the most important thing the President had to report was that a "candid and liberal experiment" had failed. That is, the overtures to the foreign governments had failed. The President laid no blame for this on any of his countrymen. The citizens in general had borne the privations of the embargo with patriotism, he said. As might have been expected, he

33 For an admirable summary of these negotiations and developments from the British point of view see Perkins, *Prologue to War*, pp. 175-177, 203-206.

34 The message of Nov. 8, 1808, is in Ford, IX, 213-225, drafts by Madison and Gallatin being given in a note. From an examination of the documents themselves it appears that TJ made a draft and sent this first to Gallatin. The latter made extensive comments on it, beginning them before the arrival of the *Hope* and completing them thereafter (LC, 32715-32718, undated). In Gallatin, *Writings*, I, 421-426, they are dated Nov. 2, 1808, but TJ sent them or some of them along with his draft to Madison, who returned them Oct. 30. Madison afterwards revised the first two paragraphs of TJ's draft in view of the dispatches brought by the *Hope* (Madison to TJ, Oct. 30, 1808 (LC, 32303; notes, LC, 32470-32475, final 3 pages omitted by Ford). TJ appears to have revised the whole. (LC, 182:20251-20255 — originally bound and numbered incorrectly. Discarded pages from original draft LC, 182:32344).

pointed out that there had been compensations. His reference to one of these, the rise of manufacturing, which was now being much talked of, was toned down at Gallatin's suggestion and left until almost the end of the message. He was now being charged with willingness to sacrifice commerce to manufacturing, and his sagacious Secretary of the Treasury wanted no contrast between them to be drawn. Jefferson himself, minimizing divisiveness, was claiming that the embargo had demonstrated to the citizenry "the necessity of uniting in support of the laws and the rights of their country."

The embargo laws were still on the books, and some people who specially disliked them said that this message clearly showed that Jefferson intended to continue them. One such commentator also expressed the opinion that "much darkness and uncertainty" prevailed in his Cabinet.[35] Whatever may have been the state of the President's mind, he did not reveal it here. He said that the decision rested with "the wisdom of Congress" what best to do in these troubled circumstances. That representative body must compare and choose between the painful alternatives. "Considering the extraordinary character of the times in which we live," he said, "our attention should unremittingly be fixed on the safety of our country." He made a last plea for the improvement of the militia system, but his report on national defenses was not unfavorable. The authorized work on fortifications was going forward, though still unfinished at New York and New Orleans where most was required. Enough gunboats had been built for the present, and the recruitment of regular soldiers was proceeding.[36] Considering the difficulties with which the administration was confronted, this was a respectable as well as a candid report. The same was true of what, pending a later and much fuller report by Gallatin, he said about finances. Including the payment to be made early in the next year, more than thirty-three and a half millions of the public debt would have been paid off, and there would be a surplus of more than eight and a half millions. He did not enter into the question whether the Treasury could support a war or a continuance of the embargo, although Gallatin had advised him that in neither case would the revenue be sufficient. Instead, looking ahead to the time when the "freedom and safety" of commerce would be restored, and anticipating further surpluses, he suggested the application of these to education and internal improvements.[37] He probably referred at this time to

[35] Samuel Taggart, Nov. 17, 1808 (*Amer. Antiq. Soc. Procs.*, XXXIII, 318).
[36] For military details, see ch. XXVIII above.
[37] On internal improvements, see ch. XXX, above.

the subject, which was so close to his heart and that of Gallatin, because it would be his last chance to do so.

Despite his reference to the future the message can be best described as a low-keyed report dealing with the past. From it no one would have supposed that these were times that tried men's souls, and it was not calculated to stir their blood. Not inappropriately, in this last annual message, the retiring President expressed to the legislators his thanks and good wishes. But in more ways than one his message was a valedictory. In view of later events it may be said to have marked the end of his presidential leadership.

⌜XXXIV⌝

Hors de Combat

A FEW days after Jefferson sent his last annual message to the federal legislature, at the beginning of what he called the congressional campaign, he let it be known privately that he would have no part in this. He described himself as now "but a spectator" on the public scene.[1] In the present situation he thought it fair, he said, "to leave to those who are to act on them the decisions they prefer." He was even more explicit a few weeks later when he said: "I have thought it right to take no part myself in proposing measures, the execution of which will devolve on my successor. I am therefore chiefly an unmeddling listener to what others say."[2] His term still had several months to run, but in the language of a later day he was a "lame-duck" President, and now that Madison's election was unquestionable he was, or claimed to be, acutely conscious of his own superfluity.

To be sure, he had never had any real doubt who his successor would be, and during the past year he may have deferred to Madison more than previously. Until he began to answer petitioners from Massachusetts, his Secretary of State rather than he had been the spokesman of the administration with respect to the embargo, and the case of the government was much more fully presented in Madison's dispatches than in anything from the President's own pen. Early in the summer the French Minister had asserted that Madison's influence became greater as the election drew near. Indeed, Turreau went so far as to say that it was necessary to act from then on "as if he were President."[3] This observation was premature, but Jefferson, who had not forgotten the obstructive actions of John Adams in the last weeks

---

[1] TJ to Lt. Gov. Levi Lincoln, Nov. 13, 1808 (Ford, IX, 227–228). The first part of this letter bore on the enforcement of the embargo in Massachusetts.

[2] TJ to George Logan, Dec. 27, 1808 (L. & B., XII, 219–220).

[3] Turreau to Champagny, June 28, 1808 (quoted by Brant, IV, 451).

of his administration, unquestionably wanted to spare his own successor all possible embarrassment. Quite properly he said: "I should not feel justified in directing measures which those who are to execute these would disapprove." He was undoubtedly thinking not only of Madison but of Gallatin, whose continued prominence in the government he assumed. No basic differences in policy between him and these devoted colleagues were voiced when he was drafting his annual message. A difference regarding tactics soon appeared, however. He had referred the crucial question of the hour to Congress without executive recommendation, but both of his trusted lieutenants were of the opinion that he should make one.

Two days after he declared himself to be a mere spectator he received from Gallatin a letter in which Madison, who was then unwell, fully concurred.[4] They both believed that "some precise and distinct course" should be pointed out to the legislature. "As to what that should be," said the Secretary of the Treasury, "we may not all perfectly agree." In fact the member of the Cabinet with whom Gallatin was least compatible, Robert Smith, the Secretary of the Navy, had already proposed to Jefferson that he recall Pinkney and Armstrong and prepare for war.[5] Continuing, Gallatin said: "I feel myself nearly as undetermined between enforcing the embargo or war as I was on our last meeting. But I think that we must (or rather you must) decide the question absolutely, so that we may point out a decisive course either way to our friends." He thought they should have a meeting — and the sooner the better — but Jefferson appears to have paid no heed whatsoever to this suggestion. There may have been meetings of executive officers which were not recorded, but no "precise and distinct course" was recommended to Congress by the President.

It can be argued that he did not really mean what he said about his role. He was always disposed to minimize his personal influence on the Legislature and, in speaking of the restrictive laws by which the embargo policy was implemented, he made a point of referring to these as congressional acts. It is conceivable that, while seeming to leave to Congress the choice between unpalatable alternatives, he expected to influence that body in devious ways and to attain his own wishes in the end. His inveterate enemies would have agreed that this was quite in his hypocritical character, and historians have often given the impression, unwittingly perhaps, that during this final congressional session he *sought* to direct the legislators even though he ultimately failed to do so. What he said privately to individual members of

4 Gallatin to TJ, Nov. 15, 1808 (*Writings*, I, 428).
5 Robert Smith to TJ, Nov. 1, 1808 (LC, 32325).

Congress in these last weeks is no more a matter of record than his own thoughts are, but the word got out that he was not committing himself on the main issue, and, while it is difficult to prove a negative, it does appear that he kept as aloof as possible from the struggle over policy during this congressional session. He was much occupied with official drudgery, especially with respect to the continued enforcement of the embargo, but he seems to have done all he could to avoid decision-making. Accordingly, he laid himself open to the charge of abdicating the responsibilities of his office.[6]

Jefferson's enemies had long contended that he could not really face a crisis. They had been saying since 1796 that his retirement from the governorship of Virginia during the Revolution at the time of Tarleton's raid was proof of this.[7] Actually he showed more courage and presence of mind than the legislators in that chaotic situation, but circumstances had caused him to look unheroic, and, facing a situation with which he could not cope, he was indubitably relieved to get out of it. One may doubt if anybody could have really coped with that situation or with the one he was now facing, but there were men of lesser stature than he who were, or seemed to be, less unhappy in a storm.

It does not appear to have been wholly fortuitous that, in a letter to his grandson in this period, he strikingly, even extravagantly, expressed his dislike of personal controversy.[8] A major purpose of this excessively didactic letter was to put this relatively innocent boy on guard against moral dangers he might encounter in Philadelphia. But, besides urging his namesake to maintain good humor and good manners, the chief executive of the United States enjoined him to avoid all disputation. One result of this advice, as the grandson afterwards reported, was to keep the boy from rushing to his grandfather's defense when attacked. In the context of its time it suggests the author's extreme distaste for the bickerings of politicians and his longing for a life marked by dispassionate reasoning and personal consideration such as he had not found in public office.

When longing to get out of the secretaryship of state, he had said: "The motion of my blood no longer keeps time with the tumult of the world."[9] At the age of fifty he had allowed himself a good deal of poetic license, but he was now sixty-five and presumably even more

---

[6] This charge is made bitterly by Henry Adams in Life of Gallatin, p. 377; and History, IV, 354–360). Adams holds, however, that in effect TJ exerted his influence to prevent change.

[7] See ch. l, p. 15, above.

[8] TJ to T. J. Randolph, Nov. 24, 1808 (Family Letters, pp. 362–365).

[9] TJ to Madison, June 9, 1793 (Ford, VI, 291).

fatigued with administration and controversy. He would unquestionably have rejoiced if he could have served under a system requiring retirement at that age. And if he had operated under a modern parliamentary system, his government might have been expected to resign when the futility of its embargo policy became known or strongly suspected. Under the rigid American system, however, he could not hope to throw off his shackles until March 4.

He had been exhausted at the end of the last congressional session, and, occupied with the enforcement of the embargo, he had not had a restful summer. During October, however, he appears to have been his usual cheerful self. Mrs. Albert Gallatin's niece, who had dinner at the President's House, described him as a "tall thin man not very dignified in his appearance but very agreeable in his manners." His face was scarcely wrinkled; he seemed very happy; he stooped very much but held his head high.[10] Toward the end of the month he was prevented from attending the races by an attack of rheumatism, but, even before he received his daughter's recommendation that he do so, he applied flannel to his aching back and toasted himself before the fire. As a result the attack lasted only four days and probably did not appreciably interfere with the preparation of his message to Congress.[11] A much longer period of confinement began about the time he received Gallatin's written suggestion that he speak more decisively respecting the embargo. He had no such misfortunes with his teeth as George Washington had, but at this juncture he appears to have had an abscess. He had an extraction and was confined to the house for about six weeks with a swollen jaw.[12]

On Christmas Day, while he was still housebound, he remarked to his ancient friend Charles Thomson of the Continental Congress that he was sensible of decline in the power of walking and that his memory was less trustworthy than in the past, but that he had "enjoyed as uniform health through life as reason could desire." In view of the activities in which he was to engage during the seventeen years after his retirement, it could hardly be claimed that his strength was seriously impaired.[13] It may be noted, however, that he was now older

[10] From "Diary of Frances Few" (*Jour. Sou. Hist.*, XXIX, 350).

[11] Letters of Oct. 25–Nov. 1, 1808, in *Family Letters*, pp. 354–356.

[12] Reference to payments of two and five dollars to Dr. Bruff (Account Book, Nov. 18, 30, 1808); TJ to Martha, Dec. 6; to Ellen Wayles, Dec. 20 (*Family Letters*, pp. 368–373). One must reconcile with these events as best one can his statement of March 21, 1819, to Dr. Vine Utley: "I have not yet lost a tooth by age" (Ford, X, 126).

[13] TJ to Chas. Thomson, Dec. 25, 1808 (Ford, IX, 234). As secretary of the Continental Congress, Thomson signed the Declaration of Independence.

than George Washington was at the corresponding point in his administration, when in Jefferson's opinion things got out of that great man's control. Years afterward, speaking of Washington in his second term, he said that "a listlessness of labor, a desire for tranquility had crept on him, and a willingness to let others act and even think for him."[14] He himself had endured no comparable physical hardships, and obviously he did not decline so fast, but in certain respects he seems to have been unwittingly describing himself during his last months in office. He was now letting others speak for him at any rate.

His physical situation at this season may have reminded him of another period of incarceration. Following his retirement from the governorship of Virginia under a cloud nearly three decades before, he had been thrown from his horse and incapacitated for six weeks.[15] That fall proved nothing about his horsemanship, which in fact was admirable, but in some sense it symbolized the state of helplessness and indignity into which fate had thrust him. Now, deprived of the daily ride by which he renewed his strength, the old Patriot was unheroically nursing his swollen jaw in the President's House. Nobody seems to have pointed out the parallel, and no doubt opinions would have differed as to whether he had been unhorsed or had voluntarily dismounted, but he was *hors de combat* in either case.

It should be observed that, while Jefferson had had influence over Congress which was to be matched by no successor in his century, his power and prestige at their highest point were not at all comparable to those of a President in the latter half of the twentieth century. It is inconceivable that even in foreign affairs he would have disregarded Congress. Even in a less critical situation one would have expected him to inform himself as best as he could of congressional opinion — that is, the opinion of the Republican majority. One way of doing that would have been to enlarge on Gallatin's suggestion by calling a conference of legislative leaders *and* executive officers. But, conscious as he was of the legislators' jealousy of their prerogatives and of the virtually universal devotion to the doctrine of separation of powers — a devotion bordering on fanaticism — he generally sought to keep his relations with congressional leaders informal and confidential. No doubt he figured that Gallatin, who was visited nightly at home by some of

[14] From the introduction to the *Anas*, dated Feb. 4, 1818 (Ford, I, 168).
[15] See *Jefferson the Virginian*, p. 358.

the most influential, could sound these men out. And, recognizing that he was nearing the end of his own resources, he may have concluded that his chief lieutenants could now handle this crucial problem better than he could anyway. He appears to have been excessively scrupulous in observing the proprieties, but, although the domestic situation was serious, the country was in no immediate danger from abroad.

His "abdication" of presidential leadership seems to have occasioned little complaint or even notice at the time. A leading Federalist congressman, Josiah Quincy of Massachusetts, referring with nostalgia to the leadership of President John Adams in his time of troubles, averred that no mighty action could be expected of the "dish of skim milk" that was now "curdling at the head of our nation."[16] But the characteristic Federalist lament was that there was too much leadership on the part of this President, not too little. Congressional Republicans, although rather disorganized at the opening of the session, do not seem to have bemoaned the lack of leadership from the Executive. This may have been because things largely followed their customary course. Committees sought counsel from departmental heads, especially Gallatin, in whose recommendations Madison concurred. In one respect, however, the situation differed importantly from that in Jefferson's heyday. He had yielded the initiative. This lay with Congress during the rest of his administration and his successor did not really regain it.

One effect of Jefferson's negative procedure was to delay matters. His foes charged him with seeking to postpone a disagreeable decision until after his term was over, and it would have been natural for him to wish that. But he was generally disposed to fall back on procrastination when in doubt, and he believed that it was still in the best interest of the country to play for time. In private he continued to say that, since submission was inconceivable, the choice lay between embargo and war. But he was willing to give his trusted lieutenants a free hand in trying to find a more palatable alternative and to permit them to get what they could out of Erskine. The net result was that, despite considerable divergence of opinion among party members and leaders in Congress, a strategy was formulated and sustained through about half of the session. Essentially it was a holding operation and it could be identified with both the party and the administration. The distinction between the outgoing and incoming administrations was imperceptible, and it is not to be supposed that Jefferson was ignored by his successors-designate. He did not claim that he wholly refrained from

---

[16] Josiah Quincy to John Adams, Dec. 15, 1808 (Quincy, *Life*, p. 146).

expressing his opinions to them, and they never denied him their full respect. But from this time onward the course of public events was determined by persons other than and forces beyond himself.

ii

New England Federalists in Congress lost no time in introducing resolutions for the unqualified repeal of the embargo. In the House the Republican majority blocked debate on the motion of Congressman Chittenden of Vermont and permanently tabled it early in the new year. In the Senate the resolution of Hillhouse of Connecticut was defeated by a strict party vote after a debate that was unusually well reported.[17] That the party line was holding fast in that chamber was shown by the votes of the New England Republicans against repeal, but both in Congress and the country the sectional alignment on this question was clearly visible. To be sure there were exceptions — such as John Randolph — but by and large Southerners supported the embargo. It was reported that this was true of even Charles Cotesworth Pinckney, recent Federalist candidate for President who chanced also to be a South Carolinian. According to other and later reports, the middle and western states were "ready to unite in any measure."[18] One reason frequently given for the relative complacency of representatives of the middle states was the growth of manufacturing in their region, especially in Pennsylvania. Senator Hillhouse of Connecticut found this an occasion for alarm, not gratification. In his opinion the embargo, which had accomplished none of its avowed purposes and could not be expected to do so, was really designed to "put down commerce and set up manufactures."[19] By contrast, William Branch Giles, the most conspicuous senatorial spokesman of the Republican establishment at this stage, claimed that Southerners endured the embargo "out of regard to *their Eastern friends*," since it made little difference to them who carried their produce to market.[20]

At Gallatin's suggestion, Jefferson had toned down the references to manufacturing in his annual message so as to avoid the impression of siding with it against commerce, but soon thereafter he added a bit of

[17] Resolution introduced in the House by Chittenden Nov. 10, 1808; permanently tabled Jan. 5, 1809 (*Annals*, 10 Cong., 2 sess., p. 982). Resolution of Hillhouse introduced in Senate Nov. 11; defeated Dec. 2 by a vote of 25 to 6 (*ibid.*, p. 230).
[18] Joseph Story to Joseph White, Jr., Jan. 4, 1809 (Story, *Life*, I, 174).
[19] In speech of Nov. 21, 1808 (*Annals*, 10 Cong., 2 sess., p. 27).
[20] Entry of Nov. 13 in the diary of Josiah Quincy, reporting a visit from Giles (Quincy, *Life*, p. 143).

tinder to this particular controversy by an action that he himself regarded as wholly patriotic. Having been told that the best fine cloth in the United States was made at the factory of Colonel David Humphreys near New Haven, he ordered enough of it to make a coat. "Homespun is become the spirit of the times," he said. "I think it an useful one, and therefore that it is a duty to encourage it by example." Whether he got cloth of deep blue, as he preferred, or had to content himself with black, is uncertain, but apparently he received it soon enough to be made up for New Year's Day. He thanked Humphreys in due course and in so doing reaffirmed certain current views of his about the economy.[21]

It can hardly be claimed that this lover of the land was greeting the industrial age with enthusiasm, but in his concern for national independence he had come to embrace the concept of economic nationalism. As an advocate of economic self-sufficiency he was quite out of sympathy with commercial men who were jealous of manufacturing. They had some ground for believing him relatively indifferent to them, for he undoubtedly regarded those engaged in the carrying trade as the main cause of the international difficulties which had beset the country. But he was chiefly grieved with them at this moment for not taking a national view of things.

The portions of the President's message relating to foreign affairs and the embargo were referred to special committees in the House and Senate respectively, and in each instance the chairman took counsel with Gallatin. The subsequent report in the House, which is commonly referred to by the name of Chairman Campbell, was written by Gallatin; and his recommendations regarding the enforcement of the laws were fully reported by Chairman Giles in the Senate.[22]

In the former document the Secretary of the Treasury, whose appointment as the next Secretary of State may have been determined on by this time, presented with great ability the American case against the British and the French. In so doing he naturally drew extensively on Madison's dispatches and he may be assumed to have spoken for them both.[23] After considering various alternatives he concluded that

---

[21] TJ to Abraham Bishop, Nov. 13 and Dec. 8, 1808; to Col. Humphreys, Jan. 20, 1809 (Ford, IX, 225–226 and note; LC, 32513). See also TJ to Thomas Leiper, Jan. 21, 1809 (L. & B., XII, 237–238).

[22] Campbell's Report of Nov. 22, 1808, is in Gallatin, *Writings*, I, 435–446, and *Annals*, 10 Cong., 2 sess., pp. 514–521. Gallatin's recommendations are in his letter of Nov. 24 to Giles (*Writings*, I, 428–435). They were reported to the Senate Dec. 8 (*Annals*, 10 Cong., 2 sess., pp. 232–236).

[23] Brant, *Madison*, p. 471, says it was practically a joint product.

they would have to choose between "abject and degrading submission, war with both nations, or a continuance and enforcement of the present suspension of commerce." This was precisely what Jefferson had said repeatedly. Memorialists from Newburyport took the position, however, that "enemies of the people" had sought to excite the belief that an embargo was the only alternative to war with Great Britain. They themselves believed that such a war would be unjust while she evinced "a disposition for an amiable settlement of all subjects of controversy," and especially when they viewed her "as almost alone maintaining a contest, on the successful issue of which depend the rights and liberties of the civilized world."[24] It need hardly be remarked that the executives in Washington could not recognize the existing British government from such descriptions.

While John Adams, also of Massachusetts, took no stock in the effort to secure redress of grievances by commercial restrictions, that generally pessimistic observer saw no escape from the evils of the situation. He told Josiah Quincy that he felt sorry for everybody. "If you continue the Embargo, the times will be hard," he said. "If you institute a total non-intercourse, the times will not be more cheerful. If you repeal the Embargo, circumstances will occur of more animation, but perhaps not more profit or more comfort. If you arm our merchantmen, there will be war. . . . If you declare war against France and England at once, this will be sublime, to be sure, and if we had a Dutch navy and a Van Tromp to sail up the Thames, and a De Ruyter to sail up the Seine, we might gain as much by it as the Dutch did when they warred against England, France, and Spain at once." He himself was prepared for hard, dull times, taking consolation in the thought that his country was better off than any other and that things could probably get no worse whatever happened.[25]

Faced with these depressing possibilities, Gallatin offered three resolutions. The first stated that the country could not, without the sacrifice of "rights, honor, and independence," submit to the edicts of the British and the French. Such a declaration might seem quite unnecessary, said the report, but at this juncture a pledge by the representatives of the nation would serve a purpose in foreign relations. The question as presented here was one of simple patriotism — whether the citizens would rally round their own government or enlist under the banners of others. Not everybody agreed that support of this resolution

[24] *Annals*, 10 Cong., 2 sess., p. 496. One of a number of petitions introduced by Congressman Livermore Nov. 17, 1808. This sentence was read twice at the request of a member who said he could not understand it.
[25] John Adams to Josiah Quincy, Nov. 25, 1808 (Quincy, *Life*, pp. 144-145).

meant approval of the embargo. Josiah Quincy took the position that the embargo itself was submission to the edicts.[26] But in the end, putting their own interpretations on this general statement, virtually everybody voted for it.

The second resolution in its first clause called for the closing of American ports to the armed vessels of both France and Great Britain, and in the second for the prohibition of all imports from both countries. These proposals represented a significant attempt to equalize the treatment of the two offending nations. British warships but not French had been excluded by Jefferson's *Chesapeake* proclamation, to Canning's annoyance, and the Non-Importation Act was directed solely against the British. A more severe attitude toward France was now fully supported by public opinion, for pro-French sentiment had practically disappeared. Since imports from France had been effectually cut off already, this application of the non-importation policy to that country was little more than a move toward theoretical consistency, but upon its face this clause signalized not only the continuance but the extension of the restrictive system. It is not surprising, therefore, that this was the part of the report — virtually the only part, in fact — that aroused real opposition. The final resolution called for taking immediate steps to put the country in a better state of defense, and everybody gave lip service to this.

Debate over Campbell's report occupied almost the entire time of the House for three weeks.[27] Opponents of the embargo availed themselves abundantly of the opportunity to express their opinions, but only against the second clause of the second resolution did they vote in considerable number, and they were decisively defeated on that.[28] Although a bill designed to carry out the purposes of the second resolution (called a non-intercourse bill) was introduced by the same committee the day after Christmas, the leaders of the majority did not press this as yet. But it appeared from these events that the incoming administration was not retreating from the policy of commercial restriction, and that thus far the party majority in the House was cooperating with it. An even firmer commitment and stronger spirit of co-operation were manifested in the Senate. In that chamber there was more interest in matters of national defense, and a bill de-

26 In the debate of Nov. 28, 1808 (*Annals*, 10 Cong., 2 sess., p. 535).

27 Nov. 27–Dec. 17, 1808 (*Annals*, 10 Cong., 2 sess., pp. 530–895).

28 Except in procedural questions, the maximum negative vote on the second clause of the second resolution was 36 against 82 (*ibid.*, pp. 393–394). Most of the debate was on the first resolution, which in the end was opposed by hardly anybody.

signed to tighten the embargo laws along the line of Gallatin's suggestions was passed before Christmas.[29] Since that bill was still pending in
the House when the year ended, we shall defer consideration of it for a
time while seeking clues to the hopes and purposes, at this stage, of the
members of the administration.

Before the end of the year Gallatin, who left more clues than any of
the others, doubted that they could maintain the embargo very long
and he was thought by some, perhaps by most, to favor war.[30] He
unquestionably preferred it to submission and he feared that submission would result if war should be long postponed. During the weeks
before Christmas, however, the argument for delay appears to have
been dominant in his mind. One inescapable consideration was the
impracticality of taking on the two mightiest powers in the world
simultaneously. But the leading members of the administration continued to hope that the international situation might change, as their
conversations with the friendly British Minister showed.

At the beginning of the congressional session, before Jefferson
declared himself a bystander and had trouble with his jaw, he had a
lengthy conversation with David Erskine.[31] He took the position that
he consistently maintained and in which he was supported by his two
major colleagues — namely, that the rejection of Pinkney's proposal
by the British (which he claimed to have found surprising) left the
United States no middle course between the "painful alternatives" of
embargo and war. On this occasion he brandished a stick and also
proffered a carrot. There was a chance, he said, that the French might
withdraw their decrees against neutral commerce on the high seas and
confine the operation of these to their own harbors. In that case the
American government could not refuse to renew commerce with
them. He went to considerable pains, however, to demonstrate that he
had never really favored the French and opposed the British. He never
could have abandoned the principle of the immunity of American
citizens from impressment, he said, but if some temporary arrangement
could have been worked out the two countries might have "shov'd
along" — a favorite expression of his, according to Erskine. He sought
to give an impression of firmness by minimizing the opposition to the
embargo, but showed quite clearly that he would have liked to work
things out with the British if he could.

[29] Dec. 21, 1808, by a vote of 20 to 7 (*ibid.*, p. 298).
[30] Nathaniel Macon to J. H. Nicholson, Dec. 4, 1808; Gallatin to Nicholson,
Dec. 29 (Gallatin, *Life*, pp. 384-385).
[31] Reported by him in a long memo, Nov. 9, 1808 (Ford, I, 335-338); by Erskine
to Canning, Nov. 10, No. 44 (FO, 5:58).

An even stronger impression of a conciliatory spirit was created by Madison and Gallatin in conversations they carried on after Jefferson lapsed into silence. Gallatin in particular sounded the friendly note, as he was in better position to do than the President and even the Secretary of State.[32] Madison expressed the opinion that when Canning saw the documents the President submitted to Congress, he would be convinced that the United States had not submitted to the French. Gallatin pointed to the purpose of equalizing the treatment of the two belligerents, as shown in the resolutions presented to the House; and, according to Erskine's report, described Madison as more friendly to the English than Jefferson, who had never been known to say anything good about them. This was an overstatement which Gallatin went to some pains afterwards to correct. Erskine was very anxious to demonstrate the friendliness of the incoming administration, and, judging from later events, his representations probably did harm rather than good. More impressed by his report of friendliness than of the determination of the government to go to war if the country was not relieved of its commercial grievances, the Foreign Minister thought the Americans would accept almost anything. Accordingly, in his later instructions Canning prescribed impossible terms, as he had in the case of the *Chesapeake*.[33] In this period, however, hope of some modification in the British Orders was encouraged by the genuinely friendly British Minister, and delay seemed desirable until some response to his representations had been received.

Writing his son-in-law the day Campbell's report was submitted, Jefferson said that the question of war might not be decided on until near the end of the session. He reported a suggestion that another diplomatic effort be made — that both belligerents be offered a categorical choice between a repeal of their edicts and war, the embargo being tightened in the meantime.[34] All of this was tentative, he said, but as between the embargo and war he told his grandson-in-law that the former would probably prevail as yet. The other alternative, "submission and tribute," was "scouted" by three-fourths of the members of Congress "from the heart." Dubbing the other fourth "schismatic," he predicted that they would support whatever proposal would lead to war with France and submission to England.[35]

---

[32] Special reference should be made to Erskine's reports to Canning on Dec. 3, 4, 1808, Nos. 46 & 47 (FO, 5:58).

[33] Perkins, *Prologue*, p. 211.

[34] TJ to TMR, Nov. 22, 1808 (*Papers, MHS*, pp. 124–125). In this period his expectations were most fully expressed in his correspondence with the male members of his family.

[35] TJ to C. L. Bankhead, Nov. 26, 1808 (*ibid.*, p. 126).

A couple of weeks later he made the surprising statement that there was a sincere desire to remove the embargo before Congress should rise, *"prevailing with everybody but the Federalists."*[36] He recognized that with the ending of the embargo they would lose their chief political talking point, but presumably he was thinking chiefly of their fear that war with the British would ensue. Like Gallatin, he was acutely aware of the difficulty of distinguishing between the two belligerents and the impracticality of fighting them both. Accordingly, he conjectured that more time might be taken to get a repeal of the offensive edicts by one nation and that Congress might meet in May or June to declare war against the other. By the beginning of the new year he believed that the congressional mind was "rallying" to that course of procedure.

Since the new year began on Sunday, the President kept open house on Monday, presumably wearing his homespun coat. According to Mrs. Gallatin's niece, the three or four hundred people who paid him the customary visit were "much dressed." While the British Minister, in court dress, was not especially impressive, the French Minister with his great mustache was superb. The President is said to have looked very happy, but he always sought to give that impression to company.[37]

Either in the early morning before his guests arrived or in the evening after they had gone, Jefferson gave a summary view of the political situation to his son-in-law.[38] He gave no indication that he was directing policy, but from his comments on the likely procedure in Congress it is obvious that he was well informed of the purposes of the party leaders. A bill was to be introduced calling for a special session in May and in the course of the debate speakers were to declare their intention regarding actions at that time — namely, the removal of the embargo; and, if the edicts of the French and British were still in effect, the issuance of letters of marque and reprisal. (These would have legalized privateering against either or both of them.) Thus these nations would be forewarned of a warlike purpose, and discouraged from persisting in their course, while the American people would be quieted by the expectation that the embargo would cease after a definite time. But he regarded the "monarchists of the North" as very threatening. It was believed, he said, that the Massachusetts legislature, meeting in the middle of the month and assured of British protection,

[36] TJ to TMR, Dec. 13, 1808 (*ibid.*, p. 130), italics added.
[37] Frances Few, entry of Jan. 2, 1809 (*Jour. Sou. Hist.*, XXIX, 357).
[38] TJ to TMR, Jan. 2, 1809 (*Papers, MHS*, pp. 130–132). Madison wrote Pinkney to much the same effect on Jan. 3 (Hunt, VIII, 40–42).

would call a convention to consider the separation of the Union, addressing the call to the whole region east of the Hudson. He was disposed to believe almost anything of New England Federalists, but a convention was certainly being talked about privately, and if not separatist in spirit it would unquestionably have been violently opposed to the existing government.[39] New England Republicans believed that if a definite day could be set when the embargo would end, a great portion of the citizens would be sufficiently satisfied and the danger of a convention would be avoided. He himself believed that this would be done, letters of marque and reprisal being issued the same day — an additional provision that New Englanders might not find acceptable since it might lead to a conflict with the British. "We must save the Union," he said, "but we wish to sacrifice as little as possible of the honor of the nation." In case of war with England he was by no means sure that country would not offer neutrality and commerce to New England and have it accepted. As though to offset these fears, this devotee of Reason still clung to the hope that England might be "wrought upon." If recent events and developments had the effect they should have on a "rational government" he believed that war could be prevented.

Although professedly only a spectator, Jefferson was doing something with his pen to encourage the faithful at home. He did not lack for messages supporting the government's policy and expressing appreciation of his services. Among these he undoubtedly set high store on resolutions from Republican citizens of Connecticut and Boston.[40] In his reply to the former, while admitting the difficulties of the moment, he pointed to the relatively favorable situation of the country — as in fact normally pessimistic John Adams had done. Thus he said with pride: "In a state of the world unparalleled in times past, and never again to be expected, according to human probabilities, no form of government has, so far, better shielded its citizens from the prevailing afflictions."[41] He frankly admitted his doubt, however, that the country could be kept out of the broils of Europe much longer. And

---

[39] Perhaps the most important letters bearing on this particular question are those of H. G. Otis to Josiah Quincy, Dec. 15, 1808 (Adams, *New England Federalism*, pp. 374-375) and to Roger Griswold, Jan. 4, 1809 (J. M. Banner, Jr., *To the Hartford Convention*, pp. 353-356).

[40] Connecticut Republicans to TJ, Nov. 4, 1808, with covering letter of Jabez Fitch, Nov. 7 (LC, 32338, 32342); William Eustis to TJ, Dec. 24, 1808, sending resolution of Republican citizens of Boston, Dec. 19 (LC, 32622).

[41] TJ to Jabez Fitch, Nov. 21, 1808 (Padover, *Complete Jefferson*, p. 539). In this work (pp. 538-542) there is a useful collection of his replies to addresses in November and December.

in his reply to his Boston supporters nearly two months later he went to pains to point out that, while time was inevitably required to carry out the policy of the government, the charge that this was a permanent policy was an absurdity.[42]

iii

Early in the session Erskine reported to Canning that all the Republican leaders in Congress had declared that the continuance of the embargo would be short; and early in the new year a resolution such as Jefferson had predicted, calling for an extra session, was introduced in the House.[43] A couple of days later he approved what has been called the Second Enforcement Act.[44] It may seem surprising that, at just this juncture, the ruling party should have grieved the opponents of the restrictive policy further by tightening the provisions of laws that were not expected to continue. Also, it may seem ironical that by this action the authority of the President should have been increased at just the time that Jefferson claimed he was trying to rid himself of it.

He saw no escape from the task of enforcement during his term of office. Furthermore, he had concluded months earlier that the successful performance of this would require an increase in executive power.[45] Accordingly, despite the fact that enforcement was better in the fall than it had been in the summer, he suggested to Gallatin that a bill to correct the demonstrated defects in the embargo laws be made ready for Congress.[46] He himself made specific proposals, but nearly all of his information on this subject had come through Gallatin, and he accepted without question that official's judgment as to what the situation required. In midsummer, when deeply discouraged, Gallatin had said: "Congress must either vest the Executive with the most arbitrary powers and sufficient force to carry the embargo into effect, or give it up altogether."[47] As a highly efficient man he expected much, and in this entire matter he and Jefferson were severely logical. They saw no middle ground. The choice was between the embargo and war, between genuine enforcement of the embargo and its abandonment; and, apparently to a greater extent in the thinking of the President than in

---

[42] TJ to Dr. William Eustis, Jan. 14, 1809 (L. & B., XII, 227–229).
[43] Erskine to Canning, Dec. 4, 1808, No. 47 (FO, 5:58); Resolution of Jan. 7, 1809 (*Annals*, 10 Cong., 2 sess., pp. 1026–1030).
[44] Jan. 9, 1809 (*ibid.*, pp. 1798–1804).
[45] See ch. XXXII, pp. 589–592, above.
[46] TJ to Gallatin, Oct. 26, 1808 (Gallatin, *Writings*, I, 420).
[47] Gallatin to TJ, July 29, 1808 (*Writings*, I, 399); see ch. XXXII, pp. 600–601, above.

that of the Secretary of the Treasury, the choice was between sacrificial patriotism and self-serving lawlessness. Jefferson's suggestion that
Gallatin prepare a bill was made before he got the discouraging dispatches from abroad, and he believed at the time that the passing of
such a measure would have a good effect in Europe without binding
Congress to a continuance of it. No doubt he held to this opinion and
remained as indignant as ever against violators of the embargo laws.
But he did not recommend to Congress the tightening of these; in the
period of passivity he had entered he did not even ask their continuance. So far as the record goes, the initiative in this matter was taken
by Senator Giles, and the recommendations by which this legislation
was guided were those of Gallatin. The enforcement bill was passed by
a majority of more than two-thirds in each house of Congress and it
was obviously supported as a party measure.[48]

The dominant opinion among the congressional leaders appears to
have been that any relaxation in the effort to enforce the embargo laws
would have been to yield to unpatriotic forces at home and to weaken
the position of the United States vis-à-vis the powers of Europe.
Undisposed to announce a retreat as yet, they chose to move forward
on the line already taken. Giles stated in the debate in the Senate that
the general sentiment at the moment was either to enforce the embargo laws or repeal them, and it was an undeniable fact that they had
decided by overwhelming vote *not* to do the latter.[49]

Besides asking Gallatin to suggest measures to render the embargo
laws more effectual, the committee inquired of him if any of the
"inconveniences" of the system could be remedied. He candidly
admitted that under such a restrictive system serious inconveniences
were unavoidable and that these "must necessarily be increased in
proportion to the opposition and efforts to evade or violate the law."
On the recommendation of this practical administrator Congress approved a large increase in the bond required of vessels engaged in
coastwise traffic — that they would carry their cargoes to domestic
ports. At the same time they were denied under virtually all circum-

[48] Gallatin's letter of Nov. 24, 1808, to Giles (*Writings*, I, 428-435) was communicated to the Senate Dec. 8 and printed as a report (*Annals*, 10 Cong., 2 sess.,
pp. 232-235). The bill, reported in two parts, Dec. 8 and Dec. 12, was passed by
the Senate, Dec. 21, by a vote of 20 to 7 (*ibid.*, p. 298). One New England
Republican, Mathewson of Rhode Island, voted with the minority; Robinson of
Vermont stuck with the majority. It was passed by the House Jan. 6, 1809, by a
vote of 71 to 32 (*ibid.*, pp. 1024-1025). The balloting began at 5:30 A.M. and ended
shortly after daybreak. There were some amendments that the Senate accepted
(*ibid.*, p. 319). It was approved by TJ on Jan. 9 (*ibid.*, pp. 1798-1804). Its
provisions are well summarized in White, *Jeffersonians*, pp. 463-464.
[49] In his speech of Dec 21, 1808 (*ibid.*, p. 276).

stances the right to plead accidents as an excuse for failure to do this.[50] But, since these severe requirements would provide ample security against the violation of the law, Gallatin observed that these vessels would be less subject to detention and arbitrary restrictions of all sorts. He foresaw that "regularly cleared" vessels would operate in greater confidence and less inconvenience under what appeared to be harsher regulations.

The greatest difficulties arose from vessels departing without clearance papers, and, in the effort to prevent their defiant violation of the law, Gallatin saw no choice but to grant the President and the collectors powers that he himself recognized as arbitrary and regarded as odious. Some of those now specifically assigned the President were designed to attain greater uniformity of procedure. They could be described by hostile critics as aggrandizements of executive authority, nonetheless. The powers granted the collectors were not quite so great as Gallatin recommended, but the permission of these officials was required for loading any vessel and, although they were not authorized to seize suspicious articles anywhere, they were authorized to do so not only on vessels but on carts or wagons whenever exportation seemed to be intended. Any person engaged in such loading could be convicted of misdemeanor, and ships violating the provisions of the law were subject to confiscation. Since all the powers of the collectors were subject to the control of the President, his recognized authority was enhanced to the point that critics could describe it as limitless; and, what was most alarming of all, he was authorized to employ such part of the navy, army, or militia as should seem necessary to enforce these laws. Not only so. He could empower others to do this.[51] The fact that Jefferson signed the law does not mean that he approved every part of it, but he does not appear to have manifested any compunctions. Thus, like his chief colleagues and the leaders of his party in Congress, he can be charged with the acceptance, in this particular situation, of the doctrine that the end justifies the means.

That doctrine is thoroughly compatible with war psychology and a major objection that Federalists raised to this legislation was that in time of peace it sought to impose a military despotism to which freemen could not submit.[52] Senator Giles, defending the measure, said that if the country was at peace it was a peace very much like war, and

---

[50] TJ specifically approved rigid requirements of this sort. See his letter to Gallatin, Dec. 7, 1808 (L. & B., XII, 208–209).

[51] Section 11.

[52] Speech of Senator Goodrich of Connecticut, Dec. 17, 1808 (*Annals*, 10 Cong., 2 sess., p. 249).

that in his judgment the situation warranted the adoption of any measure that would be justified in war.[53] This was essentially the position Jefferson had taken in the summer, and he distinguished between the sacrifice of property incident to commercial warfare and the inevitable sacrifice of life in traditional war. As long ago as the American Revolution this generally humane man had shown that he could be unforgiving of those whom he regarded as unpatriotic. On the day he sent his annual message to Congress he said privately, with obvious reference to Massachusetts, that opposition to the embargo in one quarter had "amounted almost to rebellion and treason."[54] He viewed violators of these laws with moral indignation and would have liked to make an example of them.[55]

The chief senatorial advocate of the enforcement bill displayed no tenderness toward offenders against the embargo laws. While not terming their conduct treasonable, Giles held that it partook of the character of treason. "It is, to say the least, a base abandonment of every honorable and patriotic sentiment. . . . It is violating the laws of our country, and co-operating in counteracting their effects upon our enemies for the sake of money, regardless of the consequences."[56] He stoutly denied that a military despotism was being established, as Federalists continued to claim while taunting the Republicans with inconsistency in advocating the extension of executive power. According to Giles they were merely seeking the means "necessary and proper for carrying into effect a great national and Constitutional object . . . and thus to make a last effort to preserve the peace of the nation."[57] These means now appeared to be as strong as the embargo measure itself, just as Gallatin said they had to be. The administration and ruling party had come to this point by successive steps, each of which seemed logical and necessary at the time. Senator Hillhouse of Connecticut observed that the plea of necessity had always been resorted to by tyrants.[58] Jefferson and his major colleagues do not now appear to have been tyrannical in spirit, but as one congressional opponent of this law remarked, policies need not be perpetuated because they originated in pure motives. This representative from New Jersey, who had formerly supported the embargo, believed that the

[53] Dec. 21, 1808 (*ibid.*, p. 269).

[54] TJ to Thomas Lehré, Nov. 8, 1808 (L. & B., XII, 191).

[55] See e.g., his letter of Sept. 9, 1808, to Gallatin (*ibid.*, 160). No connection has been established, however, between him and the treason trial of Frederick Hoxie to which Leonard Levy refers (*Jefferson and Civil Liberties*, pp. 131–133).

[56] *Annals*, 10 Cong., 2 sess., p. 275.

[57] *Ibid.*, p. 276.

[58] *Ibid.*, p. 297.

Southerners were insufficiently troubled by the sufferings it had brought about.[59] Though logical, honorable, and patriotic, they were chargeable at this stage with being insufficiently realistic.

The opposition was still largely limited to northeastern Federalists, and the adoption of this measure showed that, in Congress at least, Republican unity had been essentially maintained. By this act avowed champions of individual liberties had imposed on their fellow citizens the gravest economic restrictions that Americans had known since the adoption of the Constitution. A friend and supporter of Jefferson's who lived far from the seaboard and believed that the "unprincipled opposition" of the Federalists was playing into the hands of the country's enemies, described Americans in general as "avaricious, enterprising, and impatient of restraint." Accordingly, he doubted if the "prudent measures" of the government could be maintained.[60] A Congressman from Massachusetts who lived nearer the sea believed that the enforcement act could not be carried into effect and doubted if there was much belief that it ever would be.[61] Things had changed considerably since this drastic legislation was started on its course. Although the ruling party had maintained consistency in support of the commercial policy it had adopted more than a year before, it was inevitably charged with faithlessness to the "spirit of 1776." One may observe, however, that there was no return to the spirit of 1798, when High Federalism was in the ascendant. No sedition law had been passed, and the files of both Congress and the President showed that the right of petition had been preserved. Freedom of opinion was unimpaired and the right of opposition was maintained. It was being extensively exercised at just this time by the segment of the population most hostile to this legislation.

[59] James Sloan, Dec. 27, 1808 (*Annals*, 10 Cong., 2 sess., between pp. 915-930).
[60] Archibald Stuart to TJ from Staunton, Va., Dec. 23, 1808 (LC, 32617-32618).
[61] Samuel Taggart, Jan. 7, 1809 ("Letters" in *Amer. Antiq. Soc. Procs.*, XXXIII, 330).

[XXXV]

Pressures of Dissent

1808 - 1809

AMONG the protests addressed to Congress during the fall was one
from the General Court of Massachusetts, which was now under
the control of bitter enemies of the administration.[1] Whereas the Republican leaders in Washington, though recognizing that the embargo
could not be long continued in its present form, were delaying repeal
or modification in the hope of a change in the attitude of the British or
the French, the majority in the legislature of Massachusetts sought the
immediate repeal of all the embargo laws. While affirming that they
would cheerfully support a "just and necessary war," they denied the
contention of the administration that a choice must be made between
war and a continuance of the present policy. Unfortunately, however,
they did not make clear what other alternative there was besides submission. In their opinion much if not most of the present difficulty with
the British arose from the presidential proclamation, issued after the
Chesapeake affair, which forbade the entrance of British warships into
American harbors. With respect to this they supported the British
contention rather than that of their own government. By the time
their petition was read in Congress, Gallatin had already proposed that
the prohibition be extended to French warships and thus be made
genuinely neutral, but the Federalists were still charging that favoritism
was being shown the French. The pro-British sentiments of the
memorialists from Massachusetts were unmistakable and not unnaturally caused the President and others to regard them as unpatriotic.

To opponents of governmental policy such as these the tightening of
the embargo laws seemed a denial of any purpose to repeal them, or at

[1] Resolution of the Mass. General Court, read in the Senate Nov. 25, 1808
(*Annals*, 10 Cong., 2 sess., pp. 128–130).

least an indefinite postponement of such action. As John Quincy Adams quickly perceived, the enforcing act played into the hands of the extreme Federalists. In denouncing it, however, they could hardly have been more bitter than they were in observing on December 22, 1808, the first anniversary of the original measure as a day of mourning. This they did in Boston, Salem, Beverly, Newburyport, Portland, Providence, and other towns.[2] It need not be supposed that support of this action approached unanimity in these places; from Jefferson's correspondence one would judge that many of his faithful followers did not participate. Of the extreme rancor of his political enemies, however, there could be no doubt whatsoever. Thus spoke one paper of the embargo: "This illshapen brat of backstairs intrigue has now lived a year. The first thing of the kind that ever arrived at such an age. And Mr. Jefferson is the only potentate that ever lived who had either power or will to keep such a monster alive for such a length of time. It astonishes and surprises the present race of men, and will be described by generations to come with amazement." This editorial appeared in the Washington *Federalist*, but its author looked toward the region where opposition centered when he predicted that "if the fathers of this monster do not soon stifle it, a Hercules will arise in the North who will put it to rest."[3]

Shortly before and soon after the passage of the enforcing act there were numerous references in Federalist papers to the rights of petition, assembly, and remonstrance — which in fact were not imperiled or even questioned. Toward the end of January a doctrinaire Republican who was bitterly anti-British wrote Jefferson: "In any other nation on earth the leaders of the sedition now spread through the Union would long since have been conducted to the dungeon or the gibbet; I do not admire such remedies; thank God they do not belong to our code of health."[4] Although the administration could not be fairly charged with anything comparable to the Sedition Act, many expressions of the protesters might have been expected to make the author of the Declaration of Independence wince. Among these were "oppressive and arbitrary laws," "military despotism," the "spirit of 1776," and a quotation from Samuel Adams: "Resistance to arbitrary laws is duty to God." One feature of the proceedings of the various town meetings that distinguished them from those held earlier was the claim of justifi-

[2] Jennings, *American Embargo*, p. 136. In ch. VI of this work is an excellent account of opposition to the embargo with numerous quotations from newspapers.
[3] *Ibid.*, p. 137, citing the editorial of Dec. 22, 1808.
[4] William Duane to TJ, Jan. 23, 1809 (LC, 32867–32869). He favored the suspension of the functions of all the accredited agents of England in the country.

able resistance. Another was the avowal of the intention to seek redress through the state government.[5] Committees of safety and correspondence were not appointed everywhere, but it seemed that the spirit of Samuel Adams had been revived.

The change in sentiment in Washington during the second half of the congressional session can be attributed directly to opposition to the embargo laws in New England, but a change in policy was clearly indicated before any of the legislators in that region had responded to these appeals for redress. Before considering them, therefore, we should return to the capital and the leaders of the ruling party there.

Although the President, well aware of his "lame duck" status, claimed that he was playing no part in the determination of policies, he undoubtedly favored the continuance of the embargo until a last diplomatic effort could be made and would have preferred that no definite date be set for the repeal of the measure since that would weaken its effect abroad.[6] If he had been guided by his own correspondence alone, he might well have concluded that the patience of most of his countrymen had not yet run out. During the last weeks of the old year and the first of the new he received addresses and resolutions approving the policy of the government not only from the legislatures of New York, Virginia, South Carolina, and Georgia, and a town meeting in Philadelphia, but also from counties in upstate New York and Republican groups in Massachusetts, Connecticut, Maryland, and Delaware. He was well informed, however, of the intense opposition in New England and feared that either the long continuance of the embargo or war with Great Britain would imperil the Union. He may have been of divided mind, but he accepted the decision of the party leaders to hold a special session in the summer and expected the embargo to be lifted at that time although Congress had not voted that it should be.[7]

The recalcitrant New England Federalists were undisposed to wait that long and feared that they might have to wait even longer. Congressman Josiah Quincy asserted bitterly in debate that the administration had always pursued a policy of deception regarding the purposes of the embargo. Reading its mind with entire confidence, he said that

5 Boston *Columbian Centinel*, Jan. 7, 14, 18, 1809, reporting various meetings and resolutions.

6 One is reminded of the objections of the administration in the 1970's to the setting of a precise date for the withdrawal of American forces from Vietnam.

7 The bill setting the date for the special session as the fourth Monday in May was passed by the House on Jan. 20, 1808, and by the Senate on Jan. 26, but its passage, anticipated in December, was a virtual certainty by Jan. 7.

644   JEFFERSON THE PRESIDENT: SECOND TERM

coercion of England had been and still was its object and that the measure would not be abandoned until this had been attained. As for the talk of war, he described that as sheer hypocrisy. He did not believe that the majority in the House could be kicked into a declaration of war. It has been said that no Republican ever forgot or forgave this self-righteous speech. No doubt Jefferson brushed it off, expecting no better from the inner circle of his political foes, and he unquestionably regarded its author as an advocate of submission.[8]

If the embargo was to be repealed, when should this be, and what, if anything, should replace it? These questions were thrown into the cockpit less than six weeks from the end of Jefferson's term, when his friend Wilson Cary Nicholas, the representative of his congressional district, introduced a resolution in the House. This called for the repeal of the embargo on a date yet to be determined and the defense, as well as the resumption, of navigation on the high seas after that.[9] When this came up for debate, the author presented a further resolution which the House chose to divide into two parts.[10] The first related to the date of repeal, which had been left blank. He moved to insert June 1, and others moved the dates February 15 and March 4. The second part of the resolution called for the authorization of letters of marque and reprisal against nations infringing on American commercial rights. Thus, in the proposals of Nicholas, repeal was coupled, not with submission, but with action that might be expected to lead to war.

In this form the proposals may be assumed to have met the approval not only of the party leaders in Congress, the President-elect, and the Secretary of the Treasury, but also of the outgoing President.[11] The latter gentleman had not given up hope of a favorable change in the international situation, but he spoke wistfully of the ill-fated experiment he had been conducting and which now appeared to be nearing its end. Writing James Monroe, he said: "There never has been a situation of the world before, in which such endeavors as we have made would not have secured our peace. It is probable there never will be such another."[12] He could not have been expected to anticipate the world wars of the twentieth century, which were to impose on neutral

[8] Quincy's speech was delivered Jan. 19, 1809 (*Annals*, 10 Cong., 2 sess., pp. 1105–1117). See comments of Henry Adams (*History*, IV, 422–424). Among those replying to it heatedly was John W. Eppes (*Annals*, 10 Cong., 2 sess., pp. 1117–1121).
[9] Jan. 24, 1809 (*ibid.*, p. 1172).
[10] *Ibid.*, pp. 1232–1233.
[11] Brant (IV, 477) identifies the resolution as Madison's.
[12] TJ to Monroe, Jan. 28, 1809 (Ford, IX, 243).

nations problems, virtually insoluble problems, not unlike those he had been called upon to face.

The events of the next few days caused Nicholas to observe that the party leaders would have had a better chance to get what they wanted in return for the repeal of the embargo if they had not procrastinated so long. That legislator himself believed that the "only honorable course was from embargo to war," but, writing Madison within a week, he said that they must submit to the "least disgraceful" plan on which they could unite the largest number of votes. A day later Jefferson reported to his son-in-law in Virginia that "a sudden and uncontrollable revolution of opinion" had taken place, chiefly among members from New England and New York.[13] As a result of the defection of Republicans from the Northeast the date of June 1 for repeal had been rejected by the House and that of March 4 accepted. Furthermore, despite the strenuous efforts at successive party caucuses to win over the seceders, the authorization of letters of marque and reprisal was defeated. This would have been in lieu of or in anticipation of war, and it was rejected as too strong a measure. By these actions the House was not only calling for repeal of the embargo sooner than the administration and the party leaders wanted but was providing no substitute for it. In effect the representatives had voted for submission.[14]

The High Federalists continued to over-personalize this struggle. Speaking of the effort to adopt the date of March 4 for repeal, Josiah Quincy said: "Jefferson is a host, and is opposed to it, and if the wand of that magician is not broken, he will yet defeat the attempt."[15] In fact the magician's wand was not in evidence at this juncture, and the conflict could have been appropriately described in terms of party. The defeat of the motions of Nicholas was attributable to the failure to maintain Republican unity. At the time Jefferson himself referred to the defection of New Englanders and New Yorkers as unaccountable, but, a year and a half after his retirement, he ascribed it to the influence of one person, thus contributing no little to historical confusion. This person, termed by him a pseudo-Republican, was Joseph Story,

[13] Nicholas to Madison, Feb. 6, 1809 (MP, Rives Coll., 4:986); TJ to TMR, Feb. 7 (Ford, IX, 244).

[14] Following the presentation of Nicholas's revised resolution on Jan. 30, 1809, the June 1 date for repeal was defeated Feb. 2 by the decisive vote of 73 to 40, and the March 4 date was approved next day. The proposal to authorize letters of marque and reprisal was defeated Feb. 7 (*Annals*, 10 Cong., 2 sess., pp. 1328, 1334, 1350, 1421). The caucuses, of which there is virtually no record, appear to have occurred on Saturday and Sunday, Feb. 4, 5 (see Brant, IV, 478–479).

[15] Quincy to his wife, Feb. 3, 1809 (*Life*, p. 185).

later a justice of the Supreme Court, who served briefly in this Congress as the successor of Jacob Crowninshield. Jefferson stated in a private letter that Story got "complete hold" of his fellow representative from Massachusetts, Ezekiel Bacon, who became panic-stricken and communicated his panic to his colleagues, with the end result that even the "sound members" of Congress were infected.[16] Upon its face this seems an over-simplified and inadequate explanation of the episode, and actually it cannot be fully reconciled with the contemporary record. At the time, Gallatin termed Bacon a "scared Yankee," and that Republican congressman was subjected to great pressure by stalwarts of the party, especially in connection with the caucuses. At that stage, no doubt, he sought moral support from Story, then back in Massachusetts, where anti-embargo feeling was at fever heat. During the short time that representative was in Washington, however, he was highly critical of the Federalists as being opposed to everything, and, although he preferred the March fourth date for repeal, he expected to vote for June first as a good party man.[17] Story could not go along with the Federalists in regarding Southerners as hostile to commerce, and, while he referred to their reasoning as "abstract and peculiar," he described their representatives as "enlightened and liberal men."[18] He did not then view this problem as a sectionalist, and the attitude of the New England Republicans as a group, unlike that of Timothy Pickering and other Federalist Anglophiles, could not be properly labeled as unpatriotic.

Jefferson said that the defectors believed in the "alternative of repeal or civil war," as in fact he himself was inclined to do at the time, whatever he may have believed afterwards. Their position was well expressed by Orchard Cook of Massachusetts, who had much correspondence with John Quincy Adams and was akin to him in spirit. Opposing both the June date for repeal and the authorization of letters of marque and reprisal, he said: "The South say embargo or war, and the North and East say, no embargo, no war. . . . I lament that this difference of opinion exists; yet, as it does exist, we must take things as they are, and legislate accordingly. The genius and duty of Republican Governments is to make laws to suit the people, and not attempt to

[16] TJ to Henry Dearborn, July 16, 1810 (Ford, IX, 277).
[17] Letters of Story, Dec. 31, 1808–Jan. 14, 1809, in his *Life*, pp. 172–183. The account he gives in his autobiography (pp. 183–186), written a quarter of a century later, after he had seen TJ's letter to Dearborn in the first edition of the formers' writings, gives a very different impression and has been relied on too much by historians, including Henry Adams.
[18] *Ibid*., p. 182.

make the people suit the laws."[19] This was doctrine which Jefferson generally adhered to but which he did not take into sufficient account in connection with the embargo.

Not only did the Republican leadership (executive and legislative) seem to have lost control of Congress; it was showing signs of grave division within itself. It never had been united on military and naval policy. Congress continued to be unresponsive to Jefferson's recommendation of a reform of the militia system, and the failure of this cherished project may have increased his doubts of the readiness of his countrymen for war.[20] Opinion within the government had long been divided with regard to the navy. Early in the session a pro-navy group in the Senate, led by Giles and Samuel Smith and supported by the Federalists, caused the passage of a bill requiring the President to put into commission all the war vessels not then in operation, including not only the frigates but the gunboats.[21] Also, an amendment to much the same effect was attached by the Senate to a bill that the House had passed in the meantime, requiring the employment of additional naval officers and seamen.[22] Nothing came of this House bill, but that body afterwards took up the Senate bill and amended this so as to make the language less peremptory and to allow the President discretion with respect to public vessels other than the frigates.[23]

Even in this form the act represented a defeat for Gallatin, who strongly opposed these requirements, not only because of their great and immediate expense but also because of his low opinion of the effectiveness of Secretary Robert Smith. The formation of what he called the "Navy Coalition," which included Nicholas in the House, was connected with these events, and they foreshadowed the greater troubles he was to have with the Smith-Giles faction at the outset of Madison's presidency.[24] No particular significance should be attached to the fact that Jefferson signed the bill, for in his opinion the veto should be employed by a President only when he deemed a legislative action unconstitutional. There appears to be no record of any reference of his to these particular developments, but the likelihood is that

19 Jan. 31, 1809 (*Annals*, 10 Cong., 2 sess., p. 1249).
20 See ch. XXVIII, pp. 513–514 above, for the failure of his earlier efforts to reform the militia system.
21 Reported Dec. 12, 1808 (*Annals*, 10 Cong., 2 sess., pp. 238–239); passed Dec. 17 (*ibid.*, p. 241).
22 Passed by the Senate, Jan. 4, 1809 (*ibid.*, p. 306).
23 Amendments accepted by Senate, Jan. 27; bill approved Jan. 31 (*ibid.*, pp. 336–337, 1808).
24 Adams, *Life of Gallatin*, pp. 386–388.

he was closer to Gallatin than to Giles and the Smiths on this question. With the benefit of hindsight one is disposed to say that the putting of the frigates into operation would not have been amiss, though preferably this should have been done sooner and gradually. They could hardly have affected the immediate situation, however. Hence this episode is chiefly significant in showing that the situation was not under the control of the major executives.

Although the increase in the relative power of the legislature within the government during these weeks could not be doubted, Congress itself appeared to be divided and indecisive. But, as Jefferson reported to his son-in-law, the majority in that body rallied soon after the House, "in a kind of panic," voted to repeal the embargo on March 4.[25] Apparently the caucuses during the weekend, about which we know so little, were not without effect. The decision about the date of the repeal was not reversed at these meetings, and, judging from later events, no agreement was reached regarding letters of marque and reprisal, but it was decided that repeal of the embargo should not be equivalent to submission. The program to which the majority was now rallying called for limited, not total, abandonment of commercial restrictions. It called for non-intercourse with Great Britain and France. That is, the embargo was to remain in effect and their imports were to be cut off. Trade was permitted with all other countries. The treatment of the two offending powers was to be equalized, as Gallatin had recommended; the warships of both were to be excluded. As far as they were concerned, the restrictive policy was actually extended, in theory at least.[26] Gallatin had predicted that under such a system the British could easily procure American products from places with which trade was permitted, and Erskine was confident that the proposed system would be favorable to the British as against the French, but the adoption of it could be regarded as a consistent action. Thus the congressional leaders of the still-dominant party set out to salvage what they could of the policy of commercial restriction to which they stood committed. This could be described as a face-saving operation, but from the debates in Congress one gains the impression that this was a policy in which many, especially from the South and West, continued to believe.

Resolutions designed to carry out these purposes were promptly introduced in the Senate by William Branch Giles.[27] There was more

[25] TJ to TMR, Feb. 7, 1809 (Ford, IX, 244).
[26] On the caucuses, see Brant, IV, 478-479.
[27] Feb. 8, 1809 (*Annals*, 10 Cong., 2 sess., p. 345).

delay in the House because of procedural disputes, but a similar bill was reported a few days later from the Committee on Foreign Relations by Wilson Cary Nicholas in the absence of Chairman Campbell, who was ill.[28] This was debated, but it was the amended Senate bill that finally became law.

In speaking to the resolution that called for both repeal of the embargo on March 4 and non-intercourse with Great Britain and France, Giles described it as "the offspring of conciliation and of great concession" on his part.[29] He said that national honor and interest demanded nothing weaker, and he urged his colleagues to come to the session in May "in a state of readiness for war."[30] Speaking of the final bill from the point of view of Federalist Connecticut, Senator Hillhouse said that it marched them to the precipice from which the next step might plunge them into war of incalculable calamity and duration.[31] As passed by the Senate it contained a provision for letters of marque and reprisal, but the House eliminated this. By another amendment the House changed the date of repeal to March 15, in order that there would be time to inform remote sailors and shippers. The amended bill passed the House on February 27 and in this form was accepted by the Senate next day. Jefferson signed it the day after that.[32] It was generally agreed that it was not thoroughly satisfactory to anybody. The Federalists certainly did not like it. Josiah Quincy said: "Jefferson has triumphed. His intrigues have prevailed."[33] That gentleman regarded himself as a non-combatant, and in any case this was clearly an over-statement, but it does not appear that in the eyes of his contemporaries his cause had suffered a grave defeat.

ii

According to Jefferson himself, the pressure of official business on him, far from relaxing, increased as he approached his departure.[34] Part of the continuing business from which he could not escape was the enforcement of the embargo. The day after the enforcing act went

[28] Feb. 11 (*ibid.*, p. 1432).
[29] In a speech of Feb. 13 (*ibid.*, pp. 353–383).
[30] This particular resolution passed, Feb. 14, by a vote of 22 to 9 (*ibid.*, p. 409).
[31] In a speech of Feb. 21 (*ibid.*, pp. 424–436).
[32] Passed by the House by vote of 81 to 40 (*ibid.*, p. 1541); amendments accepted by Senate (*ibid.*, pp. 451–452); bill as approved March 1 (*ibid.*, pp. 1824–1830).
[33] Feb. 27, 1809 (*Life*, p. 183).
[34] TJ to Benj. Stoddert, Feb. 18, 1809 (Ford, IX, 245).

"Nonintercourse or Dignified Retirement"

Political cartoon by "Peter Pencil"
from *A History of American Graphic Humor* by William Murrell, Volume I.
Jefferson is saying: "I have stript myself rather than submit to London or
Parisian fashion."

into effect, Gallatin, with his customary efficiency and foresight, reminded him that further instructions would have to be sent the collectors, and, what is of greater interest here, that the War Department
should immediately provide directions for calling forth the militia
when needed. Gallatin believed that physical resistance to the laws was
to be expected in Massachusetts ports, especially in those distant from
the seat of the state government. Shortly after receiving this counsel
the President drafted a circular letter to the governors from the Secretary of War.[35]

In this matter Gallatin and Jefferson continued to be severely
logical. At the time neither of them expected the embargo to last in its
present form beyond June, but they regarded themselves as obligated
to enforce it as long as it was in effect, employing such additional
means as had been afforded them by law. Unfortunately, however, the
letter to the governors had a provocative effect in just the region
where the collectors were in greatest need of support. It precipitated
just the sort of conflict between state and national authorities that, as
John Quincy Adams had foreseen, the Federalist opposition wanted. In
the interest of national unity at this time of crisis it would appear that
the administration would have been wise to avoid such confrontation.
Furthermore, this was in certain respects a tactless letter. In line with
Gallatin's suggestion, it requested in the name of the President that the
governor appoint, in or near every port of entry in his state, a militia
officer on whom the collector might call when threatened with forceful resistance. But the request that the appointees be persons "of
known respect for the laws" implied that not all of the militia officers
were law-abiding. And it might have been predicted that in a state like
Massachusetts, where the righteousness of resistance to unjust laws was
being urged (as it had been in the American Revolution), the severe
castigation of violators of the embargo laws as dishonest and unprincipled would be resented.

It will be recalled that the Republicans had retained control of the
governorship of Massachusetts when the Federalists gained a majority
in the General Court. Levi Lincoln, the former lieutenant governor
who became chief executive of the state on the death of James Sullivan, had been a member of Jefferson's official family and was intensely
loyal to him and to the party. He addressed the General Court when it
reassembled on January 26, and the hostile majorities in the two
chambers replied on February 3 and February 7 respectively. Although the representatives of Massachusetts in Congress could not

[35] Gallatin to TJ, Jan. 10, 1809 (*Writings*, I, 449–450); circular letter from the
Secretary of War to the governors, Jan. 17, 1809 (Ford, IX, 237–238).

have heard of the legislative action in Boston in much less than a week, they may have anticipated it. We are chiefly concerned with it here, however, not because of any effect it may have had on legislation in Washington, but as an instance of direct conflict between the executive authority of the nation and the legislature of a state.

Governor Lincoln's address may be described in general terms as a reasoned plea for national unity.[36] While agreeing with opponents of the embargo that New Englanders were the greatest sufferers under it (a judgment which could have been contested in South Carolina or Virginia), he said that equality of effect could not be expected of legislation and that the United States was not exempt from the disasters that had befallen half the world. We may assume that the ears of most of his listeners were deaf to these words of reassurance, as no doubt they were to his assertion that a majority of New Englanders supported the government in its effort to maintain their rights and independence. Also, Lincoln questioned the competence of town meetings to pass judgment on complicated constitutional questions, and said that there were times when, a decision having been reached, there must be an end to debate. Thus he laid himself open to the charge of decrying honest dissent, which he did not really do. He did not ask for legal checks on freedom of speech, but he did stress the importance of strong public opinion in support of government.

In their replies to him both the state Senate and the House avowed devotion to the Constitution and disclaimed any thought of abandoning the Union. Both denied, however, that the time had come to end discussion of and opposition to governmental policy. Describing as unconstitutional, in certain respects, the commercial restrictions that had been imposed on them, both emphasized the role of the state in protecting the rights of its citizens. Though politely phrased, these were strong and indignant protests. Said the Senate: "The people of Massachusetts will not willingly become the victims of fruitless experiment." And the House asserted that the federal government had no right to sacrifice the interests of one section to "the prejudices, partialities, and convenience of another."

Governor Lincoln, who followed the instructions of the Secretary of War regarding the militia, was rebuked by the legislature for so doing, and, as he wrote Jefferson, he was fearful of impeachment.[37] In

---

[36] Lincoln's address of Jan. 26, 1809, is in *American Register*, V (1809), pp. 183–191, and is followed by the other essential documents bearing on this episode, pp. 191–209.

[37] Lincoln's letter of Feb. 1, 1809, about the militia, and the resolution of the legislature (*American Register*, V [1809], pp. 196–202); Lincoln to TJ, Feb. 23, 1809; received March 4 (MP, Rives Coll., 4:1003–1005).

a rather hysterical letter which Jefferson did not receive until the day he left office and which he seems to have turned over to Madison, the Governor emphasized the legality of his own actions. He regarded himself as a national agent, seeking to carry out a national purpose, and he believed that the actions of the legislature tended to the destruction of all government. He said that he could not move "prejudices stronger than mountains," and he believed that no measures opposed to Great Britain and not opposed to France would have been acceptable to those now in control of the legislature. To him it seemed that they looked for support to "smugglers, speculators, usurers, foreign hirelings, [and] men corrupted with a thirst or a glut of meretricious gain." With such men, he said, government was a fiction, and patriotism but a name.

It may be, as Henry Adams held, that at this stage the mind of Massachusetts was possessed by "a temporary insanity like the witchcraft and Quaker mania."[38] But there was substantial opposition to the legislative actions, and in form at least the various protests were kept within the bounds of legitimacy. In resolutions on the enforcement act that were passed on February 15 this measure was described as "in many respects unjust, oppressive, and unconstitutional, and as not legally binding on the citizens of this state."[39] This sounds like an invitation to civil disobedience and it may have been so intended, but in the next breath the citizens were urged to avoid individual resistance while the state was seeking redress by sending a memorial to Congress and an offer to other state legislatures to cooperate with them in seeking constitutional amendments for the protection of commerce.

The Memorial and Remonstrance of the Legislature of Massachusetts was not communicated to Congress until February 27, when the session had less than a week to run and the major decisions had already been reached.[40] It is of considerable interest, nonetheless, as an expression of opinion. Like the other protests emanating from this legislature, it described the embargo laws as unconstitutional, and it added what amounted to a rebuke to the President and his party for lack of realism. Even if commerce were less valuable and important than it

[38] Henry Adams, *History*, IV, 408–409.
[39] Resolutions of Feb. 15, 1809, are in H. V. Ames, ed., *State Documents on Federal Relations: The States and the U.S.* (1900), pp. 34–36. Ames prints extracts from the hostile responses of four state legislatures to the embargo. We do not concern ourselves here with the resolutions that were adopted by the house of representatives of Delaware, Jan. 30, 1807, but failed in the senate (*ibid.*, pp. 36–38); or with those of the legislature of Rhode Island, adopted on March 4 (*ibid.*, pp. 42–44).
[40] Feb. 27, 1809 (*A.S.P.*, *Commerce & Navigation*, I, 776–778).

654 JEFFERSON THE PRESIDENT: SECOND TERM

actually was, said these New Englanders, their habits could not be greatly and immediately changed without distressing consequences. There was ground for their claim that the government had asked too much of human nature. But these protesters had no helpful suggestions to offer. They opposed non-intercourse with Great Britain and France on the ground that it would lead to war with the former, when in their opinion war with the latter was clearly preferable. By implication they condemned the administration for failing to develop the navy, and they said that at one time they favored the arming of merchantmen. They had ceased to do so because that also might lead to war with England. In fact they bore out the contentions of John Quincy Adams and Joseph Story that the Federalists opposed everything, and what they favored amounted to submission. In their assertion of state rights, however, they did not go as far as their brethren in Connecticut.

Since that commonwealth had a Federalist governor as well as a Federalist legislature, its constituted authorities presented a united front in opposition to the request of the Secretary of War for co-operation in the enforcement of the embargo. Governor Trumbull flatly declined to make the desired appointments of officers of the militia, saying that the constitution of his state did not authorize him to do so, and that the Constitution of the United States did not authorize such a request.[41] Regarding the late enforcing law (January 9) as unconstitutional in many provisions, he thought it grossly improper for him as a state official to aid in its enforcement. He viewed the prospect as so momentous and threatening that he called the General Assembly in special session. In his address to that body he invited the members to take a view of the measures of the general government in order to ascertain if it had exceeded its constitutional authority. And he asserted that whenever the national legislature over-stepped the bounds of its powers, state legislatures had the right, and in great emergencies the duty, "to *interpose* their protecting shield between the right and liberty of the people, and the assumed power of the general government."[42] This challenge was taken up by the General Assembly, which highly approved the conduct of the Governor and adopted resolutions of considerable significance in the history of federal relations. In these the embargo laws were described as "a permanent system of measures," unprecedented in history, extending arbitrary power and infringing on the constitutional liberties of the

---

[41] Governor Trumbull to the Secretary of War, Feb. 14, 1809 (*American Register*, V [1809], pp. 178–179).

[42] Feb. 25, 1809 (*ibid.*, pp. 176–177), italics added.

people of the state.[43] Accordingly, all persons holding executive office in Connecticut were forbidden to afford aid in the enforcement of these laws. The Governor was requested to communicate the resolutions to the President, with an expression of regret that they were obliged "to assert the unquestionable rights of this state, to abstain from any agency in the execution of measures, which are unconstitutional and despotic." Also, they expressed a willingness to co-operate with Massachusetts and other commonwealths in procuring constitutional amendments.

Since these resolutions could not have reached Washington until several days after Jefferson had ceased to be commander in chief, they may have been of little more than academic interest to him. In the references to the rights and powers of states vis-à-vis the general government he could have noted some striking parallels to his own language in the Kentucky Resolutions of 1798.[44] He is not known either to have admitted this or to have denied the doctrinal similarity. If he had been put on the carpet he would have been justified in pointing out an importance difference: the protests of 1809 from Connecticut, like those from Massachusetts, were against infringements on economic freedom, while those framed by him and Madison for Kentucky and Virginia in 1798 were against infringements on freedom of speech and the press and in defense of the right of political opposition. These he regarded as more fundamental than economic freedom, although in theory he certainly favored a maximum of that. Freedom of enterprise was necessarily restricted in time of war, and, as we have seen, he regarded the country as involved in commercial warfare. Freedom of opinion, however, he regarded as illimitable, and freedom of speech as the last thing that should be restricted by society. He did not live long enough to be faced with the question of the ancestry of nullification in South Carolina, which was directed against the tariff, but no doubt he would have claimed that in spirit it was more akin to the resistance to commercial restrictions in New England than to the protests of an earlier date in Kentucky and Virginia against restrictions on expressions of opinion.

If he perceived any theoretical inconsistency in approving the embargo after having opposed the Alien and Sedition Acts, he does not appear ever to have said so. And he never ceased believing that the

---

[43] March 1, 1809 (Ames, pp. 40–42).

[44] On the Kentucky and Virginia Resolutions of 1798, see *Jefferson and the Ordeal of Liberty*, ch. XXV. TJ's authorship of the former was not made public till 1814 (*ibid.*, pp. 399–400 and notes).

policy it embodied could and should have been effective. He continued to blame the New England Federalists for making the enforcement of the embargo laws more difficult and for giving the British an exaggerated impression of American disunity. Though reconciled at the end of his administration to the partial repeal of these laws in order to preserve the Union, he appears to have never ceased regretting the necessity of this. Shortly after the War of 1812 ended, he said he had constantly maintained that "a continuance of the embargo for two months longer would have prevented our war."[45] That is, he believed that the British would have made sufficient concessions. From our present knowledge of what was going on within the British government we may doubt this. Some modifications of the Orders in Council were actually made in the spring of 1809, and the embargo may have been partly responsible for these, although the prestige-conscious ministry sought to avoid the impression of bowing to an American threat or even recognizing the existence of one. Canning may have viewed the embargo as a deterrent to concessions, and it is a fact that he did not make any until he knew that it would be partially repealed.[46] That he would have conceded enough to satisfy Jefferson and Madison seems unlikely, although a less arrogant official might have enabled the American government to save face. One can only speculate on what *might* have happened overseas.

As to the domestic effects of the embargo, Jefferson was well aware that it had given new life to the Federalists in New England. Thus far, though, their victories had been gained by relatively slight margins, as Erskine reported to Canning; and except in Connecticut their political control turned out to be precarious. The Republican party retained control in virtually all the rest of the country. The economic effects of the policy of commercial restriction could not be fully perceived while Jefferson was in office. We make no attempt to estimate them here, and one may doubt if he himself ever did so, though he could hardly have failed to observe what they were in Virginia. If he did not allow sufficiently for lost commerce and lost markets, he frequently expressed gratification, during his last months in office and the next few years, at the rise of manufacturing, believing this to be in the national interest. He may have convinced himself that in the long run the economic gain would balance the loss. But his main concern was for the honor and independence of the country. On the last Christmas day

[45] TJ to Thos. Leiper, June 12, 1815 (Ford, IX, 521). See also TJ to Dearborn, July 16, 1810 (*ibid.*, 277); and to W. B. Giles, Dec. 25, 1825 (Ford, X, 354).

[46] For an admirable account of British developments and attitudes, see Perkins, pp. 204–209.

he spent in Washington, when he was particularly dispirited, he wrote: "I feel extreme regret that an effort, made on motives which all mankind must approve, has failed in an object so much desired. I spared nothing to promote it."[47] When he left office he still regarded the embargo as the most salutary alternative to surrender or war; and, although the experiment could not be completed and had to be modified, he would not concede that it was to be regretted.

[47] TJ to Judge St. George Tucker, Dec. 25, 1808 (LC, 32625).

[XXXVI]

Exit Mr. President

SHORTLY before the last congressional session of Jefferson's administration began, the death of John Page (October 11, 1808) brought to an end a friendship that dated back to his college days and was one of the most intimate of his entire life. The event deserves mention here for its own sake, and also because his efforts to help his dying friend involved him in odd doings and considerable embarrassment.

From the beginning of his presidency, while sedulously avoiding nepotism and affirming his determination to use the appointing power without regard to ties of friendship, he was disposed to do something useful for Page. That impractical gentleman was so beloved in his own region that no one seemed likely to disapprove of favors shown him at a time when his health was bad and his need great. In his first term Jefferson was spared the risk of an unfitting appointment by his friend's relinquishment of it, and Page's immediate needs were met when his many influential friends got him elected to the relatively unexacting post of governor of Virginia. This he held for three years.

In Jefferson's second term he was appointed commissioner of loans for the state of Virginia. His friend the President described the position to him as a sinecure, and in fact its duties were of such a routine nature that a clerk could perform them. While such positions were much rarer in the United States than in England at this time, they did exist. (An effort of John W. Eppes, in the congressional session of 1803–1804, to cause the offices of commissioners of loans to be discontinued, had failed despite the support of the President and the Secretary of the Treasury.) Others besides Page drew salaries for appointive offices while somebody else did all or most of the work.[1] The action

[1] See *Jefferson the President: First Term*, pp. 86–87; TJ to Page, July 3, 1806 (Ford, VIII, 136–137n.); and, for a description of the office, White, *The Fed-*

of Jefferson in bestowing this "plum" on his old friend was indubitably legal, and no doubt it was readily condoned and even applauded in Virginia. But the appointment was not the end of the matter.

A couple of years after Page became commissioner of loans and was lying on his deathbed, Jefferson solicitously inquired if he would like his office transferred to his son Francis on the understanding that the emoluments would be for the benefit of Page's needy family. The idea was that virtually all the work would continue to be performed by a clerk.[2] Transfers of appointive offices from fathers to sons were not unknown, and Page received the proposal with the utmost gratitude. Neither he nor Judge St. George Tucker, who corresponded with Jefferson in behalf of their "common and inestimable friend" during his last days, saw anything amiss in it except that Francis, who belonged to the first set of Page's very numerous children, was not agreeable to the idea. The estimable judge had a counter-suggestion — namely, that the appointment be given to young Benjamin Harrison, who would go through the necessary motions and turn over the money to the needy family.[3] Jefferson accepted this, and Gallatin did not feel warranted in objecting. Accordingly, Harrison was given an *ad interim* appointment.[4] The problem appeared to have been solved, and Judge Tucker was impressed with "the goodness of heart of all the parties" to the arrangement. But, to Jefferson's grief and mortification, Harrison's nomination was rejected by the Senate. Jefferson explained this on two grounds: the actual work of the office was to be performed by a Federalist; and the intended disposition of the emoluments became known or suspected.[5] Both the President and the Judge thought this disposition humane and permissible, but apparently they tried to keep it secret. Thus Jefferson's actions could have been regarded as a manifestation of deceitfulness, and they do not appear to have redounded to his credit even among the senators of his own party. Despite young Harrison's rejection his commission was valid until March 3. Three days later President Madison nominated for this

---

eralists (1948), pp. 349–350, and H. C. Syrett, ed., *Papers of Alexander Hamilton*, XVI (1972), 109. On the effort of Eppes, see *Annals*, 8 Cong., 1 sess., pp. 562, 699, 952–959; TJ to Gallatin, Dec. 1, 1803 (LC, 23588). The circumstances of Page's predecessor, Meriwether Jones, were very similar to his.

[2] TJ to Page, Sept. 6, 1808 (Ford, VIII, 137*n*.).

[3] Page to TJ, Sept. 13 and 17, 1808 (LC, 32066); St. George Tucker to TJ, Oct. 5, 1808 (LC, 32174).

[4] Gallatin to TJ, Oct. 12, 1808; TJ to St. George Tucker, Oct. 13 (LC, 32201, 32204). TJ made the appointment and also received an application for the post before he learned of Page's death. Other applications promptly followed.

[5] Tucker to TJ, Oct. 23, 1808 (LC, 32258); TJ to Tucker, Dec. 8, 1808 (LC, 32512).

post Thomas Nelson, a member of a family clearly allied with the Pages. Whether he planned to support the family of Jefferson's old friend has not been revealed to this writer.[6]

In the last weeks of his presidency Jefferson made as few appointments as he could so as to leave his successor as free a hand as possible. He would have been happier if he had not made any. He was bound by certain commitments, however, and in honoring these he brought considerable criticism on himself. His nomination of Henry Dearborn as collector of the port of Boston was a case in point. This was submitted to the Senate when his own term had less than six weeks to run. Rising in the House that same day (January 25), Josiah Quincy expressed the opinion that, if not a high crime, a high misdemeanor had been committed in this connection and said that he was duty-bound to call attention to it. He claimed that, despite the desire of Benjamin Lincoln to relinquish this office because of infirmities, the President had kept it in reserve for his favorite, Henry Dearborn — who, it may be said, was no favorite of this arch-Federalist. The Congressman from Massachusetts moved that the President be asked to submit all the correspondence bearing on Lincoln's offer to resign and that a committee be appointed to investigate the whole matter. His proposals, which carried a threat of impeachment, were ridiculed by Jefferson's former secretary, William A. Burwell, and others, and were defeated by a vote of 117 to 1.[7]

In truth, Jefferson had promised the post to Dearborn in the spring of 1808 or earlier and was holding it in reserve for him while the ailing incumbent was enjoying a sinecure and his duties were being performed by his deputy. They were very ably performed, as a matter of fact, and Jefferson was indulging a Revolutionary veteran while keeping Dearborn in his own official family as long as possible. His conduct may not have been beyond reproach, but the congressmen were agreed that this case called for no investigation and warranted no threat of impeachment. Dearborn's official conduct, especially his relations with General Wilkinson, came up for scrutiny, but his nomination was confirmed by a party vote.[8] No doubt this inquiry was embarrassing to Jefferson, and the rumor that he was going to appoint Governor William Hull of Michigan Territory to succeed Dearborn aroused unfavorable comment because of his supposed connection with the

[6] March 6, 1809 (Senate Exec. Procs., II, 119).
[7] Annals, 10 Cong., 2 sess., pp. 1173-1182.
[8] See ch. XXVIII, p. 509, above, for TJ's commitment to Dearborn. In his dissertation on Dearborn, Erney describes the entire episode and gives full references (pp. 245-250).

notorious speculation in Yazoo lands. The rumor may have been unfounded and actually no successor was appointed. After the Secretary of War resigned in mid-February, the chief clerk of the department performed the duties of his office.

One annoyance of this period was occasioned by a transaction of Jefferson's which in his opinion was as innocent as any he ever engaged in. At the request of the Agricultural Society of Paris, of which he was a member and from which he had recently received the gift of a plow, he had procured from a friend a quantity of cottonseed (two tierces, he said) and had authorized the shipment of this in a public vessel that was going from New York to France. The seed was consigned to a firm in Baltimore, who had been asked by him to ship it to New York. News of the shipment got out and was taken up by Federalists as a violation of the embargo, to the embarrassment of supporters of the administration. Senator Samuel Smith, who came from Baltimore and was even more officious than usual at this stage, sent the President a comment he had recently received and suggested that the order regarding the seed be countermanded. Saying that, while willing to disregard the censure of his political enemies, he did not want to give offense to any of his supporters, Jefferson asked John Hollis, a friendly agent in Baltimore, to take possession of the seed.[9] In this letter he went to pains to describe the correspondence that went on between societies with the benevolent purpose of communicating useful information. "These societies are always at peace," he said, "however the nations may be at war. Like the republic of letters, they form a great fraternity spreading over all the earth, and their correspondence is not interrupted by any civilized nation." He was now seeking to withdraw the cottonseed from it, however, and he suggested to his correspondent that he use it in his own garden for manure. Hollis demurred at first and wondered if he could not plant it. Jefferson said that May was generally the planting time, but that as far as he himself was concerned, the sentence on the seed was irrevocable.

The most mortifying event of his last year in office took place at almost its end, when the Senate unanimously rejected his nomination of William Short as minister to Russia.[10] He had given his old secretary an *ad interim* appointment five months earlier and revealed the secret only in his last official communication to the upper branch of

[9] TJ to John Hollis, Feb. 19, 1809 (L. & B., XII, 252–254); Samuel Smith to TJ, Feb. 18, with enclosure (LC, 33053–33054). Other letters bearing on the episode are Hollis to TJ, Feb. 21 (LC, 33090) and TJ to Hollis, Feb. 23 (LC, 33093).

[10] Feb. 27, 1809 (*Senate Exec. Procs.*, II, 113).

Congress. The ostensible reason for his rebuff was that the senators saw no need for such a mission. Also, the nominee, who had spent only a few years in the country since he served with Jefferson in Paris, was regarded by many as a "mere Frenchman," and the irregularity of the President's procedure, along with his excessive secrecy, might have been expected to create resentment.

In mid-summer, 1808, Jefferson told Short that a special mission to Russia had been agreed to by the Cabinet.[11] The desire to cultivate friendly relations with that country and its ruler had been strongly expressed in his earlier correspondence with Tsar Alexander I.[12] No doubt he continued to regard the Tsar as the most liberal-minded ruler in Europe, despite that monarch's alliance with Napoleon, and he still cherished the hope that in the eventual peace negotiations Alexander would be a champion of lesser nations and neutral rights, especially maritime rights. Therefore, at just the time that the embargo was being enforced more vigorously against the chief warring powers, he wanted to make known to this potential friend the genuinely neutral position of the United States. It was not a bad idea, but, since Russia was allied with France, his political foes could have accused him of planning an anti-British move, and for this reason if for no other he thought secrecy desirable. Primarily, for reasons of secrecy, he said, it was decided that the mission should begin before, not after, the opening of the congressional session. And, although he regarded Short as an experienced and accomplished diplomat, a major reason for choosing him, no doubt, was that he could be trusted to act in confidence and was a thoroughly devoted friend.

Short carried on an extensive correspondence with Jefferson during the summer but did not confer with him or Madison in person. Though duly commissioned, he was to appear to be a private citizen, and his immediate destination was to be Paris — where he was very much at home but had not expected to stay as long as he did on this visit. After much discussion of his passage, Short, who was a bad sailor, set out from Philadelphia on October 2, 1808, in a government vessel, bearing a letter from Jefferson to the Tsar.[13] This was of a kind with those he previously wrote that potentate. Since he was at Monticello and his copies of these were in Washington, he was not able to send

[11] TJ to Short, July 6, 1808 (LC, 31643).
[12] On their correspondence, see ch. XXIV, above.
[13] TJ to the Emperor of Russia, Aug. 29, 1808 (Ford, IX, 206–207). His letter of the same date to Short (LC, 31973) is of special interest and importance. Among other letters are: Short to TJ, Sept. 4, 1808 (LC, 32012–32013); TJ to Short, Sept. 6 (L. & B., XII, 159–160); TJ to Madison, Sept. 13 (L. & B., XII, 165–166); Short to TJ, Sept. 28 (LC, 32143–32146).

them to Short to read, but he did send the Emperor's letter to him. Jefferson's undelivered letter, which closed this cycle, was inevitably couched in general terms, but it left no doubt of his desire to promote "useful intercourse and good understanding" between the two countries, and to cultivate the friendship of the sovereign whom he described as "just and magnanimous." Short, who was described here as a distinguished American citizen, was to explain the "peculiar position" and true neutrality of the United States, and the hope was tactfully expressed that, through the influence of Alexander's example, respect would be shown the character and rights of a peaceful nation. The minister who was being sent on the President's sole authority was to be a messenger of good will.

The mission was well intentioned and might have been fruitful, but it never got beyond Paris, where Short concluded that he had better remain until he learned more about developments at home.[14] Except for a letter he wrote on his arrival in Paris, Jefferson had no word from him. When the President first planned this mission, no doubt, he was confident that it would be approved by his supporters just because he recommended it, as had so generally been the case, and also because they would be presented with a *fait accompli*. He afterwards said that they (presumably he and Madison) kept back the nomination to the end of the session so that the mission might remain secret as long as possible, but this may have been a rationalization. Short did not keep it secret in Paris, where he established friendly relations with the Russian Minister. Another possible explanation of Jefferson's holding the nomination in abeyance so long is that, amid the uncertainties of this session, he perceived no time when it could be conveniently presented.

When he did get around to it his influence with the Senate had sadly eroded — partly because he was on his way out, but in part also because of other nominations he had recently made. On the very day that the Senate rejected that of Short, William Branch Giles wrote Madison that Jefferson's recent efforts in behalf of his favorites Page and Dearborn had caused the senators to be distrustful of his nominees.[15] At the moment Giles was arguing with Madison against the prospective nomination of Gallatin as secretary of state, which he believed Jefferson to be favoring, and in effect he was reading the President-elect a lecture regarding his future policy in the matter of appointments. By blocking the nomination of Gallatin, he and Samuel Smith were showing Madison where the power really was. It is significant, how-

14 I have been privileged to see an unpublished account of Short's mission by George G. Shackelford, who has made a special study of his career.
15 Giles to Madison, Feb. 27, 1809 (courtesy of the Papers of James Madison).

ever, that this influential senator, who had staunchly supported the embargo, charged the outgoing head of the party with favoritism.

Writing after Madison's inauguration, the ex-President told Short that his long absence from the country had worked to his disadvantage, but that the main reason for the action of the senators was their unwillingness to extend the diplomatic system. He reported that Madison had hastened to nominate John Quincy Adams for the post, only to have him rejected.[16] There was much more opposition to Short on personal grounds than Jefferson implied — more in fact than he may have recognized. His former secretary did not blame him for this *contretemps*, but he believed that Giles and the Smith brothers were active against him.[17]

Jefferson was surprised and pained that none of his friends in the Senate gave him the opportunity to explain things and remove objections, as they normally would have done in the past. This event showed that they no longer saw any need to consult him, and it may be said to mark the lowest point of his influence within the government.

His presidency, like his governorship of his native state a quarter of a century earlier, had ended in anticlimax, but it would be a mistake to assume that he went out of office on a wave of public disapproval. The groups that had disliked him in the first place probably disliked him more than ever; but, judging from the addresses, resolutions, and letters that poured over his desk, he had maintained a high degree of popularity with his fellow citizens. Since he received communications from Republican groups in New England, he can be said to have had messages of approval from all parts of the country. And, while the rhetorical extravagance of these writings must be discounted, they are distinctly impressive in the aggregate.

"Parson" Weems presented him with a copy of the seventh edition of his work on the private life of George Washington; and, after saying that he was not one of the multitude that adored the rising sun, he made this declaration: "Self-descending, your Excellency sets in glory." He was referring to Jefferson's declination to serve another term and could not have realized the difficulty His Excellency was having in getting through this one. The Governor of Maryland, expressing the most cordial approbation of his administration, said that it

---

[16] TJ to Short, March 8, 1809 (Ford, IX, 249–250). Actually, the Senate declined to consider the nomination of Adams. It was resubmitted and approved some months later.

[17] Short to TJ, May 27, 1809 (LC, 33313–33316).

had been "marked in every feature with wisdom, circumspection, and patriotism, and crowned with the most unparalleled prosperity." The Republicans of Bristol, Rhode Island, declared: "It is not enough for Americans to call you great; we call you good."[18]

Such sayings need not be taken at face value, and such eulogists did not view with a critical eye the events of his last months in office. The major purpose of many addresses and resolutions was to express approval of the foreign and domestic policy of the administration. Early in the year he received, in the form of a resolution, a pledge from the legislators of his own state to support the government "with the last cent of our treasure, and the last drop of our blood, in every measure either of defence or offence, which they may deem expedient to vindicate our injured honor and our violated rights."[19] The address of the Virginia Assembly that was adopted a month later by a vote of 5 to 1 was described by him as affectionate and was received with "peculiar sensibility." Written by William Wirt it had a florid style and highly laudatory tone. It thanked Jefferson "for the model of an administration conducted on the purest principles of republicanism." It listed the accomplishments of his presidency most approvingly, and it declared that, from the first moment of his resistance to foreign tyranny until now, he had shown "the same uniform and consistent character."[20] Neither he nor his administration were that pure or that consistent, but these words suggest the sort of image that was in the minds of very many of his countrymen.

There was comfort in such words as these, but his overwhelming desire was to get out of an office in which he had been fated to stay too long. On the day the Senate rejected William Short, he said in a letter to his daughter: "I look with infinite joy to the moment when I shall be ultimately moored in the midst of my affections, and free to follow the pursuits of my choice."[21] He had been saying much the same thing for many months, and in certain respects the prospects of homecoming had not brightened. Early in the year his son-in-law, whose financial plight was perennial, had written him of his desire to sell Varina, his farm below Richmond, and in response Jefferson suggested the sale of certain outlying lands of his own. Whether the proceeds went to pay

18 M. L. Weems to TJ, Feb. 1, 1809 (LC, 32940); Gov. Robt. Wright to TJ, March 3, 1809 (LC, 33167); Address of Bristol, R.I., Convention, Feb. 20, 1809 (LC, 33072-33073).
19 Jan. 6, 1809 (LC, 32753-32762).
20 Address of Feb. 6, 1809, and his reply of Feb. 16 are in Randall, III, 303-304.
21 TJ to Martha, Feb. 27, 1809 (*Family Letters*, p. 385).

Randolph's debts or his own was a matter of indifference, he said, since he considered their property "a common stock for our joint family."[22] He acknowledged with sorrow that he was about $10,000 short as the result of his presidency, and he had already made inquiries about the possibility of selling more of his own lands.[23] Also, through the agency of a friend in Richmond he procured a private loan, and Madison went on his note for another from a bank.[24] He was aware that he faced a dubious financial future, and in his letters to his daughter had much to say about the economies they must observe when he again became a private man. He continued to send money to Charles Willson Peale for his grandson, who had developed into a very serious student. Peale, returning to the painting he had long neglected because of his interest in his museum of natural history, did a portrait of Thomas Jefferson Randolph as a gift for his old friend. The solicitous grandfather received this with the utmost satisfaction, and he had the pleasure of the company of the boy himself at the end of his presidency.[25] They rode together to the Capitol on Madison's inauguration day.

On Friday, March 3, the *National Intelligencer* said: "Never will it be forgotten as long as liberty is dear to man that it was on this day that Thomas Jefferson retired from the supreme magistracy amidst the blessings and regrets of millions." To the friendly editor of this paper it seemed remarkable that one who was "crowned with popularity" and whose mind was unclouded and unweakened should be voluntarily relinquishing power that he might have kept. Samuel Harrison Smith does not seem to have observed how tired the President was.

His paper properly featured Madison in its account of inauguration day. The incoming President had a military escort such as his predecessor had not had either four or eight years earlier; and Jefferson, undramatic to the last, was attended by only his grandson as he rode down Pennsylvania Avenue. Madison's speech was no more audible than those of Jefferson had been, and the editor of the *New York Evening Post* saw in it no sign that the next President would abandon the "ruinous course" of the old one.[26]

---

[22] This expression is in his letter of Jan. 31, 1809, to TMR (*Papers, MHS*, p. 134). Other letters bearing on this topic are TMR to TJ, Jan. 6, 1809 (Edgehill-Randolph Papers, UVA); TJ to TMR, Jan. 17 (LC, 32818a).

[23] TJ to Craven Peyton, Jan. 9, 1809 (McGregor Library Collection, UVA).

[24] A more detailed discussion of his finances will necessarily be given in the final volume of this series.

[25] Peale to TJ, Feb. 21, 1809 (LC, 33088); TJ to Peale, March 10 (LC, 33191).

[26] *N.Y. Evening Post*, March 8, 1809. The inauguration was described in the *National Intelligencer*, March 6.

After the inauguration a "large concourse of ladies and gentlemen," Mr. Jefferson among them, waited upon Mr. Madison in his house. His predecessor, who had not yet finished packing and was still occupying the President's House, greeted guests there soon afterward. He also attended the inaugural ball that night — the first in the series — and talked there with John Quincy Adams, who was briefly in town on legal business. The ex-President asked the ex-Senator if he was still fond of poetry and learned that he still liked *good* poetry. Speaking for himself, Jefferson said he still enjoyed reading Homer but did not much care for Virgil.[27] He was soon to have more time for that sort of thing. According to Mrs. Samuel Harrison Smith, Jefferson (whom she quite adored) seemed very happy at these social gatherings. Despite his being described by some as venerable, one may assume that he was rather like a boy out of school.

At some time during the day he received from the citizens of Washington an address which gratified him much as that from the General Assembly of his own state had done — for these were also fellow citizens of his in a very special sense. Like others, they paid tribute to his public services, but they spoke particularly of their good fortune in having been able to know him as a man. According to the address of these citizens, their predominant feeling was that of "appreciation for the mild and endearing virtues" that had made every one of them his friend. They were not as sentimental as Mrs. Samuel Harrison Smith, who said that without this dear, good man Washington would not be Washington to her, but they left no doubt that they would miss him greatly.[28]

Although he expressed sincere regret at parting with his fellow townsmen, he devoted most of his grave valedictory to their country. "The station which we occupy among the nations of the earth is honorable, but awful," he said. "Trusted with the destinies of this solitary republic of the world, the only monument of human rights, and the sole depository of the sacred fire of freedom and self-government, from hence it is to be lighted up in other regions of the earth, if other regions of the earth shall ever become susceptible of its benign influence. All mankind ought then, with us, to rejoice in its prosperous, and sympathize in its adverse fortunes, as involving everything dear to man. And to what sacrifices of interest, or convenience, ought not these considerations to animate us? To what compromises of

[27] J. Q. Adams to Louise Catherine Adams, March 5, 1809 (*Writings*, III, 289).

[28] Margaret Bayard Smith, on Feb. 26, 1809 (*First Forty Years of Washington Society*, p. 55).

opinion and inclination to maintain harmony and union among ourselves and to preserve from all danger this hallowed ark of human hope
and happiness."[29]

In language that was to be matched by no successor until Abraham
Lincoln he was proclaiming the mission of his country; and with
greater solemnity than in his first inaugural he was invoking the spirit
of national unity in the face of greater danger than existed then. For a
variety of reasons, but chiefly because of the course of international
affairs, he had been considerably less successful in attaining and maintaining unity in his second term than in his first. He did not concede
that his policies were wrong, but other words of his suggest that at the
end of his official service he was conscious of his temperamental limitations as a public man. In a passage in a letter to Du Pont de Nemours
that was destined to be quoted many times in later years, he said:
"Nature intended me for the tranquil pursuits of science, by rendering
them my supreme delight. But the enormities of the times in which I
have lived have forced me to take a part in resisting them, and to
commit myself on the boisterous ocean of political passions."[30] Nature
conferred such a diversity of gifts on him that no one can be sure what
she specially intended him to pursue; and there could be no doubt that
during four decades he had performed with notable impressiveness, if
not always with success, in the political sphere. Nor can there be any
doubt that he found delight in the peaceful pursuit of knowledge —
any sort of knowledge — in reasonable company. In his remaining
years he was to face great personal difficulties, but, as the political man
passed into the background, the sage and builder and educational
statesman could emerge. One of the most characteristic and fruitful
periods of his life lay ahead of him. With the consent of the Madisons
he took his time in collecting his belongings and getting out of the
President's House, but he vacated it without regret, and with un-
feigned joy took the road back to Monticello.

---

[29] His reply of March 4, 1809, is in Padover, *Complete Jefferson*, pp. 552–553. A
number of his replies to addresses in the weeks surrounding his retirement are in
that work, pp. 542–563.

[30] TJ to P. S. Du Pont de Nemours, March 2, 1809 (*J.-D. Correspondence*, p.
122). It should be noted that by "science" he meant knowledge — all knowledge.

Acknowledgments

FOR assistance while preparing this volume I am deeply indebted to the National Endowment for the Humanities. This aid has been far more than material. Besides successive grants from this great agency I have received from its high officers unfailing understanding and encouragement during the slow performance of a difficult task. My old friends of the Thomas Jefferson Memorial Foundation have continued to share in this project with characteristic patience, and the American Council of Learned Societies has permitted me to avail myself of an expense account of long standing. The Rockefeller Foundation gave me a delightful month at the Villa Serbelloni at Bellagio during which I was enabled to engage in uninterrupted reflection and unimpeded writing. This enterprise has been blessed with generous and distinguished sponsorship.

Most of the manuscript materials used in this volume were originally seen by me in the Division of Manuscripts of the Library of Congress, and to that great repository I shall be forever grateful. Because of the availability of photographic materials, however, I have been able in recent years to center my research to a greater degree than hitherto on the Alderman Library of the University of Virginia. Virtually all of the writing, except for what I've done during summers on Cape Cod, has been done in the study that has been so generously provided me in that library. To list all the people there who have helped me would be quite impossible, but, besides thanking the staff as a whole, I will add a special word of appreciation to the Manuscripts Department.

Among those who have been especially responsive and helpful in providing materials from the records and collections in their charge are: Roger Bruns, assistant to the executive director of the National Historical Publications Commission, at the National Archives; Stephen T. Riley, director of the Massachusetts Historical Society; Marcus A. McCorison, director and librarian of the American Antiquarian Society; and John L. Lochhead, librarian, Mariners Museum, Newport News, Virginia.

Among those who have responded generously to requests for information from their files and have offered me wise counsel are James A. Bear, Jr., curator of Monticello; Julian P. Boyd, editor of *The Papers of Thomas Jefferson*, Princeton; and my good neighbors in the Alderman Library, Donald Jackson and Robert A. Rutland, editors respectively of *The Papers of George Washington* and *The Papers of James Madison*.

Among those who have enabled me to see valuable writings of theirs in advance of publication are Harry Ammon, biographer of James Monroe; Christopher McKee, biographer of Edward Preble; and George G. Shackelford, biographer of William Short.

For providing me with copies from the U.S. Circuit Court Records in the Federal Records Center, Boston, bearing on the Connecticut libel cases, I am grateful to Pierce Gaines, Esquire, of Fairfield, Connecticut, and his daughter.

For helpful information regarding the records of the Burr trial I am much indebted to Eppa Hunton IV of Richmond.

I have been doubly fortunate in the continued services of my part-time secretary, Katherine M. Sargeant, and my part-time research assistant, Steven H. Hochman. They have shared the labors of this entire volume, growing in skill and losing nothing in diligence through the years, and properly share with me such credit as this work may receive.

There are dozens of other people whom I ought to thank and I ask forgiveness of those I have not mentioned. My editor at Little, Brown and Company, Larned G. Bradford, has continued to bear with me patiently and to co-operate with me generously. My solicitous wife has kept me going despite the ravages of time. I trust she is not weary in well-doing nor tired of being thanked.

List of Symbols and Short Titles[1]
Most Frequently Used in Footnotes

Abernethy	*The Burr Conspiracy*, by Thomas P. Abernethy.
Account Book	Jefferson's informal account books, in various repositories. Cited by date only.
Adams, *History*	*History of the United States* (during the administrations of Jefferson and Madison), by Henry Adams. Of the nine volumes, the third and fourth chiefly concern us here.
Adams, *Memoirs*	*Memoirs of John Quincy Adams.*
AECPEU	Affaires Ètrangères, Correspondance Politique, États-Unis (transcripts in Library of Congress from French Archives).
A.H.R.	*American Historical Review.*
A.-J. Letters	*Adams-Jefferson Letters*, ed. by L. J. Cappon.
Ammon	*James Monroe: The Quest for National Identity*, by Harry Ammon.
Annals	*Annals of Congress.*
A.S.P.	*American State Papers*, ed. by Lowrie & Clarke. (Volumes entitled Foreign Relations are referred to as *A.S.P.F.R.;* those entitled Finance, Military Affairs, Naval Affairs, Public Lands, and Miscellaneous are referred to as *A.S.P., Finance*, etc.).

[1] Repositories are designated by roman capitals run together, the names of editors and authors are in roman type, and the abbreviated titles of printed works are in italics. Further details about these works, and about others frequently used but more easily identified from the references in the notes, are in the Select Critical Bibliography which follows. To avoid excess of italics in the lists, long titles are printed there in roman except in cases where a magazine or other work is italicized to distinguish it from an article in it.

Beveridge	*Life of John Marshall*, by A. J. Beveridge. References are chiefly to Vol. III.
Bixby	*Thomas Jefferson Correspondence. Printed from the Originals in the Collections of William K. Bixby.*
Boyd	*Papers of Thomas Jefferson*, ed. by Julian P. Boyd.
Brant	*James Madison*, by Irving Brant. Referred to by volume number, chiefly to Vol. IV, *Secretary of State, 1800–1809.*
Bruce	*John Randolph of Roanoke*, by W. C. Bruce.
Butterfield	*Letters of Benjamin Rush*, ed. by L. H. Butterfield.
Carter	*Territorial Papers of the United States*, ed. by C. E. Carter. The volumes dealing with particular territories are designated by number.
Cunningham	*The Jeffersonian Republicans in Power*, by Noble E. Cunningham, Jr.
D.A.B.	*Dictionary of American Biography.*
Daveiss, *View*	*A View of the President's Conduct, Concerning the Conspiracy of 1806*, by Joseph H. Daveiss.
Domestic Life	*Domestic Life of Thomas Jefferson*, by Sarah N. Randolph.
Family Letters	*The Family Letters of Thomas Jefferson*, ed. by E. M. Betts and J. A. Bear, Jr.
Farm Book	*Thomas Jefferson's Farm Book*, ed. by E. M. Betts.
FO	Dispatches of the British Ministers to the United States to the Foreign Office (transcripts in Library of Congress).
Ford	*Writings of Thomas Jefferson*, ed. by P. L. Ford (10 volumes).
Garden Book	*Thomas Jefferson's Garden Book*, annotated by E. M. Betts.
Hunt	*Writings of James Madison*, ed. by Gaillard Hunt.
I.B.M.	*Instructions to the British Ministers to the U.S., 1791–1812*, ed. by Bernard Mayo.
Jackson	*Letters of the Lewis and Clark Expedition*, ed. by Donald Jackson.

J.-D. Correspondence	*Correspondence between Thomas Jefferson and Pierre Samuel du Pont de Nemours*, ed. by Dumas Malone.
JWE	John Wayles Eppes, son-in-law of Jefferson.
King	*Life and Correspondence of Rufus King*, ed. by C. R. King. References to Vols. IV, V.
L. & B.	*Writings of Thomas Jefferson*, ed. by Lipscomb and Bergh.
LC	Library of Congress. Unless otherwise indicated, the references are to the Jefferson Papers there.
McCaleb, *Burr Conspiracy*	*The Aaron Burr Conspiracy*, by Walter F. McCaleb.
McCaleb, *New Light*	*A New Light on Aaron Burr*, by Walter F. McCaleb.
MHS	Massachusetts Historical Society. Unless otherwise indicated, the references are to the Jefferson Papers in the Coolidge Collection. See *Papers, MHS* below.
MP	Papers of James Madison, Library of Congress.
NA	National Archives, Washington, D.C.
Padover	*Thomas Jefferson and the National Capital*, ed. by S. K. Padover.
Papers, MHS	*Jefferson Papers, Collections Massachusetts Historical Society*, 7 ser., I.
Perkins	*Prologue to War*, by Bradford Perkins.
Plumer, *Memorandum*	*William Plumer's Memorandum of Proceedings in the United States Senate, 1803–1807*, ed. by E. S. Brown.
Randall	*Life of Thomas Jefferson*, by H. S. Randall (3 vols.).
Robertson	*Report of the Trials of Colonel Aaron Burr*, 1875 ed., reported by David Robertson.
Schachner	*Aaron Burr: A Biography*, by Nathan Schachner.
Senate Exec. Procs.	*Journal of the Executive Proceedings of the Senate of the United States*. Vol. II.
S.M.H.	*Writings of James Monroe*, ed. by S. M. Hamilton.

Sowerby	*Catalogue of the Library of Thomas Jefferson*, compiled by E. M. Sowerby (5 vols.).
Thwaites	*Original Journal of the Lewis and Clark Expedition, 1804–1806*, ed. by Reuben G. Thwaites.
TJ	Thomas Jefferson.
TMR	Thomas Mann Randolph, Jr., son-in-law of Jefferson.
UVA	Alderman Library, University of Virginia. Unless otherwise indicated, the references are to the Jefferson manuscripts.
Va. Mag.	*Virginia Magazine of History and Biography.*
W. & M.	*William and Mary Quarterly.*
Warren	*The Supreme Court in United States History*, by Charles Warren. References are chiefly to Vol. I.

Select Critical Bibliography

A. *Manuscripts*

The manuscript materials for this volume are basically the same as those for its immediate predecessor. I have drawn chiefly on Jefferson's own papers in the Library of Congress (LC), vols. 147–187; in the Massachusetts Historical Society (MHS); and in the Alderman Library of the University of Virginia (UVA). Although I have used the manuscripts in the large majority of cases, the papers in both of the two former collections are available on microfilm at the Alderman Library and elsewhere. Jefferson's invaluable Account Book for this period is in MHS, but photostat copies are available at LC and UVA, and I actually have one in my own study as I also have a copy of his index of letters (from LC).

Among other collections in LC which have proved useful are:

Papers of James Madison, including the Rives Collection (available on microfilm, with index). Referred to as MP.
Papers of James Monroe (available on microfilm, with index).
Papers of Joseph H. Nicholson.
Private Memoir of William A. Burwell.
Letters in Relation to Burr's Conspiracy.
Transcripts from Foreign Archives:
 Dispatches of the British Ministers to the United States to the Foreign Office, 1805–1809 (referred to as FO with the appropriate volume numbers).
 Affaires Étrangères, Correspondance Politique, États-Unis (referred to as AECPEU).

Useful collections at UVA include:

Edgehill-Randolph papers.
Carr-Cary papers.
Cabell papers.
Randolph-Garnett letterbook.
Court records of the trial of Aaron Burr (photostat copy, original in the Virginia State Library, Richmond).

The National Archives (NA) have provided various items from Records of the Department of State, Records of the Bureau of Customs, and other collections.

A microfilm edition of the papers of Albert Gallatin is now available, with abundant material on the enforcement of the embargo. Sponsored by New York University and the National Historical Publications Commission, it includes items from various repositories.

The microfilm edition of the Adams Family Papers (MHS) was used to a limited extent.

B. *Jefferson's Published Papers*

The chief collections are:

The Papers of Thomas Jefferson. Julian P. Boyd, ed. (Princeton University Press, 1950–   ). Cited as Boyd. The definitive work, projected in fifty volumes of which eighteen have been published. Since these extend only to January 24, 1791, they have been of little help in connection with TJ's presidency except in providing background material.

The Writings of Thomas Jefferson. Paul Leicester Ford, ed., 10 vols. (New York, 1892–1899). Cited as Ford and not to be confused with the same work in 12 vols.

The Writings of Thomas Jefferson. A. A. Lipscomb and A. E. Bergh, eds., 20 vols. (New York, 1903). Cited as L. & B. More extensive than Ford, but less accurate in text.

Among smaller but valuable collections may be listed:

The Jefferson Papers. Collections of the Massachusetts Historical Society, 7 ser., I (Boston, 1900). Cited as *Papers, MHS.*

Thomas Jefferson Correspondence. Printed from the Originals in the Collections of William K. Bixby. With notes by W. C. Ford (Boston, 1916). Cited as Bixby.

The Complete Jefferson. Containing His Major Writings, Published and Unpublished, Except His Letters. Saul K. Padover, ed. (New York, Duell, Sloan & Pearce, 1943).

Thomas Jefferson and the National Capital, 1783–1818. Saul K. Padover, ed. (Washington, Government Printing Office, 1946). Notes, correspondence, and reports from various repositories and publications. Referred to as Padover.

Family Letters of Thomas Jefferson. E. M. Betts and J. A. Bear, Jr., eds. (Columbia, University of Missouri Press, 1966). Correspondence between Jefferson and his daughters and grandchildren, collected from various repositories. Referred to as *Family Letters.*

The Adams-Jefferson Letters· The Complete Correspondence between Thomas Jefferson and John and Abigail Adams. Lester J. Cappon, ed., 2 vols. (Chapel Hill, University of North Carolina Press, for the Institute of Early American History and Culture at Williamsburg, 1959). Referred to as *A.-J. Letters.*

Correspondence between Thomas Jefferson and Pierre Samuel du Pont de Nemours, 1798–1817. Dumas Malone, ed., translations by Linwood Lehman (Boston, Houghton Mifflin Co., 1930). Referred to as *J.-D. Correspondence.*

"Tsar Alexander I and Jefferson: Unpublished Correspondence." N. Hans, ed. In *Slavonic & East European Review,* XXXII (December, 1953), 215–225.

"Poplar Forest: Jefferson's Legacy to His Grandson." By Norma B. Cuthbert. In *Huntington Library Quarterly,* VI (May, 1943), 333–356. Primarily correspondence between TJ and JWE.

The two following works, edited by Edwin M. Betts, continue to be invaluable:

Thomas Jefferson's Garden Book, 1766–1824, with relevant extracts from his other writings (Philadelphia, American Philosophical Society, 1944). The extracts are more important than the entries in this period. Referred to as *Garden Book.*

Thomas Jefferson's Farm Book, with commentary and relevant extracts from other writings (Princeton University Press, for the American Philosophical Society, 1953). Jefferson's agricultural activities during his presidency were limited, but his correspondence about agricultural matters is of great interest. Referred to as *Farm Book.*

Because of the personal letters and family traditions in *The Life of Thomas Jefferson* by Henry S. Randall (3 vols., New York, 1858), that distinguished work has something of the character of a source book. (Referred to as Randall.) Much of the same material is in *The Domestic Life of Thomas Jefferson* by Sarah N. Randolph (New York, 1871). Referred to as *Domestic Life.*

There is authoritative information about his major collection of books, along with his comments on them, in *Catalogue of the Library of Thomas Jefferson,* E. Millicent Sowerby, ed., 5 vols. (Washington, Library of Congress, 1952–1959). Referred to as Sowerby.

The works listed below contain original materials of the first importance which cannot be described as writings, but should be cited among Jefferson's papers:

Thomas Jefferson, Architect. Original Designs in the Collection of Thomas Jefferson Coolidge, Jr. With an essay and notes by Fiske Kimball. (Boston, printed for private distribution, 1916). A classic work.

The same, with a new introduction by Frederick D. Nichols (New York, DaCapo Press, 1968).

Thomas Jefferson's Architectural Drawings. Compiled and with commentary and a check list by Frederick D. Nichols. Revised and enlarged 2nd edn. (Boston, Massachusetts Historical Society; Charlottesville, Thomas Jefferson Memorial Foundation and University Press of Virginia, 1961). Supplements Kimball's work.

C. Official and Semi-official Collections

American State Papers. Documents, Legislative and Executive. Selected and edited, under the authority of Congress, by Walter Lowrie and Matthew St. Clair Clarke. 38 vols. (Washington, 1832–1861).

Foreign Relations. Vols. II and III (referred to as *A.S.P.F.R.*), are more frequently cited in the text than any other volumes in this official series.

Varying use has been made of volumes covering this period that are entitled Finance, Military Affairs, Naval Affairs, Public Lands, Commerce and Navigation, and Miscellaneous (referred to as *A.S.P., Finance*, etc.).

Annals of Congress, 9 and 10 Congress, 1805–1809. 5 vols. (Washington, 1852–1853). Invaluable, despite the imperfect reporting of debates. Referred to as *Annals*.

Journal of the Executive Proceedings of the Senate of the United States. Vol. II, 1805–1815 (Washington, 1828). Referred to as *Senate Exec. Procs.*

Instructions to the British Ministers to the United States, 1791–1813. Benard Mayo, ed. In *Annual Report of the American Historical Association for the Year 1936*, Vol. III (Washington, 1941). Referred to as *I.B.M.*

Treaties and Other International Acts of the United States of America. Hunter Miller, ed. Vol. II, 1776–1818 (Washington, 1931).

Territorial Papers of the United States. Clarence E. Carter, ed. Of this invaluable series (referred to as Carter), the following were specially useful for this volume:

Vol. IX: Territory of Orleans (Washington, 1940).
Vol. XIII: Territory of Louisiana-Missouri, 1803–1806 (1948).
Vol. XIV: Territory of Louisiana-Missouri, 1806–1814 (1949).

A Compilation of the Messages and Papers of the Presidents, 1789–1897. By James D. Richardson (Washington, 1896).

Documents relating to the Purchase and Exploration of Louisiana (Boston, 1904). Contains Jefferson's "Examination into the Boundaries of Louisiana," and William Dunbar's "Journal of a Voyage."

Louisiana under the Rule of Spain, France, and the United States,

1785–1807. Edited and translated by James A. Robertson. Vol. II (Cleveland, 1911).

Transactions of the American Philosophical Society Held at Philadelphia for Promoting Useful Knowledge. Especially Vol. VI (Philadelphia, 1809).

Naval Documents Related to the United States Wars with the Barbary Powers, prepared by the Office of Naval Records and Library Navy Department, under the Supervision of Dudley W. Knox. Vols. III–V (Washington, 1941–1944).

Proceedings of the General Court Martial convened for the Trial of Commodore James Barron (Washington, Navy Department, 1822).

Trials of William S. Smith and Samuel G. Ogden for Misdemeanor (New York, 1807).

The Examination of Col. Aaron Burr, before the Chief Justice of the United States . . . together with the Arguments of Council and Opinion of the Judge. [W. W. Hening and William Munford, reporters] (Richmond, 1807).

Reports of Cases Argued and Adjudged in the Supreme Court of the United States in the Years 1807 and 1808. William Cranch, reporter. Vol. IV, 3 edn. (New York, 1882).

Reports of the Trials of Colonel Aaron Burr. . . . Taken in shorthand by David Robertson. 2 vols. (Philadelphia, 1808). I have primarily cited the New York 1875 edition. Referred to as Robertson.

The Trial of Col. Aaron Burr, on an Indictment for Treason. . . . Taken in shorthand by T. Carpenter. 3 vols. (Washington, 1808). Inferior to Robertson, but includes additional material.

Burr-Blennerhassett Documents. Lesley Henshaw, ed. In *Quarterly Publication of the Historical and Philosophical Society of Ohio*, IX (January, April, 1914).

D. *Contemporary Writings*

I. CORRESPONDENCE AND OTHER PAPERS

ADAMS, HENRY. Documents relating to New England Federalism, 1800–1815 (Boston, 1877).

ADAMS, JOHN. Works. C. F. Adams, ed., 10 vols. (Boston, 1856).

ADAMS, JOHN QUINCY. Writings. Worthington C. Ford, ed. Vol. III (New York, 1914).

———. Memoirs. Charles Francis Adams, ed. Vol. I (Philadelphia, 1874). Referred to as Adams, *Memoirs*.

BAYARD, JAMES A. Papers, 1796–1815. Elizabeth Donnan, ed. In *Annual Report of the American Historical Association for the Year 1913*, Vol. II (Washington, 1915).

BENTLEY, WILLIAM. Diary of William Bentley, D.D., Pastor of the East Church, Salem, Massachusetts, Vol. III (1911).

BLENNERHASSETT, HARMAN. The Blennerhassett Papers. William Harrison Safford, ed. (Cincinnati, 1861).

BURR, AARON. Correspondence of Aaron Burr and His Daughter Theodosia. Mark Van Doren, ed. (New York, Covici-Friede, 1929).

————. Memoirs of Aaron Burr with Miscellaneous Selections from his Correspondence. By Matthew L. Davis. 2 vols. (New York, 1836–1837).

————. Some Papers of Aaron Burr. Worthington C. Ford, ed. In *Proceedings of the American Antiquarian Society*, XXIX (April, 1919), 43–128.

CABOT, GEORGE. Life and Letters. By Henry Cabot Lodge (Boston, 1878).

DUANE, WILLIAM. Letters. In *Proceedings of the Massachusetts Historical Society*, 2 ser., XX (1907), 257–394.

DUNBAR, WILLIAM. Life, Letters and Papers. Eron Rowland, ed. (Jackson, Mississippi Historical Society, 1930).

DUNLAP, WILLIAM. Diary. Vol. II, in *Collections of the New-York Historical Society for the Year 1930* (1930).

ELLICOTT, ANDREW. Life and Letters. By Catharine Matthews (New York, 1908).

FEW, FRANCES. Diary, 1808–1809. Noble E. Cunningham, Jr., ed. In *Journal of Southern History*, XXIX (August, 1963), 344–361.

GALLATIN, ALBERT. Writings. Henry Adams, ed. Vol. I (Philadelphia, 1879).

KING, RUFUS. Life and Correspondence. Charles R. King, ed. Vols. III, IV (New York, 1896–1897). Referred to as King.

LELAND, JOHN. Writings of the Late Elder John Leland . . . with additional sketches, etc. by Miss L. F. Greene (New York, 1845).

MADISON, JAMES. Writings. Gaillard Hunt, ed. 9 vols. (New York, 1900–1910). Referred to as Hunt.

————. Letters and Other Writings. 4 vols. (Washington, 1865).

MITCHILL, SAMUEL LATHAM. Dr. Mitchill's Letters from Washington, 1801–1813. In *Harper's New Monthly Magazine*, LVIII (April, 1879), 740–755.

MONROE, JAMES. Writings. S. M. Hamilton, ed. 7 vols. (New York, 1898–1903). Referred to as S.M.H.

PAINE, THOMAS. Complete Writings. Philip S. Foner, ed. 2 vols. (New York, Citadel Press, 1945).

PLUMER, WILLIAM. Memorandum of Proceedings in the United States Senate, 1803–1807. Everett S. Brown, ed. (New York, Macmillan, 1923). Referred to as Plumer, *Memorandum*.

RODNEY, THOMAS. Letters. In *Pennsylvania Magazine of History and Biography*, XLIV (1920).

Rush, Benjamin. Letters. L. H. Butterfield, ed. Vol. II (Princeton University Press, for the American Philosophical Society, 1951). Referred to as Butterfield.

Smith, Margaret Bayard. The First Forty Years of Washington Society. Gaillard Hunt, ed. (New York, 1906).

Taggart, Samuel. Letters of Samuel Taggart, Representative in Congress, 1803–1814. Introduction by George H. Haynes. In *Proceedings of the American Antiquarian Society*, XXXIII (April, 1923), Part I, covering 1803–1807, 113–226.

Taylor, John. Letters, May 11, 1793–April 19, 1823. In *John P. Branch Historical Papers of Randolph-Macon College*, II (June, 1908), 252–353.

Wilkinson, James. Memoirs of My Own Times. 3 vols. (Philadelphia, 1816).

2. TRAVELS AND EXPLORATIONS

Foster, Sir Augustus John. Jeffersonian America. Notes . . . Collected in the Years 1805–6–7 and 11–12. Edited with an introduction by Richard Beale Davis (San Marino, Huntington Library, 1954). First drafted 1833–1835.

Lewis, Meriwether, and William Clark. Letters of the Lewis and Clark Expedition, with Related Documents, 1783–1854. Donald Jackson, ed. (Urbana, University of Illinois Press, 1962). Referred to as Jackson.

———. Original Journals of the Lewis and Clark Expedition, 1804–1806. Reuben G. Thwaites, ed. 8 vols. (New York, 1904–1905).

Pike, Zebulon Montgomery. Journals. Donald Jackson, ed. 2 vols. (Norman, University of Oklahoma Press, 1966).

E. *Newspapers and Contemporary Pamphlets*

Even more in this than in the preceding volume, extensive use has been made of newspapers. Three leading Republican papers exceeded all others in value. As a source of information the most important was the *National Intelligencer*, published in Washington by Samuel Harrison Smith. This was the newspaper of record in the United States, particularly in regard to the proceedings of the federal government. Administration policies were announced and defended in its columns, yet it maintained a remarkably moderate and judicious tone. The strongest advocate of Republicanism in the nation was the Philadelphia *Aurora*, edited by William Duane, a forceful writer and an ardent partisan. Although Jefferson himself was always supported by the *Aurora*, his administration was not. Duane's conflicts with other Republicans, particularly within Pennsylvania, often diverted his paper from national issues. During Jefferson's second administration, Thomas Ritchie's Richmond *Enquirer* developed considerable national influence as the voice of the Virginia Republican party. The *Enquirer* was most important in this study for its defense of Jefferson and his party, and its reporting of the Burr conspiracy trial.

The Federalists possessed numerous well-edited newspapers, but the decline of their party outside of New England reduced the significance of the papers for this volume. Furthermore, until the enactment of the embargo, they lacked popular issues to exploit. In treating Jefferson's personal character, the Miranda expedition, and the Burr conspiracy and trial, they slipped into the worst journalistic practices of the era, printing rumors and personal slanders for partisan purposes.

In New England, where the Federalist party and press were most vigorous, Benjamin Russell's Boston *Columbian Centinel* was the most distinguished paper. In this volume, the *Centinel* and other Boston papers were consulted particularly with regard to the embargo. Certain other episodes called for special attention to the newspapers of particular regions. The Connecticut papers, used to study the libel cases there, were for both parties probably the most vituperative in the nation.

Because of the availability of newspapers in microform, it is more feasible to consult a wide variety of them today than it was in the past. As can be seen from the footnotes, numerous newspapers were consulted which are not described here. For information on many of them, see the studies of Cunningham, Fischer, and Knudsen, which are cited in section F of this bibliography. Almost all of the newspapers used are available in microform at UVA and at other major research libraries. The *Virginia Argus* was read on microfilm borrowed from the Virginia State Library at Richmond.

Pamphlets were quite important in this era, but, since their texts generally appeared in newspapers, I have generally read them there. The following were used in pamphlet form:

BRYANT, WILLIAM CULLEN. The Embargo, or Sketches of Our Times (Boston, 1808. Reprint. Gainesville, Fla., Scholars' Facsimiles and Reprints, 1955).

DAVEISS, JOSEPH HAMILTON. A View of the President's Conduct, Concerning the Conspiracy of 1806 (Frankfort, Ky., 1807. Reprint: I. J. Cox and H. A. Swineford, eds., *Quarterly Publication of the Historical and Philosophical Society of Ohio*, XII (April-June, July-Sept., 1917). Referred to as Daveiss, *View*.

FULTON, ROBERT. Torpedo War, and Submarine Explosions (New York, 1810).

GODEFROY, MAXIMILIAN. Military Reflections on Four Modes of Defence (Baltimore, 1807).

HAMPDEN. A Letter to the President of the United States, Touching the Prosecutions under his Patronage, before the Circuit Court of the District of Connecticut (New Haven, 1808).

PICKERING, TIMOTHY. Letter from the Hon. Timothy Pickering . . . Exhibiting to His Constituents, A View of the Imminent Danger of an Unnecessary and Ruinous War (1 Hartford from 2 Boston edn., 1808).

[STEPHEN, JAMES]. War in Disguise; or, The Frauds of the Neutral Flags (London, 1805).

F. *Secondary Works and Articles**

ABERNETHY, THOMAS P. The Burr Conspiracy (New York, Oxford University Press, 1954). Referred to as Abernethy.

————. The South in the New Nation, 1789–1819 (Baton Rouge, Louisiana State University Press, 1961).

ADAMS, HENRY. History of the United States of America [during the administrations of Jefferson and Madison]. 9 vols. (New York, 1889–1890). Referred to as Adams, *History*.

————. The Life of Albert Gallatin (Philadelphia, 1879).

ADAMS, JOHN QUINCY. Parties in the United States (New York, Greenberg, 1941).

ADAMS, MARY P. Jefferson's Military Policy with Special Reference to the Frontier, 1805–1809 (doctoral dissertation, University of Virginia, 1958).

ALLEN, GARDNER W. Our Navy and the Barbary Corsairs (Boston, 1905).

AMBLER, CHARLES HENRY. Thomas Ritchie: A Study in Virginia Politics (Richmond, 1913).

AMBROSE, STEPHEN E. Duty, Honor, Country: A History of West Point (Baltimore, The Johns Hopkins Press, 1966).

AMMON, HARRY. "James Monroe and the Election of 1808 in Virginia," in *William and Mary Quarterly*, 3 ser., XX (January, 1963), 33–56.

————. James Monroe: The Quest for National Identity (New York, McGraw-Hill, 1971). Referred to as Ammon.

ANDERSON, DICE R. William Branch Giles: A Study in the Politics of Virginia and the Nation from 1790 to 1830 (Menasha, Wis., 1914).

BALINKY, ALEXANDER. Albert Gallatin: Fiscal Theories and Policies (New Brunswick, Rutgers University Press, 1958).

BANNER, JAMES M., JR. To the Hartford Convention: The Federalists and the Origins of Party Politics in Massachusetts, 1789–1815 (New York, Knopf, 1970).

* This very select list contains the titles of indispensable works and others to which I am specially indebted.

BEMIS, SAMUEL FLAGG. John Quincy Adams and the Foundations of American Foreign Policy (New York, Knopf, 1949).

BEVERIDGE, ALBERT J. The Life of John Marshall. Vol. III (Boston, Houghton Mifflin, 1919). Referred to as Beveridge.

BOORSTIN, DANIEL J. The Lost World of Thomas Jefferson (New York, Holt, 1948).

BOYD, JULIAN P. "The Chasm that Separated Thomas Jefferson and John Marshall," in Essays on the American Constitution, Gottfried Dietze, ed. (Englewood Cliffs, N.J., Prentice-Hall, 1964).

BOYD, JULIAN P., and W. EDWIN HEMPHILL. The Murder of George Wythe (Williamsburg, Institute of Early American History and Culture, 1955). Two essays, reprinted from William and Mary Quarterly, 3 ser., XII (October, 1955).

BRANT, IRVING. James Madison: Secretary of State, 1801–1809 (Indianapolis, Bobbs-Merrill, 1953). Referred to as Brant, IV.

BROWN, GLENN. History of the United States Capitol. Vol. I (Washington, Government Printing Office, 1900).

BRUCE, WILLIAM CABELL. John Randolph of Roanoke. 2 edn., 2 vols. in one (New York, Putnam's, 1922). Referred to as Bruce.

BRYAN, WILHELMUS BOGART. A History of the National Capital. Vol. I, 1790–1814 (New York, 1914).

BURROUGHS, RAYMOND D., ed. The Natural History of the Lewis and Clark Expedition (East Lansing, Michigan State University Press, 1961).

BURT, A. L. The United States, Great Britain, and British North America (New Haven, Yale University Press, 1940).

BUSH, ALFRED L. The Life Portraits of Thomas Jefferson. Catalogue of an exhibition at the University of Virginia Museum of Fine Arts, April 12–26, 1962 (Charlottesville, Thomas Jefferson Memorial Foundation, 1962).

CHAPELLE, HOWARD I. The History of American Sailing Ships (New York, Norton, 1935).

———. The History of the American Sailing Navy: The Ships and Their Development (1949. Reprint. New York, Bonanza Books, 1960).

CHAPIN, BRADLEY. The American Law of Treason: Revolutionary and Early National Origins (Seattle, University of Washington Press, 1964).

CORWIN, EDWARD S. John Marshall and the Constitution (New Haven, Yale University Press, 1919).

COX, ISAAC J. The Early Exploration of Louisiana (University Studies, University of Cincinnati, 1906).

———. "The Exploration of the Louisiana Frontier, 1803–1808," in Annual Report of the American Historical Association for the Year 1904 (Washington, 1905), 151–174.

———. "General Wilkinson and His Later Intrigues with the Span-iards," in *American Historical Review*, XIX (July, 1914), 794–812.

———. The West Florida Controversy, 1798–1813 (Baltimore, The Johns Hopkins Press, 1918).

CUNNINGHAM, NOBLE E., JR. The Jeffersonian Republicans in Power: Party Operations, 1801–1809 (Chapel Hill, University of North Carolina Press, for the Institute of Early American History and Culture at Williamsburg, 1963). Referred to as Cunningham.

DE ROSIER, A. H., JR. "William Dunbar, Explorer," in *Journal of Mississippi History*, XXV (July, 1963), 165–185.

DU BOIS, W. E. B. The Suppression of the African Slave-Trade to the United States of America, 1638–1870 (1896. Reprint. New York, Schocken Books, 1969).

ERNEY, RICHARD ALTON. The Public Life of Henry Dearborn (doctoral dissertation, Columbia University, 1957).

FISCHER, DAVID H. The Revolution of American Conservatism: The Federalist Party in the Era of Jeffersonian Democracy (New York, Harper and Row, 1965).

GAINES, WILLIAM H., JR. Thomas Mann Randolph, Jefferson's Son-in-Law (Baton Rouge, Louisiana State University Press, 1966).

GOODMAN, PAUL. The Democratic-Republicans of Massachusetts (Cambridge, Harvard University Press, 1964).

GREEN, CONSTANCE MCLAUGHLIN. Washington: Village and Capital, 1800–1878 (Princeton University Press, 1962).

HAMLIN, TALBOT. Benjamin Henry Latrobe (New York, Oxford University Press, 1955).

HEATON, HERBERT. "Non-Importation, 1806–1812," in *Journal of Economic History*, I (November, 1941), 178–198.

HIGGINBOTHAM, SANFORD W. The Keystone of the Democratic Arch: Pennsylvania Politics, 1800–1816 (Harrisburg, Pennsylvania Historical and Museum Commission, 1952).

HOFSTADTER, RICHARD. The Idea of a Party System: The Rise of Legitimate Opposition in the United States, 1780–1840 (Berkeley, University of California Press, 1969).

HUNTINGTON, SAMUEL P. The Soldier and the State: The Theory and Politics of Civil-Military Relations (Cambridge, Harvard University Press, 1957).

IRWIN, RAY W. Diplomatic Relations of the United States with the Barbary Powers (Chapel Hill, University of North Carolina Press, 1931).

JACOBS, JAMES RIPLEY. The Beginning of the U.S. Army, 1783–1812 (Princeton University Press, 1947).

JENNINGS, WALTER W. The American Embargo, 1807–1809 (University of Iowa Studies, Iowa City, 1921).

JORDAN, PHILIP D. The National Road (Indianapolis, Bobbs-Merrill, 1948).

KAPLAN, LAWRENCE S. "Jefferson, the Napoleonic Wars, and the Balance of Power," in *William and Mary Quarterly*, 3 ser., XIV (April, 1957), 196–217.

KENNEDY, JOHN P. Memoirs of the Life of William Wirt. Vol. I (Philadelphia, 1850).

KIMBALL, FISKE. Thomas Jefferson, Architect (Boston, 1916).

———. "The Life Portraits of Jefferson and Their Replicas," in *Proceedings of the American Philosophical Society*, LXXXVIII (December, 1944), 497–534.

KNUDSEN, JERRY W. The Jefferson Years: Response by the Press, 1801–1809 (doctoral dissertation, University of Virginia, 1962).

KOCH, ADRIENNE. Jefferson and Madison: The Great Collaboration (New York, Knopf, 1950).

LACY, ALEX B. Jefferson and Congress: Congressional Method and Politics, 1801–1809 (doctoral dissertation, University of Virginia, 1963).

LEVY, LEONARD W. Jefferson and Civil Liberties: The Darker Side (Cambridge, Harvard University Press, 1963).

McCALEB, WALTER F. The Aaron Burr Conspiracy; and, A New Light on Aaron Burr. Expanded edn. (New York, Argosy-Antiquarian, 1966). Combines two books, the first published in 1903 and expanded in 1936, and the second published in 1963.

McKEE, CHRISTOPHER. Edward Preble: A Naval Biography, 1761–1807 (Annapolis, Naval Institute Press, 1972).

MACLEOD, JULIA H. "Jefferson and the Navy: A Defense," in *Huntington Library Quarterly*, VIII (February, 1945), 153–181.

MAHAN, ALFRED THAYER. Sea Power in Its Relation to the War of 1812 (Boston, 1905).

MALONE, DUMAS. The Public Life of Thomas Cooper, 1783–1839 (New Haven, Yale University Press, 1926. Reprint, Columbia, University of South Carolina Press, 1961).

———. Jefferson the Virginian (Boston, Little, Brown, 1948).

———. Jefferson and the Rights of Man (Boston, Little, Brown, 1951).

———. Jefferson and the Ordeal of Liberty (Boston, Little, Brown, 1962).

———. Jefferson the President: First Term, 1801–1805 (Boston, Little, Brown, 1970).

MORGAN, DONALD G. Justice William Johnson: The First Dissenter (Columbia, University of South Carolina Press, 1954).

MORISON, SAMUEL ELIOT. The Life and Letters of Harrison Gray Otis. Vol. I (Boston, 1913).

———. The Maritime History of Massachusetts, 1783–1860 (Boston, Houghton Mifflin, 1921 and 1941).

MOTT, FRANK L. Jefferson and the Press (Baton Rouge, Louisiana State University Press, 1943).

PERKINS, BRADFORD. Prologue to War: England and the United States, 1805–1812 (Berkeley, University of California Press, 1963).

PETERSON, MERRILL D. The Jefferson Image in the American Mind (New York, Oxford University Press, 1960).

———. Thomas Jefferson and the New Nation: A Biography (New York, Oxford University Press, 1970).

PRUCHA, FRANCIS PAUL. American Indian Policy in the Formative Years: The Indian Trade and Intercourse Acts, 1790–1834 (Cambridge, Harvard University Press, 1962).

PURCELL, RICHARD J. Connecticut in Transition, 1775–1818. New edn. (Middletown, Connecticut, Wesleyan University Press, 1963).

QUINCY, EDMUND. Life of Josiah Quincy (Boston, 1868).

RISJORD, NORMAN K. The Old Republicans: Southern Conservatism in the Age of Jefferson (New York, Columbia University Press, 1965).

RUBIN, ISRAEL IRA. New York State and the Long Embargo (doctoral dissertation, New York University, 1961).

SARICKS, AMBROSE. Pierre Samuel du Pont de Nemours (Lawrence, University of Kansas Press, 1965).

SCHACHNER, NATHAN. Aaron Burr: A Biography (New York, F. A. Stokes, 1937).

SEARS, LOUIS MARTIN. Jefferson and the Embargo (Durham, Duke University Press, 1927).

SHACKELFORD, GEORGE G., ed. Collected Papers to Commemorate Fifty Years of the Monticello Association of the Descendants of Thomas Jefferson (published by the association, Princeton University Press, 1965).

SHULIM, JOSEPH I. The Old Dominion and Napoleon Bonaparte (New York, Columbia University Press, 1952).

SMELSER, MARSHALL. The Democratic Republic, 1801–1805 (New York, Harper and Row, 1968).

SPAULDING, E. WILDER. His Excellency George Clinton (New York, Macmillan, 1938).

SPROUT, HAROLD and MARGARET. The Rise of American Naval Power, 1776–1918. New edn. (Princeton University Press, 1967).

STEEL, ANTHONY. "More Light on the Chesapeake," in Mariner's Mirror, XXXIX (November, 1953), 243–265.

STORY, WILLIAM WETMORE, ed. Life and Letters of Joseph Story. Vol. I (Boston, 1851).

WALTERS, RAYMOND, JR. Albert Gallatin: Jeffersonian Financier and Diplomat (New York, Macmillan, 1957).

WARREN, CHARLES. The Supreme Court in United States History. Vol. I (Boston, Little, Brown, 1922). Referred to as Warren.

WASHINGTON ACADEMY OF SCIENCES. Journal. XLIV (November, 1954). Lewis and Clark Anniversary number.

WEIGLEY, RUSSELL F. History of the United States Army (New York, Macmillan, 1967).

WHITE, LEONARD D. The Jeffersonians: A Study in Administrative History, 1801–1829 (New York, Macmillan, 1951).

WRIGHT, LOUIS B., and JULIA H. MACLEOD, "William Eaton's Relations with Aaron Burr," in *Mississippi Valley Historical Review*, XXXI (March, 1945), 523–536.

YOUNG, JAMES STERLING. The Washington Community, 1800–1828 (New York, Columbia University Press, 1966).

YOUNG, JEREMIAH S. A Political and Constitutional Study of the Cumberland Road (Chicago, 1902).

Index

Launches Lewis and Clark expedition, 172–80; receives reports of this, 188, 189, 198–201; distributes its scientific fruits, 189, 207; sponsors other exploration of tributaries of Mississippi, 192–96

Appoints James Wilkinson governor of Louisiana Territory, 216, 221; receives warnings about Aaron Burr, 223–25, 236, 237–41; orders Wilkinson to Orleans Territory, 227–28; meetings with Burr, 234, 235, 236–37; actions respecting troubles on Spanish border, 243–46; learns of conspiracy from Wilkinson, 247–51; issues proclamation against it, 251–54; interprets Burr's plans, 257, 263; asserts his guilt, 265, 334; approves Wilkinson's conduct in New Orleans, 269, 275–79; but seeks to dissociate himself from the General's high-handedness, 280–81; reports Burr's surrender, 286; plays limited part in prosecution, xvi, 300–303, 306–307, 309, 332, 341; subpoena to, moved and ordered, 314–319; his response, 320–25, 333; comments on conduct of trial, 335–36, 339, 340; second subpoena to, 343–45; actions against Luther Martin, 347–48; sends Congress copy of proceedings of court, 359; connection with Connecticut libel cases, 379–81, 383–84, 385–91

Rejects Monroe-Pinkney treaty, 398, 405, 407–10; attitude to Monroe (1807), 413–14; issues *Chesapeake* proclamation, 427–29; defense measures, 427, 432, 434, 451, 462–63; diplomatic objectives (summer of 1807), 436–37; corresponds with Tsar Alexander I, 441–42, 443–44, 446–50; receives information about British attitude, 454–57, 464; communicates it to Congress, 467–68; sends embargo message, 482–83; naval defense measures, 496–506; military measures, 507–19, 522–23

Services to architectural developments in Washington, 530–35, 537–40; avoids slavery question but recommends termination of foreign slave trade, 542–44, 546–47; maintains neutrality in contest between Madison and Monroe, 549, 551; actions for internal improvements, 553–56, 559; sends Milan decree to Congress, 561; receives communications approving embargo, 565–66; special message on negotiations with British, 566, 575; relies increasingly on Madison and Gallatin, 578–79; is given

power to suspend embargo, 579, and unexampled authority to enforce it, 580–82; activities in enforcement, 587, 589–91, 595–97, 603–604; comments on embarrassment of embargo laws, 601; replies to addresses from New England towns, 610–11; reports failure of diplomacy (1808), 619; relinquishes presidential leadership, 622–24, 626–28; expects repeal of embargo but favors delay, 634, 643; continues to share task of enforcement, 649–51; has difficulties with final appointments, 659–62; receives addresses and resolutions, 664–67; retires without regret, 668

Papers
(*see* Bibliography)

Second inaugural address, 4–9; letter on education (1805), 22; "Life and Morals of Jesus of Nazareth," 23; *Notes on Virginia,* 24, 314, 542; Garden Book, 29; annual message to Congress (1805), 69; confidential message on Spain, 70–71; instructions to Meriwether Lewis, 176–79, 184; addresses to Indians, 185–86, 191; proclamation against conspiracy (1806), 251–54; annual message to Congress (1806), 255; special message on Burr conspiracy (1807), 263–65, 267; letters to George Hay about subpoenas, 320–24, 344; annual message to Congress (1807), 352, 353, 459–61; *Chesapeake* proclamation, 427–29; embargo message, 481–82; proclamation against violation of embargo laws on Lake Champlain, 587; replies to addresses from New England towns (1808), 610–11; annual message to Congress (1808), 619–21; reply to Republican citizens of Connecticut, 635; circular letter to governors from secretary of war, 651; reply to address of citizens of Washington, 667–68

Philosophy and Opinions
(*see* Papers)

Doctrine of separation of powers, xii, 101; noninvolvement of government in religion, 7–8; freedom of press and its abuses, 8–9, 384–85; dependence of liberty on enlightenment, 22; importance of manufacturing, 24, 620, 628; nature of the fine arts, 29; prerogatives of Congress, 55–56, 464, 469; greater suitability of government to peace than war, 76; balance of